CHICANO:

The evolution
of a
people

CHICANO:
The evolution
of a
people

Renato Rosaldo   Robert A. Calvert   Gustav L. Seligmann

WINSTON PRESS 25 Groveland Terrace, Minneapolis, Minnesota
55403

WINSTON PRESS
PUBLISHER: Thomas C. Wright
EXECUTIVE EDITOR: Clifford L. Snyder
MANAGING EDITOR: Robert DeVilleneuve
DESIGNER: Guy Smalley

ACKNOWLEDGMENTS

A note of thanks is also due to Sherry DeMatteo,
Dolores Snyder, Dean Ragland, Ellen Small, Ray Gill,
Dorothea Autilio, Mary Klein, and Dr. Kenneth L.
Culver. Each has made a contribution of time and talent
toward the publication of this volume.

PREFACE

A major change has occurred in the way Chicanos, particularly the youth, view American society and their role in it. More importantly Chicanos are challenging the system, demanding that they become a part of it on equal terms with the Anglo members. This anthology explores the many facets of the changing Mexican American community.

To many Anglos, the emergence of a new Chicano came as a shock. Content and secure in their respective roles they almost instinctively feared any change; and they seemed to deny that signs pointed toward an upheaval. The thrust of history denies the *status quo,* and this book offers those unhappy individuals a partial description of a social revolution that now seemed so inevitable. The Mexican American's past has been something less than a realization of the "Great-American-Dream."

This volume does not offer solace to those who supported the *status quo,* nor succor to those who want to upend it, rather it is intended to help explain to Chicanos and to scholars how and why change came. Furthermore, this volume will serve the course of Mexican American studies in two ways: first it gives students a look at the present state of Mexican American historiography and secondly encourages others to initiate much needed research on this Nation's second largest minority. This work is not definitive: indeed none is. But this work is important in that it attempts to place a number of unrelated works into a cohesive introduction to the Mexican American experience.

Historians have ignored this large and important minority, neither integrating the Chicanos's story into the history of the nation's peoples or inexcusably, into the history of the Southwest. For example, only four major bibliographies guide students to Mexican American topics: Leo Grebler et al, *The Mexican American People: The Nation's Second Largest Minority;* the volume prepared by the Interagency Committee on Mexican Affairs; John J. Johnson et al, *The Mexican American: A Selected and Annotated Bibliography;* and Charles C. Cumberland, *The United States-Mexican Border: A Selective Guide to the Literature of the Region.* A very clear message comes through: there is plenty of room for budding young ethnic historians to carve out a niche (in some cases an empire) and spend the rest of their careers in rewarding and needed research. In all of the above, the material that could be considered history is indeed limited. For example, the Interagency Committee's effort had 1265 items; only 51 were by historians or on historical subjects. It should be indicated that in all four bibliographies the editors listed county histories and the like, and Cumberland has missed few of these.

In short never have the Mexican Americans been included as an integral part of the American past. Seldom have scholars viewed Mexican Americans as an active force in the socio-historical picture. They have been treated as slightly less than an invisible presence (but slightly). The editors believe this volume shows Chicanos in the act of fomenting their own revolution and hope to encourage other students to investigate and write a multi-ethnic history of what is in fact a multi-ethnic nation.

March 1, 1973

Renato Rosaldo
Robert A. Calvert
G. L. Seligmann

AUTHORS ACKNOWLEDGMENTS

For a volume of this size the editors obviously run up a series of debts that never fully can be paid. Tradition, however, lets us escape by acknowledging them by name. They know and we know that this is only a token; yet we offer it and it is accepted, because both sides know that no other payment can be made. We owe two general types of debts; the first are intellectual and the second, more prosaic but equally valuable, are administrative. Ward Albro of Texas A&I University and Leo Estrada and Nef Garcia of North Texas State and Abraham Hoffman of the University of Oklahoma made very useful comments not all of which were taken. We were probably wrong. Sharon O'Brien and Trisha Rainwater performed yeowomen service in preparing this volume. Mrs. Shirley Taylor and Isaura Tijerina brought order out of the chaos of our handwriting and typed neat rough drafts for us to mess up again. Lastly we must thank our editor Clifford Snyder—he knows when to push and when to wait. This makes him invaluable to his authors.

CONTENTS

3 TRYING TO CRACK THE SYSTEM 157

x   Contents

6 CONCLUSION   434

CHICANO:

The evolution
of a
people

1. INTRODUCTION:

BEGINNINGS
OF
A PEOPLE

Guy Smalley

Introduction: Beginnings Of A People

Most Americans view the various geographic regions of their nation in stereotyped images. The concept once held of the Southwest blends together an arid landscape and the sleeping Mexican, sombrero tilted to the noon-day sun. Like most folk wisdom this picture contains an element of truth. The lack of water has shaped the section's economy, and the presence of a large, culturally distinct minority has given it a unique charm. But the shy, mañana-seeking Mexican is a cultural phenomenon created by Anglo desires and not by Chicano behavior. Moreover, this Anglo fantasy is collapsing rapidly before the assault of a number of Bronze Power movements that have arisen to challenge the image. These protests, begun and matured in the Southwest, have made an indelible impression upon the national consciousness.

The story beings in the Southwest. In his pioneering and still indispensable *North From Mexico,* Cary McWilliams demonstrates vividly the tremendous debts Anglo pioneers in this region owed to the already existing Spanish presence. Arthur Campa's essay amplifies and reinforces several of McWilliams' ideas. These Hispanic Americans, as Richard Nostrand points out, compose both a population and a cultural region. The rich Hispanic legacy was constantly replenished and buttressed by Mexican immigrants. José Hernandez Alverez discusses this influx, and finally, Rodolfo Alvarez writes of the need for Chicanos to explore their cultural heritage so that they will not be doomed to relive their past.

CAREY McWilliams

Carey McWilliams (editor of THE NATION, *1955-), author of several books including* FACTORIES IN THE FIELD *(1939) and* BROTHERS UNDER THE SKIN *(1943), first published* NORTH FROM MEXICO *in 1948. This seminal study has become a classic in the field, and a model for historians interested in Chicano studies. The following selection describes the Spanish origins of the contemporary culture complex of the Southwest. Stock raising, farming, civil and common law, and many of the other unique socio-cultural traditions of the Southwest are Spanish in origin. Even the "uniquely" American cowboy is patterned after and predated by the Mexican American vaqueros. By permission of the Nation Associates and the author. From* NORTH FROM MEXICO, *Copyright © 1948.*

The Heritage Of The Southwest

Unlike the Middle West, there were no rich, fertile valleys in the Spanish borderlands; no plains which invited the plow; no lakes well stocked with fish; no rivers to be used for navigation or harnessed for power; no forests to provide lumber and fuel. The few areas capable of cultivation required irrigation in a land where water was scarce. Learning to survive in this region was a harsh and difficult undertaking. Resources had to be carefully husbanded; communications were hard to establish and difficult to maintain; and isolation magnified every aspect of the problem of settlement.

Yet the Spaniards, in a triangular relationship with Mexicans and Indians, succeeded in laying the foundations for the present-day economic structure of the region. Anglo-Americans in the Southwest have been the beneficiaries of three hundred years of experimentation, adaptation, and innovation. If one thinks of the Southwest in terms of mines, sheep, and cattle, and irrigated farming, then it is readily apparent that the underpinnings of the economy are of Spanish origin. . . .

4

HOMAGE TO THE CHURRO

Although Coronado brought the first sheep to the Southwest, the herds that were to constitute the basis of the pastoral economy of New Mexico came north in the famous *entrada* of Juan de Oñate in 1598. The raising of sheep is pre-eminently a frontier enterprise. Sheep helped to make the Spanish explorations possible for they were the mobile, marching food supply of the conquistadores. According to Messrs. Towne and Wentworth, sheep were an indispensable item in equipping every Spanish expedition to the north. From the founding of New Mexico until the Civil War, sheep fed, clothed, and supported the colonists. The only important source of cash income in the colony, sheep also served as a kind of currency. "Sheep," writes Winifred Kupper, "were the real conquerors of the Southwest."

In 1598 Spain had one of the oldest sheep cultures in the Western world. Its breeds were principally of two types: the beautiful, aristocratic *merinos* with their fine wool; and the ugly "scrubs" or *churros* long relegated to the periphery of the Spanish sheep culture. It was the scrub or *churro,* however, that the Spanish brought to the Southwest: a small, lean, ugly sheep whose wool was coarse and light in weight, seldom averaging more than a pound or a pound and a half at a shearing. But during a long period of adaptation to the semi-arid environment of Spain it had learned to hunt food and shelter, to make long marches, to survive in all sorts of weather, and to protect its lambs from wild animals. Its very "scrubbiness" made it ideally adapted to conditions in the Southwest.

The Spanish also brought to New Mexico their traditional sheep culture. Without this knowledge, based on six hundred years' experience under somewhat similar conditions, the value of the *churro* might have been negligible. There is no doubt whatever that "sheep husbandry in the United States," to quote Wentworth and Towne, "owes more to Spain than to any other nation on earth." Long prior to 1598, the Spanish had developed an extensive lore about sheep and had evolved elaborate institutions to protect and to further the sheep industry.

In Spain sheep were marched from the lowlands to the highlands and back from the highlands to the lowlands. The privilege of marching sheep in this manner had given rise to the *trashumante* system under which the rights and privileges of sheepmen were minutely regulated, defined, and safeguarded. To make this system function, an ancient organization of sheepmen had been effected known as the "Honorable Assembly of the Mesta," which has its almost precise counterpart today in the various "sheepmen's associations" in the Southwest. In Spain the various "sheep walks" were carefully laid out and defined; and what sheepmen could and could not do, on these marches, was also fixed by custom and ordinance. A somewhat similar system is in use today in the Southwest.

In short, Anglo-American sheepmen in the Southwest took over and adapted an already functioning and time-tested pattern of sheep-raising. About all they did was to enlarge the grazing areas by bringing the nomadic Indians under military control (a victory largely made possible by the introduction of the Colt revolver) and improve the breed of sheep. Apart from these contributions, they simply took over the customs, practices, institutions, personnel, and organization of an existing industry. The system of Spanish and Mexican land grants, based on larger units of land than were to be found in a non-arid environment, made possible the expansion of an industry which involved an extensive use of land resources. Similarly the practice of assigning fixed grazing rights to particular owners was Spanish in origin. Even the breeding of a heavy wool-bearing sheep came about as a result of crossing two Spanish types. For about 1820 some fine Spanish *merino* sheep were first brought to the eastern seaboard. These sheep reached the Southwest about 1876, with the general westward movement, and were then crossed with the *churro* to produce a new type ideally adjusted to the environment.

Under the Spanish system, sheep-raising was based upon a traditional social structure and a well-defined division of labor. At the base of the pyramid was the *pastor* or shepherd who was usually assigned a flock of about two thousand sheep.

Over each two or three *pastores* was a *vaquero* or mounted rider. Supervising the *vaqueros* was a *caporal* or range boss and over the *caporal* was the major-domo or superintendent. Ultimate authority rested, of course, in the owner or *patrón*. In general, this system of organization was taken over in toto by the Anglo-Americans and still prevails on the large sheep ranches of the Southwest. Between the eastern seaboard and the boundaries of the Southwest, sheep-raising was, and still is, an avocation or side-line business. Once the center of the industry had shifted to the Southwest, which was around 1870, sheep-raising became a specialized business, conducted on a large scale, by men whose sole vocation was sheep-raising. This was the Spanish system and its excellent adaptation to conditions in the Southwest is shown by the phenomenal increase in the wool clip: from 32,000 pounds in 1850, to 493,000 pounds in 1860, to 4,000,000 pounds in 1880.

New Mexico was "the ovine nursery of the nation" whose herds provided the foundation stock for the entire West. The *Californios* had never looked with particular favor on sheep-raising; in fact there were only about seventeen thousand sheep in the province in 1850. But, with the discovery of gold, large herds were driven overland from New Mexico to the mines. It is estimated that, between 1850 and 1860, more than five hundred thousand sheep were driven from New Mexico to California. Here, again, the marching qualities of the *churro* were of considerable importance. From these drives came the herds that were soon grazing in the foothills and valleys of California. It was also in California that the *churro* was crossed with the *merino* to produce the present range stock of the Western states. From California large herds were then driven eastward to the Rocky Mountain states and the new and improved breeds made their way back to New Mexico. During the 'seventies and 'eighties, large herds were driven eastward every season, grazing as they marched, to the terminal points on the rail lines from which they were then shipped to Middle Western markets. In the process of making these "drives," such states as Idaho, Utah, Colorado, Wyoming, Nevada, Arizona, and Montana were stocked with sheep.

Once this development had taken place, American wool production soared from five million pounds in 1862 to twenty-two million pounds in 1880. Increased wool production in the West meant, of course, increased factory employment in the East. The development of the sheep industry also stimulated another Western industry in which Mexicans have played a key role. For with the establishment of the first Western sugar-beet factories, the modern era of lamb-feeding came into its own. One reason for the rapid growth of the sugar-beet industry in the West was the fact that sheep could be fed and fattened on the by-products of sugar-beet production. Thus one industry neatly supplemented the other.

It was the Spaniards, of course, who taught the Indians of the Southwest to weave with wool. From 1800 to 1850 many Navajo women were employed in weaving in New Mexico and these women carried back to the tribes the skills which they had learned. From the Spaniards and Mexicans, also, the Navajo inherited the *churro* sheep. That they are today largely a pastoral people is to be traced to this early cultural borrowing. In the development of the art of weaving, however, the Spanish borrowed designs and dyes from the Indians. According to Ruth Laughlin, the Spanish brought only two dyes to New Mexico; the rest were all developed from native dyes used by the Indians. Blankets were long an important item in the barter economy of New Mexico. When trade was opened with Los Angeles by way of the Spanish Trail, one reads that New Mexico blankets were exchanged on the Coast for California horses. Blankets were also a principal item in the barter-markets of Taos and Chihuahua.

LOS PASTORES

Throughout the Southwest, the term "Mexican sheepherder" is proverbial. In the folklore of the region the solitary, superstitious, patient Mexican sheepherder is supposed to be as witless and moronic as the sheep he herds. But Mexican herdsmen are the carriers of a great tradition and it has been their skill and knowledge which has sustained the sheep industry in the West. Full of incredible lore, they can read the signs of changing weather at a glance; they know the habits of predatory animals; their knowledge of range vegetation is unrivalled; and there is little about the care of sheep that is unknown to them. In the early journals, one reads of how they trained sheep dogs by suckling pups on ewes so that the dog would learn to follow the sheep while they grazed, and return them at night to the corral. Above all, these *pastores* know how to graze a flock, guiding their movements without driving them, so that the sheep travel slowly and graze contentedly as they travel.

Living on coarse meal, goat's milk, kid's flesh and peppers, New Mexico *pastores* have tramped over most of the West in all sorts of weather and under the most difficult conditions. Until the 1890s, sheepherding was a hazardous occupation in New Mexico. One reads of Apache raids that netted five thousand sheep and of a raid in 1850 in which forty-seven thousand sheep were stolen. The most famous New Mexico Indian fighters were sheepmen. Colonel Manuel Chavez, and his *pastores,* fought the Indians for fifty years. Nor were Indians the only hazard. In California the herdsmen lived in mortal terror of bears and slept at night on raised platforms, called *tepestras,* which were built on poles eight, ten, and twelve feet above the ground.

The isolation of the shepherds was even greater than that of the other colonists in New Mexico. Something of the present-day brooding, introspective quality of the Spanish-speaking people of New Mexico can probably be traced to this experience. The notion that sheepherders are a weird lot, often driven crazy by loneliness, may be unfounded; but they are certainly the most taciturn of men. To guard against the hazards of loneliness a state law in New Mexico requires that sheepherders must be employed in pairs. Carrying their giant jews'-harps, called *bijuelas,* the *pastores* sang folk songs on the ranges of New Mexico which were of great antiquity when Columbus discovered America. No one knows the precise origin of the ancient folk play, *Los Pastores,* which has been produced in New Mexico for as long as the colony has existed. Some of the most beautiful New Mexico folk songs are, of course, the songs of the *pastores.*

Lieutenant J. H. Simpson, who travelled west in 1849, reported that the first New Mexican he sighted was "a swarthy, copper-colored young Mexican, of eighteen or twenty years of age, most miserably clad, driving the sheep before him. The morning air was keen and cold, and as he, with brimless straw hat on, a forlorn blanket about his shoulders, and pantaloons which were only an apology for such, hugged his only wrapper, his steps slow and measured, I thought he looked the very personification of patience and resignation." Whether it was the scrawny character of the sheep or the appearance of the herdsman, somehow the combination of being both a sheepherder and a Mexican came to be synonymous, to most Anglo-Americans, with the lowest possible status.

From the 1860s, bands of New Mexican sheepshearers, each with its *capitán,* made the great circle of the shearing pens from Texas to California to the Northwest and throughout the Rocky Mountain states. "I remember the Mexican sheepshearers galloping up," wrote Sarah E. Blanchard of her childhood on a ranch near Santa Paula, "and it was a time of thrilling excitement. Usually an old woman accompanied them to make tortillas and to provide them with Mexican delicacies. They were paid by ticket, so much for each fleece, and at night they gambled with these around the camp fires." Not infrequently a few Chinese sheepshearers accompanied these bands. "The shearers would come in," wrote Sarah Bixby Smith, "a gay band of Mexicans on prancing horses, decked with wonderful silver-trimmed bridles made of rawhide or braided horsehair, and saddles with high horns, sweeping stirrups, and wide expanse of beautiful tooled leather. The men themselves were dressed in black broadcloth, ruffled white shirts, high-heeled boots, and high-crowned, wide sombreros which were trimmed with silver-braided bands, and held securely in place by a cord under the nose. They would come in, fifty or sixty strong, stake out their *caballos,* put away their finery, and appear in brown overalls, red bandanas on their heads, and live and work on the ranch [in Southern California] for more than a month, so many were the sheep to be sheared." Shearers were the migratory aristocrats of the industry. They were never herdsmen, for the shearing of sheep was an exclusive vocation. Paid a wage of from five to eight cents a fleece, New Mexicans monopolized sheep-shearing until around 1890 or 1900 when the first power-driven shearing machines were introduced in California.

"The New Mexicans," wrote Twitchell, "were essentially a pastoral people." Lummis once said that sheep were "the one available utilization of New Mexico" where society was divided into two classes: those who owned sheep and those who tended sheep. Today it is said in New Mexico that those who own sheep are Spanish-Americans; those who herd them are Mexicans. From the earliest date, the great herds of New Mexico were owned by a handful of *ricos*. According to the New Mexico Guide (WPA), a few large operators still own seventy-five percent of the sheep. The Spanish governor, Bartolomé Baca, once owned two million sheep and employed 2,700 men. "El Guero" Chávez, the first governor under Mexican rule, owned a million head and Don José Leandro Perea of Bernalillo had herds of more than 250,-000. In 1880 three-fourths of the sheep of New Mexico were owned by about twenty families, sixteen of whom were families native to New Mexico. Sylvestre Mirabal, who owned 250,000 acres of grazing lands at the time of his death some years ago, was descended from a family that had raised sheep in New Mexico since 1600.

The dependence of *pastor* on *patrón* was complete and absolute. The *patrón* protected the *pastor* against the Indians and before the law. In the 1890s New Mexico *pastores* were paid a wage of from $5 to $8 per month, board included; and as late as 1940 the wage was only $35 a month. Many of the *pastores* were bound to their *patrones* by debts inherited from their fathers; even after peonage was abolished, the *partido* system by which herds were "farmed out" on shares, functioned as a thinly disguised form of peonage. "The social effects of a system of economy," writes John Russell, "wherein four-fifths of the white male population were employees of a handful of landlords have left their stamp on present-day New Mexico." Long after 1846, all the *patrón* needed to do was to say the word and his *pastores* would vote, as a group, for any candidate he recommended. "The most paternalistic form of government in

the world," writes Miss Kupper, "is a flock with a sheepherder as dictator" and the relationship between the herder and the flock is essentially that between the *patrón* and his *pastores*.

For several hundred years, thousands of New Mexico sheep were driven to points as far removed as Veracruz, Guadalajara, and Mexico City, principally for sale at the mines. After Mexico won its independence, the annual sheep drives to Chihuahua became immensely profitable and between 1839 and 1850 about two hundred thousand sheep were driven south every year. For these drives, the *ricos* would purchase the small herds of the *paisanos* who were, of course, unable to drive their sheep to market. Profits of from three hundred to four hundred percent were occasionally made on these annual drives to Mexico. With the discovery of gold in California, sheep sold for $16 a head and the drives to the West Coast took the place of the drives to Mexico. Little of this bonanza wealth ever found its way into the pockets of the *pastores*.

FROM GREGORIO DE VILLALOBOS

By a curious cultural transmutation, Anglo-Americans have long claimed credit for the origin and development of the cattle industry. No folk hero in American life has enjoyed anything like the popularity of the American cowboy. Each week millions of Americans see "Western" films and their sons and daughters will probably line up at the box-office years hence to see cowboys ride, rope, and shoot on the screen. Yet with the exception of the capital provided to expand the industry, there seems to have been nothing the American rancher or cowboy contributed to the development of cattle-raising in the Southwest.

One Gregorio de Villalobos is supposed to have shipped the first cattle to the New World. From this initial shipment to the West Indies came the stock later used to establish the great herds in Mexico and from these herds, in turn, came the cattle that Coronado drove to the Southwest. Like the lowly *churros,* the cattle that the Spanish brought to the New World were not much to look at. Light-bodied, long-legged, thin, with elongated heads and muzzles, their wide-spreading horns often measured five feet from tip to tip. "The general carriage of a Spanish cow," wrote one early-day historian, "is like that of a wild animal: she is quick, uneasy, restless, frequently on the lookout for danger, snuffing the air, moving with a high and elastic trot, and excited at the sight of a man, particularly if afoot, when she will often attack him." Such was the parent stock of the American range-cattle industry. Dating from the latter part of the eighteenth century, the cattle industry had its real beginnings in California and Texas.

When the *San Carlos* anchored in San Diego Bay on April 30, 1769, as part of the Serra expedition, some six or seven head of cattle were taken ashore: supposedly the first cattle to appear in California. Somewhat later, small herds were driven overland to California by Rivera and De Anza. So rapidly did cattle multiply in the province that the mission fathers and rancheros could count a million head by the end of the century. In fact cattle came to be regarded as a major nuisance in California. People afoot were forever dodging behind trees or jumping into ditches to escape from the wild charges of Spanish steers, regarded as more dangerous than grizzly bears. Anyone could start a herd in California, for there was no limit to the available pasture. Beef in California, like mutton in New Mexico, became a principal staple in the diet; and the hides, worked up into rawhide, were used for manifold purposes. At the Mission San José, a hundred cattle were butchered every Saturday. Cattle horns topped the fences around the wheat fields and the hides of cattle, drying in the sun, were to be seen at all seasons of the year.

With the first shipments to South American ports (1810) and the opening of the hide-and-tallow trade with Boston (1822), markets were finally found for the great surplus of cattle in California. The clipper ships, described by Dana as floating department stores, brought merchandise to exchange for the hides and tallow and a flourishing trade developed. Between 1800 and 1848 over five million hides were exported from California. It so happened, also, that the opening of the hide-and-tallow trade coincided with the beginning of the Mexican regime and the secularization of the missions. Under the impetus of this trade, the mis-

sion estates were carved up into great ranchos and stocked with cattle often plundered from the missions. By 1860 some three million were grazing on the great unfenced pastures of California. The cattle industry in California, however, had reached its zenith and had begun to decline at about the time that Texas became the cattle nursery of the nation.

Large herds were to be found in Texas at an early date but incessant Indian raids kept the industry from developing as rapidly as it did in California. In the chaotic period which followed the Texas rebellion, thousands of cattle roamed wild in the brush country between the Nueces and the Rio Grande. From an estimate of 100,000 in 1830, the number of cattle in the state increased to 382,733 in 1846. Four-fifths or more of this total was made up of so-called "Spanish cattle," for about the only cattle the Anglo-American settlers brought to Texas were a few milch cows. From these wild herds, the *cimarrones* of the brush country, came the cattle later driven to the rail terminal points in Kansas for shipment to the stockyards of Kansas City and Chicago and which were used, still later, to stock the ranges of Colorado, Wyoming, and Montana. While the Anglo-Americans may claim credit for the remarkable expansion of the cattle industry and for the conditions which made this expansion possible, the industry is indisputably Spanish in origin.

"TEN GALLON HATS"

It was the coming together, as J. Frank Dobie puts it, not in blood but in place and occupation, of the Anglo-American, the Spanish owner, and the Mexican *vaquero* that produced the Texas cowboy—"a blend, a type, new to the world." The word "cowboy" was unknown prior to 1836. "Cowboy" is the literal American equivalent of *vaquero* which is derived, of course, from *vaca* or "cow." Everything that served to characterize the American cowboy as a type was taken over from the Mexican *vaquero:* utensils and language, methods and equipment. The Spanish brought the horned saddle, to be distinguished from the English "muley" saddle, to the Southwest. Long before they came to the borderlands, the Spanish had taken this saddle over from the Moors. Along the Rio Grande, Mexican *vaqueros* made saddle stocks from the soft wood of the giant prickly pear and used a flat-topped silver horn as "big around as a soup plate." The saddle of the cowboy was merely an adaptation of this Spanish saddle. From the *vaquero,* the American cowboy took over, and adapted in his own way, the Spanish horned saddle, bridle, bit, and spur. From the *vaquero,* also, he got his lasso or lariat, cinch, halter, *mecate* or horsehair rope, "chaps" or *chaparejos,* "taps" or stirrup tips (*tapaderas*), the chin-strap for his hat (*barboquejo*), the feedbag for his horse (*morral*) and his rope halter or *bosal.* Even his famous "ten gallon hat" comes from a mistranslation of a phrase in a Spanish-Mexican *corrido "su sombrero galoneado"* which referred to a festooned or "gallooned" sombrero.

"The very language of the range," writes Mr. Dobie, "is Spanish." Such terms as bronco (from *mesteño*), mesquite, chaparral, reata, grama, huisache, retama, remuda, cavyard from the Spanish *caballada,* lariat from *la reata,* outfit or *corrida,* lasso from *lazo,* buckaroo, burro, *cinchas,* latigo, quirt (from *cuerda*), stampede (from *estampida*), hondo or hondoo for loop, calaboose (from *calabozo*), vamoose, mesa, canyon, barranca (bluff), rodeo, corral, sombrero, loco, all these, and many more, are Spanish-Mexican in origin. From the Spanish-American War, the cowboys of the Southwest brought back the word "hoosegow," or lock-up from the Spanish *juzgado.* In the borderlands, a *ranchero* (ranch) was an estate where cattle were raised; while an estate where crops were raised was a *hacienda.* Among the cowboys with whom I consorted as a youngster in Colorado, nothing was resented more keenly than the suggestion that they worked on a "farm." The words "farm" and "farmer" were anathema; they were "cowboys" who worked on a "ranch."

The Mexican ranchero loved and understood horses and often had more horses about than he had cattle. Some of the ranches in Texas had as many as a thousand head of horses and these herds, and the wild horses of the range, made the horse market in San Antonio the greatest of its kind in the world. A *manada* was a unit of horses on the range: one stallion for each twenty-five mares. The bell-mare in the herd was the *remudera.* The cowboy expression "wind-broken" is from the Spanish. The technique of horse-breaking as practiced by the American cowboy was based directly on the technique of the *domador* or professional Mexican horsebreaker.

No language in the world is so rich in hairsplitting terms to distinguish the exact color markings and characteristics of a horse as the "sagebrush" Spanish of the Southwest. The following and many similar terms are really Southwest slang, with the Spanish words being given, by long local usage, a meaning of their own: *Alazán tostado,* a chestnut sorrel; *andaluz,* a yellow horse with blond mane and tail; *azulero,* a dark blue roan; *barroso,* a smudgy dun-colored horse; *canelo,* a blue-red roan; *cebruno,* a dark brown; *grullo,* a bluish gray; *moro,* almost blue; *tordillo,* iron-gray; *palomino,* a cream-colored horse; *roano* or *ruano,* shortened to "roan," a dapple-colored horse. A "pinto" is, of course, a painted, piebald horse. An *estrello* is a horse with a star on its forehead; a *cuatralbo* is a horse with four white feet; a *potro* is an unbroken horse.

The American cowboy's elaborate lore about the rope and roping techniques was acquired directly from the Mexican *vaquero.* Roping by the forefeet was based on the *mangana* technique; while to rope by the hind feet or "to peal" was a feat also learned from the Mexicans. The Mexican expression *dale vuelta,* meaning to twist a rope about the horn of the saddle, became first "dolly welter" and, later, simply "dolly" on the Anglo-American tongue. The Mexican was an artist with knife and rope both of which he used as weapons. It was only when the Texans got the Colt revolver, about 1838, according to Dr. Webb, that they "became a terror to the Mexicans and all enemies." At a rodeo in Tucson on May 31, 1939, one José Romero, a Mexican *vaquero,* roped a full-grown golden eagle from horseback. It is also quite probable that the famous American cowboy songs are based on the *corridos* of the *vaquero.*

The great King and Kennedy ranches in Texas still rely upon Mexican vaqueros. The semi-feudal organization of these ranches, in fact, is directly patterned after the organization of the large *ranchería.* The managers are, nowadays, Anglo-

Americans; but the "hands" are Mexican—the *vaqueros,* the *caporales* or foremen, the *pasteros* or pasturetenders, and the *jinetes* or horsebreakers. "The proudest men I ever saw," is the way George Sessions Perry describes them. They still love goat-meat or *cabra* and brew the tea of the *ceniza* or sage. Spanish-speaking to a man, they sing the old *corridos* about the bordertowns, the great cattle drives, the stampedes, and the song of the *caballo fragado* or broken-down horse. Voting pretty largely as their "boss" tells them, the hands on the King ranch still refer to themselves as *Kineños.*

CORTEZ HAD A BRAND

Long prior to the appearance of the Anglo-American stockman, the Mexicans had a fully developed system of brands and brand registrations. Their brands were of three types: the *fierro* or iron; the *señal* or ear-mark; and the *venta* or sale brand. Like much of the Spanish lore about cattle and horses, brands came to Spain with the Moors. Mexican brands are of great antiquity, some of them being based on the Moorish *rúbricas,*—signs used first as a signet or signature and later added as a flourish when the writers learned to spell their names. Many Mexican brands were also copied from Indian pictographs and from symbols of the sun, the moon, and the stars. The brand used by Cortez—three Christian crosses—is said to have been the first brand used in the Americas. "There were brand books in Spain," writes Dane Coolidge, "hundreds of years ago." The Spanish had a system of registering brands which was in use in Mexico as early as 1545. When a horse or cow was sold, the old brand was "vented,"—stamped on the shoulder,—as a bill of sale; and the new brand was burned below this marking. The American law of brands and the various brand registration systems in use today are based directly on these ancient Spanish-Mexican usages.

Once a year in California the rancheros held a general roundup or *rodeo* which was presided over by one or more *Jueces del Campo* or Judges of the Plain. These judges settled all disputes over ownership and saw to it that calves were branded with the right brand. "In West Texas, New Mex-ico, Colorado, and northward," wrote Charles Howard Shinn, "wherever great cattle ranges are found today, the stockmen, in their round-ups, still follow the ancient Spanish plan; not knowing it is a heritage from a race they despise, they choose 'cattle judges' to settle disputes and uphold their decisions as final."

The well-organized and powerful cattlemen's associations of the West today are based upon the Spanish institution of the *alcaldes de la mesta.* When Austin drew up his code for the first colony in Texas, the Mexican officials added only two articles: one governing the registration of brands and the other having to do with *cimarrones* or wild cattle. As with the sheep industry, all the Anglo-Americans did was to provide capital for expansion, drive the Indians from the range, and improve the breed of cattle. The same can also be said of horses, goats, and mules. The mule industry of Missouri—once a thriving industry—was Spanish-Mexican in origin. Spanish range laws had an influence even in the Southeastern coastal part of the United States. Many Southern fence laws, range laws, and toll systems in use today are said to have grown out of customs and practices which the Spanish brought from the West Indies.

A DROP OF WATER

Just as Anglo-American settlers knew little about mining, sheep, or cattle, so they were almost wholly unfamiliar with irrigated farming. In fact there was little in Anglo-Saxon law or institutions that was applicable in the semi-arid environment of the Southwest. The Anglo-Saxon common law, with its doctrine of riparian rights, had been formed in Great Britain where water was not a problem. On the other hand, the Spanish civil law was based on a recognition of the shortage of water and the need for irrigation. The Moors had brought many of their irrigation practices and water-saving institutions to Spain in the tenth century. The similarity in environment made it possible for the Spaniards to carry over into the borderlands practices and institutions which had arisen out of the need for irrigation on the Spanish Peninsula.

The oldest irrigation systems now in use in the United States are to be found in the Rio Grande Valley in New Mexico. Here the Spanish were irrigating the bottom lands around Las Cruces when the *Mayflower* arrived at Plymouth. The Pueblo Indians were irrigating between fifteen thousand and twenty-five thousand acres in the valley when the Spaniards first appeared on the scene. Indeed there are evidences that the Indian irrigation systems of the Southwest are more than nine-hundred-years old. The Spaniards naturally had a lively interest in and respect for the accomplishments of Indians in the field of irrigation and noted, in their early journals and records, how closely Indian practices resembled those with which they were familiar. While the New Mexico colonists were familiar with irrigation, it is also apparent that they learned a great deal from the Pueblo Indians.

Irrigation is an art. To prevent wastage of precious water, soils have to be carefully prepared and levelled; and the question of when to irrigate, and to what extent, are matters learned only from long experience. "There are some arts," writes Edith Nicoll Ellison, "of which a man becomes master in the course of three hundred years or so. Levelling land is one, irrigation is another. In both these arts the Mexican is at his best. . . . With his big hoe and inherited lore, the Mexican is a valuable person." It was from the Mexican and the Indian that the Anglo-Americans learned how to irrigate.

After carefully levelling the land, the Mexicans blocked out their fields in squares, the sides of which were just high enough to hold the water. When one block was soaked—not flooded—a hole was made in the side wall of earth and the water was permitted to flow into the next square. This manner of irrigating is still known in the Southwest as "the Mexican system." The first irrigation systems in Texas, Colorado, New Mexico, Arizona and California were Mexican-Spanish in origin, if the Indian experience is excepted. It was only after the Anglo-Americans had learned to irrigate, after the Mexican-Indian manner, that they became successful irrigation farmers.

Irrigation has always been a communal enterprise. In New Mexico, the diversion dams, laterals and canals were always regarded, and are still regarded, as common property. Every spring the villagers elect a *mayordomo* who has charge of directing work on the irrigation system. A survey made by the government in 1891 revealed that in New Mexico no one was allowed to take waters from the main irrigation ditch unless he had either personally or by proxy performed the tasks assigned to him by the *mayordomo.* All work of this kind was performed by the villagers together, as a joint enterprise. The village type of agricultural settlement in both New Mexico and Utah is in part a consequence of the necessity of communal controls in irrigated farming.

The pueblo of Los Angeles, at an early date, appointed a *zanjero* to keep the main ditch or *zanja* in repair and the office was continued for many years after the American conquest. The word of the *zanjero* was supreme in all matters relating to water and took precedence over that of the alcalde, the priest, and the military commander. The *zanjero* was authorized, if necessary, to impose corvées of labor upon the population and to utilize every resource of the community to preserve the water supply. Many of these practices have a striking similarity with those of the Moors and such Spanish words as *acequia, zanja,* and *zanjero* are said to be Arabic in origin. To the borderlands, also, the Spanish brought a very considerable lore about water wells, both of the hand-drawn and water-wheel variety, and of the technique of drilling wells. Above all the Spanish colonists had an inherited social sense of the importance of water which they transmitted wherever colonies were founded.

The attempt of the Anglo-Americans to apply the doctrine of riparian rights in the arid Southwest resulted in years of conflict and litigation and retarded the development of the region. In the end most of the states were forced to repudiate the doctrine or to modify it in many important respects. The only state that had little trouble with irrigation law was New Mexico, where water rights were regulated by immemorial custom. At the present time, most of the Western states have adopted the Arid Region Doctrine, or, as it is sometimes called, the Doctrine of Appropriation. In developing this doctrine, Anglo-American jurists were no doubt influenced by the law of waters in Mexico. Under Mexican law, the government was vested with ownership of all rights in rivers and streams but could grant the use of waters to private owners. This use could be conferred on both riparian and non-riparian properties but it was customarily conferred subject to certain conditions and limitations so as to insure the maximum utilization of a limited water supply. While Walter Prescott Webb has said that the riparian rights doctrine was abandoned in the Southwest by necessity, rather than through any conscious borrowings from the civil law of Mexico, other students of the problem have shown that Mexican precedents were frequently cited in the decisions of Western courts and must, therefore, have had some influence on the formation of the present-day Doctrine of Appropriation.

Under the Spanish scheme of colonization, the pueblos were invested with certain special "pueblo rights" in respect to water. Usually four square leagues of land were set aside as communal lands belonging to the pueblo. Title to the water in streams flowing through these common lands, including the right to the underground flow, was reserved to the pueblo and its inhabitants, not only for domestic use, but for parks, trees, and non-agricultural purposes. Safeguarded by the Treaty of Guadalupe Hidalgo, these "pueblo rights" proved to be of inestimable value to the City of Los Angeles which succeeded to the rights of the former pueblo. In a famous lawsuit between the City of Los Angeles and the landowners of the San Fernando Valley, the Supreme Court of the United States finally ruled that the "pueblo rights" of the city took precedence over the common law rights of the landowners. Thus the city was given a prior claim to all waters originating within the watershed of the Los Angeles River, a claim paramount to that of all appropriators subsequent to 1781 when the pueblo was founded. One could not, therefore, estimate what the City of Los Angeles owes to the lucky circumstance that it was founded by Spanish colonists.

In general, the land-use systems developed by the Spaniards and Mexicans were much better adapted to an arid environment than were those long traditional with the Anglo-Americans. A Mexican homestead consisted of 4,470 acres: twenty-eight times the size of a homestead in the Ohio Valley. The land unit which Anglo-Americans found in the Southwest had no counterpart in the East or Middle West. It was a contribution, as Dr. Webb has said, "from Latin-America, and it came by way of Texas into the Great Plains: it was the cattle ranch." A cattle ranch might comprise two thousand or twenty thousand acres, depending on the circumstances. The Mexican idea was to give the settler some good land along a stream for farming, and considerably more land, back from the stream and not necessarily contiguous, for stock-grazing. Sometimes a three hundred-foot strip along a stream or *acequia-madre* extended fifteen miles back from the stream. Grants were never made without an adequate *porción* or portion of water. This land-use system was of major importance in the rapid development of the sheep and cattle industries in the Southwest. In 1839 Texas enacted a homestead law which was directly patterned upon the Mexican homestead. In fact, "the Texas land system," writes Dr. Webb, "had for its foundation the Mexican and Spanish system."

Property rights as between husband and wife are regulated today in California, Arizona, New Mexico, and Texas, in accordance with the Spanish *ganancial* system of community property. "Our whole system," wrote one California jurist, "by which the rights of property between husband and wife are regulated and determined is borrowed from the civil and Spanish law." When the first state constitution was adopted in California, specific provision was made for the retention of the Spanish law of community property. Of great incidental benefit to the residents of the Southwest, this system has been called "one of the most important landmarks of Spanish civilization in America." It was certainly a much more equitable system, so far as the wife was concerned, than the Anglo-Spanish common law doctrine which conferred an almost unrestricted control over the wife's property on the husband and recognized virtually no right, on her part, to property accumulated during marriage. Here, again, the needs of the West created a predisposition to accept the Spanish practice. For it has been suggested that the unequal ratio between men and women in California, when the first constitution was adopted, was an important factor in the decision to adopt the Spanish law of community property.

Any study of cultural borrowings and mutations in the Southwest must recognize that necessity has been as influential as conscious imitation. In the long run, the basic industries of the region, including mining, sheep- and cattle-raising, and irrigated farming, would have developed much as they have developed without the aid of Spanish precept and example. Peoples change their habits and customs in response to the challenge of a new environment; the question, in this instance, is one of the speed and facility with which these changes were made. On this score there can be little doubt but that the Spanish example greatly accelerated the process of cultural adaptation. For instance, studies which have been made of the California system of irrigation districts, widely imitated throughout the West, have traced the beginnings of this system to the mission establishments and their communal utilization of a limited water supply. It is also true that other cases can be cited in which the lineage of present-day institutions is uncertain and can, perhaps, never be determined. But one does not need to accept the "diffusionist" interpretation of cultural history to accord Spanish-Mexican influences due recognition in the heritage of the Southwest.

ARThUR CAMPA

Arthur Campa, (Director of the Center of Latin American Studies, University of Denver, Denver, Colorado), has been a pioneer in the study of Mexican American folklore and history. He is an expert in Latin American Studies and a Professor of Modern Languages at the University of Denver. This broadly conceived paper, read before the Rocky Mountain Social Science Association in 1971, traces the growth of class-consciousness in Mexican Americans from the treaty of Guadalupe-Hidalgo to the present. By permission of the author.

The Mexican American In Historical Perspective

The first question that arises when discussing the Mexican-American is determining who he is and, secondly, establishing the time when he appears on the American scene. The latter is more easily determined since it is based on historical fact as we shall see, but in defining the Mexican-American we find at least three views expressed by different groups of Spanish-speakers in the Southwest. Some look upon him as a cultural product, others as a racial mixture, and thirdly, he is defined as a political creation resulting from the combination of the two nationalities embodied in the term Mexican-American. The fact of the matter is that he is not any one of these three exclusively, but a combination of all three, though not in the same proportion in most cases. Culturally speaking, the Mexican-American should be by his very designation a bicultural product derived from Mexican ancestry and life in the United States. In reality, he is, more often than not, a product of Mexican folk-culture in the United States who has become a citizen by birth or by naturalization. The urban Mexican who has been wholly formed culturally in Mexico before coming to the United States does not fit into this category, and upon becoming an American citizen, he is usually assimilated at a level commensurate with his education and training, so he does not face to the same degree the problems that plague and separate the usual Mexican-American from the rest of the population.

Over the years, the Mexican part of the Mexican-American has become more the result of a traditional folk heritage. Not being reared in Mexico, he has not been provided with the opportunity to cultivate the cultural content implicit in the Spanish language, history, and art outside of the traditional folk arts, both verbal and non-verbal, inherited from his ancestors. As a result, the Mexican cultural formation of this individual is incomplete and not on a par with that which he receives from the American part of his heritage. But even the American cultural formation promised to this Mexican-American when he was made an American citizen has been sketchy and poor because he has not been able to participate as freely and as thoroughly as his Anglo-American neighbors. In spite of these inequalities, the Mexican-American's acculturation varies from a limited command of the English language and some basic notions of American institutions, to a high degree of training including the Ph.D. degree in a number of cases. This wide range produces a variety of Mexican-Americans with divergent notions of self-identity. On the whole, however, today's principal concern in our society is not the integrated individual who is already able to compete successfully in Anglo-American life, but the vast majority who across the years have not attained their corresponding place economically, socially and intellectually in the nation. As we look at the mass of Mexican-Americans, we discover that culturally they are not all uniformly alike; niether in English nor in Spanish, and that one of their justifiable demands is that they be given a better opportunity to bring themselves up to the level of accomplishment in both cultures commensurate with their personal efforts and abilities. This truly bicultural product is what many Centers of Latin American Studies in American universities try to turn out, except that by and large, the resulting Hispanists in this country are usually named Smith and Jones with a light sprinkling of Chávez and Sánchez.

Those who define the Mexican-American as a racial product usually underscore the indigenous portion of their heritage and hark back to the Aztecs before they arrived in Mexico under the Aztlan myth. This places the Mexican-Americans outside the orbit of both Spanish and English culture, and even Mexican culture as we know it today. The term some use to define this individual is *Chicano* because the word derives from the Nahuatl language. When the Mexican-American is placed in this frame of reference, he divorces himself from those Spanish-speakers who object to the connotative meaning that the term *Chicano* has had over the years and are reluctant to accept the denotative meaning ascribed to it today by the advocates of the term. This has caused a serious division among Mexican-Americans, and the gap is even wider among those who prefer the term *Hispano*. There are cases in which children who insist on calling themselves *Chicanos* have had to leave home because their parents consider this a self-denigrating term which in years past was used to refer to the lower caste Mexican. The insistence in defining the Mexican-American on racial terms with an undue emphasis on his Indian heritage courts the prejudice and discrimination that for centuries has been part of Anglo-American culture. The inconsistency of the *Chicano* name-advocates lies in that they all have Spanish or English Christian names, speak a modern European language and profess a religion that is anything but Indian. This is usually the result of using mythical notions of race combined with cultural traits and content that are diametrically opposed to the very designation adopted to represent a racial heritage removed by several centuries. Among Mexican-Americans there is also a wide range of racial mixture, from individuals who manifest a very limited amount of Indian strain to the Hispanized Indian whose features and pigmentation show the absence of Spanish heritage. Historically, their acceptance in Anglo-American society has been in direct ratio to the proportion of cognitive, aboriginal features and skin pigmentation, an attitude that has changed only superficially through the activistic demands of *Chicanos* and Mexican-Americans. Many programs and courses offered at the university level are token appeasement to the Mexican-American and *Chicano* demands with doubtful significant content.

As a political body, the Mexican-Americans came into existence after the war with Mexico when the Southwest became part of the United States. Some claimants overlook the events of history when they speak of a Mexican-American culture "which was in existence centuries before the United States came into being." This would place the Mexican-American in colonial Spanish days, long before the settlements on the eastern seaboard. Historically, American nationality was illegally conferred on the people of the Southwest by an enthusiastic General Kearney standing on the portals of the Palace of the Governors in Santa Fe, but it was properly extended to all inhabitants by Congress later on. Despite this political change, many well-known writers overlooked the American nationality of the southwestern Spanish-speakers and referred to them as "Mexicans and greasers" as is so well brought out by Cecil Robinson in his informative and well-documented book, *With the Ears of Strangers.* The term "Mexican" acquired over the years a connotation that was degrading to the people of the Southwest and as a result, many who would have used the designation willingly circumvented it by using *Hispano,* Spanish, or Latin-American. The Anglo-American newcomers continued the pejorative use of "Mexican" and resorted to such euphemisms as "Spanish" or "Castilian" when wishing to be particularly selective. Politicians and con-men always refer to the "proud Spanish or Castilian heritage" when seeking a vote or a sale. The treatment accorded to the Spanish-speakers north of the Rio Grande was in line with the attitudes behind the choice of designation.

The prejudiced connotation of the term "Mexican" persisted strongly until the advent of World War II, but it still exists in the minds of many who would despoil the Mexican-Americans of their national rights. Viewed in historical perspective, the unflattering use of the national term "Mexican" equated with inferiority, lack of ambition and unproductiveness derives from several sources. Robinson accounts for this "jaunty voice of

nationalism" by saying that "There was on the one hand the rabid racialism and mounting ferocity against the 'greaser' and on the other the pontifical tones of the doctrine of Manifest Destiny." Another reason for this negative connotation of the name "Mexican" is explained by General Manuel Mier y Terán who in 1828 was sent by the Mexican government to investigate the Anglo-Mexican colonies in Texas. He reported his chagrin over the fact that the colonists knew no other Mexicans than the northern inhabitants whom he described as ignorant and unprogressive, composed mostly of Indians and Negroes. The neglect of both Spanish and Mexican governments was largely responsible for the cultural and economic decadence of the northern fringes of the Spanish empire and later the Mexican nation. The Texas rebellion, and shortly thereafter the war with Mexico, added the emotional catalyst that merged the already conditioned mind into the pervasive prejudice that is so difficult to eradicate today. Such losses as the Alamo and the deserting of American volunteers, a good many of them members of the "Texas volunteers," at the battle of Buena Vista, won by a virtual squeak, increases the hatred of people who, to many Anglo-Americans, represent the "enemy" of 1836 and 1848. As a result, the treatment of the Mexican-American in the Southwest over the past century has been characterized by an ascending scale of neglect, apathy, discrimination, segregation, and prejudice in every sector of Anglo-American life.

The descendants of the original settlers of the upper Rio Grande who came into the Southwest in Spanish colonial days never used the term "Mexican-American," and preferred to be known as "Spanish-Americans." There is some historical justification for this choice when applied on political grounds. The issue becomes clouded when these same colonials try to base their distinction on superiority of race and culture. They lived such a short time under the Mexican flag, and were not particularly happy with the policies of the Mexican government, that they rebelled, murdered the Mexican governor, but were not successful in setting up an independent state. The occupation of New Mexico by the American army was not as hard fought as it might have been, had they been more strongly attached to the republic. The transition from Spanish subjects to American citizens (1821–1848) caused them to call themselves Spanish-American since they had been under the Spanish standard for over two centuries. In California, the settlers too became dissatisfied with the centralist policies of the new Mexican regime and became ambivalent about the Americans despite their admiration for the American constitution. Nevertheless they gave a good account of themselves and earned the respect of the Americans when they soundly defeated the same General Kearney who had taken New Mexico and had been told by Kit Carson that the *Californios* were cowardly and would run. Two Californian lances through his body convinced the General that they were not so easy to take, and in the end he became one of the *Californios* best friends.

The name "Mexican" was applied by the California settlers to the people who came into the province from Mexico after the period of settlement, and the term *cholo* was used to distinguish the undesirables who were sent north as a punitive measure. Later on, after the discovery of the mine fields, the newly-arrived Anglo-Americans continued to use the term "Mexican" as a pejorative despite the fact that they learned the mining trade, including the recovery processes of the *arrastra,* placer panning with a *batea* and the quicksilver process made possible with the mercury of the New Almaden mine discovered by a Mexican and worked by Mexicans. The national adjective "American" was never added to Mexicans anywhere in the Southwest until comparatively recent times. Mexican nationals continued to come into what was now a foreign country and their descendants eventually became American citizens automatically. During the Mexican Revolution, the figures increased considerably and with the start of World War II, large numbers were officially recruited to help with the agricultural harvests throughout the United States. The immigration figures fluctuate from a couple of thousand around the turn of the century to a quarter of a million high in the twenties. During the Depression years the number of immigrants decreased and picked up again beyond two hundred thousand in the middle fifties, but it never reached the

figure of the twenties. The constant influx of people from the border, together with the natural increase of families has built up a Mexican-American population of significant size and importance over the past century. When these numbers are added to the settlers who were already in the Southwest in 1848, the importance of this minority is readily appreciated. Estimates of Mexican-Americans in the United States vary from four million to twelve million depending on how statistics are computed.

There is one label in Mexican slang which has been used loosely for a long time for Spanish-speakers in the Southwest and which lately, in the scuffle for names, has been revived. *La Raza* freely translated means "the Race," and in this case it refers to anyone whether Spanish-American, Chicano, Mexican-American or Mexican citizens. It's an overall term which is neither denigrating nor flattering, simply an expression of fact when used in Spanish, but with a connotation of pride comparable to the term used by many groups around the world who regard their own as THE important part of the population. The Navajo Indians use the term *Dineh,* meaning "The People," that is, their people, consequently a very important designation because it singles them out. The only problem, if it is a problem, with *La Raza* is that the Spaniards use it in referring to Columbus Day which they call *El Día de la Raza,* "The Day of the Race," meaning the Spanish race, but since it is the Spanish race in connection with the discovery of the new world, there is some justification for the Spanish-speakers of North America to use it combining as they do a Spanish heritage with a new world residence.

There is an interesting historical event which took place in 1695 that suggests another name by way of compromise. When Don Diego de Vargas, the reconqueror of the province of New Mexico, established formally the village of Santa Cruz north of Santa Fe, history records that he "issued a proclamation . . . which provided for the founding of the new settlement, officially bestowing upon it the name of *Villa Nueva de Santa Cruz de Españoles Mexicanos del Rey Nuestro Señor Carlos Segundo."* Since they were all Spanish subjects inherently the old conqueror used the name *Es-*

pañoles first and secondly *Mexicanos* to indicate their place of origin, that is, they were Spaniards first and Mexicans second. He did not hyphenate their nationality. If we take a page from this record of the seventeenth century, it may be possible to use the term "American" today, as the nationality of Spanish-speakers living in the United States, and include the name "Mexican" to designate their cultural origin. Then the proper term would be "American Mexican" without a hyphen to bifurcate their nationality, and since they would then be Americans first, they would be justified in insisting on their rights and privileges as American citizens of Mexican descent, one more descent in the kaleidoscopic origin of the United States population.

Up to 1848 everything that happened in the Southwest was initiated and carried out by the Hispano-Mexicans of the day. It was therefore logical that the record of events should mention Spanish names, and that all officials and pariticpants be from the same nationality. The taking over of all administrative, trade, and cultural activities by the incoming Anglo-American naturally meant that the original settlers, in the new role of conquered and governed people, took a secondary role with minimum participation in decision making. This does not mean that the new citizens, call them what you will, ceased to exist. In fact, they were very much in evidence and have continued to be to the present time. A few of the better placed were given positions of responsibility and those who had been active in such enterprises as trade, cattle and sheep-raising, agriculture and mining continued, but the industries were now American for the most part instead of Mexican, hence little is known about them as Spanish or Mexican enterprises. This has led many to the conclusion that the inhabitants of the Southwest became complete non-entities entirely at the mercy of the newcomers. There were merchants and traders who plied their wares over the Santa Fe trail and down the old Camino Real. The Ochoas' from New Mexico and Arizona had one of the most prosperous freighting companies in the West as did the Romeros' of Las Vegas over the Santa Fe trail. The Oteros, the Armijos, the Bacas, Chávez, Mirabals, the Ortíz y Pinos and countless

others engaged in everything from merchandizing to sheep-raising on a grand scale. In California there were large estates called *ranchos* owned and managed by men bearing such names as Domínguez, Vallejo, Lugo, Pico, Guerra, Olvera and countless others until the reverses of extreme drouth and floods decimated the southern *ranchos* and the squatters and corporation lawyers took most of the land in the north. California had more abundant and richer lands to be coveted by the land-hungry Yankee who did not stop at anything in order to take possession of what he believed to be his just reward in the name of progress and Manifest Destiny. The Californio saw his land change hands under the protection of the Land Law promulgated for the purpose, and was helpless when he witnessed the broken promises and the humiliation to which he was subjected by men who professed a glowing faith in the tenets of democracy. The Californio did not disappear from the scene however; he fought back but was overwhelmed by sheer numbers and eventually sold out what property was not taken by the ruthless conqueror. Later the descendants of these same ruthless men looked back to the romance of "Spanish California" and created a cult which venerated to absurdum the memory of a romantic past they had helped to destroy. The present-day Mexican-American draws little satisfaction from the way in which the days of his ancestors are turned into gay fiestas and parades while he is far short of this image artifically created by the conscience stricken Anglo-American who incidentally profits by it.

In New Mexico the revival of her "proud and romantic heritage" did not occur until the turn of the century with the creation of the art colony of Santa Fe, but since the state did not have the available wealth of California, the "natives" plodded unnoticed and neglected. The only source of interest was the land-grants speculation and confusion through which the original settlers lost land they had come to believe was theirs, and in the end many who were landowners now worked the same lands for an Anglo-American landlord. Generally speaking, the Mexican-American whether in California, Texas or New Mexico gradually lost control of the land and with few exceptions, became a small farmer who had to supplement his income by working for the *Americanos* or for the state and county.

While the Mexican-American did not come into existence legally until the Treaty of Guadalupe Hidalgo in 1848, his ancestors had been in the Southwest for two hundred and fifty years before the arrival of the Anglo-Americans. During that time they had pushed the Spanish frontier eastward to Texas, pioneered the trail to San Antonio, had established a trade route to California across Arizona and had moved north of Taos as far as the San Luis Valley and the present city of Pueblo, Colorado. The geographer, D. W. Meinig maps out this expansion and comments on it:

> The gradual contiguous spread of Hispano Colonists during the nineteenth century is a little-known event of major importance. Overshadowed in the public mind and regional history by Indian wars, cattle kingdoms, and mining rushes, this spontaneous unspectacular folk movement impressed an indelible cultural stamp upon the life and landscape of a broad portion of this Southwest.

In the Mexican-American's search for better farming land, grazing for their cattle and sheep, and the expansion of trade with the plains Indians, they had quietly moved their families to locations which later developed into villages and cities. The ancestors of these Mexican-Americans were the real pioneers who pushed the fringes of civilization to uncharted wilderness hitherto untrod by European man.

The Anglo-American has mistakenly assumed the title of "pioneer" imbued with the hypothesis that he had extended civilization all the way from the eastern seaboard across the plains, over the mountains to the shores of the Pacific ignoring a European culture which had been in the Southwest for over two and one-half centuries. History does not apotheosize the quiet movement of the early settlers who quadrupled the area originally settled by the Conquistadores, but it does fill pages and volumes with accounts of "hardy and undaunted pioneers" who crossed over trails already known and moved into the Southwest. These newcomers learned from the inhabitants to use water for irrigation, to break the wild *mesteño* into a serviceable mount, to work the longhorn cattle of the *ranchos,* to eat *frijoles, chile* and *charqui* and to build with *adobe* in a land where lumber was non-existent. In California they learned to shout "Chispa!" not "Gold!" when they found the precious metal, and from these same Mexicans they learned to pan the streams with a *batea,* to process quartz with an *arrastra* after bringing it up from the mine over *escaleras,* and later learned to recover the gold content with the quicksilver from the Mexican-discovered mine in New Almaden. The supply lines which provided the miners with food, implements and all other necessaries were brought in by *atajos* of mules loaded by *cargadores* who later taught this art to the American army. The Anglo-Americans from the East were not really pioneers, but aggressive workers who took page after page from the Mexican culture forgotten in the history books but which, as we look back today, places the Mexican and the Mexican-American in a different perspective. This same Hispano-Mexican fought the Indian but did not try to exterminate him with the slogan "A good Indian is a dead Indian." In fact, he assimilated him, turned entire pueblos into many so-called "Spanish" villages of today. These were the real pioneers who introduced European civilization into "uncharted wildernesses" so successfully that they gave rise to the present Mexican-American mestizo.

Many Anglo-Americans, whether trappers, prospectors or traders, built upon a Mexican base much of the culture that we call today southwestern. Take the *ranchos* and the cattle industry of a century ago from the Texan, remove his *chaparreras* and *tapaderas,* relieve him of his *laso,* his *reata,* his *remuda,* his *sombrero,* his *mostrenco-*mustang, his *dally welter* and his *rodeo* and he is reduced to the midwestern farmer he was before he came into contact with the civilization that made him different from the rest of the *Americanos* of today, and incidentally, the romance of the American folk-hero, the cowboy, vanishes. Finally, in order to make the assimilation more complete, the first arrivals such as Maggoffin, Kit Carson and scores of other scouts, trappers, and traders married the charming daughters of the Oteros, Chavezes, Armijos, Lopezes, Romeros and Lunas.

When the Anglo-American conquerors took over the country from Texas to California, the new nationality of Mexican-Americans created by Congress did not fade away, though history forgot them; they became the laborers who cleared the *chaparrales* of Texas in order to expand the agricultural industry of that great state, they cultivated the cotton fields and picked the cotton at harvest-time, they picked the fruit of the California groves, they took up residence in boxcars on sidings along the railroad and laid the tracks for the freight trains and luxury passenger trains that crossed the continent, they broke horses on the now Anglo-run ranches and drove cattle over the trails. These same Mexicans became sheepherders for the sheep barons who remark that, "To educate a Mexican is to spoil a good sheepherder." When the sugar beet industry was established in Colorado, these same Mexican-Americans cultivated, topped and harvested the crops that helped to build the Great Western among others. And when war broke out, the Mexican-Americans joined to defend the soil their own ancestors conquered, but again, history speaks but lightly of the part they played in Glorieta Pass by giving Chivington a "glorious victory" over the Confederates. Again in 1898, the ranks of the Rough Riders commanded by the impetuous Teddy Roosevelt contained some unheralded Mexican-Americans and in 1918 they went back to fight in France. As wars increased in size, the proportion of men from the Southwest increased, and in World War II, the Mexican-Americans took more than their proportionate share of Congressional Medals, and they still continue to fight in far-flung battlefields today in another war not of their making. When viewed in a proper historical perspective, the Mexican-American of today with all his virtues and his defects takes on a different meaning. The fact that proportionately very few are college graduates, medical doctors, college professors, engineers and members of other professions does not alter the fact that these people have done the stoop-labor, the back-breaking work basic for the development of the industries and resources of the Southwest.

But, as George Sánchez says, they are "forgotten people" because being behind the hoe, or wielding a pick and shovel, they have gone unnoticed, they are taken for granted, unlike those men who, with more resources and opportunities at their disposal, and with no prejudice and discrimination to hold them back, are able to rise to important administrative posts where all the honors are bestowed by American society.

The closing chapter in the history of the Mexican-American began with World War II when the residents of isolated villages, small farms and city ghettos were taken across the country to training centers where they became, not Mexican-Americans, but one more serial number in the vast army of recruits. Training, working and eventually fighting alongside Anglo-Americans gave them the confidence necessary to develop their self-identity, and having shared a cause in common gave them a feeling of equality they had not enjoyed before going to war. Upon their return, they began to question the role to which they had been relegated before the war, and decided that if they could fight for their country they could also expect corresponding opportunities and treatment. Unfortunately, the old prejudices and discriminations had not totally disappeared at home, as many painfully discovered. The Mexican-Americans began to organize like they had never done before. There were G.I. Forums, Alianzas and LULACS to join and from such organizations the ascending scale of negativisms to which they had been exposed before, from apathy and neglect through prejudice and discrimination, was countered by another scale of their own, beginning with fatalism, now discarded, progressing through dissatisfaction, complaint, unrest, demand and finally today's activism. In the interim between the end of World War II and the present, enough Mexican-Americans entered the fields of medicine, research, science and technology, to say nothing of individual sports, to convince them that they were able to perform alongside those of the dominant culture as they did in the ranks of World War II. Their demand today is for the opportunities and the facilities which will enable them to share proportionately with the rest of society all the privileges and enjoyments inherent in American society. There is danger, however, that those who have become more outspoken leaders may make the demands and activism an end in themselves in order to perpetuate their role as *caudillos*. The idea is for the patient to recover even if the doctor runs out of a job, otherwise the historical perspective of the Mexican-American will become a stagnant malady in suspended animation.

Richard L. Nostrand

Richard L. Nostrand (Assistant Professor of Geography, University of Massachusetts; presently on a Post-Doctoral Fellowship at the University of Texas, Austin) used the tools and training of a geographer to define a cultural region. Students will not only gain a definition of the Hispanic-American borderland from this article, but they will see also how cultural geography aids in delineating a history of a people. The article was extracted from Professor Nostrand's dissertation, written at U.C.L.A. in 1968. By permission from the ANNALS of the Association of American Geographers, Volume 60, (1970).

The Hispanic-American Borderland: Delimitation Of An American Culture Region

People of mixed Spanish-Indian or Mexican descent, called here by the all-inclusive term "Hispanic-Americans," form a sizable and distinctive American minority group. An estimated four million Hispanic-Americans reside in the United States. Most of them speak Spanish as a mother tongue, are at least nominally Roman Catholic, and are disadvantaged socially, economically, and politically. More than eighty-seven percent of these people reside in the American Southwest.

The southwestern area where Hispanic-Americans reside has come to be known as the "borderlands." This term derives from the historian Herbert Eugene Bolton, who is credited with the "effective discovery" of the "Spanish Borderlands" (as he called them) as a name and as a field

23

of historical research. In his 1921 volume, Bolton "staked out this field," to use Caughey's words. In that volume he looked at the borderlands as the area of former Spanish and Mexican activity, for Bolton's borderlands histories ended with their inclusion within the United States. And as suggested in his subtitle, Bolton's borderlands stretched broadly across the southern United States; they even included parts of northern Mexico.

Bolton's "borderlands" term is now entrenched in the literature concerning Hispanic people, although not always as Bolton used it. Out of keeping with Bolton's usage, for example, is the common reference to the "borderlands" as the area occupied by present-day Hispanic-Americans. In this paper Bolton's term is used in the following ways: First, it is used in the singular to refer only to a part of the Southwest—the important area of Spanish-Mexican colonization in the present-day United States. Secondly, it refers to that southwestern area only after the mid-nineteenth century when the present-day international boundary was established. Thirdly, it refers only to an area which lies entirely north of the present-day international boundary. There is no borderland (as the term is used here) south of the international boundary, for the overlap of Anglo-Americans into Mexico is, by contrast, negligible. Also, the generic term "Hispanic-American" takes the place of "Spanish" as a modifier.

In the growing body of literature concerning Hispanic people to which Bolton contributed so importantly, missing are attempts to regionalize this present-day Hispanic-American borderland. An exception is Carey McWilliams' *North from Mexico,* in which the author delineated verbally the northern edge of the borderland. But McWilliams' attempts at regionalization lacked precision. Thus, after a thorough review of the literature on the United States-Mexican border area, Cumberland was able to state that "no successful attempt has yet been made" to regionalize the Spanish-Mexican Southwest. What follows is an attempt to delimit the present-day borderland —America's Hispanic culture region. Necessarily, a background discussion of the Hispanic-American precedes the attempted delimitation.

THE HISPANIC POPULATION

In 1960 the Bureau of the Census identified members of the Hispanic minority as "white persons of Spanish surname." In identifying this population, census coders were asked to compare a list of about 7,000 Spanish surnames with all census schedule names as part of the general coding procedure. The census schedule names were obtained from a twenty-five percent sample of the total population—that is, from every fourth housing unit, or in group quarters from every fourth person. Based on this sample, 3,464,999 "white persons of Spanish surname" were enumerated.

The enumeration of "white persons of Spanish surname" was restricted to the southwestern states of California, Arizona, New Mexico, Colorado, and Texas. The Bureau of the Census limited its data gathering because a preponderance of the minority lived in these five states. In 1940, when gathering data on white persons of Spanish mother tongue in all the states, the Bureau found that more than eighty-four percent of persons of Spanish mother tongue (the great majority of whom were of Mexican parentage) inhabited these five states. Thus, when "white persons of Spanish surname" was adopted for identifying Hispanic-Americans in 1950, the Bureau decided to limit its gathering of these data to the five states, and in 1960 the policy was continued.

The number of Hispanic-Americans in the balance of the United States can only be estimated. In the nonsouthwestern states the Bureau of the Census enumerated 224,934 people of Mexican stock. However, unlike the Spanish surname data which included all three nativity categories, the Mexican stock data included only the Mexican-born and native-born of Mexican or mixed parentage. Nonetheless, these Mexican stock data are useful in estimating the nonsouthwestern Hispanic population. By applying the Spanish surname ratio of foreign-born and native-born of foreign or mixed parentage populations (the equivalent in nativity to Mexican stock—45.183 percent) to the native-born of native parentage population (54.817 percent) to the nonsouthwestern Mexican stock population, the nonsouthwestern native-born of native parentage group would be an estimated 272,895. Adding to this figure the 224,934 persons of Mexican stock, the estimated Hispanic population in the balance of the United States would be 497,829. This procedure was used by Grebler, who pointed out that it assumes the existence of a similar relationship between the southwestern and nonsouthwestern nativity components.

The nonsouthwestern Hispanic population may then be estimated at approximately 500,000. This 500,000, when added to the 3,500,000 Hispanic-Americans in the Southwest, contributes to the total Hispanic population of 4,000,000. But relative to the 3,500,000, the nonsouthwestern component is small, constituting less than thirteen percent of the total. This small percentage is evidence that the Hispanic population is concentrated in the Southwest.

A DISTINCTIVE MINORITY

The minority Hispanic population is differentiated from the majority by various distinctive attributes. It is, by and large, a mestizo population, representing a fusion of Spanish (Caucasian) and Indian (Mongoloid) racial characteristics. Spanish and Indian miscegenation began in the first few decades of the sixteenth century in New Spain. Many of the migrants who made the difficult journey to the northern frontier of New Spain (and, later, of Mexico) were mestizos. Likewise, many of the migrants going from Mexico to the United States after the mid-nineteenth century were mestizos. Although individuals of the Hispanic population today run the gauntlet from Caucasian at one extreme to Mongoloid at the other, the vast majority would be characterized as mestizo.

Most Hispanic-Americans are members of the Roman Catholic Church, although data are not available on the proportion Roman Catholics represent of the entire Hispanic population. In her study of persons of Mexican descent in the unincorporated Mayfair District near the eastern boundary of San Jose, California, Clark found 70.6 percent were Roman Catholics. Heller suggested that the Roman Catholic percentage for the entire

Hispanic population was probably higher. González stated that the percentage of Roman Catholics among the New Mexican Hispanic group "was probably . . . close to 75."

Drawing upon both Spanish and Indian beliefs, the Catholicism of the Hispanic population, like that of the Mexican in Mexico, is mainly a folk Catholicism permeated with unorthodox beliefs and superstitions. Madsen, in his study of "Latin Americans" (as they call themselves locally) in four communities in Hidalgo County, Texas, related that the lower class and a large part of the middle class subscribe to folk Catholicism, but that the Catholicism of the numerically small "conservative elite" is more "orthodox and sophisticated." Whether more orthodox or more folk-oriented in its interpretation of Catholicism, the Hispanic way of life is religion-centered. This is evident in the family altar often present in the Hispanic home.

The Catholicism of the Hispanic-American is a major force in shaping his values and attitudes. One attitude shared by Hispanos is an allegiance to *La Raza,* "The Race." Carried in *La Raza,* according to Madsen, is the concept of a glorious destiny which awaits those "united by cultural and spiritual bonds derived from God." A second attitude is the Hispanic-American's fatalistic philosophy. One's fortune is predestined by God, he believes, and rather than try to overcome misfortune and control one's fate, one accepts it. Consistent with the theme of fatalism, Heller noted, is a lack of emphasis on achieving or "making good" in Anglo-American terms.

Allegiance to *La Raza* is an attitude shared by Hispanic people, and Spanish, according to Madsen, is "the primary symbol of loyalty to *La Raza.*" For the Hispanic population, Spanish is the mother tongue, the language spoken in the home. Were the Hispanic population largely Mexican-born, this might not be surprising, but in 1960 nearly eighty-five percent of this population was native-born. Thus, when data on mother tongues were gathered in the 1940 census, 91.6 percent of the second generation whites of Mexican parentage in the United States reported Spanish as their mother tongue. Moreover, from a study of records of World War II Army inductees of the Hispanic group at one training center which served the eight westernmost states, Altus found that "all trainees of Mexican ancestry speak Spanish, no matter how many generations their ancestors may have lived on what is now the soil of the United States." Data is not available on the percentage who speak Spanish as a mother tongue today. Although this percentage has probably declined from what it was in 1940, Spanish is still the mother tongue of most of the group according to Manuel.

Because Spanish is spoken in the home, the children of Hispanic families are handicapped when they first enter schools where English is the medium of instruction. Most Hispanic-Americans learn English and become bilingual; the language barrier, however, is one reason why the Hispano is disadvantaged educationally relative to the majority of the population. Grebler underscores this disadvantaged position in noting that Hispanic-Americans have a generally low attainment in formal schooling. In 1960 the median years of school completed by Spanish surname persons over twenty-five years of age in the five southwestern states was 7.1 as compared to 11.6 years for the total population.

The Hispano is also disadvantaged economically, which is made clear by considering family incomes. Using a "poverty line" of $3,000, Mittelbach and Marshall found that 34.8 percent of the 698,027 Spanish surname families in the five southwestern states in 1959 had incomes under $3,000, as compared with 19.7 percent of all 7,356,866 southwestern families. Further, the Hispanic-American is disadvantaged occupationally. In all five states the percentage of Spanish surname males in 1960 was high in operative and farm laborer categories and low in the professional and technical categories.

Hispanic people also compare unfavorably with the total population in terms of political organization and strength. As citizens who possess the right to vote, Hispanic-Americans would seemingly have political strength if only by reason of sheer voting numbers. In general, however, the Hispanic community has not organized politically to promote its interests effectively. There are exceptions—some political organization has occurred.

The League of United Latin American Citizens (LULAC), the Mexican-American Political Association (MAPA), and the Political Association of Spanish-Speaking Organizations (PASSO), to cite several more prominent examples of politically-oriented organizations, sponsor candidates and control votes. But the limited membership in such organizations attests that the Hispanic-American, in character with his strong sense of individualism and because of the social pressure and ridicule of his fellows, is typically not a joiner of political (or social) organizations.

Although the Hispano belongs to a minority confronted with problems, the problems he shares are not of equal magnitude, and the characteristics outlined above do not apply uniformly. Although Hispanic-Americans are Roman Catholic, some are more "faithful to the tenets," to use Gamio's words, and others are less so. In 1960 median years of school completed by Spanish surname persons over twenty-five years of age for the five states was 7.1, but ranged from a high of 8.6 in California to a low of 4.8 in Texas. Whereas 34.8 percent of all southwestern Spanish surname families had incomes under the $3,000 "poverty line," state percentages ranged from a low of 19.1 in California to a high of 54.6 in Texas.

Hispanic-Americans are slow to assimilate with the dominant population. Assimilation is especially slow among members of the lower socioeconomic class, whose adherence to the principles of *La Raza* is strongest; the desire for social and economic achievement (and other criteria by which assimilation is measured) becomes progressively stronger among the less numerous middle and upper classes. Perhaps no one example more forcefully demonstrates that the process of assimilation is a slow one than the retention of Spanish as the mother tongue by Hispanic people. That immigrants remain loyal to Mexico and desire not to become American citizens is further evidence. Statistics on intermarriage constitute still further evidence; in a study of the 1953 Birth Index for California, Bucchley found that endogamy among persons of Spanish surname was eighty-six percent complete, evidence of strong cohesion among the Hispanic minority.

If slow to assimilate, the Hispanic-American is, nonetheless, becoming "Anglicized." This process is perhaps most effectively demonstrated by comparing aspects of the Hispanic-American's culture with that of the Mexican in Mexico. There are, for example, differences between the two in religion. The Virgin of Guadalupe, patron saint of Mexico, is venerated among the Latin Americans of south Texas, but they "seem to lack the close personal attachment to her that is felt in Mexico." Said one Latin American:

> The Virgin of Guadalupe is very beautiful and she loves mankind but she lives in Mexico. Her people there keep her busy with their many sins. I do not think she has much time for the Texans. She is so far away.

Latin Americans of south Texas seek help instead from saints whose shrines are closer. Various Protestant sects have for some decades been actively proselytizing among the Hispanic population, and conversions to Protestantism appear to be greater among this group than among Mexicans in Mexico. Unlike the Mexican, the Hispanic-American is generally bilingual, speaking both English and Spanish. Incorporated into his Spanish are many words from English such as *aiscrin* (from ice cream), *lonchi* (from lunch), and *tiquete* (from ticket), words foreign to the inhabitant of Mexico. In Mexico individuals assume, without question, certain roles within the family, a practice which is breaking down in the Southwest. For example, it is considered improper for a woman to work outside the home in Mexico, but in the Southwest increasing numbers of Hispanic women are so employed. Madsen suggested that the Hispanic "lower-lower" class member of south Texas is "slightly more economically motivated than his Mexican counterpart." And Gamio and Burma stated that the Hispanic-American is more prone to organize socially than is the Mexican in Mexico.

HISPANIC COLONIZATION

Because of his unique attributes, the Hispanic-American is a member of a distinctive American minority. He is also a member of an old American minority, for Hispanic people have been a part of American society since the mid-nineteenth century. Indeed, Spaniards and Mexicans colonized the northern frontier of New Spain and Mexico long before it became the American Southwest.

Permanent colonization by Spaniards of their northern frontier began more than three and one-half centuries ago in an area known then as Nuevo Méjico—present-day northern New Mexico. In 1598 colonists led by Oñate set out from the frontier outpost salient, Santa Bárbara, for the upper valley of the Río Grande, to which they were attracted by reports of sedentary pueblo-dwelling Indians (Fig. 1). At one of the multi-storied adobe pueblos Oñate established his colony; the Franciscans who accompanied him set about building mission churches there and at other pueblos. In the decades which followed, presidios were built and garrisoned with soldiers, private land grants were issued, and civil pueblo communities known in New Mexico as villas were founded. Santa Fé was the earliest to be plotted (probably in the spring of 1610) and it was also the center of Spanish activity, surpassing in importance other villas such as Fernando de Taos (Taos), Santa Cruz, and Albuquerque. Save for a twelve year period following 1680, when the Spanish colonists were forced to abandon the upper Río Grande and retreat to the El Paso district (which had been settled by missionaries sent from the north in 1659), the upper Río Grande and its tributary valleys were continuously occupied from 1598 to the end of Mexican rule in the mid-nineteenth century.

A full century elapsed following Oñate's colonization before the second frontier area was permanently settled. This was the northern part of Pimería Alta, the upper country of the Pima Indians in present-day Arizona. Colonization of northern Pimería Alta came at the culmination of a century-long drive by missionaries north along the western slope of Mexico's Sierra Madre Occidental. In 1700 Mission San Xavier del Bac was founded south of present-day Tucson by the Jesuit leader Kino. Several other missions were established nearby, and following a revolt of the usually docile Pimas a presidio was erected at Tubac (1752). Franciscans replaced the Jesuits, who were expelled from Pimería Alta in 1767, and during their period of control a second presidio was built at Tucson (1776). Colonists seeking protection from the raids of Apache Indians were drawn to these presidios, and presidio-pueblo communities grew around the walls of each. Because of the formidable Apache, however, the history of northern Pimería Alta was one of continual abandonment and reoccupation of missions, ranchos (which were meanwhile granted), and other settlements, and by the time Gadsden purchased the area, effective occupation was limited to the two presidios located between the Gila River and the international boundary.

In the decade preceding the establishment of Mission San Xavier del Bac, at least one mission had a brief existence in what is today east Texas. But the permanent colonization of Texas (not including the El Paso district, which until the nineteenth century was considered part of Nuevo Méjico) awaited the settlement of Nacogdoches in 1716. Nacogdoches was the first of three early centers to which Franciscans and others travelled overland from New Spain to found missions and presidios. The second was the San Antonio center which dated from 1718 and included, in addition to missions and a presidio, a civil pueblo. The third center was founded in 1722 near the head of Lavaca Bay southeast of Victoria, but in 1749 it was reestablished on the west bank of the lower San Antonio River at Goliad. In the following decades several communities, including Laredo (1755), were settled north of the Río Grande in what was then the colony of Nuevo Santander. Besides these communities, numerous private land grants were issued between the Río Grande and the Nueces. Moreover, in the 1820s and 1830s contracts were made with empresarios for the settlement of colonists on grants of land in areas north and east of the Nueces. Although most empresarios were foreigners, several were Mexicans, the most successful being a rancher from Tamaulipas who introduced Mexican colonists to Victoria in 1824. By the mid-nineteenth century centers of Mexican colonization were widely scattered in Texas.

California was the last of the northern frontier areas to be colonized. In 1769 colonists traveling overland from the mission of Velicatá and by ship converged upon San Diego. Franciscans set about constructing a mission, and a presidio was also built. As the Spaniards moved northward along the coast, mission-presidio pairs were established within the next two decades at Monterey, San Francisco, and Santa Bárbara, in that order. Meanwhile, several civil pueblos, including San José (1777) and Los Angeles (1781), were platted, other missions were founded, and a few ranchos were granted. The important era of ranch granting, however, followed the shift to Mexican political control in 1821—a time when some 500 grants were issued. By contrast, under Mexican rule only one mission and one civil pueblo were established, the latter at Yerba Buena (1839), renamed San Francisco in 1847. With the exception of a relatively few Mexican ranchos in the Central Valley, areas which had been colonized by the end of the Mexican era were limited to the lowlands and mountain valleys of the coast.

Thus, in the territory and two states into which the Southwest was divided in the mid-nineteenth century, Spanish and Mexican settlements already established were numerous, and some were quite old. The total Mexican population was not large—an estimated 82,250. With approximately 60,000 Mexicans in 1850, New Mexico Territory was by far the most populous. Texas (including the El Paso district) and California had estimated Mexican populations of 13,750 and 7,500, respectively, although the population of California may actually have been triple the estimated 7,500 because of the so-called "Sonoran" miners who arrived and departed annually, a movement which was at its peak in 1850. Few Sonorans remained permanently in California, however, and they were not counted as part of California's resident Mexican group. Smallest was the population of northern Pimería Alta. When the purchase of that area was negotiated by James Gadsden in late 1853 only Tucson and Tubac were occupied; of these the larger was Tucson, but between them there were only 1,000 Mexicans.

With the largest and most firmly entrenched population of the Mexican frontier being in New Mexico, it is understandable that in an abortive truce called in 1847 before the conclusion of the Mexican War, Mexico was willing to cede California and to give up its claim to Texas (except for the area between the Nueces and Río Grande which it argued should be an internationalized buffer state), but it refused to cede New Mexico. Americans rejected this Mexican proposal, and in the treaty which both countries signed in 1848, Mexico was forced to cede all of New Mexico north of "the town called Paso," the northernmost large settlement of Chihuahua (present-day Ciudad Juárez), all of Texas north of the Río Grande, and all of California north of a line drawn one marine league south of the port of San Diego. The cession by Mexico of this vast tract of land, when added to that area south of the Gila purchased by Gadsden, brought under American jurisdiction some 82,250 Mexicans in widely scattered settlements. The result was the creation of a borderland.

For several decades prior to the borderland's creation, non-Mexicans had been arriving in the Southwest in numbers sufficient to engulf the Mexican. Non-Mexicans had been going to Texas since the 1820s, and by 1850 they constituted most of the 212,592 persons enumerated. Prompted by the discovery of gold in 1848, the flow to California occurred later, yet by 1850 even California had 92,597 people, most of whom were non-Mexicans. In New Mexico Territory the inflow of non-Mexicans was small, however. Although traders from the United States did go annually to Santa Fé beginning in the early 1820s, by 1850 the number of non-Mexicans was only 1,778 (of a total 61,547).

Following the turn of the nineteenth century, Hispanic settlement expanded on the northern periphery of the populous New Mexican settlement area. North of the dashed line, San Luis was founded on a small tributary to the Rio Grande in 1851, in 1854 Conejos was settled on a second tributary river, and from both San Luis and Conejos other small local villas were soon colonized. By 1861, when this corner of northeastern New Mexico Territory became a part of newly created Colorado Territory, Trinidad had also been added to the list of Hispanic communities. The northward thrust of New Mexicans in New Mexico Territory is significant because it resulted in permanent Hispanic colonization of the fifth southwestern state with a sizable Hispanic population, present-day Colorado.

Sustaining the colonization enterprises of Hispanos in Colorado was a population reservoir to the south which was growing by an excess of births over deaths. In this way and through immigration Hispanic numbers increased modestly in all of the Southwest in the latter nineteenth century. Not until the twentieth century did Hispanic numbers soar, however, a phenomenon attributed mainly to immigration. Although data on immigration suffer from manifold inadequacies, the number of recorded permanent-visa Mexican immigrants nevertheless gives some insight into the volume of flow of Mexicans to the United States. The breakdown by decade for the period after 1900 shows that during the 1920s alone nearly 500,000 immigrants arrived, and for the sixty year period over 1,000,000 arrived.

Some of the twentieth century immigrants settled in the nonsouthwestern states. They were attracted especially to cities of the Middle West—for example, to Detroit, where the Mexican colony first grew to "noticeable size" in 1918, and to Chicago, where the number of Mexicans apparently began to increase importantly the next year. Immigrants were also drawn to rural locales in the Midwestern states and to states such as Oklahoma, Kansas, Nebraska, and Wyoming. In the late 1920s McLean estimated that the nonsouthwestern Hispanic population had grown to between approximately 150,000 and 250,000. This was a temporary peak, for many returned to Mexico during the depression years of the 1930s, but in more recent decades they were once again going to the nonsouthwestern states.

The vast majority of immigrants in the twentieth century went to the southwestern states, however. Between 1910 and the early 1960s Texas and California received the largest number, the majority going to Texas in the early decades but to California more recently. Arizona, although it attracted more immigrants than California in the decade following 1910, decreased in relative importance as a destination and today ranks third to California and Texas in number of arrivals. Neither New Mexico nor Colorado was an important immigrant destination, and Colorado consistently had even fewer arrivals than New Mexico.

The influx of Mexican immigrants during the twentieth century contributed to a tremendous increase in numbers of Hispanic-Americans in the United States and especially in the Southwest, an increase which was also the result of high Hispanic birth rates. By 1960 the southwestern Hispanic population reached 3,464,999 (Table 1), and for the United States it was an estimated 4,000,000. After 1850 the number of non-Hispanic Americans in the Southwest also soared, to nearly 26,-000,000 by 1960. The Hispanic population was a minority in every state of the Southwest, and in the area as a whole Hispanos constituted 11.8 percent of the total population (Table 1).

Table 1.   Persons of Spanish Surname, by State, 1960

State	Spanish Surname Population	Percentage of Total Population
Arizona	194,356	14.9
California	1,426,538	9.1
Colorado	157,173	9.0
New Mexico	269,122	28.3
Texas	1,417,810	14.8
SOUTHWEST	3,464,999	11.8

Source: *U. S. Census of Population, 1960,* Vol. I, Chapter A, United States Summary, Table 9, and Vol. II, Persons of Spanish Surname, Table 1.

HISPANIC PATTERNS IN 1960

Initiated with the Hispanic colonization of the Southwest were processes which have shaped present-day Hispanic patterns. Before 1850 Spaniards and Mexicans pushed to the north where they planted settlements in the four present-day states which share a common border with Mexico. After 1850 Hispanic-Americans grew in number through immigration and high birth rates, and they expanded the limits of areas already settled. All the while they were increasingly outnumbered by a swelling non-Hispanic population. Thus, from processes such as initial demographic movement and colonization, subsequent immigration and areal expansion, and in-migration of non-Hispanic people, the Hispanic patterns of 1960 were created.

The twentieth century in-migration of Mexicans helped shape present-day Hispanic patterns in the Southwest. Persons born in Mexico went primarily to Texas and California, and by 1960 more than four-fifths of the total southwestern Hispanic population lived in these two states (Table 1). Thus, Hispanic numbers were relatively high in the "ends" of the Southwest, and relatively low in the middle states. Serving to "bolt down" the already heavy ends of the Southwest were the exceptionally large populations in Los Angeles and Bexar (San Antonio) counties.

Los Angeles and Bexar counties, with 576,716 and 257,090 Hispanos, respectively, represented one extreme in county populations. At the other extreme were six counties in Texas and one in California with no Hispanic-Americans. Between these two poles were the remaining 421 southwestern counties. These differences in county populations account for the highly variable local pattern.

In general, numbers of Hispanic people tend to decrease northward from the international border. With the exception of Loving and Borden counties in west central Texas, the seven counties with no Hispanic people were located distant from the border. Located equally distant from the border were counties with fewer than 500 Hispanos, but as county populations increased so, too, did proximity to the border, so that fourteen of the twenty-four counties which had populations greater than 30,000 were located within 200 miles (320 km.) of the border. Each of the other ten counties had a large urban center which undoubtedly attracted Hispanic-Americans.

Hispanic people as a percentage of the total population per county were generally low in areas such as coastal California where they had once been high, a reflection of more rapid increases in non-Hispanic people than in Hispanic people after 1850. But in two areas Hispanos had not been engulfed by non-Hispanos: north central New Mexico-south central Colorado, where Spaniards and Mexicans were the descendants of longtime colonists; and south Texas, where Mexican immigrants arrived in greater numbers than non-Mexicans during the present century. All twenty-one counties over three-fifths Hispanic in 1960 were in contiguous blocks in these two areas, and three of these (Mora, New Mexico, and Kenedy and Starr, Texas) were more than four-fifths Hispanic. These three counties held up one end of the scale of counties which graded from largely Hispanic to entirely non-Hispanic.

Hispanic percentages tend to decrease with increasing distance from the international border. The most conspicuous exception is north central New Mexico-south central Colorado. A second exception is San Benito County, California.

Each nonsouthwestern state had at least two counties with persons of Mexican stock, but large areas, notably the South, had relatively small numbers of first and second generation Mexicans. Census data are published only for counties with 1,000 or more persons of *foreign* stock, however, and the South lacks such persons. Contrasting with the South is the Middle West, where Mexican stock people were numerous. With 51,035 such individuals, Cook County, Illinois (including Chicago) was in a class by itself among the populous nonsouthwestern counties. Next in rank were two Midwestern counties, Lake, Indiana (including Gary and East Chicago) and Wayne, Michigan (including Detroit). Five of the seven counties with Mexican stock populations between 2,500 and 15,000, including Lake and Wayne, are located in the Middle West. The other two were Yakima County, Washington, and New York County, New York.

The overwhelming number of counties for which data are available wherein persons of Mexican stock accounted for less than one-half of one percent of the total population, and the otherwise low county percentages, are striking. The explanation is simply that relative to the non-Hispano, persons of Mexican stock were not numerous in the nonsouthwestern states, and in the few counties where they had numerical strength so, too, did non-Hispanic people. Yakima County is, of course, an exception, for there relatively high numbers (6,266) accounted for a very high nonsouthwestern percentage (4.3). But of all the nonsouthwestern counties, only four in addition to Yakima (Scotts Bluff, Nebraska; Washington, Idaho; Finney, Kansas; and Morrill, Nebraska) had percentages ranging between three and five, and Mexican

stock populations of these four were, by contrast, not very large.

THE HISPANIC LEGACY

Wherever Hispanic people settled, they have left their imprint in one form or another. In the nonsouthwestern states, for example, Roman Catholic churches attended by Hispanos have been named for the Virgin of Guadalupe, restaurants catering to Hispanos advertise their "Mexican food," and newspapers printed in Spanish for Hispanos are sold on the newsstands. However, in the Southwest where Spaniards and Mexicans have been longtime residents, examples of the Hispanic imprint are many times more numerous. It is in these states that the Hispanic legacy is especially rich, and "the Spanish character" has been "indelibly imprinted."

One of the more tangible aspects of the southwestern legacy is the settlement institutions prescribed for colonization of frontier areas in Spanish and Mexican law. First were the missions, which in New Mexico were churches built at Indian pueblos in much the same adobe and protruding ceiling-beam-type architecture used by the Indians. In California and Texas the missions were larger complexes, including the churches and other structures, with a quadrilateral ground plan. Accompanying the missions were presidios or fortresses garrisoned with soldiers. Grants of land, called civil pueblos, were issued to colonists who were to till the pueblo's land and live in its village platted on a rectangular grid around a central plaza. Finally, private land grants were issued to individuals, the most common being the rancho, which was made for stock raising purposes. Each of these institutions was taken to each of the four frontier areas of New Mexico, Pimería Alta, Texas, and California prior to the mid-nineteenth century.

Where they have endured to the present these institutions are visible manifestations of the Hispanic legacy. They have also played important roles in shaping present-day patterns of settlement. For example, certain missions and presidios served as foci around which large communities grew. Thus, communities which had evolved around the Tucson presidio and around the San Buenaventura mission during the Spanish-Mexican eras continued to grow into the Anglo-Hispano cities of Tucson, Arizona, and Ventura, California. Civil pueblos also served as foci for growth. San Antonio, Santa Fe, Albuquerque, San Jose, and Los Angeles were all Spanish civil pueblos, and San Francisco was a Mexican civil pueblo. Cities which grew out of civil pueblos have a central plaza with a church and sometimes a palace, as at Santa Fe. Plotted out from the plaza is a rectangular street pattern which, in some instances, has spread through the remainder of the community. Like civil pueblos, ranchos shaped various patterns; in greater Los Angeles, for example, Nelson found rancho boundaries persisting as boundaries of private land ownership, routes for roads, political boundaries (especially those of counties), railroad right of ways, power line easements, and drainage ditches.

The mission complexes characteristic of California and Texas were built in a style of architecture which has come to be known as "Spanish Colonial." Thus, the Hispanic legacy is also manifested in a tangible way in the Spanish Colonial school which has had an impact on present-day southwestern architecture. Quoting Judson:

Everywhere nowadays we see in domestic, civic and ecclesiastic buildings traces of mission influence. The complicated curving parapet or gable; the generous, wide-spreading, cloistered corridor; the patio; the small-domed, square tower; the embrasure-like arched windows ... are all features borrowed from the missions. ...

Among the more intangible aspects of the Hispanic legacy is language. Thousands of words have come from Spanish to English. So much a part of English are words such as banana, canoe, mosquito, and tobacco that people do not recognize them as being of Spanish origin. Just where these more common words were borrowed from Spanish is difficult to say, beyond the general statement that most borrowing took place in North America, but the Southwest has been important as an area of contact in the process of word borrowing from Spanish. Bentley noted this in his study of some

400 words which are less familiar in English, many of which were likely borrowed in the Southwest. Included in Bentley's study are terms for landforms such as canyon (from *cañón*), arroyo, and barranca; words for kinds of vegetation, such as chaparral, mesquite, and chamisal; words for animals and birds, such as burro and *tecolote;* words used in dress, including sombrero, reboso, and poncho; and words for foods, such as frijoles, garbanzos, and tortillas.

Literally hundreds of Spanish-language words are used in the Southwest as names of rivers, lakes, mountains, valleys, passes, cities, towns, streets, counties, and even states. In the five southwestern states there are over 1,000 Spanish-language names for towns and cities alone. Fully one-fourth of all counties in the five states, 107 of 421, have names considered linguistically to be Spanish. ...

The Hispanic legacy is rich in both its intangible and tangible aspects. It is to this legacy, and to a distinctive present-day minority population, that the Anglo-American population is exposed in the Southwest. Just as the Hispanic-American has been Anglicized, the Anglo-American has been "Hispanicized." For example, the Anglo-American has borrowed words from Spanish—adobe, bronco, corral, fandango, olla, paisano, and pinto, to name but a few. He has designated his mountains, his counties, his cities and towns with Spanish-language terms. Numerous are the communities such as two small towns in central Santa Barbara County, California—Los Olivos and Los Alamos—which were founded and named by Anglo-Americans, not Hispanic-Americans. Numerous, too, are the suburban plats which have street names taken from Spanish. The Anglo-American has borrowed from Spanish Colonial architecture in constructing his public buildings and homes. The Anglo-American has even incorporated "Mexican" food items into his diet: written alongside hamburgers and hot dogs in southwestern cafes and restaurants are tacos, enchiladas, tamales, and burritos. ...

DELIMITING THE BORDERLAND

It was assumed that the criteria for determining whether southwestern counties have significant

Hispanic populations could also be applied to the nonsouthwestern counties. Because Mexican stock represent only 45.183 percent of the total Hispanic population in nonsouthwestern counties, all Mexican stock numbers were increased by 54.817 percent, and these values were used to calculate percentages of the total population. Six nonsouthwestern counties met the 500 and five percent minima (Table 2). As none of the six was contiguous to any of the five southwestern states, the possibility that the borderland should extend beyond a southwestern state boundary in those places where it approached such a boundary was omitted. This did not exclude the possibility that these counties should be considered as outliers of the borderland, however, but for reasons noted below such as length of settlement, they were not.

In the southwestern counties, the number and percentage of Spanish surname people tend to decrease with increasing distance from the Mexican boundary. Thus, counties having Hispanic numbers and percentages greater than 500 and five in 1960 were in the southern parts of the five southwestern states, and those below these minima were in the northern parts. The first step in delimiting the borderland was to exclude those counties in northern California, Colorado, and Texas which did not meet the minimum criteria. For the same reason, four nonborderland inliers were also placed outside the borderland, although only six of the eight counties composing these inliers had both fewer than 500 Hispanic people and Hispanic percentages under five: Borden, Crane, Gillespie, Llano, Loving, and Yoakum counties, all in Texas.

Following this initial step, counties with fewer than 500 Spanish surname people but with Hispanic percentages greater than five were considered. Ten of the twenty-one counties in this status were eliminated from the borderland because of their contiguity to the large blocks of nonborderland counties in California, Colorado, and Texas. The other eleven counties were included simply because of their location within what was clearly the borderland.

Counties with Hispanic percentages under five, but whose number of Hispanic-Americans was in excess of 500 were accounted for next. Places were checked in all such counties adjacent to those meeting major criteria to determine whether concentrations of 500 or more Hispanic people existed which should be included within the borderland. Thus, in the inlier that straddles the Texas-New Mexican boundary, *Lovington* and *Hobbs* in Lea County, New Mexico, with Hispanic populations numbering 877 and 507, respectively, were considered within the borderland, whereas other places in Lea and Andrews counties, lacking a minimum of 500 Hispanic-Americans, were not. Places with 500 or more Hispanic people in counties where less than five percent of the people were Hispanic were important in the process of delimiting the borderland in all states save Arizona. . . .

Table 2. **Nonsouthwestern Counties with Minimum Hispanic Values, as Adjusted, 1960**

County	Total Hispanic Population[a]	Percentage of Total Population
Scotts Bluff, Nebraska	3,542	10.48
Yakima, Washington	13,863	9.55
Washington, Idaho	710	8.47
Finney, Kansas	1,281	7.96
Morrill, Nebraska	542	7.68
Malheur, Oregon	1,252	5.50

Source: *U. S. Census of Population, 1960*, Vol. I, Chapter A, State Parts, Table 6, and Chapter C, State Parts, Table 89.
[a]Mexican stock increased by 54.8 percent.

Amid the otherwise nonborderland counties in northern Texas and Colorado were several counties which met the minimum criteria. These counties were the basis for delimiting three borderland outliers. Ellis County in Texas met the minimum criteria and was the *raison d'être* for the outlier which includes not only *Ennis*, Ellis County's major Hispanic center, but *Dallas, Fort Worth, Denton,* and *McKinney*. The other two outliers were located in north central Colorado (including *Denver, Englewood, Lakewood, Boulder, Longmont, Fort Collins, Greeley, Brush,* and *Brighton*) and in west central Colorado (including *Fruita, Grand Junction, Paonia, Delta, Montrose,* and *Uravan*).

Large parts of counties otherwise meeting the major criteria were not included within the borderland. High mountain and desert parts of counties in eastern and southern California are good examples. The exclusion of these and other such areas is explained by the dearth of Hispanic (or any other) inhabitants. Moreover, a large area in northern Arizona has been deleted from the borderland because it contains several large Indian reservations. These two reasons for deletion loomed large in the actual drawing of the borderland boundary.

A CULTURE REGION

As delimited above the borderland is defined in terms of population criteria, but the borderland is more than the region of greatest Hispanic population concentration. Hispanic people possess a distinctive culture, and because the borderland is where this minority is concentrated, it follows that this is also where the intensity of Hispanic culture is greatest. Moreover, the borderland is where Hispanic people have been longtime colonists. It is where the Hispanic legacy is richest. It is where Anglos have been "Hispanicized." The borderland is a culture region.

This is why the six nonsouthwestern counties were not delimited as distant outliers of the borderland. It is true that the Hispanic population concentrations and corresponding cultural intensities of these counties were of greater relative importance, but the Hispanic residents of Scotts Bluff County or Yakima County or Washington County, unlike their counterparts in the borderland counties, have settled there in relatively recent times. No earlier generations of Hispanic people left a legacy in these counties. The local residents have not been significantly influenced by the Hispanic-American.

As a culture region, one would expect positive spatial correlations between the borderland and those aspects of the Hispanic legacy or present-day culture which have been mapped. Such correlations exist. To cite several examples, of the forty Roman Catholic missions which existed among the Indians of California, Arizona, New Mexico, and Texas between 1567 and 1861, thirty-seven were within the borderland. Raup and Pounds determined that the present-day distribution of Spanish-language toponyms in California was a highly

littoral phenomenon and was limited largely to the southern half of the state. With only minor exceptions the Raup-Pounds toponym pattern lies entirely within the California segment of the borderland. In their studies of religious patterns in the United States, Zelinsky and Gaustad recognized regional aspects of the largely Hispanic southwestern Roman Catholic population. Unmistakable is the correlation between the borderland and Zelinsky's "Spanish Catholic" Region; less apparent is the positive correlation between Gaustad's Roman Catholic pattern and the borderland because Gaustad's pattern is based on county units.

BORDERLAND IMPLICATIONS

The borderland places an important American minority into its spatial context. It also has meaningful areal implications for Hispanic-Americans and the larger American society. An important characteristic of the Hispanic population is that its members do not readily assimilate with the majority population. The reasons for this are numerous: residential segregation, employment in low grade occupations, and discrimination all contribute to retard assimilation. But, does the borderland provide insights as to why assimilation is slow?

Several reasons indicate that it does:

1) The borderland is the region where the large Hispanic population is concentrated, and this concentration retards assimilation.

2) The borderland is the region of greatest Hispanic cultural intensity. It is where Spanish is spoken, Spanish-language place names are widespread, and cities have grown out of civil pueblos—all factors which make the borderland an environment familiar to Hispanic-Americans and retard assimilation.

3) The borderland lies adjacent to Mexico, from which it is separated by a long land boundary, but by its very nature this boundary is no barrier; it is crossed and recrossed by Hispanic-Americans and Mexicans who maintain close contact, and in so doing retard assimilation.

4) The number of immigrants has soared in the twentieth century to increase decidedly the number of Mexicans who have joined the Hispanic population. This movement has re-inforced the institutions of Hispanic culture in the borderland. Furthermore, this influx has been recent, and time is a critical factor in the assimilation process.

5) The borderland was colonized when it was a part of New Spain and Mexico. To quote McWilliams, "we adopted the Spanish-speaking minority; they did not adopt us." To some, especially the "Spanish-American" of New Mexico and Colorado, this is an important justification for the retention of their culture.

For all these reasons, not least of which is sheer propinquity to Mexico, the borderland helps to explain the slowness of assimilation, an implication of significance for the Hispanic-American.

The Hispanic-American is disadvantaged relative to the majority population. He faces problems which are social, economic, and political in nature. The implication for the Hispanic-American (and for all of American society) is that the borderland is the areal focus of these problems.

The borderland has implications for the non-Hispanic-American. The Anglo-American resident of the borderland, because of exposure to Hispanic people and culture, has to a degree been "Hispanicized." He has selectively adopted certain Hispanic ways of life. But, held within the borderland is a wealth of Hispanic traditions and attitudes waiting to be tapped by the Anglo-American throughout the United States. . . .

JOSÉ HERNANDEZ ALVEREZ

José Hernandez Alverez (Population and Urban Research Institute of International Studies, University of California at Berkeley) utilizes his experience in migration studies to describe the patterns of migration from Mexico to the United States in the first half of the twentieth century. Most of this migration went to the Golden State, and thus set the stage for the barrio *sub-culture of post-1945 California. By permission of the author, the* JOURNAL OF INTER-AMERICAN STUDIES, *and the University of Miami Press.*

A Demographic Profile Of The Mexican Immigration To The United States, 1910–1950

During the first half of the present century, about one million Mexicans were involved in a singular instance of large scale entry into the United States. Arriving just before the influx of foreigners abated sharply, they provide an example of recent immigration. In contrast to the experience of other groups entering one or more generations before, Mexican settlement occurred during the drastic changes caused by rapid eco-nomic growth and depression, by two world wars and the nation's reorganization for modern living. Nor did the newcomers from the South follow the traditional pattern of residence and occupation. Instead of locating in the densely urban and industrial Northeast of the United States, they flowed into rural areas in the Southwest, working in agriculture, railroad construction and related activities. Except for Canadian immigrants, the

Mexicans were the only major immigrant group having relatively easy access to the home country by an overland route. Lastly, their distinctively Latin American culture has added novelty to history of immigration to the United States.

These unique features combine to provide an interesting and valuable opportunity for a demographic case study of issues such as geographic distribution, urbanization, language, education and occupational mobility. Moreover, the availability of census materials for decennial intervals from 1910 to 1950 facilitates longitudinal comparisons. It also aids in research concerning the evolution of the immigrant family structure. The Mexican group offers the advantage of having two clearly distinguishable generations during the period just mentioned. This situation permits the application of the developmental theory of family life to the entire population, thereby rendering the discovery of changes more meaningful. An approach of this kind appears to be in keeping with the general perspective of the following analysis. Our objective is to present a concise overview of as many demographic characteristics as possible, providing a single picture of the Mexican immigrant population which could serve as a point of departure for more detailed research.

GEOGRAPHIC DISPERSAL AND CONCENTRATION

In 1910 about two hundred thousand persons born in Mexico were living in the United States, mainly concentrated in the territories of Arizona and New Mexico. During the next twenty years the Mexican immigrant group increased by at least three times. By 1930, close to a million and a half persons were enumerated as born in Mexico or of Mexican parentage. At that time slightly less than 90 percent were living in the states of Arizona, California, Colorado, New Mexico and Texas. This proportion remained approximately the same up to 1950. Clearly, the primary concentration of persons of Mexican descent has been and continues to be located in the states closest to the Mexican border. In the present article, for purposes of convenience, we have chosen to call this five-state area "the Southwest."

Notable variations occurred in the spatial distribution of Mexicans within the Southwest during the period under investigation. In general, the Mexican population of California and Colorado increased at least twice as rapidly as that of Texas and New Mexico. From 1920 to 1930, the average annual increase in California was 20.4 percent and in Colorado 30.2 percent. Meanwhile the average rate of increase in Texas was 7.6 yearly and a similar percentage was recorded in New Mexico. In Arizona, only a slight increase took place during the same decade. These differences are largely due to the current of internal migration among Mexicans already living in the states of Arizona, New Mexico and Texas. This movement reached westward to the Pacific Ocean and northward to the Rocky Mountain area.

From 1910 to 1950, geographic dispersal also occurred in a direction extending northeastward to Michigan. The balance of Mexicans living outside the Southwest settled along this line of migration. Although this group never comprised more than 10 percent of the national total, their rates of increase were considerably higher than those in California and Colorado. The sudden appearance of Mexican immigrants in Illinois, Indiana, Kansas and Michigan principally represented a response to the availability of employment. About 50 percent of the Midwest settlers found jobs in manufacturing industries which were expanding rapidly in Chicago, Detroit and Gary. Similarly, opportunities in sugar beet farming and railroad construction, repair and maintenance attracted Mexicans to the rural areas of the states mentioned.

At first glance, one might expect a process of replacement in the fan of settlement. According to this hypothesis, earlier immigrants would tend to move away from traditional areas of concentration. Their experience and knowledge of the receiving nation would provide an aid and incentive for pioneering new settlements. Meanwhile, the vacancies in employment and housing left by this group would await later newcomers.

The data provided by the 1930 Census appear to disprove this conjecture. In the *Reports on Population,* replies to the question concerning year of immigration were divided into chronological groups. This procedure permits an analysis of the rates of immigrants arriving in a given period of time according to their place of residence in 1930. Among persons immigrating from 1925 to 1930 a considerably higher rate settled in the Midwest than among those who entered before 1910. Within the Southwest the rates for Arizona, New Mexico and Texas generally decline from 1911 to 1930, while successively higher rates appear in California and Colorado. About a third of the latest arrivals were residents of California, the largest proportion claimed by any state. This stands in striking contrast to the group entering the United States before 1900, 65 percent of whom were living in Texas in 1930.

Several suggestions could be made in order to explain the tendency of earlier immigrants to remain in Arizona, New Mexico and Texas while late arrivals went through and beyond these states. In general, economic opportunities outside traditional centers of concentration did not develop until the 1920s. Persons who entered the United States during this decade may have been faced with a saturation of opportunities in the original areas of settlement. They were younger and may have been attracted by the possibility of living elsewhere. These factors seem to be associated with the recruitment of Mexican laborers in cities such as San Antonio and El Paso for work outside Texas. The migration "tunnel" seems to have been reinforced by the diffusion of knowledge in Mexico concerning job opportunities in the Midwest and in California and Colorado. One of the primary vehicles of this communication was the labor contractor who traveled through Mexico seeking workers.

Recruitment of Mexican workers was almost exclusively for jobs which would relegate them to life in rural areas: agriculture, mining and railroad work. On the basis of the pattern of settlement just described one might infer that later immigrants became residents of rural areas, whereas the vast majority of those entering the United States at the turn of the century were urban dwellers. According to the statistics presented both of these assumptions seem incorrect. At one extreme, the least urban were persons immigrating before 1900, while the highest proportion of city residents occurred among the latest newcomers, those who arrived from 1925 to 1930. It must be noted, however, that the difference is not great; a range of only 7.8 percent appears among the various time intervals according to urban or rural residence in 1930. As a consistent pattern, slightly more Mexicans settled in urban areas and the urban immigrant population contained a slightly greater proportion of recent arrivals than the rural counterpart.

During the era of economic depression, from 1930 to 1940, decreases in the number of persons of Mexican birth or descent were recorded throughout the United States. The demand for immigrant labor had virtually ceased and at the beginning of this decade the entry of Mexicans diminished sharply. As hard times continued, a substantial return migration occurred, receiving an added impulse as a result of mechanical innovations in agricultural industries. This reverse movement seems to have ended after 1940; however, large-scale immigration to the United States has never been renewed. Hence, Mexicans who were residents of the United States in 1950 were largely those comprising the core that remained during the depression years and their children.

Perhaps the most important change in the geographic distribution of Mexicans in the United States from 1930 to 1950 was rapid and substantial urbanization. As indicated, immigrants arriving from 1900 to 1930 increasingly settled in urban areas; by 1930, 57.5 percent of the national total were living in cities. This trend continued and became strong during World War II and the early postwar years. As a result, in 1950 more than 70 percent of the Mexican immigrant population and their children were classified as urban dwellers. Thus, as the nationality group under study consolidated its establishment in the United States, surviving a reverse migration and producing a second generation, it also shifted away from a rural way of life.

LANGUAGE AND EDUCATION

In 1930, 55 percent of the Mexican immigrant population could not speak English. Compared with rates among other nationality groups, this percentage was extraordinarily high. However, a comparison of this nature must be qualified by noting that almost all the other immigrant groups arrived before the Mexican immigration had begun. Had a tabulation been made two or three decades before, probably data similar to the Mexican statistics of 1930 would have been gathered among Poles, Italians and Russians. Even in 1930, local concentrations of other immigrants had relatively high rates of inability to speak English. Twenty percent of the foreign-born Italian population of Rhode Island could not speak English. Slightly lower measures were recorded among French-Canadians in Maine, the Polish in the Midwest, the Finns in Michigan and Minnesota, and the Japanese living in the far west.

The language data compiled in 1930 reveal important geographic variations among Mexican immigrants. The highest rates of inability to speak English (between 57.6 and 66.2 percent) correspond to long-established settlements: Arizona, New Mexico and Texas. This is not surprising, in view of the frequent use of Spanish in many communities located in these states. The same measure was lower in California and Colorado; in the Midwest rates varied from 43.8 to 49.5 percent. Probably, immigrants who ventured forth to new areas found that knowledge of English was an important asset and the inability to communicate with the larger society a great liability. Secondly, higher rates of intermarriage with other nationality groups outside the Southwest may have contributed to a lowering of the proportion of persons unable to speak English.

Apart from the issue of regional variations, perhaps the most important implication of high rates of inability to speak English for Mexican family life is the fact that they coincided with an economic depression. While members of the second generation were being reared in the 1930s, their parents probably had extraordinary difficulties finding and keeping employment. Inability to speak English undoubtedly increased this hardship. Given these circumstances, we can assume that the language barrier represented a major impelling force for returning to Mexico. This would seem to be particularly true of late immigrants, many of whom may

not have been established by the onset of hard times.

According to the 1940 Census, relatively few Mexican immigrants raised their children with English as the prevailing language at home. This implies that, in contrast to the experience of other nationality groups, the mother language largely remained the medium of expression between generations. Therefore we could expect a different set of sociological consequences affecting the parent-child relationship as a result of the use of the host country's language. Unfortunately, data concerning bilingualism are not available; these statistics might qualify and illuminate the issue of language. The Census definition, "the principal language spoken in the home of the person in his earliest childhood," does not preclude the possibility of learning English, nor the total loss of the nationality tongue.

In addition to the difficulty concerning bilingualism, estimates of variations in the use of English as a mother tongue according to sex, urban-rural residence, regions, divisions and states are liable to a large degree of error: no population base by nationality was given for the detailed analysis of mother languages in the 1940 Census. Hence, we do not know how many persons born in Mexico or of Mexican parentage were included in the total whose mother tongue was Spanish in a given location. Within these limitations, we find that 718,980 nativeborn persons of native parentage were enumerated as having had Spanish as a mother tongue. Approximately 55 percent were living in rural areas, and 88 percent were concentrated in the South and West. The coincidence of urban-rural and regional characteristics seems to indicate that a large measure of this group consisted of third generation Mexican-Americans and persons of Mexican descent in succeeding generations. Hence, there is some statistical basis for assuming that the use of Spanish as a means of communication is not limited to the second generation.

More impressionistic evidence, such as the continuing use of Spanish in public services (radio broadcasting stations, newspapers and the like) seems to indicate that the mother language has remained an important, if not the primary medium of expression within the Mexican community. It is also likely that failure to speak English effectively has had serious implications for the education of the Mexican nationality group outside those areas where an adequate bilingual school system is available. In order to evaluate the significance of this relation, it seems important to review the scholastic achievement data for the close of the period under study.

According to the 1950 Census, about half of the foreign-born Mexican male population of the United States, fourteen years of age or older had not reached the fourth grade of elementary school. The median years of school completed varied considerably by region, urban-rural residence and age. The lowest medians correspond to immigrants forty-five years of age and older, living in rural farm areas. By way of contrast, among younger immigrants in Los Angeles, more than half had completed eight years of elementary school, the number generally considered the equivalent of a primary education in the United States.

Age differentials were not so sharply defined in the second generation and their scholastic achievement was clearly greater than that of the first. However, a considerable difference appears between city and farm and between West and South. In urban areas throughout the United States about half of the native-born had at least an elementary school education. By way of contrast, in the rural areas of the South (principally Texas), 22 percent of the second generation had never attended school. While much lower than its rural counterpart, the measure of 10 percent with no schooling in Southern cities is notably higher than the measure of 3 percent in the urban areas of the West. Hence, although as a group the second generation had surpassed the first in scholastic achievement, important segments remained at low educational levels.

At mid-century the immigrants' children who were reaching adulthood and forming families encountered a highly competitive labor market and a rapid upgrading of educational requirements for employment. Whereas their parents may have been able to earn a living with an elementary schooling, it now became important to obtain a high-school degree and, if possible, a college or university education. The educational attainment of the second generation was clearly an advance over the record for Mexican immigrants and compared favorably with that of ethnic groups with Spanish surname. However, compared with the total United States population and the second generation of other nationality groups, the Mexican-Americans scored exceedingly low. Thus, a crucial element in the complex of social and economic handicaps which beset them in the competition for employment was an unfavorable level of training. The fact that the second generation of other nationality groups scored higher than the national total seems to provide evidence that the retention of Spanish as the only or predominant language among Mexicans seriously affected their educational as well as their economic life chances.

OCCUPATIONAL AND ECONOMIC SITUATION

In order to clarify the implications of the disadvantage just described it seems important to review briefly some of the economic and employment data available for the period under investigation. The census taken in 1930 provided data in regard to the occupational distribution of the entire Mexican ethnic group, including the third and succeeding generations. These statistics indicate that most male workers of Mexican birth or ancestry were employed in the same occupations which had been an influential factor in the pattern and chronology of settlement of the first generation. Throughout the United States, agriculture, manufacturing and transportation (principally railroad work) were the leading types of employment. Mining, trade and domestic service proved to be residual classifications, while very few Mexicans were employed in public services and as clerical and professional personnel.

While the pattern just described generally applies to the Southwest, individual states show important variations. In Colorado, New Mexico and Texas, about half or more of the Mexicans were engaged in farming, a proportion higher than that in the United States as a whole. The balance of workers in Colorado also had typically rural jobs;

approximately one quarter were employed in mining and railroad work. By way of contrast, in Texas and New Mexico non-agricultural workers tended to be working in characteristically urban occupations, such as manufacturing and trade. Moreover, the proportion of farm owners and tenants was significantly higher. These differences appear to be a consequence of the relative length of establishment. In New Mexico, Texas as well as Arizona the early newcomers and their children had succeeded in obtaining property and in the peripheral services demanded by the Mexican *colonia* itself, enterprises such as barber shops, grocery stores and so forth.

The employment situation in California, a more recent settlement, differed strikingly from that of Colorado. There, many Mexicans were engaged in manufacturing, a typically urban occupation, and in construction. As a unit, these classifications overshadowed agriculture and mining. California also had the highest percentage of transportation workers not employed in railroad jobs. Thus, the original area of Mexican settlement contained a mixture of many rural workers and an assortment of urban occupations. In areas characterized by late immigration, there were extremes: Colorado, with a very large proportion of farmers and miners, California with numerous urban workers.

In the Midwestern states (Illinois, Indiana, Kansas and Michigan) there were scarcely any farmers. Here, more than half of the employed labor force were engaged in manufacturing, with approximately 30 percent working in iron and steel industries. Railroad construction, repair and maintenance constituted the only other major occupational category, taking up the balance of workers, except for a scattering of individuals in domestic service and trade. The social implications of this economic situation have been summarized as follows:

Here the colony is strikingly similar to that of the typical "foreign" settlement. ... Mexicans in Chicago and Detroit work with members of other nationality groups in highly mechanized industries. ... The boundaries of the *colonia* are not sharply defined and, in some cases, have already disappeared.

It will be recalled that this area of settlement was also characterized by late immigration, a large proportion of urban residents, intermarriage with other nationality groups and the most extensive adoption of the English language. Although only one-tenth of the United States total, the Mexican community in the Midwest provides an interesting subject for further research. A unique phenomenon within the Mexican population of the United States, it also constitutes the only group which developed in an environment similar to that of the large majority of immigrants in the United States.

The consensus of writers on the subject of Mexican immigrants in the Southwest is that their occupations in 1930 were not highly paid. Unfortunately, the 1930 census did not provide information in regard to income in the two reports concerning the foreign stock; hence, it is difficult to gauge the economic standing of the Southwest communities accurately. In the census taken ten years later, statistics were gathered concerning the value and tenure of housing. In lieu of information about occupations and income, these data provide a secondary index of the economic situation at the close of the depression years.

In 1940, about two-thirds of the population of Mexican immigrants and their children were living in rented housing. More than half of this segment paid less than ten dollars monthly rent. Assuming these figures as a point of departure, it is clear that the depression had kept or relegated the majority of Mexicans to life in some of the nation's poorest dwellings. The 1940 Census information for housing in the United States as a whole indicates that only a quarter of all tenant-occupied dwellings were renting for less than ten dollars; in urban and rural-nonfarm areas this measure was even smaller (17.4 percent). Similarly, in the renting group of the Mexican population only 13 percent spent twenty dollars a month or more for housing. By way of contrast, about half of the United States dwellings were rented for at least twenty dollars.

A similar situation appears in regard to the 30 percent of the Mexican population who were living in owner-occupied housing. In this instance, about 70 percent were living in structures valued at less than $1,000. Meanwhile, in the United States, more than 70 percent of owner-occupied dwelling had values greater than $1,000, with approximately half of the homes in urban and rural-nonfarm areas valued at more than $3,000. Thus, whether owning or renting, the Mexicans appear to have had a fairly low economic standing. Perhaps the most comparable group was that of the Negroes in urban and rural-nonfarm areas of the South. About 70 percent of the dwellings with tenants from this group were classified as renting for less than ten dollars monthly. Even in this instance, Negro rentals in metropolitan districts were substantially higher than the figure just given.

Within the Mexican nationality group generational and geographic variations appear in the data concerning housing in 1940. In general, succeedingly higher rent categories were associated with lower ratios of native to foreign born. This may imply that the second generation was experiencing greater economic hardships. Since many of the immigrants' children were beginning their own family cycle, this explanation is plausible. The same tendency in the statistics may also indicate differential birth rates among socio-economic classes of Mexican immigrants. Perhaps lower-class households were characterized by larger families. In view of the relatively young age of the second generation in certain areas of the United States, differentials in fertility seem equally plausible. These conjectures seem to merit more intensive research of a sociological nature; they bear a close relationship to the development of the Mexican family life cycle as well as to the problems which Mexicans have encountered in the United States.

Unfortunately, the 1940 Census reports provide only limited information for housing among Mexicans at regional and state levels. The data available for the city of Los Angeles follow the national configuration with two exceptions. A higher percentage of the population, both native and foreign-born, lived in rented housing. The scale of monthly rents was one step higher than the national measures and a wider distribution prevailed in the values of owner-occupied dwellings. These

findings indicate that the national statistics were probably lowered by the value of property in rural areas. They also seem to show that Mexicans living in metropolitan districts had a slightly higher social and economic standing than those living in other areas.

It will be recalled that during the decade, 1940 to 1950, many Mexicans moved to the urban centers of the United States. The occupational data which were gathered after this migration clearly demonstrate the effects of the change. In 1950, slightly more than 67 percent of employed males of both generations were living in cities. The types of employment held by these workers as well as by rural dwellers have been summarized. In urban areas, the employed labor force was characteristically scattered among the seven major divisions of urban work. The largest concentrations were at the semi-skilled levels. However, a substantial percentage, about a quarter of each nativity and age group, was composed of white-collar workers, craftsmen and professionals. By way of contrast, the rural labor force was still largely concentrated in the category of farm laborers. Even in this instance, many Mexicans were employed in jobs other than farm labor. Thus, a significant shift had occurred away from marginal employment and toward the consolidation of the nationality group in the United States social and economic life.

Important variations appear by nativity and age. In urban areas, the second generation shows a greater tendency toward clerical, sales and kindred occupations. There are also larger concentrations of native-born persons in the "operative" category. In rural areas, proportionately more immigrants were employed as farm laborers, whereas their children were more frequently engaged in occupations other than agriculture. A significant percentage of the native-born from ages 14 to 25 were working as unpaid family farm workers.

These occupational trends are reflected in the data concerning income. The newly emerging second generation and older immigrants earned considerably less than persons 25 to 44 years of age in both generations. Perhaps underemployment and marginal occupational activities account for this difference. In urban areas, the middle-aged native-born group received slightly less income than the same age group in the first generation.

It should be noted, however, that even in the case of urban immigrants from ages 25 to 44, whose median income was higher than other age and nativity groups, the amount received was not great, compared with the earnings of the general population. At mid-century, more than half of the Mexican nationality group in the United States were earning less than $2,000 yearly. In some areas and age categories, annual income was considerably less. Clearly, consolidation had not involved extraordinary economic gains for the Mexican population as a whole.

SUMMARY AND CONCLUSIONS

In the present article, an endeavor has been made to present a concise overview of the demographic data available for Mexican immigrants to the United States during the first half of the present century. Within this context, several population patterns appear:

(1) During the period of heaviest immigration (1910-1930), a geographic dispersal took place in the form of a fan of settlement, radiating about the original center of migration. This movement was disproportionately westward, to California, where employment was available for non-skilled and semi-skilled workers on produce farms and in large cities such as Los Angeles. However, an important line of settlement extended Northeastward, primarily associated with railroad construction and urban industry. Although a primary factor in the early stages of the immigration was labor recruitment for agricultural enterprises, its influence seems to have diminished as the movement developed. Proportionately more late arrivals settled in urban areas than earlier immigrants. Later immigrants also had a greater tendency to venture forth beyond the Southwest. These trends are reflected in the regional differences which appear in the ratio of native to foreign-born. At the close of large-scale immigration

in 1930, this measure was highest in urban areas and in new settlements outside of Texas, New Mexico and Arizona.

(2) From 1930 on, Mexicans of both generations became involved in an extensive process of urbanization; by 1950 only 30 percent remained living in rural areas. Proportionately more native-born persons migrated and their migration coincided with the development of the second generation in urban areas. As a result, the urban Mexican population in the early 1940s was characterized by a large number of second generation persons reaching adolescence and early adulthood. Another consequence was the emergence of the third generation beginning about 1950, the date which marks the virtual conclusion of the immigrant family life cycle and the start of the period of consolidation. Some urban centers, notably Chicago, were out of phase with the general urban pattern. In these areas, which were characterized by late immigration, the emergence of the second generation was a post-World War II phenomenon. Meanwhile, in rural areas, the pattern of generational change took place earlier and was marked by the loss of second generation persons by way of migration to cities.

(3) These regional variations in the Mexican family life cycle must be considered in relation to differences in the male-female ratio. In general, males exceeded females in the immigrant population; this disproportion was greater in rural areas, indicating a greater probability of a mixed generational or nationality marriage. A pattern similar to the general trend in rural areas appears in urban areas outside the Southwest, particularly in the Midwest. In this instance, intermarriage with other nationality groups seems to have been more common.

(4) Large differences do not appear among generations in regard to the use of English as the primary language of communication. It would seem as if the language barrier was an important factor in the return migration of Mexicans which took place during the years of economic depression (1930-1940). Deficiencies in the use of English have also been genuine handicaps in the education of the Mexican community. Despite these

difficulties the second generation clearly surpassed the first in educational achievement. They did not, however, reach a favorable level for competition with others of their own age.

(5) At the close of the era of large-scale immigration in 1930, the majority of Mexican workers in the Southwest were engaged in agriculture. By way of contrast, most Mexicans in the Central States were employed in manufacturing and urban industries. By 1950, substantial changes were evident, particularly in the Southwest, where an intensive process of urbanization had taken place. At mid-century, Mexicans were engaged in a large variety of occupations; about a quarter of the urban workers were craftsmen, professionals and white-collar workers. However, the largest concentrations were at the semi-skilled and non-skilled levels. Both housing and income data seem to indicate that this consolidation of the Mexican community into the United States population has not been attended by significant economic gains. Perhaps one of the most important factors in this limited development has been a comparatively low level of educational attainment.

Rodolfo Alvarez

In 1970, Rodolfo Alvarez (Assistant Professor of Sociology, Yale University) participated in a review symposium of THE MEXICAN-AMERICAN PEOPLE *by Leo Grabler, Joan W. Moore, and Ralph C. Guzmán. In his review of the book, Professor Alvarez delineates the developing collective consciousness of the Chicano. His review also points out the direction that he feels Chicano studies should take and new social science techniques for studying ethnic groups. By permission of the* SOCIAL SCIENCE QUARTERLY, *vol. 52 (June 1971); and the author.*

The Unique Psycho-Historical Experience Of The Mexican American People

This is the single most important book ever to attempt to understand the existential experience of the Mexican-American people. Its importance stems both from its comprehensiveness as well as from its systematic disciplinary analysis of issues treated. The two, comprehensiveness and systematic disciplinary analysis, are not separable. To-gether these attributes combine to give the volume four basic strength that no other work on Mexican Americans has had.

First, in terms of geographical area covered this is a unique, genuine, initial step toward a comprehensive understanding of the sheer facts of existence among Mexican Americans in this country.

Never before have so many demographic variables been so systematically compared among such a broad range of geographical areas in the country: the five southwestern states and one midwestern city.

Second, never before have so many disciplinary points of view been employed to "understand" variation among these demographic variables. Previous piecemeal studies, done by one or two scholars working alone, could, in general, employ only one or two disciplinary perspectives to understand very limited variations on highly limited data. In this volume a "genuine" attempt is made to take the stance of the historian, anthropologist, economist, sociologist, social-psychologist, and political scientist in the attempt to achieve a systematically organized yet relatively unabstracted presentation of the wide range of informative materials that the authors have pulled together.

Third, this work has the great added strength of being informed by the presentation of the most comprehensive and systematically comparative non-demographic data on Mexican Americans living in the two major urban centers where they constitute a sizable proportion of the population. These new comparative data on sex and family roles and other distinctly sociological and social-psychological variables will do much, not only to dispel old stereotypes, but to raise innumerable new questions that will act as intellectual launching pads for what, hopefully, will be a rich crop of young Mexican-American scholars in the next decade. For the moment, these are the most systematically collected and analyzed comparative data available on attitudes and practices of Mexican Americans living in two very different major urban centers. These materials will serve to correct what a large proportion of the few existing Mexican-American social scientists have long considered thoroughly limited, if not erroneous, small anthropological case studies of rural environments in the Southwest that have largely been the basis of generalizations on Mexican Americans. The fact of the matter is that Mexican Americans are distributed throughout most regions of the country, not just the Southwest, and, like so many other ethnic "pockets," tend to become invisible in ur-

ban areas to any but very locally knowledgeable observers.

Fourth, and finally, this volume will become the bed rock tool of research and pedagogy on Mexican Americans for decades to come. This would be true if for no other reason than because of the comprehensive and very competently constructed bibliography reflecting a variety of academic disciplines and perspectives. Similarly, the eleven appendices describing in detail research procedures used in the analysis of data treated in each of the chapters will also be a large and sturdy platform from which, hopefully, to launch many new scholars of the Mexican-American experience in the United States. Along that same optimistic line of thought, the well organized lists of tables, appendices, charts, maps, and figures all reflect care and attention to their potential future utility for other workers in the field. Because these research and pedagogical tools are so competently pulled together into one generally available work, the importance of the book is assured for any serious effort in Mexican-American Studies.

These, then, are the four basic strengths of the book. These, also, are the primary bases on which to assess its major weaknesses. Its virtues and strengths are those of commission. Its sins and weaknesses are those of omission. What the research team did, it did very well. Consideration of what they did *not* do raises questions about the structure and function of scholarship in this country and about the philosophical and existential nature of the Mexican-American experience in the United States that future generations of scholars, let alone activists for social change, will agonize to resolve. The book's potential for good, in the perspective of the larger unbounded human panorama, is very high; so is its potential for evil. The authors, of course, can not be held for the uses to which the knowledge they produce is put. However, because they are presumably "aware" social scientists they can be held accountable to make clearly explicit a sufficiently broad historical and institutional context within which their work fits so that the potential use of their work for exploitative purposes would be held to a minimum. In the following section I will contend that the authors failed to attempt that much.

LACK OF HISTORICAL PERSPECTIVE AND ITS CONSEQUENCES

The major act of omission, and therefore the major criticism that can be made of the book, is that, all excuses by the authors to the contrary notwithstanding, there is no effective, and therefore no *relevant,* historical perspective in their treatment of the Mexican-American people. It is a complete and inexcusable travesty of any notion of intellectual objectivity and all responsible social scientific disciplinary perspectives to begin such a large scale work with the year 1900. Although some little mention is made of episodes transpiring prior to 1900 in the history of what is now southwestern United States, no such references inform in any substantial way the explanations and interpretations that are made of either census or survey data pertaining to the post-1900 period. This is important because the book basically treats the Mexican-American people as if they had no special historical place on the land they occupy, despite the obvious and important identity-producing links between populations and the land they live on. Rather, despite all claims to the contrary, they are treated just as any other immigrant population in this country. Even the claims of some Mexican Americans to be a "charter minority" are made light of. The authors, of course, sense, indeed explicitly recognize, at several points, that Mexican Americans, like American Indians and blacks, occupy a very special place in the history of what is now the United States of America. Yet that recognition never enters the volume analytically. It is precisely this lack of analytical import of the special circumstances that led to the creation of a Mexican-American people that makes the exclusion of pre-1900 historical attention so important. The absence of any intellectually serious treatment of the pre-1900 historical origins of the Mexican American people preclude any subsequent issues from being effectively treated from a disciplinary point of view. In effect, then, we begin by addressing the second and third of the four basic dimensions of strength we stated in our introduction. Our second point was that never before had so many different disciplinary points of view been employed to "understand" variation among so many demographic variables. Our third point was that never before had we had such systematically collected and analyzed comparative data on attitudes in two major urban centers. Now we shall make the case that because of a lack of any effective treatment of the pre-1900 psycho-historical experience all other disciplinary interpretations given may be found wanting since they would be attempts to explain only part, the post-1900 part, of the empirical data on Mexican Americans. All such disciplinary interpretations would be more effective if they were forced to consider all data on the creation and existence of Mexican Americans *as a people* with a very special identity-giving relationship to the land; this marks them as different from all other immigrants who came as individuals, however large their collective numbers, whose identity *as a people* would be to the land of origin and not that of destination.

At this point it may make sense to ask why it might have been that the authors excluded pre-1900 historical analysis. The most obvious, probably the most sensible, answer is lack of funds; but didn't they have a substantial, indeed the largest, grant ever given for this purpose? Another might be that there simply was not available any highly competent mature historian of stature specializing in the Mexican-American people. (Were there any? If not, why not?) Yet another answer might simply be that, even if such funds and historian had been available, such an analysis was irrelevant to the authors' and the funding agency's purposes; in many instances the book reads like a sophisticated market analysis of the commercial potential of the Mexican-American population. The major author is an economist. Undoubtedly, there is an unending list of possibilities, but let us simply leave the reader with these alternatives for the moment and go on to our task. Why are the pre-1900 origins of the Mexican-American people so important?

The Mexican-American people are a creation out of imperial conquest of one nation by another through military force. This resulted in a change of international boundaries which subsequently threw the individuals living on the conquered lands into a conflict of loyalties that persists today, more than a century and a half later (depending on where the historian places the beginning of the issue it may be even longer). Imperialism is today frowned upon the world over, at least in rhetoric, if not in action. But there is no need for the current day scholarly community to be embarrassed by (and try to cover up) their own nation's yesteryear imperial intentions and actions just because such national activity is frowned upon in current day public morality. There is a certain scholarly, if not national, maturity that is made explicit by acknowledging that the past existed as it did and in not trying to hide it from consideration. All of the then powerful nations of the world were busy at their imperialistic acquisitions prior to, during, and after that historical period when United States citizens began moving into what was then called Tejas (which includes the land now called Texas), when Texas ceded from Mexico, when Texas was annexed to the United States, when the United States defeated Mexico, and when most of what is now the far western part of the country was added to the United States. Scholars can argue until the end of time as to what is (are) the more adequate explanation(s) as to why these major historical events took place. The fact of the matter is that they took place. Because these events took place they significantly affected the lives of the people who lived on the land and who believed themselves to have a collective identity with the land; an identity which gave meaning to their existence and their cultural way of life. By and large when they broke with Spain, they could change their identity and be Mexicans; both because they had already lived on the land calling themselves Mexicans as a sub-category of the larger hispanic culture and peoples and, also, because they themselves collectively committed a positive act in setting up their independence within that cultural orbit. They kept the language and most of their hispanic institutions as they had been adapted to those lands. At this point, the Mexican people of the region were to Spain much like the newly autonomous Atlantic seaboard colonials were to England when they seceded from the crown. They had language, legal institutions, and other cultural and social ties with England and saw themselves as part of that cultural orbit, but as an autonomous collective entity that came into being by a positive action on their own part to create

that relationship. A psychoanalytic interpretation of this phenomenon might be the analogy to the adolescent revolting against parental authority and eventually achieving an independent "autonomous" maturity that nevertheless maintains strong and deep socio-emotional ties with the parent. The point that I want to make is that for the new societal unit created (United States ceding from England or Mexico from Spain), there was no potentially pathological or traumatically severe change of collective identity; it was for all intents and purposes a further step in the continuous strengthening and development of a prior collective consciousness.

The coming into being of the Mexican-American people is a totally different psycho-historical experience. The Mexican-American people were created abruptly, virtually overnight, because Mexico suffered military defeat. A very large percentage of Mexico's land was taken away against its will, although the historical fact of military defeat was partially covered up through partial payments and flimsy agreements of one kind or another. Mexico was virtually powerless to disagree on any terms and simply had to accept the best deal possible under the circumstances of military defeat; that deal meant that Mexico lost any respect it might have had in the eyes of the Mexicans living on the lands annexed by the United States. Mexico couldn't protect those who would have preferred to have their land remain Mexican. Other Mexicans living on those lands may at one time or another have conceived of themselves as acting positively like other colonials by actively helping to break away from the parent society. In the future, highly competent historical work on all of these issues will contribute to our understanding of how they have subsequently affected the experiences of the Mexican-American people from their creation to the present. Historians may demonstrate to us that many Mexicans in fact may have actively and enthusiastically participated along with the new residents from the United States in the break from Mexico because they thought it would be in their own interest. However, once the break became historical fact, all "Mexicans" on the land (whether they had been for or against the break) found themselves not only losing title to their lands very rapidly through all sorts of legal and extra-legal means, but increasingly being treated as conquered, and, therefore, "inferior" people. This rapid change must, certainly, have given them a different social-psychological view of self than they had prior to the break. The break and annexation meant that they were now citizens of the United States, but surely they could not have changed their language and culture overnight merely because their lands were now the sovereign property of the United States; thus they maintained their "Mexicanness." Because their cultural ties were to Mexico, they were, in effect, "Mexicans" in the United States. As the number of "Americans" in the region increased, "Mexicans" became an ever smaller proportion of the population. They were *different* from the increasing "American" population. They were a minority. They thought, spoke, dressed, acted, and had all of the anatomical characteristics of the defeated Mexicans. In fact, were they not still "Mexicans" from the point of view of "Americans" even though they were United States citizens by virtue of the military defeat and treaties that gave sovereignty to the U.S.? For all of these reasons and more, the "Mexican" minority could be viewed as the deviants onto whom all manner of aggressions could be displaced whenever the Calvinistic desire for material acquisition was in the least frustrated. It is in this psycho-historical context that we can place the few fleeting references made by the authors (that in their context are gratuitous because irrelevant to the authors' discussions) to the rapid changeover of personal land ownership in the area from "Mexican" to "American" hands, their decline in population, and their rapid decline in social status until by 1900 most were in dependent, non-landed, low wage, employee positions—even those who had once held commanding social positions. Mexicans became a caste at the bottom of the social structure.

It is the psycho-historical experience of an unwilling break with the culture of the parent country and subsequent subjugation—all taking place on what they considered to be their land—that makes the experience of Mexican Americans different from all other ethnic populations that migrated to this country in the nineteenth and twentieth centuries. In that part of the volume

that the authors inaccurately call "historical perspectives" they pick up the Mexican-American people at about 1900 with the more or less explicit argument that that is the point in time when Mexican Americans began to appear in the Southwest in large numbers; as if an analysis were made historical merely by citing a date. The post-1900 analytical treatment of the Mexican-American people is essentially non-historical. It is non-historical because no sustained genetic explanation is given of any developmental sequence; rather, as if in an after-thought, some dated facts are cited, presumably to give some historical "perspective" to what are basically good short treatments of demographic variables from an economic point of view. The authors make no serious effort to link the experience of a large and widely dispersed "charter minority" of "strangers on their own land" to the kinds of experiences facing the post-1900 migrants from Mexico upon their arrival in southwestern United States.

The sheer social-psychological fact is that "if people define situations as real they are real in their consequences." The several waves of post-1900 migrants from Mexico were incorporated into an already thoroughly structured, thoroughly defined, social situation. Recall that even today Texas has the highest proportion of native born of native parentage population tracing its ancestry predominantly to northern European countries and subscribing primarily to fundamentalist, Calvinistic religious values. It remains for future historians to systematically investigate whether Max Weber's analysis of the tremendous acquisitive drive generated under the Calvinistic notion of the demonstration of salvation through material acquisition might help explain the national mood that led the United States to acquire half of Mexico's land. It remains also whether those historians will find enough evidence to support the similarly based thesis that the materially dispossessed "Mexicans" were viewed as manifestly not among those chosen by God to enter heaven, their defeat and dispossession being obvious indications of their unworthy nature; and, therefore, perfectly appropriate targets for aggression. However these interpretations will fare, the fact is that when successive waves of Mexican migrants arrived in the post-1900 southwestern United States they found a large materially dispossessed minority with whom they had language, custom, kinship, and all manner of qualities in common, not least of which was that they both occupied the very bottom of the social structure. It does not make sense to view these large early waves of Mexicans as similar to immigrants from other lands to the U.S. because social-psychologically the post-1900 migrant from Mexico was not like the Irish immigrant whose identity-giving land was being left behind across a large ocean. Even the physical characteristics of these lands were continuous with that of land on the Mexican side. The immigrant to New York City was not like the migrant to San Antonio "returning" to land once part of his country, where he just as likely as not might have kin dating back to that era. When he arrived in San Antonio the powerful "Anglo" population could view him and define him precisely as they already defined his kin. The migrant himself upon arriving could simply take over the social-psychological repertoire of perspectives toward self and dominant others that his kin had already thoroughly established. My argument is that the post-1900 migrant from Mexico did not have the social-psychological freedom to take on alternative roles, indeed explore alternatives in the making of roles, as did his Irish counterpart in New York City. In fact, it is very unlikely that Irish immigrants were walked through the streets of New York City in chains under armed guard on their way from the docks to the conveyances that would transport them to other areas where their manual labor was needed, as were the Mexican migrants through the streets of San Antonio. What I am trying to establish is that the experience of the post-1900 Mexican migrants as individuals was very different from the experiences of immigrants from other countries, because they were summarily treated according to thoroughly established social practices and expectations as members of a lower caste. Because they could easily be differentiated physically and culturally from the dominant population, they did not and could not have the individual freedom that other immigrants could have in trying out new roles. It is a travesty to consider post-1900 migration as comparable to immigration by other people into the United States

without a careful historical or intellectual understanding of the unique pre-1900 creation of the Mexican-American people.

At the risk of being obnoxiously pedantic, I would say that had the research team included a highly competent historian of the area and period, then a careful historical treatment of, say, 1800–1900 would have presented facts and issues about how the Mexican-American people came into being that would have greatly informed and deepened the post-1900 narrowly statistical analyses presented in the volume. This volume finds the Mexican-American people as a rootless people, but despite the magnitude of the endeavor leaves us just as rootless. If for no other reason (there are others), this lack of any true historical perspective means that *the* definitive work on the Mexican-American people is yet to be written. If the book has any value from an historical point of view it is that it points out a great scholarly lacuna that will yield a veritable intellectual gold mine to multi-disciplinary research teams consisting predominately of historians and social-psychologists. That kind of psycho-historical work is finally now being done on the black population of this country on a fairly broad scale. However, no such serious work is available on Mexican Americans or, for that matter, American Indians. This is important, of course, because, to my knowledge, the black, Mexican-American, and American Indian sub-populations are the only three against which major official and non-official sectors of this society have used organized, publicly condoned, indeed publicly financed, long-term violence.[1] The black population was not an immigrant population in the usual sense of the term since it was brought here enslaved. The American Indian (or perhaps more appropriately, Native American) population clearly did not immigrate to the United States in the usual sense of the term. What I have tried to

---

[1] Japanese Americans during WWII had a short-term intense experience with official coercion. Though that experience has certainly become part of the sub-cultural remembrances of Japanese Americans, its impact appears to have been relatively slight; they are today highly represented in higher economic positions, the professions, and the college student population.

show is that the Mexican American (who had considerable intermarriage with the Indian) was also not an immigrant population. Psycho-historically these three populations have much in common including their essentially non-immigrant status, their experience with long-term officially organized violence, and the fact that they had to be either manifestly cooperative in assuming their degraded lower caste status or cease to exist.

CONTENTS

Having dwelt at some length on the major intellectual deficiency of the study reported in this volume, we can now turn to a description of its contents and give a few indications of how the lack of historical perspective on the *creation* of the Mexican-American people seriously affects all of the interpretations of data. Furthermore, because the investigators failed to pay any attention to the peculiar psycho-historical past of the Mexican-American people, their analyses run the risk of being misused by both public and private policy makers. Also, their interpretations run the risk of becoming yet another alienating factor in the historical experience of Mexican Americans. Unless the very valuable empirical data presented in this book are interpreted with proper regard to their unique psycho-historical experience, some Mexican Americans will surely view the book as just another "market analysis" designed to exploit them; covered up, as usual, with superficially transparent "social scientific" interpretations that become more threatening to the community than similar previous interpretations, if for no other reason than because this study was carried out on such a large scale. I will make only brief suggestions of crucial places where important leads for interpretation from the point of view of a unique psycho-history occur as I describe the highlights of the contents of the book.

Part one, "The Setting," deals with the institutional context in which the study was conducted. The book opens with the following paragraph:

This book is part of the current discovery of Mexican Americans in the United States. Even the grant that made our study possible

was the first of its kind. No national foundation has ever before given funds for major research on this minority group (p.3).

Thus, the institutional context of the Mexican American has been one of being used and abused with impunity, because unnoticed in the national consciousness. Also presented is a summary statement of where the Mexican American fits in an overall socioeconomic institutional context of the country: the bottom.

Part two, "Historical Perspectives," with the distinct exception of minor passages in chapter three, ignores the pre-1900 historical origins of the Mexican-American people. The few historical references made have to do with approximations of how many Mexicans were living in what areas or with a passing reference or two about the nature of the economy prior to 1900. No effective historical explanation is given of how it came about that "... by 1900 the Mexican's role in Texas as a landless and dependent wage laborer was well established in all but a few insignificant areas" (p. 49). There is no mention at all about the reasons why the land might have switched from "Mexican" to "Anglo" personal ownership by force of arms, or by ludicrous economic bargain backed by force of arms.

Part three, "Socio-economic Conditions: A Detailed Portrait," is the strongest part of the book, both technically and analytically. Dealing with population patterns, education, income, occupation, housing and residential segregation, comparisons are made with other groups (Anglos and nonwhites) and some ingenious measures are introduced. Take out of this book these highly competent and informative contributions of the economist (not the theoretical economist, but the economic technician) and the reader would be left with a certain lack of satiation.

Part four deals with "The Individual in the Social System" and represents the most clearly sociological analysis in the book. Viewing relative social isolation (in San Antonio and Los Angeles), social class and mobility, and the family, the authors lead up to the question: Is there any sociological reason why Mexican Americans as a collectivity might not be able to participate in the national economy of the larger society if they were permitted to do so? Then, the same basic question is posed from a social-psychological perspective: family structure aside, is there any reason why Mexican Americans, as individuals, might perceive other ethnic groups in such a way as to restrict their own potential for participation in the economy; how much do Mexican Americans identify with a "Mexican" as opposed to an "American" way of life, and how do they view themselves and their potential participation in opportunities that might become available. Finally, relative assimilation by male and female Mexican Americans as indicated by intermarriage as it relates to generational differences and occupational status is discussed. The authors indicate that their findings "... suggest an assimilative potential of the Mexican-American population greater than has been commonly assumed, provided that external barriers are comparatively low" (pp. 416–17). There now exists ample evidence to hold thoroughly suspect, if not invalid, the stereotypic assertion that Mexican Americans possess distinctively traditional values and that their low socioeconomic participation in the larger society is due to lack of motivation to achieve. "Much like other Americans, and probably much like other urbanities in industrial countries, most want to get ahead in their work; they want work that gives them intrinsic satisfactions; many hope for job security and higher income" (p. 438). The authors, however, neglect to emphasize that Mexican Americans nevertheless are very earnestly searching to preserve their own culture in a *non-isolating way.* They neglect to emphasize the unique psycho-historical experience that has denied Mexican Americans their identity and through that means maintained their position at the bottom of the social structure manifestly against their will.

The authors' discussion of the sociological and social-psychological potential for assimilation would make a lot more sense if the data were interpreted in depth from the perspective of a unique psycho-history rather than from the point of view of standard, routinely mechanical comparisons as is now done. Just as a suggestion of the kind of interpretation that needs much further work let me posit the existence of four different

generations of Mexican Americans. First, there is the Creation Generation that suffered the unique pre-1900 psycho-historical experience of which I have made so much. This, in a sense, is the betrayed generation: betrayed by Mexico as well as by the United States. Second, there is the Migrant Generation between 1900 and, roughly, World War II. This generation had its cultural orientation and loyalties invested in Mexico for several reasons; upon arriving in the U.S. it experienced the normal nostalgia that all immigrants tend to have for the old country, but, in addition, it met with harsh social rejection and isolation that made that cultural loyalty all the stronger. Third, there is the Mexican-American Generation dating roughly between the Second World War and the war in Vietnam. This generation had its cultural orientation and loyalties invested in the United States. As members of this generation were achieving maturity they were asking their parents: What did Mexico ever do for you? You were poor there, your exodus reduced the unemployment rate in Mexico, you sent part of your hard earned wages back to relatives which improved Mexico's dollar balance of payments, and what did Mexico do for you except help labor contractors and unscrupulous southwestern officials to further exploit you? I am an "American" who happens to be of Mexican descent. I'm going to participate fully in this society because, like descendants of immigrants from so many other lands, I was born here and my country will guarantee me all the rights and protections of a free and loyal citizen. Fourth, there is the Chicano Generation, currently in its early stages of development. This generation is more affluent than all previous Mexican-American generations; i.e., it has benefited from its modern U.S. citizenship more than all previous generations. However, it is feeling the pains of social rejection; the pains of perceiving itself as disadvantaged. Studies like the one under review are presenting those in the Chicano Generation with evidence that leads them to believe that they have been socially betrayed by the United States. Members of the Chicano Generation are therefore saying to the previous generation: "So you are a loyal 'American' willing to die for your country in the last three or four wars; what did your country ever do for you? If you are such an 'American' how come your country gives you even less education than other disadvantaged minorities, permits you only low status occupations, allows you to become a disproportionately large part of casualties in war, and socially rejects you from the most prestigious circles? As for me, I am a Chicano, I am rooted in this land, I am the creation of a unique psycho-historical experience. I trace part of my identity to Mexican culture and part to United States culture, but most importantly my identity is tied up with those contested lands called Atzlán! My most valid claim to existential reality is not the false pride and unrequited loyalty of either the Migrant Generation or the Mexican American Generation. Rather, I trace my beginning to the original contest over the lands of Atzlán, to the more valid psycho-historical experience of the Creation Generation. I have a right to intermarriage if I wish, to higher education, to economic achievement, and to my own measure of political self-determination within this society. I have a unique psycho-historical experience that I have a right to know about and to cultivate as part of my distinctive cultural heritage. Unlike the Migrant Generation I will not look back in ignorance to a culture that all too willingly abandoned me. Unlike the Mexican-American Generation I will not in ignorance be satisfied with a culture that gives me a few crumbs at the bottom of the social structure even if that is more than my parents had. Instead, with complete self-awareness I will challenge the future and make my own place in this pluralistic society."

Part five, "The Role of Churches," is thoroughly professional in analytic presentation and only infrequently appears to have an implicitly favorable orientation toward religious organizations. These chapters seem intent on excusing long-standing small scale and ineffective church efforts on behalf of the Mexican-American population, or even outright hostility toward Mexican Americans, through bland writing or by explanations that make reference to lack of church resources.

Part six, "Political Interaction," deals with governmental agencies, voluntary associations, political leadership, and political efficacy of the Mexican-American community. Traditional interaction between Mexican Americans and all manner of governmental agencies (public health, employment, police, etc.), whether in a rural or an urban context, can be generally characterized by the statement of a "local under-sheriff":

> We protect our farmers here in Kern County. They are our best people. They are always with us. They keep the county going. They put us here and they can put us out again so we serve them. But the Mexicans are trash. They have no standard of living. We herd them like pigs. (p. 532)

Survey respondents had a low level of awareness of most ethnic voluntary associations; community leadership has tended to be highly localized and ineffective. These chapters, like the entire book, raise an unending series of anomalies and questions for further research. It is puzzling, for example, that political efficacy has been higher in Texas despite the greater isolation of the Mexican-American community, its greater harrassment by police and other government agencies, poll tax and voter registration procedures which frighten and repulse, much lower rates of naturalization, and the general lower level of economic development, as compared to California where political efficacy has been much lower despite significant advantages over Texas on virtually all other dimensions. On this and a number of other issues, the volume does the academy a great service by opening up whole areas for interdisciplinary research. On this particular issue, for example, anthropologists and sociologists working together might raise the question of how it is that social and cultural structures interact. Mexican Americans in Texas experience a much more exclusive, some would say repressive, cultural structure on the part of the dominant "Anglo" population than they do in California. Their own culture has retained much more of a traditional character. Yet, even though they face a much more open social structure in California they have made deeper political inroads in Texas. Does the sociological maxim "outgroup antagonism, ingroup solidarity" help explain these contrasting phenomena?

Here, again, is a case where the peculiar psycho-historical experience can help explain the political defeat of the Creation Generation, the continuing political inertness of the Migrant Generation, and the nascent political ineffectiveness of the Mexican-American generation. Because the earliest waves of the Migrant Generation were most intense in Texas, the Mexican-American Generation would have developed there first. The psycho-historical experience was more intense in Texas than in California (majoritarian society was more hostile and rejecting as well as culturally and religiously more homogenous); i.e., outgroup antagonism was more obvious and concerted, therefore ingroup political solidarity was somewhat more effective. But the relatively more open social and cultural structure of California, while it may have increased the political ineffectiveness of the Mexican-American Generation there, has brought about the faster development of the Chicano Generation because the greater economic and educational achievement made possible by freer structures has permitted greater introspection and search for roots. The introspectiveness of the Chicano Generation allows it to differentiate itself from its preceding generations. Local Chicano leaders appear to intuitively select one or another of the major preceding generational foci as a basis on which to take a stance. How they differentiate their current actions and perspectives from that preceding period tends to give that particular leader his distinct identity and goals. It is almost as if each of the major currently identifiable leadership styles had its roots in a given historical era—analogous to the way some current biological species might have their initial appearance traceable to a particular geologic period. For example, Reies Tijerina's activities seem to be linked to the land claims which were the central focus of the Creation Generation. Rodolfo (Corky) González has come to be known as a proponent of "cultural nationalism" which links his central activities to the major focus of the Migrant Generation with its cultural orientation to Mexico. José Ángel Gutiérrez has tended to emphasize political effectiveness within approved structures thus linking his activities to the central focus of the Mexican-American Generation. However, as leadership styles within the Chicano Generation, all of these different political movements have a common image of the future: full participation in this pluralistic society through self-determined action.

Now that widespread consciousness-of-kind has developed among some Mexican Americans in California, the avant garde of the Chicano Generation, it remains to be seen whether they can become the most politically effective sector ever. That effectiveness will probably not be possible without an organized joining of forces between rural and urban Mexican Americans there. It may be that that organized example will be the sine qua non to a national Chicano consciousness and effectiveness. Such an event may require the cultivation of a highly sophisticated, cooperative, urban, executive leadership counterpart to that of César Chávez. I say "leadership" because if the Chicano Generation is to be able to achieve any significant measure of political efficacy it will have to develop a diffuse leadership cadre capable of action within a pluralistic democracy in an urban industrial context. So far César Chávez's activities and intellectual perspectives seem to be the only ones clearly based on the Chicano Generation. His movement clearly seeks to utilize the levers of power in a modern urban industrial society and is not detered by cultural ties to Mexico in seeking its objectives. However, it has not yet been parlayed effectively from a rural to an urban context (where most Mexican Americans live), or from fundamentally narrow economic objectives to general political objectives. The major point to be made here is that each of the nascent leadership styles tends to define a major definitional facet of the Chicano Generation by its contradistinction to an earlier period.

SOME CONCLUDING REMARKS

The major thesis in this review article has been that what was done in the study reported in this volume was technically expert, but what was not done mars its intellectual value.

On the one hand, I have been unqualified in my statement concerning the central role that this volume will play in the development of Mexican-American studies in the next decade. Just as important will be the major role that the study has already been playing and will continue to play in the formation of national, state, and local policy toward Mexican Americans. Additionally, the volume is playing and will continue to play a major role in the developing cultural, political, and economic consciousness among Mexican Americans themselves.

On the other hand, it must be emphatically said that the book's potential for evil is very great because of its lack of theoretical and interpretive aspirations. It remains to be seen what will be the effect of omitting the pre-1900 psycho-historical origins of the Mexican-American people from consideration. What must be said here is that since the book is likely to play a disproportionate role in Mexican-American studies programs and in the consequent consciousness of young Mexican Americans, it is imperative that this volume not be viewed as the definitive work on the subject. It is a factual compendium, a very useful research and pedagogical tool, but what interpretive prespectives it presents on the data are mechanistically standardized. As such it may lead young Mexican Americans, and their sympathetic majority counterparts, merely to strive for some mechanical equalization of material standards among the Mexican-American people and both majority citizens of the United States and members of other minority groups. That would be one more betrayal of the Mexican American people as a people. What is needed is extensive historical, social-psychological, as well as other disciplinary work to fully develop knowledge of self which is such a necessary precondition to self-determination. Unless students are systematically exposed in depth to the study of their peculiar psycho-historical past, they will be done the great disservice of being left as yet another rootless generation of Mexican Americans. Without such counterbalancing study both Mexican Americans and public policy makers are likely to be led, on the one hand, to actions that will be destructive to Mexican Americans as a people, and on the other hand to policies that will continue, albeit in more subtle forms, the exploitative relationship between the dominant society and the Mexican-American minority.

When viewed as a fertile, formally uncultivated, underdeveloped domestic economic market, the Mexican-American people became ripe for exploitation by well capitalized users of the highly sophisticated market analyses contained in this book. Never before have the dimensions of the Mexican-American community been so carefully mapped out in such a useful way for anyone interested in determining what appeals to what proportion of the Mexican-American people in which communities and what are the prospects that they will be able to afford it, if they are properly appealed to through which communications media. These data are, of course, like all knowledge, useful for a variety of other purposes. However, the absence of any effective treatment of their history stands as a monumentally significant obstacle to usage of these data for purposes beneficial to the Mexican-American people. I can but recall George Santayana: "Those who cannot remember the past are condemned to repeat it!" Or, if you will, in the words of an old Mexican proverb: "El flojo y el pendejo andan dos veces el camino!" From the Creation Generation to the Chicano Generation every generation of Mexican Americans has, in ignorance, been reliving its history. BASTA! BASTA! BASTA!

2.

ACQUIESCENCE AND ADJUSTMENT

Acquiescence And Adjustment

As the preceding section indicates, one element of the many Mexican American sterotypes is their passivity. Too often, perhaps through oversight, scholarship has reinforced this false image. A current generation of Southwestern scholars are now actively revising this view. They assert that what appeared as passiveness was a cultural difference that reflected Anglo aggressiveness and goals. The rejection took several forms. Usually the Hispanic population neither accepted nor openly opposed Anglo mores. Rather, they tried adapting to the more aggressive behavior patterns by at times merely ignoring them or—in extreme cases—sacrificing material holdings to the new settlers in order to retain Hispanic cultural values. Thus, in the first stage of the struggle to preserve their native culture before the assault of the gringo, Mexican Americans acquiesced when necessary, adjusted somewhat, but at all costs maintained their ethnic uniqueness.

Mexican intellectuals feared, as Gene Brack demonstrates, that the American occupation of the Southwest might destroy existing Hispanic culture. The next selections verify the accuracy of these forebodings. In the first essay Paul Horgan provides valuable insights and descriptions of daily life and material culture of nineteenth-century Mexican Americans; while in the second George Sánchez relates how this different culture enabled "ruthless politicians and merchants" to exploit an indigenous population through the use of the new and unfamiliar Anglo laws and traditions. This exploitation was not unique to New Mexico. For, as Leonard Pitt points out, the discovery of gold in California lured thousands of Anglos to that state, and in turn they subjugated the local population.

Subjugated peoples, however, can act as well as be acted upon, and too many scholars have forgotten this fact. In his excellent discussion of the *Cibolaros* and the *Comancheros,* Charles Kenner shows that the Mexican American was a first-rate frontiersman, while Rosenbaum demonstrates that the Hispanic New Mexican population was not always passive. One can gain valuable insights into the nature of prejudice by contrasting Kenner's frontiersman with Américo Parades' story of the Anglo-Texas concept of the Chicano as treacherous, cowardly, and morally degenerate. This racial prejudice made assimilation all but impossible, and drove the Hispano ever inward; seeking rewards and refuge from within his own culture. One form of this cultural isolation is discussed by Juan Gomez—while Warren A. Beck tells of both the isolation of the upstate New Mexico villages, and of the rejection of Anglo mores by the *Penitentes,* an outgrowth of Spanish Catholicism. The harsh impact of racial prejudice, and such religious aberrations as the *Penitentes* are explored in Raymond Mulligan's "New York Foundlings at Clifton-Morenci." This essay chronicles a classic example of the worst sort of racial discrimination.

59

GENE M. BRACK

*Gene M. Brack (Associate Professor of History, New Mexico State University) is a specialist in the area of United States-Mexican diplomatic relations, 1821–1848. This study, published originally in WESTERN HISTORICAL QUARTERLY (April, 1970), points out the revisionist path his work is taking. Professor Brack argues that by the 1840s Mexican intellectuals feared Anglo-Saxon cultural domination would be the inevitable result of American expansionism in the Southwest, and therefore the intelligentsia became staunch advocates of war. The Mexican Press perpetuated the war climate by reporting Anglo-America's racist tendencies, and the ill treatment afforded to both the Indian and the blacks. It was justifiably believed that the same treatment would be given to the Mexican.
By permission of the WESTERN HISTORICAL QUARTERLY (April 1970), pp 161–174; and the author.*

Mexican Opinion, American Racism, And The War Of 1846

When Mexican forces attacked a detachment of General Zachary Taylor's army on the east bank of the Rio Grande in April 1846, President James K. Polk justified a declaration of war against Mexico with the charge that "American blood" had been shed upon "American soil." The clash culminated two decades of abrasive relations between the United States and Mexico. By 1846 the most palpable cause of contention was the rapid expansion of the United States toward the borderlands of Mexico. The Polk administration appeared determined to carry forward a program of expansion which would ultimately embrace much of northern Mexico. The Mexican government seemed equally determined to avoid losing any part of her national domain. For nine years Mexico had refused to recognize Texas independence and more recently had rejected Polk's offer to purchase upper California. Failing to gain concessions by peaceful means, Polk then made a show of force: it did not fit the purpose of the president's war message to acknowledge that the boundary between the United States and Mexico was undetermined, the area between the Nueces and Rio Grande rivers being disputed territory rather than "American soil"; that for weeks the mouth of the Rio Grande had laid under an American blockade; that an American squadron hovered near Vera Cruz; or that an American "exploratory" expedition had entered upper California.

Merely to cite American provocations does not wholly explain Mexico's reaction. Her decision to fight rather than surrender territory by any means was a momentous one for both countries, yet since the publication in 1919 of Justin H. Smith's *The War with Mexico,* American writers have given scant attention to the factors that may have influenced Mexico's course of action. Smith explained that the decision was in large measure based upon Mexican confidence in their military superiority; believing their army larger and more powerful, Mexicans also remembered that the United States had demonstrated martial ineptitude during the War of 1812. Thus, according to Smith, Mexicans sought war, for, "vain and superficial, they did not realize their weakness."

But for years Mexico had vowed to respond to American annexation of Texas with an immediate declaration of war against the United States. Therefore, if she sought war, why did Mexico not launch it in 1845 when Texas joined the American Union? It was the administration of José Joaquín de Herrera, who had become president in December 1844, that determined Mexico's response to annexation. Herrera's alternatives were to preserve peace by simply recognizing the irrevocable loss of Texas, or to act upon the threats of previous administrations and to declare war. The president appeared obligated to pursue the latter course, not only because of Mexico's previously announced position, but also because the revolution that brought Herrera to power had as an important purpose the creation of a government that would take a firm stand against the United States.

Herrera nevertheless wished to avoid war. He explained his position in a pamphlet which declared that it served the true interests of the country to preserve peace, that there was no longer any hope of recovering Texas, and that war, in Mexico's present circumstances, would lead to disaster. In accordance with Herrera's conciliatory policy, the government agreed in October of 1845 to admit an American envoy. Such a measure required support from outside the administration, however, and in November 1845 the foreign secretary sent a circular letter to local officials throughout Mexico soliciting their cooperation. The secretary agreed that Mexico had ample justification for declaring war, but he realized also that the country lacked the means to support an army hundreds of miles away on the distant frontier. The northern divisions could scarcely maintain their garrisons, let alone take the offensive. The secretary informed the local officials that Mexico could depend upon neither military nor financial support from other nations, and that in such circumstances the administration believed it expedient to avoid disaster by peacefully ceding an underpopulated part of Mexico's immense territory.

Thwarted by the combined opposition of the press, an aroused public, and rival political factions, Herrera's appeals went unheeded. When the American envoy arrived late in 1845 he was refused recognition, nominally because his credentials were improper, actually because Herrera could not afford further to offend public opinion by negotiating with a representative of the United States. The concession failed to save Herrera. He had assumed a moderate position when Mexicans would accept no course but a militant one. In December 1845 he was overthrown by General Mariano Paredes y Arrillaga. But the new president was also unable to breathe energy into a bankrupt and divided people.

When Paredes seized power he was aware of the nation's impotence. During the summer of 1845, while commanding a large body of the Mexican army at San Luis Potosí, Paredes himself had predicted that a clash with the United States would disgrace his nation before the eyes of the world. And correspondents from the capitol had informed Paredes that, for lack of funds, the army could not be strengthened.

During the summer and fall of 1845 Paredes had received frequent communications from General Mariano Arista, commanding Mexican forces on the northern frontier, informing him of Mexican weakness along the Rio Grande. In July Arista wrote that the army was in a state of "dreadful misery"; an advance upon Texas was out of the question, because the army lacked the means of bare subsistence. To Arista the frontier appeared threatened, and he wrote that he would do what he could to protect it, but that it was impossible to defend the nation with "hungry and naked" troops. He felt that he would weaken his army even more by sending a brigade to protect the department of Coahuila; to guard the entire line of the Rio Grande appeared impossible. Arista informed Paredes that he was convinced that the United States intended to attack and that Mexico would be defeated and then "dominated by Americans."

In October Arista wrote that he was desperate, his troops were hungry and that "the situation was very sad." Apparently preparing to advance upon Matamoros, the gringos had seized all of the passages across the Nueces, and Arista could do nothing to prevent it. The autumn weather was frigid, his men had neither coats nor blankets. They were perishing from cold and hunger, and yet the "public writers" had declared war.

Thus Arista, who would be ordered in the spring of 1846 to initiate hostilities, appeared more apprehensive than bellicose. And Paredes, regardless of his intentions when he entered the presidency, knew that Mexico was vulnerable and did not order an attack until seriously provoked by the United States. Arista's lament that the public writers had declared war clearly underscores the role of the press and of public opinion in creating the paradoxical situation confronted successively by the administrations of Herrera and Paredes. And within the tangled web of events that led to war it is particularly significant that American officials were aware of the paradox.

Prior to the termination of official diplomatic relations in the spring of 1845, the American minister at Mexico had informed his government that Mexican opinion was so decidedly hostile to the United States that Mexican leaders were considered traitorous unless they appeared to cater to that opinion. In one of his last despatches from Mexico, the American minister reported that the Mexicans who realized war would be "ruinous" and "disastrous" were compelled "to join the public clamor, in order to maintain their positions."

When formal relations were terminated, the Polk administration continued to receive despatches from its consul and from William Parrott, its "confidential agent" in Mexico City. Both repeatedly informed their government that Mexican opinion favored war, but that Mexican officials, realizing their army was weak, and the treasury empty, would stop short of fighting. In the summer of 1845 the American consul reported that the present Mexican government had no intention of declaring war. Nor did he think the opposition, should it come to power, would "ever seriously think of entering into a war (in earnest) with the United States." Parrott informed the Polk administration of Arista's weakness when he reported in September that the Mexican general had no more than three thousand men to defend a line of "about 140 leagues," and thus could have no hope of success even if he did intend to launch an attack.

From such reports the Polk administration must have known that Mexican officials sought to avoid war if possible; it also must have known that public opinion in Mexico limited the options of Mexican leaders. But by ordering General Taylor to the Rio Grande and by taking other hostile measures during the winter and spring of 1845–1846, was not the Polk administration further inflaming Mexican opinion and restricting the freedom of action of the Mexican government? It might be argued that the Slidell mission offered peace to Mexico, but Paredes logically defended his dismissal of Slidell by stating that the presence of an American army on the Rio Grande and of an American fleet in Mexican waters prohibited negotiations. To the Mexican president it appeared that by intimidating Mexico the United States hoped to acquire territory for the asking. Paredes was trapped by forces beyond his control: his countrymen demanded war, and the actions of the United States apparently left him no room for maneuvering. The only alternative was to surrender territory to the Americans, and that was clearly unacceptable.

The historian must approach public opinion with great care. Modern devices measure it none too accurately, and when one is dealing with scattered fragments of the past, the difficulties are enormously increased. But if the foregoing is a reasonably accurate reconstruction of the circumstances leading to the Mexican War, it becomes important to devote more than passing attention to the factors that created a climate of opinion so rigidly hostile toward the United States that it led Mexico into a war for which she was dubiously prepared. In other words, it becomes important to know why the alternative—ceding territory to the United States—was so abhorrent to Mexicans.

At least a partial explanation may be that some Mexicans, like many Americans of that period, discerned a relationship between American expansion and racist elements within the United States. They were aware that many Americans looked upon Mexicans as inferior beings; the implications, when combined with the American desire for Mexican soil, were frightening. Americans apparently had no respect for the culture of those whom they considered inferior. They had been merciless in their treatment of the Indian. The Negro, also deemed inferior, had been reduced to a brutal form of servitude. Similar treatment probably awaited Mexicans should their northern departments fall under American control. The Americans failed to respect his agreements with the Indian; he could hardly be relied upon to be trustworthy when dealing with Mexicans. Perhaps this is what many Mexicans had in mind when they insisted that should Texas and California be lost, other Mexican territory would soon follow.

During the two decades prior to the war, Mexicans often criticized the United States for proclaiming humanitarian principles while driving the Indian from his land and condoning slavery. The degree to which the United States was prepared officially to defend slavery became apparent to Mexicans in the 1820s when Joel Poinsett, the first American minister to Mexico, introduced the subject while negotiating a treaty of limits between the two countries. Mexicans questioned a clause in the treaty providing for the detention of escaped slaves. They maintained that public opinion in Mexico would be outraged by the proposed clause. Poinsett reasoned that the border ought to be settled by a law-abiding population and suggested that slaveowners were an especially orderly and desirable class. The treaty was eventually ratified without the offending clause, but Poinsett's arguments in its defense revealed to Mexico the ardor with which the United States would support the rights of its citizens to own human property.

Accounts of Poinsett's activities, as well as of other matters pertaining to the United States, were disseminated in newspapers throughout Mexico. Each important faction in Mexican politics usually had one or more newspapers to articulate its position, and these newspapers were widely distributed. In *tertulias*—informal discussions, often held in taverns—a literate Mexican might read aloud to his non-reading friends; all would then discuss the topics of the day. The United States was among the topics. Much of the information in Mexican newspapers was likely to be doctored and misleading, but they did place the subject of the United States frequently before the public.

Typical of the kind of information that began appearing in the Mexican press during the 1820s was an anecdote describing a tyrannical Virginia slaveholder who ordered an old black man to hit a recaptured slave three hundred times, whereupon the old man fatally stabbed first the owner and then himself. At this time Mexicans also began to reveal an interest in American treatment of the Indian. The important conservative newspaper *El Sol* printed a letter written by John C. Calhoun in which the American cabinet official recommended sending Indians to uninhabited western regions. The Mexican editor urged his countrymen to take note of the matter not only because it seemed to reflect the American attitude toward Indians, but also because it portended future danger to the frontier of Mexico. The same newspaper later printed a letter written by an unidentified American citizen who criticized his government's Indian policy for being too lenient. Making treaties and compensating Indians for their lost land, he thought, only created needless expense. Instead of negotiating with the Indian, the United States should simply force the Indian to submit. It was absurd to purchase land from those who failed to cultivate it, for in this way the savages became the "depositories of the wealth that resulted from the progress and industry of the white population." The Mexican editor declared the letter typical of the American attitude toward the Indians. In 1840 *El Mosquito Mexicano* told its readers that Branch Archer of the Texas government favored the conquest of all Mexico and was known to have said that Mexicans, like the Indians, should give way to the energetic force of the Anglo-Americans.

El Amigo del Pueblo was a liberal organ whose editors were friendly toward the United States, but it too expressed concern at the systematic demoralization of the Indian by Americans. It reported in 1828 that it was the objective of the United States to expand to the Pacific. The process would eventually threaten Mexican territory, but presently the chief victim was the Indian. He was first deprived of his lands by a combination of deceit and force, and then his institutions were shattered. In this way a noble, brave, fiercely independent soul was reduced to a state of utter degradation. And Spaniards also had been insulted, cheated and robbed by the United States in the course of acquiring Florida. Therefore Mexicans should be concerned at the rapid approach of Americans toward the frontier.

Mexicans expressed alarm with increasing frequency at the threat of American expansion and at the growing realization that American condescension toward others included Mexicans. As early as 1822 the first Mexican minister at Washington warned his government that the Americans were an arrogant people who thought of Mexicans as inferiors. *El Sol* reported in 1826 that John Randolph in a senate speech insisted that his countrymen ought not to associate as equals with the people of Latin America, some of whom had descended from Africans. The Mexican editor believed that Randolph's view was typical of the "fanatical intolerance" that prevailed in the United States.

An article in *La Aguila Mexicana* stressed American contempt for the civilization and culture of Indians, who were called savages because their customs were different from those of the Anglo-Saxons. The writer was certain that Americans viewed Mexicans in the same way. An anonymous Mexican who claimed to have resided for a time in New Orleans reported in the newspaper *El Correo* that Americans seemed totally disinterested in understanding Mexicans; the American press gave more attention to "Persians and to Asian Tartars" than to Mexicans, and any notice accorded their southern neighbors was invariably insulting. Shortly before the Texas revolution *El Mosquito Mexicano* declared that the "refined egoism" of the white race caused Americans to treat persons of color with utter contempt and to assume the right to oppress them. The paper warned that Mexicans had much to fear from a people capable of such cruelty.

Manuel Eduardo de Gorostiza, Mexican minister to the United States during the Texas revolution, was the leading man of letters in Mexico and an experienced diplomat. Arriving in Washington in 1836 he was shocked to hear widespread statements of hatred and contempt for Mexico. Treated rudely by the Jackson administration, Gorostiza returned to Mexico and published a pamphlet criticizing Americans for their complicity in the Texas revolution and for their condescending attitude toward Mexicans. In 1840 Gorostiza urged the Mexican government not to surrender its claim to Texas. For Gorostiza there was a clear link between the expansionism of the United States and racism. He thought that Mexicans should make every sacrifice to retain Texas because they stood in danger of losing not only that territory, but also "sooner or later," their "nationality." The struggle to halt American expansion was a "war of race, of religion, of language, and of customs."

José Mariá Tornel y Mendivel, Mexico's secretary of war during the revolution in Texas, wrote in 1837 that the colossus of the north was obviously guilty of fomenting the revolt. He thought that it was the "roving spirit" of the Anglo-Saxon people that impelled them to sweep aside whatever stood in the way of their aggrandizement.

Like Gorostiza, Tornel was disturbed by American arrogance in their relations with Mexicans. In their treatment of Gorostiza, their encroachment upon Mexican territory, in statements by American officials and in the American press, there was ample evidence that many in the United States looked upon Mexicans as inferiors, possessing no rights that an American need respect.

The church also seemed threatened. A pamphlet published in Puebla following the Texas revolution warned that when the United States acquired Mexican territory "the Catholic religion will disappear from Mexican soil." Mexicans, like the Indians in the United States, would be deprived of the last traces of their civilization. *El Mosquito Mexicano* declared that the American advance toward Mexico involved more than the mere loss of Mexican territory; it threatened "the safety of the Catholic religion." A newspaper published in northern Mexico stated that it was essential to prevent American encroachments because a new religion would be established upon Mexican soil. Mexican citizens would be "sold as beasts" since "their color was not as white as that of their conquerors." *El Mosquito Mexicano* editors believed that the Catholic Church in Mexico faced the same danger from the United States as that of "the English under Henry VIII, the Irish under William, and Quebec under Wolfe."

Mexican editors often supported their allegations of American condescension with evidence drawn from newspapers published in the United States. The official gazette of the department of Tamaulipas reported in 1836 that a New Orleans newspaper had declared the Texas revolution to be one of the most notable events of modern times. The American paper had gone on to say that greater events would follow because "the superiority of the Anglo-American over the primitive inhabitants" of Mexico was so clearly manifest that it "presaged the conquest of Mexico itself." *El Diario* alleged that certain American newspapers had proclaimed that within ten years an "Anglo-Saxon" would be president of Mexico because Mexicans were incapable of governing themselves. A New York newspaper had said that fighting Mexicans was similar to "coon hunting." *El Siglo Diez y Nueve* expressed shock at the patronizing attitude of American journalists who believed that Mexico deserved to be conquered by those who were more industrious and efficient than her present inhabitants. Both *El Diario* and *El Mosquito Mexicano* reprinted an unidentified Texan's speech that encouraged his fellow Texans to support the conquest of Mexico. He was reported to have said cowardly Mexican troops would abandon the population and "immense wealth" might be seized from Mexican churches and from contributions imposed upon a "vagrant, corrupt, and lascivious clergy"; that such a conquest would undoubtedly expand the limits of slavery was said to be an additional advantage.

If any Mexican newspaper could be termed pro-American during these years, it would be the influential *El Siglo Diez y Nueve,* but in analyzing the differences separating the two countries, *El Siglo* also recognized the element of racism. The new world, it said, was divided between two distinct races, the Spanish and the English. Each had won its independence from colonial powers and had established almost identical institutions, but the two peoples had become strangers, if not enemies. Their laws, ideas, religion and customs were different: one was Catholic, generous, warlike and impetuous; the other Protestant, calculating, businesslike, astute. That the two should struggle when they made contact, as in Texas, was not strange. *El Siglo* found it particularly annoying that Americans should judge Mexico so unsympathetically. Mexico's history made it difficult for her to advance as rapidly as the United States, yet Americans assumed that her slow progress was a mark of inferiority. American newspapers spoke of Mexicans as "savage, barbaric, immoral and corrupt." These words might describe an individual criminal but not an entire community. *El Siglo* hoped that Americans would recognize that the generality of Mexicans was no more lawless than the people of New York, for example, which though highly civilized also harbored immoral and corrupt individuals.

Despite their moderation the editors of *El Siglo* nonetheless felt that Mexico must not surrender its claim to Texas. The fact that Americans in Texas owned slaves and professed opinions about the inferiority of all men "not of their race" made their defeat necessary. And by 1844 *El Siglo* had lent its voice to those who warned that the United States threatened the very existence of Mexico. Lacking respect for other civilizations, the United States, according to *El Siglo,* conquered only to acquire land, giving no thought to improving the condition of the conquered. Some American politicians had declared themselves in favor of exterminating the "odious Spanish race" along with their religion. These Americans shared eccentric beliefs and professed the most contradictory doctrines. They could be terrorized by the predictions of insane religious fanatics, and they proclaimed liberty for all and yet had virtually annihilated the Indian. Given the chance, they would do the same to Mexicans. Americans would not be content with merely acquiring Mexican territory; they would only be satisfied when they had destroyed the "Mexican Race."

Until 1844 Mexicans did not exhibit a significant interest in American elections. The annexation of Texas was, of course, a leading issue in the presidential campaign of that year, and Mexicans, realizing that forces were at work in the United States which affected their vital interests, followed the campaign with much foreboding. To *El Siglo* the threat of Texas annexation was the most serious question to confront Mexico since independence. The loss of Texas would be a "mortal blow," indicating that Mexicans were incapable of preserving the nation bequested to them by an earlier generation. Instead of passing as it should into the hands of those who shared the same "memories and language," Texas would be controlled by a "rival and enemy" race. To lose Texas would mean not only losing the value of the land, it would also mean establishing upon Mexican soil the "superiority of the Anglo-Saxon race." *El Diario* declared that the outcome of the election mattered little because all Americans, regardless of party, viewed Mexicans as vile, inept, degraded creatures. Regardless of who their president might be, Americans were determined to expand their dominion to include Mexico. The question before Mexico was obvious; "To be or not to be?" Americans recognized neither the rights of the Indians they had destroyed, nor of the Negroes, nor of Mexicans, whose territory they clearly intended to seize. Every action taken by the United States in relation to Texas was covered in the Mexican press. Readers were persistently reminded that the loss of Texas would lead to even greater losses in the future. Much of the diplomatic correspondence between the two nations was printed, and in almost every instance the Mexican editors pointed to the apparent relationship between American slavery and expansionism.

A pamphlet of 1845, urging Mexicans to fight for Texas, declared that Americans were energetic and ruthless in pursuing their objectives. They had displayed remarkable efficiency in eradicating their Indians and could be relied upon to treat Mexicans in the same way. *El Estandarte Nacional* perhaps best summarized the Mexican attitude in April of 1845: to make territorial concessions would open the door to the "triumph of the Anglo-Saxon race," the enslavement of the Mexican people, the destruction of their language and customs, to the loss of what was most "dear and precious, their nationality."

The cumulative effect of these and similar observations contributed to the creation of a public opinion that by the spring of 1846 was so rigidly opposed to American expansion that it forced Mexico into a war that she was not likely to win. Many of the pronouncements demanding war in order to "defend the national honor" (pronouncements often quoted by American writers who blame Mexico for the war) may be dismissed as chauvinistic appeals of demagogic politicians, ambitious soldiers, or irresponsible journalists, or as attempts to pursue private ends by exploiting anti-Americanism. But these demands struck a responsive chord among Mexicans who, rightly or wrongly, from their knowledge of the racist nature of American society, had come to fear the extinction of Mexican civilization should the United States acquire dominion in Mexico.

PAUL HORGAN

Paul Horgan has written twelve novels, ten other works of fiction and eleven works of non-fiction. THE GREAT RIVER: THE RIO GRANDE IN NORTH AMERICAN HISTORY (1954–1955; two volumes) won the Pulitzer and Bancroft prizes. THE HEROIC TRIAD (1970) came from Mr. Horgan's aforementioned THE GREAT RIVER, but concentrates on the three peoples—the Indian, the Mexican-American, and the Anglo—who settled in the area surrounding the Rio Grande. The following selection from THE HEROIC TRIAD movingly depicts the Hacienda life and family customs of the Spanish peoples in New Mexico. From THE HEROIC TRIAD by Paul Horgan. Copyright © 1954, 1955, 1970 by Paul Horgan. Reprinted by permission of Holt, Rinehart and Winston, Inc.

Life In New Mexico

LAND AND HOUSE

The riverside groves were deep and cast a sweet chilling shade. In their silence, their dampness in the low ground, the composite sound of the river reached far along the cottonwood or poplar aisles. Silky flow could be heard, and little incidents of suck and seep, and the murmur of ducks talking, and the blurred clap of wings as a blue heron clambered slowly from mud bar to sky. Willow stands made little green rooms open to the air. Cutting through the boskies, the main ditch opened its mouth upstream at the riverbank to take in flow for irrigation. It was a ditch perhaps six feet broad, four feet deep. It had wooden gates and sluices. From its artery ran narrow shallow veins to the various fields. When the light was low and the earth was darkening, these little channels looked to hold quicksilver. In full noon, their water was seen to be heavy with mud, brown and sluggish.

But their work was visible in the green of the fields, which gave cool air to anyone who rode by

67

them. Feed for animals grew there, and vegetables for the families who lived beyond the fields that separated them from the river. Orchards lay at the end of the field. Facing anywhere, the immediate land was flat. A few miles away mountains rose up, and against their hazy screens the slim poplars and broad cottonwoods of the foreground were dark. The clear deserts beyond the valley were cooked by the sun to give off an herby sweetness in the air, which travelled to the groves and fields and, mixing with their blue dampness and the rich muddy breath of the river, made an earthy smell that caused a pang of well-being and memory of place in those who now and then inhaled with sudden awareness.

The farms lay in narrow strips inland from the river. The earliest New Mexico grant under title was given in 1685. Where several clustered side by side, there were common enterprises. Cattle and sheep were grazed in the foothills rising away from the bottom lands, and tended for all by herders from not one farm but several. Corrals lay near to the house.

The house of a big hacienda was an image in earth of the family. Through generations it grew as the family grew. Its life faced inward. The outer walls were blind against the open country with its Indian dangers, and were entered by wide covered passageways as deep as a room, and barred with heavy wooden doors that were secured with massive iron locks. Within, the rooms all opened on a patio in which trees grew, that in time towered over the roofs. Where the clay hives of the classic Indian towns grew upward in terrace above terrace, the hacienda, built of the same materials, and using many of the pueblo's details in style and method, expanded along the ground in a single story. Beginning with one system of rooms about a square patio, the house, as new lives came, grew into another patio, and even another. The walls were often three feet thick, built of weighty adobe blocks and plastered with earth mixed with straw. Ceiling beams were peeled tree poles, and between them were laid peeled sapling sticks, often in a herringbone pattern. Windows facing the patio held sections of selenite or small panes of imported glass, and were shuttered with carved wooden panels, hung from iron or leather hinges or upon round wooden pegs fitted into carved wooden rings. The floors were of packed earth. Within the patios, an extension of the roof made a porch on all sides that was supported with wooden pillars and carved, scrolled corbels. In their plan—a succession of squares, either extended in line or grouped in checkerboard—the great earth houses might recall in their humble way the grille of the Escorial Palace.

In feudal containment, the river house threw its high clay wall around all the purposes and needs of its life. There was a great room, or *sala,* for grand occasions—dances, receptions, family gatherings. A family chapel sat at one corner of the oldest patio, and over its door might be a belfry with a bell from Mexico. Each parental bedroom was also a sitting room with its own fireplace. The kitchen was a long room where the family sat down to meals. Near it were long dark storerooms in one of which meat and game were hung. In another, dried fruits were stored, and piñones in bags, and grain of wheat and corn in jars. Beyond the walls of these rooms, and reached by a heavy rear gate, sparkled a little ditch, bringing a vein of water from the main ditch that drank of the river. Rooms for servants ran along the rear. A blacksmith shop with forge, anvil, and leather bellows and a tool house with carpentry supplies and hides stood side by side in a work patio, where pens for chickens and sheep, a stable for horses and a shed for milk cows closed the square. The soft lumber of the cottonwood, that yet weathered so well, turning a silvery gray and drying to hardness, was used for posts, rails, pegs, and joists.

The interior walls of the dwelling rooms and the inside patio walls were finished in a glowing white plaster of gesso, or gypsum, which occurred in deposits near the river, as at Cochiti. It was powdered and mixed with water, and applied by the family women with a soft pad of woolly sheepskin, in a craft that was common to the Moors of North Africa, the Spaniards of the homeland, and the Indians of the river pueblos. Around the base of the walls, rising two feet above the floor, a dado was painted with plaster made from the most colorful hue of the local earth—red or yellow or sienna—as a shield for the pure white walls against the dust of the floor. Where black earth could be found, it was mixed with fine sand and moisture until it could be spread on the floors in a smooth thin surface. When it dried hard, it was polished with the bare palm of the hand until it shone again.

In its essential form, the room was simple, and very close to the Indian's. The Indian at first lived on his floor. Later he made an earthen bench that hugged his wall, and if he sat, he had his wall to lean against. His very house was his furniture. The humble Spaniard made his earthen bench too, and in using it was tied to his wall. But the rich Spaniard moved away from the wall to the free center of the room, where he placed furniture, which was heavy, dark, and formal. Its character reflected his. If he sat in his chair, he must sit bolt upright, for the seat was narrow and shallow, its back straight, its arms high and hard, its legs tall. No matter how rich the materials that shaped it—carved wood, polychromed leather, Valencian velvet, Italian fringe and gold bullion lace, Peruvian serge—his repose was fixed in a discomfort that seemed proper to his decorum. His luxuries, even if he was rich, were spiritual, not material. . . . In penance—an opinion that could be detected in many Spanish ways of life—in penance resided virtue. It was only suitable that even wealth brought its discomforts to be suffered in patience.

What grandeurs he allowed himself represented the Spanish colonist's pride more than his joy in luxury. There were beauties to be enjoyed in many of the objects accumulated in the river valley by a patriarchal family, and sentiments to be told over as heirlooms descended. Placed against the stark earthen walls of a valley house, imported furnishings and precious objects even at their richest never seemed out of place. Inlaid woods, gold leaf, velvets, crystal, pure silver, turned the master's rooms, which in form were like those of a pueblo, into the apartments of a Castilian palace. Profuse trade with the Indies brought European articles to New Spain, and some of these found their way to the northern kingdom, where they made references of nostalgia, pride, and respect for the past.

In the *sala* was a pair of Castilian *vargueños*—Spain's only invention in furniture—which were wooden chests honeycombed with little drawers and compartments, supported by high legs, and carved, inlaid with ivory and nacre, and studded with worked metals. There were tall straight chairs with leather seats, and stiff armchairs in crimson velvet rubbed pale at the edges. A long narrow table, so high that it could not be slouched over, recalling the style and discipline of the monastery, stood in the middle of the room. Along the unbroken whitewashed wall facing the patio windows across the room was a continuous bench made of wall-earth. It was covered with Indian-made blankets. Above it, for its whole length, fixed to the wall, was a strip of Dutch cotton cloth to protect from the whitewash the shoulders of those who leaned back as they sat. At one end of the room was a wide, deep fireplace. Its hearth was made of flagstones. Heavy iron fire tools stood by its maw. In its chimney face there might have been a design of Valencian tiles, showing birds, leaf and flower forms in dark red and white, or an animal drama, such as a wolf eating a rabbit. If the family had armorial bearings, these were displayed in Valencian blue and white tile. Near the fireplace, on the floor, sat a Mexican chest with heavy iron hinges, lock, and handles. Its panels were like little scenes in a theater, painted in brilliant colors, and illustrating stories of common knowledge. Many mirrors hung along the walls, some framed in gold leaf over carved wood, some in tortoise shell and ivory, some in little facets of mirror set in mosaic along the frame. The Mexico-Orient trade brought curious, gleaming fabrics from China, and for its rarity and strange richness of gold and silver thread, a strip of Chinese brocade was sometimes hung flat on the white wall. By daylight the room was cool and dim, for the patio windows were deep and low, and shaded outside by the overhang of the porch. The room was lighted at night by candles, held in iron candelabra, or others carved of wood, covered with gesso, and finished with gold leaf. The establishment was clean.

This was because there were enough servants and because the lady of the house was an energetic and demanding housekeeper. The bedroom that she shared with her husband revealed her duties and her preoccupations. The bed was big enough for two—thinly mattressed, covered with a richly embroidered spread done in native yarns by the mistress, who copied flowers off a Chinese shawl—and presided over at its head by a blue and gilt statue of Our Lady of Guadalupe. Clothes were kept in chests of leather studded with brass nails, or of carved unpainted wood. Indian rugs were on the hand-rubbed floor. There was a fireplace, and by the window stood a small worktable and a chair where the matriarch spent hours at her work. On the table was her mother-of-pearl needle case. Next to it was a Moorish box of tortoise shell, ivory, and teakwood, which held her silver scissors, a little penknife, her spools of thread, her gold thimble, and a magnifying glass in a silver-gilt handle. There she embroidered altar cloths, bedspreads, tablecloths, linens, and taught her daughters her skill. If they married, each must know, as she had known, how to work on handkerchiefs with strands of her own hair the name of her husband. They must be able to embroider with beads. She kept little glass phials filled with beads of different colors and with them made scenes, flowers, birds, and sentiments on muslin strips. Vestments had to be embroidered and repaired. There was a rage for poodles in eighteenth-century polite society, for the King of Spain was a French Bourbon and the poodle was a French dog. Ladies —in Mexico and New Mexico—sewed elaborate little backgrounds into which tiny china poodles could be stitched, and the whole framed and displayed in the *sala.* Callers admired these objects and spoke of them as "very European"—always the highest compliment a colonial could pay. A pair of silver daggers lay on the bedroom table. On the deep window sill were a copper bowl and pitcher, and by them stood a dark blue drinking glass ornamented with golden roses and an inscription in gold that said "My Love." In a corner was a long row of boots belonging to the master, a pair for every task, as they showed, from walking in the river mud, to riding spurred, to dancing in the *sala.* In the same corner leaned a musket that was always loaded. On a wall of the bedroom hung a likeness of Our Lady of Succor, embroidered on red velvet in lifelike colors, her robe studded with baroque pearls. She was the patroness of the river kingdom. It was impossible to pass her a dozen

times a day without each time in half-awareness wafting to her a thought, a prayer, for protection for the house, its lives, and all its possessions.

The kitchen was in many ways the richest room in the house. Its graduated copper pots, hanging above the fireplace and its iron oven, shone like treasure. On its wooden shelves gleamed rows of dishes and glass. There was blue glass from Puebla —pitchers, mugs, goblets. There were cups and tumblers and vases of glass, milk-white and clear and colored, from La Granja de San Ildefonso in the province of Toledo. There were deep cups and saucers of Talavera pottery out of which to drink chocolate, and large breakfast bowls of the same ware. Porcelain from China, Majolica from Mexico, jugs and bowls from the pueblos of the river stood on wooden shelves to tiled ledges in the kitchen. Wood was used for utensils too, long trough-shaped *bateas,* or bowls, in which clothes were washed, or vegetables, or dishes. Large trays and bread plates were fashioned out of cottonwood and, after use, were washed and set on edge to drain and dry. From much handling through many years, they were good to touch—smooth, softly polished, and loved through work. The kitchen furniture was not so grand as that in the *sala.* It was of plainly made, unfinished wood— long table, chairs, and benches. Against a wall stood several *trasteros.* These were tall cabinets with locked double doors whose upper panels were latticed, or pierced in designs, and inlaid with mosaic patterns of common straw that gleamed like gold. Through these openwork panels shone the highlights of the family silver. When the *trastero* doors were unlocked and swung open, the shelves revealed large silver platters, trays, and bowls standing on edge. There were piles of silver dinner plates, and rows of cups and saucers, mugs, pitchers, chocolate pots; knives, forks, and spoons. Some of it was made in Spain, and bore Spanish hallmarks; much of it in Mexico. All of it was heavy, almost pure in its silver content and, except for any blazons proudly belonging to the family, plain. Light struck from its surface as from water, with a faint suggestion of ripple that added richness of texture to weight of substance. Though massive, the silver pieces had grace, and though treasured, they bore the little pits and dents of daily use. To eat in the kitchen, off silver —in this were both the Spaniard's earthy simplicity and his pride.

His spirit he took across the main patio to the family chapel, entering through panelled doors that held the carved keys of Saint Peter and the Spanish Crown, side by side, the Two Majesties. The chapel was a small, plain room with an alter at the end. A crucifix of dark wood stood on the alter between candlesticks. The body of Christ was carved to show His agony, with drops of blood in relief and painted red, at brow, side, hands, and feet—symbol of a sacrifice never to be forgotten by the family, and lesson to sustain them in their own commonplace daily sufferings. The altar was clothed in a frontal of imported velvet or brocade; or if such was not to be had, in a *colcha* embroidery done at home, of dyed yarns, representing large flowers, leaves, and fruit. The family's favorite saints, in various representations, stood on pedestals or hung on the walls in paintings. To them, in mute appeal for aid in particular causes, were affixed little votive images called *milagros*. If a hand was injured, if an ear ached, if rheumatism crippled a leg; if a cow was sick; if sheep were threatened by mountain lions, little silver likenesses of these members or creatures were pinned to a saint in perpetual intercession for relief. A thoughtful household, obtaining these from Mexico, kept a supply on hand in a little velvet-covered casket and produced them as needed. The head of the household conducted family prayers in the chapel, and when the priest came, the altar was dressed with wild flowers and lighted with extra candles; a set of vestments kept for the purpose was produced; and all heard Mass. Those families who lived near towns went on Sunday to the town church. Albuquerque in the latter half of the eighteenth century was empty all week, but on Sunday was alive with the families who rode or drove from the river farms to attend services at Saint Philip of Neri's.

FASHION

They wore their best for such an occasion. Indian servants kept their traditional dress, which showed little change since the Spanish colonization, except for woollen blankets which they had learned to make. Half-castes, and the poor soldiery serving time in New Mexico instead of in prison, and an occasional trail-driver, and the valley farm-hands appeared in red, blue, or brown suits made of *jerga*, a coarse woollen serge woven in the province. Their hats were flat-brimmed like those of Cordova. The Spanish cloak was replaced by the Mexican serape, which in turn came from the Indian's shoulder blanket. The men's jackets were long-skirted and full-sleeved, and their trouser legs now reached to the foot, having dropped from the knee. All wore boots. A sash wrapped several times about the waist replaced a belt and held small weapons of blade or barrel. The wives of such humble men wore voluminous skirts of *jerga*, and shirts as elaborate as they could afford, over which were sleeveless little coats. On their heads and shoulders the women wore shawls, or rebozos, of bright solid colors, which they folded in a large triangle, and whose points they crossed at the throat to be thrown over the shoulders. The shawls were fringed, and the length of the fringe determined the worth of the article, and the wealth, the position, of its owner.

The leading families—those who called themselves *gentes de razón,* "those who use reason," "the educated ones," "the right people,"—had a handsome variety of dress to choose from, with many colors and precious materials. The men wore fine linen shirts and underclothes. Their suits were of velvet, or of thin soft leather, or French serge, heavy with gold or silver cording in elaborate traceries, and buttoned with gold or silver or diamond-paste buttons. A skirted coat, a short waistcoat, and long skintight trousers buttoned the whole length of the leg from waist to ankle made up such a suit. With it went small arms— dagger, pistol, short sword; a tightly woven serape large enough to cover the whole body when unfolded and slipped over the head by a slit in the center; and a hat, whether a tricorne edged with ostrich plumage, or a cordovan hat with a high crown banded in many rows of gold lace, either sometimes worn over a silk kerchief tied tightly over the head like a cap, and recalling the scarf worn under a steel helmet.

Women of the rich houses followed the fashion of Spain, which changed slowly, so that even if they were far away in time and distance from Madrid and the court, they were in the style in their tight bodices and long sleeves, their low necks, their pinched high waists and their spreading, shining skirts of heavy silk or satin, over which laces were cascaded and looped. They had a choice of rebozos, whether one of white lace, or one of China silk heavy with embroidered scarlet and yellow flowers and green leaves and blue shading and long red fringe, or one of silk that fell like water in plain solid colors, including black, or finally, one of black lace with its designs like the shadows of rose leaves. From their little ivory and velvet caskets they could choose their jewels—emerald and pearl and amethyst and gold earrings, bracelets, rings, and pins; and rose-cut diamonds from Ceylon set in clusters like bouquets; and a Paris-style lorgnette with mother-of-pearl and gold handles with which to follow the Missal and edify an Indian; and gold chains and flexible gold fish and pure gold tassels by the cunning goldsmiths of Germany. If such finery picked up its share of dust in the far valley, still it spoke formally of the proper way to live, wherever.

FAMILY AND WORK

For in its own scale the family was as rigid and formal as the court of the King in respect to authority, reverence, and responsibility. So long as he lived the father was the lord, to be obeyed, respected, and loved. In turn he must provide the goods of life to those for whose lives he was responsible, and lead them wisely, and guide their work. The mother, in rich family or poor, was the lady of all, and worked harder than any at the endless household duties. Reverence was due to her, for she brought life and gave it to the world, and in doing so through the years received wisdom to which all would do well to listen. If her lord died before her, she until her death was the head of the family, and to the love and respect paid to her was now to be added obedience. Her ways were the right ways, no matter what the world tried to teach. She knew them without learning. Often in the colonial family, if the father represented the earth's life and its work of seasons and its secrets of strength, the mother was the fire and the spirit, the divined imagination at the heart of things, which she seemed the older she lived to perceive the more brightly. Her sons and daughters dared to risk humor with her, though rarely with their father. The grandchildren and great-grandchildren—for the families in their homemade sustenances were long-lived—stood in awe of their august forebears.

Relationships were stabilized, and each had its appropriate manner. Matrons of equal age and degree on meeting leaned their faces side by side and each kissed the air murmuring a politeness. Men, in greeting, formally folded each other in their arms, making two quick little slaps on the shoulder. Once a man declared himself *compadre* —"co-father" or fellow godfather—with another man, he was bound in a friendship that had a sacred duty to remain unbroken. A community in which such fellowships were intershared by all the men was certain of its own harmony, for to break it was almost sacrilegious, and could occur only through tragedy or passion.

When prayers in the chapel were finished for the day, all filed out past the senior member of the family who had led the prayers, and kissed his hand, genuflecting, in veneration of age. Arriving in a jolting, heavy carriage slung on leather straps, a great-aunt would come to stay with a rich family. She was received by the assembled relatives to whom she gave the most formal greeting. She stiffly put the tips of her small fingers, heavily jewelled, on the shoulders of each in turn. Her Indian maid followed her from the carriage, and men carried her shallow trunk of tanned rawhide that was stitched together in lozenges and squares, showing red flannel in between. The household soon learned her eccentric custom of crying out "Ave Maria" to anyone who took her notice. Who heard her was supposed to pause, cross his arms, and recite the whole prayer silently. She invited certain ones to join her in a compact of the Ave Maria. Hooking her right little finger in that of her friend, she led in reciting a charm:

"How many hours has the day,
Has Hail Mary whom we pray."

If she made a compact as *comadre,* or "co-mother," "sister god-mother," with another woman, they chanted together:

"Flower basket, scatter never
In this life and in the next,
We'll be *comadres* forever.

Tra-la-la and tra-la-loo
Whoever becomes *comadre*
Divides her heart in two."

To repudiate a shocking statement or action, the cross was invoked by putting the right thumb upright across the right forefinger held level, and saying *"Pongote la cruz"*—"I put the cross on you!"

Children, who wore miniatures of their parents' clothes, early echoed their parents' formality. They soon learned to stop crying over trifles. In their grave, dark, pearly faces with their large black eyes were reflected the animal repose, the spiritual certitude, and the mind's government that so generally marked the temperaments of their elders. These were qualities of order that could be shattered by passion or debauched by folly; but they survived, if not in the individual, then in the ideals of the conservative life he came from, in which the family, however large, remained tightly woven together; and in which a pride of inheritance gave rich and poor alike a dignity becoming to the heirs of Columbus and Cortés and Coronado and Oñate and Vargas, whose deeds and graces begot not only kingdoms but characters. In even his simplest acts the colonial Spaniard seemed to proclaim his proud heritage. For his beliefs and ways required a certain accompaniment of style; and in a remote land, poor in itself, style took effort to maintain. Behind the style of the big river households there was much work, for the men out of doors, for the women within.

While children played in the patio, under the prattling cottonwoods, and talked to their parrots, the mother had many tasks to oversee. For her embroidery and knitting, there was wool to be dyed. Favorite colors came in the Mexican trade —reds and blues from cochineal, indigo, and bra-zilwood. But these were scarce, and the old Indian dyes, used for centuries on sacred feathers and kachina masks, now colored the threads for embroidering bedspreads, altar cloths, upholstery, and clothing: yellow from rabbit brush, blue from larkspur, pink from the tag alder, blue-green from copper ore. Wool from brown and black sheep was used unchanged. With homespun yarns the women knitted stockings and wove brown and white rugs for the slippery floors. They made toilet soap from animal fats, adding melon seeds, rosemary, wild-rose leaves and bran starch, and grinding the whole mixture to paste, forming it in cakes, and setting them in the sun to dry. To make pomade for their hair, they mixed strained beef marrow, powdered rose leaves, and rosemary. If their skin was too swarthy, they bleached it with a paste prepared from wild raspberry juice mixed with powdered eggshells or ashes of elkhorns, soaked rice, and melon seeds. To hold curls in place, they used thick sugar-water. The women made candles, dipping a long cotton string into melted tallow or beeswax and hanging it up to cool. When it was cool, they dipped it again, and again, until the candle was as big as they liked. In the spring, they gathered up the blankets in the house, heaped them on a cart and drove them to the river to be washed. By the riverside a fire was built, water was heated in big copper kettles, and yucca root was beaten and thrown into a long wooden trough into which hot water was poured. The women, bare-armed and barefooted, knelt by the trough and flailed the water until they made suds. The blankets were then immersed, rubbed, and wrung until the country's unfading dye colors came clear again. At the river's edge while mockingbirds, larks, and blackbirds swept above them with excitement, they rinsed the heavy cloths in the current, and then spread them in the meadow grass to dry.

If extra help was needed, women came from nearby families, but never to work for pay. Their men would have been offended to have money offered to their women. When the work was done, and the visitors returned home, they were willing to accept a little gift, of "whatever was handy." This had pride, remembering the pretensions of the starving hidalgos of long ago, and also good sense, if on another day the helpers needed help.

Food and drink took much work to produce. The women made spiced wine, simmered in an earthen pot for a day with spices and sugar, sealed with a ring of fresh dough. Sweet cookies were made with twenty-four egg yolks. On a heated metate stone, dense chocolate was made by grinding cocoa beans, stick cinnamon, pecans, and maple sugar—all imported—into a paste which was dried and cut into cakes. Cooked with thick whole milk, these made the black chocolate drink which was served at breakfast, and at four in the afternoon with cookies. The finest tortillas—large, thin, round corncakes—were made from blue corn meal. Three of these, layered with slices of pink onion and curls of yellow cheese and sprinkled with green lettuce and swimming in cooked red chili pepper sauce, made a favorite dish. When men butchered beeves or hogs in the work patio, the beef was cut in strips and dried in the sun, the pork was sliced and soaked in a juice of red chilis, sharp with garlic and salt. Pork fat was diced and fried in deep fat to make cracklings, which were used in place of bacon. A soupbone was used not once but many times, and was even passed from one poor family to another to boil with beans. Women harvested grapes, which they washed, drained in a basket, and hung in a storeroom from the beams to dry into raisins. In the fall, as the Pueblo people had done for centuries, the hacienda women cut up sweet pumpkins and melons, setting the pieces out on stakes to dry. Squashes and plums were dried on cloths spread over the flat roofs. When the cane was mature in the fall, it was time to make syrup, and all helped. Against an outdoor wall near the kitchen was a long oven made of earthen bricks. In its top were six round holes under which a fire was kept hot. The days were often cool and the evenings cold, and as the work was long, bonfires were kept burning to give warmth and light while men with wooden mauls pounded the fresh cane on fat logs, reducing it to a pulp. The pulp was put into a wide barrel, into which a round heavy press was fitted. To the press a long slender timber was attached so that it could rock free like a seesaw. Here now was boys' work, and two climbed on each end of the timber, and

as they rode up and down in privileged delight, the press rose and fell, squeezing juice from the pulp which ran through a hole in the barrel's side into a wooden trough. Women took up the juice in dippers made of cut gourds, strained it into clay jars, and set these, six at a time, to boil on the oven until the juice was red and clear. In the bonfirelight after dusk all was animated, purposeful, and satisfactory, and when the first jar was ready, a sample of the syrup was passed about to be tasted by those who had helped to produce it.

The great families had Indian slaves. These were housed with the paid servants, and given lessons in catechism, and promised their freedom so soon as they might be, in the judgment of their owners, civilized enough to sustain it. They were allowed to marry, and their children were born free under the law. Female slaves were ladies' maids and kitchen helpers. Male slaves worked in the fields and among the animal herds. So few goods came by wagon train that the province had to sustain itself, and the raising of cattle and sheep, and the growing of good were the main concern of all. Crops, said a Franciscan survey, were "so limited that each inhabitant scarcely raises enough for himself." But by the middle of the eighteenth century there were millions of sheep grazing on the sparse slopes of the watershed. Between two hundred thousand and five hundred thousand sheep were driven every year to Mexico for sale. The grasses struggled for life in ordinary years and in dry years barely showed. The colonials looked at their hills and shook their heads. It was all very much like Spain, a condition of natural life that seemed impossible to govern. The tilted lands were growing more barren; the torrents—when it did rain—swept faster and cut deeper; the earth ran into the tributaries and into the river, piling up silt on the river floor; the river spilled over its old banks and made swamps on good farm land, and a man could only bow his head and invoke patience. Inherited practice had a firm hold upon him, at the expense of understanding the forces that his use of the land released in violence. Rain made grass, and he lifted up his eyes to look for rain. No other answer occurred to him. Animals had to eat. They had to stay on his own range or be stolen by roving Indians. He watched his sheep for signs of rain, for though they rarely gamboled, they would do so if rain were in the air. Before a rain, said the shepherds, a sheep would draw himself up and bleat and shake himself as though already wet. Before a rain, said the cowherders, a cow would throw her hind legs and bawl.

In May men rode out from the hacienda to help with lambing at the sheep camps. There were always goats with the herds, and when the men returned, they brought home kidskins of long, silky white hair. These were delivered to the mistress, who had them washed with soap and water. When they were dry, cooked sheep brains were rubbed into the hairless side. Set into the sun, the skins became soaked as the brains melted. Washed again, they were dried and worked by hand until they were soft as cloth and pure white. Some were dyed in brilliant colors and used as little hearth-rugs in the bedrooms, to keep the feet warm while dressing and undressing by the fire.

All houses kept horses to ride, burros to carry packs, and mules to pull the massive wagons and carriages. Wheels were greased with a homemade lubricant of fat mixed with pine tar. When a family carriage went travelling, it was accompanied by armed outriders and postilions, not for style but for protection against waylaying Indians.

Where water power could be had from a ditch brought close to the house, a mill was set up in a room twelve feet square. The ditchwater turned a wooden wheel outside the walls, and beyond it fell booming into a pool, shaded by willows and huge hairy sunflowers, where the youths of the household bathed and swam. Inside the walls an axle from the wheel turned a massive wooden gear that revolved a pole fixed to a grinding stone. Hanging from the ceiling was a stiff bullhide hopper from which grain fell in a steady stream into the hole of the turning stone and was ground against a circular flat stone eighteen inches thick that was bound to the floor, and enclosed in a bin. The meal was taken from the bin, sacked, and sent to the house, where kitchenmaids spread it out on a large white cloth upon the floor. They sifted it through a swiss-cloth sieve that was made to rise and fall on a smooth pole held upright. One sifting prepared the flour for whole-wheat bread; a second, through a finer sieve, for pastries. This work began with a prayer, before the maids loosed their prattle. Later, setting the dough for bread, they murmured the name of the Holy Trinity, and marked the soft loaves with a cross, to insure a good baking.

After the harvest in the fall, and the threshing of beans, peas, and grains, orders were given by the master for a wagon to set out for the salines beyond the eastern mountains, where the household would obtain its year's supply of salt. As winter came on, outdoor work lessened, and wandering laborers were seen no more till spring. But others came. A tailor might stay for weeks, while he made suits for the family men. A shoemaker might appear with his boxes and tools to repair boots and make new ones with tough bullhide for the foot, and fine Cordovan leather for the tops. Now and then a startling creature or two would appear, dressed in wild stripes and shimmering and chiming with jewelry. These would be gypsies —Turks or Arabs—who came selling medals and rosaries, which they swore came from the Holy Land. Glaring strangely, they smiled over the secret which all knew they had, which was the power to put evil spells. Apprehensively they were made guests, their holy trash was purchased, and presently they moved on to the mingled relief and regret of the family, who saw so few visitors. An occasional government officer would appear from Viceroy's court in Mexico on his way to Santa Fe, and make himself at home. He was treated with respect, for Spaniards accepted authority. They might be skeptical and willing to change the authority under which they lived, but authority there must be. Even if the travelling official gave himself airs—which the farther he went from the capital seemed to grow grander—his hosts smiled. Many odd things came with the law, but the law was powerfully implanted in them from long ago, and its flourishes were in fact a pleasure instead of a nuisance. In any case, hospitality to the visitor was a sacred tradition, and every comfort, all exquisite courtesy were his no matter who he might be. And when off the dusty riverside trails there came a guest who brought with him more than his own simple claim as a man, who in fact was a legal and spiritual descendant of the Twelve Apostles, then the household outdid itself.

Three times during the eighteenth century the successive Bishops of Durango travelled from their cathedral city in New Spain to Santa Fe, the most outlandish town in their province. Each moved by heavy carriage, accompanied by baggage carts, a mounted guard, and various clergy. The Bishop made use of the hospitality of the great river houses. The chapel was thrown open, decorated, and lavishly lighted. His mitre, crozier, and cope were taken from their leather hampers; he was vested; he gave Benediction at the altar and, touring the premises, he blessed the house. Children were told off to be prepared for confirmation, which he would administer on his return from Santa Fe. The kitchen buzzed like a hive and steamed like a hot spring. The whole house sparkled and shone. It was like receiving royalty to have the Bishop and his train. Every last finery from the great cities to the south and over the seas was brought out, and every local grace was displayed with anxiety. The Lord Bishop was gratified, and weighed homage for its true value, which was the pleasure it brought the giver, not the receiver. When he entered his carriage again in his worn black with edges of purple, he looked only like a country priest, and when he drove off on his squealing wheels, he left whirling eddies of thought behind him. According to their temperaments, some members of the household, at this contact of the great world, were more content; others more dissatisfied, with the homely labors, loves, and beauties of family life in the valley.

In late November the yearly market caravan began to assemble, starting at the northernmost river towns, and coming down the valley to pick up wagons at each stop on its way to Mexico. The wagons were loaded with goods and covered with lashed wagon sheets. The cargoes included woollen blankets, dried meat, tanned buffalo and deer hides, strings of red and green chili. These articles would be sold or traded for products of Mexico, the Philippines, China, South America, and Europe. Silver and gold money found its way each year into the province when the train returned. But for the most part, transactions in New Mexico were completed in goods of the country, for almost no hard money circulated. A system of four kinds of pesos, dollars, came to custom among the people: silver dollars, which were very scarce, worth eight *reales,* "royals," or about an ounce of silver; "dollars of the future," worth six royals; "old" dollars, worth four royals; and "dollars of land," worth two royals. As all were called dollars, the Indians and simpler people accepted all as equal; but the traders always reckoned what they bought in "dollars of the land," or cheapest value, and what they sold in silver dollars, or highest value. It was a monetary system based on coinage but activated through barter. Blankets, hides, livestock changed hands instead of money. . . .

FEAST DAYS

There were more joyful occasions, and these they made for themselves in the river households. Religious feast days were celebrated with gaiety as well as devotion. In March there were prayers to San Isidro, patron of farmers, when the irrigation ditches were cleared of their golden winter stubble. If a ditch served several families, men from each came to do their share. The weeds were ignited. All day the ditches were watched to see that fire did not spread to the fields. Food was taken out to the watchers, and picnics for all the family sometimes followed. The ditch fires showed after dusk and were guarded all night. At home, the children, before going to bed, went to the heavy patio gates and looked through the cracks at the magic glow across the fields. On June twenty-fourth the water in the river and the ditches was declared holy, for this was the feast day of Saint John, who had baptized Jesus in the river Jordan. Early after sunup the women and girls went to the ditches or to the river and bathed. Good health would follow. When they returned, little children went and then youths and men. This order was observed out of decency, for they were people extremely modest and would not go to bathe in mingled sexes.

The great feast of Christmas was celebrated with food, song, prayer, theatre, and firelight. Special delicacies came out of the kitchen—fried tarts of mincemeat and piñon nuts, white corn tamales, sweet cakes. Little bands of young singers, called the Oremus Boys, went from house to house in the villages, or in a hacienda toured the living quarters, knocking at each door, before which they sang Christmas songs. When their song was done, they received freshly baked sweetmeats. The housetop was illuminated with dozens of lanterns burning candles. All day before Christmas special fires were laid of piñon sticks, in squares of four, and rising to eight or ten rows high. These were placed to outline the plan of a rambling house, or the road of a village, and even the profile of nearby hills. When darkness fell, they were lighted, and in their orderly distribution, gallant columns of spark and smoke, and spirited crackle, they made a spectacle that delighted all. But they had more purpose than this. By the very signal of that firelight, the Holy Child born that night was to find His way to the homes of those who had made the fires. Boys ran among the bonfires, jumped over them, and dared rebuke. It came, in the form of the *Abuelo* (grandfather), or Bogeyman, who appeared once a year, always at Christmas, to threaten boys with punishment for badness. He carried a great whip which he cracked after them over the bonfires. He was a fright in tatters, with a false voice and a made-up face. They dreaded and dared him, laughingly. He chased them home where he made them kneel down and say their prayers. When he left, they burst out again into the sharp clear night where the aromatic piñon smoke smelled so sweet under a whole sky quivering with stars of Bethlehem.

It was not a season of personal gifts. The greater gift of the infant Jesus came to all in joyful renewal. In the great *sala*, by candlelight, after much whispered preparation, at one end of the room a company of family players appeared in costume to enact the tale of the Nativity, in many scenes, before the rest of the household and guests and neighbors. The shepherds told in verse of the star in the sky. The three kings appeared in finery with their gold, frankincense, and myrrh. At the door of an inn, someone knocked and sang, and all knew it was Saint Joseph.

> Where is there lodging
> For these wandering ones
> Who come so tired
> From long hard roads?

To this the landlord replied:

> Who knocks at the door
> In imprudent disturbance,
> Forgetting how late,
> And awakes all the house?

In the audience all knew what was coming but the littlest ones, and they learned and would never forget, as Saint Joseph sang:

> Sir, I beg of you
> In all your charity
> To give shelter to this Lady.

It was anguish to know the sufferings of that small and Holy Family when the landlord, reminding all of what mankind was capable, answered in his hardness:

> My house awaits
> Him who has money.
> May God help him
> Who has none.

So the scene shifted to a stable where, through a window, an ox and a mule put their heads, and where, attended by angels and visited by the three kings, the Child of the world was born again in the midst of homely music and passionate belief.

At midnight the patio was alight with fires and all moved to the chapel for services. Sometimes a priest from the town church was on hand, and held midnight Mass. At the elevation of the Host, the bell was rung, and with a hot coal a special salute was touched off from gunpowder poured on the blacksmith's anvil and covered by a big flagstone.

WEDDING FEASTS

Other than fixed feast days, marriages were the highest occasions. There was no courtship. One day the father of a promising youth, accompanied by the boy's godfather or best friend, called upon the father of a suitable girl and presented a letter, or made a formal speech, proposing marriage between the two young people. No answer was expected immediately. Pleasantries were exchanged over cups of chocolate, and the callers withdrew. After a few weeks, the call was returned, with a refusal or an acceptance. If accepted, the bridegroom may have heard something earlier that told him of his happiness, for the house of the bride's family would be redecorated throughout for the wedding, and news of unusual activity in her household perhaps travelled. Neighboring families might be joined by the marriage, or families living far apart. Cousins in the second and third degree frequently married, for the great families took pride in keeping intact their pure Castilian blood, and to do so, where there were fewer Spanish than mixed strains, would marry within the clan. Once the date had been agreed upon, preparations went forward too in the groom's family, until at last they were ready to set out for the home of the bride. They went in their jarring carriage. In a wagon behind them came the groom's contributions to the wedding—all the food for the feast and cooks to prepare it; the leather trunks carrying the bride's wedding gown and her whole trousseau; and other gifts.

When they arrived, the groom's parents were given the freedom of the house, for they were to be in charge of the whole wedding festivity. The godparents of both bride and groom were there too, and would serve as best man and matron of honor, and counsel the young couple until they were married. Marriage was a sacrament. The godparents had solemn duties in connection with such a great stage in life. The betrothal took place as soon as the wedding party was complete. All relatives gathered in the *sala*, where the families came together. The bride's father brought her forward and presented her to the groom's father saying, "Here is she whom you sought." The groom's father introduced her to all his own people, and then introduced the groom to all her family. It was possible that this was the first meeting of the betrothed. All then turned toward the bride's godfather, before whom the young couple knelt down on white cushions, while he solemnized the engagement by putting a rosary of corals or pearls— the two precious sea growths from the faraway Pacific—first over the groom's head and then over the bride's.

Now the trunks were brought in from the groom's wagon and presented to the bride. They were taken unopened to her bedroom, where a few privileged girls could see their contents with her. Happiness and importance filled the air now as the preparations for the wedding went rapidly ahead. It would follow the next day. The bride stood for her godmother to see if the wedding dress needed alteration, and tried on all the other clothes. The visiting cooks went to work, helped by the resident cooks. The mud ovens outdoors were heated up. The groom's comestibles were noticed, to determine if he was generous or stingy. Musicians arrived. Lanterns were put everywhere in the open. If the time of year permitted, the patio was decorated and used. Pine boughs were tied to the posts of the *portal* all around the court. Guests kept coming to stay. Kegs of wine, flagons of brandy from El Paso were set about. If the chapel was large enough for all, the wedding would take place there; but if it wasn't, an altar was set up in the patio or the *sala*, where the priest could administer the sacrament of holy matrimony. He would do this only with the provision that at the first opportunity the married couple must come to town, bringing their godparents, to hear a nuptial Mass and receive the blessing in church.

At last all was ready, and the engaged youth and maiden, who though under the same roof since their betrothal had kept away from each other, now met again before the altar in the evening, accompanied by their godparents. They were married in candlelight, with the hand-shaped earthen walls of their family about them, and a burden upon them of solemn commitment. Tensions broke when the vows were done. All gathered in the *sala* for the wedding feast. Now a river house had put forth another reach of growth and promise of the future, all in proper observance of ways that were as old as memory. In her white silk wedding dress the bride went on the arm of her husband in his rich silver-braided suit and his lace-ruffled shirt. Everyone came past to embrace them, and then the feast began. Roast chicken basted in spiced wine and stuffed with meat, piñons, and raisins; baked hams; ribs of beef; fresh bread of blue meal; cookies, cakes, sweets; beakers of chocolate and flasks of wine, bowls of hot chili; platters of tortillas, all stood upon extra tables draped to the floor with lace curtains. All feasted.

Then came music, and dark eyes fired up. The *sala* was cleared, while the musicians tuned up on two or three violins, a guitar, and a *guitarrón,* or bass guitar. Servants came to spread clean wheat straw on the earth floor to keep dust from rising, or stood by with jars of water from which to sprinkle the floor between dances. In the candlelight the faces of the women, heavily powdered with Mexican white lead, looked an ashen violet, in which their eyes were dark caves deeply harboring the ardent emotion of the occasion. The orchestra struck up. They danced quadrilles and minuets, whose figures drew all dancers into fleeting touch with each other. There were paired dances, like *la raspa,* with its heel thunderings and its laughing fast walk. There were marching dances, accompanied by spoken verses invented on the spot by someone who was famous as an improvisor. He would go to stand before a guest, bow, and without an instant's groping for what to say, recite an improvised ballad of eight-syllabled lines paying compliment to his subject whom he faced. He celebrated the beauty, charm, and talent of the bride, weaving in episodes of her childhood, alluding to her gallant ancestry, and promising her a dazzling future. The groom he saluted in another decima as a superb horseman and buffalo hunter, or trail-driver, or heir of an illustrious house. Sometimes he sang a riddle poem, and all tried to guess the answer.

While the dancing went on, the bride had an obligation to fulfill. Retiring from the floor in her wedding dress, she reappeared presently in another gown from her trousseau, and later in another, and another. Everyone was eager to see what she had been given. Politely and proudly she gratified them. They fingered her silks and examined the set of jewels given her by the groom— matching earrings, necklace, bracelets, combs, brooches, of gold inlaid with enamel, or seed pearls, rose diamonds, amethysts, or garnets.

Before midnight the bride retired not to reappear. Her maiden friends and her godmother went with her. The groom drank with the men in whose company he now belonged, while boys watched and nudged. The dancing continued, and humor went around. The groom's father, calling above the noise in the hot, hard-plastered room, urged everyone to keep right on enjoying themselves. Presently the groom managed to slip away. In the bridal chamber the ladies admitted him and left him with his bride. Across the patio the merriment continued. Voices were singing. Someone shouted a refrain. The violins jigged along in a remote monotonous sing, and the gulping throb of the *guitarrón* was like a pulse of mindless joy in the night.

So the river society renewed, celebrated, and blessed itself.

On the following day the groom took his bride home to his father's house, where new rooms would be added as their home, in which they would have privacy, even as they shared the communal life of the hacienda.

When the children were born of the marriage, they were baptized as soon as possible. There was no greater token of love than to dedicate them to God. If they died in infancy, grief was put aside for a sort of exalted rejoicing that in their christened innocence they had been gathered straightway to God in heaven. If they lived, they were cherished. As they grew, like all children, they aped in their play what grownups did; but very early they were given tasks to do, and a little boy worked at a miniature share of his father's work, in field, corral, or shed; and a little girl learned at sewing table, or in kitchen. They were an observant part of all the family's large or small occasions. The largest of these was death.

MORTALITY

There were sombre relish and conviviality in how death was received in the river kingdom. The Spaniard-Mexican had a black mind and a morbid tradition. Philip II lived in him for centuries. Death was the gateway to an eternal life, whether, by his own choice, in heaven or hell. Its symbols were always before him. They clattered in gaiety on All Souls' Day—skeletons, candy skulls, tiny trick coffins like a jack-in-the-box—and they presided over him daily in all the painted and bloody agonies of his household saints. He did not fear death more than most men, but more than most, he was an informed critic of the emotions of mortality, and at proper times summoned them forth for their own sake, gave them style, and so became their master.

When death from natural causes was seen to be coming, the family could only do its best to make the victim comfortable. There were no physicians anywhere on the river excepting the pueblo medicine doctors, and their concepts were too alien to Spanish life to be taken seriously. The parish priest was sent for if he was within reach. To die in sanctity was the most real of necessities. All prayers and observances were made. If the dying belonged to the sodality of Our Lady of Mount Carmel (who was the divine inspiration of Saint John of the Cross as theologian and poet), he knew that he might not die until once more he felt the earth. At his request a brick of clay was brought him to touch. Touching it, he believed his final struggles would be eased. His dear ones watched by his bed. When the last hour came, they sent for the *resador*, who always led prayers aloud at devotional services. He now had a duty to perform, and he came to join the watchers. He was an expert at knowing the exact moment of death. Relying on his wide experience and his natural gifts, he kept his gaze upon the dying face; and when he recognized the first veil of final mystery as it came, he cried loudly three times, as was his duty, the name of Jesus. At the moment of death, the soul took flight to its Savior's name. The best friend of the deceased or the oldest man present closed the eyes. Men dressed the corpse if it was that of a man; women if that of a woman, or a child.

And now that death was among them, the bereaved women screamed in grief. They did it as a form of artistry. They threw themselves from side to side and wailed formless words. This was expected of them, a mortal politeness that was understood and even judged. In obscure wisdom they set out to exhaust, to cure grief through its own excesses. Now and then in the midst of their working clamor, their interest might be seized by something beyond. They paused and gazed while their shrieks fell to whimpers. They were lost like staring children; and then, as always, life moved, their fixity was broken, and with a shake of the head they came back to their duty and redoubled their lamentations. Private loss became an experience to share in full measure with all who would partake of it. A woman shrieking and throwing herself required other women to hold her and give comfort. These in turn needed friends to relieve them at their enervating work. The whole society of women worked toward the seemliness of the event.

Men built the coffin of raw wood. The corpse was laid in it, and then with lighted candles at head and feet was placed on view in the *sala* for the wake, or *velorio*. All who could, attended to watch all night, while prayers were recited in unison, hymns of devotion to the patron saint were sung, and memories of the dead were exchanged. At midnight supper was served. The household was thronged and busy. Such an occasion was so much enjoyed that wakes were held even without death present. These were solemnized in honor of appropriate saints throughout the year. Men singing traditional laments in procession brought saintly statues from the church or the chapel, and communal meditations on death were observed as for a recent bereavement. A wake for a deceased person sometimes continued for two nights and was ended with burial. If the family lived near town, the coffin was borne to the parish church for a Requiem Mass, after which it was buried in the floor of the church while all present sang dolefully together. If the family lived far in the country, burial took place in the family chapel or in a cemetery upland from the river, out of reach of swampy soil. A fence of wooden pickets with ornamental tips stood around the family graveyard. A cairn of stones was put at the head of the grave to support a wooden cross. Late in the eighteenth century itinerant stone carvers sometimes appeared in the river settlements, and were hired to make a monument. One family, at Belén, had a carved stone mausoleum, built by sculptors who were brought from Italy. The funeral of a child was gay and impish, reflecting the happy fact that it died without sin. Dressed in white and decked with flowers and bright ribbons, the corpse was carried along in a procession that all but danced. The local musicians played furiously on their violins the tunes which everyone knew at their fandangos. The marchers chattered and laughed. Grief was out of place for one who had left the temptations of the world and already knew heavenly bliss. . . .

In their first century on the river, Spaniards had brought their saints from Europe—large church paintings and carved images in the styles of the High Renaissance. In them along with piety echoed the civilized richness of court and cathedral, and through them shone conventions of drawing, modelling, and painting that adored the human body in its beauty, and strove to immortalize it with every elegance. The exuberance of patronal society was raised in works of art, even in religious themes, to a dazzling splendor, through superb techniques. Greek ideals of pagan beauty were revived to celebrate the persons and events of the Christian Church. Through imported works of art, European sophistication presided over the worship of the river Spaniards and Indians in their rude adobe churches—until the terror of 1680. And then in one overwhelming gust of hatred, the Indians destroyed every vestige of the Spanish spirit that could be burned, ripped, or uprooted, and the European likenesses of Christ, the Holy Family, and the saints disappeared from their places of reverence in the homes and churches of the river. After their return to their impoverished kingdom, the colonists and the friars restored what they could of their property. But the Crown had lost interest in spending money on New Mexico. The Franciscan order on its own could afford only the most meagre of supplies to keep the missions alive. The barest necessities of life were all that came north in the wagon trains. The river kingdom began to recede more and more into its northern remoteness with every year as the home government in Spain found itself increasingly absorbed and on the defensive in European affairs. Imperial Spain was slowly bled of its life flow, and almost all the goods of life along the river were now created locally. Among these were the very saints themselves.

For, one way or another, there had to be saints in every house, chapel, and mission, and if there were no saints from Europe, once again, the Franciscan friars—who, when necessary, could do anything—filled the need. They painted sacred pictures on buffalo skins. They remembered mannerisms of drawing and of coloring out of Europe, and their first efforts reflected these. On little tablets of wood they painted saints that could be hung up on a wall. Out of columns of cottonwood they carved statues, which they colored. The friars fiercely preserved the seemliness of religious places by founding a local school of saint makers. They taught what they knew about drawing, painting, and carving to those among their people who showed aptitude. As the eighteenth century passed, and the friars were gradually withdrawn, the work was left wholly with laymen. Born in the river world, they knew no direct European influence. A recognized profession of saint maker grew up, to create an original contribution of the Rio Grande to the art of the world.

It was an art that sought the universal divine, and expressed it through the humble daily likeness of the saint maker's own people. If this was the inevitable formula for the artist anywhere, then it was the qualifying locality, and the nature of style, that made the Rio Grande saints unique. The faces and postures of those saints were those that prevailed in the bosky farms of the river—little cramped gestures without grace and yet tense with spirit; poor thin faces with great eyes that had always looked on poverty and in the mystery of hardship had found an identity with the divine. If the actors in the penitential events of Holy Week were fixed suddenly in their stark attitudes, with their dark eyes, their angled arms, their gaunt bodies, black hair, pale olive skins, and brilliant lips, there, suddenly, would be seen the attitudes of the religious art of the Spanish Rio Grande. The *santos* at once gave and received a staring piety that exactly expressed the spirit of faith in all its vast, yet intimate, simplicity.

In time the saint maker became a familiar figure as he travelled up and down the river with his pack mule whose panniers contained a selection of saints to be sold at the rich houses or in the poor villages. He had tablets, or *retablos,* ranging in size from about four by six inches to about twelve by eighteen. He made these by first smoothing the wooden surface, then coating it with several washes of gypsum like that used on the walls of rooms. He ground his own pigments. Black came from charcoal; reds, browns and orange from iron ores; yellows from ochreous clay; blue and green, which faded, from the copper ores used by the Indians for their kachina painting. For his medium he used water and egg yolk, and, much later, oil. He drew the outline of his saint in black or dark brown, and then filled in the color. His tablet often had an ornamental painted border, and at the top, a lunette carved in shell-like flutings. He tied a rawhide thong through a little hole by which to hang the tablet on the wall.

In his pack there were wooden figures fashioned in the round that stood from a few inches to several feet tall. These he called bultos. He made them like dolls. The torso was of one piece, the arms and legs of others that were attached, sometimes by sockets, sometimes by strips of muslin pasted as hinges. He covered the face and body with his gypsum wash, and then painted the features and the flesh. Every saint had his attribute by which he was recognized—Michael with his sword and the scales of justice, Raphael and his fish, Peter and his keys, Veronica and her veil, John with his long cruciform staff and his lamb. The saint maker carved such attributes separately, and affixed them to the figure. He worked to make his creations as lifelike as possible. If his bodily proportions were inaccurate, and the modelling of face and hands and feet faulty, it was only because his skill was not equal to his intention. But the passion that begot his works had more power to express than his technical ignorance had to constrain. His failures in realism did not deny life to his works— the life that he breathed into them out of the depth of his feeling, the power of his faith, and his desire to please his customers. He was an artist for whose production there existed a lively demand throughout the society he was part of. This condition gave him dignity and fulfillment as man as well as artist. Fully integrated among his fellows, he gave in his work not only his own vision but theirs; and when he re-imagined their life in the presence of their reality, he became the means by which their society perpetuated its own image in art.

It was odd, but it was true, that though he had a set of severe conventions for painting faces, they never came out exactly alike, but had striking originality in characterization; and yet, however individual they might be, all his faces were unmistakably Spanish. He gave them deep porched eyes, heavily rimmed with black, and thick, arching black eyebrows, and coal-black hair. The women's faces he finished with a paint that made them look like matrons made up for fandangos, with the ash-violet complexions that came from their lead powder. To his portraits of Christ and other masculine saints, he gave beards, painted in shiny black. He often attached real hair to the heads of both male and female statues, and sometimes did not carve their clothing but made it out of cloth soaked in gypsum wash, arranged in folds when wet, and painted when stiffly dry.

Looking at the Mother of God bought from a saint maker, the owners could often see the living mother of their mud house in the valley. One statue showed her in sorrow, with a black rebozo, her brows lifted in pity above mica eyes, her full mouth trembling on the very taste of the grief that swelled in her round cheeks, with their touches of pink paint, and her full throat. Her dress was painted and so were its buttons, embroidery, and the rosary about her waist. Her hands were unduly large, and looked rough with work. Another divine-and-earthly mother had a calm, knowing gaze, above a great nose and a mouth shadowed with a wise smile, that seemed to rest upon daily concerns of husband, children, cooking pots, and domestic animals. A Saint Raphael holding his fish was a heavy-browed youth with huge eyes full of the joy of the fisherman who has taken his catch out of the river beyond his family fields. In the right hand of a Saint Joseph was his flowered staff that bore a cluster of yucca blossoms. In his other arm he held the infant Jesus, whose almond eyes and painted smile recalled the Mongol antiquity of the river Indians. The saint himself wore a look of grave, untutored wisdom in Indian fixity. In a crucifix were all the exhaustion, dryness, filthiness of caked wound and scab, the rivulets of painted blood, that countless people had seen on the village Christs of their own hill. His arms and legs were bound to the cross with miniature strips of cloth. In another carved Christ, with real hair hanging lank, the local face was focused in staring rapture upon universal mystery unseen but believed. In another Christ, recumbent in a wooden cage symbolic of the tomb, the carved and painted mouth with a row of revealed tiny teeth was fixed open upon a silent unending scream. The power in his face was like that in the open-mouthed masks of those clay figures buried with the dead in ancient Mexico. The Holy Trinity was represented by three bodies, joined, and three heads, as identical as the saint maker could make them, and the face of all was the square face of a handsome bearded farmer with roughly chiselled features, who in obedience and patience drew the term of his life out of the river earth. So in countless examples, stiff, angular, almost coerced into eloquence, the saints in tablet and statue spoke with passionate directness of the daily life whose daily need had called them forth in all their anguished divinity.

Though they had an awesome character, they had also an intimate personality. A favorite household saint was almost a member of the family, constantly included in the making of decisions, and consulted a dozen times a day in the comfort of half-thought and daydream. "What shall I do?" The *santo* would send the right answer. "May my harvest be good!" The *santo* would arrange it. "If the baby would only get well!" The *santo* must save it. "If I could only be loved!" The *santo*—if it was a legitimate love—might bless it. Living as such a personality, the *santo* was subject not only to reverence but on occasion to displeasure, when prayerful requests were not answered. Then the *santo* was turned with its face to the wall, or put away in a trunk, until the request was answered, or its purpose dwindled through passing time. Addresses to the saints now and then took on an Indian character. When storms came, an Indian cook in a Spanish house went out the door and, recalling the sacred use of corn meal in the pueblos, threw a handful of salt to the sky, making the shape of a cross, and praying:

> Saint Barbara, holy maid,
> Save us, Lady,
> In thunder and lightning afraid.

PROVINCIALS

So in simplicity of spirit, and in direct productive life upon the land, with the most laborious of methods, the life of the hacienda valley took its way far from the great world. Out in the world, revolutions in psychology, and government, and science were creating new concepts of living. But Spain, the mother country, consciously closed herself to these; and barely a ripple of late eighteenth-century European movement reached the river kingdom. The machine was being discovered as a power in civilization. Technology was born. Industry entered upon violent growth. But not in Spain, and not in the far valley of the Spanish river of North America. The Spanish had no gift for technology, generally speaking. Though the pure sciences were studied, their application was left to other nations. But even Spain's rich tradition of scholarly education did not reach to the river frontier. There were no schools for the haciendas, and no colleges. Even the Franciscan classes in the pueblo missions were disappearing in the last colonial century, as the teachers were withdrawn. Children of the river families learned what they could from their parents. This meant a sufficient skill at the jobs of working the land and saving the soul. But it brought little for the life of the mind. There was no printing press in New Mexico before the 1830s. The only books that came in the trade caravans went to the friars, and were of a professional religious nature, with perhaps a copy or two of the poems of Sister Juana Inés de la Cruz, Mexico's intellectual nun. An occasional youth was taught to read, write, and consider philosophy by a priest who guided him toward a vocation in the religious life and presently sent him to a seminary in Mexico. For the rest, only sons of the richest river families could hope for a formal education. Such young men were sent to Mexico City to college or to Spain. They were promising scholars. Baron von Humboldt in Mexico found "that the young men who have distinguished themselves by their rapid progress in the exact sciences came for a great part from the northernmost provinces of New Spain," where because of constant guard against wild Indians they had led "a singularly active life, which has to be spent mostly on horseback." When they came home, they might become leaders in local politics and enjoy the prestige of having seen the world. But the local horizons and ways of river prevailed over the sons as over the fathers. Now and then a proud daughter of a hacienda was taken south with the autumn wagons to be educated in a convent where she would learn the crafts of ladyship. In due course she would return to her family, ready to marry an eligible young man and maintain with him the combination of domestic grace and primitive husbandry that characterized life in the river estates.

For the rest, it was a life that had its arts. If these did not blaze and tremble with the peculiar acrid glory of Spain at her greatest, they yet glowed behind the sombre patience of the people like coals dying under ashes. If their spirit longed for poetry, it had to be content with the doggerel rhymes at dances, and in the place names of the land, like the name given to the mountains between Galisteo and the Rio Grande, which were called the Sierra de Dolores. In such a place name the Spaniards met the landscape of their souls. Their theatre was made of the artless plays enacted by amateurs at Christmas and in Holy Week with deep religious meaning. Their music sounded in the simple scratches of violins at parties, funerals, the wail of the flageolet in the Penitential passion, the singing of High Mass, the celebration of love and adventure in ballads. Their painting and sculpture showed in the saints made in the valley. Their architecture rose out of earth forms in the universal style of the adobe house and church. All expression in art was integrated in the occasions and forms of local living in the long valley. It was all unprofessional and traditional, and none of it was produced for its own sake, but always to serve primarily an intimate function of the society. As the ways of life were taken from the local earth, the texture of living more and more showed the face of local tradition with its Indian source. The river house, Indian dress, dyes, articles of trade, seasonal ceremonies like the opening of the ditches in spring, the drying of succulent foods, the kivalike form and secrecy of the *morada,* the bogeyman who benevolently scared children into goodness—such details stood for the gradual absorption of the Spaniards into the ancient environment where they came to conquer and remained to submit.

Did they see themselves in their long procession through the colonial centuries—thirsty for discovery, but often scornful of what they found; bearers of truths which all too often they bestowed with cruelty; lionhearted and greedy-minded; masters of great wildernesses that yet mastered them in the end?

Those who lived in the haciendas and villages of the river illustrated a last chapter of what it meant to be provincial in the Spanish empire. Through three centuries the colonials knew first how it was to move farther away from Spain; and then from Cuba, then from Mexico City, then from Culiacán; and from the big monasteries of New Biscay and Coahuila to the Rio Grande. Every stage brought reduced movement, less color, luxury, amenity, worldly importance in all things. In time, remote from their sources, the colonists lived on hearsay instead of communion. Folk artisanship replaced skilled professional craftsmanship. Barter substituted for money. Home-butchered animals instead of prepared commodities sustained life. Custom overshadowed law. It was a civilization falling asleep—remembering instead of creating, and then forgetting; and then learning the barest lessons of the new environment, until meagre local knowledge had to serve in place of the grandeurs of the source. As they were native lessons, so were they appropriate, but as their products in objects and ways were primitive, they were matters of marvel at what was produced not with so much skill, but with so little. A grand energy, a great civilization, having reached heights of expression in the arts of painting, poetry, architecture, faith, and arms, subsided across the world into the culture of the folk. Defeated by distance and time, the Rio Grande Spaniards finally lived as the Pueblo Indians lived—in a fixed, traditional present.

What they preserved were their distinction and grace of person and manner—all that was left of the Golden Age whose other attributes had once been so glorious, so powerful in two hemispheres.

And yet in their daily realities they found content. Escorials and armadas and missions over the seas were all very well, but now there was enough to do just to sustain life. All about them was a land whose forms of mountains, desert, and valley seemed to prefigure eternity. The brilliant sky called out life on the hacienda by day; and at night, with tasks done, and reviewed in prayer, and promised for the morrow, all seemed as it should be, with the sound of frogs and crickets, and the seep and suck of the river going forever by, and the cool breath of the fields, and the heavy sweet smell of the river mud, and the voluminous quiet of the cottonwood domes. The haciendas fell asleep under a blessing of nature.

George I. Sánchez

George I. Sánchez (Director of the Center of International Education at the University of Texas at Austin) in many ways both exemplifies and was the precursor of Mexican American awareness. Coming from a rural New Mexican background, Professor Sánchez earned a B. A. at age 24, and in 1934 received his Doctorate from Berkeley. By this time he was already writing to Senator Bronson Cutting urging bi-lingual education in New Mexico. In 1940, his first book, FORGOTTEN PEOPLE, *was published. The excerpt from that book describes how in late-nineteenth century the native New Mexican became part of "the Forgotten People."* From FORGOTTEN PEOPLE: A STUDY OF NEW MEXICANS. *By permission of the author.*

Stepchildren Of A Nation

"We come among you for your benefit, not for your injury."——Kearny, August 15, 1846.

With these words, General Stephen Watts Kearny addressed the people of Las Vegas as he took possession in the name of the United States. Four days later he told the assembled populace at Santa Fe: "We come as friends, to better your conditions . . . you are now become American citizens.

. . . I am your governor—henceforth look to me for protection."

The common people of New Mexico did not, of course, comprehend the true significance of these words. It was a matter of indifference to them as to who was governor or what promises were made. They had seen officials come and go. They felt no attachment to a far-off Mexican government and, for years, had suffered at the hands of ruthless officials named to represent first Spain

86

and then Mexico. They had become hardened to political oppression. Since their governor, Manuel Armijo, had deserted them, it was immaterial to them who was named to hold his office. They cared little whether the governorship was filled by appointment, by usurpation, or by conquest. They, as always in the past, expected to continue in their traditional humble way of life. *Qué importa!* What does it matter!

There were those among the New Mexicans, however, who appreciated the meaning of the events of the American Occupation. They were educated, knew of the outside world, had visited in Mexico, and had traded with the American settlements and outposts. They were aware that, under the American Democracy, the condition of the New Mexican could be improved. They appreciated the promise of a new day. They were not unwilling that New Mexicans should become Americans. . . .

For years prior to the American Occupation the people of New Mexico had felt the effects of political bickerings among their officials. Revolts had been incited, a governor was murdered and his successor summarily executed, and justice juggled for personal privilege and profit. Private and political rights had been made the football in the contests that arose between conflicting interests. Political leaders were often at odds with the clergy. Land and water rights were carelessly used to obtain the allegiance of this or that sector of the population or of individuals. Civic affairs were in a deplorable condition.

The years immediately following the American Occupation proved disappointing to those who had expected that the new order would bring them relief from this situation. For five years the people of the region were denied territorial government. Civil and military powers became hopelessly entangled. The judiciary established by the military was, in some instances, of doubtful competence and integrity. Army officials and their appointees exceeded their authority, violated their instructions from Washington, and were active in factional political movements.

After the treaty of peace in 1848, and until the organization of territorial government in 1851, the administration of public affairs in New Mexico was in turmoil. The region was neither territory nor state. Not only were Mexican laws not in force but the Congress of the United States had failed to provide for the regulation of the affairs of New Mexicans. As a lawyer of that period has stated:

> As it is, a *de facto* government obtains here of a most anomalous character, having no parallel in our (American) history, opposed to the spirit and genius of our institutions and laws, and unrecognized by any competent authority.

Thus was American government introduced to the New Mexican. Instead of receiving the relief and security which he sorely needed, he was embroiled in factional political strife, was subjected to the bewildering tug-of-war of political pressures, and was assigned prerogatives and responsibilities which were not only meaningless to him but which were of questionable validity. A populace, ignorant of modern ways, was thrown into a situation which would task the most enlightened societies. Centuries behind the times, without a democratic tradition, unaware of their rights and status, and incapable of voicing their views and feelings, they became cannon fodder for political guns.

The tragedy of this introduction was not solely a civic one. The opening of the area to American commerce opened the door to economic competition of a scale, and on a basis, far beyond the comprehension of the natives. Business relationships, legal technicalities, and sharp practices soon began to take their toll of the economic resources of the people. Urged to exercise their rights as free citizens, they, in their ignorance, entered into agreements which lost them their birthright.

Ruthless politicians and merchants acquired their stock, their water rights, their land. The land grants became involved in legal battles. Was a grant genuine, was it tax free, was it correctly administered, was it registered? Who were the grantees, who the descendants, where the boundaries, and by whose authority? Defenseless before the onslaught of an intangible, yet superior force, the economic foundations of New Mexican life were undermined and began to crumble. As their economy deteriorated so did the people, for their way of life was based on, and identified with, the agrarian economy which they had built through many generations.

Far-seeing leaders sought to bring about reforms that would stem the tide of political and economic regression. The memorable address of Governor Donaciano Vigil to the first Legislative Assembly (1847) indicates that native leaders had envisioned a plan for the incorporation of the New Mexican into the American fold. On that occasion he advocated reforms that would safeguard public revenues, that would protect the Indian, and that would give the small farmer adequate water rights. Above everything, he was interested in education for his people. Governor Vigil's ideas with reference to public education reflect a clear insight into the foundations of democracy. In the same address referred to above he said:

> If your government here is to be republican, if it is to be based upon democratic-republican principles, and if the will of the majority is to be one day the law of the land and the government of the people, it is evident, for this will be properly exercised, that the people must be enlightened and instructed. And it is particularly important in a country, where the right of suffrage is accorded and secured to all, that all should be instructed and that every man should be able to read to inform himself of the passing events of the day and of the matters interesting to his country and government. This is the age of improvement, both in government and society, and it more particularly becomes us, when commencing, as it were, a new order of things, to profit by and promote such improvements, and they can only be encouraged and promoted by diffusing knowledge and instruction among the people. The diffuson of knowledge breaks down antiquated prejudices and distinctions, introduces the people of all countries to a more intimate and attached acquaintance, and is calculated to cultivate these sympathies among the masses in all nations which induce comparison and insure improvement. The

world at large is advancing and how can we profit by the advance unless the people are educated? It is true that the available means which could be applied at present to the cause of education are small, but for the promotion of so desirable an object they might be both increased and economized. All that the Legislature can do in the cause of education for the people is most earnestly pressed upon them and will meet with my hearty approval and cooperation.

This abiding faith in education he shared with other leaders such as Father Antonio Martínez, of whom more will be said later. Twitchell, in characterizing Governor Vigil, gives us an insight into the activities of progressive native leaders of the times when he says:

> Governor Vigil was found on the side of the people as against the imperious exactions and oppressions of the priests, as well as against those of the politicians, both of whom were alike resting as an incubus upon the country in 1846, rock-rooted and moss-grown, in contradistinction of the most sacred rights and privileges of humanity, by the authority and prestige of nearly three centuries of church and state combined. Not only his voice, but his pen, were frequently brought to this service, as sundry pamphlets and newspaper articles still extant attest. He found no fault with the people for their unfortunate surroundings. He regarded the situation as the result of a vicious system, for which they were not responsible, and which was their misfortune.
>
> He had an abiding faith that, with enlarged powers, with education, as free men, they would relegate this system to the rear and, in the end, entirely free themselves from their oppressors.

Though that Legislative Assembly was of doubtful legality, it passed ten acts. Among these was one creating a state university and setting forth measures for its support. These acts were not enforced and it is not until some fifty years later that we find the beginnings of a public school system for the territory, the counsels of Vigil, of Martínez, and of other leaders notwithstanding. The degree to which this fundamental aspect of cultural incorporation was neglected can be deduced from educational data for the latter part of the century.

Before 1890, there were virtually no public schools in the territory and education had been left largely to private and church endeavor. In 1853, the Sisters of Loretto had opened at Santa Fe the Academy of Our Lady of Light, which, by 1890, had had a maximum enrollment of fifty boarders. During that period, this Order opened several other boarding schools for girls elsewhere in the territory and, in connection with them, accepted a few day students. The Christian Brothers had established the College of San Miguel in Santa Fe in 1859. In connection with this boarding school the Brothers carried on a free day school where, through the years, several hundred children received instruction. Later they opened the La Salle Institute at Las Vegas and a school in Bernalillo. In 1892, these schools enrolled about 350 children. These schools, together with a few other small private and denominational centers, constituted the chief educational institutions for the first forty years after the Treaty of Guadalupe Hidalgo. To them came students from over the territory, from Arizona, Texas, Colorado, and Mexico.

The University, the College of Agriculture and Mechanic Arts, and the School of Mines were created in 1889. These schools opened their doors in 1892, 1890, and 1895, respectively. In 1893, the Legislature created the Normal School at Silver City, which opened in 1894, the Military Institute at Roswell, and the Normal School at Las Vegas. Both of the latter institutions opened in 1898. By 1905, these schools enrolled almost a thousand students and employed seventy-eight teachers.

After 1890, considerable progress was made in establishing public schools. Nevertheless, this progress was purely relative. As late as 1903, more than half of the school population was not in attendance in any school. In 1900, an average of $4.94 per capita was spent for the children enrolled in rural schools, of which $3.72 was for teachers' salaries. The rural schools had more than half of the enrollment in the territory. At that time, school terms, town and rural, averaged four and a half months and teachers' salaries less than $250 per year. Over 24 percent of the native white males of voting age were illiterate in 1900.

It is quite apparent that this situation was not conducive to the development of a people long isolated from Western civilization. That native leaders realized this is evidenced by such statements as those made by J. Francisco Chaves, territorial superintendent of public instruction, in his report to the governor in 1901. . . .

In commenting on the inadequacy of school facilities among the rural people he argued that:

> There should be a more equitable distribution of the school funds to the end that the work in the lower grades and primary schools in the rural districts shall be systematized, their general standard raised and placed upon a more substantial footing. The facts as they exist indicate the urgent need of some such action, even if there should result, for the time being, a curtailment in the further development of the higher educational institutions, for unless the schools of the lower grade are given careful fostering care these higher educational institutions of learning will ere very long have quite grown away from and beyond the reach of their usefulness as a part of our common school system, and as time elapses we shall more than ever witness the humiliating spectacle of that which is now partially apparent—taxpayers of New Mexico supplying funds devoted largely to the higher training of youth from Texas, Mexico, and Arizona, even from California and Missouri, while their own children are yet poorly served in the lower grade schools and wholly unable to qualify for admission to the higher institutions.

At the same time, Superintendent Chaves urged that Congress take cognizance of the educational situation in the territory and come to its aid. Referring to federal land grants made to New Mexico, he stated:

> It was tardy justice indeed that brought to New Mexico the original grant. How small

and niggardly it all appears now that we have witnessed what the federal government is doing for its newly acquired Porto Rican, Cuban and Philippine territory in the lavish expenditure of public moneys for the educational equipment of the masses. We in New Mexico have for years past more than liberally taxed ourselves for common school purposes, and yet we need to utilize every possible resource to carry on the work, now so auspiciously under way, and to that end I would suggest that no further time be lost in placing our just demands properly before Congress. . . . After having examined critically into the present needs of our school system and especially the need of adequate school homes in the rural districts, we feel that it would be an inexcusable lapse of public duty to remain silent, and it is hoped that every friend of good government and good schools who may read this page will use what influence he or she may have among friends in Congress toward procuring this additional concession of public land for so worthy a purpose as popular education of the masses of our people, so cruelly neglected by the parent government since as long ago as 1850.

Though Congress made grants of land to the territory for educational purposes, the national government never made due recognition of its responsibilities to the native people of the region it acquired from Mexico. It failed to take note of the fact that those people were, in effect, subject peoples of a culture and of a way of life radically different from that into which they were suddenly and unwittingly thrust by a treaty. The government also failed to appreciate the fact that the territory lacked the economic resources, the leadership, and the administrative devices necessary to launch an effective program of cultural rehabilitation.

As late as 1905, the territory could raise only half a million dollars for public education. This sum equalled only $11 per pupil enrolled in all common and higher schools and less than $7 per child between the ages of five and twenty-one. Of this latter amount, less than twenty-five cents

came from the income from federal land grants! In the light of the backward condition in which the people found themselves, it is unthinkable that such a pittance would go far in making them Americans.

What has been said of education can be said with equal or greater force about other public services intended to raise the cultural level of a society. Health programs, the administration of justice, economic competition and development, the exercise of suffrage, land use and management —the vital aspects of the social and economic incorporation of a people were left up to the doubtful ministrations of improvised leadership. The New Mexican was placed at the mercy of those political and economic forces, of those vested interests, that could control the machinery of local government. In an area of cultural unsophistication and of economic inadequacy, he was expected to lift himself up by his own bootstraps.

Whereas the adoption of the New Mexican has been a casual matter to the United States, the New Mexican quickly and wholeheartedly accepted his foster parent. The American Occupation took place without the firing of a shot and without any bloodshed or disturbance whatsoever. The abortive revolt at Taos in 1847 can be attributed to a few malcontents who did not have the sympathies of the native leaders or of the masses. The response made by New Mexico during the Civil War showed the loyalty of the people to the central government. The temper of that loyalty is best illustrated by the words of Colonel Manuel Antonio Chávez, a truly great Indian-fighter, frontiersman, and soldier of the West. On being offered a commission in the Confederate Army, he said: ". . . When I took the oath of allegiance to the United States, I swore to protect the American flag, and if my services are needed I shall give them to the country of my adoption and her flag."

The Spanish-American War and the World War, likewise, gave New Mexicans an opportunity to evidence their loyalty. In the World War, New Mexico had more volunteers per capita than any other state. Sixty percent of these volunteers were of Spanish descent. As a matter of fact, New Mexico had so many volunteers that there were not enough able-bodied citizens left to fill the draft quota!

Thus have an humble people reacted to their adoption. Loyal and uncomplaining, they have sought to carry on in the face of forces beyond their ken. In view of the circumstances already referred to, it is not to wonder that they have been unable to span completely the cultural and economic gap between their traditional way of life and modern America. The progress that has been made serves but to suggest the levels that might have been attained had a neglectful parent been more considerate of her children—stepchildren that the nation adopted through treaty.

.

LEONARD Pitt

Leonard Pitt (Professor of History, San Fernando Valley State College, California) won the 1967 Commonwealth Club Award for THE DECLINE OF THE CALIFORNIOS (1966). *In the selections that follow he writes of the relationships between the Anglos, native Californians, and recent immigrants from Mexico in the California mine fields. Pitt tells of how, by 1852, after the Anglos gained numerical superiority, the combination of discriminatory legislation and violence by white Americans drove the Californios and Mexicans from the fields.*
Originally published by the University of California Press; reprinted by permission of The Regents of the University of California.

Greasers In The Diggings: Californians And Sonorans Under Attack

As news of the discovery [of gold] spread in 1848, Californios speedily converged on the Sierra from all directions and, in a sense, made up for lost time. The experience of the Angeleños was typical. With Don Antonio Coronel taking on the function of patrón, the thirty Californios, Sonorans, and Indian servants had good luck from the outset. They immediately enticed some mountain tribesmen to accept baubles in exchange for gold nuggets and, after spying out the Indians' trove and plying them with more trinkets, they obtained their digging labor into the bargain. In one day Antonio himself ended up with 45 ounces of gold; Dolores Sepúlveda found a 12-ounce nugget; and Señor Valdez discovered a boulder buried only three feet down which had once blocked the flow of an ancient alluvial stream and produced a towelful of nuggets in a short time. He sold his claim to Lorenzo Soto, who took out a whopping 52 pounds of gold in eight days and then sold it to Señor Machado, who also became rich. Even a Sonoran servant became fabulously wealthy overnight.

In all, about 1,300 native Californians mined gold in 1848, the year of the bonanzas. If they had missed the opportunity to discover Sierra gold in the past, they did not do so now; nearness to the placers gave them the head start on the thousands of prospectors still getting their wits together for the voyage halfway around the world. The Californios had additional advantages in knowing precisely where and how to find gold and in gladly pooling their resources and dividing their labor. As a result, the organized Californians, though less numerous than the 4,000 individualistic Yankees in the mines that year, probably extracted as much gold as they. Coronel, a struggling Mexican schoolteacher, had pocketed enough gold to become a prominent landowner, viticulturist, and community leader. He and many other Californios resolved to make a second expedition the next year. They dismissed the news that a few Californios had been harried from their claims by fist-swinging Oregon Yankees, who refused to acknowledge that the Treaty of Guadalupe Hidalgo granted some Mexicans full citizenship: in 1848 "everything ended peacefully."

In the year that followed, the story changed drastically. Coronel's return trip to the mines began badly, with a near-fatal brawl in a Sonoma saloon. One day he and *compadre* Juan Padilla were waiting for the wet January weather to clear, when a former Bear Flagger began to bully Padilla for having served as Bernardo García's henchman in the wartime atrocity against Cowie and Fowler. Padilla insisted that the charge was a lie, and the American replied with an assault. After a severe beating, Padilla lay in an upstairs room, hovering near death for several weeks, while below his accuser continued to threaten his life. Only Coronel's good reputation and the intercession of friendly Americans restrained the former Bear Flagger.

After nursing his friend back to life, Coronel returned to the Sierra. He fell in among Chileans, Mexicans, and Germans doing well at dry digging until confronted with posters declaring that foreigners had no right to be there and must leave the mines at once; resistance would be met by force. Although this threat never materialized, excitement mounted. In a nearby camp, a Mexican gambler's tent had been raided, and some Yankees accused five foreigners of stealing 5 pounds of gold. Coronel's associates doubted the accusation against at least one apparently honorable man and raised 5 pounds of gold to offer as ransom. Coronel conferred with a Yankee delegation and gave them the gold. The delegates then retired to consider the offer but never re-emerged from the drunken and agitated crowd, which by then numbered into the hundreds. The money did no good; all five prisoners were convicted and flogged at once, and two of them, a Frenchman and a Chilean, were charged with a previous murder and robbery. Guilty or not, the pair scarcely understood enough of the proceedings to reply to the accusations. When Coronel next saw them they were standing in a cart, lashed together back to back and pinned with a note warning away defenders such as might come from Coronel's camp. A horse then jolted the cart from under the men, and California had witnessed its first lynching. That incident resulted, Coronel thought, from a declining gold supply and the Yankees' increasing jealousy of successful Spanish Americans.

As quickly as possible Don Antonio led his group away from the newly named "Hangtown," and resettled in the remote northern mines. But even there a hundred gringos appeared with the gruff announcement that the entire riverbed belonged exclusively to Americans who would tolerate no foreigners. Furious, some of Coronel's people who had reached the limit of their endurance planned armed resistance, even at the cost of their lives, but Coronel held back and sadly announced, "For me gold mining is finished."

By July many other Californios had cause to echo Coronel's words. As the only true native-born citizens they did have a legitimate place in the mines, yet they knew no way to convince 100,-

000 hostile strangers of this truth. Fisticuffs or hand combat simply was not the Californians' style. Consequently, one of them carried into the field of combat a safe-conduct pass, signed by the army's secretary of state, which certified him as a bona fide citizen deserving of every right and privilege, of every lawful aid and protection. What good the pass did is not recorded, but the attacks mounted. For most Californios, the best answer was to go home and stay there; "Don't go to the mines on any account," one *paisano* advised another. Out of pride, which prevented them from being converted into aliens by Yankee rogues and upstarts, few Californians ventured back into the maelstom after 1849.

Musing over the gold rush from a safe distance, the Californians once more concluded that outsiders were, by and large, despicable. Mariano Vallejo said of the forty-niners without sparing any nationality, "The good ones were few and the wicked many." Hugo Reid ticked off the list of troublemakers:

> ... vagabonds from every quarter of the globe. Scoundrels from nowhere, rascals from Oregon, pickpockets from New York, accomplished gentlemen from Europe, interlopers from Lima and Chile, Mexican thieves, gamblers of no particular spot, and assassins manufactured in Hell for the expressed purpose of converting highways and biways into theatres of blood; then, last but not least, Judge Lynch with his thousand arms, thousand sightless eyes, and five-hundred lying tongues.

The Californians now simply reverted to their customary circular logic, which held that evil came from outsiders, that outsiders were mostly evil, and that evil mothered evil. In no other way could they explain the ugly behavior of so many people, especially Americanos.

After a century of slow population growth, during which the arrival of twenty-five cholos or fifty Americans seemed a momentous occasion, suddenly and without warning California faced one of the swiftest, largest, and most varied folk migra-

tions of all time. More newcomers now arrived each day in California than had formerly come in a decade. Briefly told, the story of the Californians in the gold rush is their encounter with 100,000 newcomers in the single year of 1849—80,000 Yankees, 8,000 Mexicans, 5,000 South Americans, and several thousand miscellaneous Europeans—and with numbers that swelled to a quarter million by 1852. Even assuming the goodwill of every last one of these strangers, they outnumbered the Californians ten and fifteen times over and reduced them to feelings of insignificance.

It is the destiny of ethnic groups in the United States to be thrown together with people of "their own kind" whom they neither know nor particularly like—perhaps even despise. This was the lot of the Californios in 1849, with the massive migration of Latin Americans. It was bad enough that by 1850 the Mexican cholos outnumbered the 15,000 Californios; even worse, angry Yankees simply refused to recognize any real distinctions between Latin Americans. Whether from California, Chile, Peru, or Mexico, whether residents of twenty years' standing or immigrants of one week, all the Spanish-speaking were lumped together as "interlopers" and "greasers." In this molding, the Californians, who had always kept aloof from cholos and earlier had won some grudging respect from the Yankees, lost most heavily. Their reputation as a people more heroic, handsome, and civilized than other "Spaniards" now dissolved. Their proximity to the greasers between 1849 and 1852 put them in actual jeopardy of their lives. In essence then, the Latin-American immigrants were a sort of catalyst whose presence caused the sudden and permanent dissolution of the social elements.

The biggest waves of Latin Americans came from Chile and northern Mexico. The Chileans excelled in baking and bricklaying and other skills and thus found themselves in especially great demand in California. They settled down at the foot of San Francisco's Telegraph Hill, in a place called "Little Chile," or went into the mines to dig, until expelled by the Yankees.

Even more prominent and numerous were the northern Mexicans. Distinguishable from other Latin Americans by their billowy white pantaloons, broad sandals, and sombreros, the

"Sonoranians" or "Sonorans," as the Yankees called them, first entered the Sierra late in 1848, after either trudging across the Colorado deserts or sailing via Mazatlán. Some had sojourned in California earlier; in 1842, well before the advent of James Marshall, a Sonoran had discovered gold near San Fernando Mission. More visibly mestizo, less consciously Spanish than the Californians, they seemed "primitive" by local standards. Apache raiders kept them from their own mines and pastures, so that the Sonorans pounced on the California discovery as a panacea. The northern Mexican patróns themselves encouraged the migration of the peons by sponsoring expeditions of twenty or thirty underlings at a time, giving them full upkeep in return for half of their gold findings in California. The migration included so broad a spectrum of the population of Sonora and Sinaloa and was so large and continuous through 1850, that it compelled the governors of northern Mexico to admonish repeatedly about the dangers of life on gringo soil.

The Sonorans came on swiftly, heedless of any warning, knowing that they had vital services to offer California—as prospectors and hired hands, as supply merchants and mule skinners, also as monte gamblers and prostitutes. The leading merchants of Altar and Horcasitas, Sonoran towns near the international boundary, stripped their shelves in the spring of 1849, loaded up every available pack animal, and scurried for the mines. There they sold everything they had brought, dug some gold, and shortly left their followers to return to Sonora for new stock or for quick investment in Mexican securities—much of this accomplished before most of the Yankee Argonauts had even arrived.

Sonorans gravitated mainly toward the San Joaquin River tributaries, called the "southern mines" or "dry diggings," especially near a spot named in their honor, Sonora. Here they introduced Yankees to many of the rudimentary mining techniques that typified the early gold rush era. Sonorans somehow would probe the topsoil with knives and bring up nuggets, or work the *batea* (pan) to great advantage. Where water was scarce and quartz plentiful, as in the southern mines, they had the endurance to sit for hours and winnow dirt in their serapes, sometimes using their own gargantuan breath if the wind died down. They could also improvise the *arastra* (mill), consisting of a mule harnessed to a long spoke treading in a circle and grinding ore under a heavy, flat boulder. Others eventually caught on to those techniques and machines and later surpassed them, but the Sonorans' sixth sense for finding gold and their willingness to endure physical hardship gave them great advantages. Talent made them conspicuously "lucky"—and, therefore,—subject to attack by jealous Yankees.

Although the Californios quietly withdrew from the Sierra and left the field to the Mexicans and the Yankees, the scene in the mines deserved their closest attention. For, the mines became the staging ground for widespread attacks on their ranchos and pueblos, the rehearsal place for broad-scale assaults on the Spanish-speaking.

The problem of precisely how to react to the remaining "Spaniards" made the Yankees squirm. They shifted from violence to legislation, from legislation to litigation, and back again to violence. Some wished to exploit, others to expel, and still others to control the Latin Americans. On occasion, some Yankees even proposed allowing them completely free access to the mines.

It would have given small comfort to Coronel, Vallejo, Reid, and other Californios to learn that good and decent men had inspired the purge trials of the winter and spring of 1849. Yet, in truth, a great deal of antiforeigner agitation originated from the most reputable new citizens—army officers, lawyers, merchants, clergy, and public officials. It is a fact that the first organized and officially sanctioned outburst against Spanish Americans came from three hundred "white-collar" Yankees. While stranded in Panama in January, 1849, on their way to San Francisco, they heard distressing rumors that "foreign plunderers" from all over the Pacific littoral had already siphoned off $4 million worth of gold in California; how much remained for "true citizens" thus was problematic. On a slight provocation, the Yankees called a public meeting to deal sternly with the interlopers. No less a dignitary than the justice of the Oregon Territory presided over the gathering, and in the background hovered General Persifor

F. Smith, traveling to Monterey to take charge of the army. Smith drafted a circular declaring that, in California, he would "consider everyone who is not a citizen of the United States, who enters upon public land and digs for gold as a trespasser." This declaration won him three hundred vows of support.

The miners, who twice confronted Coronel with the charge that "foreigners" had "no right" to dig gold, were simply enforcing Smith's hastily improvised "doctrine of trespass." In April, vigilantes at Sutter's Mill drove away masses of Chileans, Mexicans, and Peruvians; and during a similar purge along the Sacramento River on the Fourth of July lives were lost, property was destroyed, and foreigners' goods were sold at auction. More than a thousand victims, mainly Chileans, came pouring down into San Francisco shortly afterward, many of them embarking for home. "General Smith is blamed by everyone as the sole cause of the outrage."

Smith beat a hasty retreat when he discovered that the consequences of the plunderers' activities had been grossly overrated: gold was still plentiful, and most of the dust already exported from California had found its way into the hands of American supply merchants. His successor, Brigadier General Bennet Riley, rode through the mines trying to undo some of the damage caused by the doctrine of trespass by telling Americans that technically all diggers were guests on government land, and that thereafter none should be denied access to its bounty.

Resentment against the "greasers" mounted, however, a product of deep and abiding feelings of nationalism, racism, and despair over the debasement of free labor. The nationalism was partly a hangover from the war. Some men imagined seeing "whole battalions, armed to the teeth . . . moving through the heart of Mexico . . . gotten up by the great capitalists and friends of Santa Anna . . . rising in one solid mass whose cry is 'California's recovery or death!'" Yankee veterans unhappy in the diggings and nostalgic for army comradery saw in the coming of the "greasers" the pretext for a "muss," whether for mayhem or for merriment. Northern Europeans—the Irish in particular—and Australians became implacable

foes of the Spanish Americans, more so perhaps than many native-born citizens of the United States. The notorious San Francisco gang, the "Hounds," for example, which was staffed by former New York Volunteers and Australians, took particular delight in attacking the Chileans who came to San Francisco after fleeing enemies in the mountains.

The forty-niner's xenophobia also stemmed from fear of unfair economic competition. Back home, one could normally see who became rich, how rich, and by what means; a community could use institutional means to regulate the process and keep it fair. But on the periphery of civilization, controls broke down: men sometimes prospered by unfair means; the population upsurge, the ceaseless shuffling of men from camp to camp, and their scrambling for the top of the social ladder defied control by ordinary methods. Thus the forty-niner improvised new devices, even vigilante justice.

Fear of economic competition had some basis in reality. Sonoran peddlers marched into the mines and sold 10,000 pack mules in three years, thereby depressing the prices of mules (from $500 to $150 a head in a matter of weeks) and of freight rates (from $75 to $7 per hundredweight in two months). This reversal of fortunes evoked no complaint from the Yankee miners, who could buy onions, potatoes, and other supplies all the more cheaply and had come to associate Mexican mule bells with savory cooking odors and a few cheap comforts of life; but it brought, in 1850, a pained outcry from Stockton entrepreneurs, who sought mass expulsion of their business rivals. Moreover, when the Mexicans set to work as peons in the employ of their patróns, they did make themselves the target of the prospectors. Miners who began muttering against the Mexicans and plotting violence felt keenly conscious that the Spanish Americans were cheapening the value of labor.

The treatment of immigrant Spanish Americans in the mines hinged also on the slavery question. They came into California precisely when the Yankees felt most irritated on this score and could see most clearly the parallels between Negroes and their masters, on the one hand, and peons and patróns, on the other. Yankee prospectors ejected from the mines with equal vigor any combination of bondsmen and masters. In July a prominent Texan, Thomas Jefferson Green, and his slaves were unceremoniously tossed out of Rose Bar on the Yuba River. The prospectors put into effect a local code prohibiting the mining operations of all master-servant teams, whatever their relationship. Three months later this provision cost the life of a Chilean and led to the ear cropping and whipping of Chileans and Mexicans who tried to oppose it.

With California's entry into the Union as a free state, the plight of the Spanish Americans in the mines worsened momentarily. Their protagonists proclaimed that, if slaves were prohibited from the mines, then so should be the "refuse population from Chile, Peru and Mexico and other parts of the world [who are] . . . as bad as any of the free negroes of the North, or the worst slaves of the South." The apparent inconsistency in immigration policy annoyed both the friends and the enemies of slavery. In the first California legislature, nativists freely categorized the Pacific immigrants as a race whose morality and intelligence stood "but one degree above the beasts of the field." The State Assembly, in no uncertain terms (by a vote of twenty-two to two), asked Congress to bar from the mines all persons of foreign birth, *even* naturalized citizens.

This extreme nativism soon brought about its own backlash. A fraction of the entrepreneurs in the mines began to worry less about the alleged dangers of unlimited immigration or of competition from "foreign capitalists" and more about the "disgregated, fractioned, broken up" techniques of mining; more about the possibilities of investing capital and hiring Mexican laborers, and less about expelling the interlopers. Usually outshouted at public meetings and outvoted in the legislature, this Yankee faction nonetheless had on its side the logic of economy and the ear of a few outspoken politicians who began a campaign to exploit, rather than exclude, aliens.

Advocates of this new position were most numerous and effective in the southern mines. There, the Sonorans evicted from the northern placers late in 1849 found relative safety, hiring themselves out to Yankees who maintained loaded pistols, "cool eyes . . . [and] steady nerves" against possible opposition by other Yankees. The Yankee patróns especially appreciated the Sonorans' skill and willingness to work for a daily wage of a dollar in food and a fraction of gold. "Greasers" worked speedily, when prompted, although work itself— and riches or savings—bored them, and gambling, drinking, dancing, and indolence cut down their work time. The argument ran as follows: The American, "with all his impatience of control, his impetuous temperament, his ambitions and yearning will . . . [never] be content to deny himself the pleasure of civilized life in the states for the sake of $4.00 to $3.00 per day, to develop the resources of the dry diggings"; the Mexican, on the other hand, is "milder in spirit, more contented to endure, more willing to suffer, more weak spirited, if you please," but for those very reasons he is the man for the job. Although a mere "hewer of wood and drawer of water," he would unlock California's wealth much as the Negro had done in the South. American freight shippers at the same time learned that the Mexican *arrieros* (mule skinners) were the most reliable of hired hands—skillful, proud of their work, and sure to get the pack train through the worst blizzard, over the toughest mountain trail. A genuine paternal fondness sometimes linked the arriero and his new Yankee patrón.

Yankee tradesmen of the southern mines came to see the Spanish Americans as particularly good customers. It occurred to them that, in contrast with the stingy Yankee who saved his money and sent it home, the Latin American invariably wanted to take home goods, not money; he spent all he had. Just as the Spaniard's eccentric work habits could be turned to the operator's profit, so could his spendthrift tendencies be turned to the advantage of the merchant. General Riley discovered that "Americans, by their superior intelligence and shrewdness in business, generally contrived to turn to their own benefit the earnings of Mexicans, Chileans and Peruvians."

The tension between Yankee and Latin-American miners climaxed in the Foreign Miners' Tax Law of 1850, one of the most original if benighted laws ever passed in a California legislature.

Thomas Jefferson Green, its author, boasted that he personally could "maintain a better stomach at the killing of a Mexican" than at the crushing of a body louse. A Texan, he had come to this opinion in a Mexican prison while brooding over the failure of a filibustering expedition. After a harrowing escape from the prison, Green published an account of his exploits, together with a tirade against all things Mexican (and Negro) and a proposal that the United States swallow up all of Mexico. He had come to California in the hope of using slaves to plant cotton, although the episode at the Yuba River smashed that idea completely. Because he had served in three Southern legislatures, however, and had a good reputation among Southerners, he easily won election as state senator from Sacramento.

Green had legendary powers of persuasion, even over men who disliked his social ideals. It was he who always gained adjournment of the California Senate to "more comfortable surroundings"— namely, his own bar—and thus earned his colleagues the sobriquet, "Legislature of the Thousand Drinks." In his tax bill—a kind of personal rejoiner to the men who had expelled him from Rose Bar for attempting to use Negro bondsmen —he proposed to issue mining permits to foreigners at a cost of $20 monthly (he later reduced it to $16). This tax, he thought, would bolster the bankrupt state treasury by $200,000 each month and would also encourage Yankee operators to buy licenses for their operatives, and to employ them "at a fair rate . . . until the labor is performed according to contract." The law would delight Americans no end and discourage mob action, or what Green grandly called "the interruption of the stronger power which is in the people." This possibility so neatly wrapped up all the nagging problems of labor competition, foreign monopolies, taxation, bondage, immigration, and mob violence that the Assembly passed it nineteen to four and the Senate seven to four; the latter house, by a vote of eleven to two, also gave Green a special commendation for originating so "splendid" a plan.

Although later condemned as an intemperate and malicious act, "conceived in drink and brought forth in jollity," the Foreign Miners' Tax Law actually had quite sober intentions. Its main difficulty was that instead of flatly trying to either exploit, expel, or give free rein to the foreign-born, it tried to straddle the issue. It promised something for everybody: the prospector would be able to evict all "unprotected" aliens, the operator would be able to undercut the "agents of foreign money to pay its bills (among them, the expense vouchers of the legislature), the collectors would make a commission of $3 on each permit sold, and the immigrants themselves could claim the protection of the law if they paid their tax. On the face of it, one could hardly have asked for a more equitable solution.

Yet the Foreign Miners' Tax Law hardly worked that way at all. In Tuolumne County, where most of the potential taxpayers were entrenched, the impost caused outright defiance. Printed posters immediately denounced the tax and implored its intended victims to "put a bridle in the mouths of that horde who call themselves citizens of the United States, thereby profaning that country." Two French radicals, schooled in the Revolution of 1848, engineered a rebellion and for its success needed the cooperation of the Mexicans. Although the Mexicans were gun-shy, they nevertheless went to tell the Yankees what was on the mind of all non-Yankees. An impressive array of 4,000 "aliens"—mostly Mexicans—congregated on the outskirts of Sonora on Sunday, May 19, to consider proper action against the law, which was to take effect the next day. To the collector's face the delegation flatly declared that the foreign-born might pay $3 or even $5 monthly, but not $20—a token sum for protection against rowdies, but not an entire fortune monthly. When the collector held his ground and demanded the full amount, most foreigners fled the town. One remaining Mexican threatened the sheriff, or so it seemed to the bystander who killed him with a bowie knife. Local officials prohibited merchants from selling supplies to any foreign miners and spread an alarm to nearby camps to call up reinforcements for the forthcoming "war" at the county seat.

One hundred and fifty war veterans promptly stopped work at Mormon Gulch, selected a captain, put on the remains of their uniforms, and, with regimental colors high, marched to Sonora for action. Sonora received them warmly with fulsome speeches, food, and free liquor. By nightfall the town seethed with inevitable rumors of Mexican incendiarism, assassination, and massacre. Officers posted pickets, stored weapons, and briefed the men for the next day's action. Sonora was under martial law.

Next morning, into the diggings marched four hundred Americans—a moving "engine of terror" —heading for Columbia Camp, the foreigners' headquarters. They collected tax money from a few affluent aliens and chased the rest away, with a warning to vacate the mines. One trooper recalls seeing "men, women and children—all packed up and moving, bag and baggage. Tents were being pulled down, houses and hovels gutted of their contents; mules, horses and jackasses were being hastily packed, while crowds were already in full retreat." The posse finally arrested the two "hotheaded Frenchmen . . . of the red republican order," who started everything, fined them $5 for "treason," and dismissed them. Thus ended the "muss." The men liquored up for the road, hoisted the Stars and Stripes to the top of a pine tree, fired off a salute, and headed for home. Next day, about five hundred French and German forty-eighters stormed into Sonora shouting revolutionary slogans and vowing to liberate the Frenchmen. Upon hearing that the pair had been freed, the would-be liberators dispersed sheepishly.

Sonora had just about recovered from the excitement of this "French Revolution" when a new attack broke over the heads of the Spanish-speaking. A series of robberies and violent deaths came to light near town in which the victims were Yankees and the murder weapons *riatas;* this made it easy to blame "foreigners of Spanish-American origin." Next, a Sonoran and his three Yaqui Indian retainers were caught burning two bodies and would have been lynched, but for the timely intervention of the justice of the peace and the sheriff, who remanded the prisoners to the district court. On the morning of the court trial (July 15), the Mormon Gulch veterans again descended on Sonora in military order and spoiling for action. Informed that the prisoners might be hirelings of a "notorious Mexican chief" at Green Flat, they marched there, rounded up practically every

male in sight, herded them back to Sonora, and literally corralled them for safekeeping overnight. In the morning, the justice of the peace investigated the "caze of murther against 110 Greasers . . . captured by 80 brave Americans," but, having determined that the Mexicans were innocent newcomers, he let them go. After a momentary riot scene in the courtroom, the Sonoran, on bended knees, convinced the jury that he and his Indians had killed no one but had accidentally discovered the bodies and were trying to dispose of them according to Yaqui burial custom. The crowd dispersed grudgingly.

Unhappily, another gruesome death, uncovered the very next day, again made Sonora the prey of every rumor incriminating Latin Americans. Since all previous measures had failed to stop the atrocities, it was proposed to cleanse the hillsides thoroughly of every Spanish American with the least tinge of "evil." The present emergency demanded that "all Mexicans should suffer for a few." The "better element" of Yankees in the southern mines, who normally recoiled from drastic measures, now feared that their territory was fast acquiring the reputation of a bandit refuge, which was bad for business, and felt impelled to join the broadside attack. Outshouting one dissenting voice, a large public meeting in Sonora voted to force all foreigners to deposit their arms with Americans and apply for permits of good conduct. All Latin Americans, except "respectable characters," were given fifteen days in which to depart. The Mormon Gulch veterans set to work enforcing these dicta with gusto.

The screening plan to expel the "obnoxious" Spanish Americans worked well. It reduced the danger of *bandido* attack and frightened off economic rivals. Between May and August, from five to fifteen thousand foreign-born diggers scattered from the southern mines. Mexicans went elsewhere looking for surcease of trouble but were dogged everywhere; eventually, they came streaming out of the Sierra, some showing signs of "pinching want." Even those who paid the extortionate $20 found that it bought very little protection, for if the collector neglected his monthly rounds their certificates lapsed, and if the Americans of one county refused to honor permits bought in another, the Spanish-speaking had little recourse but to leave. They knew that they alone of all foreign miners were being subjected to the tax: when they taunted the collectors to tax Irishmen, Frenchmen, and other Europeans they received no satisfactory reply. Masqueraders posing as collectors came into Mexican camps, solemnly tore up valid permits, and demanded money for new ones; when rebuffed, they auctioned off the victim's dirt and installed in his claim a "loyal citizen." One imposter carried off his charade so well at Don Pedro's Bar that he convinced a posse to help him chase away forty peons and their patrón and killed two Mexicans in the action, before his identity was uncovered.

Even when seeking an escape from California, Mexicans found the Americans lying in wait for them. On the Colorado River, a United States Army lieutenant had express orders "to make all Sonorans passing out of California with gold, pay a duty . . . and for my trouble, to put the whole of it in my pocket." A troop of California militiamen blandly confiscated from homebound Sonorans more than a hundred "stolen" mules and horses, ignoring the brand marks proving ownership and compelling the Mexicans to walk 300 miles, including 100 miles across desert.

In the preceding year misunderstanding, fear, and hatred had created an atmosphere so hostile to "Sonorans" as to sanction fraud and murder. Nonetheless, the argument for both protecting and exploiting the foreign miners once more gathered strength. The earliest and most effective counterattack against prejudice was made by the San Francisco Vigilance Committee of 1849, which summarily expelled the "Hounds" from town and made amends to the Chileans who had been tormented by them. Thereafter many individuals took up the cause, speaking in behalf of civil law or laissez-faire competition or on grounds of simple revulsion against mob violence. Among those spokesmen were judges, editors, lawyers, a sheriff, a brigadier general, merchants, mine operators, and the French consul. Several sympathetic collectors ceased selling permits. Even the state attorney general disliked the tax so thoroughly that he refused to defend the collector prosecuted in the California Supreme Court and ignored the governor's threat to prosecute him for dereliction of duty.

Xenophobia had injured its perpetrators as well as its victims. As Mexicans fled the southern mines in 1850, the profits of Yankee merchants plunged alarmingly. Eight-dollar crowbars in one afternoon dropped to fifty cents; a plot of land worth several thousand dollars went begging "for a few bits." Out of sheer dollars-and-cents self-interest, if nothing else, businessmen collected money, hired a lawyer to sue the local collector, and circulated a mass petition asking the governor to lower the impost to $5; all but one merchant signed the document. In July and August, after the second wave of expulsions caused retail losses as high as $10,000 a day in three southern counties, merchants who had helped expel the "evil characters" during the bandit scare became aware that *all* Mexicans were fleeing, not merely the undesirables. A crowd gathered at Georgetown, down the road from Sonora, and went on record as denouncing antiforeigner vigilantes and as supporting civil law. As a result the Stockton *Times* reported that the screening plan enforced at Mormon Gulch and elsewhere was "speedily held in contempt."

These forces had planned to persuade the governor to reduce the tax, the legislature to repeal it, or, best of all, the courts to nullify it. In the state Supreme Court they pleaded that it infringed the exclusive right of the federal government to govern federal lands and abridged the protection granted to aliens by the state constitution and by two treaties with Mexico. Neither of these arguments, however, swayed the high tribunal, which advanced a philosophy of states' rights in all matters relating to the federal government. Two Southern attorneys convinced the court that a state (1) could rightfully tax federal lands, unless specifically prohibited from doing so, and (2) had police powers to defend itself against undesirables. The court, in effect, agreed with the author of the tax act, Green, who had grandly declared that congressional inaction on the California mines had thrown the state back onto "universal laws . . . higher, greater, and stronger than the written constitution." Gratuitously, the court added that even had the law violated a treaty— which had not been demonstrated—it might still be valid, for state laws could take precedence over treaties. Thus the Spanish Americans had unknowingly become the victims of the imponderable and pervasive sectional controversies of the day.

Notwithstanding its new judicial seal of approval, the tax was a practical failure, as even its original supporters admitted. The Mexican was not the Negro slave; California was not Texas. The governor, aware that the tax was reaping more resentment than revenue, cut the rate to $20 for four months. Even after this corrective, however, the state obtained only $30,000 instead of an expected $2,400,000. The collector in a county that had 15,000 potential taxpayers, sold only 525 permits and was so harrassed on his job that he resigned. By 1851 Stockton's leading citizens had developed such loathing for the tax—"a law for the killing of children to get their fat"—that they decided to rally the entire county and lobby in the state capital to obtain its repeal. This they accomplished early in 1851.

The tax had failed to make the state wealthy, to prevent mob action, and to convert immigrants into hirelings as promised. It had eliminated the Latin Americans already in California and curtailed new immigration, a result that did not altogether fill the original bill. Now, having pushed the tax aside, the boosters of the foreign miners hoped to summon them back and make amends. The Yankees had a sudden vision that with the law gone, tens of thousands of Latin Americans would come flooding out of Mexico and Chile and the California towns and wash up into the southern mines, thus opening a new era in gold mining.

That dream failed to materialize, however, since the Spanish Americans by now mistrusted the Yankees and suspected that gold was giving out. They withdrew to Los Angeles and other villages or returned home, informing their countrymen of the dangers of venturing forth into California. Of course, small parties of Spanish Americans continued to enter the diggings, rummaging about on their own hook and staying alert to the possibility of trouble. The one lone Mexican patrón who dared bring in peons in 1852 stood out so conspicuously that he became the center of an international incident. His case made the complete circuit to Mexico City, Washington, and back to California. The district attorney investigated it for the United States Secretary of War, who determined that, although the crowd of Americans who stopped the Mexican was "wholly unprincipled and deserving of punishment," Mexican nationals should seek reparations in the state courts, since the federal government took no responsibility for riots. Thereafter, no patrón was courageous or indiscreet enough to enter the mines, and the Yankee triumph over "foreign capitalists" and "slaves" was complete.

In the long view of California history, the Mexican miners represent merely a link in a long chain of migrants who reach across the "Spanish borderland." They unwittingly followed the trail blazed by the Spanish soldier Juan Bautista Anza and used later by Mexican cholos and colonists. They foreshadowed the coming of the "wetbacks" and the *braceros* in the twentieth century. As ever, the Mexicans met with mixed success in California, often defeat. They did find some gold, but had to fight for every ounce. That they escaped Yankee bondage was perhaps the most fortunate thing that happened to them.

The migration of the Mexican forty-niners affected the Californios in two ways: for one thing, it put the Yankees in an ugly frame of mind toward all the Spanish-speaking, including the native-born; for another, it sent the newcomers into the established old communities of California, where they fused imperceptibly with those born there. This tended to break down the old and somewhat artificial distinction between "native Californians" and "Mexicans." The fusion went on continuously thereafter.

The Mexican newcomers had, however, one major advantage over their California-born brethren; whereas they could ultimately evade the gringo enemy by returning home, the Californios, attacked on their own soil, could not.

AMÉRICO PAREDES

*Américo Paredes (Professor of English and Anthropology,
The University of Texas at Austin, Texas) is an
internationally known folklorist. His scholarly works include
the well-known "WITH HIS PISTOL IN HIS HAND": A
BORDER BALLAD AND ITS HERO (1958). This book
presents a different oral tradition than the usual Anglo one.
The point of greatest variance in historical traditions
probably centers on the folk myths of the Texas Rangers. In
the following selection from "WITH HIS PISTOL IN HIS
HAND," Professor Paredes writes of the Chicanos' relations
with the Rangers in the early twentieth century.
From: Américo Paredes, "WITH HIS PISTOL IN HIS
HAND": A BORDER BALLAD AND ITS HERO (University
of Texas Press, 1958).*

With A Pistol In His Hand

Most of the Border people did not live in the towns. The typical community was the ranch or the ranching village. Here lived small, tightly knit groups whose basic social structure was the family or the clan. The early settlements had begun as great ranches, but succeeding generations multiplied the number of owners of each of the original land grants. The earliest practice was to divide the grant among the original owner's children. Later many descendants simply held the land in com-mon, grouping their houses in small villages around what had been the ancestral home. In time almost everyone in any given area came to be related to everyone else.

The cohesiveness of the Border communities owed a great deal to geography. Nuevo Santander was settled comparatively late because of its isolated location. In 1846 it took Taylor a month to move his troops the 160 miles from Corpus Christi to Brownsville. In 1900 communications had im-

102

proved but little, and it was not until 1904 that a railroad connected Brownsville with trans-Nueces areas, while a paved highway did not join Matamoros with the interior of Mexico until the 1940s.

The brush around Brownsville in the 1870s was so heavy that herds of stolen beef or horses could be hidden a few miles from town in perfect secrecy. Even in the late 1920s the thick chaparral isolated many parts of the Border. Ranches and farms that are now within sight of each other across a flat, dusty cotton land were remote in those days of winding trails through the brush. The nearest neighbors were across the river, and most north-bank communities were in fact extensions of those on the south bank.

The simple pastoral life led by most Border people fostered a natural equality among men. Much has been written about the democratizing influence of a horse culture. More important was the fact that on the Border the landowner lived and worked upon his land. There was almost no gap between the owner and his cowhand, who often was related to him anyway. The simplicity of the life led by both employer and employee also helped make them feel that they were not different kinds of men, even if one was richer than the other.

Border economy was largely self-sufficient. Corn, beans, melons, and vegetables were planted on the fertile, easily irrigated lands at the river's edge. Sheep and goats were also raised in quantity. For these more menial, pedestrian tasks the peon was employed in earlier days. The peon was usually a *fuereño*, an "outsider" from central Mexico, but on the Border he was not a serf. *Peón* in Nuevo Santander had preserved much of its old meaning of "man on foot." The gap between the peon and the vaquero was not extreme, though the man on horseback had a job with more prestige, one which was considered to involve more danger and more skill.

The peon, however, could and did rise in the social scale. People along the Border who like to remember genealogies and study family trees can tell of instances in which a man came to the Border as a peon (today he would be called a *bracero*) and ended his life as a vaquero, while his son began life as a vaquero and ended it as a small land-

owner, and the grandson married into the old family that had employed his grandfather—the whole process taking place before the Madero Revolution. In few parts of Greater Mexico before 1910 could people of all degrees—including landowners—have circulated and obviously enjoyed the story of Juan, the peon who knew his right, and who not only outwitted his landowning employer but gave him a good beating besides, so that the landowner afterward would never hire a peon who "walked like Juan."

This is not to say that there was democracy on the Border as Americans recognize it or that the average Borderer had been influenced by eighteenth-century ideas about the rights of man. Social conduct was regulated and formal, and men lived under a patriarchal system that made them conscious of degree. The original settlements had been made on a patriarchal basis, with the "captain" of each community playing the part of father to his people.

Town life became more complex, but in rural areas the eldest member of the family remained the final authority, exercising more real power than the church or the state. There was a domestic hierarchy in which the representative of God on earth was the father. Obedience depended on custom and training rather than force, but a father's curse was thought to be the most terrible thing on earth.

A grown son with a family of his own could not smoke in his father's presence, much less talk back to him. Elder brothers and elder cousins received a corresponding respect, with the eldest brother having almost parental authority over the younger. It was disrespectful to address an older brother, especially the eldest, by his name. He was called "Brother" and addressed in the formal *usted* used for the parents. In referring to him, one mentioned him as "My Brother So-and-So," never by his name alone.

Such customs are only now disappearing among some of the old Border families. In the summer of 1954 I was present while a tough inspector of rural police questioned some suspects in a little south-bank Border town. He was sitting carelessly in his chair, smoking a cigarette, when he heard his father's voice in an outer room. The man straightened up in his chair, hurriedly threw his cigarette out the window, and fanned away the smoke with his hat before turning back to the prisoners.

If the mother was a strong character, she could very well receive the same sort of respect as the father. In his study of Juan N. Cortina, Charles W. Goldfinch recounts an incident which was far from being an isolated case. After his border raider period Cortina was forced to abandon Texas, and he became an officer in the Mexican army. At the same time his desertion of his wife set him at odds with his mother. Later Cortina returned to the Border and was reconciled with his mother. "They met just across from her ranch on the Mexican side of the river. As they met, the son handed his mother his riding crop and, as he knelt before her, in the presence of his officers, she whipped him across the shoulders. Then the chastised son, Brigadier General Cortina, arose and embraced his mother."

These same parent-child customs formerly were applied to the community, when the community was an extended family. Decisions were made, arguments were settled, and sanctions were decided upon by the old men of the group, with the leader usually being the patriarch, the eldest son of the eldest son, so that primogeniture played its part in social organization though it did not often do so in the inheritance of property.

The patriarchal system not only made the Border community more cohesive, by emphasizing its clanlike characteristics, but it also minimized outside interference, because it allowed the community to govern itself to a great extent. If officials saw fit to appoint an *encargado* to represent the state, they usually chose the patriarch, merely giving official recognition to a choice already made by custom.

Thus the Rio Grande people lived in tight little groups—usually straddling the river—surrounded by an alien world. From the north came the *gringo,* which term meant "foreigner." From the south came the *fuereño,* or outsider, as the Mexican of the interior was called. Nuevo Santander had been settled as a way station to Texas, but there was no heavy traffic over these routes, except during wartime. Even in the larger towns the inhabitants ignored strangers for the most part,

while the people of the remoter communities were oblivious of them altogether. The era of border conflict was to bring greater numbers of outsiders to the Border, but most Borderers treated them either as transients or as social excrescences. During the American Civil War and the Mexican Empire, Matamoros became a cosmopolitan city without affecting appreciably the life of the villages and ranches around it. On the north bank it took several generations for the new English-speaking owners of the country to make an impression on the old mores. The Border Mexican simply ignored strangers, except when disturbed by violence or some other transgression of what he believed was "the right." In the wildest years of the Border, the swirl of events and the coming and going of strange faces was but froth on the surface of life.

In such closely knit groups most tasks and amusements were engaged in communally. Roundups and brandings were community projects, undertaken according to the advice of the old men. When the river was in flood, the patriarchal council decided whether the levees should be opened to irrigate the fields or whether they should be reinforced to keep the water out, and the work of levee-building or irrigation was carried out by the community as a whole. Planting and harvesting were individual for the most part, but the exchange of the best fruits of the harvest (though all raised the same things) was a usual practice. In the 1920s, when I used to spend my summers in one of the south-bank ranch communities, the communal provision of fresh beef was still a standard practice. Each family slaughtered in turn and distributed the meat among the rest, ensuring a supply of fresh beef every week.

Amusements were also communal, though the statement in no way should suggest the "dancing, singing throng" creating as a group. Group singing, in fact, was rare. The community got together, usually at the patriarch's house, to enjoy the performance of individuals, though sometimes all the individuals in a group might participate in turn.

The dance played but little part in Border folkways, though in the twentieth century the Mexicanized polka has become something very close to a native folk form. Native folk dances were not produced, nor were they imported from fringe areas like southern Tamaulipas, where the *huapango* was danced. Polkas, mazurkas, waltzes, lancers, *contra-danzas,* and other forms then in vogue were preferred. Many Border families had prejudices against dancing. It brought the sexes too close together and gave rise to quarrels and bloody fights among the men. There were community dances at public spots and some private dances in the homes, usually to celebrate weddings, but the dance on the Border was a modern importation, reflecting European vogues.

Horse racing was, of course, a favorite sport among the men. In the home, amusements usually took the form of singing, the presentation of religious plays at Christmas, tableaux, and the like. This material came from oral tradition. Literacy among the old Border families was relatively high, but the reading habit of the Protestant Anglo-Saxon, fostered on a veneration of the written words in the Bible, was foreign to the Borderer. His religion was oral and traditional.

On most occasions the common amusement was singing to the accompaniment of the guitar: in the informal community gatherings, where the song alternated with the tale; at weddings, which had their own special songs, the *golondrinas;* at Christmastime, with its *pastorelas* and *aguinaldos;* and even at some kinds of funerals, those of infants, at which special songs were sung to the guitar.

The Nuevo Santander people also sang ballads. Some were songs remembered from their Spanish origins, and perhaps an occasional ballad came to them from the older frontier colony of Nuevo Mexico. But chiefly they made their own. They committed their daily affairs and their history to the ballad form: the fights against the Indians, the horse races, and the domestic triumphs and tragedies—and later the border conflicts and the civil wars. The ballads, and the tradition of ballad-making as well, were handed down from father to son, and thus the people of the Lower Rio Grande developed a truly native balladry.

It was the Treaty of Guadalupe that added the final element to Rio Grande society, a border. The river, which had been a focal point, became a dividing line. Men were expected to consider their relatives and closest neighbors, the people just across the river, as foreigners in a foreign land. A restless and acquisitive people, exercising the rights of conquest, disturbed the old ways.

Out of the conflict that arose on the new border came men like Gregorio Cortez. Legends were told about these men, and ballads were sung in their memory. And this state of affairs persisted for one hundred years after Santa Anna stormed the Alamo.

MIER, THE ALAMO, AND GOLIAD

In the conflict along the Rio Grande, the English-speaking Texan (whom we shall call the Anglo-Texan for short) disappoints us in a folkloristic sense. He produces no border balladry. His contribution to the literature of border conflict is a set of attitudes and beliefs about the Mexican which form a legend of their own and are the complement to the *corrido,* the Border-Mexican ballad of border conflict. The Anglo-Texan legend may be summarized under half a dozen points.

1. The Mexican is cruel by nature. The Texan must in self-defense treat the Mexican cruelly, since that is the only treatment the Mexican understands.

2. The Mexican is cowardly and treacherous, and no match for the Texan. He can get the better of the Texan only by stabbing him in the back or by ganging up on him with a crowd of accomplices.

3. Thievery is second nature in the Mexican, especially horse and cattle rustling, and on the whole he is about as degenerate a specimen of humanity as may be found anywhere.

4. The degeneracy of the Mexican is due to his mixed blood, though the elements in the mixture were inferior to begin with. He is descended from the Spaniard, a second-rate type of European, and from the equally substandard Indian of Mexico, who must not be confused with the noble savages of North America.

5. The Mexican has always recognized the Texan as his superior and thinks of him as belonging to a race separate from other Americans.

6. The Texan has no equal anywhere, but within Texas itself there developed a special breed

of men, the Texas Rangers, in whom the Texan's qualities reached their culmination.

This legend is not found in the cowboy ballads, in the play-party songs, or the folk tales of the people of Texas. Orally one finds it in the anecdote and in some sentimental verse of nonfolk origin. It is in print—in newspapers, magazines, and books —that it has been circulated most. In books it has had its greatest influence and its longest life. The earliest were the war propaganda works of the 1830s and 1840s about Mexican "atrocities" in Texas, a principal aim of which was to overcome Northern antipathy toward the approaching war with Mexico. After 1848, the same attitudes were perpetuated in the works, many of them autobiographical, about the adventurers and other men of action who took part in the border conflict on the American side. A good and an early example is the following passage from *Sketches of the Campaign in Northern Mexico,* by an officer of Ohio volunteers.

> The inhabitants of the valley of the Rio Grande are chiefly occupied in raising stock. . . . But a pastoral life, generally so propitious to purity of morals and strength of constitution, does not appear to have produced its usually happy effect upon that people . . . vile rancheros; the majority of whom are so vicious and degraded that one can hardly believe that the light of Christianity has ever dawned upon them.

In more recent years it has often been the writer of history textbooks and the author of scholarly works who have lent their prestige to the legend. This is what the most distinguished historian Texas has produced had to say about the Mexican in 1935.

> Without disparagement, it may be said that there is a cruel streak in the Mexican nature, or so the history of Texas would lead one to believe. This cruelty may be a heritage from the Spanish of the Inquisition; it may, and doubtless should, be attributed partly to the Indian blood. . . . The Mexican warrior . . . was, on the whole, inferior to the Comanche and wholly unequal to the Texan. The whine of the leaden slugs stirred in him an irresistible impulse to travel with rather than against the music. He won more victories over the Texans by parley than by force of arms. For making promises—and for breaking them—he had no peer.

Professor Webb does not mean to be disparaging. One wonders what his opinion might have been when he was in a less scholarly mood and not looking at the Mexican from the objective point of view of the historian. In another distinguished work, *The Great Plains,* Dr. Webb develops similar aspects of the legend. The Spanish "failure" on the Great Plains is blamed partly on the Spanish character. More damaging still was miscegenation with the Mexican Indian, "whose blood, when compared with that of the Plains Indian, was as ditch water." On the other hand, American success on the Great Plains was due to the "pure American stock," the "foreign element" having settled elsewhere.

How can one classify the Texas legend—as fact, as folklore, or as still something else? The records of frontier life after 1848 are full of instances of cruelty and inhumanity. But by far the majority of the acts of cruelty are ascribed by American writers themselves to men of their own race. The victims, on the other hand, were very often Mexicans. There is always the implication it was "defensive cruelty," or that the Mexicans were being punished for their inhumanity to Texans at the Alamo, Mier, and Goliad.

There probably is not an army (not excepting those of the United States) that has not been accused of "atrocities" during wartime. It is remarkable, then, that those atrocities said to have occurred in connection with the Alamo, Goliad, and the Mier expedition are universally attributed not to the Mexican army as a whole but to their commander, Santa Anna. Even more noteworthy is the fact that Santa Anna's orders were protested by his officers, who incurred the dictator's wrath by pleading for the prisoners in their charge. In at least two other cases (not celebrated in Texas history) Santa Anna's officers were successful in their pleading, and Texan lives were spared. Both Texan and Mexican accounts agree that the executions evoked horror among many Mexicans witnessing them—officers, civilians, and common soldiers.

Had Santa Anna lived in the twentieth century, he would have called the atrocities with which he is charged "war crimes trials." There is a fundamental difference, though, between his executions of Texan prisoners and the hangings of Japanese army officers like General Yamashita at the end of the Pacific War. Santa Anna usually was in a rage when he ordered his victims shot. The Japanese were never hanged without the ceremony of a trial—a refinement, one must conclude, belonging to a more civilized age and a more enlightened people.

Meanwhile, Texas-Mexicans died at the Alamo and fought at San Jacinto on the Texan side. The Rio Grande people, because of their Federalist and autonomist views, were sympathetic to the Texas republic until Texans began to invade their properties south of the Nueces. The truth seems to be that the old war propaganda concerning the Alamo, Goliad, and Mier later provided a convenient justification for outrages committed on the Border by Texans of certain types, so convenient an excuse that it was artificially prolonged for almost a century. And had the Alamo, Goliad, and Mier not existed, they would have been invented, as indeed they seem to have been in part.

The Texan had an undeniable superiority over the Mexican in the matter of weapons. The Texan was armed with the rifle and the revolver. The ranchero fought with the implements of his cowherding trade, the rope and the knife, counting himself lucky if he owned a rusty old musket and a charge of powder. Lead was scarce, old pieces of iron being used for bullets. Possession of even a weapon of this kind was illegal after 1835, when Santa Anna disarmed the militia, leaving the frontier at the mercy of Indians and Texans. Against them the ranchero had to depend on surprise and superior horsemanship. Until the Mexican acquired the revolver and learned how to use it, a revolver-armed Texan could indeed be worth a half-dozen Mexicans; but one may wonder whether cowards will fight under such handicaps

as did the Borderers. The Rio Grande people not only defended themselves with inadequate armament; they often made incursions into hostile territory armed with lances, knives, and old swords.

The belief in the Mexican's treachery was related to that of his cowardice. As with the Mexican's supposed cruelty, one finds the belief perpetuated as a justification for outrage. Long after Mexicans acquired the revolver, "peace officers" in the Nueces-Rio Grande territory continued to believe (or pretended to do so) that no Mexican unaided could best a Texan in a fair fight. The killing of innocent Mexicans as "accomplices" became standard procedure—especially with the Texas Rangers—whenever a Border Mexican shot an American. The practice had an important influence on Border balladry and on the lives of men such as Gregorio Cortez.

The picture of the Mexican as an inveterate thief, especially of horses and cattle, is of interest to the psychologist as well as to the folklorist. The cattle industry of the Southwest had its origin in the Nueces-Rio Grande area, with the stock and the ranches of the Rio Grande rancheros. The "cattle barons" built up their fortunes at the expense of the Border Mexican by means which were far from ethical. One notes that the white Southerner took his slave women as concubines and then created an image of the male Negro as a sex fiend. In the same way he appears to have taken the Mexican's property and then made him out a thief.

The story that the Mexican thought of the Texan as being apart and distinguished him from other Americans belongs with the post cards depicting the United States as an appendage of Texas. To the Border Mexicans at least, Texans are indistinguishable from other Americans, and *tejano* is used for the Texas-Mexican, except perhaps among the more sophisticated. The story that the Mexican believes he could lick the United States if it were not for Texas also must be classed as pure fiction. The Border Mexican does distinguish the Ranger from other Americans, but his belief is that if it were not for the United States Army he would have run the Rangers out of the country a long time ago.

Theories of racial purity have fallen somewhat into disrepute since the end of World War II. So has the romantic idea that Li Po and Einstein were inferior to Genghis Khan and Hitler because the latter were bloodier and therefore manlier. There is interest from a folkloristic point of view, however, in the glorification of the Plains savage at the expense of the semicivilized, sedentary Indian of Mexico. The noble savage very early crept into American folklore in the form of tales and songs about eloquent Indian chiefs and beautiful Indian princesses. Such stories appear to have had their origin in areas where Indians had completely disappeared. On the frontier the legend seems to have been dichotomized. After the 1870s, when the Indian danger was past, it was possible to idealize the Plains savage. But the "Mexican problem" remained. A distinction was drawn between the noble Plains Indian and the degenerate ancestor of the Mexican.

The legend has taken a firm grip on the American imagination. In the Southwest one finds Americans of Mexican descent attempting to hide their Indian blood by calling themselves Spanish, while Americans of other origins often boast of having Comanche, Cherokee, or other wild Indian blood, all royal of course. The belief also had its practical aspects in reaffirming Mexican racial inferiority. The Comanche did not consider Mexican blood inferior. Mexican captives were often adopted into the tribe, as were captives of other races. But the Comanche had never read the Bible or John Locke. He could rob, kill, or enslave without feeling the need of racial prejudices to justify his actions.

Even a cursory analysis shows the justification value of the Texas legend and gives us a clue to one of the reasons for its survival. Goldfinch puts most Americans coming into the Brownsville-Matamoros area after the Mexican War into two categories: those who had no personal feeling against the Mexicans but who were ruthless in their efforts to acquire a fortune quickly, and those who, inclined to be brutal to everyone, found in the Mexican's defenseless state after the war an easy and safe outlet for their brutality. It was to the interest of these two types that the legend about the Mexican be perpetuated. As long as the major-

ity of the population accepted it as fact, men of this kind could rob, cheat, or kill the Border Mexican without suffering sanctions either from the law or from public opinion. And if the Mexican retaliated, the law stepped in to defend or to avenge his persecutors.

In 1838 Texas "cowboys" were making expeditions down to the Rio Grande to help the Rio Grande people fight Santa Anna. In between alliances they stole their allies' cattle. McArthur states that their stealing was "condemned by some" but that it was "justified by the majority on the ground that the Mexicans belonged to a hostile nation, from whom the Texans had received and were still receiving many injuries; and that they would treat the Texans worse if it were in their power to do so." In the 1850s and 1860s when the filibuster William Walker—a Tennessean—operated in Central America, he did so to the cry of "Remember the Alamo!" Al Capone in the 1920s, sending his men off to take care of some German shopkeeper who had failed to kick in, might just as well have cried, "Remember Caporetto, boys! Remember the Piave!" But perhaps Scarface Al lacked a sense of history.

This does not explain why the legend finds support among the literate and the educated. The explanation may lie in the paucity of Texas literature until very recent times. Other peoples have been stirred up by skillfully written war propaganda, but after the war they have usually turned to other reading, if they have a rich literature from which to draw. J. Frank Dobie has said that if he "were asked what theme of Texas life has been most movingly and dramatically recorded ... I should name the experiences of Texans as prisoners to the Mexicans. If it is true that the best writing done about Texas until recent times was ancient war propaganda directed against the Mexicans, it is not strange that the prejudices of those early days should have been preserved among the literate. The relative lack of perspective and of maturity of mind that Mr. Dobie himself deplored as late as 1952 in writers about the Southwest also played its part.

Is the Texas legend folklore? The elements of folklore are there. One catches glimpses of the "false Scot" and the "cruel Moor," half-hidden among the local color. Behind the super-human Ranger are Beowulf, Roland, and the Cid, slaying hundreds. The idea that one's own clan or tribe is unique is probably inherent in certain stages of human development. Some times the enemy is forced to recognize the excellence of the hero. Achilles' armor and the Cid's corpse win battles; the Spanish hosts admit the valor of Brave Lord Willoughby, the Englishman; and the Rangers recognize the worth of Jacinto Treviño, the Mexican.

The difference, and a fundamental one, between folklore and the Texas legend is that the latter is not usually found in the oral traditions of those groups of Texas people that one might consider folk. It appears in two widely dissimilar places: in the written works of the literary and the educated and orally among a class of rootless adventurers who have used the legend for very practical purposes. One must classify the Texas legend as pseudo folklore. Disguised as fact, it still plays a major role in Texas history. Under the guise of local pride, it appears in its most blatant forms in the "professional" Texan.

THE TEXAS RANGERS

The group of men who were most responsible for putting the Texan's pseudo folklore into deeds were the Texas Rangers. They were part of the legend themselves, its apotheosis as it were. If all the books written about the Rangers were put one on top of the other, the resulting pile would be almost as tall as some of the tales that they contain. The Rangers have been pictured as a fearless, almost super-human breed of men, capable of incredible feats. It may take a company of militia to quell a riot, but one Ranger was said to be enough for one mob. Evildoers, especially Mexican ones, were said to quail at the mere mention of the name. To the Ranger is given the credit for ending lawlessness and disorder along the Rio Grande.

The Ranger did make a name for himself along the Border. The word *rinche,* from "ranger," is an important one in Border folklore. It has been extended to cover not only the Rangers but any other Americans armed and mounted and looking for Mexicans to kill. Possemen and border patrolmen were also *rinches,* and even Pershing's cav-

alry is so called in Lower Border variants of ballads about the pursuit of Villa. The official Texas Rangers are known as the *rinches de la Kineña* or Rangers of King Ranch, in accordance with the Borderer's belief that the Rangers were the personal strong-arm men of Richard King and the other "cattle barons."

What the Border Mexican thought about the Ranger is best illustrated by means of sayings and anecdotes. Here are a few that are typical.

1. The Texas Ranger always carries a rusty old gun in his saddlebags. This is for use when he kills an unarmed Mexican. He drops the gun beside the body and then claims he killed the Mexican in self-defense and after a furious battle.

2. When he has to kill an armed Mexican, the Ranger tries to catch him asleep, or he shoots the Mexican in the back.

3. If it weren't for the American soldiers, the Rangers wouldn't dare come to the Border. The Ranger always runs and hides behind the soldiers when real trouble starts.

4. Once an army detachment was chasing a raider, and they were led by a couple of Rangers. The Mexican went into the brush. The Rangers galloped up to the place, pointed it out, and then stepped back to let the soldiers go in first.

5. Two Rangers are out looking for a Mexican horse thief. They strike his trail, follow it for a while, and then turn at right angles and ride until they meet a half-dozen Mexican laborers walking home from the fields. These they shoot with their deadly Colts. Then they go to the nearest town and send back a report to Austin: "In pursuit of horse thieves we encountered a band of Mexicans, and though outnumbered we succeeded in killing a dozen of them after a hard fight, without loss to ourselves. It is believed that others of the band escaped and are making for the Rio Grande." And as one can see, except for a few omissions and some slight exaggeration, the report is true in its basic details. Austin is satisfied that all is well on the Border. The Rangers add to their reputation as a fearless, hard-fighting breed of men; and the real horse thief stays out of the surrounding territory for some time, for fear he may meet up with the Rangers suddenly on some lonely road one day, and they may mistake him for a laborer.

I do not claim for these little tidbits the documented authenticity that Ranger historians claim for their stories. What we have here is frankly partisan and exaggerated without a doubt, but it does throw some light on Mexican attitudes toward the Ranger which many Texans may scarcely suspect. And it may be that these attitudes are not without some basis in fact.

The Rangers have been known to exaggerate not only the numbers of Mexicans they engaged but those they actually killed and whose bodies could be produced, presumably. In 1859 Cortina was defeated by a combined force of American soldiers and Texas Rangers. Army Major Heintzelman placed Cortina's losses at sixty; Ranger Captain Ford estimated them at two hundred. In 1875 Ranger Captain McNelly climaxed his Red Raid on the Rio Grande by wiping out a band of alleged cattle rustlers at Palo Alto. McNelly reported fifteen dead; eight bodies were brought into Brownsville. One more instance should suffice. In 1915 a band of about forty *sediciosos* (seditionists) under Aniceto Pizaña raided Norias in King Ranch. Three days later they were said to have been surrounded a mile from the Rio Grande and wiped out to the last man by a force of Rangers and deputies. About ten years later, just when accounts of this Ranger exploit were getting into print, I remember seeing Aniceto Pizaña at a wedding on the south bank of the Rio Grande. He looked very much alive, and in 1954 I was told he was living. Living too in the little towns on the south bank are a number of the Norias raiders.

It also seems a well-established fact that the Rangers often killed Mexicans who had nothing to do with the criminals they were after. Some actually were shot by mistake, according to the Ranger method of shooting first and asking questions afterwards. But perhaps the majority of the innocent Mexicans who died at Ranger hands were killed much more deliberately than that. A wholesale butchery of "accomplices" was effected twice during Border History by the Rangers, after the Cortina uprising in 1859 and during the Pizaña uprising of 1915. Professor Webb calls the retaliatory killings of 1915 an "orgy of bloodshed [in which] the Texas Rangers played a prominent part." He sets the number of Mexicans killed be-

tween 500 and 5,000. This was merely an intensification of an established practice which was carried on during less troubled years on a smaller scale.

Several motives must have been involved in the Ranger practice of killing innocent Mexicans as accomplices of the wrong doers they could not catch. The most obvious one was "revenge by proxy," as Professor Webb calls it, a precedent set by Bigfoot Wallace, who as a member of Hays's Rangers in the Mexican War killed as many inoffensive Mexicans as he could to avenge his imprisonment after the Mier expedition. A more practical motive was the fact that terror makes an occupied country submissive, something the Germans knew when they executed hostages in the occupied countries of Europe during World War II. A third motive may have been the Ranger weakness for sending impressive reports to Austin about their activities on the Border. The killing of innocent persons attracted unfavorable official notice only when it was extremely overdone.

In 1954 Mrs. Josefina Flores de Garza of Brownsville gave me some idea how it felt to be on the receiving end of the Ranger "orgy of bloodshed" of 1915. At that time Mrs. Garza was a girl of eighteen, the eldest of a family that included two younger boys in their teens and several small children. The family lived on a ranch near Harlingen, north of Brownsville. When the Ranger "executions" began, other Mexican ranchers sought refuge in town. The elder Flores refused to abandon his ranch, telling his children, *"El que nada debe nada teme."* (He who is guilty of nothing fears nothing.)

The Rangers arrived one day, surrounded the place and searched the outbuildings. The family waited in the house. Then the Rangers called the elder Flores out. He stepped to the door, and they shot him down. His two boys ran to him when he fell, and they were shot as they bent over their father. Then the Rangers came into the house and looked around. One of them saw a new pair of chaps, liked them, and took them with him. They left immediately afterwards.

From other sources I learned that the shock drove Josefina Flores temporarily insane. For two days her mother lived in the house with a brood of terrified youngsters, her deranged eldest daughter, and the corpses of her husband and her sons. Then a detachment of United States soldiers passed through, looking for raiders. They buried the bodies and got the family into town.

The daughter recovered her sanity after some time, but it still upsets her a great deal to talk about the killings. And, though forty years have passed, she still seems to be afraid that if she says something critical about the Rangers they will come and do her harm. Apparently Ranger terror did its work well, on the peaceful and the inoffensive.

Except in the movies, ruthlessness and a penchant for stretching the truth do not in themselves imply a lack of courage. The Borderer's belief that all Rangers are shooters-in-the-back is of the same stuff as the Texan belief that all Mexicans are backstabbers. There is evidence, however, that not all Rangers lived up to their reputation as a fearless breed of men. Their basic techniques of ambush, surprise, and shooting first—with the resultant "mistake" killings of innocent bystanders—made them operate at times in ways that the average city policeman would be ashamed to imitate. The "shoot first and ask questions later" method of the Rangers has been romanticized into something dashing and daring, in technicolor, on a wide screen, and with Gary Cooper in the title role. Pierce's *Brief History* gives us an example of the way the method worked in actuality.

On May 17, 1885, Sergt. B. D. Lindsay and six men from Company D frontier battalion of rangers, while scouting near the Rio Grande for escaped Mexican convicts, saw two Mexicans riding along. . . . As the horses suited the description of those alleged to be in possession of the convicts, and under the impression that these two were the men he was after, Lindsay called to them to halt, and at once opened fire on them. The elder Mexican fell to the ground with his horse, but the younger, firing from behind the dead animal, shot Private Sieker through the heart, killing him instantly. B. C. Reilly was shot through both thighs and badly wounded. The Mexicans stood their ground until the arrival of men from the ranch of a deputy-sheriff named Prudencio Herrera, who . . . insisted that the two Mexicans were well known and highly respected citizens and refused to turn them over to the rangers. . . . The citizens of Laredo . . . were indignant over the act of the rangers in shooting on Gonzalez, claiming that he was a well-known citizen of good repute, and alleging that the rangers would have killed them at the outset but for the fact that they defended themselves. The rangers, on the other hand, claimed that unless they would have proceeded as they did, should the Mexicans have been the criminals they were really after they, the rangers, would have been fired on first.

There is unanswerable logic in the Ranger sergeant's argument, if one concedes him his basic premise: that a Mexican's life is of little value anyway. But this picture of seven Texas Rangers, feeling so defenseless in the face of two Mexicans that they must fire at them on sight, because the Mexicans might be mean and shoot at them first, is somewhat disillusioning to those of us who have grown up with the tradition of the lone Ranger getting off the train and telling the station hangers-on, "Of course they sent one Ranger. There's just one riot, isn't there?" Almost every week one reads of ordinary city policemen who capture desperate criminals—sometimes singlehandedly—without having to shoot first.

Sometimes the "shoot first" method led to even more serious consequences, and many a would-be Mexican-killer got his head blown off by a comrade who was eager to get in the first shot and mistook his own men for Mexicans while they waited in ambush. Perhaps "shoot first and ask questions afterwards" is not the right name for this custom. "Shoot first and then see what you're shooting at" may be a better name. As such it has not been limited to the Texas Rangers. All over the United States during the deer season, Sunday hunters go out and shoot first.

Then there is the story about Alfredo Cerda, killed on Brownsville's main street in 1902. The Cerdas were prosperous ranchers near Brownsville, but it was their misfortune to live next to one of the "cattle barons" who was not through expanding yet. One day three Texas Rangers came down from Austin and "executed" the elder Cerda and one of his sons as cattle rustlers. The youngest son fled across the river, and thus the Cerda ranch was vacated. Five months later the remaining son, Alfredo Cerda, crossed over to Brownsville. He died the same day, shot down by a Ranger's gun.

Marcelo Garza, Sr., of Brownsville is no teller of folktales. He is a respected businessman, one of Brownsville's most highly regarded citizens of Mexican descent. Mr. Garza claims to have been an eyewitness to the shooting of the youngest Cerda. In 1902, Mr. Garza says, he was a clerk at the Tomás Fernández store on Elizabeth Street. A Ranger whom Mr. Garza identifies as "Bekar" shot Alfredo, Mr. Garza relates, as Cerda sat in the doorway of the Fernández store talking to Don Tomás, the owner. The Ranger used a rifle to kill Cerda, who was unarmed, "stalking him like a wild animal." After the shooting the Ranger ran into a nearby saloon, where other Rangers awaited him, and the group went out the back way and sought refuge with the federal troops in Fort Brown, to escape a mob of indignant citizens. The same story had been told to me long before by my father, now deceased. He was not a witness to the shooting but claimed to have seen the chasing of the Rangers into Fort Brown.

Professor Webb mentions the shooting in 1902 of an Alfredo Cerda in Brownsville by Ranger A. Y. Baker. He gives no details. Mr. Dobie also mentions an A. Y. Baker, "a famous ranger and sheriff of the border country," as the man responsible for the "extermination" of the unexterminated raiders of Norias.

The methods of the Rangers are often justified as means to an end, the stamping out of lawlessness on the Border. This coin too has another face. Many Borderers will argue that the army and local law enforcement agencies were the ones that pacified the Border, that far from pacifying the area Ranger activities stirred it up, that instead of eliminating lawlessness along the Rio Grande the Rangers were for many years a primary cause of it. It is pointed out that it was the army that defeated the major border raiders and the local authorities that took care of thieves and smugglers.

The notorious Lugo brothers were captured and executed by Cortina, the border raider. Mariano Reséndez, the famous smuggler, was taken by Mexican troops. Octaviano Zapata, the Union guerrilla leader during the Civil War, was defeated and slain by Texas-Mexican Confederates under Captain Antonio Benavides. After the Civil War, when released Confederate soldiers and lawless characters were disturbing the Border, citizens did not call for Rangers but organized a company of Texas-Mexicans under Captain Benavides to do their own pacifying.

That the Rangers stirred up more trouble than they put down is an opinion that has been expressed by less partisan sources. Goldfinch quotes a Captain Ricketts of the United States Army, who was sent by the War Department to investigate Cortina's revolt, as saying that "conditions that brought federal troops to Brownsville had been nourished but not improved by demonstrations on the part of some Rangers and citizens." In 1913 State Representative Cox of Ellis attempted to eliminate the Ranger force by striking out their appropriation from the budget. Cox declared "that there is more danger from the Rangers than from the men they are supposed to hunt down; that there is no authority of law for the Ranger force; that they are the most irresponsible officers in the State." John Garner, future Vice-President of the United States, was among those who early in the twentieth century advocated abolishing the Ranger force. •

In *The Texas Rangers* Professor Webb notes that on the Border after 1848 the Mexican was "victimized by the law," that "the old landholding families found their titles in jeopardy and if they did not lose in the courts they lost to their American lawyers," and again that "the Mexicans suffered not only in their persons but in their property." What he fails to note is that this lawless law was enforced principally by the Texas Rangers. It was the Rangers who could and did furnish the fortune-making adventurer with services not rendered by the United States Army or local sheriffs. And that is why from the point of view of the makers of fortunes the Rangers were so important to the "pacification" of the Border.

The Rangers and those who imitated their methods undoubtedly exacerbated the cultural conflict on the Border rather than allayed it. The assimilation of the north-bank Border people into the American commonwealth was necessary to any effective pacification of the Border. Ranger operations did much to impede that end. They created in the Border Mexican a deep and understandable hostility for American authority; they drew Border communities even closer together than they had been, though at that time they were beginning to disintegrate under the impact of new conditions.

Terror cowed the more inoffensive Mexican, but it also added to the roll of bandits and raiders many high-spirited individuals who would have otherwise remained peaceful and useful citizens. These were the heroes of the Border folk. People sang *corridos* about these men who, in the language of the ballads, "each with his pistol defended his right."

CHARLES KENNER

Charles Kenner (Professor of History, Arkansas State University) has spent several years studying the Hispanic-New Mexican's activities on the frontier. His research has produced one book—HISTORY OF NEW MEXICAN–PLAINS INDIAN RELATIONS, 1969. This work presents the New Mexican as an excellent frontiersman. In this original essay Professor Kenner elaborates on New Mexican-Comanche relations, pointing out that unlike the Anglos, native New Mexicans lived at peace with the Indian, trading in goods as well as ideas. Kenner's description of these traders, the "Comancheros," and the "Ciboleros," the New Mexican buffalo hunters, further demonstrates the ability of the New Mexican as a superb plainsman and hunter. This essay is based on material found in chapters four, five, and six of A HISTORY OF THE NEW MEXICAN–PLAINS INDIAN RELATIONS (Norman, University of Oklahoma Press, 1969).

The Eastern New Mexico Frontier During The 1850s

One of the forgotten sagas of Southwestern history was the alliance between the New Mexicans and the Comanches that existed unbroken after 1786. Individuals of each race visited freely in the villages of the other; New Mexicans voluntarily abandoned their homeland to live with the Indians; and, significantly, Comanches, likewise settled down in New Mexican plazas with New Mexican wives. New Mexican governors "confirmed" and pensioned Comanche chiefs and joined with them in campaigns against the hated Apaches. So firm and close were the ties that not

114

even the intrusion of Anglo traders upset the alliance which would persist until the Anglo conquest of the Southwest forcibly ended it in the 1870s.

Despite the capture of Santa Fe in 1846, several years elapsed before the Anglo officers, sitting uneasily in Santa Fe's Palace of the Governors, took notice of the strange alliance between the savage and the peon. In June, 1851, a squadron of troops that had been dispatched to check an American merchant's complaint that the Comanches had entered the Pecos Valley in large numbers found "the inhabitants in their fields and everything quiet, no one having any fear of the Comanches." Colonel John Munroe, the troop commander, shrewdly recognized that since the residents at Anton Chico and the other settlements on the Pecos carried on a continual trade with the Comanches, it was to their interest to preserve peace with them.

While the Comanches engaged in considerable trade during their visits, a much greater commerce was carried on in the Comanche camps by itinerant traders known as *Comancheros.* Their activities were so widescale that as early as 1820 Stephen Long, an American officer trekking across the Southwest, reported that a well-beaten trail containing more than twenty bridle paths followed the Canadian River eastward from New Mexico toward the plains. By the 1840s the *Comanchero* traffic had broadened the pack trails observed by Long into full-fledged cart roads. Lieutenant J. W. Albert, who in 1845 led an official exploration down the Canadian, stated that the trail had "the appearance" of a wagon road. Four years later, Captain Randolph B. Marcy, after guiding a group of Forty-niners from Van Buren, Arkansas, to Santa Fe, described the *Comanchero* trail as "the old Mexican cartroad." A gold seeker with Marcy's caravan was more explicit. Along the upper Canadian, he wrote, "you find large, broad wagon trails made by the . . . Comanche traders, which lead you to the settlements."

In addition to going to the Comanche country in Texas, the *Comancheros* sought also to trade with the Cheyennes of Colorado. But here they faced formidable opposition from Anglo traders who resided among these Indians. "Uncle John" Smith, an American squawman who exercised a great

deal of influence over the Cheyennes, was one of the most persistent of the New Mexicans' tormentors. He forced all traders coming to "his Indian village" to pay tribute to him before they were allowed to barter. On one occasion a group of "strange Mexicans" refused. Smith thereupon ordered the Cheyennes to dump the goods of the "cowering Mexicans" onto the ground and to help themselves. Ordered out of the camp, the *Comancheros* left, according to Smith's youthful friend, Lewis Garrard, "crossing themselves and uttering thanks to Heaven for having retained their scalps." Thereafter, Garrard related, the "poor Greasers" promised Smith "every third robe" for his permission to trade.

Anglo officials seldom failed to take advantage of any opportunity to condemn the *Comancheros,* even calling them "a reckless band of desperadoes," and charging them with using their influence to "keep up the hostile feeling against the whites." On occasions, however, they were pleased to use them in the rescue of American captives. In 1849, for example, Mexican traders were employed unsuccessfully in an attempt to ransom a Mrs. Jane White and her daughter from Jicarilla Apaches. Despite this failure, several Americans including Mrs. Sarah Horn, a Mrs. Harris, and Nelson Lee owed their lives to friendly Mexican traders.

Typical of these rescues was the story of Mrs. Jane Wilson, a young Texas farmwife whose husband had been killed by Indians in the summer of 1853 while they were en route to California. While Mrs. Wilson was returning to East Texas with a small wagon train, she and her two teenaged brothers-in-law were captured by Comanches. After twenty-five days of brutal maltreatment, she escaped, only to face quick and certain starvation on the barren plains. After being reduced to "a mere skeleton," she met a small party of *Comancheros,* who tended her "in every possible manner," clothed her in men's apparel, and secreted her with some provisions in a hollow tree. Then they went on to the Comanche camp, hoping to ransom her young brothers-in-law. By the time they returned eight days later, unsuccessful in their quest for the boys, Mrs. Wilson was so weak that they had to pack her on an Indian travois. They turned her over to an American family at Fort Union and were rewarded with forty dollars by David Meriwether, the new superintendent of Indian affairs in New Mexico.

Meriwether was satisfied and Judge W. W. H. Davis stated that the conduct of the *Comancheros* was "such as entitle them to all praise," but Colonel Philip St. George Cooke, commander at Fort Union, dourly condemned the traders because they did not also "rescue or redeem" the two boys. Cooke expressed a deep suspicion of such "friendly intercourse with these aggressive savages," but he did not explain what might have been Mrs. Wilson's fate had the *Comancheros* not found her. Meriwether dispatched the *Comancheros* on a mission to rescue the two boys, but the attempt was unnecessary. Both had already been ransomed by other traders of the plains. Congress later appropriated one thousand dollars to reward the rescuers of the boys, a generous sum compared to the forty dollars doled out to the *Comancheros* for Mrs. Wilson.

Equally mistrusted and suspected as the activities of the *Comancheros* by the military officials were the operations of the New Mexican buffalo hunters, the famed *ciboleros*. These expert lancers had journeyed to the plains to hunt for decades —apparently without encountering hostility from the Indians. But by the 1850s, whether due to a decrease in the buffalo numbers or the influence of Anglo traders, the Cheyennes suddenly sought to stop *cibolero* hunting in Colorado. In the fall of 1853, a large party of New Mexicans who failed to find the buffalo herds along the Canadian River continued northeastward until they located them between the Cimarron and Arkansas rivers. During the hunt, two Cheyennes and a New Mexican were killed in a skirmish. The New Mexicans claimed that the fight began when three Cheyennes attempted to steal some of their horses; the Cheyennes, that "the Mexicans caught two of our young men by themselves and killed them."

A military investigation concluded that the Indian version was the more accurate. After the buffalo hunters reached the hunting grounds, Lieutenant J. E. Maxwell reported, a small party led by a youth named Salazar—son of the Damasio

Salazar who had brutally maltreated the members of the Texan-Santa Fe expedition in 1841—split off from the main group and later attacked three visiting Cheyennes "to obtain their horses." Their treachery backfired, however, for young Salazar was killed and one of the Indians escaped. Salazar's comrades then fled to New Mexico. They escaped, but the infuriated Cheyennes retaliated against the main body of *ciboleros,* who had known nothing of the altercation, by capturing eighty or more head of oxen and wrecking about twenty carts.

The Indians were so warmly supported by William Bent, the influential proprietor of Bent's Fort, and by Thomas Fitzpatrick, the veteran mountain man serving as the agent for the Cheyennes, that suspicions are raised that the two were using the incident to rid themselves of troublesome competitors for buffalo robes. Fitzpatrick highhandedly gave the Cheyennes permission "to take the property of the Mexican hunters" and sell it to the Anglo traders about Bent's Fort. For his part, Bent penned a letter to Governor Meriwether, presenting the Cheyenne case against the New Mexicans. Claiming that hundreds of *ciboleros* had been roaming through their country in violation of their treaty rights, the Indians (or Bent) demanded immediate compensation for Salazar's treacherous act: "If the Mexicans will send us the pipe of peace and something to reward the parents of the two young men we will bury the tomahawk, but if not we will kill them when we see them." The missive was signed: "Your children the Cheyennes." In a personal postscript, Bent assured Meriwether that "from what I can learn . . . the Mexicans were to blame in this case."

Although the Cheyennes had promised not "to hurt one hair on the head of our friends the Americans," Governor Meriwether was deeply alarmed. He asked Bent to tell the Indians that "any attack upon the Mexicans of New Mexico will . . . be punished by me as though the same had been made upon the Americans." He rejected the Cheyenne claim that the New Mexican hunters were trespassing, pointing out that by the Treaty of Fort Laramie in 1851 the Cheyennes had been assigned the land between the Arkansas and North Platte rivers while the dispute with the *ciboleros* had occurred south of the Arkansas. The "whole American people," he threatened, would punish the Cheyennes if they went to war.

Meriwether, however, did not have the support of the Army. Colonel John Garland, commander of the troops in New Mexico, felt that the Cheyennes were justified in their complaints. Since the *ciboleros* killed off the game upon which the Indians depended for subsistence, the latter, he argued, were forced to choose among breaking up the hunting parties, depredating upon the settlements, or starving to death. He made no apparent effort to protect the frontier from the threatened attacks.

In the spring of 1854 the Cheyennes more than made good their threats. In a series of raids they killed, according to Colonel Garland, fourteen New Mexicans in San Miguel County alone. True to their word, the Cheyennes harmed not a single one of their "friends, the Americans." In turn, the American officers, instead of resisting them, merely philosophized, in Colonel Cooke's words, that it was "reasonably to be expected" that the Plains Indians "should commit depredations on this frontier" because of the

> serious depredations committed by the inhabitants of the Territory on them: Viz. the annual destruction of buffalo within their country (attended by occasional murder) in defiance of law and express treaty obligations; and I have information of repeated complaints and warnings by them to Americans passing-through their country.

Apparently New Mexicans were fair game for any Indians who chose to attack them.

In addition to the killings, the Cheyennes kidnaped eleven boys from the vicinity of Tecolote and Las Vegas. Governor Meriwether, while en route to St. Louis during the summer of 1854, met a party of Cheyennes who openly boasted that they had committed the depredations and carried off the prisoners. Unable to carry out his threat to punish the Indians, Meriwether asked the New Cheyenne agent, J. W. Whitfield, to try to procure the release of the captives. Upon returning to Santa Fe, Meriwether perceived something of the pathetic impact of the raids when an old peon,

"very poorly clad" and in "very bad health," walked sixty miles to inquire about his two sons, who had been among the kidnaped youths.

Meanwhile, Agent Whitfield, with a "liberal present," had bribed the Cheyennes into releasing two of the Mexican captives, "very interesting children" who had aroused his sympathies. Despite this show of compassion, Whitfield realistically pointed out: "We cannot establish the precedent of buying Mexican prisoners, if we were . . . only to pay for what the Indians now have in my Agency it would Bankrupt your Treasury— I am certain the Comanches and Kiowas have one thousand."

While the killing and kidnaping of New Mexicans by Cheyennes might be overlooked, it soon became apparent that the stealing of a few Anglo beeves by Comanches called for massive military retaliation. Until 1855 the military in New Mexico had had no trouble with the Comanches, but by then two developments had set the stage for a clash of alien cultures. Anglo ranchers began moving onto the eastern border of New Mexico: Lucien Maxwell and Samuel Watrous into the upper Canadian Valley and Alexander Hatch, James M. Giddings, and Preston Beck into the Pecos Valley below Anton Chico. Simultaneously, large numbers of Comanches were being forced to retire toward the New Mexican frontier. In 1855 Colonel John Garland, commander of the Department of New Mexico, complained that Comanches "driven from Texas" were hovering about the eastern border. Later in the year, Governor Meriwether was visited by Comanches who claimed that they "had been driven from their homeland by the Osages" and stated that they wished to remain permanently in New Mexico. Meriwether ordered them to return to Texas, but to no avail.

A rash of minor incidents accompanied the Comanche intrusion. In May, the bands of Chiefs Sanaco and Pahanca visited the Pecos settlements and voluntarily surrendered a prisoner, but on their departure they "broke up" the ranch of Beck and Giddings. The following month, some three hundred Comanches stopped at the same ranch and proceeded to hold a barbecue, for which they "borrowed" two oxen, one calf, one "fine American boar hog," twenty-nine pigs, and sixteen chickens. One of the women at the ranch tried to stop them from killing the chickens, but they nonchalantly drove her away with two arrow shots and went ahead with their feast. Upon being asked about the incident later, the Comanche chiefs blamed it upon "bad Indians" whom they could not control.

In July a band of Kotsoteka Comanches visited Lucien Maxwell's ranch on Rayado Creek and, according to Maxwell, killed two hundred sheep, stole a mule and all the loose ranch property, took several articles from his employees, and arrogantly promised to return when "the corn was ripe." Despite the hostility of the Comanches, several things about the "raid" puzzled Governor Meriwether: Maxwell had voluntarily given the Comanches food and clothing, he had admitted trading horses with them *after* the occurrence of the alleged depredations, and the Indians, when intercepted by soldiers, had displayed a certificate of "good conduct" signed by Maxwell. The Comanches obviously did not consider these incidents as raids. For generations they had helped themselves to foodstuffs while visiting in New Mexico, and the native New Mexicans had learned to accept their dinner stops with grace. The Anglo ranchers, however, stridently demanded military protection.

In response to the complaints, Colonel Garland in September dispatched Major J. H. Brooks and 150 soldiers to the eastern frontier with instructions to warn the Comanches against hovering around the borders of New Mexico and to attack them if they committed any act "worthy of chastisement." Although this order was temporarily suspended a week later because the troops were not "properly instructed and disciplined," the roles had been cast for the drama to be played during the balance of the decade. The Comanches would continue to visit the New Mexican frontier settlements, the American inhabitants to protest, and the military to oppose the Indian incursions. Silent onlookers at first, the native New Mexicans would gradually align with the Comanches.

Resuming their unwelcomed dinner visits in September, 1856, some Comanches under Chief Esaquipa camped on the Gallinas River and

helped themselves to the corn on Alexander Hatch's newly established ranch. Hatch persuaded them to leave by giving them an ox and "some other staples," but then other parties, including some Kiowas on their way to raid the Navahos, stopped at the ranch and demanded food. As a result, the military claimed, Hatch "suffered much from the loss of corn, whole fields of which the Indians . . . destroyed."

Besieged by both Hatch and James Giddings' for protection, Garland sent Captain W. L. Elliott to survey the area for a suitable fort site. Elliott found that Giddings ranch on the Pecos far below Antón Chico had little stock, few residents, and fewer signs of Indians. On the other hand, Hatch's ranch, located on the Gallinas River thirteen miles northeast of Antón Chico, offered an excellent site. Its buildings, Elliott reported, would afford "comfortable shelter" for a company of troops and their horses, there were ample water and firewood, and Hatch had enough corn (despite the inroads of the Indians!) to supply the troops through the winter.

The establishment of the new post, known simply as Hatch's Ranch, was a boon both to Alexander Hatch personally and to the entire eastern frontier. The troops not only protected Hatch's corn fields and stock but, according to Lieutenant J. H. Beale, a young army engineer who visited the post in 1858, they furnished him with a lucrative market: that year Hatch "had already collected some ten thousand bushels of corn which he was selling at over one dollar a bushel *to the government*" and also making "large profits by taking contracts for the delivery of grain or selling it at his house." Hatch profited further from his unique arrangement with the military by serving as sutler for the garrison. Other Anglo ranchers, emboldened by the existence of the fort, moved to the Gallinas Valley, and soon an influx of New Mexican settlers moved in to minister to the thirsts and appetites of off-duty soldiers. Pleasantly situated on the Gallinas three miles above Hatch's Ranch, the New Mexican settlement, Chaparito, became one of the strongholds of the *Comancheros*.

Perhaps because of the presence of the garrison, the New Mexican frontier was relatively peaceful during 1857. A few "friendly" Kiowas stopped at Giddings' and Beck's ranch in early February, but they left after being given some beef. J. L. Collins, the new superintendent of Indian affairs in New Mexico, was not entirely pleased when a few Comanches visited the New Mexican plazas and treated the residents in a "menacing manner," but, he hastened to add, they complied peacefully when warned by the military to leave. Later in the year, some Kiowas, questioned by Indian agent Robert Miller about a few depredations near Las Vegas, readily admitted committing the crimes and promised to "return in kind" what had been stolen.

Underneath the apparent tranquility, the Comanches were becoming increasingly resentful of the intruding Anglo ranchers. Years later, an old frontiersman recalled meeting in 1857 a grim-faced Comanche chief who declared that while he lived he would allow no settlements east of the Gallinas. With the exception of one or two inconclusive encounters, the eastern frontier remained calm until March, 1858, when the Comanches suddenly unleashed their pent-up fury on the encroachers. Samuel Watrous, lured by the deceptive quiet of the previous year, had sent his foreman, a man named Bunsham, to establish a ranch on the Canadian River about 130 miles below Fort Union. When Bunsham rejected their ultimatum to abandon the ranch, the Comanches decided to make an example of him. Three New Mexicans who had long lived among the Comanches secured jobs at the ranch; a few days later, four Indians arrived and pretended they wished to trade. After the renegade New Mexicans lured Bunsham from his house, the Comanches speedily cut him down, burned the ranch buildings, and ran off the stock. They allowed Bunsham's legitimate Mexican ranch hands to return unharmed to the settlements with instructions to tell the Americans that "they should not settle there, for the Comanches would kill any who attempted it."

To emphasize that the raid was not the act of a few impetuous young braves, the Comanche leaders sent word to the American officers that the destruction of the ranch "had been resolved on in council beforehand"; they also reaffirmed their determination to prevent settlements east of Hatch's Ranch. Although he responded to the raid by reinforcing the garrison at Hatch's Ranch,

Colonel Garland's reaction was remarkably mild: the attack "was expected by many, and Mr. Watrous was advised not to undertake a settlement so distant from protection."

The following year, when the Anglos undertook to survey the Canadian Valley, the Comanches dramatically re-emphasized their opposition to the eastward expansion of the settlements. R. E. Clements, the contractor for the survey, began the task in early July despite warnings not to proceed without military protection. The Comanches, understanding quite well that the surveyors' chains would be followed by settlers, immediately dispatched a war party which, without firing a shot, captured the government group. For four hours the Comanches debated the Americans' fate while Clements feverently promised to abandon the survey if spared and his New Mexican employees (whose own safety was never in jeopardy) likewise pleaded for his life. After taking all the surveyors' property and sternly warning them that he could call together five hundred warriors "by one smoke," the Comanche leader ordered Clements' release. With the army still unable to furnish an escort, Clements, to the apparent disappointment of no one, called off the survey. As Superintendent Collins pointed out, no settlement could be established in the Canadian Valley without the protection of a fort. When a fort is located there, he asserted, "it will be time enough to complete the surveys."

In the autumn of 1859 the Comanches launched their most serious attacks yet on the New Mexican frontier, hitting for the first time the New Mexican *rancheros* as well as the Anglos. Striking the ranch of Don Feliciano Guterous in the *Cañon de Quele* on November 20, they drove off the herders and butchered a large number of sheep. Four days later they attacked the ranch of Don Felíz Chávez on the Rio Conchas, "seized and stripped the herders," killed two head of cattle, and destroyed the ranch property. These were not isolated cases; all along the frontier the Comanches swarmed, killing cattle, stealing horses, and pillaging. But out of respect for their traditional friendship with the New Mexicans, they did not kill a single herder. That would come if their warnings went unheeded.

Stepping up its efforts in response to the pleas of the frontiersmen, the military was seriously handicapped by false reports from New Mexican traders as to the whereabouts of the Indians. Many of the officers soon felt that the New Mexicans, in the words of Lieutenant Colonel J. V. Reeve, were "a set of villainous vagabonds" aiding the Indians. All efforts to intercept incoming Comanches were futile until June, 1860, when a force of fifty infantrymen surprised about one hundred Indians en route to trade at the Mexican towns on the Pecos. At a range of only 150 yards, the troopers fired a volley that killed three or four and wounded others, but the rest of the Indians escaped. Levi Keithly, an Indian agent who was at Hatch's Ranch, later claimed that the Indians had not merited the punishment. The Comanches, he insisted, had come in with their families and pack animals to trade and when fired upon had run off "without making any hostile demonstration."

Meanwhile, the military commanders were planning an ambitious offensive down the Canadian to punish the Comanches for their raids. Major C. F. Ruff assembled six companies (almost 300 men) at Hatch's Ranch and prepared to "make a pursuit" after Indians and "attack" them. From the inception of his campaign, however, the native New Mexicans, aware of the threat to their friendly relations and commerce with the Comanches, tried to sabotage the Canadian expedition. A *Comanchero* told Major J. S. Simonson at Fort Union on June 7 that the Comanches and Kiowas were camped in great numbers on the Cimarron Ciba, ten or fifteen miles from Lucien Maxwell's ranch. Simonson, however, refused to believe the report and instead charged that there was "not a doubt" that the Indians were "well posted" by the New Mexicans on the movements of the troops and the strength of the garrisons in eastern New Mexico.

Major Ruff, however, was less suspicious of the *Comancheros*. Having left Hatch's Ranch on June 1, he established a subdepot, naming it Camp Jackson, sixty miles to the east on the Canadian. Assured by "various sources" that six to twelve thousand Comanches were camped on the Pecos River below the Bosque Redondo, Ruff on June 8 altered his plans and led his force southwestward to the junction of the Pecos with the Rio Hondo below present Roswell. He found neither Indians nor "Indian signs." To add to his frustration, so many of his horses broke down because of a mysterious disease called "black-tongue" and the lack of forage that half his command had to walk back. Finally arriving at Camp Jackson on July 4, the duped commander vented his fury on the New Mexicans who had led him astray:

> The representations were made by men who live by trading with the Comanche Indians, and who deprecate the loss of that trade . . . more than they seek our friendship; lying Mexicans who never tell the truth if a falsehood can possibly be made to answer the purpose.

Lieutenant J. V. Dubois, one of Ruff's subordinates, was more lyrical and only slightly less impassioned in confiding his outraged feelings to his diary: "Alas for those who put their trust in Mexicans. . . . There is no truth in them. Their evident intention was to take us away from the Indians and they have succeeded.

Major Ruff's troubles had only begun. Leaving the depot again on July 10, he proceeded down the Canadian with 225 cavalrymen and two ex-*Comanchero* guides whom he apparently was determined to use as scapegoats for his failures. The fourth day out, he encountered six Indians who raised a white flag and rode around in a small circle—the Comanche sign that they desired a peaceful talk. Ruff, however, having nothing of a "friendly character" to say to them, ignored their overtures and pressed on in search of their village. His New Mexican guides led him almost directly to a large Comanche camp, which he destroyed, but the Comanches scattered in three directions. After exhausting his horses (which were still in poor shape and no match for the lean Indian ponies) in vain pursuit, Ruff, ever ready with an excuse, blamed all his failures on the two *Comanchero* guides:

> It is a matter of keenest regret, to feel assured as I do, that our failure to capture, or destroy this entire body of Indians . . . is

solely to be attributed to a want of Guides, had I had with me, six good Guides who knew the country, not afraid to proceed a mile or two in advance of my column, there could be no doubt whatever that the surprise and destruction of this large body of Indians would have been completed.

Unwilling to concede defeat, Ruff followed doggedly after the elusive Indians, hoping to surprise them by a night attack. But his *Mexican* guides, he discovered to his disgust, could not trail at night and thus he lost another opportunity for "inflicting full and summary chastisement." After camping for a time at William Bent's old adobe fort about twenty miles east of present Stinnett, Texas, Ruff reluctantly turned back. With only 139 of 293 horses still serviceable, he dared not venture farther because of his lack of guides, grass, and water.

Upon returning to Hatch's Ranch, Ruff, his health temporarily broken by the arduous campaign, relinquished his command to Colonel A. L. Porter, who energetically refitted the expedition and resumed the search for the Comanches. Taking a lesson from Ruff's unfortunate experience with *Comanchero* guides, Porter replaced them with Antoine Leroux, a veteran Mountain Man who was confident that he could find the Indians. In an effort to surprise the Comanches, Porter moved in a sweeping circle northeastward to the Rabbit Ear Mountains, then southeastward into the Canadian Valley, and back to the New Mexican settlements—without seeing a single Comanche. Baffled by their repeated failures, the military leaders reluctantly called off the campaign.

Soon afterward, a band of Comanches, including many women and children, unwisely traveled to Chaparito to trade. The officer at Hatch's Ranch, seeing his chance to avenge the humiliations of the preceding summer, dispatched a select body of troops, who found the Indians asleep in the courtyard of Don Felíz Ulibarri, a local *rico*. Opening fire, the soldiers killed two and wounded one of the Indians before the survivors could take refuge in Ulibarri's house. The troops then appropriated the horses and mules of the Comanches and reportedly sold them the next day in Las

Vegas. The *Santa Fe Weekly Gazette,* in describing this bizarre episode, vehemently denounced the action: "There is a culpability on those who ordered the attack that will not be readily cleared up. The Indians were among the whites on a peaceful trading expedition . . . the attack as made was unjustifiable and wanton . . . a miserable military exploit."

In retaliation for this wanton attack, the Comanches struck anew at the frontier ranches. Within a few days, they had captured more than a thousand head of cattle in the Canadian Valley, including the entire government herd of 460 head. When stealing the government's cattle, the Comanches, cognizant that their vendetta was with the Anglos, carefully refrained from harming the New Mexican herdsmen, telling them that if they remained quiet they would not be injured but that if they interfered they would all be killed. Despite a belated cavalry pursuit, the Indians escaped unscathed with the cattle.

In early 1861 a military force under Lieutenant Colonel George B. Crittenden surprised and destroyed a Comanche camp on the Cimarron River, although all but ten of the Indians escaped. The Comanches thereupon sent word by several returning *Comancheros* that they desired a peace conference and Colonel W. W. Loring, the new commander of New Mexico who was concerned about the crisis caused by secession, answered their request affirmatively. On May 10 and 11, the conference was held at Alamo Gordo Creek, a small tributary of the Pecos, with the government represented by Captain R. A. Wainwright and Superintendent Collins and the Indians by Chiefs Esaquipa, Pluma de Aguilar, and Paracasqua. In return for an armistice, the Comanches, willing to pay almost any price for peace, promised to stop their depredations, to stay away from wagon trains on the Santa Fe Trail, to keep away from the settlements of eastern New Mexico, and to trade only at Fort Union or at "such places as shall be designated by proper authorities." Seeking to sever the intimate relations between them and the New Mexicans, Wainwright and Collins warned the Comanches that "if they listened to any other people" besides the military or acted upon their advice, they would "get in trouble."

The truce thus established collapsed almost immediately. Failing to grasp the full implications of the treaty, Chief Esaquipa, only a few days after signing it, led a trading party to Chaparito. Captain Thomas Duncan, the commander at Hatch's Ranch, ordered the Comanches to return at once to the plains. Evidently they did not promptly oblige, for Duncan attacked as soon as he "got his men ready." Although the Indians fled wildly in all directions, the troops succeeded in killing one, wounding three, and capturing two. This unwarranted attack once more alarmed the frontier settlers, who feared that the Indians would make reprisals against them. Levi Keithly, who was ranching on the Pecos, anxiously wrote that "one of my peons today saw Comanches not more than a mile from my house evidently acting as spies, one of them having come to him and inquired in regard to the soldiers, and as to how many persons were living in certain houses. Fortunately, the Comanches chose to move to their summer hunting grounds on the Arkansas.

The American officials and the settlers differed sharply on the causes for the sudden collapse of the treaty. The Comanches would have remained away from the settlements, Superintendent Collins maintained, but for the intervention of some traders, "a lot of scoundrels who contribute more to the encouragement of Indians depredations than all other causes combined." Rancher Keithly, realizing that the Comanches could not be expected to stay away from the New Mexican settlements, asserted that the unwise attacks by the troops were responsible for most of the Indian hostilities. Three times, he later wrote, he had

seen peaceful Comanche trading parties fired upon: "They came with friendly intentions and it was my opinion at the time that they were badly treated." The argument that the soldiers had provoked much of the trouble on the frontier was seemingly verified when the troops were withdrawn from the area at the outbreak of the Civil War. With the soldiers out of the way, the New Mexicans and Comanches resumed their old-time trade relationships.

The alliance could not be tolerated by the Anglos. For a few short years during the Civil War trade flourished on a wider scale than ever. But a flurry of Indian raids on the Santa Fe Trail produced an all-out military campaign against the Comanches and Kiowas in late 1864. The New Mexicans protested vociferously but vainly that war with the Comanches was "entirely uncalled for" and *Comancheros* warned the Plains Indians of the advance of Kit Carson's force. They were then able to turn back the Anglos at the Battle of Adobe Walls. Incensed by this action the military sought to completely eradicate the *Comanchero* trade, but to little avail. For another ten years, the traders carried on an immense commerce in stolen Texas cattle that actually hit its peak during the late 1860s. They thereby inspired the Comanches to take a heavy toll upon the advancing American frontiersmen. By the mid 1870s, however, irresistible military force had converted their Indian associates into miserable, reservation-confined paupers. With this development, the books were closed forever upon both the *Comanchero* trade and the strangest alliance of southwestern annals.

JUAN GOMEZ-Q

Juan Gomez-Q (Professor of History, University of California, Los Angeles) has written a brief introduction to the famous PLAN OF SAN DIEGO, TEXAS, STATE OF TEXAS. *Professor Gomez-Q, however, places the plan in a broader historical prospective than it usually appears and urges the student to place this and like phenomena in their proper historic and cultural perspectives.* From AZTLÁN-CHICANO JOURNAL OF THE SOCIAL SCIENCES AND THE ARTS, *Vol. 1 (Spring 1970.) By permission of the author.*

Plan De San Diego Reviewed

Given the number of *Planes* published by Chicano movement organizations, there may be interest in shedding light on the Plan de San Diego, principal document of an irredentist movement of the early twentieth century. Although there has been some writing on the subject, research has been limited and based on American sources and documented hearsay. Possible Mexican sources deserve thorough investigation. Thus, although the more sensational aspects of the Plan have readily caught the attention of those who wish to rationalize racial persecution, little has been studied about the larger social and economic context in which the Plan arose, the concepts which underlaid this liberation movement, and the repercussions which followed its implementation. Certainly, after the facts are compiled and examined, a critical analysis of its significance, if any, for our times would have merit.

South of Alice on U.S. Highway 59 in countryside common to the Southwest and the Mexican North amidst llanos and mesquites, is the small town of San Diego, Texas, with a population of 2,500. Today it is a quiet community of stone, adobe, and sun. It has a history of Mexicans, cattle, Rangers and racial conflict. In January of 1915 one Basilio Ramos was captured and taken to Brownsville, Texas. Among his personal papers was found

123

the Plan de San Diego, which, he allegedly testified, had been transmitted to him by a friend while in jail in Monterrey, Mexico. He was accused of conspiracy against the United States government, later the case was dismissed and with it the Plan, this despite actions and rumors along the border. During the years 1914-1915, Mexicans, citizens of the United States and Mexico, conceived, wrote and attempted to implement a manifesto of liberation which they entitled the Plan de San Diego. The Plan called for a general uprising on February 20, 1915 in which the Mexican people of the Southwest would reconquer territories stolen in 1836 and 1848; Anglos and Mexican traitors were to be dealt with harshly. Importantly the Plan had clauses addressed to the black, the Indian and the Oriental in which provisions were made for their freedom and national autonomy. Under a junta-like organization, an interim Republic was to be established with perhaps an eventual reannexation to Mexico, if desired. This Plan, so alarming to the Texans, can best be understood in the light of the historic, economic and social conditions of the Mexicans in the Southwest at the time; the repression suffered and the revolutionary hopes of the Mexicans and the racism, brutality, and fear of the Anglo populace.

The early twentieth century was a time of expectations and troubles for the Mexican people. To the south Mexicans were moving in rhythm with one of the surges for justice and the fulfillment of revolutionary ideals which have periodically convulsed peoples throughout history. These ideals were not confined to Mexico, and there was a great deal of activity in the Southwest. Agitation and strikes were occurring in rural and urban areas: in the mines, on the railroads, and among the fields. Followers of Ricardo Flores Magon had been organizing in the Southwest since 1906 and had prepared several armed efforts. The activities of the Magonistas were known in both Anglo and Mexican communities. The prosperity that had been enjoyed from the spill over the border of revolutionary money soon receded and the economic dislocations caused by the revolution were now suffered. This coincided with a state-wide recession in Texas as the previous "boom" slowed. Concurrently Anglo hostility became more severe

than normal for Texas. Fear was spreading among the Anglo population, as killings, lynchings and other violent acts were committed by Anglo vigilantes and law men against the Mexican populace. As the Mexican community was hopeful and resentful, the Anglo community was fearful and vindictive. In a well-known pattern of association, the Mexicans, radical activities, and the current foreign enemy were linked together in the mind of the dominant sector. Out of this atmosphere of distrust, hysteria and violence appeared the Plan de San Diego, a plan which mirrored many of the Mexican hopes, and galvanized the worst of Anglo fears. Thus the actions taken in the name of the Plan, and the reactions to it, must be seen in the light of Mexican agitation, Anglo fear and a long history of violent conflict between the two peoples.

Doubts concerning the authorship of the Plan, notwithstanding, military actions did occur which were related to the Plan's proposals. Later, after the capture of Ramos and the seizure of his documents, came notice of a junta organizing in Laredo within the framework outlined in the Plan. This activity seems to have had urban and rural support as insurgent leaders such as Aniceto Pizáño and Luis de la Rosa, Mexicans native to Texas, directed armed organized bands of from 25-100 men in a series of actions in the lower Rio Grande Valley. Gaining momentum, by July of 1915, the irredentist movement began to attract widespread attention as raids and encounters became a daily occurrence. From reports given at the time, these well-organized groups, which often averaged 50 men, raided, destroyed bridges and engaged in numerous encounters with Texas Rangers, posses, and the United States Army. An indication of the influence of the Plan can be seen in reports of battles where the flag of the Plan de San Diego was carried. A number of Anglos were killed, yet the executions were not random.

The rural struggle of the Mexicans gained support in urban areas also. On August 30 in San Antonio, Texas, twenty-eight men were arrested following a riot between police and Mexicans. The Mexicans reportedly shouted that the time had come to rise and kill the Anglo. Identified as adherents of the Plan de San Diego, they were accused of treason, and there was widespread fear of a Mexican uprising in the area. There were also numerous actions throughout the Southwest at the time, and although there is no conclusive evidence of their connection with the Plan, their actions may have arisen from convictions which inspired the Plan de San Diego. The irredentist movement seems to have been spreading, and gaining in size and momentum.

Although Anglos at first disregarded the Plan de San Diego, they became more and more alarmed as the raids in the Lower Valley increased. As usual in the Southwest, Anglo fear and self-interest was manifested by brutal vigilante action and economic reprisals. Taking advantage of unsettled conditions, persons made profit. Of course then, as later, peace officers suspended the laws where Mexicans were concerned, and joined and often led in the hunt of Mexicans, allegedly raiders. The major participants in these actions, the Texas Rangers, were considered unsavory even by the military who worried lest the prestige of the Army be tarnished by association. General Funston, commander of the Army in that area, pointed out the difficulty of cooperating with "peace officers who are such scoundrels," and refused to "tolerate such malicious deviltry and so flagrant an attempt to make matters worse." The Rangers in fact seemed to have been a major cause for the border trouble. Four years later Representative J. T. Canales of Brownsville courageously charged the Rangers with shooting Mexicans in jail without trials, and said that "the Rangers had been the cause of most of the border trouble, because the families of the victims of the Rangers' lawlessness turned to banditry to avenge their relatives." During these vigilante actions many Mexicans were killed and lynched as their homes were burned, arms seized, and the people forcibly removed to urban areas. Out of fear and because of forced migrations, over half of the Valley's population left, and the economy of that area was virtually destroyed. This condition of war existed until October when the border patrols on both sides increased, and the raids declined.

Much doubt and conjecture surrounds the Plan de San Diego in all its aspects. For historical analogy, perhaps one must look to the "Republic" of the Rio Grande in 1847. The authorship of the Plan, crucial from a certain speculative point of view, is in question. Some feel Carranza devised the Plan as part of a series of actions designed to gain diplomatic recognition of the United States; if so, it seems odd he would risk incurring the wrath of the American government who had invaded Mexico often and who currently held an area of Veracruz. It has also been suggested that Germany devised the Plan in an effort to draw the attention of the United States away from Europe. Webb hints that a prominent Texan may have encouraged the Plan to further personal interests. The evidence used to present these three views has not been documented, only assessed. There is, however, a possibility that the Plan de San Diego was what it purported itself to be, a *Plan* by Mexicans in Texas to reclaim the Southwest and liberate the oppressed people living within its border.

Looking at the Plan de San Diego itself one can speculate on a number of points, which may tend to indicate Mexican-American authorship. The Plan makes an historic claim to the areas of the Southwest as a unity, and it was stipulated that the area would become an independent republic. Reannexation with Mexico might occur, *if expedient.* This seems to indicate that the claim was being made for and by the Southwest as an entity which was not conceived of being an intrinsic part of either the United States and Mexico. The obvious collective junta-like leadership under which the new republic was to be governed was and is often typical of Southwest organizations. Another important aspect of the Plan is the attention paid to other oppressed groups in the area; the blacks, the Indians, and the Orientals. It seems that the concern expressed for them would more likely arise from a group who had suffered the same experiences rather than those who had not. Clauses 5, 6, and 7, harsh as they may seem, can best be understood in view of the brutal racial relations between Anglos and Mexicans, and the bitter feeling of the latter towards members of their own community who collaborated with the Anglo civilians, politicians and peace officers.

The Plan of San Diego can be examined best as a response and a reaction within a particular set of circumstances. To the scholar and the interested community organizer, the principal question should focus on factors leading up to it, its conceptual assumptions, its operational phase, and the repercussions. In isolation the Plan is an antiquarian's curiosity, within its proper historical context: there is history from which we can learn.

Provisional Directorate of the Plan of San Diego, Texas.

PLAN OF SAN DIEGO, TEXAS, STATE OF TEXAS, JANUARY 6th, 1915.

We who in turn sign our names, assembled in the REVOLUTIONARY PLOT OF SAN DIEGO, TEXAS, solemnly promise each other, on our word of honor, that we will fulfill, and cause to be fulfilled and complied with, all the clauses and provisions stipulated in this document, and execute the orders and the wishes emanating from the PROVISIONAL DIRECTORATE of this movement, and recognize as military Chief of the same, Mr. Augustin S. Garza, guaranteeing with our lives the faithful accomplishment of what is here agreed upon.

1. On the 20th day of February 1915, at two o'clock in the morning, we will arise in arms against the Government and country of the United States of North America, ONE AS ALL AND ALL AS ONE, proclaiming the liberty of the individuals of the black race and its independence of Yankee tyranny which has held us in iniquitous slavery since remote times; and at the same time and in the same manner we will proclaim the independence and segregation of the States bordering upon the Mexican Nation, which are: TEXAS, NEW MEXICO, ARIZONA, COLORADO, AND UPPER CALIFORNIA, OF WHICH States the Republic of MEXICO was robbed in a most perfidious manner by North American imperialism.

2. In order to render the foregoing clause effective, the necessary army corps will be formed, under the immediate command of military leaders named by the SUPREME REVOLUTIONARY CONGRESS OF SAN DIEGO, TEXAS, which shall have full power to designate a SUPREME CHIEF, who shall be at the head of said army. The banner which shall guide us in this enterprise shall be red, with a white diagonal fringe, and bearing the following inscription: "EQUALITY AND INDEPENDENCE" and none of the subordinate leaders or subalterns shall use any other flag (except only the white flag for signals). The aforesaid army shall be known by the name of: "LIBERATING ARMY FOR RACES AND PEOPLES."

3. Each one of the chiefs shall do his utmost by whatever means possible to get possession of the arms and funds of the cities which he has beforehand been designated to capture, in order that our cause may be provided with resources to continue to fight with proper success. The said leaders each being required to render account of everything to his superiors, in order that the latter may dispose of it in the proper manner.

4. The leader who may take a city must immediately name and appoint municipal authorities, in order that they may preserve order and assist in every way possible the revolutionary movement. In case the Capital of any State which we are endeavoring to liberate be captured, there will be named in the same manner superior municipal authorities, for the same purpose.

5. It is strictly forbidden to hold prisoners, either special prisoners (civilians) or soldiers; and the only time that should be spent in dealing with them is that which is absolutely necessary to demand funds (loans) of them; and whether these demands be successful or not, they shall be shot immediately without any pretext.

6. Every stranger who shall be found armed and who cannot prove his right to carry arms, shall be summarily executed, regardless of his race or nationality.

7. Every North American over sixteen years of age shall be put to death; and only the aged men, the women, and the children shall be respected; and on no account shall the traitors to our race be spared or respected.

8. THE APACHES of Arizona, as well as the INDIANS (RED SKINS) of the Territory, shall be given every guarantee; and their lands which have been taken from them shall be returned to them to the end that they may assist us in the cause which we defend.

9. All appointments and grades in our army which are exercised by subordinate officers (subalterns) shall be examined (recognized) by the superior officers. There shall likewise be recognized the grades of leaders of other complots which may not be connected with this, and who may wish to cooperate with us; also those who may affiliate with us later.

10. The movement having gathered force, and once having possessed ourselves of the States above alluded to, we shall proclaim them an INDEPENDENT REPUBLIC, later requesting (if it be thought expedient) annexation to MEXICO, without concerning ourselves at that time about the form of Government which may control the destinies of the common mother country.

11. When we shall have obtained independence for the negroes, we shall grant them a banner, which they themselves be permitted to select, and we shall aid them in obtaining six States of the American Union, which States border upon those already mentioned, and they may form from these six States a Republic that they may, therefore, be independent.

12. None of the leaders shall have power to make terms with the enemy, without first communicating with the superior officers of the army, bearing in mind that this is a war without quarter;

nor shall any leader enroll in his ranks any stranger, unless said stranger belong to the Latin, the Negro or the Japanese race.

13. It is understood that none of the members of this COMPLOT (or any one who may come in later), shall, upon the definite triumph of the cause which we defend, fail to recognize their superiors, nor shall they aid others who, with bastard designs, may endeavor to destroy what has been accomplished by such great work.

14. As soon as possible, each local society (junta) shall nominate delegates who shall meet at a time and place beforehand designated, for the purpose of nominating a PERMANENT DIRECTORATE OF THE REVOLUTIONARY MOVEMENT. At this meeting shall be determined and worked out in detail the powers and duties of the PERMANENT DIRECTORATE, and this REVOLUTIONARY PLAN may be revised or amended.

15. It is understood among those who may follow this movement that we will carry as a singing voice the independence of the negroes, placing obligations upon both races; and that, on no account will we accept aid, either moral or pecuniary, from the Government of Mexico, and it need not consider itself under any obligations in this, our movement.

"EQUALITY AND INDEPENDENCE"

San Diego, Texas, Jan. 6, 1915.

President,
Signed, L. Farrigno.
Signed, Augustin S. Garza, Com.

Signed, Manuel Flores
Signed, B. Ramos, Jr.

Secretary,
Signed, A. Gonzales, Lawyer
Signed, A. A. Saenz,
Saloon Keeper
Signed, E. Cisneros
Signed, A. C. Alamraz.

ROBERT J. ROSENBAUM

In the following essay, Robert Rosenbaum discusses the LAS GORRAS BLANCAS *movement, its successes, and finally its ultimate failure. Dr. Rosenbaum questions the historical generalizations that the mexicanos simply yielded control in New Mexico, via attrition, to the always increasing Anglo population. In fact, as evidenced by the Las Gorras Blancas, the mexicanos strenuously resisted, sometimes violently, the effects anglo presence had on their lives and culture.*
By permission of the author.

Las Gorras Blancas
Of San Miguel County, 1889–1890

On the morning of April 27, 1889, the owners of a ranch near San Geronimo, twelve miles west of Las Vegas, awoke to find their four miles of new barbed wire fence cut. Cut is a mild word. It was destroyed, the fence posts chopped to kindling and the wire strewn in glittering fragments. The partners—two English adventurers trying their luck at Wild West ranching—were the first victims of a civil war that raged across San Miguel County for the next eighteen months. Wearing white masks or caps—*gorras blancas*—bands of native New Mexicans—*mexicanos*—struck at night, lev-

eling fences, destroying crops, burning buildings, and, not infrequently, shooting people.[1] By the summer of 1890, according to one English language newspaper, *Las Gorras Blancas* had brought business in Las Vegas to a standstill.

Until very recently, historians ignored this intense conflict between *mexicano* and *americano*. Histories depict the progress of Anglo-Americans in New Mexico Territory as a process of attrition. Anglo entrepreneurs had connections in Washington, access to capital and command of technological innovations, and they formed momentary alliances of convenience with New Mexican *ricos* who possessed great influence over the predominately *mexicano* electorate, and who owned, controlled or could facilitate access to, natural resources, primarily land. In this view, New Mexico's history describes an erratic succession of continually realigning factions. Gradually, through immigration, Americanization and the accumulated weight of minor victories, Anglos gained a secure advantage, although they never entirely eliminated Hispanos from power.[2]

This is a very simplified summary of the traditional interpretation, and I do not quarrel with it as a concise generalization. But if not used cautiously, this generalization leads to an incomplete and incorrect explanation. It presumes that the *ricos* controlled the bulk of the *mexicano* population with almost feudal ease. Without questioning how the *ricos* got and maintained their power, it leaves the impression that *las masas de los hombres pobres,* to use the phrase of a sympathetic Spanish language newspaper, were passive, fatalistic peons and that the Hispanic side of the territorial chronicle can be told completely by studying the actions of the elite. By focusing only on the most visible Hispanos, this interpretation provides for neither overt resistance against the Anglo newcomer, nor for the tensions which clearly existed between native New Mexicans.

The year and a half of raiding by *Las Gorras Blancas* raises serious questions of this picture. *Las Gorras Blancas* dramatically resisted changes that the *americano* presence threatened their lives. Moreover, *los hombres pobres* filled the ranks of the nightriders, and they did not hesitate to attack *mexicanos* as well as *americanos* who threatened traditional relationships.

Chicano activists have attacked the role American historians usually assign to Mexican-Americans. In response, two studies of *Las Gorras Blancas* appeared in recent months. One, by Andrew Bancroft Schlesinger, was published in the Spring 1971 issue of the *Journal of Mexican-American History;* Robert Larson, delivered the second at the last meeting of the Organization of American Historians. Both studies emphasize the violent, widespread and relatively long-lived nature of the movement, and, therefore, provide a clear corrective to the placid, *mañana*-oriented peon stereotype. But neither, I believe, penetrates very deeply into the culture of *los hombres pobres,* and moreover, both tend to fall back on the Knights of Labor and incipient Populism as explanations for the outbreaks of violent resistance. By doing this, both Mr. Schlesinger and Mr. Larson imply that *Las Gorras Blancas* were an outgrowth of Anglo radical ideologies; that without Anglo know-how, *los hombres pobres* would have placidly stepped aside.

When viewed against the background of their culture, *Las Gorras Blancas* do not stand out as an atypical phenomenon caused by outside agitators. The dominant issue—land use and ownership—came directly from the traditions of *los hombres pobres.* The membership and leadership of local bands followed traditional patterns, and the tactics used by the angry men, warnings followed by violent, destructive raids, were culturally sanctioned, acceptable methods to *los hombres pobres* for facing a crisis. *Las Gorras Blancas* do stand out as the most wide-spread, well-organized and effective instance of *mexicano* resistance to *americano* control during New Mexico's territorial years. There was a close correlation in membership and leadership with the Knights of Labor, and the agitation of *Las Gorras Blancas* helped lead to the formation of *El Partido del Pueblo Unido,* a new political party in the county that made common cause with the Populists, for a time.[3] But *Las Gorras Blancas* were an attempt by *los hombres pobres* of San Miguel County to cope with damaging changes to their way of life. When these threats had been quieted, in their eyes, *los hombres pobres* stopped riding and the *politicos* took over. *Los hombres pobres* ultimately lost because nothing in their culture taught them how to deal with the gradual, subtle tactics that their opponents adopted after the era of nightriding.[4]

No observer, past or present, denies that most of the raiders were poor *mexicanos.* "Hot-headed Mexicans . . . the most ignorant people on the face of the earth," according to one frightened Anglo land speculator; "a simple, pastoral people [protesting] the establishment of large landed estates," wrote a sympathetic Anglo judge. In warnings nailed to offending fences, and in a declaration posted throughout Las Vegas, *Las Gorras Blancas* called themselves "The People . . . especially of the helpless class," and challenged anyone who doubted that they were law-abiding citizens to "come out to our homes and see the hunger and desolation we are suffering."

In 1890, San Miguel County had a population of more than 24,000. Las Vegas boasted 5200 residents, about equally divided between *mexicano* and *americano.* As the metropolis of east-central New Mexico, Las Vegas attracted the most Anglos and the most wealth in the county. *Mexicanos* dominated the countryside, and they were poor. More than two-thirds of the heads of households in the county owned property—real and personal— with a combined value of less than $300.[5]

That most native New Mexicans were poor comes as no surprise to anyone vaguely familiar with New Mexico. But *los hombres pobres* of San Miguel County enjoyed a self-sufficiency and were possessed of a vigor that belies their reference to themselves as the "helpless class." These characteristics were rooted in the pattern of Hispanic settlement of the region, a pattern *Las Gorras Blancas* fought to maintain.

One of the dominant institutions in the native New Mexican way of life for San Miguel County was the community land grant. Between 1794 and 1846, Spain and Mexico awarded fourteen tracts in the region. Six were community grants. In 1890, almost eighty percent of the county's population lived within the boundaries of these six grants.[6]

Basically, Spain and Mexico used the community land grant to encourage and regulate settlement by *los hombres pobres.* Upon petition by a group, the governor would award a specific tract of land, bounded by prominent landmarks. In the San Miguel county, the grants were usually quite large, often more than 300,000 acres. The grantees chose a specific site on the grant for their village, including irrigated fields. House lots and farming lands were divided equitably and held in private ownership. The remainder of the grant was owned in common, free to all, for grazing, watering places, firewood, timber and building materials. The grant was open to additional settlement, and other villages could be established on the same grant, with the same pattern of house lots and fields owned privately and with equal access to the grant's common land. Provisions were made for local government, especially for regulating the irrigation system, usually under the jurisdiction of a *mayordomo de acequia,* or ditch boss.

The community grants awarded in east-central New Mexico envisioned a society of homogeneous people following a mixed economy of farming and grazing. Often the settlers drew lots for the initial distribution of homesites and irrigable fields, and they were charged to work in harmony "with that union which in their government they must preserve." To the Anglo-American eye, the grant documents picture a Hispanic and cooperative variation on the Jeffersonian image of the sturdy yeoman farmer.

Spain and Mexico did not follow the homogeneous community pattern perfectly, and it was not the only one they used to settle New Mexico's eastern frontier. After all, eight of the fourteen grants in the region were private awards. Large sheep and cattle ranchers grazed their stock on the eastern grasslands, altering the homogeneous form; merchants and Indian traders also contributed to a *rico* class whose wealth and influence reached across the region and across the territory.

Conflicts disturbed the harmony on the grants. Feuds broke out over rights on the common grazing land; village sometimes fought village for irrigation water. Rare was the village not divided into two factions, often along family lines. Despite these tensions, life followed a predictable course until the eighteen-eighties. Disputes occurred for relative advantage within an accepted framework.

This framework rested on personality, influence, power and custom. Land, the basic resource, fell into two catagories: the privately owned house lots and fields, and the vague common land. Custom, need and power determined who used the common land; it was not precisely measured and carefully tagged with the name of an owner.

Local landmarks bounded the horizons of most *mexicanos. Ricos* coped with the larger regional and territorial problems, and *los hombres pobres* were glad to let them. *Ricos* built followings through persuasion, force or economic sanction, but usually they gained supporters by offering immediate, tangible benefits, and they left the autonomy of the village relatively untouched.[7]

By the eighteen-eighties, *americano* influence in San Miguel County threatened the pattern of several generations. The threat came in two forms: direct competition and changes in the rules of the game. Not only were *los extranjeros*—the foreigners—taking up resources and occupying positions of power, but the *ricos*—those who had traditionally coped with the larger than local problems, were working with the newcomers. Using their influence in the *mexicano* communities, the *ricos* became political *jefes*. Using the power that came from winning votes, the *jefes* tried to maintain their position as the leaders of local society and to reap profit in the changing system. But by behaving in Anglo ways, many wealthy *mexicanos* fell victim to *Las Gorras Blancas*.

All aspects of the *americano* presence threatened the way of life for *los hombres pobres*, but none as obviously and with such immediate damage as the threat to the common land. To the Anglo-American, land must be precisely measured and it must belong to some owner—be it an individual, a corporation or a government. Rights and obligations on land that was, in some sense, public, had to be clearly spelled out; public land, in any case, was a temporary condition of governmental stewardship, waiting to be apportioned privately upon demand. The *americano* in New Mexico found it difficult to comprehend, and harder to tolerate, the idea of community owned land—vague in limits, open to common use, and on which rights were defined by custom and ownership devolved upon some imperfectly described communal body.

The attack on *los hombres pobres'* common land came from three directions. Anglo entrepreneurs saw in the tangled land grant situation an opportunity to acquire large landed estates free from the regulations of the General Land Office; ambitious and agile *ricos* did the same by using their facility in both cultures. Anglo ranchers and homesteaders looked at the common land, saw it as unoccupied and unclaimed, and tried to file on it as part of the public domain. Whether homesteader, speculator or *rico*, many people claimed large tracts on the common land and built fences where none had stood before.

For *los hombres pobres*, fencing the common land was not just a violation of the natural order of things, it meant disaster. San Miguel County did not have enough productive farm land to support the people; the common land, the grazing land, was necessary for survival. By 1889, a crisis had developed.

Los hombres pobres responded to the crisis as their culture and history taught. Angry men joined in the villages around local leaders. Some communities might be solidly behind the movement, others were divided. In one, the *mayordomo de acequia* might be the leader, in another, a personable quasi-bandit used to a high risk life might attract a following.[8] Whatever the local variations in leaders and membership, all had common grievances and a shared sense of outrage.

All bands also agreed about tactics. The settlements had long faced the threats of hostile Indians; military engagements were a thing of the recent past.[9] Violent defense had been part of the community effort for a long time. Even more telling, violence was an accepted solution to major personal and civil problems. In a society regulated by custom, with few institutional controls from above, violence was often the only alternative to capitulation. Many disputes—individual fights, family feuds, or competition between villages for grazing land or irrigation water—had been settled by force of arms.[10]

Thus, there is nothing exceptional about the self-defense aspects of *Las Gorras Blancas* in terms of *mexicano* culture. In a society that encouraged cooperative effort, in a society that saw violence as, in the words of the *Las Vegas Daily Optic*, "the only speedy and adequate remedy at their command," it is not startling to find groups ready to use violence for the common good. But *Las Gorras Blancas* do stand out: no other movement was as widespread and as well-organized; no other movement achieved the same degree of success, at least in the short run. In addition, *Las Gorras Blancas* stand out because of their connection with the Knights of Labor and their relationship to *El Partido del Pueblo*.

The blending of the grievances and tactics of *los hombres pobres* with a labor union and an insurgent political party was accomplished by an exceptional man, Juan José Herrera. Through Herrera's efforts, *Las Gorras Blancas* organized effectively enough to gain momentary victory by August 1890.

Herrera was born in New Mexico and lived in San Miguel County for a time. He left Las Vegas in 1866, reportedly because of an affair with a married woman. Little is known about his activities between his departure from Las Vegas and the outbreaks of fence cutting, although family tradition says that he spent some time in Colorado and Utah and that he had probably joined the Knights in Colorado. In any event, by 1888, Herrera returned to San Miguel County holding a commission from the Knights as district organizer for New Mexico. He differed from *los hombres pobres* in terms of education and experience, but Herrera knew, understood and sympathized with the *mexicanos* of San Miguel County.[11]

Herrera used the Knights of Labor to unify local groups of active men into a widespread organization. He established twenty local assemblies in San Miguel County, and moved into the neighboring counties of Santa Fé and Bernalillo. *Mexicanos* joined the Knights for several reasons. The union had long opposed land speculation and large land-owners. In 1887, the Las Vegas local assembly helped form the Las Vegas Land Grant Defense Association to raise money for the legal expenses of some *mexicanos* whose rights on the Las Vegas Grant were challenged by an *americano* cattle company.[12] The Knight's stand on land, their support during the trial, and the fact that the district organizer was a *mexicano* help account for the appeal of the order.

Herrera coordinated, he did not create. *Los hombres pobres* had the issues, the local organizations and the tactics; Herrera provided encouragement and an organizational superstructure that facilitated communication.[13] He also added some additional targets and demands; in the spring of 1890, almost a year after the raiding began, *Las Gorras Blancas* started to burn bridges and tear up tracks on the Atchison, Topeka and Santa Fé Railroad, to threaten section hands, to order teamsters to strike, and to proclaim against the corrupt system of "partisan 'bossism' " developed by the *jefes politicos*. But as Herrera organized assemblies, and as *Las Gorras Blancas* activity increased in intensity, land remained the issue that cemented the local groups together.[14]

Herrera did not have universal success. In some villages, the old people who will talk about the fence cutters say that *Las Gorras Blancas* and the Knights of Labor were the same: "*Las Gorras Blancas* was just a nickname," they explain, "but they preferred to be called *Los Caballeros de Labor.*" In other villages, *Las Gorras Blancas* were recruited through the Knights, but functioned separately and secretly from the local assembly. And in some areas, *Las Gorras Blancas* gained no ground. But the combination of *mexicano* outrage and Herrera's organizational skills momentarily halted the *americano* advance.

By the summer of 1890, few fences remained standing, lumbermen no longer cut timber on the common land, few new settlers came to the county, and the legal authorities were powerless. Violence and secrecy, coupled with public opinion that agreed with the moral position, if not the tactics, of *Las Gorras Blancas,* led to a stalemate. Territorial Governor L. B. Prince summarized the situation for the Secretary of the Interior. As the organization was secret, the governor explained, it was difficult to know for whom to issue a warrant; as the fence-cutters were violent, it was difficult to find witnesses who would make a sworn statement "even for a large consideration"; as juries were chosen from the same class that made up the nightriders, conviction seemed unlikely. Furthermore, lamented Prince, many of the "best citizens" sympathized with the fence cutters, thus preventing that "strong public sentiment which we ought to have as an aid in suppressing these outrages."

With the fences down, *Las Gorras Blancas* stopped riding. On August 25, 1890, the *Las Vegas Optic* published a call for delegates to the county convention of a new political party. A mixed bag of Las Vegas *politicos*—unhappy Republican *jefes,* Anglo Democrats, and young, ambitious *mexicanos*—gathered under the banner of *El Partido del Pueblo.* They capitalized on the issues and organization of *Las Gorras Blancas,* and controlled the county for the next four years. But the switch from violent to electoral politics signalled defeat for *los hombres pobres*. It was defeat by attrition, by piecemeal machinations. Local bands of *Las Gorras Blancas* rode sporadically, at least until 1926, as *los extranjeros* continued to usurp chunks of common land.[15] But the threat to grant land was never as pervasive as it was during the eighteen-eighties, and resistance never again achieved the cohesion that it had enjoyed during the eighteen months of 1889 and 1890.

Ultimately, *Las Gorras Blancas* failed. But their story demonstrates that some *mexicanos* in New Mexico possessed an energy and an awareness of their self-interest that has often been slighted. *Las Gorras Blancas* responded to a clear threat to their way of life; both their momentary success and ultimate defeat lay with many related causes. The task facing historians is to sort out these factors, and this must be done by examining history from the perspectives of all involved. Not only will this approach more accurately portray the Mexican-American—and I do not mean to minimize the importance of that correction—but it will also lead to a better understanding of the processes of cultural confrontation, accommodation and assimilation. The United States encompasses many cultures. Studying the American West in terms of all of the cultures active in it should shed light on the causes of passivity and resistance, acquiescence and rebellion, compromise and revolution. And, this approach is necessary in order to discharge one of the historians primary obligations, which is "to try to understand the actions of past men as they understood them . . ."

NOTES

1. I have taken poetic license in describing the destruction of the fence. It is justified because of two factors. There is ample documentation that the White Caps did destroy fences in this manner. Furthermore, there was, and still is, a distinction between cutting a passageway, viewed by the fence owner as much the same as such "acts of God" as fallen trees, and in destroying a fence. For a modern comment on the distinction, see Richard Gardner *¡Grito!,* (New York, 1970), pp. 64-65.

White Caps and White Capping are beginning to come under study, thanks in part to Richard Maxwell Brown's mention of them in "Historical Patterns of Violence in America," pp. 62–65, 67, in Hugh Davis Graham and Ted Robert Gurr, eds., *Violence in America* (New York, 1969). Brown sums up White Capping in general as a "spontaneous movement for the moral regulation of the poor whites and ne'er-do-wells of the rural American countryside," although he acknowledges that in New Mexico, White Caps fought land enclosure. Whatever national relationships between White Caps in various parts of the country will be discovered by further research, it is clear that in New Mexico they arose from local problems and used traditional tactics. Even the name was given to them by Anglos, although they accepted it readily. See draft of a report by Prince to Secretary of the Interior John Noble, Prince Papers.

2. Howard R. Lamar, *The Far Southwest* (New Haven, 1966) and Robert W. Larson, *New Mexico's Quest for Statehood,* (Albuquerque, 1968) are the most recent and most exhaustive territorial political histories. Both Lamar and Larson look at New Mexico from the top, analyzing alliances and quarrels among the territorial magnates. Such a view is useful, indeed indispensable, but it does not plumb the depths of social, economic, and political relationships. A book that does attempt an in-depth analysis for the twentieth century is Jack E. Holmes' *Politics in New Mexico,* (Albuquerque, 1967). All three studies tend to ignore such movements of resistance that did materialize because such movements were local in impact and uniformly unsuccessful.

3. No one at the time admitted to being a member of *Las Gorras Blancas,* and their opponents' frequent assertions that they were identical must be treated skeptically. Many kinds of evidence, however, indicate that there was a close correlation, but not 100 percent duplication, between the nightriders and the Knights. Sixty-eight people were arrested for fence-cutting (none convicted), and at least five were Knights. There is a strong correlation between areas that welcomed the Knights, areas embroiled in the land disputes, and White Cap raids. As the Knights of Labor spread, so did raiding. Furthermore, Pinkerton Operative Charles Siringo joined the Knights in 1891 in an attempt to trace the unsuccessful assassins of territorial senator J. A. Anchetta; Siringo reported that many of the White Caps were members of the Knights, but that the raiders functioned separately from the union. (See Anchetta Shooting Folder, Prince Papers, especially Siringo to Prince, April 30, 1891.) Oral tradition on the grants in San Miguel and Guadalupe counties supports the relationship between the Knights and the White Caps; many informants said that the two organizations were identical, and volunteered that their fathers had ridden with them.

The connection between *El Partido del Pueblo* and the Knights is easier to establish—it was self-admitted by both organizations. The party represented a realignment of *politicos* who sought to fill the power vacuum created by the legal authorities' inability to suppress *Las Gorras Blancas.* The party capitalized on the issues of land and "partisan 'bossism' " raised by the White Caps, and added the national anti-capitalist themes soon to coalesce around the People's Party. *El Partido del Pueblo Unido* was created before, and functioned separately from, the Populists, although the two parties did join forces for the county election of 1892. Despite its rhetoric, and the sincere efforts of some of its leaders, *El Partido* essentially followed politics as usual, albeit with a self-consciously *mexicano* theme, and *los hombres pobres* fared little better under the new regime. Traditional enmities erupted in 1894, precipatating another realignment, and brought the short life of *El Partido del Pueblo* to an end.

4. The case of the San Miguel del Bado Grant graphically illustrates the subtle tactics that cost *los hombres pobres* most of their land. Congress formed the U. S. Court of Private Land Claims in 1891, and shortly thereafter residents on the grant brought suit before that tribunal to establish that the San Miguel Grant was a community grant. The court so ruled in 1894, but did not clearly state the quantity of land involved. After almost ten years of debate and appeal, only 5,024 acres, the land under ditch, was allowed. By depriving the residents of 310,000 acres of common land, the economic utility of the grant was destroyed—the farming land alone could not support the people.

5. George I. Sánchez in *Forgotten People* (Albuquerque, 1940) estimated the population of Spanish descent of San Miguel County in 1938 to be 83 percent (p. 30). It is safe to assume that in 1890, the *mexicano* peoples made up between 83 and 90 percent of San Miguel's population.

According to territorial statute, each head of household or property owner was allowed a $300 exemption. The San Miguel County Assessment Rolls for 1890 (in NMSRCA) reveal about 2000 taxpayers, of whom over one-half were Anglos. Furthermore, many of the wealthiest property owners were either land and cattle companies or absentee land speculators.

6. Eleventh Census (1890). Arrived at by computing the population of the precincts known to be in the six community grants. Two qualifications must be noted. I was unable to locate three of the precincts; they could well be on these grants. Second, the town of Las Vegas, or more properly the two communities of East and West Las Vegas, is on the Las Vegas Grant. If its 5200 residents are subtracted from the county's total, almost 58 percent of the county's people live on these six grants. While there are good arguments for treating Las Vegas as a unique case, it must be remembered that many residents of Las Vegas had an interest in the grant, and that a faction in the town wanted the town to control and administer the whole grant.

7. Jack E. Holmes, *Politics in New Mexico,* pp. 17–33, goes to some length to refute what he calls the "Procrustean synthesis" of the works of Margaret Mead and Lyle Saunders and the *patron* or *jefe politico* dominated peon stereotype. What Holmes argues, and what my own research supports, is that the *patrones* and *jefes politicos* had to compete for their constituencies, that they did so by offering rewards that made sense to *los hombres pobres.* These rewards could be money, the erasure of a debt, prestige, patronage jobs, freedom from police harassment, etc.

8. For example, the head of *Las Gorras Blancas* in El Llano on the Antonchico Grant was the *mayordomo de acequia,* Manuel Gonzales, while two miles up the Pecos in Antonchico, a "mean, bad man" named Nicolas Ortega led the nightriders. Interviews with the grandsons of the two men, Don Miguel Gonzales and Don Ramon Ortega, February 18, 1972.

9. All grant documents stress defense as an important part of the communal effort and stipulate that the settlers had to be properly armed. Comanches and Apaches were fresh memories; many still remember the Texas-Santa Fé expedition of 1841, or Sibley's column during the Civil War.

10. In addition to examples of conflict already cited, the oral tradition of the people abounds with tales of personal courage, particularly in the face of insulting Texas cowboys, and of feuds between families. Many such events have been recorded in *corridos*—ballads—similar to The Ballad of Gregorio Cortez that has been ably examined by Américo Paredes ("With his pistol in his hand," Austin, 1958). The phrase *mucho hombre*—much of a man—punctuates the telling of these stories.

Las Gorras Blancas were not free from this tradition of conflict; often White Cap bands fought each other over which fences to cut. In addition, not all of the fence cutting and barn burning during this period could be attributed to the "secret gathering of fence cutters," for the turmoil produced by the White Caps provided perfect cover for the settling of personal grudges, a fact recognized by Governor Prince. See Prince to Noble, draft of report, Prince Papers.

11. John K. Martin, Frank C. Ogden and J. B. Allen to T. V. Powderly, August 8, 1890, and Miguel Salazar to Prince, July 23, 1890, Prince Papers. Robert Larson interviewed two of Herrera's descendants and included a summary of their statements in his paper. "The 'White Caps' of New Mexico: The Political and Ethnic Origins of Western Violence," delivered on April 6, 1972, in Washington, D.C. Herrera alluded to the charge of adultery in a letter published in the *Optic* on April 9, 1890, and again in his own newspaper, *El Defensor del Pueblo* (Albuquerque) on December 19, 1891.

Although Herrera had been a bit of a wanderer, his two brothers, Pablo and Nicanca, had remained in the county, as had many other relatives. Herrera was no stranger to *los hombres pobres* of San Miguel County.

12. The case in question was Phillip Millhiser et al. versus José Léon Padilla et al. The Knights of Labor in Las Vegas, at that time mostly Anglo, were perfectly willing to side with *mexicanos* against large landowners, but they viewed the land as public domain, not as part of a community grant. Therefore, when the *mexicanos* became violent, agitated for the land as theirs alone, and became increasingly anti-Anglo, the Anglo Knights grew uneasy and tried to disassociate themselves from the movement. See Martin et al. to Powderly, August 8, 1890, Prince Papers.

13. To illustrate this point: Herrera organized an assembly at Genova in the northeastern portion of the county. The local leader of the new assembly was Don Emiterio Gallegos, a rancher whose property was valued in excess of $8000 in 1890. Gallegos faced competition from Anglo cattle companies, and saw in the Knights a source of political power, both violent and electoral, that would protect his interests.

14. Despite this expansion of targets, over 60 percent of the attacks during the summer of 1890 were directed against landholders. It should also be noted that the railroad cut across grant land, that lumbermen cut timber on the grant's common land, and that both the railroad and its employees were relatively unprotected points of the *americano* enemy. While *los hombres pobres* probably thought higher wages were a good idea, and while they probably relished attacking the *jefes,* one should move cautiously before equating these tactics with other union movements. Perhaps Herrera was strongly committed to these issues, but it is by no means clear that *los hombres pobres* shared this committment. Equally plausible is the argument that Herrera saw these points as weaknesses in the American armor, and was primarily trying to inflict pain rather than trying to achieve any real change in the labor situation.

15. The White Caps did not die away completely. Some kind of organization persisted through the 1890s, with varying membership, and they rode again, en masse, through Antonchico in 1903, and again against the Preston Beck Grant in the mid-1920s. Interviews with Dwight Duran, Don Eduardo Montano, Don and Doña Antonio Ruiz, Don Manuel Lucero, Don Francisco Sena, Don George Jaramillo, Pedro Delgado, Don Roman Ortega and Don H. H. Mondragon, February 11, 15, 18, 1972.

WARREN A. BECK

Warren A. Beck (Professor of History, California State College, Fullerton) originally specialized in the history of Guatemala. While teaching at Eastern New Mexico State University, he became interested in that state's history, and subsequently wrote NEW MEXICO: A HISTORY OF FOUR CENTURIES *(1962) and co-edited* AN HISTORICAL ATLAS OF NEW MEXICO *(1968). In this original essay Professor Beck has put his broad background in Latin American and Spanish history to good use in showing that the Penitente experience is not a uniquely New Mexican phenomenon. By permission of the author.*

The Penitentes Of New Mexico

Los Hermanos Penitentes of Los Hermanos de Sangre de Cristo is a religious brotherhood found among the Spanish-American citizens in New Mexico, in Southern Colorado, and in contiguous territory across the border of Mexico. They practiced flagellation and the actual dramatization of the Biblical story of the Passion. Their rites during the Lenten season have attracted much attention from many observers, usually Protestants who found their ceremonies so different from what their church practiced. In addition to their religious function, which is of primary importance, the Penitentes have exercised a charitable role among their members, have been directly involved in politics, have even played a judicial role in some communities, and have provided the primary social outlet for their members.

Because most of its members have, in the past, been illiterate, and because of the secret nature of the association, it has been extremely difficult to obtain accurate information about the group. The same problems one would encounter in seeking accurate knowledge about secret lodges, where most traditions are handed down by word of mouth, is the kind of difficulty encountered in a study of the Penitentes. Complicating the prob-

137

lem of obtaining authentic knowledge is the fact that many observers were most unsympathetic to the practices of the order and, therefore, in recording the rites, permitted their biases to enter. Then, too, there are great differences between individual chapters, so generalizations concerning the order are extremely risky.

Each community has its own organization of Penitentes which may or may not have contact with neighboring groups. Over each chapter is a President or the Hermano Mayor, who is normally elected every year or, in some cases, is even elected for life. Assisting him is a group of other officers, each of whom has a particular duty to perform in much the same manner as in many modern fraternal organizations. These officers and older brothers make up the Brothers of Light or *Hermanos de Luz.* Their name is derived from the fact that they carried the candles to illuminate the ceremonies. They do not participate in the public ceremonies, but are there mainly to supervise the rites. The brothers who whipped themselves were called *Los Hermanos de Sangre de Cristo* or the Brothers of the Blood of Christ. In a subordinate but also important role is the female organization known as the *Auxiliadoras de la Morada.* They are the wives, widows, or daughters of the Hermanos. Their primary duties are the physical care of the Morada, the nursing and care of the sick members of the chapter, the preparation of meals during the ceremonies of Holy Week, and attendance at and preparation of *la cena,* the supper, during wakes. The women may participate in the rites during Holy Week, but in general they do not.

A Morada is a meeting place of the order, and one was found in most communities. It is a small one-story building, without windows, and with only one door, and can be identified by the crude wooden cross that stands in the front of it. Originally, Moradas were the chapter houses located in villages, often adjacent to the Roman Catholic Church, but they were later moved to isolated locations to get them away from the curious. These chapter houses were originally intended as chapels, and for this reason had altars draped in black and sometimes decorated with skulls cut out of white cloth. Human skulls, candles and crucifixes, statues of the saints, of the Holy Mother,

and the Christus were kept there. In addition, the heavy wooden crosses carried in the processional, the whips *(disciplina),* chains, special clothing, the cart of death, and other material used in the ceremonies were stored in the Moradas.

The monumental religious expression of the Penitentes is concerned with the Lenten season. The ceremonies usually begin on Wednesday of Holy Week when the members gather at the Morada, usually staying there until Easter Sunday. Although rites vary, one is the enactment of the entire Passion story, the betrayal of Judas, Pilate's role, and the procession to Golgotha, climaxed by the crucifixion of Christ.

Beginning on Wednesday evening, the ceremonies go far into the night and are continued on Thursday evening. Naturally, the high point in the processional was the crucifixion on Friday. The men in the procession wore black caps and white trousers, and in some instances, black hoods to conceal their faces. Their backs were bare and as they marched they whipped themselves until the blood flowed, and when they were no longer able to continue, friends assisted them in their self-torture. As the men marched, they were accompanied by a weird music including the wail of the *pito,* the whirling of a wooden rattle called a *matraca,* the rattling of chains and tin cans, and in some chapters, the use of a drum. In the processional was a crude wagon which carried a skeleton, or a figurine of a skeleton representing death. Struggling to carry a huge cross, perhaps weighing a hundred pounds, came the Christ. Originally, the crucifixion took place at the Morada, but in more recent times it has been done in isolated places so as to escape the curious. In some instances, a wooden figurine of Christ was fastened to the cross in place of a man. It has been claimed by some observers that the man enacting the role of Christ is nailed to the cross, but it is more probable that he is tied by rawhide thongs.

Membership in the Penitentes is open to all practicing Catholics. Some Protestants, especially if they are friends of the community or politicians, have been given honorary membership, and, more recently, many have joined for strictly political purposes. Women were at one time members but were not permitted to participate in the public ceremonies, although they probably did private penance. As most of the Spanish-Americans at one time belonged to the society, it is obvious that its potential political power was tremendous. Perhaps the most apt comparison, for purposes of understanding its political role, is with the Ku Klux Klan in the South in the post-Civil War period.

The word of the head brother is law, and if he instructs members of the order to vote Republican, they do so. It was thus inevitable that politicians of both parties should vigorously court the Penitentes, or at least not do anything to antagonize them. Although it cannot be proved, it is more than likely that the virtually solid Republican support by the Spanish-Americans was delivered through the backing of the Penitentes. It is alleged that at one time no one could be elected to public office in New Mexico without the blessing of the society.

The political strength of the early Penitentes is usually associated with the Taos uprising in 1847. The fact that the participants in this revolt went to their death without revealing the possible complicity of Padre Martinez would indicate that their lips were sealed by the vows of the society. Later, the political prowess of the Penitentes was displayed in the election of the former priest, Gallegos, to several terms as New Mexico's territorial delegate to Congress, in spite of vigorous opposition. The selection of Padre Martinez as president of the council of the first territorial legislature in 1850 is further evidence of their power.

Though again adequate proof is lacking, it is generally believed within New Mexico that the political power of the Penitentes has lasted well into the twentieth century. For obvious reasons the extent of that power today is not known. Archbishop Salpointe was closer to the truth than he knew when he commented that the Penitente Society "has degenerated so that it is nothing today but an anomalous body of simple credulous men, under the guidance of unscrupulous politicians. Their leaders encouraged them, despite the admonitions of the church, in the practice of their unbecoming so-called devotions in order to secure their votes for the times of political elections." One authority explaining the opposition to the Ro-

man Catholic Church claims that "The members of this dissident religious sect can be compared to the Methodists and Anabaptists of the lower classes of England, who defied the established church that had allied itself to such an extent with the wealthy and the privileged." In some communities there were both Republican and Democratic moradas, and the activities of the society were interwoven with politics.

At one time the political power of the society was so great that it virtually administered justice itself. In Spanish-American countries it was almost certain that a member of the society would appear on a jury. And when one considers that the Penitentes are sworn to assist and protect one another, even to the extent of perjury in the courts, it is obvious that it would be difficult if not impossible to administer justice involving them. Instances abound in which the sheriff, the local judge, or other leading officials were Penitentes, and thus would not press a case against a member. Even in the twentieth century there is a record of an attempt of the Penitentes to intimidate a federal court.

This is not to suggest that culprits go unpunished. During the virtual absence of law enforcement in Mexican times, the Penitentes developed their own system of punishment, and have preferred to use it rather than surrender their members to what they consider foreign courts. First of all, since they believe that a man can atone for his sins by doing penance, backsliding brothers apply the whip to their naked backs the more vigorously. The Penitentes even have their own courts where they hear criminal cases. Some are expelled from the order and their right hip cut three times with a flint so that everyone will know that their offense was great. Inmates at the state prison at Santa Fe who were members of the Penitentes could be easily identified by such markings.

The fraternal and benevolent role of the society remained in most communities. Members would cooperate in time of need to assist those who were sick or who had suffered some disaster or another. Frequently, they arranged for the burial of the dead when priests were not available. They took care of widows and orphans or aided a disabled member to till his fields or tend his flocks. Visitors have seen moradas that were well stocked with supplies held in a common storehouse to be used only in time of communal need.

During the nineteenth century the Penitente Society was the center of social activity of the community. What little relaxation there was from the toil of everyday life was furnished by members of the society. And thus they have unwittingly preserved the cultural heritage of the Spain that is no more, for many of the plays given by the society have their roots in sixteenth century Spain. These plays, based upon Biblical texts, have been handed down from one generation to another and are still produced in isolated villages, the parts learned from memory, for most of the actors cannot read. There are also many poems that are preserved in the same manner.

What were the origins of the Penitentes? Some have attributed the movement to the Indian influence. Others have claimed that it represented a degeneration of the lay Third Order of St. Francis. Still others have traced its beginnings back to the practices of the flagellants of the Middle Ages, while a few authorities see the Penitentes as an outgrowth of the confraternities of Spain. Some even contend that it is indigenous to New Mexico.

The Spanish attempted to find Christian influences among the Indians and noted many similarities between their pagan religious rites and Christian practices. This search undoubtedly influenced the early missionaries to accept Indian religious practices and incorporate them with those of the Roman Catholic Church. Some would even go so far as to contend that the Church only superimposed a thin veneer of Christianity over a pagan base. Anita Brenner in *Idols Behind Altars,* a book whose title indicates its basic theme, contends that Indian elements have fused with Christian. Such a synthesis had continued so that the statuary of Christianity has simply been substituted for pagan idols and in many cases even have pagan names. Those who dismiss Indian influences on the Penitentes stress the fact that the Pueblo Indians of New Mexico abhor torture and considered the practice of self-flogging as ridiculous. Fray Benavides, in his reports in the missions in 1630, related an Indian's reaction to practices of flagellation: "You Spaniards and Christians, how

crazy you are! . . . You want to teach us that we be crazy also! . . . You Christians are so crazy that you go altogether, flogging yourselves like crazy people in the streets shedding your blood. And you must wish that this Pueblo to be crazy also!" And a traveler of a later day told of an Indian remarking upon seeing the Penitente rites on Good Friday: "Spanish very mad today. Do much fool things today."

However, this attitude of the Pueblo Indians does not necessarily represent the attitude of all Indians. The Aztecs used whipping and self-torture as a means of initiation into various sects, but whipping is not self-flagellation, and the purifying ritual of the Indians has no similarity to the expiating, self-scourging of the Penitentes in an effort to attain communion with a personal God. Yet, the possibility exists that through the process of acculturation the Spanish who settled New Mexico may have picked up some of the practices of self-torture from the Aztecs. For doing their rituals, even the native gashed his ears and parts of his body with blades of obsidian. The Penitentes, in order to mark their members, used the same kind of stone to make a small cross on their backs. Such positive identifying marks were reported to have been seen on young men inducted into the armed forces as late as World War II.

Many authorities have attributed the origin of the Penitentes of New Mexico to the Flagellante. Practicing flagellation for the expiation of sin or as a means of exalted devotion is found in most religions, and was common in Christianity from the Apostolic Era. Self-inflicted punishment was encouraged as evidence of greater faith during the Middle Ages. In 1056 the Bishop of Ostra gave official approval to the practice and thus "pious men of every rank and condition in life were seen armed with whips, rods, thongs and besoms, lacerating their own bodies in order to merit a share of divine favor."

Fraternities devoted to regular public flagellation appeared in Italy in 1210, and rapidly spread throughout southern Europe. The great mass of people assumed that through such self-torture man could expiate sin and attain a mystical communion with God. The description of some of their ceremonies could easily have been those of New Mexico's Penitentes: "Then they began disciplining themselves with their scourges, which were armed with knots and four iron points, all the while singing the usual psalm of the invocation of our Lord, and other psalms; three of them . . . with a sonorous voice, regulated the chant of the others, and disciplined themselves in the same manner." Flagellation fraternities were also common in France in the sixteenth century and were commented upon by Montaigne in 1580.

Flagellation was such an accepted part of the monastic life of Spain that it was seldom commented on by the observers of the day. Leading Spanish mystics such as Saint Teresa of Avila and St. John of the Cross emphasized the importance of flagellation. Ignatius Loyola, the founder of the Society of Jesus and perhaps Spain's leading churchman, stressed self-chastisement as a part of devotional exercises. Cervantes refers to the processions of flagellants in a manner that suggests they were very common in his day. The fact that Oñate, the conquistador of New Mexico, was observed flogging himself in 1589 has been used as proof of how flagellation was brought to New Mexico. Thus, one can assume that flagellation was extensively practiced in the Hispano church and was brought to the New World and ultimately to New Mexico.

Franciscan origin is, perhaps, the most widely accepted theory accounting for the New Mexican Penitentes. Bolstering this contention has been the fact that the Franciscans had responsibility for the missionary work in that province until the early nineteenth century. The Third Order of St. Francis, or tertiaries, were laity who followed ordinary occupations but yet were permitted to participate in certain works of the Church. But aside from the fact that both the Third Order and the Penitentes were found in New Mexico, there is little that the two groups have in common. The Franciscan group did not permit the kind of penance practiced by the Penitentes and was much closer to Church authorities. Even the Roman Catholic authorities in nineteenth century New Mexico believed that the Penitentes were a degenerate form of the Third Order of St. Francis. Helping to perpetuate this idea has been the fact that the Third Order was also called the Order of Penance.

Some authorities contend that New Mexico's Penitentes grew out of the *cofradias* or confraternities of Spain. The purpose of these associations was to engage in temporal works of charity such as helping the needy, arranging for the administration of the last sacraments, getting people out of jail, assisting at funerals, caring for widows and orphans, or arranging for masses for deceased members. Members were usually of the same trade or profession and might also be members of the same guild or *gremio*. With the passage of time the guild and confraternity frequently became synonymous and spiritual and economic welfare became joined. In the seventeenth and eighteenth centuries the economic practices of the guilds came increasingly under attack so the term *hermandad* or brotherhood came into usage. Some of these organizations became wealthy, built hospitals for their members, provided dowries for orphan daughters, and pensions for the aged. The association provided the basic social outlet for its members with the year's ceremonial climax being the fiesta held in honor of the patron saint of the brotherhood. The image of the patron saint was carried in procession during Holy Week with members of the group engaging in self-mortification. The continuance of the confraternities in modern Seville carry on some of these traditions.

This Spanish confraternity was transplanted to the New World where it took root and flourished. Some were associated with religious orders, a primary function being the care and support of hospitals or similar institutions. Priests encouraged confraternities among Indians to better propagate the faith, to encourage proper care of church images, and to promote religious festivals. The existence of 2,928 confraternities and 231 brotherhoods in the diocese of Guatemala in 1774 attest to their popularity. The care of the patron saint's image and the mutual benefits enjoyed by members were strikingly similar to the Penitentes of New Mexico. The Guatemala associations were so powerful that both church and state tried in vain to curb them.

A careful reading of the records of the confraternities of Mexico also reveal a striking similarity with New Mexico's Penitentes. They discharged charitable functions among their members, cared for the image of their saint and the Christus, marched in procession during Holy Week, and practiced flagellation. They exercised greatest power in the more isolated geographic areas such as in the present state of Michoacan. In fact, in this area they were claimed to be as completely in political control as the Ku Klux Klan in the post-Civil War American South. Study of the Inquisition records show that that body received numerous complaints that confraternities engaged in excessive flagellation and other practices similar to those of the Penitentes.

Fray Angelico Chávez, an able observer of the New Mexico scene, denies that the Penitentes have any Spanish origin and claims that their practices were imported into New Mexico from New Spain (Mexico) between 1777 and 1833. This assumption rests upon the fact that a detailed survey of the missions of New Mexico made in 1777 fails to mention the Penitentes while another report in 1833 does. The Bishop of Durango condemned the group in Santa Cruz in the latter year: "A Brotherhood of Penitentes, already existing for a goodly number of years; but without any authorization or even the knowledge of the bishops, who definitely would not have given their consent for such a Brotherhood ... since the excesses of very indiscreet corporal penances which they are accustomed to practice on some days of the year, and even publicly, are so contrary to the spirit of Religion and the regulations of Holy Church ... We strictly command, laying it on the conscience of our present and future pastors of this villa, that they must never in the future permit such reunions of Penitentes under any pretext whatsoever." The Bishop concluded by banning the Brotherhood forever. Fray Chávez also believes that the organization was brought from Mexico between 1790 and 1820. Thus, he claims: "this makes the Penitentes a late New Mexico phenomenon of the half-century prior to the American occupation of 1846, and definitely not a society and movement inherited from the first two centuries of New Mexico as a Spanish Kingdom."

The similarity to the earlier confraternities of Seville and the fact that the music of the Penitentes was definitely Andalucian in character Fray Chávez explains as resulting from the order being a late transplant: "Some individual, or more than one, came to New Mexico from New Spain (soon to become Mexico), or from some other Spanish colony to the South, where such penitential societies had long existed. Such individuals had belonged to such a society, to be able to impart its organization and ritual to their new neighbors here in New Mexico. And if we consider the New Mexicans' own medieval-Spanish religious background at the time, a feeling made more acute by living for generations so close to the essentials of life and death in a stark land, the soil was most fertile and ready for such a transplant." Such a claim is creditable in view of the fact that such penitential societies were common throughout the Spanish-speaking world at that time. One weakness of Fray Chávez's conclusion is that the practices of the Penitentes may have been so accepted that they were not commented upon by Fray Francisco Atanasio Dominguez when he made his report in 1777. In fact, much of the knowledge we have of their practices have resulted from reports of outsiders who found the flagellation processions most unusual.

The claim that the Penitentes were a late transplant to New Mexico is viable in light of the religious atmosphere of eighteenth century Spain. The long period of decline of religious fervour associated with the Spanish Catholic Reformation was partially halted by the work of a remarkable Jesuit, Pedro de Calatayud (1689–1773). Banned by ill health from missionary work in America, he became Spain's greatest religious orator of the century. Author of several works stressing the Christian life, he was at his best conducting missions where his preaching topics stressed practical Christian advice. In his effectiveness Father Calatayud could be compared to the eighteenth century German pietists Philip Spener and Herman Franck or to the English clerics John Wesley and George Whitefield. There was even some similarity to the American of the twentieth century, the Reverend Billy Graham.

As part of his preaching missions which, it was claimed, attracted audiences in the thousands, Father Calatayud stressed religious processionals of the faithful. During such displays of piety flagellation was practiced, sometimes to an extent which prompted church disapproval. As the Jesuits encouraged flagellation throughout the Spanish world, it can be assumed that devoted followers of so prominent a cleric as Calatayud brought his practices to the New World so that they ultimately reached New Mexico.

Regardless of the exact origin of the Penitentes they are, as one observer has ably put it, "related intimately to, and drawn from, the traditional and persistent Hispanic culture of New Mexico." An anthropologist uses six institutional values to define social values common to Hispanic culture and all six can be found among the Penitentes. "Paternalism" is present in the relationship of the members-at-large to the officers of the organization. "Familism" is found in the organizational structure and in the extension of social benefits to the whole community. "Dramatism" is revealed in the emphasis upon and participation of individuals in the elaborate ritual of the order. "Fatalism" is in the focus upon the death of Christ on the cross to the neglect of other religious values, the preoccupation with funerals, and the presence of death symbols in most *moradas.* Finally, "traditionalism" is depicted in the retention of religious ceremonies that have been abandoned elsewhere.

Further evidence that the Penitentes are a distinct product of Spanish culture is provided by the fact that similar practices abound in the Spanish-speaking world. For flagellation, as well as simulated crucifixion, is practiced in many parts of Mexico, South America, the Philippines, the Argentine and in Puerto Rico. In addition, such practices are still common in contemporary Spain. Thus, the Penitentes of New Mexico are true representatives of Spanish religious thought and Spanish culture in general.

The Penitentes of New Mexico were able to retain their traditions while similar organizations in other parts of the Spanish world were changing. This was true because of the remoteness from authority of the mountain vastness of the northern part of the state. Then too, the growth of the Peni-

tentes of New Mexico was a result of historical factors unrelated to the Church. Beginning with the ousting of Spain from Mexico in 1821, the territory went through a long period of transition wherein the simple social mores of the natives were constantly subject to change. First, their priests were largely driven out by the Mexicans, (as they were Spanish nationals), creating a spiritual vacuum which the Penitente order attempted to fill. Officials of the group soon performed many of the functions of priests. Frequently the Hermano Mayor was also the local alcalde. And as the old way of life was consistently threatened with change, the Penitentes became "an organization of the common man against his masters—a brotherhood with temporal benefits and a pure solidarity and secretness." Although its religious basis remained predominant, the absence of qualified clerical supervision led to a perversion of its teaching and practices, which the Catholic Church was to later have much difficulty in controlling. In fact, when Bishop Lamy arrived in the mid-nineteenth century, the reforms which he tried to put into operation were bitterly opposed by the few native priests in New Mexico whose concept of Christianity was vastly different from that of their French supervisor and they were supported in their opposition by the Penitentes.

Not only did the Penitentes preserve their Spanish religious heritage, they also quite effectively preserved their cultural heritage, especially in terms of music and art. The earliest Spanish missionaries to the New World quickly discovered the importance of music as a means by which the Indians could be induced to accept Christianity. Both vocal and instrumental music were used effectively, and it is probable that music was taught more extensively to the natives than any other subject. The enthusiasm with which the Indians could be taught their catechism with music led to a stress upon its use. The first European music teacher to come into New Mexico was Percival de Quinanes, who came to Mexico between 1598 and 1604. He even brought an organ with him to the remote colonies.

Music played a key role in the religious rites of the Penitentes. Apparently, the only universal musical instrument used by them was the pito. This reedlike flute has been used down through the ages to imitate the reactions of people to tragedy. The music produced by the pito had a wailing sound that echoed and reechoed through the countryside and could be heard for great distances. Indispensable during the processionals during Holy Week, it was also used when the Penitentes observed their wakes *(velorios)* or at the religious rites they held on Saint's days. The matraca was the only other instrument extensively employed in the Penitente rites. The latter was a type of wooden rattle composed of a stiff stick slipping over a notched wheel which made a large cracking sound. However, some Penitente chapters also used the drum.

Most of the singing of the Penitentes was a cappella. Hymns were collected in copybooks in most chapters. However, as few people could read, the usual pattern was for the children to learn their hymns early in life and pass them on to the succeeding generation. The New Mexican *alabado* is a hymn which begins with the words "alabada sea" (praise be in honor of the blessed sacrament). Through the passage of time, the word came to suggest any religious hymn, so the technical explanation is no longer applicable in New Mexico. Many of the hymns are simply the Penitential psalms. Because of the lack of a written tradition, the same hymns may be sung to different music in different communities and even have different words.

Some of the hymns have an untold number of verses which reflect local improvisation. Some even were undoubtedly written by the natives. But most were brought in from the outside. There were regular Catholic hymns that the Penitentes or their ancestors may have learned from the priests. Many *alabados* originated in fifteenth or sixteenth century Spain. The music for these hymns is reminiscent of the Gregorian chants, "but often with a wilder, more primitive strain, particularly in the case of songs sung by an individual Penitente, which suddenly startle the listener with the piercing note of the *saeta,* 'arrow song' of Seville—undoubtedly of Moorish origin." Friar Chávez concurs in this origin; "Their hymns and alabados are also Sevillan, both in metric form and in their minor-key cadences, as well as in their uninhibited manner of delivery. It is the *Cante Jondo,* a deep singing brought up from the very depths of being, a cry wrenched from the soul as in a fit of paroxysm, and trailing off in unexpected tones and half-tones." Another observer comments that while traveling through the villages of old Castille, he was frequently surprised to find that a New Mexican tune which he had learned in childhood was almost identical to one still used in Castille. Some of the songs of the Penitentes undoubtedly saw their origin in Jewish canticles. The theological content of the hymns was decidedly limited and the brief verses were intended to be sung repeatedly during the lengthy ceremonies, especially during the passion season.

However, as important as music was, art was the most significant cultural expression of the Penitentes. As Unamuno contends: "The highest artistic expression of . . . Spanish Catholicism is in the art that is most material, tangible, and permanent, . . . in sculpture and painting, in the quest of Velasquez, that Christ who is ever dying, yet never finishes dying, in order that he may give us life." And the sacred art of the Penitentes of northern New Mexico ably portrays the depth of human religious feeling of simple people. As one observer has commented: "It embodies not only the mood of Medievalism, but the asceticism of El Greco, the grief imbued in the Gothic, and the Miserere of Rouault, as well as the stark simplicity of the frescos in the catacombs beneath Rome, that were tantamount to prayers and offerings for the salvation of the deceased." The tradition of Spanish folk religion is ably expressed in the artistic creations of the simple Penitente in his quest for oneness with God. Penitente art may be favorably contrasted to the Russian icon wherein the simple peasant was able to reveal his inner religious feelings, the nobility of his soul, and the depth of this thought on religious matters. Into their artistic creations the Penitentes put their love of God and the feelings they had for His suffering son. In doing so, they were also putting in their own fears: their fears of the harsh life they were forced to undergo on earth and the fears they had of hell. Their art reflects the depth of religious feeling so ably expressed in their enactment of the crucifixion: a rite wherein they vicariously suffered with their Lord.

Charles Lummis has referred to New Mexico as the land of *Poco Tiempo,* or literally, the land where time has stood still. This cultural isolation is the only thing that accounts for the preservation of the religious folk art of the region. As a recent article remarks "religious art in the Rio Grande Valley was tucked away in a time capsule—nicely insulated against foreign influences, in a sort of cultural hypnosis. Even church authority was missing, thanks to the ecclesiastical squabble with civil administration, ending in the desecularization of the clergy. Outmoded concepts sometimes continued in fashion, oblivious to officialdom; the Holy Trinity represented as three identical personages—a Byzantine concept—had been banned by Pope Benedict XIV in 1745. The news failed to impress the New Mexican faithful where this heretical version flourished throughout the nineteenth century." Of course, the purpose of such art amongst a predominantly illiterate people was reflected in the words of St. Augustine when he spoke of sacred pictures as the "books of the simple."

In this ability to preserve their Spanish heritage in religion, music and art through the centuries, the Penitentes of New Mexico are similar to other people who have been untouched by changing habits and customs. In recent years, studies have shown that in the hill country of Appalachia in the United States there has been preserved songs, mannerisms of speech, and folkways that date back to seventeenth century England. The Penitentes, in some of their practices, may be unique but, in general, they can be best understood for their preservation of Spanish traditions into the twentieth century. The Spaniard in Spain had retreated into the castle of his own person during the period of the Moorish occupation and resisted acculturation. In this, he was not totally successful as he was unquestionably influenced by his conqueror. Similarly the New Mexican, isolated in his mountain vastness, sought to preserve the Hispanic civilization that he had brought with him.

Raymond Mulligan

*Raymond Mulligan (Chairman of the Department of Public Administration, University of Arizona) has written extensively on Arizona history and government. In the following article, Professor Mulligan discusses the racial and religious prejudice surrounding the efforts of a well-meaning priest to place forty anglo orphans in Mexican American homes. The Gallic priest discovered that the social conditions in Clifton-Morenci, Arizona, were such that the Anglo population would willingly resort to violence to preserve the "whiteness" of the children.
By permission of ARIZONA AND THE WEST Vol. VI (Summer 1964), pp. 104–118.*

New York Foundlings At Clifton-Morenci: Social Justice In Arizona Territory

Of all the themes employed by students of the frontier, few deal with children—and practically none with dependent or orphaned children. Buried, however, among the records of children's aid societies and foundling homes are interesting and dramatic accounts that point up the role these agencies played in the history of the American West. Particularly revealing of the operations, and the difficulties, involved in the placing of children in foster homes was the attempt in 1904 by the New York Foundling Hospital to settle forty of its charges in the Clifton-Morenci area of Arizona. As it happened, this episode proved to be more than a simple matter of placing travel-weary foundlings in foster homes. Before the children were settled satisfactorily, the home-finding process was inter-

146

rupted by howling mobs, armed deputies, and angry lawyers, and by pronouncements of the Territorial Supreme Court. President Theodore Roosevelt, as well as Governor Alexander O. Brodie, became involved in the affair, and for a time it appeared that even the Arizona Rangers would be called into action to restore order and recover the children. The case of the New York foundlings not only illustrates some of the problems that characterized the history of child welfare in the United States, but also offers insights into the workings of formal and informal justice in Arizona at the turn of the century.

The agency that sent the foundlings to Arizona in 1904 was only one of many such organizations that long had been engaged in locating homes for dependent children. As early as 1852 the New York Children's Aid Society had pioneered the use of the free foster home system. This organization was founded by Charles Brace, who had been greatly moved by the conditions of the children of the poor in New York City, many of whom were growing up in idleness, vice, and crime. At that time, and for many years afterward, thousands of homeless, neglected, and dependent children thronged the streets of the larger Eastern cities, with very few individuals concerned with their plight. It was an age of deadening poverty for the poor, with concomitant high birth, death, and mortality rates, sprawling slums, rampant vice, few compulsory school laws, and an almost complete absence of welfare programs of any significance.

Although an advocate for the shelter, religious training, recreation, schooling, and remunerative work for dependent children, Brace felt that the one solution for the homeless child, and even the children of the poor, was the placing of these children in foster homes in rural areas of America. In 1853 he began writing to farmers, mechanics, and manufacturers in rural areas, requesting that they take children into their homes. From responses to this appeal, and to others which followed, he obtained a list of applicants, and was soon making individual placements. In 1854, Brace expanded his operations to include the sending of large groups of children to one locality—a practice that continued until 1929. From 1853 to 1894 the Soci-

ety placed more than 20,000 children, a majority of them being accepted by families living in Southern and Western states. Indeed, these areas appeared to have offered the most hospitable welcome, as well as the right combination of Christian charity and need for youthful labor.

That the placing-out process did not operate without unforeseen difficulties was vividly borne out in the case of the New York foundlings sent to the mining towns of Clifton and Morenci, Arizona, in the fall of 1904. The Foundling Hospital had learned of the availability of desirable homes in these towns from Father Constant Mandin, who temporarily was in charge of the Clifton-Morenci parish during the absence of Father Peter Timmerman, the resident priest. Father Mandin had only been in the United States ten months, spoke English with difficulty, and being a true Frenchman apparently had all the Gallic obliviousness of his countrymen to racial and ethnic distinctions that were not generally appreciated in Arizona in 1904. He had announced the contents of a circular from the agency to his congregation, and soon had requests for children of both sexes. The priest is alleged to have informed the agency that forty children could be placed in the homes of his congregation, which he represented to be of Spanish background, but who spoke English.

In response to the application, the Foundling Hospital made arrangements to send forty children to Arizona. The children were of "Anglo-Saxon race," and, as requested by the priest, were chosen from among these in the institution who were fairest and lightest in complexion. They were said to have been of unusual beauty and attractiveness, and varied in age from eighteen months to five years. Attached to the clothing of each child was a tag which carried a number, his name and date of birth, and the name of the person to whom he was consigned. In addition, on each child's shirtwaist his name was beautifully embroidered. To the family receiving a child, the Sister Superior sent a letter, instructing the head of the household, within a week after the child arrived, to fill out and return an enclosed blank, giving the name of the child, and the name, occupation, and post office address of the foster parents. The foster parents also were asked to write yearly, about May 1, concerning the child's progress.

Late Saturday evening, October 1, 1904, forty children, accompanied by three members of the Sisters of Charity order, three nurses, and G. Whitney Swayne, agent for the Foundling Hospital, reached Clifton in a special railroad car. At that time, the towns of Clifton and Morenci were not well-ordered communities. For example, the residential district in Morenci was called Helltown, while the business section was composed principally of saloons and dance halls. It was referred to as the toughest town in the Territory. One writer referred to the inhabitants with a few exceptions to be somewhat less refined than the copper smelters found in the area. During the previous year, 1903, twenty-five of the twenty-six Arizona Rangers then in service had been called to Morenci to keep order during a strike in the mines.

Gathered at the station awaiting the arrival of the train was a crowd of Spanish-speaking and English-speaking residents, together with several Chinese. The news already had circulated that a number of foundlings were to arrive, and would be distributed to "Mexican" families. When Father Mandin came into the special car, he was met by a barrage of questions. Sister Anna Michella immediately inquired as to what sort of people the foster parents were, and he is alleged to have replied that they were all good moral American citizens who had no children of their own. Their homes were all that could be wished for. Noticing that some of the people were not as fair in color as she had hoped for, or expected, the nun is purported to have asked if there were any "half breeds" among them—and he said "No." The Foundling Hospital, Sister Michella then stated, had a rule that the children always were placed on trial until such time as the homes could be visited by the sisters. If any of the homes were not as expected, the children would be removed. Apparently satisfied by the priest's replies, the hospital representatives began taking the children from the car. When the question of the disposition of the foundlings was raised by persons in the crowd, Swayne stated that there would be no decisions made that night. It was later stated that he even assured one of the women who pressed him on the matter that the following morning she would have an opportunity to make an application for one of the children.

That night, however, sixteen children were placed with foster parents in Clifton. As required by the Foundling Hospital, the parents had purchased clothes for the children and had agreed to pay part of their fare from New York. The total expenses varied from $30.00 to $40.00 per child. Because money changed hands during the course of the transfer of the children from hospital authorities to parents that evening, a story became widespread that the children were sold like cattle. The following morning, Sunday, Swayne secured wheeled conveyances and with Father Mandin and the sisters took the remaining twenty-four children to Morenci for distribution among the families there who had agreed to accept them.

At a latter date it was claimed that the persons in Clifton and Morenci who received the children were wholly unfit to be entrusted with them. They were said to have been of the lowest class of "half-breed Mexican Indians"—persons who were impecunious, illiterate, unacquainted with the English language, vicious, and in several instances, prostitutes and persons of notorious character. Many had children of their own, whom they were unable properly to support. Sister Michella, who was responsible for carrying out the instructions of the hospital, was said to have been so struck by the unfitness of the foster parents that in three instances she gave them up "with tears streaming from her eyes." Apparently she was not satisfied with the families to whom the foundlings were delivered, but felt that she could not override the authority of the priest.

On Sunday morning, while Swayne and his party were en route to Morenci, the residents of Clifton learned that the children had been placed in Mexican homes. An informal conference of citizens hurriedly was called to discuss the matter, and a committee of two was appointed to go to Morenci and ascertain from Father Mandin and Swayne their purposes. They also were to be informed of the excitement caused by the children being placed with "half-breed Indian" families.

This committee was composed of Jeff Dunagan, a deputy sheriff, and Thomas Simpson. Dunagan and Simpson arrived in Morenci shortly after two o'clock in the afternoon, and went immediately to see Charles E. Mills, the superintendent of the Detroit Copper Company and one of the leading citizens of the town. With him they went in search of Swayne, whom they found at the hotel. Dunagan and Simpson later testified that in response to their inquiries, Swayne said that he knew his business, and did not propose to be dictated to by others. The children "had been placed, and would stay placed." Dunagan telephoned the information to Clifton that they had seen Swayne, and that the agent would do nothing.

Dunagan's report resulted in a second meeting being called that day in Clifton. Hundreds of persons, including women and children, crowded into Liberty Hall, which stood on the present site of the Phelps Dodge store. After several speeches, it was decided that a committee of twenty-five should be chosen to take possession of the foundlings in Clifton, regardless of the objections of the foster parents. This vigilante group, some of whom were armed, acted swiftly and ruthlessly, although it was later stated that the children were "voluntarily" surrendered to the committee. When taken from their foster homes, the children were said to have been in a filthy condition, covered with vermin, and with two or three exceptions, ill and nauseated from the effects of coarse Mexican beans, chiles, watermelons, and other "improper" food which had been fed them. In some instances beer and whiskey had been given them to drink.

By evening the children had been collected at the Clifton Hotel. It was raining, and the crowd had increased and was in an angry mood. There was talk of lynching both the priest and the agent. The women present took charge of the foundlings, and secured medical care and attention for them. An informal selection process then began. A Morenci doctor picked out a child, a Clifton official selected another. When one wide-eyed little girl looked at the wife of the hotel owner and said, "Mama," the woman opened her arms and claimed the child as her very own. On the next day, the remaining children were placed with Anglo families in Clifton.

Early Monday morning, October 3, Swayne and Father Mandin reached Clifton with Dunagan and Simpson. They found that more than two hundred citizens had assembled. That evening there was another meeting. There was a great deal of excitement manifested at the gathering, but there was no act of violence. Many persons, however, did crowd around Swayne, hurling threats of a general character—threats such as "Make him leave town!" "Tar and feather him!" and "Hang him!" Only the intervention of deputies John (Hard Times) Parks and Lee Hobbs saved Swayne from violence. Both Swayne and Father Mandin made statements to the group. Apprehensive that he might receive bodily harm, Swayne assured the citizens that the children had been placed only temporarily. The sisters would remain for two or three weeks, and if they found any of the children in improper homes, they would remove them. He protested against the seizing of the children without his consent or that of the sisters. The following day more meetings were held at which both the priest and the agent were present. At the conclusion of the proceedings, the citizens chose to be firm, and not give up the foundlings to the hospital representatives. It was feared that if so returned, the children might be again placed in equally unfit homes of Mexican families elsewhere.

In Morenci the same indignation arose among the Anglo citizens, and much of the same course was pursued as in Clifton. Charles E. Mills and others called upon the sisters and upon the agent, remonstrating against permitting twenty-four of the children to remain in Morenci with the people to whom they had been distributed. As a result of these remonstrances, and a strong statement by Mills that the local residents would not suffer the children so to remain, Father Mandin and Swayne visited the Mexicans having the children, obtained a surrender of them, and brought them to the local hotel. These foundlings, with the exception of the three who were turned over at Dunagan's request to certain Morenci residents, were then delivered to the sisters. Sister Michella and Swayne later stated that they would not have left the three children in Morenci except that they believed that the citizens would have refused to release the children to them. Several days later, the nuns, the nurses, and twenty-one of the children boarded the train at Clifton for the East.

On October 18, the sisters arrived in New York City mentally and physically exhausted, having been delayed en route by washouts on the railroads. They said that they had had a terrifying experience. Mobs in Arizona had threatened to shoot them because they had sought to place the foundlings with Catholic Mexican families. Swayne had narrowly escaped lynching. On October 5 a "committee of citizens" had accompanied the agent to the train advising him not to return. Father Mandin had been forced to leave Clifton the day before. One of the nuns gave the following story to a reporter:

> At Clifton we left 16 children, and the others at Morenci, 18 miles distant, and over a hard mountain road. Some of the children were taken to refined, dependable, prosperous Spanish people, whose homes were neat and clean.
>
> On Sunday night we were called from the rooms of our hotel in Morenci. In the street a sheriff sat on horseback, armed with a revolver, like the other men. Women called us vile names, and some of them put pistols to our heads. They said there was no law in that town; that they made their own laws. We were told to get the children from the Spaniards and leave by Tuesday morning. If we did not we would be killed. We got the children, but nineteen of the twenty-four were taken from the nurses by force and put, I understand, into the families of Americans.
>
> When we reached Clifton we were compelled to take once more that trying journey to Morenci and obtain the five children left there. When we left Arizona we had 21 children, who were taken by Dr. Swain [Swayne] into Illinois, where we had many applications for them.

The Foundling Hospital, it also was reported, planned to make an appeal to the federal authorities for recovery of the children.

As early as October 16, the families in Clifton and Morenci holding the foundlings began making application in the probate court at Solomonville, the county seat of Graham County, for letters of guardianship. These requests for adoption papers were granted in the matter of a few days by Probate Judge Peter C. Little. Arizona attorneys familiar with the case were of the opinion that the Foundling Hospital had lost all right to the children by abandoning, or placing, them with incompetent and unworthy people. The Mexican foster parents were the only ones who had a standing in court, but as they now probably did not want the children, it was unlikely that they would try to recover them.

On November 5 Governor Brodie arrived in Clifton. Although his purpose was to speak before a political rally, the rumor quickly spread that he had come with instructions from President Roosevelt to collect the children and send them back to New York. It was stated that Brodie was expecting trouble, and had instructed Captain Tom Rynning, of the Arizona Rangers at Douglas, to be ready to quell any disturbances. The Governor met the women who had assumed charge of the children, and visited the homes of the Mexican families where the children originally had been placed. At the conclusion of his investigation, he wired an informal report to Washington.

When news of the happenings in Clifton reached New York, the Foundling Hospital went into the courts to recover the children. An appeal of Judge Little's decision was filed in the district court at Solomonville, and pending this appeal the institution made application through its Arizona attorneys, Eugene S. Ives, of Tucson, and Thomas D. Bennett, of Bisbee, to the Supreme Court of Arizona for writs of habeas corpus to secure custody of the children.

On January 12, 1905, in Phoenix a hearing was begun before the Supreme Court regarding the writs. The attorneys waxed eloquent before a courtroom crowded with anxious residents from Clifton and Morenci, the children under question, and interested spectators. Walter Bennett, of the influential firm of Kibbey, Bennett, and Bennett, paraded a host of witnesses before the court. The nuns, Swayne, and the parents who had filed adoption papers for the children were asked to testify. The nuns, it was reported, broke down under questioning and blamed the priest. Swayne was evasive. According to one Mexican parent who had received a child, several of the Mexican families had been forced to take children "under the orders of the padre." As the hearing dragged on, the local papers made much of the plight of the children:

One woman, the possessor of a beautiful little girl, sat at lunch in a restaurant and cried when she thought of the possibility of an adverse decision. "I would rather," she said, "give up my right arm than lose her." One little boy, stopping with his foster father and mother at a hotel, grew sleepy ... and when his father told him to go to sleep, he said: "Won't you watch me so the Mexicans can't get me."

Scrubbed and in their Sunday best, the children were seen frequently on the streets of Phoenix. Wherever they went they found "admiring crowds." In the courtroom, several of the foundlings were seated in conspicuous locations for all to see. Toward the end of the hearing Bennett injected the issue of religion into the discussion. To neutralize any attempt by opposing counsels to raise the question of religious discrimination, he pointed out that several of his clients were Catholics and that they had applied for, but had been refused children by the priest.

Thomas D. Bennett presented the argument for the Foundling Hospital. While the attorney for the Clifton residents had based his case on the welfare of the children, the counsel for the institution pressed for consideration of the legal points involved. His statements were brief, and noticeably lacking in fervor. Few witnesses appeared. The fact that the better known of the two attorneys retained by the Foundling Hospital, Eugene S. Ives, failed to enter the hearing until near the end, added to the feeling of futility that pervaded the statements made before the court by his partner.

After a week of hearings, the Court took the case under advisement. On January 21 a decision was rendered. In his pronouncement, Chief Justice Edward Kent took issue with the point made by counsel that it would be to the interest of the

children "to take them to the East, and there place them in homes far removed from the knowledge of their antecedents. . . ." In strong-rhetoric, he asserted:

. . . these present foster parents—persons of some means and education—from the day when with humanitarian impulse, and actuated by motives of sympathy for their pitiful condition, they assisted in the rescue of these little children from the evil into which they had fallen, down to the time of their attendance at this trial, at cost of much time and money, in their loving care and attention, have shown that more than ordinary ties of affection bind them to the children, and that in no other homes that can be found for them are they so likely to fare as well. We feel that it is for their best interests that no change be made in their custody, and that, if anywhere, here in the changing West, the land of opportunity and hope, these children, as they grow to manhood and womanhood, will have the fullest opportunity that it is possible for them to have to be judged, not upon the unfortunate condition of birth, but upon the record they themselves shall make, and the character they shall develop.

Kent stated that at the time of the controversy, neither the Foundling Hospital nor the Clifton families had a right to the children. The Foundling Hospital certainly had no right because its charter specified they were to care for, not dispose of, the children. The new parents had legally adopted the foundlings and now legally owned them, he asserted.

Although Judge Kent dismissed the writs filed in the case, the Foundling Hospital, because of the interstate nature of the litigation, was able to appeal the decision to the United States Supreme Court. The appeal was based on the question of "personal freedom" arising from the habeas corpus petitions. Both John Gatti, whose charge, William Norton, was the object of the test case, and Henry Hill, the wealthiest parent involved, went east to attend the hearing; Hill furnished most of the money to fight the Foundling Hospital.

The task of preparing for the appeal proved tedious. By March 3, Ives had received the stenographic minutes of the proceedings at Solomonville, and had prepared a statement of facts "in the nature of a special verdict for our supreme court to find. . . ." He sent this statement to Charles E. Miller, the attorney for the Foundling Hospital in New York, who made certain alterations and returned it. On March 17, Ives forwarded the statement to Justice Kent in Phoenix. Kent suggested changes, and late in March, attorney Walter Bennett corrected the statement further. Finally, early in April Ives sent the revised statement to Miller. The efforts of the Foundling Hospital, however, came to naught. On December 3, 1906, the Supreme Court dismissed the case as "not appealable" to the high court, thereby reaffirming the decision of the lower court. The Anglo families in Clifton and Morenci had won final custody of the children.

In reviewing the court decisions and the newspaper accounts in Arizona of the foundling case, it is interesting to note that the question of religion received little attention. Each party in the case resorted to the legality of its own position, while the court based its decision on the welfare of the children involved. However, as the children were undoubtedly Catholics and originally were placed in homes of this faith, one cannot help but wondering if the Foundling Hospital were not fighting two battles: it not only was fighting the forceful removal of the children from its control, but also was fighting to preserve the religion of the children. In the history of child welfare in the United States, one of the reasons for the establishment of private institutions for dependent and neglected children, or even delinquent children, was to give children care under the religious auspices of their parents, and thus to keep them from losing their ancestral faith. The Foundling Hospital evidently was operating under this principle in its original placement of the children, although it did not make an issue of it during the court procedures, nor did the court make mention of it in its paean to the ultimate foster parents.

In many ways, the circumstances surrounding the placement of the foundlings in the Clifton-Morenci parish was unfortunate. It was unfortu-nate because of the socio-economic background of the families and the contrasting ethnic social systems of the children and their foster parents. As foster home placement should represent an opportunity for the children involved, the original placements, considering all the factors in the case, did not appear to offer opportunities for the foundlings. Furthermore, the introduction of mob justice was unfortunate. Without this popular upheaveal, the nuns perhaps would have visited the original foster homes, and according to the rules of the Foundling Hospital, could have reclaimed the children, if they found the homes and families unsuitable.

Finally, the Territorial Supreme Court was slightly ethnocentric in handling the case. Certainly the foundlings were forceably and illegally removed from the original foster parents and the Foundling Hospital representatives. The court chose to ignore this, referring to the mob action as "committee meetings" and the surrendering of the children to armed groups as "volunteer" action. The spirit of the frontier in all its ramifications played a larger role in the court decision than abstract justice. The collection and return of all the children in Morenci, except three, to the nuns, was a sane and civilized action—and perhaps the wisest solution to the case. If a similar plan had been followed in Clifton, little Phoebe would not have been dragged out in a rainstorm at night to become a candidate for pneumonia and death.

Contrary to the statistics carried by some of the newspapers, only seventeen of the original forty children were involved in the court cases. The Foundling Hospital recovered twenty-one and subsequently placed them in homes in the Midwest. One child died, as had been noted. These calculations leave one child unaccounted for. It was reported that a Mexican family disappeared with one of the children during the wild and rainy night the foundlings were being gathered up by the aroused residents of Clifton. The family was purported to have returned to the community some time later with a red-haired female child, who upon maturity worked as a maid. The tale, which has been referred to as "The Mystery of the Red-Haired Maid," may account for the fortieth child.

3.

TRYING TO CRACK THE SYSTEM

Trying To Crack The System

Section Two of this book ended with a poignant example of the massive racial prejudice that created an enormous barrier to the Mexican Americans' aspirations throughout the Southwest. Only in New Mexico did many Chicanos vote, and there primarily because Anglos could control their ballot. In the mid-1920s, other Chicanos became more active politically, too. Sizable numbers of Mexican Americans realized by then that the "American Dream" of cultural diversity and material well-being had not included them. Rather than a multi-racial culture, Anglos offered prejudice; rather than prosperity, Mexican Americans found abject poverty. Thus throughout the Southwest they sought ways to crack the system and enter into the economic mainstream.

"The system," however, asked for technological skills that few Mexican Americans possessed. This lack of training and racial antagonisms condemned most Chicanos either to the poverty of migrant farm labor or some other equally menial and unrewarding employment. Ernesto Galarza sets the scene for exploitative economics in "California, the Uncommonwealth." Faustino Solis, in the following selection, traces the history of these conditions into the 1970s. The next three essays—one from the *Monthly Labor Review*, Charles Wollenberg's account of "Huelga," and Harold A. Shapiro's story of the pecan shellers in San Anto-

nio, Texas—describe attempts to ameliorate such conditions through strikes. These strikes had some success when immediate demands were met, but long-range ones, such as collective bargaining rights, were not. Undoubtedly the strikes did aid in creating a feeling of class consciousness that Bronze Power advocates would draw upon in the future. But strikes did not bring most Mexican Americans into the "American Dream."

Other activities besides strikes expressed the discontent of Chicanos. The young particularly resented the blatant prejudice all around them, but they had not received cultural traditions to help them cope with racism. One result was the *Pachuco* phenomenon of the mid-1940s. Octavio Paz and George I. Sánchez, in two fine essays, the latter contemporary to that period, discuss this reaction of the rootless, young Mexican American although others reacted more traditionally to the Anglo world. Consequently, this section of the reader ends with what amounts to a micro-study of New Mexico. The last four selections, by George Sánchez, Charles P. Loomis, Clark Knowlton, and Jack E. Holmes tell of a rural people entering into the twentieth century life and politics. In their endeavors the *Hispanos* attained some individual successes; yet as a class they failed to "crack the system."

ERNESTO GALARZA

Ernesto Galarza (born in Tepic, Mexico; author, educator, and labor organizer) worked as day laborer, harvest hand, and cannery worker in the central valley of California. Professor Galarza came from the "lower part" of Sacramento to earn a Ph.D. at Columbia University. He has written extensively on problems of labor organization and migrant workers. His latest book, SPIDERS IN THE HOUSE AND WORKERS IN THE FIELD, *was published by the University of Notre Dame Press in 1970. The following selection from his well-known* MERCHANTS OF LABOR *(1964) describes the economic and working conditions of the Bracero and the native-born Mexican American in the Calfiornia farm lands prior to World War II. It is not a pretty story.*

Reprinted from MERCHANTS OF LABOR: THE MEXICAN BRACERO STORY, *by Ernesto Galarza. By permission of McNally & Loftin, Publishers.*

California, The Uncommonwealth

California was given its name by the Spanish writer, Rodrigues de Montalvo, early in the 16th century. He wrote of a fabled island inhabited only by women who waited somewhere in the imagination of chivalry for the coming of the *conquistador.* Three centuries of exploration finally brought soldiers and priests to the real California—Alta, a massive addition to the colonial empire bordering the Pacific for a thousand miles; and Baja, a stringy peninsula dangling off the west coast of New Spain.

California remained unsettled and undefended. While feudalism marked time south of the Rio Grande, the Americans marched on north of it. As their traders and scouts explored the continent to the water's edge they thought of possibilities other than those of commerce. William Shaler, a Yankee skipper, wrote in 1808 after a business voyage to the Pacific Coast: "The conquest of this country would be absolutely nothing. It would fall without an utterance to the most inconsequential force." And it did. The American armed forces landed in

158

Monterey Bay in July, 1846, occupied the town, raised their flag and proclaimed California a part of the United States.

About a third of the area they annexed was embraced in the great Central Valley. This unbroken alluvial plain spread from the Tehachapi range in the south to the foot of Mount Shasta in the north. The Sierra Nevada raised a snowcapped windbreak against the winter winds from the east, while the coast ranges bowed low to give passage to the beneficent Pacific rains. The valley was nearly 400 miles long and 100 miles wide. More than a dozen rivers—the American, Mokolumne, San Joaquin, Kings, Kern and others—scoured the mountains and laid deep sedimentary deposits on the floor of the elliptical bowl, endowing it with a solid underfooting of rich earth.

To the south and west of California's Big Dish a fringe of smaller valleys, pocketed by the hills, added to the agricultural potential of the state, extending the range and variety of its soils and climate. Farming was possible somewhere almost throughout the year. The Americans soon discovered to their great delight and profit that the growing season in many parts exceeded 240 days. In the level deserts, once water was brought to them, plants could be cultivated and their fruits harvested throughout the year.

The Spanish kings had given away this land to their deserving subjects in abundant lots. Rancho San Antonio, whose boundaries included the land on which the cities of Berkeley, Oakland and Alameda were to rise, was given in 1820 to Sergeant Luis Peralta, a veteran of the DeAnza expedition of 1776. José de la Guerra's four ranches in Santa Barbara totalled more than 215,000 acres. Over 400 grants were issued under Mexican rule between 1833 and 1846 for small tracts of 4,000 acres and large ones of 300,000. In 1848 something like 8,000,000 acres were held by 800 *rancheros,* who called their little empires by names holy, hopeful, mocking or vulgar—*Las Virgenes* (The Virgins), *Buena Vista* (Pleasant View), *Salsipuedes* (Get out if you can), *Las Pulgas* (The Flees).

These generous portions of real estate passed into the hands of practical, ambitious men who had only a limited interest in the past. The rancho way of life, so far as the earth and its uses were concerned, died fast. Its memory remained embalmed only in romance—the yearly pageants of Santa Barbara, the cool seclusion of the missions, the musical place names of cities and resorts, and the schmaltzy revival of bandit tales like those of Joaquin Murrieta and Tiburcio Vasquez.

The new land plungers and speculators impressed on California its characteristic of land ownership on a large scale. Men like Henry Miller and William G. Chapman appreciated two things about the *ranchero:* that he had owned the earth in a big way and that it was not too difficult to separate him from it by force, cunning and politics. They appropriated the most and the best of the public domain. Six operators, including the well-known Chapman, Miller and Lux, laid out and made good their claims to 1,250,000 acres.

Between the speculators and the railroad companies, which received more than eleven million acres of real property in grants, practically all of the public domain in the state was absorbed. The prior rights they held, the volume of capital they controlled and the political influence they enjoyed gave them the commanding lead in California agriculture which they never lost. From them descended such enterprises as the Kern County Land Company, organized in 1874. In 1883 the Newhall-Saugus Land Company put into modern production a tract of several thousand acres in Los Angeles County. Coming much later but in no wise handicapped for that reason Joseph DiGiorgio in 1919 staked out a farm of over 10,000 acres in Kern County, southeast of Bakersfield. The perimeter of this ranch, which was one in a chain of large holdings running from the Imperial desert to the upper Sacramento Valley, measured nineteen miles. These "places," like the El Solyo Ranch and the orchards of the California Packing Corporation, became the hubs of resources, production and influence. In 1889 the larger commercial farms were already showing what such advantages were worth. One-sixth of the farms in the state produced slightly more than two-thirds of the crops, by value.

Corporate commerical agriculture abandoned the narrow base on which the farm economy had rested in the two previous stages of stock raising and grain production. The possibilities were grasped of the single cash crop produced with hired labor at relatively high cost in the expectation of large profits. This became the way of life. Farming, taking the state as a whole, developed into a variety fair of domestic staples and exotic delicacies—wheat, corn, beets, Chilean clover, Ararat olives, Andalusian oranges, French prunes and Mexican avocados.

The speedy success of commercial farming settled these important matters: (a) It consigned the family farm to a diminishing place in the economic scheme of things; (b) it bound the industry to the mass markets; and (c) it made harvesting dependent on high seasonal peaks of hand labor.

It had been expected that the completion of the railroads would bring an influx of settlers who would work the land in small holdings. This migration, so it was supposed, would break up the large estates. Land squatting was for many years the means by which it was sought to bring this about; but squatting was bitterly fought by those who had already tightened their hold on the shattered heritage of the *rancheros*. American agrariansim of the eastern variety did not succeed either in fighting or buying its way into a respectable partnership, much less a leading position, in the basic economy.

In this new economy individual subsistence or local self-sufficiency had no place. These were the traits of the backward *hacienda* system, with its traditional plaza fairs, its barter for use, its petty bargaining, its niggardly balancing of limited production and still more limited desires. Commercial farming on a technological basis required the mass market already being provided by industrial areas at home and abroad. The farm wealth with which California began to burst after the gold boom flattened demanded proportionate outlets in national and international consumption.

Technology was making the necessary connections. The ice-making machine was invented in 1851 and the refrigerated freight car in 1868. A year later the Central Pacific Railroad was finished and in less than twenty years entire freight trains with iced produce were moving over the Sierras toward the great common market of the east. The threat to the unity of this market was turned back by the victory of the North in the Civil War. The defeat of the plantation system with its chattel slavery secured for industrial agriculture an open market for its cash crops as broad, wide and rich as the nation itself.

The dependence on seasonal farm labor in numbers out of all proportion to the year-round work force became a characteristic of commercial agriculture. This necessity could diminish only as mechanization was able to take over the harvest tasks of picking, cutting, pulling, topping, sorting, sacking or boxing; and mechanization was slow in adapting itself to many of these tasks. The result was a highly characteristic curve of demand for seasonal labor with sharp peaks and long depressions between. This pattern became fixed. Technology improved, but production also expanded, and the specialized croppers of California seemingly could never match their everlasting manpower shortages at harvest time. In 1946 the figures for Kern and Fresno counties and for the state recapitulated the trend of decades. Kern County needed 1,750 seasonal and transient workers in March and 15,880 in November. Fresno County had work for 250 seasonals in April and for 32,710 in September. For the state as a whole the extremes of seasonal hiring in the fields ran from 68,000 in March to 244,880 in September.

This peculiar range of job opportunities required adult workers whose level of living was on a par with the limited income that they could make in four or five months of employment. Between the harvests such workers were expected to drift back to the "skid rows," the shanty towns and the grubby settlements that ringed many cities. This was the pulse beat of work and life for the California casual, and it had been familiar so long that farmers came to regard it as "one of the natural laws of economics."

What commercial agriculture had to offer its seasonal laborers in the way of a living was determined by the employers. These terms seemed attractive to Mexico's poor. Indeed, in the light of the conditions they faced at home, they were enticing. They stimulated the current of migration that set in before the close of the Diaz regime and rose by leaps thereafter.

MIGRATION BY DRIFT

The treaty of Guadalupe-Hidalgo of 1848 left between the two countries a barrier to migration consisting of a desert 400 miles wide. From the south the Mexican central plateau slopes into the Rio Grande Valley over rugged terrain through which neither rivers nor pleasant prairies make passage convenient. Northwestward the Sierra Madre Occidental encloses the nation, its ranges backstopped by badlands of mesquite and sand. The narrow strip of coastal plain between Mazatlan and Guaymas, a possible migrant route, also is sealed at the northern end by the desert. Along its length population was sparse and roads non-existent. Passage was barred by hostile tribes and the hot climate was uninviting to the dwellers of the temperate uplands.

Thus the two nations remained back-to-back until Porfirio Diaz and foreign capital opened pathways through these barriers. Between 1880 and 1910 nearly 15,000 miles of railways were constructed to carry gold, silver, copper, lead and other minerals abroad. Some of these export routes connected the mines of Durango, Zacatecas, Chihuahua and Sonora with the American terminals of Eagle Pass, El Paso, Douglas and Nogales, which became the gateways as well for the export of livestock, petroleum and agricultural products.

The freight trains that carried this traffic could not avoid disturbing the sluggish feudalism through which they rumbled. Railroading competed for the indentured peons who were often ransomed from the *haciendas* to work as track hands. Construction camps sprang up along the right-of-way in a lengthening chain of outposts along which ex-miners as well as ex-peons moved. The American smelters lying just north of the border drew upon these trickles of manpower for the dirty work of handling the ores, creating permanent settlements where the laborers could work, pause, learn a few English words and weigh their chances for better living farther north. The progress of construction and transport quickened a sense of looseness, an awareness of the possibilities of movement, along their course. At its far end there was dollar work to be found, no more agreeable than the menial tasks of the *hacienda,* but payable in hard currency that outmatched the *peso* two to one.

As civil war spread over the republic after 1911 a major exodus from the countryside began. Landowners fled to the large cities, principally the capital, followed by hundreds of thousands of refugees who could find no work. This was one of the two great shifts that were to change radically the population patterns, until then overwhelmingly rural. The other current was in the direction of the United States, now accessible by rail. It moved in the dilapidated coaches with which the Mexican lines had been equipped by their foreign builders, in cabooses fitted with scant privacy, on engine tenders and on flat cars for the steerage trade. *"A la capital o al norte"* (to Mexico City or to the border) became the alternatives for the refugees from the cross-fires of revolution.

The dream of a few became a reality for hundreds of thousands. In 1902 migration to Texas of Mexican farm laborers was sizable enough to attract national attention. According to a contemporary report, 400 men left one community in Zacatecas to seek work north of the Rio Grande. In June of the following year 672 *braceros* passed through Ciudad Juarez on their way over the border and in February 1910 the number was 2,380. The total number of migrants reported at points of exit between Ciudad Juarez and Matamoros was 1,000 per month. In the last ten years of the 19th century 971 Mexicans were reported as immigrants to the United States. In the first decade of the 20th, more than 49,000 were admitted.

The Liberal Party of Mexico, which lighted the fuse under Diaz, declared in 1906 that "spoliation and tyranny" had brought about "the depopulation of Mexico" as "thousands of our fellow countrymen have had to cross the border in flight." The Party promised that "all Mexicans residing abroad will be repatriated and given land that they may cultivate."

It was a feeble promise and it was made too late. Emigration increased steadily. Between 1911 and 1921 the number of legal entries to the United States rose to nearly 250,000. From 1921 to 1930 a peak was reached with a total of 459,287 persons, the admissions receding to 22,319 for the decade 1931–1940 as a consequence of the depression in the United States. During World War I immigration had been stimulated by a liberal interpretation of the law. The Department of Justice suspended the contract-labor prohibitions, head tax and illiteracy test. As a result of these concessions during the fiscal year which ended June 30, 1919, over 20,000 Mexican workers were temporarily admitted, many for employment in California. Altogether 72,862 agricultural laborers entered the United States during the war and immediately after. Of these 21,400 were reported as deserters by the Department of Justice.

Combining the numbers of immigrants officially recorded by the Department of Justice with those who entered illegally, well over 1,000,000 Mexicans crossed the border between 1900 and 1940. They settled principally in southern Texas, Arizona and California. Census figures for 1940 showed that over a million and a half Mexicans resided in the borderlands and the more remote states into which they had scattered.

This massive trend enlarged on an unprecedented scale the population of the towns on the Mexican side of the frontier. Between 1940 and 1950 Tijuana's population increased from 16,846 to 59,117 and Mexicali's from 18,775 to 63,830. Matamoros had 15,699 residents at the beginning of this period, 43,830 at the end of it; Ciudad Juarez, 48,881 as compared with 121,903, 1960. Taken together these border cities formed a labor pool secondary to the *colonias* of California and Texas.

The centers of population strung along both sides of the border constituted the great farm labor reservoir of the southwest. Within the borderlands recruiting, transportation, border crossing and contractor hiring kept the Mexican supply attuned to American demand. From the south the reservoir was continuously replenished by new arrivals, among them the seasonal cotton pickers who remained in the Rio Grande Valley after the harvest. On its northern front it was constantly depleted as the older migrants pushed on to get away from the lower wages and the harsh competitiveness of the areas nearer Mexico. It was here that the Wetbacks exerted the greatest pressure,

spreading until they were to be found throughout California and in many central and eastern states.

The conditions for the development of the Wetback traffic were the following: the concentration of workers in large numbers and in dire need immediately south of the border; facilities to enter and remain in the United States for the duration of the job; the offer of employment by American farmers; the absence of criminal penalties for hiring persons who had entered the country clandestinely; the protective coloration offered by the Mexican *colonias;* the services of Mexican intermediaries; and a tolerant or indifferent public opinion.

Wages, of course, played an important part in stimulating the flow of illegal labor. However low they might seem by American standards they were more than attractive by Mexican ones. In the 1940s some farmers paid 60 cents a day without board or housing. Ten years later an official of the U.S. Department of Labor noted that in the lower Rio Grande Wetbacks could be hired for 15 cents an hour, which was half the wage commonly demanded by resident local labor. In California wage rates in general were affected by what a Wetback would work for. He was glad to accept 40 cents an hour in the Imperial Valley as late as 1954. "The Wetback," Department of Justice agents reported, "was at the mercy of the employers in terms of wages and housing." He could be paid practically any wage his employer might choose.

Farmers found the Wetbacks as anxious to please as they were willing to endure. From among them the employer selected the more able workers for tasks requiring skill, such as irrigating or tractor driving. They became differentiated from the common run of illegals, serving in specialized operations and becoming stable, regular employees. The employer would make unusual efforts to keep them and to arrange for their return if by chance they were picked up by the Border Patrol. Many of these "specials," as they were called, eventually obtained immigration visas with the assistance of their employers. There are no reliable data on this class of farm laborers any more than there are on Wetbacks in general, but it can be supposed that they numbered between 6,000 and 8,000 throughout California before the *bracero* program got under way in 1942.

Among the Wetbacks there were not only peasants but also miners, bricklayers, truck drivers, weavers, chauffeurs and other skilled craftsmen. They were often enticed from the fields by canners, processors and packers at wage rates which were likewise lower than those for which local semi-skilled labor could be obtained. This transition was made easier by the fact that often packing was done in the fields, where men could be shifted without regard for job classifications or wage differentials. The transfer of Wetbacks from field to town was a natural one, although attended by greater risks of arrest and deportation.

Through these higher level employments many a Wetback discovered more promising chances to improve his lot. In the fruit and vegetable packing sheds he obtained a social security card, something which he had not been able to secure as a menial field hand. This, and the higher pay, encouraged him to seek work beyond the sheds, a search in which he was encouraged by non-agricultural employers who were themselves looking for men willing to accept lower than standard wages. Thus the Wetback soon was to be found in restaurants, hotels, laundries, garages, building construction, domestic service, mills, brick factories and railway maintenance. In short, the Wetback, growing in numbers and experience, tended to show all the adaptive powers of a capable human being, useful and exploitable in a variety of trades and occupations.

The Wetback infiltration was geographic as well as occupational. Its base was the borderlands and its range the central and northern counties of California, where the pay was higher and the climate more agreeable. Those who were not transplanted thither by labor traffickers made their own way, starting at dusk from their hideaways in the Imperial Valley to avoid the blistering sun of the desert. The way of the Wetbacks led around the Salton Sea and by the main irrigation canals, along which they could often be seen, trudging in single file through the twilight, the shadowy figures of an animated frieze framed by dusty tamarisks and purple mountains. From Imperial and San Diego the illegals set out, sometimes in autos or trucks,

paying for the ride as much as $100 deductible from future wages. They spread to the lettuce fields of Monterey, the orchards of San Joaquin and the beet fields of Yolo and Sacramento. The number of Wetbacks in the state during the harvest peak of 1952 was probably not under 60,000.

The stable portion of the Mexican population, the people who called themselves *locales,* was to be found in the rural and suburban *colonias.* By 1940 there were over 200 of these communities throughout the state. The largest of them was Belvedere Gardens and the adjacent Boyle Heights, dismal suburbs within the city limits of Los Angeles in which more than 200,000 Mexicans had settled. Others were hardly more than hamlets, like Cucamonga in the heart of the citrus country and Mendota, a huddle of tents and shanties midway on the west side of the Central Valley. Hardly a town of any size or pretensions—Delano, Hanford, Brawley, Sacramento, San Diego, Fresno—failed to acquire between 1900 and 1940 its Mexican *colonia* on the weathered side of the railroad tracks. In 1930 it was estimated that 28,000 foreign-born Mexicans were living in the Imperial Valley; 96,000 in Los Angeles County; 16,000 in Fresno; 14,000 in Ventura; 10,000 in Santa Barbara and 10,000 in Orange. The Spanish-speaking population of California was given as 416,000 persons in the census of 1940. The settlements in which they lived had a well-defined economic and social function. They were relatively stable labor pools into which recent arrivals from Mexico fitted easily.

The period from 1900 to 1940 was one of migration by drift, in contrast with the administered migration of the *bracero* that was to begin in 1942. It was a migration propelled by political turbulence in Mexico, channeled across the desert and brought into junior partnership with the capital that was ready to transform vast and barren lands to the uses of commerical agriculture. Legally or otherwise the migrants crossed the border, palping their way, seeking new roots, guided and manipulated by turns through no design or plan. *Locales* they became after a time, resident farm laborers who became less desirable as they grew in understanding of the ways of an aggressive and powerful industry. Mingling with the Wetbacks in the *colonias* they were, on the whole, an ignored generation, subdued clusters of individuals rather than men and women in or progressing toward community.

The farm labor force of California which had been put together between 1860 and 1940 in racial layers consisted in its larger part of Mexicans who were easily molded to the established requirements and controls. In normal peace times it could do well enough without industry-wide planning. Although the system was slack and wasteful it clung to the methods of management characteristic of the labor pool.

THE POOLING OF FARM LABOR

Located on the western edge of the continent and on the eastern rim of the Pacific basin, California agriculture is strategically positioned with respect to the manpower stocks of China, Japan, the Philippines, the Mississippi Valley and Mexico. The industry, with its heavy and abrupt peak loads, had particular reason to "never forget," George Santayana's reminder "that among the raw materials of industry one of the most important is man." The harvest hands that were to be found in those areas were both raw and plentiful. They were recruited in a succession of ethnic waves that displaced one another.

The first to be brought in were the Chinese, initially for work on the railways and in the mines. As the gold boom passed and the transcontinental lines were completed—and as racial hostility mounted—the "coolies" moved into agriculture. In 1886, according to an estimate cited by Carey McWilliams, 30,000 Chinese worked as harvest hands typically grouped in gangs under a headman. The passage of the Chinese Exclusion Act prevented the continuous renewal of this source of labor and California farmers, after unsuccessful experiments with southern Negroes and a premature look at the possibilities of Mexicans, turned to Japan.

The Japanese became an important factor in agriculture between 1890 and 1910, during which period their number in the United States increased from slightly over 2,000 to more than 72,-

000. They served a long apprenticeship in the truck farms of Monterey and San Joaquin, spreading gradually over the state. Being not only indefatigable wage laborers but skillful farmers as well, they leased and eventually owned land, managing it in their own right. In 1920 they were established in Fresno, Los Angeles and Imperial counties. By becoming more intractable as field laborers and more numerous as growers the Japanese, like the Chinese, became the target of bitter racial hostility. Japanese exclusion in turn became a rousing political issue and again farm employers had to look elsewhere for harvest hands.

The successors to the Japanese were the Filipinos, recruited in the Islands or from the surplus of plantation workers in Hawaii. In the mid-1920s they were arriving in California at the rate of more than 4,000 a year. By 1930 they represented a labor force of 25,000 single men, concentrated in the San Joaquin and Salinas valleys, where they became the base labor force in asparagus, lettuce, grapes and truck crops. Though they never equalled in numbers either the Chinese or Japanese, the Filipinos were no less important as competitors for farm work at the low end of the wage scale. Ill feeling brewed against the wiry, agile "boys" who moved about in tight crews, working faster and harder than was called for by a fair day's wages for a fair day's labor. Before 1930 riots against them broke out in Tulare, Watsonville, Stockton and Imperial. Once again, agriculture had touched the limits of another alien reservoir.

At about the same time, however, the ill wind that was dusting the plains of the lower Mississippi began to blow providently for agribusiness. The great trek of southern Americans, white and Negro, out of Oklahoma and Arkansas was beginning. Nearly 130,000 entered the state as farm workers, concentrating on the south end of the Central Valley and spilling over into Salinas and Imperial. Steinbeck found them in the canvas and tin can tenements of Weedpatch, Arvin, Strathmore and Cotton Road. Their arrival, according to Professor Walter Goldschmidt, brought for the first time native white American families to "the army of cheap labor that is requisite for the continued functioning of the industrialized agriculture of California."

The continued expansion of commercial farming, racial antagonisms, the inevitable maturing of greenhorns into canny sellers of their labor, and the seepage of discontented and experienced workers out of the labor pool became the indicators of a perpetual shortage of agricultural manpower. Clearly not more than one generation of newcomers could be counted on to accept farm employment on any terms. The experience of a few years at the most was enough to convince them that they were worth more than they were getting. But unlike the skilled craftsmen in industry and the service trades, the alien farm hands were never able to organize their own labor market in order to bargain on relatively even terms. The world of labor was for them a pool into which they were dumped in large numbers; within which they were impounded by effective barriers of language, custom, and alienation; and from which they escaped only when racial antagonism dried up their jobs or competing industries offered them a way out.

The pool was conceived in practice, if not in theory, as an allocation to California of a portion of a self-renewing stock of raw labor. It sources were international—Kyoto, Canton, Manila, Oahu, Michoacan and the Ozarks. Selection at the point of supply was merely a matter of sorting out enough hands to fill the vacuum at the point of demand in Lodi, Tracy, Watsonville, Delano or Brawley.

The labor pool so constituted was supposed to be, ideally, frozen at the periphery and completely fluid at the center. It was the common resource of an entire industry, not of a single enterprise. No particular worker was committed to a given employer; and all employers, within the limits of a gentlemanly understanding concerning wages and other conditions, could dip into the pool. This was an important condition, for it made the immigrants the concern and responsibility of no one employer. What happened to them and how they lived, or what burdens they placed on the community in general, could in no way be held against the industry as a whole or any of its members individually. The pool at its best was insulated from the general labor market. American workers would not normally be willing to enter it; the immigrants could not easily leave it.

The basic function of the labor pool was to assure a surplus of manpower. Its effects were therapeutic as well as economic. Commercial farmers suffer from an occupational nervousness around harvest time that is inflicted on them by two unpredictable powers: the weather and the market. The ups and downs of temperature and price determine the difference between a successful "deal" and a disastrous one. A margin of extra harvest hands offered insurance in two respects. It guaranteed the gathering of the crop and, by keeping the supply rather than the demand side competitive, held wages down. Thus, the normal fever of a harvest "deal" was reduced.

The concept of the pool became another one of those "natural laws of economics" which are the theoretical stock-in-trade of agribusiness. William J. Monahan, a journalist who understood the theory, defined it with unusual candor as "a multilayer system of workers, including a bottom echelon of poorly paid harvest workers who have been used in seasonal labor in a mass employment technique." This bottom echelon was described as "an ample and fluid supply of labor" by the voice of commercial farming, the *Western Grower and Shipper.* The Farm Placement Service of the California Department of Employment shared this point of view. In the Department's Bulletin on the Stockton labor market for April 1957 it was stated that "there is a need for migratory workers to build up the dwindling labor pool in the area."

Labor recruiting associations were a natural outgrowth of the requirements of pool maintenance. It was early realized that among the joint interests of all commercial growers was the encouragement of favorable conditions for the labor supply. There was general agreement on what those conditions should be, for specialized crops affected by them presented the same difficulties of labor pricing, recruitment, management and control. The farm labor association emerged out of these circumstances.

Among the earliest of them was the Valley Fruit Growers Association of Fresno, which in 1917 brought together 3,000 growers "for the distribution of farm labor in the raisin districts to meet distress labor requirements." The Agricultural Labor Bureau of San Joaquin County was incorporated in 1926 to assist its grower members in obtaining labor. In the southern part of the state the Agricultural Producers Labor Committee was constituted to serve the needs of producers and packers of walnuts, avocados, oranges, lemons and miscellaneous vegetables. Wherever seasonal labor was a prime concern similar agencies were established. By 1946 there were 74 labor bureaus representing the interests of growers in every major crop in all the important production centers of California.

The procurement and distribution of seasonal workers was by no means the whole of the task which the labor bureaus set themselves. Equally vital was the stabilization of wages, which tended to rise in spite of the pool effects when workers stayed only through the peak of the picking, when they were pirated or when they presented more or less concerted demands for higher pay. The standardization of wage rates to meet such difficulties became a primary object of the labor bureau. In 1921 the Valley Fruit Growers of San Joaquin announced a uniform wage scale in grapes on which its members had agreed.

From the outset the Agricultural Labor Bureau considered it as one of its most important functions to obtain the consensus of its associates on picking rates, which were then published as the rates that would prevail. A representative of California cotton interests described the procedures as follows: "There is a custom ... for farmers to gather together prior to harvest and discuss a uniform picking rate of wages ... after that scale has been arrived at ... not only us but other financing agencies ... assist them to conform to that." "The proliferation," wrote Lloyd H. Fisher in 1953, "of wage fixing organizations in California agriculture is so extensive and all-embracing that there would be no reason short of illiteracy combined with serious defects of hearing for any farmer to be unaware of the 'prevailing wage' for any commodity in any season."

The labor bureaus found that they could keep most of the farm labor contractors in line by the use of the published wage rates. The yardstick was applied to individual farmers and to intermediaries, who would not ordinarily risk their standing with their patrons by deviating from the schedules. The contractors carried no weight in the labor associations and were regarded by individual employers chiefly as the instruments by which labor pirating was carried out. Usually the contractor played the role of apologist of the wage schedules to the workers, his stock arguments being that "the farmers have to pay what everybody else pays" and that "the market won't let them pay any more."

The containment of wages worked smoothly enough over the long run, but it was a standing grievance among workers, who also blamed the employers and contractors for encouraging Wetbacks and pitting one racial group against another in the fields. Occasionally passive resistance turned into angry protest and when there was leadership to direct it, the labor associations responded with systematic violence.

To organize such violence was, among others, one of the purposes of the Associated Farmers, constituted in 1934 "to foster and encourage respect for and to maintain law and order, to promote the prompt, orderly and efficient administration of justice" and to assist employers in securing the undisturbed picking and transportation of their crops. The Associated Farmers, a statewide organization, was joined by local committees of farmers and their retainers who during the emergencies practically enforced the dictates of the labor bureaus. Behind the Associated Farmers and the vigilante committees there stood the less conspicuous commodity federations, whose leadership was in close touch through interlocking directorates that extended their lines of communication into every major power center in the state.

The enforcers were unquestionably successful in keeping the labor pool under control and wages on the level. The 1928 strike of the *Confederacion de Uniones Obreras* was defeated by arrests and deportations. The threatened loss of the melon crop in the Imperial Valley "led the local authorities," as Professor Robert Glass Cleland noted, "to use extra-constitutional methods in dealing with strikers." The cotton strike of 1933 was broken by organized violence. In Lodi the angry farmers, literally up in arms, declared themselves against trial by jury in labor litigation "as reminiscent of medievalism" and a pastime for boneheads. In Brawley in 1934 a meeting of workers was invaded by police officers who attacked with tear gas and clubs. Sheriff's deputies and special guards numbering more than 400 put down the 1936 strike in Orange County. The Filipinos in Salinas were overwhelmed by mass violence and back-stage maneuvers. The Mexican strikers in Santa Paula were evicted in 1941 in large numbers and their places given to dust bowl refugees. Professor Cleland summarized his view of wage controls and their enforcement tersely. He wrote in 1947: "California's industrial agriculture can exhibit all the customary weapons ... gas, goon squads, propaganda, bribery."

The labor force conceived as a pool, recruited from the surplus stock of people in Asia, Mexico, and the backward counties of the United States, held together by mass coercion, was adequate for the needs of a democracy at peace. A spreading world war, however, was drawing the United States into its vortex, and California agriculture was sucked mightily into it. Mobilization and the production crisis at once threatened to tax its manpower, upset its wage structure, possibly give a smaller and more compact labor force some measure of economic leverage, and unsettle in unforseen ways the existing private controls. It was this crisis that led directly to the first migrant labor agreement between the United States and Mexico, and eventually to managed migration under Public Law 78.

THE MANPOWER CRISIS OF 1942

According to the United States census California had in 1940 a farm labor force of 243,000 persons, of whom slightly more than 105,000 were hired workers. Of the hired force approximately 25 percent were seasonal, principally resident Mexicans and southern Americans, migrants from out of the state, intra-state migrants and Wetbacks. Of the Asian laborers the Chinese had disappeared as a

factor in agricultural employment but there remained thousands of Filipinos, Japanese and Hindustani who dedicated themselves to special crops in limited areas of their own choice.

These were the agricultural manpower resources of the state upon which the demands of war production pressed. Farm employers were aware that those demands would strain the imperfections of the labor pool, bringing new and perhaps far more serious worries.

Among those imperfections the worst was that the immigrant farm laborer, whether he came from Mindanao, Oklahoma or Zacatecas, could not be bound permanently to the industry or to any particular segment or member of it. Agriculture was being continuously drained of manual labor by manufacturing, transportation and the service trades. These offered opportunities for better jobs which alert farm workers bid for. Industry and the service trades were expanding, their draft on the farm labor bank threatening to keep pace with accelerating war demands.

Within agriculture itself, in spite of the watchfulness of the labor bureaus, competition for workers was never thoroughly stabilized. The gentlemen's agreements on wage schedules did not prevent individual growers from hiring away their neighbor's help in the pinches of harvest. Pirating continued, especially where Wetbacks were concerned, through intermediaries of employers who were either too busy or too sensible to give personal offense to their peers by being caught stealing.

The enticement of laborers was not limited to local raiding. California's employers had to be ever watchful against the lure of higher farm wages in Oregon and Washington. The war, moreover, disrupted one important sector of agricultural production when in 1942 the evacuation of the Japanese population of the Pacific coast began. This had the double effect of removing field workers who were notably industrious, and of displacing farm families whose labor contributed importantly in certain crops. These imbalances in the supply of labor and the demands of production were accentuated by the growth of war industry —shipbuilding, aircraft, steel and oil refining. The new plants and shops in San Francisco, Vallejo,

San Pedro, and San Diego drew thousands of migrants away from the Central Valley.

From the point of view of commercial farmers, particularly of the relatively small percentage who used the major part of the seasonal labor, the war not only threatened to subtract from existing manpower but also to add to costs by breaking wages from their old moorings. Higher wages were almost certain to follow from the better competitive position of the men and women who remained at farm work. In the decade preceding Pearl Harbor farm pay had indeed shown a tendency to rise, though not precisely in a breakthrough. The gap with industrial wages showed a mild but disquieting tendency to close.

To head off this trend district and area committees were set up under Federal authority, the committees being composed of prominent growers and processors "who were actually instrumental in setting out the policies for the administration of ceiling orders." Through these committees certain crops were given protection against wages pressures. The rising curve of the preceding decade was pegged. In asparagus and tomatoes wages not only levelled off, they were actually rolled back. The lower limit of the rollback was fixed at 50 cents per hour, defined as the substandard minimum rate.

The success of agricultural employers in arresting wage increases for the duration of the war was an important accomplishment. Aside from the immediate economic benefits of the stabilization of the harvest costs close to or even below 1940 levels, the local area and crop committees were a device that permitted commercial farming to take over the structure of control while the labor bureaus and associations were in abeyance for the duration of the war.

This was, however, only a temporary state of affairs. The transition from war to peace could prove as difficult as the adjustment from peace to war. Farm workers might renew their pre-war organizing activity, which had in great part caused the rise in wages already noted. The migrant workers from the southern states had proved to be both clamorous and belligerent. Thousands of farm workers would be returning to the fields from the war plants of the coast with union experience and new ideas on how to get more for their labor. The Asian labor stock was closed for an indefinite time. Controls would be removed from prices, but so would they from wages.

However useful controls were in keeping things tidy while farm employers pondered these matters, they were not addressed to the most critical problem of all. New sources of manpower had to be found. This was not only because of the real drains on the farm labor supply by military service and the attractions of industry; the pool had to be resupplied if the anticipated tensions were to be avoided. In 1942 farmers were already complaining over the loss of crops that might ensue if the labor shortage became more critical; they were also aware that losses other than financial ones— the intangible perquisites that go with social class domination—could be sustained if the pool were not refilled with proper workers.

The decision to turn to Mexico for such a supply was not hastily made. It was no longer a simple matter of opening the border and allowing the Mexicans to enter wherever they might choose and at whatever seasons of the year. Deliberate planning was required in an economic area in which it had never been welcome. Such planning could not be carried out by the private agencies of commercial agriculture as they existed with the speed and in the manner which would respond to wartime needs. It required the participation of the Federal Government. This was a departure that would have to be carefully considered by men committed wholeheartedly to self-helping free enterprise.

It was necessary to consider with great prudence the terms and conditions upon which labor would be made available. Terms and conditions for the employment of agricultural workers had never been subject to question or negotiation in California agriculture. There had been occasional bargaining between farmers and crew leaders. In their dealings with some labor contractors there had also developed a semblance of hiring by contract. But these instances were not typical. What standards there were before the war, so far as wages were concerned, were set up by the labor bureaus. In matters such as transportation and housing, employers brooked little interference except such as they agreed to among themselves as gentlemen, or such as was tactfully exercised by state agencies under the law. Standards set up for foreign workers in particular could easily become standards in general, and it was strongly suspected by agricultural spokesmen that such minimum requirements would be used as an excuse for extending to domestic laborers forms of protection which had never been conceded.

These and other shoals through which planned migration under official auspices would have to sail were not the figments of the imagination of suspicious men. They were hazards to be reckoned with. Their location had been marked in the course of a long and successful navigation. If they were to be risked because workers were becoming scarcer the chances were not to be taken lightly.

There were, on the other hand, certain enticements for an adventurous change in policy. Planned migration could provide orderly recruitment. It would guarantee a supply of men selected according to the requirements of the employers. Minimum wage standards in any event would be predetermined, opening an area yet to be explored jointly by government and employers. The labor force thus assembled would not be an organized one in the trade-union sense. Growers in the central and northern areas of the state would be assured an equitable share of the manpower provided. Public funds would be spent in initiating and maintaining planned migration, meaning that the financial burdens of such a program would be greatly lightened if not altogether removed through Federal subsidies. Furthermore, Mexicans recruited under official standards or minimum requirements could be prevented "from listening to the siren call of the shipyards," and the blandishments of higher-wage industry in general. Finally, these workers could be sent home at the end of the harvest.

By the beginning of the summer of 1941 requests were already being pressed on Federal agencies in Washington by cotton and beet growers in Arizona, New Mexico and Texas. California farmers, estimating their needs at 30,000 men for 1942, had asked the state government for approval of certifications. The California Field Crops Corporation had been organized to negotiate the recruitment of 3,000 Mexicans, all of them for employment in the beet fields. The orange and lemon industry growers were asking for 50,000 Mexicans to be delivered at the rate of 10,000 a month, an influx that would have overshadowed that of the gold rush. Like the beet growers, the orangemen held that they could not meet the stepped-up production schedules unless Mexicans were provided. On the same note of urgency, the Southern Pacific Railroad petitioned for 5,000 recruits for maintenance-of-way operations.

Even before the Japanese attack on Pearl Harbor in December 1941 it was clear from the number of Mexicans wanted, the importance of the industries asking for them and the pressures that employer organizations were marshalling that a decision had been made by leaders of commercial farming, supported by railroad corporations. This decision was to draw upon the stock of labor in Mexico to meet the manpower deficit for the duration of the war, and to do so through the agencies of the Federal Government. It was a high policy choice, an emergency measure which became permanent, a sharp veer from drift to management in immigration and farm labor procurement.

FAUSTINA SOLIS

Faustina Solis (Associate Professor, Department of Community Medicine, University of California at San Diego) has not only won distinction in the academic world, but she has also attained practical experience with the Farm Workers Health Service; California Department of Public Health. Professor Solis draws upon her academic and professional training to delineate problems that farm workers encounter and suggests how social work methods may help to alleviate them.

Socioeconomic And Cultural Conditions Of Migrant Workers

The plaintive and indignant cry of the migrant farm worker is at last being heard in our rapidly advancing technological society. For many years the humanistic goals of the United States have seemed incompatible with the indifference manifested toward the deplorable living and working conditions of the migrant population. The insig-

170

nificant power of this group, as well as the fact that field workers are usually recruited from among those ranking lowest in socioeconomic status, have enabled the nation to dismiss collectively the hardships imposed by the migrant way of life.

It is not the purpose of this article to dwell in detail on the plight and problems of the seasonal and agricultural migratory populations; their hardships have been grippingly and dramatically reported since the early 1900s. The purpose is to delineate major socioeconomic and cultural factors that are basic for an understanding of the farm workers' efforts to utilize services and mobilize their own quests for a viable community. Focus will be on the worker of Mexican descent or the citizens of Mexico living or working in the Southwest.

Unfortunately, statistics concerning the agricultural migratory population are generally unreliable. Data collection methods are questionable because most sources of information document a partial sample of the population. Ethnic, age, and sex distribution is usually not available, and the counts on migrants are not consistently kept for peak and low harvest months. A discussion of the ethnic backgrounds of migratory workers before the Senate Subcommittee on Migratory Labor in April 1970 suggested that only 40 percent of the labor force is made up of members of minority groups (Mexican and black). This estimate undoubtedly ignores the increases in commuter, "green carder" (resident alien), and illegal entry migrants from Mexico.

HISTORICAL OVERVIEW

The increasing need for a constant labor supply for the developing agricultural areas in the country, particularly in the southwestern states, initiated the importation of foreign laborers primarily from China, Japan, and the Philippines from the late 1870s through the 1920s. The Mexican immigrants hired as laborers at the turn of the century were primarily employed as members of "extra gangs" and as section hands on the railroads. Approximately 90 percent of the Mexicans emigrating to the United States between 1920 and 1928 were unskilled laborers. A "cheap" farm labor supply therefore became readily available.

During the mid-1930s, residents of the Great Plains states and other areas, who either fled from the drought or sought employment during the depression era, constituted another significant supply of migrant farm laborers to the West. Thousands of people from Oklahoma, Arkansas, Texas, Arizona, Missouri, and Kansas moved westward to augment an already burgeoning labor supply.

In 1942 foreign labor importation legislation was passed as an emergency measure to assure the harvesting of crops during the war years. The *bracero* (farm laborer) imported from Mexico produced a dependable labor supply in California and other southwestern states for over twenty years. Following the repeal of this legislation in 1964, attention had to be directed toward hiring the existing domestic labor supply. The foreign labor importation legislation had given rise to expressed dissatisfaction by domestic farm workers. Contractual benefits guaranteed to the *bracero* but not available to the domestic worker were a minimum wage, housing, medical care, and transportation to and from the border. There were instances, however, when contractual agreements were violated and exploitative maneuverings resulted against *braceros*.

UNIONIZATION OF FARM WORKERS

The National Labor Relations Act, enacted in 1935, excluded agricultural workers from its basic coverage, which guaranteed the right to organize or not, to bargain collectively through representation of choice, and to engage in those activities that promoted mutual assistance and protection. The reasons for excluding the agricultural labor force from the enforcement of this act have never been quite clear, although it is generally assumed that the exclusion stemmed from political rather than from administrative factors. The farm lobby was powerful and strongly opposed this legislation.

Despite the lack of substantive support from the National Labor Relations Board, which is responsible for the enforcement of the act, sporadic attempts were made in the last four decades to organize farm labor. These efforts resulted in repeated failures, which perhaps were due to the fact that trade union methods were used to organize workers. Because most farm workers were unfamiliar with these techniques, it was necessary to import professional organizers who invariably left the area defeated by such overwhelming obstacles as politically powerful farmers, forming ruthless opposition that at times threatened their lives, and a farm labor force, grossly lacking in organizational skills and caught desperately in a struggle for survival.

These professional organizers failed not because they lacked organizational prowess or commitment but because they were unwilling to modify their approach for agricultural workers. They failed to observe how the workers' strong social and cultural values were inconsistent with the patterns of trade unionism, and most important, they did not develop able leadership within the ranks of farm laborers themselves.

In the early 1960s, two important developments took place in farm worker organization. Both took place in California, the setting for numerous past unionization efforts and particularly suitable for union organizing because of several factors: (1) the state employs more farm workers and pays higher wages than other states; (2) agriculture is one of the states's top industries because of its gross receipts; and (3) there is year-round and seasonal harvesting, as well as a large variety of crops grown.

The first important development occurred in 1960, when the Agricultural Workers Organizing Committee (AWOC), in an attempt to seek more effective methods of stimulating unionization, directed its efforts to include labor contractors. At about the same time César Chávez organized the National Farm Workers Association (NFWA). Chávez believed that the initial job of the association was to organize farm workers in a community of interests and endeavors that would insure in them a greater sense of self-worth and confidence and would enrich the quality of their family and community lives. Integrated into the plan was the development of leadership on various levels of activities. The organization was formed intentionally as an association because many workers had witnessed or experienced punitive measures following abortive attempts at union organization and were thus fearful of unions. Chávez's efforts were more effective because of his identification with the ethnic and cultural patterns of the farm labor force. He was keenly aware of the long process of community evolvement that would have to precede the constructive participation of the farm worker. Formal programs of community training in management and organizational skills were launched. When the first labor dispute arose in Delano in 1965, the NFWA had the backing of a small but strong contingent of farm workers well aware of the price their commitment would cost them and their families.

In 1966 a merger of AWOC and NFWA resulted in the United Farm Workers Organizing Committee (UFWOC). Members are primarily California resident farm workers—seasonal and migrant. It would not have been organizationally feasible to concentrate on interstate migrants as a resource for early membership, although these workers are joining the committee in increasing numbers.

Simultaneous with the activities to seek nationwide support for La Causa was the necessary task of recruiting professional and nonprofessional staff and volunteers to organize in those areas still unfamiliar to the workers—effective picketing, organization of boycotts, use of mass media communications, and fund raising. Grass-roots impact was demonstrated in the setting of priorities in union negotiations, in the implementation of the Robert Kennedy Health Plan, and in the continuing development of Forty Acres, a community complex of employment, social, legal, and health services operated and maintained by union membership.

The present UFWOC membership, which is not so numerous as the general public might surmise, may constitute less than 15 percent of the total agricultural force in California. There are significant numbers of farm workers who are not UFWOC sympathizers and others who remain distrustful of unionization. It is significant, however, that the reawakening of the public conscience to long-standing injustices took place only when farm workers could express themselves through an organization.

CURRENT CONDITIONS

The more than one million migrant agricultural workers and their dependents in this country—including the blacks and Puerto Ricans who are currently available as farm workers on the eastern seaboard and in the middle western states—have estimated annual family incomes ranging from $1,400 to $3,600. During harvest periods the families may not be eligible for public assistance or medical care. They continue to live in substandard, dilapidated housing with inadequate sanitation facilities and are exposed to environmental hazards that breed disease. Local educational programs and attitudes of school personnel discourage rather than encourage the participation of the migratory children and youth in the schools. The rate of infant mortality and the incidence of morbidity of certain disease categories are higher than in any other occupational group. Occupational injuries in agriculture are second only to those in the construction industry.

Migrant workers are usually surrounded by a society that is insensitive to them, to their problems, and to their aspirations, values, and needs. They have no political power because their mobility and economic struggles do not allow them to establish the community cohesiveness that is essential both to organization and to the mobilization of political effort. Migrant farm workers are discriminated against by the dominant group and often by their own ethnic group. Historically they have been considered desirable as laborers but not as citizens. It is, therefore, difficult for this population to believe that perseverance and hard work will insure financial success.

EMPLOYMENT PATTERNS

Four general types of migrant farm laborers can be identified according to employment patterns: (1) United States resident families that have depended on migrancy in agricultural work for two or three successive generations and consider themselves locked into the system for the future; (2) seasonal agricultural workers who do not wish to pursue their lives as farm workers but whose circumstances, such as their limited skills and their responsibility for support of their families, allow little time and funds to pursue other educational, training, or employment endeavors; (3) workers who want to stop doing farm work but must reenter the migrant labor force periodically because of fluctuations in the general labor market; and (4)

workers whose homes are in Mexico or "green carders" whose earnings in the United States are considerably higher than the wages they could possibly earn in Mexico. Attitudes toward farm labor will vary within the group, depending on mobility patterns, distances traveled, and opportunities for upgrading of employment in home base areas. Not all farm workers consider their plight irreversible. The spectrum of attitudes is wide, ranging from quiet resignation to demonstrated impatience for raising the status and opportunities for farm workers through organizational methods. Workers as a whole do not consider farm labor a degrading occupation, but they do consider the conditions under which they work degrading.

Competition and some animosity exist between local seasonal agricultural workers and workers from Mexico. The worker whose home base is Mexico tends to express less dissatisfaction with his working and living conditions. He isolates himself more from the domestic migrant community and the community at large. His lack of proficiency in English, as well as the strangeness of institutional structures, creates for him a world of uncertainties. He relies heavily on his countrymen and relatives for advice.

Migrants whose homes are in Texas and Arizona usually establish a pattern of mobility built through their own experiences or through envoys who make explorative visits to evaluate promising harvest areas and to make housing arrangements. The ability to negotiate employment is one general indicator of the worker and his family's increasing ability to identify opportunities and services within the communities. Families or individuals who negotiate their work through labor contractors and crew leaders narrow their interaction with the community and know less about their benefits because they depend on employers to assist them.

Workers on the move are seldom known to take risks. They have developed a communications system for passing along information regarding matters that enhance or threaten their economic survival. Unlike most of the single men who travel alone, families traveling separately tend to follow the itineraries of other families from their home states. Migrant workers do not always take unfamiliar co-workers into their confidence, and therefore important helpful information may not reach all workers in one specific location. Workers also may not divulge even innocuous information about neighbors and relatives; they do not wish to give information that may be used against one or all of them at some future date.

Although the origin of residence may differ considerably in the groupings described, the economic plight is severe for all. Even for those workers who regularly return to the same fields of harvest with the same employers, economic uncertainty looms annually. The winter months cause an accumulation of debts—particularly for food, transportation, and emergency medical care. There is always talk about whether winter frosts, too much rain, or an early spring will ruin crops or will precipitate their ripening. Reaching a harvest area to find that a crop may be two or three weeks late for picking can be catastrophic for a family whose financial resources at hand may not be sufficient to cover one weeks's living costs.

In recent years alternative considerations have been given to planning for family mobility. As a result, there has been an array of groupings—single, unattached men or women, partial families that may include one older person to care for the very young, and total families, especially when contracts are made for "family crops." Family crops include selected tree crops, such as cherries, and row crops, such as berries and cucumbers; farmers with these crops can usually employ all family members who are able to work.

The family that travels together may not always stay together. The Mexican family resists camping in orchards, river beds, or ditches, but, when there is a need for two or more units in a crowded farm labor center, some members of the family may have to be distributed among relatives and friends not residing in the center. The family computes its earnings as a group. In fact, it is not uncommon for the father to compute all earnings under his social security number, not understanding the individual benefits that may accrue to all other members if each were to use his own number. Accepting

wage deductions today for benefits in the far future is a difficult concept, particularly when the future, as well as the benefits, is undependable and uncertain.

SOCIAL AND CULTURAL CONSIDERATIONS

Common to most farm worker groupings is the dominance of Mexican tradition, with its more conservative behavior patterns. Because mobility does not encourage close and intimate friendships, there tends to be great reliance on family dependency and independence from the surrounding community. The reluctance of some parents to send children to school may be based on economic need. Nevertheless, the economic need may be a guise to keep children and youth from losing respect for their families and their cultural inheritance, which many parents believe to be the primary mission of some schools. As Chicanos, these parents have experienced discrimination on many levels, and their perception of continued harassment colors the degree to which they will allow any intervention with their families. Generally, however, they hope for improved opportunities for their children and, therefore, support educational endeavors. Departure from and return to the home base are planned with schooling in mind, and it is not infrequent for adolescents to be sent home with younger children so that they can start school while their parents remain to pick the autumn harvest.

If one were to generalize about this population, one could say that migrants are individualistic and self-sufficient. Their physical pain or emotional agony must be unbearable before they seek assistance; for their children, however, they will often seek help earlier. Their endurance tolerance is such that children, rarely hearing their parents complain of their hurts, will also endure pain and discomfort.

Individuals and families that follow the crops learn to adapt to new surroundings but maintain their own system of values. The farm worker acknowledges his fear and despair, at times expressing powerlessness to effect change in his life. His demands and his expectations are minimal. His approach to services, when they do exist, is one of skepticism. He is unable to adjust to the values of those providing services, which, in essence, he is expected to do, although reciprocal understanding is not always evident. He is often described by agency workers as unobtrusive, undemanding, and easy to work with. His demeanor may well be a method for limiting unwelcome intrusions into his life.

PATTERNS OF SERVICES

Although services have been provided sporadically for migrant populations for several decades, they have been limited in scope and usually have been under the auspices of voluntary agencies. Unless special funds are appropriated, public services appear to be incidental, accidental, or provided to meet only certain crisis situations. Agencies, as well as communities, do not consider specialized services for migrants important. They too believe that migrants should be educated to avail themselves of all mainstream services as do other citizens. In reality, of course, migrants cannot be compared to other citizens.

In the last decade, legislation enacted on behalf of the poor has earmarked funds for seasonal and agricultural workers and their families. Particularly important have been the Migrant Health Act of 1963, the Economic Opportunity Act of 1964, and federal grants for compensatory education, which provide special educational programs to migrant children. The latter include remedial education as well as preschool and day care services; day care facilities have offered social services as a fringe program component in some areas.

Needless to say, funding for crucially needed programs has been discouragingly limited and uncertain. Health funds available cannot possibly provide comprehensive health care for even 15 percent of the population in need. Because these funds, representing a decided improvement, are so limited, sponsors of services tend to concentrate their efforts in farm labor centers and definable migrant streams. In those states in which seasonal and migratory populations do not follow a stream but are dispersed over large geographic areas, hundreds of families remain unreached during peak harvest months.

Rural areas traditionally structure programs using the philosophy of service and staffing models of the urban areas and ignoring the following special features of the rural areas: lack of public transportation, distances, political barriers, and dearth of professional manpower. Little consideration is given to programming for people on the move, although all society has become increasingly mobile. Social services are often designed for long-term activity. Families are not trusted to diagnose their own problems, and the service process is therefore unnecessarily prolonged and ineffectual. Services are expensive for the client even when he does not pay a fee. Free care is costly when the family must pay expenses for private transportation, interpreting, child care, and meals.

Broken appointments and failure to follow through with referrals are especially frustrating to professionals, but many professional workers are unaware that referrals undergo a series of procedural steps when they involve migrants or residents new to an area. Before a final disposition is made, the referral is usually discussed both with family members and friends or relatives whom the individual trusts.

A public health nurse could not understand a note that was left for her by a bilingual community health worker, which read: "Mrs. G has not had time to talk with Mrs. C about your referral to the clinic; therefore, at her request, I cancelled her appointment for today's clinic." The explanation is quite simple when it is understood. Mrs. G would like to consider following through with the referral, enough to seek the counsel of her friend, Mrs. C. If her friend has not attended the clinic, she would locate, if possible, more than one person who had attended and would report on the services. Mrs. G could then make her decision on the basis of additional knowledge.

Contributing to the lack of communication between social workers and migrant clients are the differing definitions they give to the word *crisis,* which reflect, of course, basic differences in their value systems. A family may experience severe anxiety and panic because it will not be in Texas when a relative is scheduled to arrive. The social worker may be more concerned about the fact that the family is not seeking needed medical care for a particular condition.

The description that migrants and other poor people give of agencies is noteworthy. While working as project director at the Farm Workers Health Service, Berkeley, California, the writer was assigned a Spanish-speaking international social worker for placement. As an orientation to a California rural community, the worker was asked to assess the need for a day care center in a specific migrant neighborhood. Purposefully no explanation was given to her of voluntary and public agencies and how they function in the state. She was to learn about services from the people in the community. After two weeks she called the writer, troubled that the people did not know what a social worker was and that many of them did not know that public services, such as public health services, existed. She was also troubled by the fact that most people identified an agency through the services received from the efforts of a particular worker rather than through an understanding, even theoretical, of the scope of services provided by the agency. From what families reported, she had identified youth corrections as residential centers for emotionally disturbed youth and the welfare department as a correctional system. Most astounding to her were the number of serious problems that had gone unattended because they were either not identified or because the family resisted acknowledging them to professionals in the neighborhood, fearing that it would lose all power to make decisions.

Attitudes toward recipients of service are also reflected in facilities and their arrangements. Poor people and those who work with them are the endurance testers for facilities that are inadequately equipped, crowded, unattractive, and depressing but that are expected to provide quality services. Complaints lodged against facilities center primarily on the reception areas, in which clients are stripped of all their dignity. The lack of privacy—a luxury that many families cannot afford in their own housing arrangements—is more acutely experienced when they seek assistance.

THE SOCIAL WORK TASK

The task facing social work today is immense and its position is precarious.

When a class of our citizens—farm workers—are not able to drive its roots into a community; when they can be driven out of farm labor camps, as they were after World War II; when they can be told there are literally 200 crop areas in California where they can expect no lodging if they are traveling with their families, [this] obviously creates the atmosphere in which services—social services—are needed, including social assistance and public health. . . . The migrant farm workers are a sand dune, and the winds that blow them from place to place are deliberately created by social and economic forces in our society.

Although there has been inordinate and sometimes unjust criticism made of social work and its role in these changing times—particularly in economically deprived areas—there is also restiveness within the ranks of the profession itself. This restiveness threatens the profession even more than accusations made by the communities. It certainly demands a response. The dissatisfaction is not related to a specific agency or to a group of social workers whatever their specialty might be; it relates to the profession as a whole.

Is social work demonstrating a concerned, active, and assertive role in relation to broad social issues? It is folly to respond defensively to irresponsible accusations, but it is apparent that there is a societal and professional demand for reorganizing and redirecting skills. The duality of responsibility to the individual and to the community becomes even more intense because it is no longer possible to ignore the physical, social, and political reality of people's lives while trying to concentrate on symptoms and conditions that are created in great part by society. Social work can and must, through its advocacy programs, bring into partnership the providers and consumers of service. It must help to reorganize and reorder national and regional priorities for planning, programming, and implementing service mechanisms.

Migrant workers and the general farm labor community are striving for an opportunity to experience freedom in establishing a community that will allow the enjoyment of collective economic advantages, humane support, emotional and cultural contacts, and mutual understanding. The field of social work has keys to open the storehouse of limitless possibilities of assistance, advocacy, and action on behalf of people. The power that turns the keys, however, is not merely an understanding of individual and social behavior and social work methods but a disciplined commitment to people throughout cycles of social change.

The MONTHLY LABOR REVIEW *is an official publication of the Bureau of Labor Statistics. Its articles are written anonymously and are descriptive rather than analytical. This article, based on Professor Paul S. Taylor's studies of Mexican labor in California, describes labor and working conditions immediately prior to "Huelga," 1928. By permission of the* MONTHLY LABOR REVIEW.

Industrial Relations And Labor Conditions

MEXICAN LABOR IN THE IMPERIAL VALLEY, CALIF.

About 20,000, or more than a third of the people in Imperial County, Calif., are Mexicans and they constitute an inextricable part of the social and economic life of this agricultural community. An investigation of Mexican labor in this section of the country was made in the spring and early summer of 1927. The results of this inquiry and the conclusions based thereon are brought together by Paul S. Taylor in volume 6 of the University of California publications in economics, which is the first of a series of studies being conducted "as a project of

the committee on scientific aspects of human migration of the Social Science Research Council." Some of the findings of this initial study are presented here.

A table showing race distribution of the elementary school children in Imperial County lists 54.7 percent of the Mexican children enrolled in such schools as born in the United States, which fact is indicative of the "increasing stabilization" of the Mexican population in that section of the country. Mr. Taylor declares that this permanent group is

178

immensely "more important numerically than the group which crosses the line for seasonal work in the valley and returns to Mexico when the season ends, and of infinitely greater social significance to the United States, for these are becoming a permanent part of the culture of the valley."

About 50 percent of the Mexicans of the Imperial Valley are town residents; however, most of those who reside in the towns are agricultural laborers whose homes are located near the ranches on which they work. During fruit and grape-picking seasons, from July through September or even longer, probably a majority of the Mexicans close their town homes and migrate to the San Joaquin Valley and other parts of California. Also, the rural Mexican populations shift their location according to crop conditions, the harvest labor group leading in mobility. Such labor may not be in the same section for more than two months at a time. Individuals in this group migrate even more rapidly. Another group is constituted of semipermanent rural residents whose stability depends upon the somewhat constant labor requirements of certain crops. Alfalfa, on account of its eight or nine cuttings per annum and the fact that dairying is dependent upon it, contributes more to the labor stability of the valley than any other crop.

The distribution of Mexicans in the valley, then, is a shifting phenomenon. Its explanation is principally in terms of crops, both at present and historically at the formative years of town building. Towns located in the center of the valley have generally had the advantage of location and of a larger tributary area, and so have drawn heavy Mexican populations. But location within an area of intensive agriculture is the most important condition for building up a Mexican colony.

ECONOMIC SIDE OF THE VALLEY'S AGRICULTURE

Although the valley soil is rich and the money returns on the crops are high in good years, absentee ownership, tenant farming, and generally unstable conditions characterize agriculture in this part of California. According to the United States census, tenant farming in the State of California decreased between 1910 and 1925 from 20.6 to 14.7 percent, while in Imperial County in the same period it increased from 31.8 to 46.7 percent. The majority of melon and lettuce growers are companies which came into the valley as commission merchants. Recently these companies have leased the land themselves to grow truck crops, subleasing it in small tracts or turning over small acreages to foremen or managers or operating their own holdings.

The housing, machinery, labor, and other farm requirements under intensive cultivation are entirely different from those under extensive agriculture. Considerable dislocation is caused at the beginning and close of vegetable leases. The crop-lease rotation system followed in the valley, which in many cases is practically crop-lease farm rotation, "adds one more shifting element to the general instability." Mexicans are employed mainly to meet the highly seasonal calls for hand-labor gangs. Present conditions are not favorable for establishing a class of either white or Mexican resident working farm owners, and there is considerable difference of opinion as to the desirability of building up such a class of residents. Urban interests, especially financial and mercantile, are strongly in favor of doing so, while the large growers stress the economy of production on a large scale.

THE LABOR MARKET AND WAGES

In 1927 Mexican laborers were being used to some extent in nearly all the agricultural operations in the valley.

It is in the truck crops, however, that Mexicans predominate heavily—melon and lettuce harvesting and picking tomatoes and peas. They pick cotton, they harvest nearly all the milo maize by hand labor, and they pick grapefruit. The grapefruit crop is not at present a cause of heavy demand for Mexicans, but its importance is increasing as new trees come into bearing. Cleaning the heavy silt deposits from irrigating ditches is done by Mexican hand labor throughout most of the year. August, otherwise a slack month, marks considerable activity in ditch cleaning. The larger ditches are of course dredged by machinery. The importance of ditch cleaning is indicated by the fact that the annual cost of this work is estimated at $3 per acre.

It is not at all easy to determine the labor requirements for a given crop or for all crops at a particular period. The heaviest demands for Mexican workers in the valley are in January and February, at the time of the lettuce harvest, and from May to mid-July, when melons are harvested.

The current daily wage rate in the valley for Mexican general ranch workers is from $2.50 to $3, usually for nine hours of labor. These rates are exclusive of board and vary with the employer, the worker, and the proximity of a labor market.

Rates per hour are ordinarily from 30 to 35 cents, but in certain years at harvest time they have been as high as 45 cents. One large ranch, which employs Mexican workers the year round, pays $50 a month with board and $80 a month without board. White ranch laborers are usually paid 50 cents or $1 a day more than Mexicans. Housing is sometimes provided for Mexican workers.

The following are the rates of pay for different kinds of agricultural work in the valley: For irrigating the usual rate is $3 per day; for asparagus harvesting, principally by Filipinos, $2.75 per day; cotton picking, 1¼ to 2 cents per pound; grapefruit picking, 40 cents per hour; lettuce harvesting, 30 cents per hour; cantaloupe harvesting, 13 to 15 cents per crate.

In the valley and also in other localities the statement is frequently made that "Mexican labor is not good on hour work, only on piecework." It is usual for certain crops to use Mexican labor under contract at so much per acre, per ton, or per crate, in order to get the results by this method of payment that are secured under hour work by "driving" or "supervision." Nearly all the large vegetable and melon growers, however, prefer to pay their labor by the hour. Each worker is assigned to a row and when a whole gang is operating together in this way under a supervisor the individual laborer's pace becomes conspicuous if

he does not conform to that of the gang. When the men are hired for piecework close inspection is more necessary.

In the cantaloupe season earnings per day are often high; amounts as high as $5 to $7 are ordinarily reported by both the Mexicans and the growers. In exceptional cases, with long hours, daily earnings have been reported as high as $12 to $14. It is evident, however, according to the author, that "high daily earnings are not a very reliable index of seasonal earnings."

It is extremely difficult to determine with any approach to exactitude the annual earnings of Mexican laborers. The varying bases of payment, the irregularity of employment, the lack of uniformity in rates paid in different portions of the valley and by different employers, the migrations of the Mexicans over the State and into Arizona, make any exact computation exceptionally difficult. Barring that small minority of Mexicans regularly employed by the same employers the year round, a fair estimate of the annual earnings of a Mexican laborer of Imperial Valley is from $600 to a possible $800. In some cases his housing is furnished, or he can construct his own, rent free, on a ditch bank, or he may own or rent a small "shack" in a town, or during the course of a single year he may live in all of these ways.

A detailed study of Mexican migration is to be embodied in another report. In the monograph under review, however, some little space is given to this subject. Among the statements made in this connection the following is of special interest:

The major portion of the migratory Mexicans, and these constitute probably half or more of the Mexicans of the valley, join in the great migration to the San Joaquin Valley to work in grapes, cotton, apricots, peaches, and prunes. This tide of Mexican labor moves north principally by automobile on the State highways. It flows not only over the San Joaquin Valley, which absorbs the major number, but over all the valleys of the State as far north as San Francisco and even beyond. At the close of the season most of it flows again southward.

VIEWPOINTS ON MEXICAN LABOR

Opinions vary on the matter of the desirability of Mexican labor. Among those quoted as representative of the range of opinion is that of a man who has been familiar for years with agriculture in the valley, who states that "Mexican labor is good labor, and we couldn't get any other class of labor for anything like the same money. * * * About 30 percent of Mexican labor is first class and makes good gang pushers. Mexican gang pushers are better than white, and are paid 25 cents per day extra."

A large grower declares: "Mexicans are much to be preferred to whites. Once fixed, they are permanent and reliable. I do not think they are good for other types of labor."

A field man for a large-scale grower of lettuce and cantaloupes says: "Mexicans are very satisfactory. They offer no disciplinary problem, but require constant supervision and driving." On the other hand, a young rancher from Wisconsin who employs white labor "can't understand why some ranchers are able to say 'My Mexicans are good.'" A foreman with steady year-round Mexican workers on a large alfalfa and cattle ranch reported that his men when teaming, "fresnoing" (leveling land), or irrigating, worked "best if left alone," and that they kept up "a steady gait."

Not all Mexican labor in Imperial Valley agriculture is gang labor, although the heaviest demands are for this type. This is the chief explanation of the frequency with which one is told of the necessity for driving. Some Mexicans are used for general ranch labor, for irrigating, teaming, "fresnoing" (leveling land). In Imperial Valley Mexicans are less often spoken well of as teamsters than in San Joaquin Valley. In very few cases do Mexicans drive tractors. The consensus of opinion of ranchers large and small, however, is that only the small minority of Mexicans are fitted for these types of labor at the present time.

WAGE CLAIMS

In 1926 in the San Diego Imperial district almost all the complaints made by the Mexicans to the California labor commissioner were wage complaints. The inability of employers to pay is the principal reason for the nonpayment of wages. These employers for the most part are contractors or lessees. A lessee's position is a precarious one, as often he has no property and if his crop fails he has no assets to attach. The owner is not responsible for a lessee's debts and the worker gets nothing. "Probably nothing short of a bond for the payment of wages would fully protect the wage earners."

A Valley Labor Union

In April, 1928, less than 12 months after the field survey of the present study was closed, a Mexican union was formed under the name of Union of United Workers of the Imperial Valley (Inc.). This title was shortly afterwards changed to Mexican Mutual Aid Society of Imperial Valley. The organization, however, is primarily a union. Its formation was suggested by the former Mexican Consul at Calexico, who had been called upon by the Mexicans to settle so many labor claims that he had come to the conclusion that the organization of a union might remedy the situation. A very interesting account of an incipient strike following the refusal of certain demands of the union is included in Mr. Taylor's monograph.

The upshot of the situation was that the "strike," which was never really a strike, was broken up; the pickers generally found their demands for better wages, for ice and sacks, acceded to, cases against practically all of the sixty-odd Mexicans arrested were dismissed, only four or five who pleaded guilty to technical violations on minor charges being given suspended sentences. One of these, a Mexican born in Arizona, agreed to leave the country for the period of his suspended sentence as a result of an agreement with the district attorney. The Mexicans in the union came out of the affair with a sense of unjust treatment, but with optimism for the future.

The resentment against the sheriff seems in no way to have become attached to the growers, many of whom, particularly the large companies, the Mexicans hold in high esteem.

Careful inquiry has failed to disclose the slightest evidence of violence or "uprising," or to yield the least support to the charge that the union is "red" or communistic.

With a few exceptions, Mexican labor is not found in trades which ordinarily come within the scope of unionized labor.

Housing of Agricultural Laborers

The State Housing Commission's inspectors try to enforce certain minimum standards in the housing of agricultural labor in the valley; for example, the flooring of tents for workers in the lettuce season, the provision of beds, screened cook houses and toilets, baking facilities, and garbage disposal. Up to the time the study was made (1927) the inspectors had had a great deal of difficulty in attempting to maintain such standards, which were far from being "universally observed." Among the factors militating against good housing conditions are "the atmosphere of impermanence which characterizes the valley," the desert climate which does not call for the same kind of construction as in other sections of the State, the highly seasonal nature of the valley's agricultural work on which Mexican labor is used, and the fact that Mexican families are unusually large, which make for overcrowding unless additional space is provided.

A man familiar with the condition of the valley outlines the situation as follows:

The Mexicans are satisfied to live anywhere. It is hard to get white labor to do the work and live as they do. Our intensive labor and short seasons make standard housing prohibitive for the Mexicans with their large families. We couldn't employ Mexicans at the housing standards of others. Nevertheless, we must make some improvements to meet the better housing which other sections of the State are beginning to offer to Mexicans.

The growers' attitude toward the housing inspectors' activities range from indifference to unmistakable opposition. Nevertheless, in some cases a genuine attempt has been made, especially by two or three large companies, to raise their housing standards.

From the standpoint of health, however, the dependence on ditch water for drinking purposes is even more of a menace than the character of the housing. According to the health officer of the county, the use of such water is accountable for gastrointestinal complaints and some typhoid fever.

MEXICANS AS SOCIAL CHARGES

One of the outstanding objections to the immigration of Mexican manual workers is that many of them become public charges. Whatever may be the situation in other sections of the country, the support of poverty-stricken Mexicans does not seem to be a heavy burden on the Imperial Valley community. Indeed, an appreciable part of Mexican relief is provided by the Mexicans themselves through organizations and also through unorganized means of assistance which Mexican workers commonly extend to each other in times of need.

The chief reasons why Imperial Valley Mexicans do not become objects of charity in the same measure as in some other places are these: "The community is almost entirely rural or dependent upon agriculture. It is not difficult to find some place to live rent free, if not with friends, then along some ditch bank. Mexicans who live in ranch camps are commonly allowed to continue to live there without charge during the dull season.

Ownership of Property

While the rapid development of home ownership in the towns is one of the most significant aspects of the Mexican labor situation in the Imperial Valley, there was no indication in 1927 of any movement among the Mexicans in the valley toward the ownership of the land which they were cultivating.

Mexicans in Independent Business

As yet there is no evidence that Mexican immigrants whose parents belong to the working class are competing with Americans in independent business or even establishing substantial business undertakings for their own race. Almost all of the Mexican merchants who are successful in conducting their stores on modern American business lines are middle or upper class Mexicans.

Education

Nearly all of the Mexican children of school age in the Imperial Valley attend school. Up to the present, however, merely a handful have gone on to high schools. In the past public education in the valley has made very little change in the occupational status of the Mexicans living there, but there are indications of a gradually increasing appreciation of schools by the Mexican children, resulting mainly from contact with these institutions. Furthermore, parents and growers are showing "a greater willingness to cooperate in enforcement of the law" in regard to school attendance.

Isolation

In the valley towns, with the exception of Calexico, Mexicans live in colonies entirely apart from Americans.

The reasons for this separation are several. In the first place, most of the Mexicans outside of Calexico are poor, and poverty leaves them little choice of residence outside of the cheapest quarters. Furthermore, there is the natural tendency to gravitate toward the places where, in a strange land, others of one's language, class, and culture may be found. Finally, there is the social pressure from the American community, which generally does not desire Mexicans as neighbors. A symptom of this pressure is the race restriction sometimes included in the deeds to property.

Socially the line of demarcation between Americans and Mexicans is as sharply defined as the segregation of their homes. More or less separation of American and Mexican school children is found in half a dozen schools in valley towns, and in certain rural schools separate rooms are assigned for "Americanization" or "opportunity" classes which are almost wholly Mexican.

The segregation of school children upon a racial basis is illegal. It may be done, however, by making a school district coincide with a Mexican colony and establishing a school in that section. The rigidity of the practice of separation varies in different localities. In one town at least, Mexicans with high American social and educational standards are sometimes allowed to transfer to American schools. In another town even upper-class Mexicans were refused transfers.

For the most part, Mexicans raise "no serious objection to separation." It is reported, however, that "the belief that they would be obliged to continue in the east-side school was deterring some Mexicans above the age limit of compulsory attendance from prolonging their education."

Among the factors contributing to the segregation of Mexican children in the schools are: The difference between the American and Mexican standards of personal cleanliness, dread of diseases resulting from uncleanliness, race consciousness, and violent fluctuations in the number of children of migratory workers attending school. The migratory group being principally Mexicans, it is convenient to isolate the problem on a racial basis. Moreover, educational authorities have pointed out that this segregation of the Mexican children shields them from American social prejudice and also from discouragement arising from the realization of their slower progress in school as a result of language or other handicaps.

There is almost no social intercourse between Americans and Mexicans, even in the town of Calexico, and the isolation of rural Mexicans from the American population is even greater than that of the Mexicans in the towns.

Mexicans are proud and sensitive to the prejudice against them. They keep to themselves the more because of consciousness of social ostracism instead of hurling themselves aggressively against it. In some cases, particularly, but not exclusively, among those who are above or are trying to rise above the lower levels of the Mexican population, there are defense reactions to the American prejudices in the form of sensitiveness to the American-made stigma of being "Mexican" or not being "white."

On the whole, the Mexican laborers of the Imperial Valley constitute a class apart with a culture of its own. Social ostracism is maintained by the combination of racial class and cultural differences, and this social ostracism in turn fortifies and renders more stable the differences upon which it is built up. The early immigrants from Europe to the United States who formed colonies in our large industrial centers and the Mexican migration to the Imperial Valley are both working-class migrations. The Mexican migration differs from the European mainly "in that it is rural and in that it involves a strong consciousness of racial difference." These differences tend to heighten "the domicilary and social isolation" of the Mexicans of the Imperial Valley, retard the convergence of the two cultures (or the elimination of one), and delay "the blurring of the class line."

charles Wollenberg

Charles Wollenberg (Chairman of the Department of History, Laney College, Oakland, California) is representative of the younger generation of historians who are primarily interested in ethnic history. The next article tells of the background and condition of Huelga, 1928. Copyright © 1969 by the Pacific Coast Branch, American Historical Association. Reprinted from PACIFIC HISTORICAL REVIEW, Vol 38 Number 1, pp. 45–58, by permission of the Branch.

Huelga, 1928 Style: The Imperial Valley Cantaloupe Workers' Strike

The Imperial Valley cantaloupe workers' strike of 1928 has been all but ignored by California historians. As a labor dispute, it is dwarfed in scope and drama by the Wheatland strike of 1913 and the virtual class warfare of the 1930s. Unlike these more spectacular conflicts in California's fields, the 1928 strike was a purely local affair, staged by Imperial Valley workers with little or no aid from outside organizations. It was broken easily, in part because of organizational weaknesses, but primarily through threats and force by the valley's growers and law enforcement officials. Nevertheless, the strike stands as an important event in California history. It was the first attempt at a major work-stoppage organized by Mexican farm workers in modern California. It is important to note that this attempt occurred nearly forty years before the current struggle in Delano and nearly fifteen years before the beginning of the formal *bracero* program. The strike of the Imperial cantaloupe workers in 1928 is part of a long and sometimes bitter heritage of conflict between Mexican agricultural workers and their employers in rural California.[1] The basic economic and social conditions that caused the Imperial Valley strike already were well established in 1928, and the Delano *Huelga* indicates that these conditions still exist in California's fields.

During the first week of May 1928, the Imperial Valley was preparing for the harvest of the cantaloupe, its most valuable crop. As early as April 26, the first crate of ripe melons was shipped out of the valley, destined for President Calvin Coolidge at the White House. On May 4 another crate was sent to Washington, this time addressed to Senator Hiram Johnson, leader of the fight for congressional approval of the Boulder Dam Project, a cause dear to the hearts of Imperial growers. By May 5 the valley had filled its first railroad car with ripe melons. Extensive harvesting was expected to begin on Monday, May 7. Work would continue until the middle of July, by which time more than fourteen thousand carloads of Imperial cantaloupes would have been shipped to all parts of the United States.

But on many of the valley's ranches extensive harvesting did not, in fact, begin on May 7. At the Sears Brothers Ranch near Brawley, about half the crew of Mexican field laborers refused to work unless they were paid a piece-work wage of fifteen cents per standard crate of melons. Since the harvesters already had been contracted to work at a thirteen and one-half cent rate, the employer, E. L. Sears, turned down the demand for higher wages. The rebels tried to prevent the other workers from going into the fields. A confused, bilingual argument ensued and, eventually, Sears sent out for the county sheriff. The strikers were dispersed, and four of them were arrested for disturbing the peace. Similar incidents occurred at other Imperial Valley ranches that Monday morning, and by afternoon knots of excited Mexicans were discussing the day's events on the street corners and in

the pool halls of the valley's towns. On Tuesday the eighth and Wednesday the ninth few field workers reported for harvest duty. The local press reported that between two and three thousand workers were idle.

At the time, Imperial County's agriculture was dependent on Mexican labor. During the first decade of the twentieth century, extensive irrigation projects had opened Imperial desert land to cultivation. The original agricultural pioneers of those years had utilized American Indian, "white," and Oriental labor. Between 1910 and 1920, there was a steady increase in acreage under cultivation, particularly in crops (melons, lettuce, and cotton) which needed a large labor force. While World War I created a substantial growth in the demand for these crops, it also created a shortage of native agricultural labor. By this time, Chinese and Japanese were moving into occupations that were more lucrative than field work. Thus, by 1910, Imperial growers were being forced to look to Mexico as a new source of labor. A revolutionary upheaval had created social and political chaos in some parts of Mexico, conditions that helped to stimulate migration to the United States. By 1920 Mexicans dominated the valley's harvest work and, at the time of the 1928 strike, persons of Mexican descent comprised about ninety percent of Imperial County's field labor force.

Although the valley's Mexican population originally came to the United States as temporary migrants, by 1928 the great bulk of that population had become year-around residents of Imperial County. About twenty thousand people, one-third of the county's total population, were persons of Mexican descent. Virtually all economically active Mexicans living in the valley were field laborers. Some of them spent a few weeks each year in other agricultural regions of California and the Southwest, but they lived most of the year in Imperial Valley towns and worked most of the year in Imperial Valley fields. During the height of the harvest season for the area's two major crops, lettuce and cantaloupes, the resident work-force was supplemented by some temporary migrants from elsewhere. But most, if not all, of the workers who struck in 1928 were residents of Imperial County.

---

[1] For the purposes of this paper, "Mexican" refers to farm laborers of Mexican descent.

The major employers of agricultural labor in the valley were large landholders—either individuals or corporations which owned or leased large holdings. Such growers needed big work crews, and rather than take the trouble to hire great numbers of workers directly, the growers utilized the services of labor contractors. Contractors were often men of Mexican descent who organized work crews, collected wages from employers, and distributed the money to workers. In return for these services, contractors normally were allowed to deduct for themselves one-half cent per standard crate of melons from the pay of their workers. They distributed wages at the end of each workweek, withholding the first week's pay until the end of the harvest. Thus, after the last workweek, the contractor owed the workers two weeks' pay. When the workers tried to collect this last installment, it was not uncommon for the contractor to disappear.

Uncollected wages was not the only difficulty Mexican workers experienced. Dr. Paul S. Taylor of the University of California made a thorough study of the valley's Mexican population in 1927. He found that the average Mexican field worker earned only six to eight hundred dollars per year. Such a worker housed his family in a one or two-room shack, usually on the outskirts of one of the valley's towns. Most of the Mexican dwellings had no plumbing or sanitation facilities. Mexican children in most Imperial County communities attended segregated elementary schools.

By 1928, then, Mexican workers had become an integral part of the Imperial Valley's economic and social system. They provided the growers with a source of cheap labor, and organizations representing growers acted energetically to protect this labor source. The federal immigration laws of the 1920s allowed Mexican nationals to enter and live in the United States, providing they paid fees amounting to about eighteen dollars on entry. An estimated seventy-five percent of the Mexicans living in the Imperial Valley in 1926 had not paid these fees and thus were illegal residents of the United States. When it was rumored that the Immigration Service was planning to deport such persons, the Associated Labor Bureau, an employment agency founded by and for Imperial

growers, began a campaign to "persuade" Mexican workers to pay their fees retroactively. The deportations never occurred, but many workers were forced to pay immigration fees through involuntary wage deductions.

In the early months of 1928, growers faced another threat to their supply of Mexican labor. Legislation applying the 1924 immigration qutoa system to Mexico and the rest of the Western Hemisphere was introduced by Congressman John Box of Texas. Imperial County's Western Growers Protective Association joined with similar organizations in California, Arizona, and Texas to fight the Box bill. The association's executive secretary, Calexico banker Chester Moore, spent six weeks in Washington lobbying against the measure. In the middle of March 1928, Moore happily reported that the Box bill was buried in committee and would remain that way for the rest of the 1928 congressional session.

While Imperial County growers were exerting pressure to protect their labor force, the county's Mexican workers were organizing a union. The original idea of the union seems to have come from Carlos Ariza, Mexican Vice Consul at Calexico. In his official position, Ariza received many complaints from workers about defaulting contractors and poor working conditions. In early 1928 he decided that a union might protect the workers' interests, and discussed his idea with members of the valley's Mexican community. In the middle of April, these discussions led to the formation of the Union of United Workers of the Imperial Valley. On April 22 Ariza, now a private attorney, filed incorporation papers for the new organization. Offices were established in Brawley and El Centro, dues were set at one dollar per month, and an executive committee was chosen. By the time of the strike, the union claimed a membership of 2,754 persons, all of Mexican descent.

It appears that Vice Consul Ariza was the only "outside agitator" who played a role in the organization of the Union of United Workers. The union's leadership seems to have come from two *mutualistas,* or mutual aid societies that had long existed in the Imperial Valley. The *Sociedad Mutualista Benito Juárez of El Centro* (established

1919) and the *Sociedad Mutualista Hidalgo* of Brawley (established 1921) had memberships composed largely of Mexican agricultural workers. The two *mutualistas* provided small payments to their members in case of illness, injury, or unemployment. In return, members paid dues of two dollars per month. The two organizations were also the centers of the valley's Mexican social life, sponsoring dances and patriotic celebrations on Mexican holidays. The *mutualistas* served as natural cores around which the Mexican labor union formed.

The Union of United Workers took its first important action on May 3, 1928, when the organization's executive committee sent letters containing specific requests for improvements in wages and working conditions to the valley's growers and to the Chambers of Commerce of Brawley and El Centro. Among the requests was one for a piece-rate of fifteen cents per standard crate of cantaloupes or an hourly wage of seventy-five cents. The growers also were asked to supply free picking sacks and ice, to deposit withheld wages in commercial banks rather than to turn such monies over to contractors, and to assume responsibility for payment of workmen's compensation (the contractors traditionally had had this obligation).

The union's letters were either rejected or ignored. Dr. Louis Bloch, statistician for the state Bureau of Industrial Relations, found that most growers had little objection to the fifteen-cent wage, but considered most of the other requests to be "exorbitant." Bloch also found that growers were determined not to recognize or negotiate with a labor union. The Brawley *News* reported that growers felt that granting the union's "reasonable requests" simply would open the door for "unreasonable demands." "With a union there is no limit."

It does not seem that the union leadership intended to call a strike if its requests were not met. The letters to the growers were polite and did not contain any threats of work-stoppage. On May 8, the day after the initial incidents occurred at the Sears Brother Ranch, the Brawley *News,* published a letter signed by Union President Ramón Mireles which denied that the union was urging workers to stay out of the fields. Mireles claimed that his organization wished "to work in conformity with the laws" and "would gladly see agitators that try to commit unlawful acts punished." But at the same time that this conciliatory statement was being published in English-language papers, a leaflet in Spanish was being distributed which contained a different message. This document boasted of the union's strength and belittled growers' threats that strike-breakers would be brought in from outside of the valley. Thus the union disassociated itself from the strike in English, while buttressing the spirits of the strikers in Spanish.

This apparent contradiction may have been clever public relations work, or it may have reflected divisions within the union leadership. But, in any case, it does not appear that the union executive committee ever issued a clear statement of either support of condemnation of the strike. The letter published in the Brawley *News* called for law and order, but it did not admit that the strike was illegal. The letter also denied that the union had urged workers to strike, but it did not ask them to return to the fields. The Spanish-language leaflet bolstered striker morale, but did not specifically call upon workers to remain off the job. There is no evidence that the union issued any more published statements after May 8. On May 10, Imperial County Sheriff Charles L. Gillett closed the organization's offices and banned further meetings for the duration of the emergency. On the fifteenth, the union changed its name to the Mexican Mutual Aid Society of the Imperial Valley, perhaps in an effort to improve the organization's "image" and disassociate it from what by then was a clearly unsuccessful strike.

On the surface, anyway, the union as an organization does not seem to have either planned or led the strike. The work-stoppages of May 7 and May 8 may have been spontaneous actions by informal groups of workers who probably were union members. Perhaps some individuals resolved not to work for less than the pay-scale requested by the union.

These workers, "agitators" as they were called by the growers, persuaded others to join them, thus creating such incidents as the one at Sears Brothers Ranch. When news of the scattered walkouts spread throughout the valley, most of the other harvest workers may have joined the strike out of conviction, fear of ostracism, or a combination of both motives. This picture of a "spontaneous strike" can only be tentative, since there is little available record of the attitudes and conflicts within the valley's Mexican community during the first weeks of May 1928. Nevertheless, the picture of a spontaneous strike fits available evidence, and it is consistent with the conclusions contained in the best contemporary source—Dr. Louis Bloch's official report to the Bureau of Industrial Relations.

The valley's growers seemed to be psychologically unprepared for a strike of Mexican laborers. Many employers had come to believe that "their" Mexicans were content and peaceful. One California rancher had testified before a congressional committee in February 1928 that a Mexican worker "never causes trouble except when he indulges in intoxicants." Dr. Bloch concluded that Imperial growers considered their Mexican workers to be "bovine and tractable individuals." Thus, it was not difficult for many Imperial Valley residents to believe that the strike had been caused by alien forces which had subverted the passive, happy workers.

One grower claimed that "agitators or communists or whatever they are ... have come with their comrade stuff and with threats have intimidated the workers." Imperial County Sheriff Charles L. Gillett believed that the strike had been caused by "reds and radicals." An Imperial Valley *Press* headline declared: "Radicals to Blame." The Imperial Valley *Farmer* warned that "agitators" might be planning "dangerous and violent acts." And from the Los Angeles *Times* came a report that I. W. W. members are in back of the movement." (Later the *Times'* headline writer forgot about the Wobblies and decided that "Agitators from Old Mexico" had caused the disturbance.)

In spite of the frequency of such charges, there is no evidence indicating that the Imperial Valley strike was fomented by "outside agitators" or members of radical organizations. A spokesman for the workers claimed that "we are not a bunch of Bolsheviks or I. W. W.'s." He and his fellow laborers had organized a union to gain "better wages for the benefit of our families." Dr. Bloch accepted these claims; moreover, the local press, which gave extensive coverage to the legal hearings of "agitators" who were arrested as a result of the strike, made no mention of any attempt by the County District Attorney to prove that the defendants were members of radical organizations or that they were non-residents of the Imperial Valley.

Such questions, however, must have seemed academic to most Imperial County growers on May 8. Their major concern was to persuade workers to return to the fields. On that day anonymous leaflets, reportedly printed in "illiterate Spanish," appeared throughout the valley. They warned the workers to "be careful." "If you fail to cooperate, the same men who have given their time and money to get you into this country and protect you here, the same men, will turn against you." Some of the leaflets contained alleged copies of telegrams in which Texas and Arizona employment agencies assured Imperial Valley growers that "thousands" of new workers could be brought to California within thirty-six hours.

Along with these threats came action by Imperial County's law enforcement officials. Perhaps the attitude of these public servants was best summarized by District Attorney Elmer Heald: "Imperial Valley melon growers have millions of dollars invested in a highly perishable crop, and every resource of law enforcement machinery is to be used in harvesting the crop." On Tuesday, May 8, the County Board of Supervisors ordered Sheriff Gillett to "arrest agitators." Gillett also was given authority to add forty deputies to his staff, which he did, in part, by swearing in field bosses from some of the largest ranches. The sheriff also told Mexican workers in the Imperial Valley that, if they were not satisfied with conditions in the United States, they could go back to Mexico. Both Gillett and Heald warned that trouble-makers would be referred to the United States Immigration Service for possible deportation.

Sheriff Gillett believed that "Mexicans are excitable and if idle will gather into groups to their own detriment as well as hindering work in the fields." Given these premises, the sheriff's tactics were obvious: he would see to it that Mexicans in the

Imperial Valley neither "remained idle" nor "gathered into groups." On Tuesday, May 8, Gillett arrested about thirty Mexicans for "loitering about the streets of El Centro." Learning that the union was planning a membership meeting in Brawley that evening, he announced that he would be "chairman of that meeting." One half hour after the sheriff arrived at the gathering, "there were few Mexicans left in the vicinity." On May 13, a Mexican newspaper distributor in Brawley was arrested for allegedly writing on his billboard, "Forty-eight Mexicans in jail—What for?—Nothing."

Dr. Bloch could not resist injecting a bit of subtle humor into his official report when he described the activities of Imperial County's sheriff. "Prompted by an intuitive sense of justice and spurred on by the requirements of the occasion, . . . [Gillett] sallied forth immediately to bring order out of the chaos which threatened to engulf the land of the cantaloupes." And, indeed, Gillett's zeal did at times lead him into embarrassing situations. On the afternoon of May 8, he saw a group of Mexicans gathering outside the county courthouse in El Centro. Fearing the worst, the sheriff arrested the group, only to discover that it was a delegation of workers invited to discuss the crisis with District Attorney Heald. On the evening of May 10, Gillett entered the Martinez Pool Hall in Westmoreland and ordered patrons to vacate the premises. The patrons, led by Mrs. Francisca Rodriguez, responded by throwing the sheriff into the street. Gillett recovered his dignity, gathered reinforcements, and returned to arrest four persons, including Mrs. Rodriguez. The sheriff later claimed there had been one thousand people in the pool hall; Mrs. Rodriguez put the figure at six.

But if Gillett's actions sometimes were humorous, they were also effective. By May 11, at least fifty persons of Mexican descent had been arrested. The offices of the Union of United Workers had been closed for the duration of the emergency, and so were five pool halls frequented by a Mexican clientele. All "congregations of foreigners" in the Imperial Valley were prohibited. The sheriff claimed to have a "secret service" operating in the valley's Mexican neighborhoods in order to identify agitators and troublemakers. Louis

Bloch concluded that "the Sheriff's decisiveness in rounding up and incarcerating actual and potential disturbers of the peace undoubtedly had the effect of stopping a movement which might have resulted in an effective general strike and in heavy losses to the growers."

During the week of May 14, as the cases of arrested workers came up for hearing, attention shifted from Gillett to District Attorney Elmer Heald. In some instances, prisoners may have been released after a night or two in jail, without formal charges being brought against them. However, by Monday, May 14, there were still about fifty workers in custody on charges of vagrancy and disturbing the peace. Bail had been set at between $250 and $1,000 and there is no indication that any prisoners had been able to post bond. But Elmer Heald had no intention of keeping Imperial County's jails filled with harvest workers. He wished only that the Mexicans would go back to work and stay out of trouble. Thus the prisoners were offered six-month suspended sentences if they would plead guilty and promise to return to the fields. As Heald explained, "if the judge would hold them on bail, they would enter pleas of guilty next day and would go to work and behave themselves."

In view of the high bail schedules, many workers had no choice but to accept Heald's offer. However, on the fifteenth, Alfred Blaisdell, a Calexico attorney hired by the Mexican consulate, entered the case on behalf of the defendants. Blaisdell advised his clients to refuse the prosecutor's terms, and on May 15 and 16 Blaisdell instituted *habeus corpus* proceedings in an attempt to free the prisoners. He argued that the trials had been delayed too long and bail set too high. He also suggested that Gillette and Heald be cited for contempt of court. On the fifteenth Blaisdell was unable to obtain freedom for several prisoners held in Brawley. But on the sixteenth he did win the release of thirty-three prisoners in Westmoreland. The decision was hardly a landmark for civil liberties. Justice of the Peace F. T. Cook decided that the city of Westmoreland no longer could afford to feed thirty-three prisoners.

By the time of the hearings, the strike had been broken. Harvest work seems to have been seriously hampered from Monday, May 7, to Thursday, May 10. On Saturday, the twelfth, the Imperial Valley *Press* reported "all quiet in labor circles," and the Brawley *News* announced that "the strike, so-called, seems to have passed into history." The growers do not appear to have sustained major losses as a result of the work-stoppage. An unusual spell of cool weather kept the melons from ripening too quickly and, by the time that temperatures rose on the twelfth, the strike had been broken. By May 18 more than one hundred and fifty carloads of melons a day were being shipped by rail out of the valley. Between the first and twenty-third of May, a total of 1,855 carloads left the valley, a record harvest for that period.

Yet, from the workers' point of view, the strike was not a complete failure. On Saturday, May 12, the Brawley *News* proudly claimed that the conflict had ended "with no yielding on the part of the employer." However, another article on the same page admitted that S. A. Gerrard, one of the valley's largest growers, had "reached a compromise with the workers." Dr. Bloch found that most growers eventually agreed to pay the fifteen-cent per crate wage originally requested by the union. But most of the other requests were ignored, and in no case was the union recognized as a bargaining agent.

Dr. Bloch, himself, played a major role in informing the state government of the difficulties encountered by Imperial Valley workers. His report to the Bureau of Industrial Relations emphasized the inequities of the contract system. During December of 1928, Bloch and bureau chief W. J. French came to the Imperial Valley to persuade growers to readjust their labor arrangements. A joint grower-bureau committee wrote a "standard picking agreement," which all growers were encouraged to use during the 1929 harvests. The agreement's most important features were those calling for the elimination of withheld wages and the direct distribution of wages to the workers by growers rather than by contractors.

The strike also strengthened the position of those who wished to limit further immigration of Mexicans into the United States. After learning of the disturbance in the Imperial Valley, Congressman Box reaffirmed his conviction that, since

"Mexico is by far the most bolshevistic country in the Western Hemisphere," Mexicans "constitute a bad element to have imported into the United States." Although the Box bill had been killed for the 1928 congressional session, its supporters planned to try once more in 1930 (a try that would again fail).

By the beginning of 1929, an informed observer such as Dr. Bloch could be cautiously optimistic about the future of Mexican farm workers in the Imperial Valley. The state government had taken action to alleviate some of the workers' difficulties. Federal restriction of Mexican immigration certainly would have improved the bargaining position of the valley's resident Mexicans. And workers had shown a willingness to form labor unions and strike for better wages and working conditions.

But Bloch could not foresee the events which, for the next thirty-seven years, would weaken the ability of Mexican field workers to improve their economic and social positions in California. The depression of the 1930s created a disastrous drop in wage rates and caused the introduction of hundreds of thousands of Anglo workers into the field-labor market. Violent strikes organized by outside radical groups occurred in the valley during the thirties but were not successful. World War II helped create the bracero program, which gave California growers a government guarantee of cheap migrant labor from Mexico. Not until Congress ended the importation of *braceros* in 1965 did anything approximating the agricultural labor situation of the 1920s return to rural California. Perhaps, then, it is no accident that in September of 1965 Mexican workers in Delano again walked out of California fields.

This paper has sought to emphasize that the conflict between California farmers and their Mexican workers has a heritage of more than forty years. In spite of the pioneering published works of writers such as Paul S. Taylor and Carey McWilliams, current events in Delano too often are treated as if they have no historical perspective. If we are to understand fully the Delano conflict, we also must understand the role that people of Mexican descent have played in rural California for more than a generation. We must know more about the organizations and institutions that were developing in the *barrios* of California towns during the twenties. We must have a better understanding of the part Mexican workers played in the great agricultural strikes of the 1930s. Certainly we should be studying the impact of the bracero program upon resident Mexican laborers in the forties and fifties. And we need studies of past conflicts between Mexicans and other ethnic groups engaged in field labor. Finally, the entire history of Mexican field labor must be placed within the context of the larger story of migrant workers and agricultural development in California's fields.

HAROLD A. Shapiro

Harold A. Shapiro (The University of Texas) writes of one of the first strikes by Chicanos in Texas. This strike brought to the Mexican American workers a mixed economic victory, but it did increase the awareness in the Chicano community of the powers of joint action.
By permission of the SOUTHWESTERN SOCIAL SCIENCE QUARTERLY, *Vol. 32 (March 1952), pp. 229–244.*

The Pecan Shellers Of San Antonio, Texas

San Antonio has been the center of the pecan-shelling industry for more than fifty years. G. A. Duerler, candy-maker and soft-drink concocter, pioneered the way in the closing years of the 19th century. Soon he was shelling more meats than he needed for his delicacies, and the excess was disposed of in national markets.

Initially the shelling process was performed by hand, but the introduction and development of machinery proceeded rapidly among all of the major operators. The mechanization of plants in St. Louis and in other cities progressed even during the Great Depression era. In San Antonio, however, the trend toward more modern production methods was reversed; for a vast army of migratory agricultural laborers and thousands of immigrants gravitated to San Antonio, the "capital of the Mexico that lies within the United States." They were unskilled, illiterate Mexican peasants, unaccustomed to urban life and to the American standard of living. They welcomed the opportunity for employment at any price.

Quick to perceive a competitive advantage over their machine-minded rivals, San Antonio's entrepreneurs, under the leadership of the Southern Pecan Shelling Company, inverted the technological process. Machines were displaced by men. Thousands of Mexican peons were hired at amazingly low piece-work rates. Pecan shelling in the city became an exclusively hand operation. And the Southern Company, although it was not established until 1926, soon dominated the pecan industry, not only in San Antonio, but in the country at large. By the early 1930s it handled fully 50 percent of the total seedling pecan crop in the United States.

A corollary of the hand-shelling technique was the contracting system. Under this procedure Southern and other large concerns bought the nuts from farmers and dealers and transferred them to 'independent' contractors. The latter directly employed crackers and pickers to process the pecans, and reconveyed them to the companies. The contractors were to all intents and purposes employees of the big operators, who controlled the supply of nuts and set the prices for shelling, but the polite fiction was maintained that the contractors were private entrepreneurs—in business for themselves. Their true economic status was excellently illustrated when one of them was arrested and convicted in County Court for violation of the state child labor laws. The contractor had worked his eleven year old daughter in his factory because, as he told the Court, the child's earnings were needed for the support of the family.

Primitive working and sanitary conditions prevailed in the contractors' plants. Frequently as many as 100 pickers toiled in a room 25 by 40 feet. Illumination was poor; ventilation was inadequate and the fine dust from the pecans hung in the air except when doors or windows were opened in warm weather. Inside flush toilets and even running water were a rarity until 1936 when a city health ordinance compelled all plants to install these luxuries. The statutes also required health examinations for all food handlers, but at least one case is on record of a known syphilitic who secured a job shelling pecans immediately after successfully passing the health department's physical examination.

Shelling was often a family affair and no effort was expended to exclude children. They fingered the nuts as they worked or played about the premises. Sometimes the families took their work home, in spite of health department restrictions to the contrary, and all members of the household spent their leisure hours picking away in the discomfort of their own living quarters.

Home-shelling was a doubly convenient procedure since the pecan industry was concentrated on the West Side of the city, an area of four square miles wherein fully two-thirds of the community's Mexican inhabitants resided. The section was and is one of the most extensive slum areas found anywhere in the United States. The only vital substances that ever thrived in the area are the germs of tuberculosis and infant diarrhea. Thousands of human beings living in decrepit wooden shacks or in crowded corrals, breathlessly shelled pecans in a race with starvation. In these homes, which lacked toilets and running water and which rented for as little as fifty cents a week, pecans were shelled and picked for the fastidious tables of northern and eastern gourmets.

Pecan shelling is a highly seasonal industry. The nut crop matures in the fall. Peak employment is maintained through the winter and early spring months and skeleton crews function during the late spring and summer.

Fluctuations in the level of employment make it difficult to measure the size of the working force. The only reasonably accurate record is provided by the city health authorities who administered the requisite health examinations and issued permits to the pecan workers. At one time (1938) over 12,000 individuals employed in 110 different plants were registered. If the shellers without health cards are added to those legally working, their numbers would undoubtedly total 15,000 or more. Ten thousand of them were employed by the Southern Pecan Shelling Company.

Wages were unbelievably low. The owner of the Southern Company testified at a Regional Labor Board hearing in 1934 that his employees were paid three cents per pound for small pieces and five cents per pound for halves and that the usual worker could shell eight pounds in an eight hour day. At that rate the average sheller earned less than $2.00 per week.

Another report, this one by an NRA investigator, on the wages of 1,030 employees of 14 San Antonio contractors disclosed average earnings during December, 1934, of $1.29 per week for

34.8 hours of work. Pickers and cleaners averaged three and five cents per hour, respectively. Some operators paid as little as two cents per pound in 1933–34. The rates went up the next year to five cents for pieces and six cents for halves but dropped to three and four cents the following season. From 1936 to 1938 the five and six cent scale generally prevailed.

A former secretary of one of the pecan shellers' unions insists that wages plummeted to one cent per pound for pieces and one and one-half cents for halves at the depth of the depression. On that basis even the "champions" could earn no more than $1.50 per week; some of the less skilled received only sixteen cents for a week's labor. But whatever the exact amount, the weekly stipend was invariably enclosed in a yellow pay envelope appropriately inscribed with the bankers' dictum: "Let a Bank Account shelter you on that Rainy Day! The Acorn from which wealth grows is— Savings!"

It may be difficult for an outside observer to understand how the shellers and their families managed to survive, but it was no mystery to the president of the Southern Company. He explained to government officials that five cents per day was sufficient to support the Mexican pecan shellers because they ate a good many pecans while they worked. Since no limit was set on the amount they could eat, money incomes could be used for any additional wants that the shellers might wish to satisfy.

Another of the Company's officers spoke in a different vein. He claimed that if the shellers made 75 cents by three o'clock, they would go home, for they did not care to make much money. They were satisfied to earn little, and besides, they had a nice warm place to work and could visit with their friends while they earned.

In 1938 two government analysts probed into the details of the shellers' lives in an effort to understand how they actually lived. Five hundred and twelve Mexican pecan workers and their families were interviewed. Four out of every ten of them had been working "in pecans" for at least eight years. Median yearly income was $251 for a family of 4.6 persons; only 2 percent of the families had incomes of $900 or more. The mean weekly

income reported by individuals in pecan work was $2.73; for all jobs reported by the shellers' families, the mean income was $3.01 for a 51-hour week. The average family studied had two wage earners with a total income of 69 cents per day.

Seventy-seven percent of the pecan workers paid rental for their houses at an average rental of $4.49 per month. Over 5 percent of the "renters" paid no rent at all; they lived with relatives or in deserted or make-shift shacks. An additional 8 percent paid from one to two dollars rent per month.

Nine percent of the shellers had flush toilets; 39 percent had old-fashioned pit privies; evidently the others possessed no toilet facilities or shared communal privies with their neighbors. Only 25 percent illuminated their dwellings electrically; the rest used kerosene lamps.

Of the shellers interviewed 17 percent were born in San Antonio; 50 percent came to the city between 1911 and 1930. Hence most of them were long-standing residents of the community.

Out of the 512 pecan-shelling families, 450, or 88 percent, received some income from "sources other than employment" during 1938. The aid came from the Guadalupe Church food depot, the CIO soup kitchen or from the agency distributing federal surplus commodities.

There were 867 children of school ages in the families studied. Only 55 percent attended the full school term and only 62 percent attended school at all in 1938. Among the shellers who worked also as migrant laborers, 22 percent of the children eleven to thirteen years of age did not attend school; in the nonmigratory group the corresponding figure was 11 percent.

As primitive as their existence was, however, most of the workers succeeded in surviving the darkest days of the 1930s. The Southern Pecan Shelling Company also managed to weather the depression. In a two year period its net realization exceeded $500,000—not too disheartening a return for an enterprise with a very nominal capital outlay for plant and equipment. During the same years workers who shelled the pecans for the Company continued to be a public charge. WPA relief, church aid and private charity bridged the gap between their slender earnings and starvation.

At that time, when the national government through the NIRA was attempting to stabilize the pecan industry and to raise wages, two rival labor unions competed for the patronage of the shellers. One, *El Nogal*, a truly independent union, claimed a membership of nearly 4,000 between 1933 and 1936. It tried to extract dues of five cents a month from the members, but the secretary conceded that half of them did not pay. The other, the Pecan Shelling Workers' Union of San Antonio, was financially supported by the President of the Southern Company. It was practically a one man affair conducted by Magdaleno Rodriguez, who was characterized by an NRA representative as a "fugitive from justice, a citizen of Mexico and a labor agitator who betrays his workers."

Rodriguez, purporting to represent 9,500 workers, joined the shelling companies in protesting against the establishment of an NRA code for the pecan industry. He insisted that the proposed minimum wage of 15 cents per hour would double labor costs in San Antonio's shelleries and put the operators out of business. The code was never effective. Northern and southern operators disagreed on the proposed level of wages and also on the question of a North-South wage differential. Thus the status quo was maintained in the city's most infamous industry.

After the abortive attempt under the NRA to boost the earnings of the pecan shellers, little or no attention was directed to their lowly state by government representatives. Piece rates ranged from three to eight cents per pound and the living conditions of the shellers varied from miserable to increasingly miserable.

Both "independent" unions were singularly ineffective; a docile labor force became still more passive. But apparently their docility was only a surface manifestation, for on Feb. 1, 1938, at the peak of the season, thousands of shellers left their work tables in protest over a one cent per pound reduction in rates.

San Antonio has never witnessed an industrial dispute of like magnitude. Fully half of all of the pecan workers, scattered among 130 plants in the western portion of the city, "hit the pavement" (unpaved dirt roads would be more accurate in this case). More than 1,000 pickets were arrested during the course of the strike on charges ranging from "blocking the sidewalks" to "disturbing the peace" and "congregating in unlawful assemblies." Within the first two weeks tear gas was used at least a half-dozen times to disperse the throngs that milled about the shelleries.

From the outset the city officials, Mayor Quin, Police Commissioner Wright and Chief of Police Kilday, fought the pickets with all weapons, legal and otherwise. An obscure city ordinance of doubtful constitutionality was invoked to prevent the pickets from carrying signs:

> . . . it shall be unlawful for any person to carry . . . through any public street . . . any advertising sign, until said sign shall first have been submitted to the City Marshal, and a permit given for said carrying.

A "City Marshal" had to approve of all signs carried by pickets—but there was no "City Marshal" in San Antonio at that time. The office had been eliminated many years before.

The illegal sign, prima facie evidence of intent to picket in violation of police orders, read:

> This Shop
> UNFAIR
> Pecan Workers
> Local No. 172
> C.I.O.

This was the crime for which strikers were arrested in wholesale lots and fined $10 and costs—for carrying advertising signs without a city permit.

The Bexar County sheriff tendered a less unique interpretation of the law. He held that picketing was legal and announced that strikers would be unmolested as long as they created no disturbance. Thus peaceful picketing of the few shelling plants outside of the city limits continued.

Police Chief Owen Kilday's interference with the strike was not confined to the pickets themselves. When J. Austin Beasley, a CIO organizer arrived in San Antonio to take over the leadership of the strike, he was promptly jailed by Kilday's minions. The Chief asserted that Beasley was wanted by postal authorities in El Paso, though the San Antonio postmaster and FBI office denied requesting Beasley's arrest. He was released the next morning when Kilday concluded that the postal officials did not want Beasley after all. Harassment by the police continued, nonetheless.

Throughout the 37-day dispute Chief Kilday insisted that no strike existed. When Donald Henderson of the United Cannery, Agricultural, Packing and Allied Workers Union (Ucapawa) arrived in San Antonio, the Chief stated: "He is an intruder down here that hasn't 600 or 700 followers in the pecan industry. You call it a strike; I call it a disturbance out of Washington, D.C." Actually, when Henderson came to the city, he took the strike leadership away from fiery Emma Tenayuca, San Antonio's most renowned Communist, and turned it over to Beasley, whose political sympathies were unknown in San Antonio.

Ucapawa had entered the fray after the presumably spontaneous walkout by the remnants of the "independent" unions. Lacking trained leaders they welcomed turning over the conduct of the strike to the CIO. By the middle of February the CIO union stated that more than 6,000 of the 12,-000 shellers had applied for membership in the union and that about 3,000 paid dues during the strike period.

But Chief Kilday was adamant. He continued his strike suppression activities to prevent, as he put it, a "communistic revolution" among the pecan shellers. "I branded the leadership as communistic and I still think so." When a union attorney queried Kilday as to his authority to judge the leadership, the Chief pontifically exclaimed: "It is my duty to interfere with revolution, and communism is revolution."

Dr. Edwin Elliott, regional director of the National Labor Relations Board, also interposed objection to police actions. Again Kilday argued that "if the strike was won under its present leadership, 25,000 workers on the West Side would fall into the Communist Party." Dr. Elliott suggested that it was not Kilday's function to keep 25,000 people out of the Communist Party, but the Chief averred that he would make it his function.

The crusade proceeded. Based on his definition: "A Communist is a person who believes in living

in a community on the government and tearing down all religion," Kilday packed "his" jail in a manner remindful of the "Black Hole of Calcutta." At one time almost 250 men were confined in a jail section with a normal capacity of 60 persons.

Five prominent women of the community inspected the Kilday domain in an effort to determine precisely the conditions under which the pecan shellers were held. It was discovered that the shellers were not allowed the privilege of using the runway between the cells as were burglars, drunks and pickpockets. Eight to 18 men were kept night and day in cells built to accommodate four persons. Female prisoners were packed in like fashion. As many as 33 women were confined to a cell designed for six people. Prostitutes and pecan shellers resided in the same cell. And although 90 percent of the prostitutes suffered from infectious venereal diseases, all cellmates shared a common toilet and the lone drinking cup.

The inquisitorial methods of the police department were greeted with general approbation by the "respectable" element of San Antonio. The Mexican Chamber of Commerce, the Lulac (League of United Latin-American Citizens), and Archbishop Drossaerts refused to support the strike under Henderson's leadership. The Archbishop commended the police for their actions against "communistic influences," but somewhat paradoxically he also called upon employers to raise wages, because he said, low wages breed communism. At a lower level in the hierarchy Reverend John Lopez had a different solution for the problems of the pecan shellers. He urged them to return to the principles of the church, for the church was a friend of the working masses. Not to be outdone, the members of the San Antonio Ministers' Association, in their demand for a prompt settlement of the strike, insisted that "all Communistic, Fascist or any un-American elements not be parties of the settlement." They neglected to define their terms, however.

The newspapers also joined the chorus. The *San Antonio Express* editorialized:

To all appearances, outside influences were mainly responsible for the strike. Paid agents from the Committee for Industrial Organization, and Communist agitators before them, convinced the pecan shellers that they were being treated unfairly. . . .

Chief of Police Kilday—knowing the CIO —did well to take firm action to prevent serious disorders.

No one will begrudge the pecan shellers a better living wage, if that be possible without destroying the industry.

Government investigators were less sympathetic with Kilday's machinations. The State Industrial Commission, ordered by Governor Allred to conduct public hearings in San Antonio, reported unanimously that police interference with peaceful assembly and picketing was without justification. Dr. Elliott, NLRB observer at the hearings, concluded that "there has been a misuse of police authority in handling the strike." The Governor himself took exception to some of the acts charged against the police of San Antonio: refusing to permit strikers to congregate peacefully on vacant lots hired by them for that purpose; grabbing union buttons from the strikers and trampling them underfoot; and forcing people to become "scabs" under threat of deportation.

But the forces of "law and order" prevailed. Even the soup kitchens set up to provide free food for the strikers were ordered closed because they allegedly violated the city health ordinances.

The shellers finally sought to put "the law" to work for themselves; they prayed for a temporary restraining injunction to enjoin police interference with peaceful picketing. The plea was rejected by Judge S. G. Tayloe of the 45th District Court, who rendered his decision in a six-page opinion—immediately upon the termination of oral arguments! The magistrate explained to open-mouthed attorneys that he had awakened at four o'clock that morning to "write his views," with the mental reservation that the oral arguments might change his mind. They didn't. The judge's early morning stint was preserved for posterity if not for precedent.

The Tayloe opinion is a classic example of the legal mind at work and a faithful reproduction of the mind-set of San Antonio's "better element."

The judge reviewed the evidence and agreed that "the average wage of these workers is so small as only to provoke pity and compassion." Tayloe continued—his sympathies no longer in doubt:

The evidence shows that probably many hundreds of persons have been engaged in the strike and have on various occasions been arrested and the evidence for the plaintiffs shows that on three or four occasions excessive force was used by the arresting officers resulting in painful injuries to such persons. However, none have been sent to a hospital for treatment.

The Judge conceded that:

There can be no doubt about the right of the strikers to cease work and also to attempt peaceably to persuade other workers to cease their work and to also attempt to dissuade other persons from entering into the employ of their former employers.

With the undoubted right of the strikers to peacefully picket firmly established, the justice proceeded to explain to the pecan shellers why they did not possess this right after all.

The assembling in one place of a large number of pickets incensed by a spirit of resentment to grievances, whether real or imaginary, tends to produce disorder and become a menace to the public peace, as well as an interference with orderly traffic and use of the streets by others, and I cannot think that the Legislature has transcended its rightful powers or violated any natural, constitutional or other lawful rights in enacting or authorizing the enactment of such preventative measures.

In effect, then, the judge said that although there was no doubt about the right of the shellers to picket, there was also no doubt about their not having that right. And anyway, His Honor concluded, granting of the injunction would cause too great a strain on the minds of the police officers:

To grant an injunction of the nature sought would put every city peace officer in peril of contempt proceeding for violation of the injunction and would require such officer to so determine difficult and doubtful questions as to his authority in many cases.

Apparently it was far better, in all cases where the officer was undecided, to send the suspect to jail and ask questions later.

A dramatic sidelight to the case developed the night before judgment was pronounced. A "bomb" was found in the basement of the County Court House—directly below the room in which the case was being tried. Military experts insisted that the lethal object was a homemade incendiary. Newspaper headlines screamed that the "bomb" was potent and explosive. The "bomb" was "exploded" and proved to be a "dud" several days later—after the judge rendered his decision— when a Court House clerk, who worked in a vault in the basement, asserted that he had seen the object every day for nearly two years. It was being used as a weight to swing a basement door shut.

Two more weeks of unrest followed the court decision. Finally on March 9th, after 37 days of strife, the opposing forces consented to submit their cases to a board of arbitration. Local Union No. 172 of Ucapawa was recognized as agent for all employees in the industry for purposes of arbitration. The board, composed of Jack Horkheimer, owner of the Alamo Pecan Company, the Reverend Marcus Hogue of Austin, representing the union, and Mayor Tom Miller of Austin, neutral member, rendered its decision on April 13th.

In the words of the press: "The settlement was a compromise, leaning in favor of the operators." The wage scale of five cents per pound for pieces and six cents for halves, which was instituted immediately prior to the strike and which precipitated the walkout, was to be continued through May 31st. During the slack season, June 1st to November 1st, an increase of one-half cent per pound was ordered. The employers in turn agreed to recognize Local No. 172 as sole bargaining agent in any plant upon proof that it represented a majority of the employees in that plant. The latter, incidentally, was nothing more than the employers' legal obligation under terms of the National Labor Relations Act.

Contracts were duly consummated with all major operators. When the contracts expired, new agreements were negotiated with 13 operators who normally employed some 8,000 workers; even Southern Pecan Company fell into line. The new contracts, signed in the fall of 1938, provided for a closed shop, a check-off system, grievance machinery and piece rates of seven and eight cents per pound. The wage scale was to apply only if the industry could obtain an exemption from the minimum wage rates set by the Fair Labor Standards Act which had recently been passed by the federal Congress. Otherwise, of course, the statutory minimum of 25 cents per hour would prevail.

The union joined the Southern Pecan Shelling Company and the other operators in maintaining that pecan shelling involved the processing of an agricultural product; that San Antonio and all of Texas were within the area of production for pecans; hence exempt from the provisions of the minimum wage law.

When its plea was rejected, the Southern Company petitioned for a learning period of three months during which time 2,500 to 3,000 workers were to be trained to operate its newly installed machine-shelling equipment. In lieu of the statutory 25 cents per hour the Company offered to pay 15 cents per hour to the learners while they absorbed the intricacies of machine production. Southern claimed that the learning period was necessary because "there is no labor available, trained, skilled or experienced for machine operations. The entire processing operation must be learned." The request was not selfish but represented an effort to absorb the displaced workers. "The application is made to prevent the curtailment of employment opportunities," said the Company.

The Wage and Hour Division of the U.S. Department of Labor conducted public hearings in San Antonio before acting on the Company's application. Except for one other employer, representatives of the industry were unanimously opposed to the "learning period." E. M. Funston of St. Louis, Southern's largest competitor, testified that a beginner did not require more than a week to become an efficient sheller or picker. A Chicago operator, representing an association of 21 houses, agreed. A Texas sheller insisted that he could break in and develop a new worker in two days, while an agent of the manufacturer who installed the machines at the Southern Company argued that an experienced hand-picker would reach average proficiency the same day that he commenced work with the new machines.

Everett Looney of the Texas Industrial Commission and Mayor Tom Miller of Austin, both of whom had previous contact with the shelling industry in San Antonio, urged favorable consideration of the application. They believed that a training period for shellers was essential. The union's business agent concurred, although several pecan workers trained in the old hand-picking process testified that they thought they could become proficient at the new processes in from two to ten days' time.

The Wage and Hour Division employed an experienced management consultant and expert in manufacturing processes to examine the new mechanized operations. He noted that when a plant is mechanized, the cracking and shaking operations loosen a proportion of the meats and remove and draw off a portion of the shells, depositing the pieces and halves in separate receptacles. The meats so freed involved no picking labor costs. The expert also stated that careful attention to the economics of operation is heightened when wages are raised and that improved lighting would add to efficiency and productivity of workers. These, however, were management problems and a reflection of its efficiency. Furthermore, it would be easier to obtain efficient pickers, for the adoption of machines reduces the number of workers needed and leaves a wider choice in the selection of personnel.

The hearing officer concluded that the Southern Company's request should be denied. He decided that since there were between 7,000 and 10,000 experienced pickers in San Antonio, it would not be too difficult for the Company to recruit the 2,500 or 3,000 workers needed for machine operations. The evidence was conclusive that not more than one week was required to train a beginner. What Southern lacked was not experienced workers but rather the technical management personnel to supervise the operation of the new equipment. It was for the training of these officials that the 90-day training period was desired. If the training period were granted, "the worker would pay in substandard wages for a part of the cost of training management and mechanizing the factory. It would make pecan pickers take a pay cut to compensate management while it is putting itself through a learner period."

Several other firms sought exemption from the provisions of the Wage and Hour law. One operator from Weatherford, Texas, claimed that he sold pecans in the shell to townspeople and farmers and later bought back the picked meats. He denied violating either the spirit or the letter of the law, since he sold the pecans and bought the meats back again "at the market price." Thus the homeworkers earned a profit, not a wage.

Another employer claimed exemption from the law on the grounds that he rented seats in his plant to the workers. He sold them pecans in the morning and bought back the shelled nuts in the afternoon.

A third employer took a different approach.

The Mexicans don't want much money. . . . Compared to those shanties they live in, the pecan shelleries are fine. They are glad to have a warm place to sit in the winter. They can be warm while they're shelling pecans, they can talk to their friends while they're working, their kids come in after school and play because it's better than going home. If they get hungry they can eat pecans.

If they put the 25 cent minimum wage law over on us, all these Mexicans will be replaced by white girls. The Mexicans have no business here anyway. They flock into San Antonio with their kind, and they cause labor troubles or go on relief at the expense of the taxpayer.

Despite their contentions the larger operators at least were forced to pay their workers the legal minimum wage. By March of 1939 the Southern Pecan Shelling Company employed 1,800 shellers at the 25-cent minimum. Three months later the number of employees covered by the statutory minimum dropped to 800 and a like number labored in smaller plants which were evading the law.

Employment in the industry continued to decline. By 1941 Southern's labor force fell to 600 members. In 1950 the Southern Company, which at one time had employed 10,000 workers at the peak of the season, hired only 350 production employees during its busiest periods. Total output was somewhat less than it had been in 1938, but Southern was still one of the largest operators in the United States.

The effect of the minimum wage law on the pecan industry in San Antonio is readily apparent. The earnings of those who continued in employment doubled and in some cases tripled. However, approximately 5,000 of the less skillful shellers lost their jobs almost immediately and 5,000 more were let out within the next few years. They were either replaced by machines, as described above, or they left the industry along with the "straggler enterprises" which were forced out of existence by the increase in production costs. Two labor economists observed in this regard that in the entire United States the only major group of workers displaced as a direct result of the minimum wage law was in the pecan-shelling industry.

Thus, regardless of humanitarian or other justification for the statutory setting of minimum employment standards, thousands of individuals in San Antonio became "unemployable" as a result. It was a boon to the younger, more vigorous and productive of the pecan workers. One wage earner in a family could earn as much as two or three had done before. But the old and the feeble, most of whom were unable to speak English and many of whom were excluded from public assistance because of their alien citizenship, were removed from the employed labor force. Few employers found them "productive" enough to warrant paying them the legal minimum wage.

A small segment of these "displaced persons" was absorbed by the Finck Cigar Company, which ostensibly confines its activities to the State of Texas, hence is not "covered" by the federal law. Finck never lacks a labor supply. Even during periods of high levels of employment, several thousand persons, otherwise "unemployable," compete for the few hundred jobs available at 25 cents per hour.

Not only has employment in the pecan industry, at one time the most important employer of San Antonio labor, declined to a point of relative insignificance, but the industry's companion of ten years' standing—the union—has completely vanished. The Pecan Workers' Branch of Local Union 172, which was conceived during the 1938 dispute, disappeared from the scene in 1948. It passed without fanfare and with little public mourning. In fact so quietly did death come that many union leaders in San Antonio were unaware of the funeral.

Even while it lived, however, the union led a rather uneventful existence after its initial fight for recognition. In the early 1940s the union minimum wage was the statutory minimum of 40 cents per hour. Contractual relations were maintained with the major operators; all followed the actions of the acknowledged leader, the Southern Company. Minor gains were achieved and harmony reigned in the industry.

Illusions of prosperity were soon shattered by a combination of events that destroyed the pecan shellers' union in the city. The first blows were delivered over a three year period but the impact was not felt until the end of that period. The Food, Tobacco and Agricultural Workers International (CIO), successors to Ucapawa, had headquartered its regional director in San Antonio. Located there, he could keep a watchful eye on the pecan local. When the regional office was moved to another city, however, close supervision of the activities in San Antonio was no longer exercised. Leadership of the local gravitated into the hands of two English-speaking Mexican girls, wise to the ways of the business world. Their first devious act was to discontinue the regular business meetings of the union. Then, since the "check-off" was in effect, their sole duties consisted of calling for the union dues at the companys' offices. A membership of 600 to 800 was maintained and dues approximating $700 were collected monthly. But the International was informed that merely 25 or 30 members were active and per capita taxes were paid for that number only. In lieu of the balance

202

of the funds due the international, a doleful tale of declining membership was remitted to central headquarters. Literally thousands of dollars were pocketed by the local president and secretary of the union. When the fraud was discovered, the officers left for parts unknown and the local union was left with an empty treasury.

The union was not ready to succumb, however. Regional director Harry Koger was returned to San Antonio to help repair the damage to the union and to its treasury. At that point a second warning knell was sounded. H. B. Zachry, a construction contractor with twenty years' experience in resisting the demands of the building trades unions, purchased the Southern Pecan Shelling Company.

Zachry had never signed a union contract and vowed that he never would. Though many of his fellow-contractors operated union shops and 90 percent of the commercial construction in San Antonio was union work, Zachry remained outside of the fold. Pecan union leaders were understand-

ably disturbed. The largest plant in town had a change of ownership, and the new proprietor, as he informed this writer, was "inherently opposed to union contracts."

When the existing contract with the pecan union ran out in 1946, the unexpected happened. Not only did Zachry agree to continue contractual relations, but he also conceded a five cent per hour raise to Koger, the union negotiator. Koger was jubilant, since this was the first union contract that Zachry had ever signed. It was also his last. The following year Zachry refused to renew the agreement. The union was in no position to protest. A strike threat was an empty weapon. A loosely knit organization whose members were not accustomed to attending union meetings and were not indoctrinated with union principles could not survive in a hostile atmosphere. Since the issue was not one of wages, the pecan shellers were content to let the union expire. And when it expired, so also did the anomolous epoch of pecan shelling in San Antonio.

OCTAVIO PAZ

Octavio Paz (philosopher, poet, and present ambassador from Mexico to India) won international acclaim with his superb book THE LABYRINTH OF SOLITUDE (1950). *This book both probes and defines the culture and character of Mexico. In the first chapter of the book Professor Paz draws a distinction between the character of the Mexican American, shaped by his North American environment, and his kinsmen to the South. The selection below is from that chapter and describes Paz's view of the* Pachuco *phenomenon.*

Reprinted by permission of Grove Press, Inc. Translated by Lysander Kemp. Copyright © 1961 by Grove Press, Inc.

The Pachuco And Other Extremes

When I arrived in the United States I lived for a while in Los Angeles, a city inhabited by over a million persons of Mexican origin. At first sight, the visitor is surprised not only by the purity of the sky and the ugliness of the dispersed and ostentatious buildings, but also by the city's vaguely Mexican atmosphere, which cannot be captured in words or concepts. This Mexicanism—delight in decorations, carelessness and pomp, negligence, passion and reserve—floats in the air. I say "floats" because it never mixes or unites with the other world, the North American world based on precision and efficiency. It floats, without offering any opposition; it hovers, blown here and there by the wind, sometimes breaking up like a cloud, sometimes standing erect like a rising skyrocket. It creeps, it wrinkles, it expands and contracts; it sleeps or dreams; it is ragged but beautiful. It floats, never quite existing, never quite vanishing.

Something of the same sort characterizes the Mexicans you see in the streets. They have lived in the city for many years, wearing the same clothes and speaking the same language as the other inhabitants, and they feel ashamed of their origin;

203

yet no one would mistake them for authentic North Americans. I refuse to believe that physical features are as important as is commonly thought. What distinguishes them, I think, is their furtive, restless air: they act like persons who are wearing disguises, who are afraid of a stranger's look because it could strip them and leave them stark naked. When you talk with them, you observe that their sensibilities are like a pendulum, but a pendulum that has lost its reason and swings violently and erratically back and forth. This spiritual condition, or lack of a spirit, has given birth to a type known as the *pachuco.* The *pachucos* are youths, for the most part of Mexican origin, who form gangs in Southern cities; they can be identified by their language and behavior as well as by the clothing they affect. They are instinctive rebels, and North American racism has vented its wrath on them more than once. But the *pachucos* do not attempt to vindicate their race or the nationality of their forebears. Their attitude reveals an obstinate, almost fanatical will-to-be, but this will affirms nothing specific except their determination—it is an ambiguous one, as we will see—not to be like those around them. The *pachuco* does not want to become a Mexican again; at the same time he does not want to blend into the life of North America. His whole being is sheer negative impulse, a tangle of contradictions, an enigma. Even his very name is enigmatic: *pachuco,* a word of uncertain derivation, saying nothing and saying everything. It is a strange word with no definite meaning; or, to be more exact, it is charged like all popular creations with a diversity of meanings. Whether we like it or not, these persons are Mexicans, are one of the extremes at which the Mexican can arrive.

Since the *pachuco* cannot adapt himself to a civilization which, for its part, rejects him, he finds no answer to the hostility surrounding him except this angry affirmation of his personality. Other groups react differently. The Negroes, for example, oppressed by racial intolerance, try to "pass" as whites and thus enter society. They want to be like other people. The Mexicans have suffered a less violent rejection, but instead of attempting a problematical adjustment to society, the *pachuco* actually flaunts his differences. The purpose of his grotesque dandyism and anarchic behavior is not so much to point out the injustice and incapacity of a society that has failed to assimilate him as it is to demonstrate his personal will to remain different.

It is not important to examine the causes of this conflict, and even less so to ask whether or not it has a solution. There are minorities in many parts of the world who do not enjoy the same opportunities as the rest of the population. The important thing is this stubborn desire to be different, this anguished tension with which the lone Mexican—an orphan lacking both protectors and positive values—displays his differences. The *pachuco* has lost his whole inheritance: language, religion, customs, beliefs. He is left with only a body and a soul with which to confront the elements, defenseless against the stares of everyone. His disguise is a protection, but it also differentiates and isolates him: it both hides him and points him out.

His deliberately aesthetic clothing, whose significance is too obvious to require discussion, should not be mistaken for the outfit of a special group or sect. *Pachuquismo* is an open society, and this in a country full of cults and tribal costumes, all intended to satisfy the middle-class North American's desire to share in something more vital and solid than the abstract morality of the "American Way of Life." The clothing of the *pachuco* is not a uniform or a ritual attire. It is simply a fashion, and like all fashions it is based on novelty—the mother of death, as Leopardi said—and imitation.

Its novelty consists in its exaggeration. The *pachuco* carries fashion to its ultimate consequences and turns it into something aesthetic. One of the principles that rules in North American fashions is that clothing must be comfortable, and the *pachuco,* by changing ordinary apparel into art, makes it "impractical." Hence it negates the very principles of the model that inspired it. Hence its aggressiveness.

This rebelliousness is only an empty gesture, because it is an exaggeration of the models against which he is trying to rebel, rather than a return to the dress of his forebears or the creation of a new style of his own. Eccentrics usually emphasize their decision to break away from society—either to form new and more tightly closed groups or to assert their individuality—through their way of dressing. In the case of the *pachuco* there is an obvious ambiguity: his clothing spotlights and isolates him, but at the same time it pays homage to the society he is attempting to deny.

This duality is also expressed in another, perhaps profounder way: the *pachuco* is an impassive and sinister clown whose purpose is to cause terror instead of laughter. His sadistic attitude is allied with a desire for self-abasement which in my opinion constitutes the very foundation of his character: he knows that it is dangerous to stand out and that his behavior irritates society, but nevertheless he seeks and attracts persecution and scandal. It is the only way he can establish a more vital relationship with the society he is antagonizing. As a victim, he can occupy a place in the world that previously had ignored him; as a delinquent, he can become one of its wicked heroes.

I believe that the North American's irritation results from his seeing the *pachuco* as a mythological figure and therefore, in effect, a danger. His dangerousness lies in his singularity. Everyone agrees in finding something hybrid about him, something disturbing and fascinating. He is surrounded by an aura of ambivalent notions: his singularity seems to be nourished by powers that are alternately evil and beneficent. Some people credit him with unusual erotic prowess; others consider him perverted but still aggressive. He is a symbol of love and joy or of horror and loathing, an embodiment of liberty, of disorder, of the forbidden. He is someone who ought to be destroyed. He is also someone with whom any contact must be made in secret, in the darkness.

The *pachuco* is impassive and contemptuous, allowing all these contradictory impressions to accumulate around him until finally, with a certain painful satisfaction, he sees them explode into a tavern fight or a raid by the police or a riot. And then, in suffering persecution, he becomes his true self, his supremely naked self, as a pariah, a man who belongs nowhere. The circle that began with provocation has completed itself and he is ready now for redemption, for his entrance into the society that rejected him. He has been its sin and its

scandal, but now that he is a victim it recognizes him at last for what he really is: its product, its son. At last he has found new parents.

The *pachuco* tries to enter North American society in secret and daring ways, but he impedes his own efforts. Having been cut off from his traditional culture, he asserts himself for a moment as a solitary and challenging figure. He denies both the society from which he originated and that of North America. When he thrusts himself outward, it is not to unite with what surrounds him but rather to defy it. This is a suicidal gesture, because the *pachuco* does not affirm or defend anything except his exasperated will-not-to-be. He is not divulging his most intimate feelings: he is revealing an ulcer, exhibiting a wound. A wound that is also a grotesque, capricious, barbaric adornment. A wound that laughs at itself and decks itself out for the hunt. The *pachuco* is the prey of society, but instead of hiding he adorns himself to attract the hunter's attention. Persecution redeems him and breaks his solitude: his salvation depends on his becoming part of the very society he appears to deny. Solitude and sin, communion and health become synonymous terms.

If this is what happens to persons who have long since left their homeland, who can hardly speak the language of their forebears, and whose secret roots, those that connect a man with his culture, have almost withered away, what is there to say about the rest of us when we visit the United States? Our reaction is not so unhealthy, but after our first dazzled impressions of that country's grandeur, we all instinctively assume a critical attitude. I remember that when I commented to a Mexican friend on the loveliness of Berkeley, she said: "Yes, it's very lovely, but I don't belong here. Even the birds speak English. How can I enjoy a flower if I don't know its right name, its English name, the name that has fused with its colors and petals, the name that's the same thing as the flower? If I say *bugambilia* to you, you think of the bougainvillaea vines you've seen in your own village, with their purple, liturgical flowers, climbing around an ash tree or hanging from a wall in the afternoon sunlight. They're a part of your being, your culture. They're what you remember long after you've seemed to forget them. It's very lovely here, but it isn't mine, because whatever saying it for me . . . or to me, either."

Yes, we withdraw into ourselves, we deepen and aggravate our awareness of everything that separates or isolates or differentiates us. And we increase our solitude by refusing to seek out our compatriots, perhaps because we fear we will see ourselves in them, perhaps because of a painful, defensive unwillingness to share our intimate feelings. The Mexican succumbs very easily to sentimental effusions, and therefore he shuns them. We live closed up within ourselves, like those taciturn adolescents—I will add in passing that I hardly met any of the sort among North American youths—who are custodians of a secret that they guard behind scowling expressions, but that only waits for the opportune moment in which to reveal itself.

I am not going to expand my description of these feelings or discuss the states of depression or frenzy (or often both) that accompany them. They are all apt to lead to unexpected explosions, which destroy a precarious equilibrium based on the imposition of forms that oppress or mutilate us. Our sense of inferiority—real or imagined—might be explained at least partly by the reserve with which the Mexican faces other people and the unpredictable violence with which his repressed emotions break through his mask of impassivity. But his solitude is vaster and profounder than his sense of inferiority. It is impossible to equate these two attitudes: when you sense that you are alone, it does not mean that you feel inferior, but rather that you feel you are different. Also, a sense of inferiority may sometimes be an illusion, but solitude is a hard fact. We are truly different. And we are truly alone.

This is not the moment to analyze our profound sense of solitude, which alternately affirms and denies itself in melancholy and rejoicing, silence and sheer noise, gratuitous crimes and religious fervor. Man is alone everywhere.

George I. Sánchez

George I. Sánchez (see p. 86) in an essay in the now defunct journal COMMON GROUND *(Autumn 1943) gave perhaps the best contemporary account of the discrimination and background of the wartime "Zoot Suit Riots."*
By permission of the author and COMMON GROUND.
With the permission of the American Council for Nationalities Service.

Pachucos In The Making

Widespread attention has been drawn to the Los Angeles, California, gangs of zoot-suited, socially maladjusted, "Mexican" youngsters known as "pachucos." Mixed with the intelligent efforts and genuine concern of some public officials and laymen over the disgraceful situation which has been allowed to develop in the Los Angeles area, there is also much sanctimonious "locking of barn doors after the horses have been stolen" sort of expression and action by those whose past lack of interest and whose official negligence bred the juvenile delinquency which now plagues that city's officialdom, hinders the program of the armed forces, and embarrasses the United States before Latin America and the world.

The seed for the pachucos was sown a decade or more ago by unintelligent educational measures, by discriminatory social and economic practices, by provincial smugness and self-assigned "racial" superiority. Today we reap the whirlwind in youth whose greatest crime was to be born into an environment which, through various kinds and degrees of social ostracism and prejudicial economic subjugation, made them a caste apart, fair prey to the cancer of gangsterism. The crimes of these youths should be appropriately punished, yes. But what of the society which is an accessory before and after the fact?

Almost ten years ago, I raised this issue in an article in the Journal of Applied Psychology: "The frequent prostitution of democratic ideals to the cause of expediency, politics, vested interests, ignorance, class and 'race' prejudice, and to indifference and inefficiency is a sad commentary on the

207

intelligence and justice of a society that makes claims to those very progressive democratic ideals. The dual system of education presented in 'Mexican' and 'white' schools, the family system of contract labor, social and economic discrimination, educational negligence on the part of local and state authorities, 'homogeneous grouping' to mask professional inefficiency—all point to the need for greater insight into a problem which is inherent in a 'melting pot' society. The progress of our country is dependent upon the most efficient utilization of the heterogeneous masses which constitute its population—the degree to which the 2,000,000 or more Spanish-speaking people, and their increment, are permitted to develop is the extent to which the nation should expect returns from that section of its public."

When the pachuco "crime wave" broke last year, I communicated with the Office of War Information: "I understand that a grand jury is looking into the 'Mexican' problem in Los Angeles and that there seems to be considerable misunderstanding as to the causes of the gang activities of Mexican youth in that area. I hear also that much ado is being made about 'Aztec forebears,' 'blood lust,' and similar claptrap in interpreting the behavior of these citizens. It would be indeed unfortunate if this grand jury investigation were to go off on a tangent, witchhunting in anthropological antecedents for causes which, in reality, lie right under the noses of the public service agencies in Los Angeles County."

Subsequent developments have borne out the fears implied above. And still, in June of this year, the Los Angeles City Council could think of no better answer to the deep-rooted negligence of public service agencies than to deliberate over an ordinance outlawing zoot suits! The segregatory attitudes and practices, and the vicious economic exploitation directed against the "Mexican" in California in the past—not zoot suits—are responsible for the pachucos of today.

The pseudo-science of the Los Angeles official who is quoted as reporting to the Grand Jury on the Sleepy Lagoon murder case that "Mexican" youths are motivated to crime by certain biological or "racial" characteristics would be laughable if it were not so tragic, so dangerous, and, worse still, so typical of biased attitudes and misguided thinking which are reflected in the practices not only of California communities but also elsewhere in this country.

The genesis of *pachuquismo* is an open book to those who care to look into the situations facing Spanish-speaking people in many parts of the Southwest. Arizona, Colorado, Texas, and, to a much lesser degree, even New Mexico have conditions analogous to those which have nurtured the California riots. In some communities in each of these states, "Mexican" is a term of opprobrium applied to anyone with a Spanish name—citizen and alien alike, of mestizo blood or of "pure white" Spanish colonial antecedents. In many places these people are denied service in restaurants, barber shops, and stores. Public parks and swimming pools, some of which were built by federal funds, are often closed to them. Some churches, court houses, and public hospitals have been known to segregate them from "whites." Separate, and usually shockingly inferior, segregated "Mexican" schools have been set up for their children. Discriminatory employment practices and wage scales, even in war industries (the President's Executive Order 8802 and his Committee on Fair Employment Practice to the contrary notwithstanding), are still used to "keep the 'Mexican' in his place."

An affidavit from California before me says that when a Spanish-name citizen of this country, in response to a public advertisement by a national railroad company, applied for a job, "he was told by the foreman, 'I have orders from the general foreman not to hire Mexican help.' On inquiry as to why Mexicans were not being employed, this foreman states as follows: that the Mexicans got drunk on the job, did not keep up with their work, caused trouble, and that the shops were open only to white labor; that if Mexicans wanted to work with the company they could work on the section gangs." Apparently drunkenness, laziness, etc. were tolerated on the section gangs!

A Texas friend says that the Mexicans in her town had been ordered out of the parks and that Mexicans were mistreated there. Another report tells of a group of school children of Mexican and Latin American origin who went to a neighboring town "to spend the day and to attend a celebration. . . . They decided to go swimming in a public swimming pool and they were denied entrance thereto because they were of Latin American and Mexican origin, although they permitted two Japanese children . . . to enter said swimming pool." The Chancellor of a Mexican Consulate "was expelled with his wife and children from the —— swimming pool in the town of ——, Texas; the only reason given for the expulsion was that they were Mexicans." In another town "the teacher took the Latin American school children to a park . . . she was told by the keeper of the park to get out as this park was not for the use of the Mexicans."

In the course of a hike, a Scoutmaster and his troop of Boy Scouts, all in uniform, were ordered out of a public park where they had stopped to rest, because they were "Mexicans." A group of American citizens of Mexican descent, on the verge of joining the Army, "were denied entrance to the swimming pools because they were 'Latin Americans'." Soldiers in the uniform of the United States Army have been refused service in public places because they were "Mexicans," several of them having been ejected when they insisted on buying a cup of coffee, a hamburger, or a bottle of beer.

A newspaper from a West Texas city states: "City Police Chief —— today issued a request that all persons except negroes [sic] and Latin Americans stay out of the swimming hole at the —— Street crossing on the —— (river). 'This portion of the river was fixed by the city especially as a swimming pool for negroes [sic] and Latin Americans. Many other people, not knowing this, are using it also. We'd appreciate their quitting the pool and leaving it to the persons for whom it was planned,' Chief —— said."

A pathetic letter from a descendant of the colonial settlers of Texas states: "Do you think there is any hope of getting our problems solved? We wish you would do something to help us. We are being mistreated here every time we turn around. We are not allowed in cafes, movies, restaurants. Even Latin Americans in United States Army uniforms are sometimes told they can't see a show because the Mexican side is full. In the public schools our children are segregated. They are given only half a day's school because of the teacher shortage, while the others have full-time classes. There is no teacher shortage for them. Please tell us if there is anything to do about it. We wrote a letter to the Office of Civilian Defense, Washington, D.C. But we haven't heard from them. We don't know if that is the right place to write to or not."

A Mexican Consul reports that "there were signs posted by the —— County authorities as follows: 'For Colored and Mexicans,' and in the Church named the —— was this sign: 'For Whites' and another 'For Mexicans.' Mexicans are not permitted to attend this church on Sundays." Not only in civic affairs and in Christian worship but even after death, the "Mexican" is segregated. It is reported: "in many cemeteries, whether owned by county authorities, by private individuals or corporations, or by religious organization . . . the bodies of 'Mexicans' are denied the right to burial. . . ." In those cemeteries where such bodies are recieved "they are assigned a separate plot of land, far enough from the plot destined for the so-called 'whites' so as to be sure that the bodies of the so-called 'whites' will not be contaminated by the presence of the bodies of the 'Mexicans'."

A traveler on a transcontinental bus stated that "the bus stopped at —— (town) so that the passengers could eat at a restaurant known as Hotel ——. He observed that everyone else was served except him. When he inquired why he was not waited on, he was advised that Mexicans were not served at said place." Another report points out "that [high school] seniors graduating at —— (town) were segregated at a banquet given them. The tables for the Latin Americans were placed in a separate locality from that reserved for the Anglo Americans."

A newspaper story tells of the building of a new theater in a west Texas City: "Today the cost already had moved past the $40,000 mark and the seating capacity had been raised to 1,100 including 250 on the balcony where the colored and Latin American movie fans will be accommodated." The Mexican colony from the city of —— reports that "the toilets in the courthouse bear a sign which reads 'For Whites—Mexicans Keep Out'."

In another town, on the Fourth of July, "several hundred citizens of the United States of Mexican extraction were told over the loud speaker that they should go home because the dance being held in a public square was for white people only. Among the persons ejected were many wearing United States soldier's uniforms." At still another place, again on the Fourth of July, at an American Legion dance, Spanish-name veterans of World War I were asked to leave because the dance was for "whites" only.

The constitution and by-laws of the so-called "White Man's Union" of a certain county in Texas provide that only "white" citizens shall be eligible for membership. These regulations state: "The term White Citizen, as provided herein, shall not include any Mexican, who is not of full Spanish blood. Only persons who are white citizens . . . shall be permitted to vote at any primary or other election held by this association." These regulations are also enforced in the Democratic primaries, the election machinery of the primaries being in the control of this "White Man's Union." Who, indeed, could prove that he is of "full Spanish blood," assuming, for argument's sake, that a mestizo or Indian, otherwise qualified, can be thus disfranchised! It should be noted that the primary election is the election in such overwhelmingly Democratic counties as this.

Many communities provide a separate school for children of Spanish names. These "Mexican schools," are established ostensibly for "pedagogical reasons," thinly veiled excuses which do not conform with either the science of education or the facts in the case. Judging from current practice, these pseudo-pedagogical reasons call for short school terms, ramshackle school buildings, poorly paid and untrained teachers, and all varieties of prejudicial discrimination. The "language handicap" reason, so glibly advanced as the chief pedagogical excuse for the segregation of these school children, is extended to apply to all Spanish-name youngsters regardless of the fact that some of them know more English and more about other school subjects than the children from whom they are segregated. In addition some of these Spanish-name children know no Spanish whatsoever, coming from homes where only English has been spoken for two generations or more.

The community mores suggested in the above illustrations do not reflect simply the attitudes of untutored masses. Equally glaring, un-American practices are carried on by those of privileged social and economic status. The basic real estate contracts in many subdivisions in several Texas cities provide that "neither they nor their heirs, executors, administrators or assigns, shall sell or lease any portion of said property to any person of Negro blood, or Mexicans." Another far too common provision in deeds stipulates that: "No lot or part of lot in said addition at any time may be occupied by or used by any person except those of the Caucasian race. . . . This provision shall be so construed as excluding from occupancy in said subdivision Mexicans, Latin Americans, Negroes, and people of the yellow race." Wealthy, highly educated, prominent Latin Americans, some citizens of the United States and some citizens of prestige of Mexico and of other Latin American countries, have been refused the right to purchase or occupy property in those subdivisions. A Vice Consul of Mexico was requested to move out of a house in a city in Texas, "on the ground that, in that subdivision, properties could not be sold or rented to 'Mexicans'." A letter from a Mexican Consul to the mayor of a large city, referring to another such "incident," states: "It is with much regret that I am constrained to bring to your attention a matter that has caused a great deal of ill will and disappointment to the Mexican colony in —— by reason of the fact that one of the most outstanding Mexican families in —— was refused the right to acquire a place in which to live at —— [street address] in —— [subdivision] within the limits of the city of ——, on the sole ground that the purchaser was a Mexican.

"I need not call to your attention the position which Mr. —— owner of the —— Company holds in this community. I can point out no other person who stands higher in the estimation of both the Mexican and the American People, who is a prominent civic leader and a successful business man. Certainly, a great injustice has been done in thus humiliating him and his family, which is a matter that reflects the attitude of many people residing in several sections of —— [the city], where similar obnoxious clauses are included in the deeds."

These acts by otherwise intelligent people cannot be excused simply on the basis that they are motivated by commercial considerations. The same kind of acts are committed by public officials. During the second registration for the Selective Service in a large city in Texas, the officer in charge gave a story to the press in which he announced that arrangements had been made to register Negroes, Latin Americans, and "whites" in separate rooms of the County Courthouse. Fortunately, vigorous protest brought about a satisfactory correction. The Selective Service procedure in certain places has forced American citizens of Spanish name to be classified as "Mexican" in the questionnaire which states: "3. My race is — White; —Negro; —Oriental; —Indian —Filipino. Other (Specify) —." An attorney in a border city writes: "It appears that the persons in charge of filling out the blanks at the reception center are guided only by the sound of the name. If the name is Spanish, then they classify the selectee as 'Mexican'; if it is 'American' then the classification is, of course, 'White.' One of the latest cases is that of a son of ——. His name is —— [Spanish]; the mother is an Anglo American. . . . He was classified 'Mexican' because of the name ——; yet, in the same group, another young boy, with an American or English name was classified 'White' even though he has Mexican and perhaps even Negro blood." [The mother in the latter case is "Mexican" and the father "Anglo." It is to be noted that, through the intervention of national offices, orders have recently gone out calling for the cessation of such classification.

Applicants for positions listed by the United States Employment Service are frequently told their applications cannot be received because they are "Mexican" and would not be eligible. Insult is added to injury when, after the employers have subjected the "Mexican" to discriminatory wage scales, the other employees bring about their segregation. A report on oil workers points out that two refineries, "notwithstanding the fact that they have Government war contracts, pay from 10 to 13 cents an hour less to the 'Mexican' workers than the salary paid to Anglo-Saxon workers for the same kind of work. They keep separate toilet-rooms, separate drinking water faucets, and separate bathrooms for the 'Mexicans'. . . ."

One of my assistants reports the situation in a border community, which "has contributed to the limit in manpower. Many of its young men enlisted in various branches of the service before they were drafted. As a result, Latin American boys from —— [town] are at present all over the world. . . . A short time ago, a group of young Latin American girls . . . (all of them having brothers and sweethearts in the service) called Mr. ——, manager of the USO, by phone, and asked how they went about becoming USO hostesses." They were told just to come down and register, but when the spokesman said "there was a group of twelve Latin American girls who wished to offer their services, he said 'Oh, wait a minute. In that case you will have to see Father —— (priest at —— Church) who is organizing a Latin American USO.' The girls didn't like the sound of it, but they contacted the priest who told them he knew nothing about USO activities, and confirmed their belief that a Latin American USO, if established, would only be another form of segregation to which they should not subscribe."

Upon investigating the above matter, we were informed, in effect, that the local USO itself had no jurisdiction in the matter since it was entirely up to the Girls Service Organization as to whom they would admit for membership. My assistant states: "It is understandable that the sisters and sweethearts of these boys should feel not only a keen disappointment but a deep humiliation at what is to them a refusal of the opportunity to do their rightful part, as American citizens, in furthering the war effort to which their loved ones are daily dedicating their lives."

Two years ago six friends wrote me as follows: "The undersigned write you so that, if you find it possible, you will make for us before the appropriate department an energetic protest for the humiliating treatment which we received. It happens that we were named by the Selective Service committee to undergo the examination for soldiers, and an employee of the draft board took us to eat at — Cafe. We were refused service solely because we were of Mexican descent. After that we were taken to Hotel —— where we were served in an empty room. . . . As you will see this is not in accord with reason and justice and we fear that this is probably the work of fifth columnists who handicap the efforts of the government."

On July 12, 1941, before the pachuco question had become a matter of general interest, a Spanish American from California summarized the situation this way: "The so-called 'Mexican Problem' is not in fact a Mexican problem. It is a problem foisted by American mercenary interests upon the American people. It is an American problem made in the U.S.A." He was protesting the movement then on foot to permit the indiscriminate and wholesale importation of laborers from Mexico. In response to such protests steps were taken by the governments of the United States and of Mexico to protect both the imported alien and the residents of this area from the evils inherent in such letting down of the bars, evils of which ample evidence was furnished during World War I under similar circumstances. Today, however, the pressure of vested interests is finding loopholes in that enlightened policy and, again, the bars are rapidly being let down.

Si Casady of McAllen, Texas, in an editorial in the Valley Evening Monitor hits the nail on the head when he says: ". . . there is a type of individual who does not understand and appreciate the very real dangers inherent in racial discrimination. This type of individual does not understand that his own right to enjoy life, his own liberty, the very existence of this nation and all the other free nations of the world depend utterly and completely on the fundamental principle that no man, because of race, has any right to put his foot upon the neck of any other man. The racial discrimination problem has been kept daintily out of sight for so long in the [Rio Grande] Valley that it cannot now be solved overnight. Instead of dragging it out into the sunlight where it could be left lying until all the nauseous fumes of hypocrisy and bigotry had dissipated, we have shoved the problem down into the cellar like an idiot child, hoping the neighbors would not notice its existence."

In two illuminating articles, Carey McWilliams, earlier in this magazine, has made a brilliant and forceful presentation of the "Mexican problem." Before him, Dr. Paul S. Taylor of the University of California and Dr. H. T. Manuel of the University of Texas had also clearly pointed out the evils inherent in the mistreatment of Spanish-speaking people. This writer and other students of the problem have, over the past twenty years, repeatedly pointed out the dangers and have continuously insisted on adequate remedial measures. Neglect on the part of public service agencies lies at the root of the disturbances which we observe today. Those disturbances, serious as they are, simply presage even worse effects in the future unless adequate remedial measures are undertaken immediately.

What would be the nature of these remedial measures? The malady suggests the cure. Where negative and un-American practices now prevail, undertake positive, equitable, American action. This is not as difficult as it appears at first blush. While unfavorable popular attitudes and community customs are difficult to correct and though there are many elusive factors back of the prejudicial situations I have referred to, the people involved are susceptible to sound guidance and leadership—particularly to that of their duly selected officials and of well-established civic organizations. Furthermore, I am sure that much of the mistreatment of Spanish-speaking people would not take place were it not for the fact that the common people take their cue from the discriminatory acts (of commission or omission) of their public officials.

The establishment of segregated schools for "Mexicans" lays the foundation for most of the prejudice and discrimination. Local and state educational authorities have the power to institute satisfactory remedies. There is no legal requirement in any state calling for the organization of such schools. There are all sorts of legal mandates to the contrary. Forthright action by school authorities could remove these blots on American education in a very brief period of time. As an illustration of how this may be done in Texas, consider this provision adopted by the State Legislature in 1943: "The State Board of Education with the approval of the State Superintendent of Public Instruction shall have the authority to withhold the per capita apportionment to any school district at any time that a discrimination between groups of white scholastics exists."

The exclusion of "Mexicans" from public places,

solely on the basis of "race" (legally, they are "white"), can be stopped through the enforcement of such provisions as that embodied in the legislative Concurrent Resolution adopted in Texas a few months ago: "1. All persons of the Caucasian Race within the jurisdiction of this State are entitled to the full and equal accommodations, advantages, facilities, and privileges of all public places of business or amusement, subject only to the conditions and limitations established by law, and rules and regulations applicable alike to all persons of the Caucasian Race. 2. Whoever denies to any person the full advantages, facilities, and privileges enumerated in the preceding paragraph or who aids or incites such denial or whoever makes any discrimination, distinction, or restriction except for good cause applicable alike to all persons if the Caucasian Race, respecting accommodations, advantages, facilities, and privileges of all public places of business, or whoever aids or incites such discrimination, distinction, or restriction shall be considered as violating the good neighbor policy of our State." Vigorous action by public officials in enforcing this mandate in Texas, and similar legal provisions in other states, would go far in solving this fundamental phase of the whole "Mexican" question.

These illustrations of specific remedial action could be multiplied by reference to legal mandates as to suffrage, jury service, practices in war industries, etc. Public officials—local, state, and federal—have in their hands the power to correct the discriminatory practices which lie at the root of prejudicial attitudes and actions on the part of some sectors of the public. I have the fullest confidence that the great majority of Americans would applaud the enforcement of those legal mandates.

The Spanish-speaking people of the United States need to be incorporated into, and made fully participating members of, the American way of life. The "Mexican" needs education, he needs vocational training and placement in American industry on an American basis, he needs active encouragement to participate in civic affairs and to discharge his civic obligations, and he needs constant protection by public officials from the pitfalls into which his cultural differences may lead him or into which he may be forced by unthinking sectors of the public.

The record, briefly reported here, of oppressive self-righteousness and the "incidents" to which it has led is an appalling one. Even more frightening are the prospects of a future when such cheaply hatched social attitudes and practices come home to roost as the full-fledged and expensive spectres of crime, disease, ignorance, internal discord, and international enmity. One generation's sins of "racial" oppression on the part of a majority sector of the population are indeed visited upon its progeny, many fold. The fruits of "racial" discrimination are boomerangs—seeds which breed, in the majority group, fascism and tolerance of the concentration camp for "inferior races." The vicious practices referred to above do harm to the "Mexican," yes. However, infinitely more harm is done to the group which perpetrates or tolerates the practices. The pachuco is a symbol not of the guilt of an oppressed "Mexican" minority but of a cancerous growth within the majority group which is gnawing at the vitals of democracy and the American way of life. The pachuco and his feminine counterpart, the *cholitsa*, are spawn of a neglectful society—not the products of an humble minority people who are defenseless before their enforced humiliation.

George I. Sánchez

George I. Sánchez (see p. 86) in this second selection from FORGOTTEN PEOPLE *shows that even though the Hispano fared better in New Mexico than in other Southwestern states, "better" is truly a relative term. By permission of the author.*

The New Mexican Today

The descendants of the Spanish colonists of New Mexico are to be found in every walk of life. The conditions arising out of the adjustments which resulted from the development of the region within the last ninety years have had varying effects upon the populace. Some managed to retain their land holdings and are in comfortable circumstances as farmers and as ranchers. Some have taken advantage of new economic opportunities and have proven successful in business. A few have seized upon educational advantages and are to be found in the professions and in government. Many make their living as clerks and as skilled workers.

While due recognition must be made of the successful manner in which some members of the group have adapted themselves to the new environment, it is to be observed that the great masses of the people constitute a severely handicapped social and economic minority. Generally speaking, their status is one of privation and want, of cultural inadequacy and of bewilderment. Neglected for more than two hundred years as Spanish colonials and Mexicans, their cultural situation was not greatly improved by the territorial regime. In fact, the little improvement that took place through the limited educational efforts that were made in their behalf was more than offset by the social and economic decline that resulted from the influx of new people and of a new economic order.

The evidence of decline and deterioration is best observed in situations faced by those rural sections of the state where New Mexicans represent a substantial sector of the population, though such evidence is not lacking in the towns and cities. Almost a hundred years after becoming American citizens, a broad gap still separates them from the culture which surrounds them. In

214

lieu of adequate instruction, they have clung to their language, their customs, their agricultural practices. Though no fault can be found with a society because it seeks to perpetuate worthy elements of its culture, it is to be regretted that, in this instance, the process has not been accompanied by suitable adaptations.

The New Mexican often carries on inferior and obsolete practices and beliefs because he has been permitted, and forced, to remain in isolation. Of necessity, he has persisted in a traditional way of life that is below current standards. His language has suffered by disuse, yet he has had little chance to learn to use English effectively. His social status reflects his economic insufficiency. His lack of education handicaps him in the exercise of his political power. That same lack makes him a public charge once he has lost his land, his traditional source of livelihood. Midst the wreckage of his economy and his culture, and unprepared for the new order of things, he is pathetic in his helplessness—a stranger in his own home.

The task of portraying the present status of the citizens of Spanish descent in New Mexico is one that exceeds the bounds of this limited report. Those who are familiar with the area and its people recognize that the task is a difficult and a highly complicated one. There are many ramifications of the questions involved, and issues arising from those questions present perplexing social and economic problems. It needs to be pointed out that no organized effort has ever been made to compile and present information with reference to these questions. Isolated agencies and individuals have made researches and, on occasion, have inaugurated action programs of limited scope. At no time, however, have these efforts been coördinated nor has joint study ever been given to the various phases of the minority problem of the area by those who have devoted time and effort to its study.

In each of fifteen (of the thirty-one) counties this element comprises 50 percent or more of the population. These fifteen counties have almost three-fifths of all the people in the state. In each of seven counties, (Taos, Rio Arriba, Mora, San Miguel, Valencia, Sandoval, and Socorro) the Spanish-speaking people constitute more than 80 percent of the population. In the light of the observations made above, these figures suggest the severity of the situation faced in these areas. A brief survey of readily available facts will illustrate the nature of this situation.

The United States census of 1930 revealed that 13.3 percent of the people in New Mexico were illiterate. When compared with other states, New Mexico ranks third from the lowest in literacy. Though sparsely populated, the state is twenty-second in number of illiterates. As might be expected, the counties with the highest proportions of Spanish-speaking people also tend to have the highest illiteracy rates. This is true even when illiteracy rates are corrected for the Indian population.

New Mexico has more than fourteen people for each daily newspaper, giving her a rank of forty-seventh among the states. The state has about one-sixth-of-a-volume-in-public-libraries per capita, in which item New Mexico has a rank of thirty-eight, though her rank is still lower when the circulation of such volumes is taken into consideration. There is an almost total absence of literature in rural areas. The people of those areas are also the least able to afford radios, have fewer means and opportunities for social contacts, and are served by the poorest schools. In addition, the rural New Mexican has had the least contact with English and with the culture represented by that language. And so on almost endlessly, the inherent inertia of the situation breaking down with exasperating slowness.

The educational level of the Spanish-speaking population is most vividly portrayed by school statistics. Though children from this sector of the population constitute one-half of the public school enrollment, they make up less than one-fifth of the enrollment in the twelfth grade. Of almost sixty thousand Spanish-speaking children enrolled in school, more than half are in the first three grades. Over one-third of the total enrollment of these children is found in the first grade. In every grade beyond the first, more than 55 percent of the children are more than two years over-age for their grade. Generally speaking, the achievement of the Spanish-speaking child in school subjects is not only far below national standards but also below state averages.

The explanation for these conditions is to be found in the nature and quality of the educational facilities available to these children. In the counties with the largest proportions of Spanish-speaking people, school terms are shorter, teachers are less well prepared and their salaries are lower, and materials of instruction and school buildings are inferior to those found elsewhere in the state. As a matter of fact, careful analysis reveals that as the percentage of Spanish-speaking population increases, educational opportunity decreases.

The special nature of the problem of educating this cultural minority has never been properly recognized by federal and state governments. Educational practices in New Mexico have been patterned after those developed in the Middle West and in the East for peoples and conditions vastly different from those obtaining here. The selection of educational officials by popular election is a practice that is particularly incongruous in this situation. So is the district system. The use of standard curricula, books, and materials among these children is a ridiculous procedure.

The language problem illustrates the inadequacy of current instructional practices. Imagine the Spanish-speaking child's introduction to American education! He comes to school, not only without a word of English but without the environmental experience upon which school life is based. He cannot speak to the teacher and is unable to understand what goes on about him in the classroom. He finally submits to rote learning, parroting words and processes in self-defense. To him, school life is artificial. He submits to it during class hours, only partially digesting the information which the teacher has tried to impart. Of course he learns English and the school subjects imperfectly! The school program is based on the fallacious assumption that the children come from English-speaking homes—homes that reflect American cultural standards and traditions.

The unresponsiveness of the school to the environment of New Mexican children tends to force them out of school. Most of these children leave school before they have learned enough to help them become effective in improving their environmental conditions. They leave school not only without an adequate knowledge of English but without the rudiments of education in health and work habits, in social practices and personal duties. It is conceivable that, with superior teachers and instructional materials, considerable improvement can be brought about even under the handicap of present administrative and curricular defects. However, superior teachers cost money and these people are poor. The counties with the largest Spanish-speaking population are also the poorest counties in the state—the higher the percentage of Spanish-speaking people in a county, the lower the per capita assessed valuation. Not only that, but the distribution of state school revenues tends to accentuate rather than to reduce this handicap.

In the school year 1937–1938 New Mexico spent $51 per pupil in average daily attendance for the total current expenses of the public schools. That year, each of the four counties with the highest percentage of Spanish-speaking population spent less than $35 per pupil—less than half the amount spent by the county with the highest expenditures. As suggested above, this discrepancy is due in large part to the inequitable manner in which state school revenues are distributed. For example, the first distribution of the state public school equalization fund in the 1939–40 school year gives the four most "Spanish" counties less than $50 per classroom unit. In that distribution, the average for the state is about $90, one county (among the lowest in proportion of Spanish-speaking population) receiving about $160 per unit. Several counties (all with a low percentage of native population) received well over $100 per unit.

The educational policy followed in New Mexico is startling in its ineptitude. It seems almost unbelievable that, insisting as we do that the American of Spanish descent learn English, we give him less opportunity to learn that language than is given to any other group in the state. The state, in its educational policy, compounds the understandable cultural handicap suffered by the New Mexican because of his background. It would be truly remarkable if, in the face of these obstacles, he should achieve cultural success.

The inadequacy of the provisions made for the support and administration of public education is illustrative of the failure of government to meet the problems presented by the New Mexican. This inadequacy is apparent in all fields of public service. Vital statistics are of particular significance in this connection. Whereas the infant mortality rate for the nation is 51 for every 1,000 live births, the rate in New Mexico is 125.9. Thirteen of the counties have an infant mortality rate of less than 100, eighteen counties have rates ranging from 104.8 to 167! It is significant to note that the ten counties that have the highest infant mortality rates in the state are counties where more than half of the population is Spanish-speaking.

New Mexico, with a death rate of 13.8, has almost three more deaths per 1,000 of population than the nation at large. All of the ten counties, except one, having the highest death rates (from 14.7 to 22.1 per thousand) are counties where the people of Spanish descent constitute more than half of the population. The lack of health services in these counties is made evident by the fact that in Mora County almost 80 percent of the deaths were from *unknown* causes! In Taos and Sandoval this percentage was sixty-nine. The rank of the counties of the state on percentage of deaths from unknown causes corresponds very closely to their rank on percentage of population of Spanish extraction!

These facts serve merely to emphasize the general observation that the descendants of the colonizers of New Mexico constitute an underprivileged socio-economic minority in the state. As the common day laborer and subsistence farmer, the economic status of the native New Mexican puts him at the disadvantage felt by similar classes elsewhere in the country. In addition, it is quite apparent that, in New Mexico, this group suffers additional handicaps that are products of the cultural gap that separates the New Mexican from other Americans.

Health practices are often guided by medieval traditions and superstitions. These beliefs range from such matters as credence in the Evil Eye to faith in incompetent mid-wives and *curanderos* (herb doctors)—to say nothing of homely remedies, patent medicines, and general ignorance of modern health practices. Many of these people still live in the seventeenth century, in so far as matters of health are concerned. It is easy to understand why this is so. Modern health standards were developed in Western civilization *after* these people went into isolation. When the Spaniards came into New Mexico in the sixteenth and seventeeth centuries they came with the beliefs and standards of that time. Since then they have had no opportunity to learn of new developments in that field. They have, perforce, continued practicing the only standards they know. It is not at all remarkable that, being so far behind the times in health knowledge, these people should lag behind current trends in health status. Indeed, it would be remarkable if they did not. What is startling is that so little has been done to improve these conditions.

What has been said about the cultural handicap in the field of health applies to civic activities and to other social practices as well. It is not a matter of wonder that, lacking the leadership and the instruments of progress, a society should not be progressive. The persistence of outmoded practices and beliefs among a people is remarkable when those practices and beliefs are, in truth, outmoded. As has been suggested before, the incorporation into the American fold of the people adopted by the United States through the Treaty of Guadalupe Hidalgo has been left largely up to them. Through trial and error, by casual contacts with other Americans, and with their coöperation, some progress has been achieved, notably within the last two decades. Even so, as indicated by the figures cited in the matters of education and health, the American of Spanish descent in New Mexico is still behind the times. Left largely to his own resources, he has, of course, been unable to outmode his own standards and traditions.

Those who have doubts as to the immensity of the problem of bridging the gap between the culture of the New Mexican and that of modern America might turn to the Indian problem for a singularly appropriate analogous situation. Confronted with virtually the same handicaps facing the New Mexican, the Indian is still far removed from the standards of American society in spite of the tremendous special efforts that have been made in his behalf. Private societies and individuals have championed his cause, seek to protect him in his rights, and act as political pressure groups in his behalf. The federal government gives him schools, lands, health service, legal service, guidance and supervision. Under special protection and unhampered by taxation, his disadvantage in the face of American culture is materially reduced.

The special nature of the Indian's cultural status and of his place in American history has given our national government just cause for according him special protection and assistance. Yet, the Indian still lags behind his neighbors in educational level, in health standards, and in general standards of living. It is not surprising that his oldest neighbor, the New Mexican, who labors under much the same handicaps of isolation and cultural difference, should find it difficult to adjust to this new, and very foreign, way of life. The New Mexican has had no societies pleading his case. He has not had access to special legal services nor has his health been ministered to by competent public agencies. No one has given special consideration to his agricultural problems. Instead of safeguarding him in his land and water rights, government has inadvertently deprived him of those rights through taxation, through the expansion of Indian lands, and by placing him at the mercy of unrestricted economic competition. His schools are what he has made them. His community life has not been given supervision and has broken down before the weight of a new order.

Since this region became a part of the United States, the usual political and public service agencies have been established without due regard for the fact that these people were not only not American culturally but were handicapped by centuries of isolation. Unfortunately, while their status as subject peoples was but little different from that of the Indians, this status was not recognized and the proper measures for their incorporation into American practices and institutions were not taken. Their education was left wholly up to them. In an area of cultural unsophistication and of limited material resources, this meant virtual social abandonment. It meant, also, that the weaknesses of the American social and economic

structure would become over-emphasized in this region for lack of the normal popular checks against excesses and miscarriages.

Citizenship and suffrage of the New Mexican did not constitute the means for his self-regeneration. He did not, and still does not, know the nature of his problems nor the techniques for their solution. The value of his vote as an instrument of reform is decreased by his lack of understanding of issues and goals, of political tactics, and of party politics. Because of this he has proven ineffective in bringing about necessary governmental changes even though he is politically powerful from the standpoint of numbers. More often than not he sees little connection between candidates for office and his own welfare. Elections are disassociated from the vital factors of making a living, from education, from health. As a consequence, political leaders and office-holders show an amazing indifference to the major needs of these people. Too often it appears that these leaders feel that they have discharged their obligation to the New Mexican when they have graded a road in his county or when they have hired some of his friends as clerks and laborers at his expense.

This has been the tenor of self-government in New Mexico. The progress that has been made has been haphazard and slow in its development. Only as popular education has spread have reforms been instituted. Bossism and machine politics based on the spoils system on a crude scale is still the rule, however. The time for a major attack through government upon the social and economic ills facing the New Mexican is yet in the future. An educated electorate and a conscientious leadership are the prerequisites.

Too often the problem presented by these people today is regarded simply as a "bi-lingual" problem—one wherein language differences are of primary importance. It is much more than that. The problem is one of culture contacts and conflicts—one wherein traditional cultural and geographic isolation accentuate the normal problems presented by incorporation and aggravate the deficiencies of an undeveloped economy and of a frontier social structure.

Without minimizing the importance of the problems presented by native New Mexicans in cosmopolitan centers, rather assuming that the rural field offers a valuable approach to those problems, the rural New Mexican constitutes the major issue in acculturation in this area. In migratory labor communities, or in permanent rural settlements which are predominately Spanish-speaking, his social and economic situation offers the most serious obstacles to incorporation. Living in isolation, he is not only removed from the normal social contacts which would tend to improve his condition, but he is highly inaccessible, physically and culturally, to the public agencies of incorporation. In the one case, he lives in the home of his colonial ancestors, unprepared to participate successfully in current affairs and unresponsive to the goals and values of his fellow Americans. In the other case, he labors in the sheep camps, in the vegetable and cotton fields, and in the fruit groves —a piecework cropper with no permanent roots in the community and, because of his condition, offering little opportunity to the normal public service organizations. In either case, these people are society's stepchildren—forgotten people on the "other side of the railroad tracks."

New Mexico was inducted into territorial status, and later into statehood, on the basic assumption that the region embraced those social and economic resources that would enable it to attain a level of social welfare comparable to that of other regions within the United States. It is the sense of this study that such an assumption was a fallacious one. That assumption was not made in the case of the Indian, of the Filipino, or of the Puerto Rican. It seems just and proper that, in the case of the New Mexican, as in those other instances, due regard should have been given to the special character of the problems he presented. It should be recognized that technical citizenship, alone, was no solution to those problems.

In so far as the special nature of his problems are concerned, the New Mexican has been in a position comparable to that of those other subject peoples. The fact that he occupied an area contiguous to the American Union did not materially change this situation. To all intents and purposes he was a foreigner—a foreigner whose background reflected a long-outmoded Western civilization that had undergone many generations of special adaptation to the region. Because of this adaptation and due to isolation, the New Mexican was virtually indigenous to New Mexico. Like the Indian, the Puerto Rican and the Filipino, his problems merited special consideration. In his case, and in his case alone, such consideration was not forthcoming from the national government.

In health, wealth, and education, the New Mexican holds the lowest position of any large group in the state. Furthermore, the measures being undertaken to remedy his condition are less effective in his case than they are for other sectors of the population. This lack of effectiveness is due to three fundamental causes: (1) the measures are not adapted to his needs; (2) his cultural inertia is greater; and (3) the measures are inequitable and tend to discriminate against him. This latter deficiency is easily verified, particularly in the field of education.

The very nature of state and county government in New Mexico militates against an adequate approach to the problems herein suggested. The New Mexican's needs are great, yet he is least able to afford the services that will meet those needs. In addition, his cultural status makes him less effective in voicing his needs before county, state, and federal governments than is the case with any other large group in the state. This ineffectiveness is evidenced in the officials he selects for both state and county offices and in their after-election indifference to his vital problems.

In summarizing the viewpoint herein presented, it needs to be said that the generally inferior status held by the native New Mexican today is, in large measure, a result of the failure of the United States to recognize the special character of the social responsibility it assumed when it brought these people forcibly into the American society. Granting them technical citizenship did not discharge that responsibility. The legal right to "life, liberty, and the pursuit of happiness" is an empty privilege when the bare essentials of Americanism and of social welfare are wanting.

CHARLES P. Loomis

Charles P. Loomis (Department Chairman of Sociology and Anthropology, Michigan State University) was one of the first sociologists to concentrate on rural sociology. He edited and helped found the JOURNAL OF RURAL SOCIOLOGY. *In 1939 he and Olen Leonard began their seminal study of the village of El Cerrito, New Mexico. This study was published by the United States Department of Agriculture and is rightly regarded as a classic work in rural sociology. In this article, Professor Loomis returns to El Cerrito fifteen years later and describes the disintegration of an isolated village caused by the technology of modern America. Reprinted by permission from* NEW MEXICO HISTORICAL REVIEW, *Vol 33, No 1 (January 1958).*

El Cerrito, New Mexico:
A Changing Village

Isolated in the high mesas of New Mexico, the village of El Cerrito, thirty miles from Las Vegas, New Mexico, was originally studied in 1939. For over a decade and a half this original study has been the standard reference describing the life and culture of the Spanish-speaking people living in the rural areas of the southwestern United States. During the past decade of prosperity and

good wages, however, phenomenal changes have taken place as a result of the migration of these people from isolated villages to the cities. In an effort to understand these changes, a restudy of El Cerrito was undertaken during the summer of 1956.

Historical background. Although there is no detailed historical record of the origin of El

Cerrito, it is known that the date of present occupancy goes back well over a century. All villagers in El Cerrito are of native or Spanish-American stock, descendants of Conquistadores and the indigenous population with which they mixed. The Spanish heritage of livestock raising, language, family and church which are still strong was blended with the Indian heritage of such cultural traits as the irrigation ditch and its dam, the use of adobe for building, crops and foods, and the methods and tools of farming.

Most of the present residents are descendants of people who migrated to El Cerrito from San Miguel, twelve miles north of El Cerrito on the Pecos river from which both villages and many other similar ones both above and below derive their irrigation water. The original settlers in the area knew more about stock raising than farming. Their forefathers had passed up good arable land in their trek eastward to the Las Vegas area, thus named because it appeared to be good grazing land. Over the last fifty or so years most of the twenty to thirty families who have owned property in the village at any one time were dependent upon the several stockmen of the village for wages as herdsmen. Formerly in this setting as elsewhere in the Spanish Borderlands a well-regulated and organized system developed in the village so that available work was distributed in accordance with need to those not regularly on the "patron's payroll." But this patron-villager relationship is a thing of the past because practically all patrons and others of Spanish-speaking ancestry have lost their grazing lands and like the other villagers must seek work outside the village.

Now as in the past the majority of the families actually living in El Cerrito own and operate from ten to forty acres of dry-farming land plus one to four acres of irrigated land. Most of the land is used for subsistence farming and garden crops producing little if any cash income. Most of the irrigated land owned by villagers was a part of the original land grant handed down from the original San Miguel del Bado Grant. Other dry land was added by homesteading and some purchases. Only one family now living in the village has enough land without renting for a family-sized stock farm or ranch. This family owns some 2,000 acres of mesa land upon which graze about a hundred head of cattle. Only this family has any appreciable cash income from agriculture.

Fifty years ago the people of El Cerrito and elsewhere in north-central New Mexico possessed vast holdings of land used for grazing. Secondarily, small irrigated plots were set aside for subsistence agriculture purposes. Today the outlying mesa which once supported the livestock industry has been transferred to other hands. Thus most remaining units are the small, irrigated plots that were never of adequate size and fertility to support a family.

The great exodus. According to demographic theories which attempt to explain migration, continued depression in the village and continued prosperity outside should lead to out-migration. Of course, solidary communities with a high level of integration such as El Cerrito may resist the pressure longer than others. At the time of the first study in 1940 there were 26 family units in El Cerrito. Today there remain only four family units and four old couples whose children have gone elsewhere to live. Fifteen families have locked their doors, boarded up the windows, and left to work at year-around jobs elsewhere. Further, three families have died out. Thus about one-fourth of the people who were in El Cerrito in 1940 remain there today, and these are predominantly older people.

Such an exodus takes the very heart and soul out of a community. El Cerrito is a prime example. An older person said, "When we die El Cerrito is gone, and that won't be long now." This is really not true because there are two younger families with farming and ranching units large enough to support them, especially if eventually those who have left decide to sell or rent their land to them. Two other families with older parents have sons who may take over their units, and one family has moved to another ranch some 50 miles away and uses the El Cerrito products there. Nevertheless, a community with many old people reflects a different set of aspirations than a community of young people. Even during the depression the community with its young people furnished not nearly such a gloomy and pessimistic prospect as do the older people now during prosperity. A decade and a half ago one out of every ten was over 55 and one out of every fifteen over 65. Now one out of every three is over 55 and one out of every seven is 65 and over.

In the previous study great stress was placed upon the importance of the family to the individual and community. What has this exodus done to the family? How has the family functioned during this period of near crisis? We shall discuss this in relation to the social systems of the village. Suffice it here to say that of those whose destinations are known almost four out of five have gone to the one city of Pueblo, Colorado. Another twelve live in cities near Pueblo and all are more or less in constant contact with one another. All return or plan to return to El Cerrito even if less frequently than formerly. Thus, in exodus as when the homes in the village were full, the family remains the strongest sub-system.

COMMUNICATION AND INTERACTION— PRINCIPAL SYSTEMS AND PROCESSES

The community's sub-systems. As is well known few societies manifest stronger community integration than the Spanish-speaking villages of the Southwestern United States. This is in general true despite bitter cleavages common in many villages but from which El Cerrito has been free for many years. Community-wide rites of passage and activities such as weddings and funerals, church ceremonies, cooperative irrigation clearing activities, dances, Christmas school programs, school closing programs in the old days involved most members. However, in the last decades with most of the able bodied working men and their families away the community as a social system is not at all what it once was. No longer are there school programs because loss of population has brought about the closing of the school. No longer are there dances because the school building where dances were originally held has been sold and is no longer available and because there are fewer young people who want to dance. Other community-wide social events which continue are so small and lacking in the original enthusiasm that a villager said "it is only the skin and bones of the old El Cerrito."

The family. In few societies does the family have a more prominent place among the social systems and organizations than does the family in Spanish and Latin American culture. In the villages the family remains the basic channel through which all organized activities must flow. At an early age the child learns that almost no responsibility is greater than that of loyalty to and support of the family. The various status-roles of family members pattern life somewhat differently than they do in Anglo communities in the same area. Formerly unmarried girls and boys did not mingle except at dances or in situations providing parental supervision. Girls in El Cerrito were not even allowed to walk away from the village unchaperoned. Now that the first eight grades of the school in El Cerrito have been transferred upstream to the larger village of Villanueva the control necessary for the separation of the sexes is somewhat relaxed. The parents who frequently bemoan the weakening of controls realize that children must meet somehow if they are to marry. Actually girls and boys meet more or less clandestinely in Villanueva, Las Vegas or elsewhere. Mating no longer has the parental supervision it once did. Originally marriages were arranged by the parents when a youth expressed an interest in a girl whom he had seen at dances, in the school or elsewhere. Now the village for the first time in its history has a woman with children deserted by the father of the children. One of the daughters of a respected family, the mother originally met the father in town. The deserted girl has returned with her children to live with her parents, who had little to say about her marriage. An older lady said, "Children going outside for recreation is bad for their morals. They come to respect their parents less." As will be indicated later, not only are the customs leading to marriage changing but the status-roles of parents and children are changing. On the whole they are changing in the direction of the lower class Anglo family.

During the early years of the great depression it was the extended family which provided the main support of the frequently hungry and poverty stricken villagers of El Cerrito. Later during the New Deal, relief, WPA work, and many other provisions made available from governmental sources saved them from real starvation. But the family contacts of the isolated villagers in the county seat and elsewhere provided the information necessary to make these resources and facilities available.

Now during prosperity many of the families have moved together to Colorado and many work in the same plants. Family systems which once sought out the relief and WPA jobs and other temporary work opportunities now report more permanent job opportunities and provide the security required in the transition from isolated village to metropolitan life. In fact most large cities in the Southwest are interlaced with cliques of Spanish-speaking people who once lived in villages. At the present El Cerrito is closer in terms of family ties to Pueblo, Colorado, a city of 70,000, which is 263 miles distant, than it is to other towns and cities which are closer geographically. Family and village ties have helped remove the dozens of people who had no future in El Cerrito. Now that they are removed they unite through what we shall later describe as polite separatism to preserve the Latin-American culture which El Cerrito through geographic isolation preserved from Anglo culture for so many generations.

The Church. Although El Cerrito has never had a resident priest, the Catholic tradition has always been strong and no Protestants have ever lived there permanently. The church is still the best kept and appearing building in the village, and as in most Spanish-speaking communities is centrally located in the plaza. Probably there has been less change in the religious activities of the village than in those of any other social system. Services are held at least once a week by the villagers themselves with the priest from Villanueva conducting mass once a month. Two sisters accompany the priest once a month to teach the children their catechism. During the months of May, June and October the local people hold daily services in the church to which the women and just a few men are regular attendants. As previously the chief church celebration and for that matter village celebration is that of the "Function," held in the fall or winter in honor of its Patron Saint. Whereas previously the ceremony lasted two days with feasts, it now lasts only one

day. The feasts are served and ritual and ceremony arranged by the two local church officials, *"Mayordomos de la copia,"* appointed each year by their predecessors and approved by the priest. Whereas previously between one hundred and two hundred participated now the number is only 25 to 50. The greatest change in the activities of the church is in the number and composition of those who attend resulting from the change in the composition of the village. Some of the pews which were filled regularly a quarter of a century ago have been vacated by death but the church still has many older members because it is they and only a handful of younger families who have remained.

The Ditch Association. From an economic point of view there is no community-wide social system of as much importance as the ditch association. It is certainly the oldest community organization. Its function is that of controlling, maintaining, cleaning, and repairing the irrigation system, the most important components of which are the dam and the main ditch. The dam, built on the principle of those found in use by the Indians hundreds of years ago when the Spanish arrived and consisting of stones and brush which are dropped in the river about a mile above the village, is in constant danger of being washed out. The rather long ditch leading from the dam located upstream to the fields around the village requires regular cleaning and repairing, particularly in the spring. About a quarter of a century ago each man was assessed one day's labor for each acre of irrigated land. Since the great decline in the village population the assessment is not so great, one day of work for every two acres of land. Those absent or for other reasons not able to work must pay three dollars per day for a substitute. The *mayordomo* of the ditch, or the ditch boss, and the ditch board or commission, composed of the president, secretary and treasurer, are still elected annually by popular vote in the village. The Board makes or changes rules regarding the ditch and the mayordomo or ditch boss supervises all work done on the ditch during the year. Only the ditch boss does not contribute the regular quota of hand labor—his status-role requiring executive functions. Whereas earlier the annual spring cleaning of the ditch was the occasion of considerable festivity usually lasting about two days, this is somewhat less true now. It is a job to get finished, and there are fewer to do the work and to make merry. Today as earlier many villagers wish that a government program might improve the ancient irrigation system, making it possible to raise the water higher and prevent the inevitable loss of crops when a flood washes out the dam.

The school. When asked what has been the most important event affecting the community during the last five years, several villagers mentioned the closing of the school by the County Board of Education because there were insufficient children of school age in the village to support a school. In 1940 two teachers were regularly employed to teach at the village school. Today the 14 children in El Cerrito are transported by bus to the school in the nearest village, Villanueva, over a dangerous and rocky road which in many other parts of the country would be considered practically impassable. Most of the villagers with children said they worried when they were en route to and from and at the Villanueva school during the long days. This would have caused even more anxiety a decade and a half ago when children and women seldom left the village.

Several villagers mentioned the great loss when the County Board of Education sold the school building. One room of this building is now used as a dwelling, the other room is used as a storage space for hay. The closed school with its desks, covered with jack-knife carved initials, under a pile of hay must produce nostalgia for those who learned to read and write, attended village dances, met their present spouses, participated in local political meetings, and all the other non-religious functions of the village there of earlier time. In fact for the author the image of the school house with its screens partly ripped off, hay protruding from a partly opened door, and the broken flag pole symbolized an almost deserted village, a village which is dying. No longer do parents and children peer out of windows ready to send the children off to school upon the irregular arrival of the teachers. No longer do parents expect them home for a brief period of lunch at noon after

which they scampered back to school. Now the school bus arrives regularly and children must be ready or be left behind.

The Well Association. Until 1949 all water used for drinking, cooking, washing and bathing was carried in buckets from the irrigation ditch. Throughout the area this general practice resulted in many New Mexican counties having very high death rates, especially among young children, due to dysentery. Typhoid was endemic in many places and old and young alike in many villages suffered chronic diarrhea. In 1956 when families in El Cerrito were asked what the most important events in the village were in the last years many answered, "The water project." It is interesting to note why they believe this to be true. The State Health Department officials are agreed that the main function of the well program is that of improving the health of the villages. The villagers, when questioned why they thought the attainment of the well and water system was so important, never once gave this reason. The reasons given were: The water tastes better, beans and other foods cooked in it taste better, it is softer, it avoids the effort and trouble getting the water from the ditch, too often the ditch water is muddy and must settle for too long a period before it is used. Several villagers claimed the ditch water was perfectly healthy, this notwithstanding the fact that there have been deaths in the village from typhoid, although usually not attended by a doctor. Most people commented upon the fact that the water from the Pecos river is harder and does not taste as good as the water from the well.

A law passed in the 1949 state legislature resulting from Senate Bill No. 58 states that villages may form a "Mutual Domestic Water Consumers Association" which will provide for the installation of sanitary domestic water facilities, thus eliminating the present hazardous practices involved in the use of ditch water, open shallow wells, creeks, and rivers which are subject to contamination and, therefore, are injurious to public health. The law further specifies that "the persons so associating, their successors and those who may thereafter become members of said association, shall constitute a body corporate by the name set forth in such certificate and by such name may sue and be sued, and shall have capacity to make contracts, acquire, hold, enjoy, dispose of and convey property real and personal and to do any other act or thing necessary or proper for carrying out the purposes of their organization; provided, however, that such association created by this Act shall not have power to become indebted or issue bonds of any kind." Although El Cerrito and other similar villages had earlier held land grants under corporate arrangements based upon Spanish and Mexican law, this is the first time El Cerrito has entered such a contractual arrangement under State law.

The San Miguel County health officials in Las Vegas and Santa Fe were surprised that little El Cerrito, isolated and without electricity as it was then, should be one of the first of the area to carry through negotiations and actually organize, prepare articles of incorporation and execute incorporation of an Association making the facilities available under the Corporation Commission of the state. In an effort to explain why this little conservative and isolated community applied in June of the year the law was passed and had its water supply in the same month, an official commented as follows:

> El Cerrito unlike many villages does not have factional strife which is a frequent hindrance to the villages of the area interested in this program. There were no wells there originally so that no one already had water. In Villanueva, for example, there was both factional strife so common in these villages and some families already had wells. Some of the better-to-do people who had wells were opposed to a community project. El Cerrito is more like La Cueva—just one big family. La Cueva got theirs easily, too. Also Luis Aragon, a leader there in El Cerrito, pushed it. He is progressive and aggressive.

There is the further fact that El Cerrito has sent its share of migrants to Las Vegas, the county seat, and some of these people keep tab on what goes on in the court house and state legislature. This rural-urban linkage through relatives is used in politics and was very important in getting relief

and making use of other facilities during the depression.

Although villagers from El Cerrito initiated action by talking with County Department of Health officials, a representative of the county office initiated the project in the village by holding a public meeting at which all who attended signed an application and a contract specifying among other things that

> We agree to contribute all unskilled labor, such skilled labor as is available and desirable and all local materials such as sand, gravel, stone, timbers, vigas, adobes and any other materials it is feasible and desirable to obtain locally.

The state of New Mexico paid $3,444.43 for the engineering and geological services in planning the well, for its digging, and for the equipment including the gas engine, pump, tank, etc. The people contributed $1,939.00 in cooperative labor, digging the trenches within which to lay the lead pipes and in materials such as adobe, vigas, etc. Twenty-one families, most of whom are not now living in the village, paid the $1.00 membership fee and only one family in the village now uses the ditch water. This family is a member but claims that it cannot afford to make the main connection to the house.

Maintaining the pump. Typical of the Well Association and life in the village is the manner in which it is maintained and operated. The gasoline tank on the pump holds two gallons of gasoline which will fill the water reservoir tank holding a thousand or so gallons of water. When the pump stops because the gasoline tank is dry, the secretary-treasurer sends a child to collect either five or ten cents from each family to purchase gasoline for the next filling. Five cents is collected if the reserve water tank is only half empty and only one gallon of gas is needed to fill it. The child collects ten cents from each family if two gallons of gas are needed to fill the tank.

In 1956 the well was idle for two months because no one could make the repairs required for the engine and the pump. This and the insistence of the County Department of Health officials in Las Vegas prompted the officials including the president, vice president, a secretary-treasurer and two other commissioners to begin levying a $1.00 a month upkeep charge from the eight members now in the village and using the water. This forms a reserve fund which the secretary-treasurer keeps for an emergency. Many of the villagers believe the one dollar a month collected by the secretary-treasurer is used for paying off an indebtedness. This is an interesting misapprehension on the part of these villagers because the people are not under obligation to pay for the well but only to maintain it.

According to the records in the County Health Department in Las Vegas there are ten inside connections and six or eight washing machines in the village. There are as yet no inside toilets or baths. The county health officials say that in other villages almost all families who get water soon get washing machines, and as funds are available, toilet and bath equipment is bought piece by piece.

The community.   A decade and a half ago El Cerrito was described as an example of the convergence of neighborhood and community, a grouping within which almost every one of the two dozen or so families could claim at least a third cousin relationship with every other. Sociometric interaction charts described several powerful extended family groupings all linked to one another. Now, with three quarters of the people away from the village most of the time and several families gone permanently, El Cerrito is becoming merely a neighborhood in the trade center community of Las Vegas, New Mexico.

El Cerrito remains a community in the sense described by writers such as Brownell and Mead who see the small community as an arena for the nurture and development of the ideal socialized personality, the internalizing of the generalized other, the basic unit of strong healthy nations. However, unlike most other such neighborhoods it is isolated geographically and culturally and, except for the linkages through family ties to those working in the large centers, remains a closed system in many respects.

SOCIAL PROCESSES

Social-cultural linkage with the outside world.
The third most important event in the village in the last decade and a half, after the organization of the Well Association and the closing of the school, according to the people, was the coming of electricity. In 1952 an engineer of the Rural Electrical Administration located in Mora, from which the REA cooperative of the area is operated, visited the village and called a meeting of those who wanted electricity. At this meeting seven members signed an agreement to the effect that if the line were extended to El Cerrito they would install lights. Two families then argued against bringing this facility to the village and refused to sign the agreement, saying they could not afford the service. Both have since joined the cooperative and become users of electricity. The minimum monthly rate per family in El Cerrito is four dollars—fifty cents more than in neighboring Villanueva because El Cerrito is more inaccessible and farther from the center of distribution. Older people and some younger people, too, worry about the payments which could not be made if children working away were to lose their jobs or if another depression came such as they suffered in the thirties. Thus the fixed payments of $4.00 minimum per month for electricity per family (some must now pay over $10.00), $1.00 for water and then the many other installment payments for the second hand car, the refrigerator, the washing machine, television set, or other items indicate the linkage of this once isolated, subsistence village to the greater society. The coming of electricity was the final link which brought the outside world into El Cerrito. Most of the remaining families have viewed television in the home of the one family which has a set bought on the installment plan.

Comparing El Cerrito now with El Cerrito a decade and a half ago, it is the closeness of the linkage of the once isolated village to the greater society which most impresses the visitor. This linkage, in spite of a difficult road and considerable distance, is now firmly established. A decade and a half ago there were two radios serviced by electricity from batteries when their owners could afford them. These radios functioned only on occasion and were frequently out of order. Now practically all have radios or easy access to them. Then two old automobiles and two antiquated trucks were the only motored transportation to Las Vegas. Usually families with no auto or truck needing to go to town paid $3.00 to the owner for the privilege of riding into town and back with his purchases. After a trip to town was arranged those not needing to go were carried for less than the $3.00. Today all families with younger people own a car and/or a truck. Most families go to town once a week and the cost of riding with a neighbor has been reduced to $1.50. Families working in Colorado or in other places return occasionally to check on their property and the many members of families now living in the village return more frequently. These latter especially send back money and bring various electricial gadgets, even refrigerators, radios and other large items.

After a decade and a half of ever accelerating and ramifying social-cultural linkages El Cerrito, still isolated geographically, and separated from the urban world by a stretch of road which, especially after rains, would frighten most drivers from other regions, now accepts the values of groupings in Las Vegas, Pueblo, Denver and Albuquerque above those of the village. For all except the few families who remain El Cerrito, which they still affectionately call *La Placita,* is little more than a possible haven during unemployment or a possible depression. All the older families and many of the younger people know that it could not serve as a haven during another depression unless the government provided the equivalent of PWA work jobs and other relief payments. Increased use of automobiles and trucks, radio, television and more frequent contacts in Las Vegas and the more remote centers which provide more and more year-round employment have now linked El Cerrito to the major social systems of the nation and world.

During the field work on the original study over a decade and a half ago the author lived with a family and came to know intimately two boys in their teens. In his diary written then is the following:

Bene and I prepared to to go Las Vegas. He was to see about an NYA job. . . . When Christiano (the father) sent his son with two pails of provisions and a shabby old pasteboard suitcase to Vegas for 15 days, he gave him much fatherly advice. Bene is about 20. The father showed real emotion. Tears stood thick in his eyes and ran down his cheeks.

The same scene was repeated earlier when the author took the younger brother of Bene for an overnight trip to Las Vegas and Santa Fe—the first such visit he had had in his life. A decade and a half ago this usually happened when sons or daughters left the village. Although family ties are practically as strong as ever today, the weekly contacts of most families with Las Vegas by car and truck, the daily school bus trips to Villanueva, mass media and many other contacts would make the above notes out of keeping with life today. Social-cultural linkage with the outside world has been achieved.

Boundary maintenance. Polite separatism characterizes the basic nature of boundary maintenance of Spanish-speaking groups in New Mexico. The evolution of this pattern is complex and has developed over the many decades of Anglo-Hispano interaction. In a brief space we can only sketch certain aspects of the evolution of polite separatism as a boundary maintaining device. Suffice it to say that even before the annexation of New Mexico by the United States in 1848 and in ever-accelerating measure thereafter, "invading" Anglos who generally maintained an exalted belief in their own superiority pushed their business and other interests in ' the Anglo way," that is, through the application of shrewd, often sharp, practices. Against this aggressive and industrious Anglo enterprise the natives were unable to compete. Spanish-speaking stockmen lost their grazing lands and watering facilities, business men lost their trade in the keen competition. Moreover, in the village centers such as Socorro, Taos, Santa Fe and Albuquerque,

"Houses were opened for the indulgence of every wicked passion; and each midnight hour heralded new violent and often bloody scenes for the fast filling record of crime. The peaceable Mexicans hastened to pack up their little store of worldly wealth, and, with their wives and children, fled from the rapidly depopulating village.

The results of this interaction have been summarized by Zeleny:

The average Spanish-American drawing what security he needs from the family, community and church, as an individual possesses "a serenity, a lack of competitive zeal, and a contented enjoyment of leisure and simple pleasures which makes him stand in contrast to the more tense, aggressive Anglo-American. ... The reaction against their treatment by the Anglos as well as the conflict of cultural differences and values have tended to provoke attitudes among the Spanish-American group that have reinforced the pattern of social separatism. The Spanish-Americans have voluntarily remained aloof from social intercourse with the Anglos in part because of hostile attitudes toward them. From the time Anglo-Americans first appeared in New Mexico they were called 'Gringos' a term of contempt referring to them as foreigners or intruders, a group unlearned in the ways of the country.

Through the device of polite separatism El Cerrito and the many similar villages retain their Spanish heritage despite the fact that most of the people who live there now work outside in the Anglo dominated urban cultures. Actually for generations this pattern of outside work has prevailed. Previously the most common outside participation was in Spanish-speaking section gangs on railroads, groups of Spanish-speaking people working in harvest fields and tending sugar beets, or in mines where the work groups were largely Spanish-speaking. Now the principal migrations are to the industrial centers of Colorado and infiltration with Anglo workers is more common. Nevertheless, the device of polite separatism results in groups of El Cerrito villagers living and maintaining contacts on and off the job in Pueblo, Denver and Albuquerque. Boundary maintenance makes acculturation to the national culture very slow indeed.

Olen Leonard and the author as Anglos spent many months of patient and constant effort to gain acceptance in El Cerrito in the thirties. Some contact has been retained in the intervening years. but the author was again impressed upon re-entering the village at the effectiveness of polite separatism as a boundary maintaining device. If we had not invested the many months of helpful effort in cultivating the friendship of the villagers, and if they had not learned in the fifteen years since the field work that we meant no harm, our reception would have been that of polite contact and avoidance. The original study and the camera report of the United States Department of Agriculture had been circulated in the village and by Senator Dennis Chavez in New Mexico generally, so that our status-roles as non-hostile but objective investigators were legitimized. On the revisit two New Mexican Spanish-speaking graduate students accompanied the author, and even their activities were viewed with suspicion until people learned that they were helping on the re-study of the village. In terms of the basic cultural and social components of El Cerrito, the device of polite separatism has been an effective boundary maintaining device. Social-cultural linkage to the society outside has not meant that the basic value orientation and social structure has changed greatly.

Decision making.   Decision making on a community level in El Cerrito now and fifteen years ago differs from that in many other Spanish-speaking villages. This was emphasized by the county Health Department officials who worked in the village while the well association was organized. As indicated above the New Mexico Department of Health is attempting through what amounts to outright subsidy to introduce community pumps into villages where the hazard of sickness is great because drinking water is taken from surface water sources. Typically the villages are torn by bitter inter-family feuds. In such villages if one group begins negotiations for a well it inevitably meets the opposition of the traditional opposing group. Negotiations may thus be held at a stalemate for months or even years.

As stated in the original study, the two leading families in El Cerrito long ago carried their feud to the point of actual murder and severe beatings. Both families lost heavily in sheep and money and one finally withdrew from the village. The termination of the feud and the subsequent unity accounts for the fact that El Cerrito was one of the first villages in the region to agree to install a community well and join the REA cooperative and that never has difficulty in the election of officials for managing the most important community cooperative, the ditch association. Today as in previous generations all officers except the appointive church officials are elected by popular vote.

In the case of the village decision to organize the well association and install water, the initiator was the head of a family which is now the number two family of the village in terms of wealth and the only owner of a television set. Through almost unbelievable energy and thrift this family has moved from a position of dire poverty to that of being relatively well-to-do. A decade and a half ago he would not have been the chief decision maker of the village in an activity of this kind. Then the leading families spoke of him somewhat disparagingly as a striver and one too interested in his own advancement. Then, although he could not speak English well, the author thought his motivation in this respect stemmed from sentiments more typically Anglo than that of the leading families. Today this man, who fifteen years ago was considered as a bit overly ambitious for the village and not a key person, is without question one of the three leading men in decision making in most all community-wide decisions.

Communication. Communication as in earlier times within the village is primarily by word of mouth. The author's revisit to the village was known and evaluated in a very short time after his arrival. Visiting is still the most common form of pastime and recreation and is going on most of the waking hours and especially after church and other community gatherings. Since the closing of the school, the discontinuance of dancing and school entertainments, and the decrease in the number of full-time residents, com-

munication and interaction opportunities are provided mostly through visiting. The return of relatives frequently without notice provides a time of intense interaction for the larger family group involved. Now that so many families are away, and since many do not write, a family may return to find those kin away whom they most wanted to visit. For example, on the door of the house in which the author lived in the thirties, now boarded up because the family is in Pueblo, Colorado, is the following inscription in pencil: "We came to see you and found you had left. Flora." However, since coming and going is mostly by families and since larger family groupings usually go outside to the same larger city, frequently working in the same plant, the coming and going of individuals are generally known to those most concerned.

Language. Whereas fifteen years ago few of the villagers could speak English now most young people, many of whom have served in the armed forces in various parts of the world or have attended the relatively good schools in Villanueva, can speak English. Likewise the many who have migrated to work and who remain in areas where English is spoken on the job have more practice in it and speak well. Thus one villager who scarely speaks English commenting about his three sons said, "Cirilio was with the Army in Europe, Candido went with the Army to Africa and the Orient, and Teodoro was with the Navy. I wish I had learned the English my boys know. We would all be better off."

Incidentally El Cerrito differs from many Spanish-speaking New Mexican towns and villages which lost many sons in the Philippine Islands. The National Guard units sent to the Philippine Islands were made up of people living close enough to centers such as Las Vegas with armories in which to drill weekly. El Cerrito and similar villages were too isolated for this and had no national guard.

VALUES AND STRUCTURAL ELEMENTS OF THE VILLAGE

Some Changes in Ends and Norms. Fifteen years ago the people of El Cerrito would argue the advantages of life in their village with almost anyone. Although many knew that only a few could gain their chief livelihood there, most truly believed it was the best place they knew to live and bring up children. Men working in section gangs on the railroads, in beetfields to the north or later in various plants during the war longed for the day they would return to El Cerrito. Now all this has changed. Only three or four families want to stay permanently and they doubt that many of those working away will return permanently. The tendency noted in the thirties to glorify the village's past still exists but now beside these past glories is placed a gloomy future. "There is little left. No dances, just a few people. There is little going on." Each longs to visit friends and relatives on weekly trips to Las Vegas or to visit with relatives in Pueblo, Colorado, Denver, or Albuquerque.

In summary we may say that as villagers in El Cerrito attempt to consider the changes they will or should accomplish through community-wide cooperation, that is, the ends and objectives of the community, they report a gloomy prospect. Some hope that there might develop some industry or employment so the people could earn a living and remain a part of the community, but most believe little short of a miracle will produce this. Aside from the pessimistic view of the future, villagers are anxious, as in the past, to cooperate in any way to improve the life of the village. As the children become more acculturated to outside ways a sort of marginality in the effectiveness of the old and new norms apply. People are uneasy about an apparent development of immorality in terms of old Latino norms and manifest uncertain and ambivalent attitudes toward Anglo norms, which some are adopting and with which more are in contact.

Some changes in status-roles and social rank.

In the village itself such status-roles as those of father, mother, grandparents have remained relatively unchanged. Age and those who are parents and grandparents are still respected. However, in the urban centers to which the larger family units have gone, the villagers are accepting more and more the Anglo's low evaluation of all those who do not earn, including the grandparents and older persons. In the village, however, several of the grandparents are provided with grandchildren to help them with chores and housework. In the urban centers all indications are that with the husband away on the job, the Anglo pattern of increasing social rank and status for wives and mothers from villages such as El Cerrito is an inevitable development. Men on the job are no longer independent. The Spanish-speaking woman, like Anglo women but unlike her sisters who remain in the village, can and does contradict her husband at home, particularly regarding the socialization of the children. The urbanized village woman may demand and have time and money of her own to spend as she wishes. She can and is often expected to dress stylishly and to wear makeup. In fact, in contrast to earlier practices, adolescent and younger women are now doing this in villages such as El Cerrito. Older women and younger children follow the norms of status-roles in the villages but children in adolescence are less strictly supervised. The adolescent children are often the chief linkage the parents have with Anglo culture.

In El Cerrito with the loss of the school the important status-roles of the teachers, members of the school board and pertinent relations to the county school system with its organization disappeared. The various officials of the Ditch Association, Well Association, the non-resident priest, the mayordomos of the church and the justice of the peace are, as a decade and a half ago, the chief status-roles. As indicated above in the discussion of decision making, one family through great industry and thrift has increased its rank in the village. However, the villagers when they move to larger centers enter the lower classes. Only a few become skilled laborers and attain upper-lower class status.

Changes in Social Power. In recent generations no person or family in El Cerrito has had great power as have some of the Spanish-speaking dons and well-to-do leaders elsewhere. No family owns more than a few thousand dollars worth of property. Nevertheless, through able management of political resources based upon available votes the leaders of the village still make their demands felt. This happened when effort was exerted to get the well and when electricity was requested from REA. Relatives from the village are numerous, and although the posts in county offices are not high nor many, politicians do not like to disregard even the smallest villages such as El Cerrito with its many kinship linkages throughout the area. It must be admitted, however, that the decrease of population in the village, particularly the loss to other states, has lessened its voting strength and power in politics.

Sanctions. Since villagers frequent the larger centers and since there are fewer resources in the village by way of recreation and entertainment, the former negative and positive sanctions of gossip and fear of local disapproval no longer have the efficacy they once had. Thus although most families contribute their quota of labor to the Ditch Association, four resident families among the twenty-one have not paid the monthly levy made by the Well Association. The power of local disapproval of the others is insufficient to make them contribute even though they are able. We doubt that a decade and a half ago these four families would thus deviate. As in the past there are no law enforcement officials in the village and none are needed.

Facilities. From a community point of view there have been substantial losses in facilities since the thirties. There is no village school, no place in which meetings such as the one held for the organization of the Well Association can be held. There is no place for community dances. The chief gains are the well installation and electric light facilities. The road to Las Vegas is some but not much improved. Individual families have improved levels of living through the addition of various facilities such as washing machines, refrigerators, radios and other appliances. Three families own tractors and some motorized farm equipment whereas fifteen years ago there were none in the village. As mentioned earlier, fifteen

years ago there were only two dilapidated cars and two old trucks in the village. Now all extended families have a car and/or a truck, or older people have children with such vehicles.

Territoriality. El Cerrito itself has not changed its geographic boundaries, and families do not go further for work than was the case fifteen years ago. However, as mentioned previously the village has heavy and perhaps permanent anchorage points, expecially in Pueblo. Also several families from the village live in Albuquerque, Denver, and Las Vegas. Considering the strong family ties and other frequent interaction this means that in many ways the actual community of El Cerrito extends now to these distant points.

SUMMARY AND CONCLUSIONS

In the decade and a half since the original study of El Cerrito, a typical isolated Spanish-speaking village in San Miguel County, New Mexico, work opportunities outside the village coupled with continued contraction of local resources and opportunities have finally produced a major exodus. Although working outside the village is nothing new in El Cerrito, the pattern has changed greatly. Whereas formerly males worked on ranches, railroads, in mines and elsewhere a few months and then returned to the village, now many families have left to live the year around away from the village. The exodus has resulted in the loss of three quarters of the population, the school, and most hope for the future of the community. The outside contacts and linkages are producing fundamental changes in the social structure and value orientations of both those who remain in the village and especially those who have left for the urban centers.

CLARK S. KNOWLTON

*Clark S. Knowlton (Director of the Institute for the Study of
Social Problems, University of Utah, Salt Lake City)
specialized in the study of the village cultures of Northern
New Mexico. Professor Knowlton, as in the preceding essay,
describes how the intrusion of English-speaking culture and
technology destroyed the traditional cultural patterns in the
small villages. In this selection from SOCIAL FORCES,
(October 1962) Professor Knowlton explains why the
traditional patron-peon system is collapsing, and discusses
why no other leadership pattern had evolved to fill that
vacuum.
By permission of the University of North Carolina Press.*

Patron-Peon Pattern Among The Spanish Americans Of New Mexico

In this paper an endeavor will be made to delineate the role and structure of the patron-peon pattern in the rural social organization of the Spanish American people of northern New Mexico and southern Colorado, the changes that have taken place in this system, and the social and cultural implications of these changes. Living for the most part in rural farming villages, the Spanish Americans are a unique ethnic group different in language, culture, and historical experience from other Spanish-speaking groups in the United States.

The rural Spanish American social organization structured upon the interlocking institutions and patterns of an extended patriarchal family, the Roman Catholic Church, the independent self-sufficient farming village, and the patron-peon system has been until recently quite resistant to acculturation toward the dominant English-speaking society.

232

This resistance has been further intensified by the unfortunate historical experiences of the Spanish Americans. Stripped of much of their land by English-speaking Americans, exploited economically, treated with contempt and prejudice by many and forced into a subordinate social and economic position within their own state, they have reacted in the past by withdrawing from all but essential social, political and economic contacts with the dominant English-speaking group.

The cultural and social isolation of the Spanish Americans lasted until the depression of the 1930s. Mass unemployment, serious loss of land and water rights, growing population pressure upon a narrowing resource base, the temporary termination of traditional occupations such as migrant agricultural labor, sheepherding, and track work for the railroad destroyed the independent self-sufficient nature of the Spanish American villages. The villagers, unable to maintain themselves by their customary economic activities, were forced to accept economic assistance from the government agencies. Through these agencies, large numbers of the Spanish Americans became dependent upon the larger English-speaking world outside the village.

The destruction of the village economic structure was accompanied by a serious weakening of its social integration. The gradual erosion of the extended patriarchal family, the slow decline in the influence of the Roman Catholic Church, the intrusion of Protestant denominations, the destruction of the patron-peon system, the development of an educational system dominated by Anglo values, the draft of young men into the military service during World War II and the Korean War, the accelerated rise of new social and economic expectations, the development of a massive emigration movement away from the villages and into the urban areas of the West, and the rise of large urban centers on the fringes of the Spanish American area not only threaten the existence of the traditional village culture but the survival of the Spanish American culture as a separate cultural entity. A culture that has managed to survive almost three centuries of vicissitudes has now entered a period of such rapid economic, social, and cultural changes that its continued existence is perhaps problematical.

One of the first cultural patterns that began to break down under the impact of the invading English-speaking culture was the patron-peon system. Among the Spanish Americans, the patron was and is a person who is able to provide employment, social and economic security, and leadership to those who must work for a living. He is usually a person of substance belonging to a family that is socially prominent in the area. His position as a patron is not based primarily upon his personal characteristics, but rather upon his ability to perform the institutionalized role of a patron.

Two basic types of a patron evolved in the Spanish American culture area. One was the large powerful landholder so characteristic of much of Latin America. This type developed primarily in the cattle and sheep ranching areas of southern and eastern New Mexico, although scattered patron families of this type were, and are, found in other sections of the state.

The second and more common type of patron was the village patron encountered at one time in almost every Spanish American village. The Spanish American land owning system was not in general characterized by the concentration of land in the hands of a few. It was marked by the predominance of self-sufficient agricultural villages inhabited by small independent landowners owning plots of irrigated land and possessing grazing rights on the village commons.

In the sections of New Mexico where the large landholder did become the dominant social, political, and economic figure, a way of life was created that had much in common with the latifundias of Latin America. The landowner lived in a massive fortified ranchhouse. Grouped around the ranchhouse were the church and the homes of the peons. This nucleus formed a self-sufficient socioeconomic unit isolated to a large degree from the outside world and completely dependent upon the landowner, the powerful patron.

The labor force on the ranches was largely composed of workers held in debt peonage. Legal in New Mexico until it was abolished by a special act of Congress in 1867, debt peonage was defined as a voluntary service for debt involving no loss of civil rights, no sale of another person, and no legal obligations inherited by the children.

Under the law, a debtor who could not pay his debts was obligated to work them out at a rate set by the patron. He could be sent to jail only if his creditor refused to accept his labor service. As a result, the peon was in almost life-time servitude. Wages were low, and essentials had to be purchased at high prices from the landowner.

The system of debt peonage provided economic security at the cost of personal freedom. Many poor families deliberately went into debt in order to secure assistance and protection from a patron in exchange for their labor. Peonage, although banned by law, continued to exist in New Mexico until very recently.

The basic relationship between the landowning patron and the peon was not wholly economic in nature. In many respects, it resembled the lord and vassal system of the Middle Ages. The patron was responsible for the entire economic and social well-being of his peons and their families. He provided them with employment and took care of the sick, the orphaned, and the widowed. He became the godfather of the peon children at baptism. His peons were protected if they became involved with the law. He also financed church activities and supported religious and secular fiestas. The peons in return gave absolute obedience and loyalty to the patron. Loyalty was regarded as the cardinal virtue of a peon.

In summary, the patron-peon relationship rested upon a foundation of unexpressed but clearly understood set of reciprocal obligations as well as respect for the personal dignity of the patron and of the peon. If either the patron or the peon failed to comply with his duties and obligations, the sense of reciprocal obligation was broken.

The village patron was in quite a different position from the large landholder. He was more apt to be a merchant, a political or military leader, or an individual respected by his fellow villagers because of his wealth, social position, political contacts, family background, or his wisdom and knowledge. His position as a patron did not depend upon landownership but rather upon his ability to provide employment to village members and to command their respect and loyalty.

The position of the village patron was not as secure as that of the powerful landholder. The villagers were not peons caught in a network of debts. They were independent farmers who for various reasons voluntarily respected a village individual and his family as patrons and yielded them more authority and respect than they did to other village families. If the village patron were unable to maintain his dominant position in the village, he lost his patron position and might be replaced by another individual.

The village patron, as long as he respected the customs and traditions of the village, was granted authority and prestige as the village leader. As such he represented the village in its dealings with other villages and with higher political authority. He had the power to call out village members to repair roads and irrigation ditches, to build schools and churches and to perform other types of communal labor. As a patron he was expected to provide for the unemployed, the hungry, the aged, the sick, the orphaned, the widowed, and for those in trouble. He also settled disputes between villagers, and his decisions were final.

If no priests lived in the village, the patron usually took over church responsibilities and became the lay religious leader of the village. He frequently was invited to become a leader among the Penitentes. In a priestless village the authority of the patron was much greater than it would be in a village where he shared his authority with the priest.

In villages with resident priests, the influence and power of the patron did not extend to matters of religion, morality, or the family. Authority in those areas rested with the religious patron, the priest. The relationship between the priest and the patron was one of uneasy equality. Because of personality factors, one or the other usually dominated. When they competed for village dominance, the village was apt to be divided into quarreling factions.

Both the village patron and the landholding patron were expected to be generous, hospitable, brave, courageous and to display qualities of leadership. They were required to respect the personal dignity and honor of those who followed them. To some degree the reputation of the village and of the peon depended upon the personality and the behavior of the patron. The patron who could not hold the respect of his peons or of his fellow villagers was in serious danger of losing his position.

The patron-peon relationship rested upon values and attitudes that for the most part still exist and in a large measure still determine the attitudes of Spanish Americans toward government, political activities, welfare , employment, and patterns of leadership. Among these values are the following: (1) a blind loyalty toward ethnic leaders that is frequently reflected in voting patterns; (2) a tendency to endeavor to enter into a secure political or economic position of dependency upon a prominent political leader or a person with wealth; (3) a reluctance among many to make decisions and a tendency to postpone decisions as long as possible; (4) dislike of competition and of personal initiative so important to English-speaking Americans; (5) a preference for a stable hierarchical social system with well-defined statuses and roles; (6) a preference for friendly person-to-person primary relationships rather than the formal impersonal relationships of our urbanized world, and (7) a strong dislike for and resistance to social and cultural changes. These values strongly handicap the adjustment of large numbers of Spanish Americans to the urbanized industrialized society into which so many of them are now moving.

In the rural villages where native Spanish American patrons are still found with some degree of power, wealth, and authority, there is little cultural breakdown or social disorganization. Resistance toward acculturation and toward Anglo control of the political, social and economic life of the area remains strong. Social and cultural change are much slower than in the villages where the local patrons have disappeared. These latter villages are marked by factionalism, lack of leadership, weakened village unity, increase in social disorganization, and accelerated social and cultural change.

Under serious and constant Anglo-American pressures, the Spanish patron-peon pattern rapidly weakened and then disintegrated in the first half of the twentieth century. The large landholders were the first to suffer. Stripped of their lands by violence, fraud, legal deceptions, excessive land taxes, unwise use of credit, and the problems of adjustment to a strange and unfamiliar fiscal and political system, they have almost completely disappeared as an important cultural and economic element in the present socioeconomic structure of New Mexico.

Almost all of the range land in New Mexico has passed into the hands of Anglo-Americans. The majority of these new landholders who employ Spanish American workers refuse to accept the role of the patron that had formerly accompanied large landholdings. They endeavor to regulate their employee relationships upon the traditional Anglo concept of cash payment for labor rendered. Once the salary is paid, the Anglo employer feels no further obligation toward his employees. The Spanish American workers, unable to comprehend the formal distant impersonality of their Anglo employers, become bewildered and resentful. They frequently retaliate by gossip, apathy, or by leaving their employment without notice.

A few Anglo ranchers or landholders for one reason or another may endeavor to fulfill the role of the patron. Many of them, failing to understand the nexus of reciprocal obligations that underly the system, become unknowingly the subject of ridicule and even of exploitation on the part of their Spanish American workers. A few who develop insight into the values of the patron-peon system and fulfill the reciprocal obligations may be accepted as patrons and given the complete unconditional loyalty of their Spanish American workers and neighbors. A very few who learn Spanish may acquire a devoted following among the Spanish American and in time do become important political leaders in the state of New Mexico.

Although the village patrons have survived somewhat better than the large landholders, their influence has been sharply reduced by the intruding Anglo-American merchant, politician, school teacher, and social worker. Of all of these groups, the merchant perhaps has played the major role in weakening the authority and power of the village patron. The merchant came to make money and seldom participated in the community life of the Spanish American rural village. Because of superior business methods, better wholesale and credit contacts, and the support of other Anglo merchants, he was usually able to drive out of business any competing Spanish-owned store. As he neither understood nor sympathized with the cultural patterns of the Spanish Americans, it was difficult for either the priest or the patron to establish a working relationship with him. Yet, neither could ignore him. By the liberal extension of credit, the encouragement of new wants, and the purchase of village products, the average merchant came in time to dominate the economic life of the village.

The village families gradually became financially dependent upon the merchant. Many patron families, unaccustomed to the aggressive and frequently ruthless business methods of the Anglo merchant, lost their lands to him. Thus the merchant, without realizing himself what was happening, gradually destroyed the economic position of the patron and seriously weakened the social integration of the village. The merchant seldom was able to assume the obligations and duties of a patron and when the Spanish American patron disappeared, the village was left without leadership. The merchant took from the village economically and contributed little in return to the social or cultural life of the community.

Only in the area of politics have the Spanish Americans been able to preserve a position of relative equality with the English-speaking group. Anglo politicians have had to adopt Spanish American political customs in the Spanish-speaking area of New Mexico in order to secure the vote of the local inhabitants. They have also had to accept Spanish American politicians who could control that vote and award them suitably for political support.

Over the course of years since New Mexico became a part of the United States, an informal pattern of superordination-subordination developed. The higher political positions in the state such as governor, senator, or congressman were reserved for the Anglo politicians. The Spanish Americans had reserved for them the subordinate positions such as lieutenant governor, secretary of state, and the local county, and village positions. This pattern of accommodation has tended to break down since World War II.

The Spanish American politician, in order to retain influence and power, had to deliver blocs of votes in every election. In order to obtain these votes he had to fulfill the role of a patron to the best of his ability. A political patron is known as a *jefe politico* in the Spanish American areas of the state. Each village has come to possess its local *jefe politico* who interacts politically with county and regional political leaders. Many of these political bosses are from the old patron families, while others are men who have moved up from the lower classes in areas where the former patrons have disappeared.

The *jefe politico* with less power and influence than the old patron struggles to carry out the role of a patron in his village or county. As he controls almost every public position in his area, he is able to reward his followers with employment and other forms of patronage and to deny public employment to his opponents. In northern New Mexico, where nonpolitical employment is scarce, the ability of a political leader to provide or to deny employment permits him to exercise considerable power.

The authority and the power of the political boss is also enhanced by the voting habits of the Spanish American voter. The loyalty of such a voter is seldom given to a political party. It rather belongs to the political leader. If the *jefe politico* switches from one party to another, his supporters will follow him.

The *jefe politico* is seldom concerned with the more important economic, social, or cultural problems of his people. He is deeply involved in "bread and butter politics." In a literal sense, he is for sale to the state political leader who will award him the most patronage to distribute to his followers and money with which to buy votes. The result is that the serious problems facing the Spanish American people at present tend to be ignored by both local and state politicians, whether Spanish or Anglo.

In northern New Mexico the *jefe politico* is still a powerful figure in the rural villages. In other sections of the state, he has tended to disappear. The increase in the English-speaking vote, the rise of a more educated and politically sophisticated younger generation of Spanish American voters, the increased extension of federal programs beyond the ability of the *jefe politico* to control, and the slow and halting movement toward a state civil service in time will probably reduce and perhaps even liquidate his authority.

In summary, the decline of the patron-peon pattern has left a vacuum in the social organization and value system of the Spanish Americans that as yet has not been filled. The traditional patterns of leadership and of decision making, responsibility for the poor and the weak, the solution of family and of group conflicts, the financing of church, school, and other communal activities, and of maintaining ethnic and village unity are disintegrating. No adequate substitute patterns have as yet appeared.

Perhaps the greatest crisis of the Spanish Ameri-

cans caused by the decline of the patron-peon pattern is that of leadership. The Spanish Americans in general are marked by extreme factionalism. It is difficult for them to cooperate in communal endeavors or to follow the patterns of problem solving and decision making of their Anglo neighbors. Spanish Americans who do accept Anglo procedures find themselves isolated from their own people who will not follow them. The masses still admire and prefer the patron. Unfortunately, today it is extremely difficult for any Spanish American to acquire the wealth, the social position, and the power necessary to become a patron. The result is that today there are few effective Spanish American economic, political, or cultural leaders in New Mexico.

JACK E. Holmes

Jack E. Holmes, (Professor of Political Science, University of Tennessee at Knoxville) has had a successful career in governmental service as well as in teaching and research. In New Mexico, for example, he directed the Legislative Council Service, became a practical politician, and served as a special assistant to the Republican state committee. Professor Holmes uses both his practical and professional training to analyze the political strengths and weaknesses of the New Mexico Chicanos as a voting block. Since the reading of the paper at the Southwestern Social Science Meeting in 1967, Dr. Holmes' book, POLITICS IN NEW MEXICO (1967), has been published. By permission of the author.

Success And Failure: The Limits Of New Mexico's Hispanic Politics

Although it is seldom the case elsewhere in the nation, the Hispanic citizenry of New Mexico has long possessed and wielded political power. Bolstered by the state's constitution, embedded in the statutes, sustained by organization and a high level of voting, and maintained out of a conviction of its utility, that political capacity has led to an endless debate centering upon two questions: First, what are its key cultural and institutional linkages? Second, is it, or is it not, a power well-founded and well used?

New Mexico's example is obviously of more than local or even academic importance in view of the current struggles for political leverage in the United States of such culturally differentiated groups as Negroes, Puerto Ricans, and long-time

238

residents of Appalachia to catch up in a "techno-logical society" which may be becoming increas-ingly marked by group differentials and personal deprivations stemming from differentials in cul-tural and individual access to the "knowledge in-dustry" and all that it implies.

Now the questions of the ends and means of political capacity are not at all foreign to Hispanic action or discussion in New Mexico, but the ques-tions as posed are generally matters for discussion in circles other than those of the Spanish Ameri-can; for, although the debate is reflected in politi-cal speeches and the newspapers, it finds it chief expression in private discourse, *belles lettres,* and scholarly investigation. But, wherever found, the discussion lies so close to emotion and to values concerning ends and means that its utility for heu-ristic analysis is apt to be foreclosed by the very terms of the debate.

Interwoven in many discussions of the political role and activity of New Mexico's Hispanic citi-zenry is the thought that somehow or other the Spanish American has failed to pursue rational goals in his own interest. Thus, Sanchez remarks in his study of Taos County:

> The Taoseño constitutes over 90 percent of the total population. . . . He elects the public officials. He controls the public affairs in the county and wields the political power of the county in state affairs. The leadership for this political influence of the Taoseño has too of-ten come from those of his own group who haven't the background of experience or of training or the inclination to use this influ-ence effectively on behalf of the people.

In other contexts or writings the implication is plain that political mentors have failed, and per-haps deliberately, to provide a political environ-ment and style of debate in which the Hispanic voter would be induced or required to accept all of the rational, political-economic, and social goals of the larger society so that he might prosper by striving for the achieving "success" as others do. In still other prescriptions, it is clear, the political system and its members, both Anglo and Hispanic, are scored because they have failed to foster and perpetuate the values and ways of life thought to be common (as of some uncertain date) to the Spanish American.

Nor have the most widely used sociological and anthropological field studies clarified the political and policy matters so long under debate. The stud-ies cited agree on the profound importance of family, and generally regard it both as the unit upon which the Hispanic villages are based and as an essential instrument in the control of the indi-vidual's relations with other institutions. The roles of church and *patrón* are also heavily stressed, although, in some, the *patrón* (sometimes "good" or at least kindly) is distinguished from the *jefe politico,* the political leader or boss (usually "bad"). All stress the infrequency of other types of social or interest groups and organizations. Opin-ions among the various authors concerning the extent of knowledge, interest, and effectiveness in politics of Hispanic voters differ a great deal, and in several reports there is a strong flavor of the pejorative in discussions of the state's system of politics. Writings based upon first-hand knowl-edge are not numerous, but from them there has been derived a somewhat Procrustean synthesis exemplified in works of Margaret Mead and Lyle Saunders.

According to this synthesis, villages were iso-lated from each other and the village economy was semicommunal. Land was cultivated by large family groups incorporating several generations; tools and equipment were freely shared and bor-rowed as were labor and products. And thus, al-though the village community was highly self-sufficient, the individuals in it were not. The economic unit was the community, not the indi-vidual." Within the village, family and church were the dominant institutions. Family and village often tended to be almost synonymous, while reli-gion—"a devout Catholicism"—was the center, "the core of all institutional activity." The third institution was the *patrón* system. "A large land-owner, a person of wealth, an influential politician —anyone with prestige, power, resources, and a sense of obligation toward a given community might become a *patrón*." He was a person "with whom the villagers assumed a reciprocal relation-ship of mutual assistance and dependency." Mead sees the *patrón* as the link between the village and the larger community, and in this respect the *patrón* even supercedes the father or oldest family male, important though he be in the family scheme of things. Says Mead: "The *patrón* system reproduces the family picture for the community, and the *patrón* holds the position ascribed to the father in Spanish-American culture. To be Spanish American is to be a father or to be dependent, or both, in different contexts. . . . The older, in general, are in authority over the younger, men over women, and, to some extent, the rich over the poor." Further, "There are no voluntary associations here, with elected leaders."

The conventional analysis implies a prevailing tendency to preservation of a condition of internal social equilibrium centered upon traditional concerns and the person of the *patrón*. A picture emerges of tightly-knit villages in which there is a normal inclination to a political unanimity reflecting an underlying social unanimity—a condition leading, in stable times, to a local one-party dominance maintained by the *patrón* in his role of father figure and conservator of village solidarity. A one-party stance results from the normal equilibrium of the village, and a two-party balance of around 50 percent is divisive of the community. Consequently, a response to external forces of change, or a shift in the party allegiance of the *patrón* implies a major change so that, for example, the village once 80 per cent Republican changes, if it does, to an equally one-sided Democratic vote. Similar changes may come as a result of the activities of a *jefe politico,* but this actor is indifferent to the preservation of the core values of the community. The *jefe* merely seeks, and frequently finds, a vote he can easily control and move from party to party.

A curious alignment of circumstance, and of questions and answers, is apparent in various studies of Hispanic communities of the state. Most of the villages studied were quite naturally targets of opportunity chosen for their availability to the researcher, or for the inappropriateness to concerns in which matters political were more or less incidental. None of the authors cited bothered to count the votes. In the selection of the places studied there was, of necessity, no grand design by which to fit a cross section of villages into the slots of a carefully wrought sample. But, as a fortuitously random sample, the villages studied comprise by quite improbable chance a statistical oddity producing a skewed result. So, too, do inferences drawn from the *patrón* conception. That *patrones* and local political bosses have long existed in New Mexico is beyond dispute, but neither their supposed frequency nor power accounts for the electoral or organizational pattern the political record discloses. (The results which might be anticipated from the foregoing systems of analysis appear in New Mexico only in areas in which Hispanic voters are a local minority; but, in those cases more conventional explanations appear to suffice.)

In the face of such prescriptions and expectations there is little cause for wonder that from some quarter or other New Mexico's Hispanic voter is apt to be criticized because he has (all unknowingly) failed to solve by his politics a dilemma of culture, economics, and public policy that continues to engage the best efforts of our Oscar Lewises and Michael Harringtons.

HOW HAS HE FARED, AND WHY?

There should be little doubt (as I shall attempt here to demonstrate) that New Mexico's Hispanic voters have solved a portion of their problems in that they have developed a redoubtable political expertise and maintained a political power that is roughly proportionate to their number. But underlying a part of the generalized indictment of the goals of that power and expertise, and of the extent and kind of social and economic well-being that the state has accorded its Spanish-American citizens, is undeniable evidence that by almost every measure of material wealth the typical resident of the Hispanic community fares less well than other citizens. In listings of counties by their per capita income, for example, those of predominantly Hispanic population have for years tended to cluster near the bottom. Welfare payments per capita are just as consistently at the highest in the same areas.

Some of the factors in this lag can be accounted for in economic terms. The land grants on which the early day pastoral economy was based tended to be disrupted or to pass into other hands; federal land reservations for the national forests reduced grazing resources by making them subject in part to the claims of others; the unreserved and unprotected lands of the public domain were subjected to a damaging over-grazing by all comers in the decades near the turn of the century. The irrigable lands available to the traditional talents and funds of late nineteenth-century New Mexico were too few and too poor to support an agriculture similar to that of the Midwest, even if its products had been able to compete in the distant markets. The additional water rights later made available by reclamation projects were almost always, due to gravity and the availability or irrigable land, down-stream rights located far from the northern areas of settlement, and those downstream rights were usually acquired and exercised by those who had the relatively large amounts of capital required.

That the traditional areas of Hispanic settlement in the northern counties are not those favored by the current state of the arts, by nature, or by the economy is increasingly apparent. Except for Valencia and Dona Aña, the counties of Hispanic settlement are suffering either relative or absolute population losses just as are those other and "Anglo" counties whose economies are dependent upon the same factors. Of major investment other than agricultural the typical Hispanic county has attracted it generally in the fugitive form of limited or relatively short-lived mining enterprises. There was a time when a form of "mercantile capitalism" served to convert the produce of the area into goods and exchange. In that era of 1875-1920, the residents of the northern counties apparently registered economic gains that were as great as those made elsewhere in the state, but the forces that finally impelled such firms as the Charles Ilfeld Company to migrate from Las Vegas to Albuquerque were those which made Albuquerque a transportation and investment center while they reduced the northern counties' relative productivity or attractiveness for new capital. If cultural considerations or limited community aspirations are laid aside as agents of cause, these areas are "depressed" or underproductive in the sense economists usually employ the terms, and the problems they present are essentially the problems that have been made familiar in cut-over areas of the northern forested states, the mining areas of West Virginia, areas of non-competitive crop lands such as in portions of Maine or Pennsylvania, and numerous local areas of chronic underemployment in Appalachia and the Southern states.

HISPANIC VOTES AND VOTING

Institutions of Hispanic origin had been functioning in New Mexico for over 200 years before the area became a Territory of the United States in 1846. It was then, and long remained, a pastoral and irrigated farm economy which increasingly based its social organization on villages comprising the nucleus of land grants which, in the earlier periods, were generally to individuals and, in the later, to community associations. By 1900, the 195,000 residents of the Territory were still concentrated in the traditional areas of settlement along the Rio Grande and 67 percent of the population lived in the Hispanic counties of Bernalillo, Doña Ana, Mora, Rio Arriba, San Miguel, Sante Fe, Socorro, Taos, and Valencia. As late as 1915, native-born Spanish Americans numbered 57 percent of the state's total population and constituted 75 percent or more of the population of eleven counties, between 50 and 75 percent in three, and from 25 to 50 percent in four others of the state's twenty-six counties. And by this time many were townsmen of Santa Fe, Las Cruces, Albuquerque, and Las Vegas. By 1950, the increasingly urbanized residents of Hispanic surname had dropped to 37 percent in the state, and only ten of the thirty-two counties could muster an Hispanic majority. By 1960, only six counties of the mountainous north still had a Spanish-American majority and the Hispanic portion of the total was only 27.5 percent. The present day population of over a million is concentrated in nine counties and the state is one of the nation's most urbanized.

Albuquerque and Bernalillo County now cast about 30 percent of the state's ballots, the block of six contiguous counties of the southeast border regions which have long been called "Little Texas" cast about 22 percent, and the 10 or eleven counties in which Hispanic politics is most influential still cast from 25 to 30 percent of the votes.

During the Territorial era the only statewide election was that for delegate to Congress. Democratic candidates won six of the thirteen elections of 1884-1908, and the Democratic percentage of the two-party vote ranged from 37 to 56 percent for a mean of 48 percent. Nor have the narrow limits set by the Territory been exceeded by the gubernatorial and presidential elections of fifty years of statehood, for each has normally ranged well within the limits of 40 to 60 percent.

From 1900 through 1928 only one Hispanic county—Valencia—could cast a lopsided Republican vote, in three or four it could frequently reach the 60 percent which became almost a limit, and in four or five others Republicans could normally win but with the narrowest of margins. Voting rates in the Hispanic counties were usually the highest and most stable in the state, and provided the thin margins by which the Republican party controlled the legislature (which had a critical number of its members elected from multi-county districts) and managed to elect about half of its gubernatorial candidates from 1911 until 1930. No personal or party monopolies of power existed in the typical Hispanic county. There were, of course, small areas such as precincts or villages in which a man or a family might for a time maintain a hegemony of authority, but even in these there were typically alternative sets of leadership in active competition; and everywhere, save in Valencia County, Democrats maintained fully staffed precinct and county organizations. So tight and durable was this party competition, so complete the commitment of its voters, that the Theodore Roosevelt and LaFollette candidacies made a respectable showing in only two of the hispanic counties of the day—Bernallilo and Sanoval.

If there were, in fact, numerous *patrones* or bosses prior to 1932 in the precincts treated in the literature cited above or in the much larger set of precincts in the northern counties, then one might conjecture that a majority of *patrón* and *gente* alike were quite content to be Republicans, yet there were only a score or so of 223 precincts in which *patrones* seem to have been in residence.

A series of firm party majorities is an unreliable clue to a vote controlled by a local boss or organization; for to be found across the land are unbossed clusters of voters who maintain an astonishing party loyalty. The more frequently rewarding indicator of electoral faction, boss, or machine is a highly flexible series of votes. Behavior of the embattled precincts of Mora, Rio Arriba, San Miguel, Santa Fe, and Taos counties in the state's northern Hispanic heartland provides evidence permitting a tentative judgment of the incidence of controlled voting. The paired elections of 1920 and 1936—bridging the career of the Republican maverick, Senator Bronson M. Cutting, and the shift from the Republican hegemony to the Roosevelt sweep of the Hispanic counties are the measure here.

To Republicans, 1920 was a sound and satisfying year; 1936 brought a bonanza to Democratic candidates and a lasting realignment of voter loyalties. One hundred of 148 rural and small-town precincts yielded Democratic gains ranging from 1 to 30 percentage points—changes of an order which should raise no eyebrows. More likely as fiefdom of *jefe* or *patrón* are precincts which moved in sharp opposition to the trend, or those which gave the long-term trend and party switch an extraordinary support. Twelve precincts flouted the Democratic trend and reduced the party's vote by 10 to 34 percentage points; a score produced Democratic gains of 30 to 65 points. Some were precincts in which politics was strongly influenced by the Penitentes—Catholic groups verging on apostasy, and serving the sociological functions of a sodality. Others were probably only indulging a passion for politics. A few at either extreme of party change were doubtless producing their notable shifts at the behest of some local family or leader. Whatever the nature of the psychological and sociological variables involved, the voters and political institutions of the five counties produced a classic example of a smooth and fluid partisan shift.

The most frequent Democratic percentage in 1920 was in the 30-40 percent range; in 1936 the mode moved 20 points to the 50-60 range. More germane to the argument is the point that the number of precincts with an extremely lop-sided party preference was small in each election. Seventy per cent of the precincts fell within the range of 30 to 70 percent Democratic in 1920; in 1936 that range accounted for 89 percent of the precincts.

If one plots time series graphs of the party vote for governor in the ten counties still half or more Hispanic in 1950, each shows an individualistic tempo of party change over the series of elections from 1911 through 1964. In each case, whatever the slopes of the regression line for the series, the series is remarkably linear, and in all but three cases the 50-year range (plus or minus standard error of estimate times 2) about the regression line is 12 percentage points or less. Table 1 sets out the appropriate data for the ten counties.

Table 1.   Long-Term Shift in Party Strength and Variability of the Party Vote in Ten Hispanic Counties, Gubernatorial Vote, 1911-1964

County	Democratic Percentage Points Gained-Lost	Regression Line Values		Variability Rating $(2S_y)$
		1911	1964	
1. Valencia	39.2	19.5	58.7	14.3
2. Rio Arriba	18.0	39.3	57.3	11.8
3. Socorro	16.7	38.0	54.7	12.0
4. Taos	14.8	40.0	54.8	10.9
5. San Miguel	14.5	40.4	54.9	10.8
6. Santa Fe	13.3	40.5	53.8	12.4
7. Sandoval	12.1	44.0	56.1	14.2
8. Dona Ana	8.7	46.1	54.8	15.7
9. Guadalupe	6.3	46.9	53.2	9.8
10. Mora	-6.3	50.3	44.0	10.1
Ten Counties as a Unit	14.1	40.4	54.5	8.8

Source: New Mexico *Blue Books* and *Official Returns*. Secretary of State, State of New Mexico. The first two gubernatorial elections bridged a five-year term; thereafter elections were held at two-year intervals.

The trend vote shown for the group of Hispanic counties in 1911 is 40 percent for the Democratic candidate for governor, and by 1964 the ten counties had moved 14 percentage points to produce a group trend line "majority" of 55 percent. The five counties heading the list in the table, however, registered Democratic gains ranging from 15 percent to 39 percent. The movement of this

half of the Hispanic counties has been so steadily toward the Democratic party's candidates that there is some likelihood that they may march past the border of a 45-55 percent electoral range well into the province of that party. Mora is the sole anomaly among the Hispanic counties—a stranger at the end of the procession.

The variability score of the Hispanic counties as a group is only 9 points. Yet these counties differ greatly in their individual ratings of party stability —from 16 percentage points in the case of Doña Ana down to 10 in the case of Guadalupe—measures indicating that the several counties have frequently evinced differing reactions to candidates, issues, or campaign tactics. The 1948 and 1950 elections illustrate the matter. The Democratic gain from 1948 to 1950 for the ten counties was 4.2 percentage points; but in Doña Ana, the largest, richest, and most variable, local issues brought out an imposing vote and the Democratic margin there declined by 20 percentage points, a factor sufficient to limit the change of the group.

INSTITUTIONAL ROOTS OF POLITICAL SKILLS

A cagey knowledge of the mechanics and nuances of politics is not inborn. Nor is that knowledge necessarily an ingredient of a social heritage, although it may be fostered by relevant institutions and perfected by a succession of generations. In New Mexico's case, scarcely two generations separate the Kearney Code of the Military occupation of 1846 and the 1910 constitution, but sixty-four years were enough; for the pupils were apt, the tutors were proficient and in dire need of votes, and institutions already at hand had long fostered political skills. At the beginning, the anecdote goes, the young men of Taos asked their famed, and unfrocked, politician-priest what kind of government the United States was. Padre Martinez replied that it was a republic, and added that a republic was a "burro on which lawyers jog along better than priests." At the close of the Territorial era, Col. Venceslao Jarmillo, Republican state chairman, had occasion to address his party's convention. Colonel Jarmillo stressed protection, particularly of the sheep industry, called President Taft a statesman, and went into the "race issue" with a suave reminder to his Anglo colleagues of the party's dependence upon Hispanic votes. The period of tutelage had ended.

The key factors and institutions underlying this prompt and efficient accommodation to a new political system are not those usually accorded sociological primacy. Elemental agencies such as church and family dominate an intricate and diffuse range of activities and relationships, but in New Mexico's case provide only the broadest of contexts for political analysis. There had evolved a notable emphasis upon political institutions and processes—an emphasis probably entirely compatible with central elements of the Hispanic subculture. The emerging system had made crucial adjustments with a minimum of strain. In the critical Territorial years, the lawmaking process was American and Anglo-Saxon, but the majority of legislators was Hispanic, and the leadership of both parties was representative of both cultural groups. Statutes governing descent and distribution of property, marital and family matters, and the control of land and water rights promptly became a blend of the continental and the common law.

So the acculturating—the politicizing—institutions at issue here are those of a lesser scope: those called into existence to cope with matters of a specific focus. The assignment of herd or guard duty, determination of the type and priority of repairs to an irrigation system, the assignment of water rights, and the organization of joint ventures of several families were all of an order of activity likely to result in specific institutional arrangements. Any account of the mechanisms of social control and cooperation of the typical Hispanic village of the northern counties must include an elective system for the governance of the economic essentials of land and water.

The land grant technique was brought from Spain to Mexico and New Mexico where, in the latter, according to sources cited by Sanchez, there were twelve grants of less than 1,000 acres; thirty-five of 50,000 to 100,000 acres; and nineteen grants of more than 100,000 acres. Sanchez notes that many of the grants, including some made to individuals, became the property of the community, while others were made initially to the community in which:

> Only the homesteads and farming lands were owned privately. The rest of the land was owned in common and was managed by a community board of directors. Grazing and water rights were assigned by community boards or councils. . . . This system of land use and management became the dominant factor in the economic and social life of the settlers.

A review of the statutes governing land grants and acequias indicates that the political and administrative training received in the typical land grant community or irrigation system must have been significant. According to the 1897 codification of acequia statutes, all rivers and streams were declared public, and acequias were "bodies corporate, with power to sue or to be sued as such." Officers were three commissioners and one mayordomo (ditch boss), each of whom had to be the owner of an interest in the ditch. Officers were elected annually, and the commissioners were vested with authority to assess fatigue work. Statutes confirming self-government of the land grants were similar, and any ten or more owners in common could petition to be vested with corporate powers. Each person owning any interest in the grant could vote in the biennial elections for the board of nine trustees. Trustees could act in the corporate name, make rules and regulations, impose assessments, and determine grazing allotments. The land grants also often provided for the election of one or more graziers or herders.

There has also long existed in New Mexico a lay religious and fraternal organization called the Penitent Brothers of Jesus of Nazareth, or *Los Hermanos Penitentes.* The chapels of the Brothers early became schools for politics, and a formidable counterweight to other institutions both sacred and secular.

It appears that the origin of the organization was similar or related to that of the secular Tertiaries of Saint Francis in Europe, and it is probable that characteristics of New Mexico's Penitentes such as chapel self-government and flagellation were also importations drawn from Europe. On the occasion, in 1947, of the acceptance by a group of Penitente chapels of the authority of the Church (and after a full century of Church efforts to impose its guidance upon the Brotherhood), Archbishop Edwin V. Byrne of Santa Fe wrote that the older probably had its beginnings in New Mexico when the Franciscan padres left by order of the new government of Mexico.

> Groups among the faithful tried to keep up Catholic practices, without priestly guidance, and, though certain excesses crept in, it is to these groups of Penitential Brethren that we owe, in a manner, the preservation of the faith in those hard and trying times.
> But why do we make this declaration now? Precisely because many, even Catholics, harbor an erroneous notion concerning this association. It cannot be denied that the association itself is at fault because of certain excesses and abuses in the past. There are still scattered instances of individual bad lives, as in other societies, and this or that group still makes of itself a political football, thus giving a bad name to the brethren.

Fergusson's history relates that "It was in the rugged upper valley that the fraternity of the Penitent Brothers, wholly a plebian organization, had its headquarters and its greatest strength." Each morada was a highly organized social entity (and a few among the 135 remaining in 1960 appear to be so even today). During the century or so when they operated outside of the mantle of the Church, a fully staffed morada elected ten officers at the annual elections. The ritual attendant upon the religious observances, the practice of self-flagellation, and the judicial responsibilities of the morada each required the presence of specialized officers. Lummis lists four officers whose capacities were directed to the rituals of flagellation or worship. There was also an *enfermero* who attended the sick, a *celador* or warden who attended to the morada and executed sentences imposed for a misdeed, a teacher of novices, a *mandatario* or

collector, and a secretary. The chief officer of each morada, the *hermano mayor,* or older brother, might be young but he was a man of broad authority. Normally elected for one-year terms, he had the duty of general overseeing of the other officers, served as a court in disputes between members, and represented the morada before official agencies or outside parties.

Most writers who have described some facet or other of Penitente practice or villages have stressed that the organization has generally drawn its members from "the poorer men of the community—probably those whose interests are least well represented by the *patrón,* and whose influence is otherwise negligible." Fray Angelico indicates that the rituals of the Hermanos were public in the early days and that the men of the moradas provided the priestless villages with religious ceremonies for "which they greatly hungered," but that not all, by any means, of the villages were members. Nor was membership restricted by the poor to the poor.

> The *ricos* and more sophisticated men, if they joined at all, tended to be only "brothers of light" ... content to light the way for the more simple and sincere brethren and their scourging, and, after the American occupation, to peddle them as voteblocks at the polls.

It is difficult to separate fact from legend in an accounting of the politics of the Brotherhood. According to some sources the Penitente vote was "deliverable" and highly subject to manipulation. According to others, it was a vote inflexibly controlled by the Republican party. Probably it was neither. A manipulable vote is most useful to a party machine when it is seeking to control its own primaries, but New Mexico did not adopt a primary law until 1939. And a dominant party normally seeks to make its general election vote as high and stable as possible. If the general election vote of the Penitente precincts had been inflexibly dominated by the Republican party, it is improbable that officers of both parties would have felt impelled to expend in them as much time and effort as they did. Much more likely, insofar as I could find from lengthy analyses of the voting returns, is the proposition that the Penitente precincts contained a vote just large enough, and just variable enough, to make them a marginal factor critical in the electoral strategies of both parties. Within the northern counties of the state's Hispanic heartland, political leaders, whether of the Brotherhood or not, were unquestionably "powerful," but they were so only in the limited sense in which authority must have due regard for supportive factions. The scattered groups of Penitentes were too pervasive; and, probably, too much a functioning part of the Republican party to permit them consistently to behave, as politicians would view it, with a feckless opportunism. But, since the Penitentes were a minority in the localized Hispanic group which, in turn, was a part of the structure of a statewide party, they apparently sometimes did as the policy permits such groups to do: that is, use their weight as a balance of power within the party and between the parties and other groups as well.

In brief, the men of the moradas played the game *con gusto* and in the expectation that their vote or convention support would be courted. If that vote was ever a vendible commodity, in the sense that it could be made to break away from tradition, and friends and neighbors, then it was an angular and difficult thing to package, wrap, and consign. But when elections are close, then a few hundred votes bulk as large on the horizons of politicians as the Rockies to the westward traveler, and the presence of a man or cadre who can move them is apt to be the source of legends as glittering as those spun by travelers returned from El Dorado.

Sixty-four years of practice in the ways of Gringo politics ended in 1910 with the writing of a constitution containing some extraordinary guarantees of Spanish-American civic and political rights. To assess those features of the constitution as measure and result simply of Hispanic political power and skill would not, of course, be altogether accurate, for the legal position accorded this "minority" was an institutional product fashioned by a partisan grouping in which the Hispanic members were

merely one of several essential elements. One half of the seventy Republican delegates to the one-hundred member convention were Spanish American. The other half included a dozen or so Republicans of the rank and file, but most were key figures in the Republican Old Guard who were thoroughly representative of the dominant economic interests of the state. Nor was it an accident that the indispensable member of the Old Guard leadership of the convention was Solomon Luna—spokesman and leader of the Hispanic members who "formed a comparatively solid block welded by a common interest . . . the preservation of their traditional way of life and the language of their fathers."

The camaraderie of political fellowship and many lasting personal attachments are not to be discounted, but the relationship binding Anglo representatives of mining, railroad, and commercial interests to Hispanic members of party and convention had earlier become less one of mutual than of complimentary needs. In seeking its goals, each side was profoundly aware that it needed the support of the other. For their part of the bargain, Hispanic members achieved a constitution which should remove any doubt that the nexus between politics, economics, and group power had long been clear to a decisive, if not large, number of Hispanic citizens.

The objection might be raised that the convention action on the provisions establishing the guarantees of Hispanic civic and political rights merely demonstrates that a limited group of political leaders required those provisions. There is strong evidence, however, that Anglo and Hispanic voters alike were either aware of readily induced to become aware of the underlying issues.

The vote on the 1912 amendment to remove the congressionally required qualification that office holders and legislators be able to read and write English, and the vote on the congressionally required "Blue Ballot" amendment to make the constitution easier of amendment are contrasted in Table 2. The sharply negative correlation of the two elections is clearly dependent upon the proportions of Hispanic and Anglo voters in the various counties.

Table 2.   Relation of Vote on Two Culturally Relevant Constitutional
Amendments to "Anglo-Hispanic" Population Proportions

Percent Population Hispanic[a]	Number of Counties	Percent of Voters for Gov. and Pres. Voting on Measures		Percent Voting Yes[b]	
		1911	1912	1911 "Blue Ballot"	1912 Removal of Literacy Qualification
0-24.9	9	95	81	83	31
25-74.9	10[c]	92	80	57	67
75-100	7	96	94	45	88

[a]*New Mexico Blue Book*, 1915, p. 142.
[b]Derived from New Mexico Blue Book, 1917, pp. 221 and 227.
[c]Union County 1911 vote not available on "Blue Ballot".

For lack of space to present more of the state's political archeology relevant at this juncture, I have to revert to a rather dogmatic summary. The evidence is clear that the politics of most of Hispanic New Mexico came long ago to parallel the politics of other two-party areas in the United States; where the Hispanic citizenry is a localized minority, it maintains a devotion to political activity, but it then generally becomes more aligned with the Democratic party than is the norm in the state. In either case, if the ethnic flavor differs somewhat from that in most states, it is mainly in the spicing, much as good native chili differs from clam chowder. And Hispanic political strength is so firmly embedded in the institutions and traditions of the state that only continued and drastic losses in relative numbers will readily alter it. There are a few other points, however, that bear upon the questions whether that political power has been or could be used to gain an optimum social advantage.

MECHANISMS AND GOALS

Generally, the well-to-do, the urban, and the counties once the outposts of the politics of the South are becoming steadily more Republican; New Mexico's laboratory and research areas show a highly variable but surprising inclination to turn, at critical times, to a Republican vote; and the relatively poor Hispanic and Catholic counties, those heavily engaged in the extractive industries,

and the other counties of lower income have moved steadily toward an increased Democratic vote.

Increments or losses in party strength in the Hispanic counties are far more uniform at all levels of the ticket than they are in other counties of the state; schools and related institutions are more openly politicized, and school and local elections typically draw heavy turnouts only in the Hispanic counties. And, although the Hispanic counties are highly cognizant of issues and personalities in national politics, they are unique in that long-term party shifts or realignments of the voters and factions can frequently be foreshadowed in the voting for county offices.

Party machinery in the Hispanic counties and precincts is highly organized and fully staffed. In spite of the primary—which Hispanic leaders stoutly resisted for years—partly is still normally able to determine nominations. Unfortunately, so much weight and emphasis is given to local office that Hispanic legislators frequently serve only while waiting their turn for a local or statewide office. As I have hinted above, moreover, there is the strong possibility that the very intensity and competitiveness of politics in the Hispanic counties and some of their urban neighborhoods (and, as it may develop in some Indian communities) will continue to limit the uses to which state and local government can be put. The endless factional maneuverings, the use of office primarily to support and reward factions, the personal and narrowly political obligations which successful candidates for the legislature have apparently so often assumed as the price of their election, and the exceedingly close and personal involvement of leaders and potential leaders in their own communities—all these things operate to limit the capacity of Spanish Americans to use their political power to obtain an increased advantage for their communities. (There is little reason to suppose that other disadvantaged groups and communities have behaved—or will—much differently.) A more objective factor—reapportionment has also reduced Hispanic legislative weight to about a half of what it was early in the state's history, but reapportionment and a large number of single-member districts will serve to increase the number and stabilize the positions of Hispanic legislators from the larger urbanizing areas.

And early in the state's history, the ethos of neither the Anglo Old Guard nor that of their Hispanic colleagues and adherents was geared to devising governmental machinery or politics which would commit state or local government to broad programmatic goals in which government would be instrumental in achieving broad social goals of the sort we now associate with the New and Fair Deal movements. After World War II, however, Hispanic legislators twice deserted party lines almost to a man to secure a Fair Employment Practices Act and a Civil Rights Commission. And increasingly a related division grows in the legislature. Young college-trained Anglo legislators from the urban areas seek increasingly to hold stable existing governmental programs while they exert great effort and ingenuity to increase the operational capacity and efficiency of the legislature and the state government generally. They are conservatives who seek only operational change. Hispanic legislators are relatively cool to those efforts—efficiency means such things as merit systems, denigration of overt partisanship, etc.—and increasingly turn their attention to the programmatic outlook and content of government. But they do not yet pursue these matters with intensity of purpose, and they are not so organized within or without the legislature that they can institutionalize their efforts for a long-range pursuit of the goals they are learning to formualte and articulate. To the degree that they do, they can perhaps become the driving force of a form of positive liberalism still strange to New Mexico.

Chances are good, I think, that Hispanic New Mexico and the newly enfranchised Indian voters will be a force for programmatic change.

It is a loose, rather than a tight and rigidly structured political environment in which New Mexicans live, and the economy, with its tax structure, no doubt permits of more than it has recently produced for ameliorative programs. Hispanic spokesmen seem to be increasingly aware of the requirements for education and personal mobility in an increasingly technological order. Many of the new legislators will be relatively secure in their new little constituencies, and if, as statistical probabilities of such matters lead me to anticipate, a fair number of them are responsible and intelligent men, they will be in a position to exert a strong leverage upon the legislature and state government. And, assuming a continuance of the legislature's proclivity to create its own standards and environment as well as to provide the arena in which prospective governors and congressmen may demonstrate their capacity, the legislature should continue to provide a situation in which a mere handful of astute and adroit individuals could utilize its processes to produce some startling achievements. I am willing to suggest, in short, that the lively community and communications mechanisms the Hispanic voters have so long used can be deliberately turned to developing and exploiting a politics geared to change rather than to stasis. These are autonomous communities with a dynamics of their own.

A few men with a knowledge of the complex mechanics of legislation, and the ability and willingness to operate at the administrative and legislative levels in the manner developed by the better interest group lobbyists, could exert an enormous influence. Such skills are always badly needed wherever policy is determined, and their availability, always for a suitable—not too high—bargaining price, plus the leverage exerted at critical moments by minority group voters, could sometimes be decisive. If such a development should occur it might do so as a result of accident or social forces rather than conscious action, but there is nothing in the politics of the state which should necessarily preclude it. In this milieu an Hispanic or Indian Adam Clayton Powell could be disastrous, but an Hispanic Lyndon Johnson or programmatically inclined legislator with the skills of the Old Guard's Charles Springer could move the political mountains; and, if nothing else were at hand, he could do it with the materials of group politics already available. To create the optimal system even momentarily is probably a problem that can never be solved. To create an improved situation for a group is quite another matter, although it would probably require assumption of the heavy burden of mutual responsibility.

4.

THE BEGINNINGS
OF
BRONZE POWER

The Beginnings Of Bronze Power

Section III closed with a micro-study which pointed out that in New Mexico, at least, some talented Chicanos could succeed by traditional means. The slowness of this sort of success, if it came at all, grated upon the more militant. Furthermore, to many it seemed that the best way to crack the system was to become a cultural "Anglo." In short, one made it faster if he obliterated his past. To many Chicanos the fee was too dear, particularly since white hyphenated groups had not paid it.

Beginning in the early 1960s, the apparent inflexibility of Anglo culture caused unrest to grow in the *barrios*, both urban and rural, of the Southwest. Other factors fueled this dissatisfaction—the Black Power revolt, political confidence gained from such experiences as the "Viva Kennedy Clubs," and the flow of federal anti-poverty funds down to the local level created new Chicano leadership. The incendiary spark that fired the new spirit the most, however, was the impatience of youth with the slowness of change. They became the army that gave life to a movement diverse in tactics but united into a specific goal—the material betterment of the Chicano without sacrificing his inherited culture—or a demand for Bronze Power.

Fernando Peñalosa chronicles many of the circumstances necessitating Brown Power in "The Changing Mexican American in Southern California" and its sequel. Then the reader may explore four individual examples of the new Chicano movement. Francis L. Swadesh writes of the *Alianza* as a leader of social improvement in New Mexico; Joan London and Henry Anderson contribute a sketch of Ernesto Galarza, an early union organizer; Luis Valdez praises the radical implications and accomplishments of NFWA; and César Chávez recounts the problems of organizing that Union. Then the reader is asked to turn to Texas and political activity in the Valley. In two essays John Shockley looks at the Crystal City story. The first portrays the optimism that the political victories of 1963 inspired and the disillusionment that followed when not all the goals were obtained. The second records a new revolution in 1970; one led by new organizations, staffed with more militant chicanos, who have more confidence in confronting the gringo. The revolution has not swept the Valley. Indeed—as David Fishlow's poignant sketch, "Pancho Flores is Dead," demonstrates—the Chicano still faces a long, harsh struggle in moving into American society.

Brown Power advocates are exploring other methods for Mexican American advancement besides politics and organizations. Essays by Clark Knowlton and Jorge Lara-Braud call for Hispano gains brought about by the more traditional governmental actions. Yet these men certainly do not reject Bronze Power. Indeed Knowlton's demands that Mexican Americans receive compensation for lost Spanish land grants and that the government take steps to preserve Hispano culture in New Mexico is a very far sighted approach

253

that Anglos may still, and most certainly would have ten years ago, reject out of hand. Bi-lingual education, the subject of Lara-Braud's essay, is now demanded by all young militant Chicanos. The same pride that demands bi-lingual education prompted the last essay in the section—Jesus Luna's autobiographical sketch. The excellent subject material in the essay is justification enough for its inclusion in this book, but even more than that, the author is an example of a new breed of intellectual coming from the Bronze Power movement: one who is brown and proud of it.

FeRNaNdo PeÑalosa

Fernando Peñalosa (Professor of Sociology at California State College at Long Beach), has long been concerned with the differences between the concept of Mexican Americans held by sociologists and the reality of the life situation of Chicanos. In two articles, reprinted from SOCIOLOGY AND SOCIAL RESEARCH, *Professor Peñalosa first builds a model to refute the usual textbook picture of a Mexican American minority as being largely unskilled farm laborers. He argues, instead, that the Anglo-Mexican cast system was breaking down as a result of increased opportunities. Three years later in 1970, the emergence of Chicano militancy in the barrios forced him to re-think his earlier position. He articulates his new view in the second article. The student should note not only the changing position of Dr. Peñalosa, but the historical perspective that these essays give to the Chicano movement.*
From SOCIOLOGY AND SOCIAL RESEARCH, *Vol. 51, (July, 1967).*

The Changing Mexican American In Southern California

INTRODUCTION[1]

One of the hazards of any empirical science such as sociology is the constant temptation to reify what is essentially a statistical concept or a theoretical construct of the researcher. When such a model is essentially homologous with empirical reality, little theoretical or practical harm may come from reification. But when the model is essentially static, while the empirical reality with which the model is putatively homologous is in fact in a process of dynamic change, either the theoretical or the practical consequences, or both, may be unfortunate. It may safely be asserted that the concept or construct "Mexican-American population" as ordinarily found in the sociological lit-

[1]The practical definition which has been used by the writer in his researches in southern California is as follows: A Mexican-American is considered to be any person permanently residing in the United States who is descended from Spanish-speaking persons permanently residing in Mexico, and who in childhood and youth was enculturated into Mexican-American subculture.

erature frequently manifests a significant gap with empirical reality.

The most often used, and undoubtedly the best, approximation to the parameters of this population relies on a count of the Spanish-surname population, particularly in the states of the Southwest. But while the term "Spanish-surname population" is operationally definable, the terms "Mexican-American population" or "Mexican-American community" are not so easily controlled. Existentially there is no Mexican-American community as such, nor is there such a "thing" as Mexican-American culture. The group is fragmentized socially, culturally, ideologically, and organizationally. It is characterized by extremely important social-class, regional, and rural-urban differences. Partially because of the great regional variations of this ethnic group, this paper will be concerned primarily with southern California, one of the areas of greatest concentration of this population in the Southwest.

THE MEXICAN-AMERICAN POPULATION

Despite or perhaps because of its extreme fragmentation, there is significant evidence of increased self-consciousness of the group as it struggles through a crisis for self-identity. A perennial topic of discussion in Mexican organizations, as well as in talks given by Mexican-American leaders before Anglo groups is, "What shall we call ourselves?" In various regional and personal contexts this minority group is often called "Spanish-Americans," "Spanish," "Spanish-speaking people," "Latin-Americans," "Latinos," "Hispanos," etc. In southern California the most prevalent term used is "Mexican-American." This term, however, has little currency outside of southern California, and even in the latter area there is some dissatisfaction with the term. In recent years there has been an increase in use of the expression "Americans of Mexican descent" at the expense of the term "Mexican-American." Yet these terms are not in any strict sense synonymous, but realistically represent two quite different segments of the population under discussion. Persons of Mexican descent who were not at one time enculturated into the subculture of some Mexican-American

neighborhood are best labelled "Americans of Mexican descent" rather than "Mexican-Americans." The former do not constitute an ethnic minority group as do the latter. Another recent trend is that the attempt to disguise Mexican ethnic origin by self-identification as "Spanish" appears to be on the wane.

At the present time, in southern California as in the Southwest as a whole, the Mexican-American population is increasing more rapidly than the white population as a whole and only slightly less rapidly than the Negro population. In southern California the Spanish surname population increased 92.3 percent between 1950 and 1960, but more than 100 percent in Los Angeles (100.5) and nearby Orange (122.0) counties. The result is that the Mexican-American continues to be the largest minority group in southern California. In 1960 there were 870,600 Mexican-Americans in the eight southern California counties. It is probably now well over 1,000,000. This population is 78.8 percent native-born. The fact that immigrants from Mexico during 1955–60 accounted for 5.1 percent of California's Spanish surname population five years and over in 1960 indicates that natural increase is not the only significant factor contributing to the population's growth. Since 78.0 percent of the Mexican-Americans in southern California in 1960 were under the age of 35, this young population has a very high growth potential. Undoubtedly this fast growing segment of California's population will become numerically and proportionally even more important in the future.

ATTENUATION OF TRADITIONAL CULTURE PATTERNS

The standard accounts of Mexican-Americans stress their relatively high degree of cultural conservatism. This population is partially indigenous to the region, since it was largely responsible for settling the Southwest before its acquisition by the United States from Mexico in 1848. The continuing waves of immigrants, largely rural lower-class in background, from Mexico have been of much larger dimensions than the flow of acculturated individuals into the mainstream of American life.

Thus it has been that persons of Mexican descent have resided in southern California for almost two hundred years and many have largely retained their language and culture over this long span of time.

The primary reasons would seem to be the nearness of the country of emigration and the failure of the public school system to teach an adequate command of the English language and the other skills necessary for successful entry into the occupational world. As a result Mexican-Americans have had to compete economically with a continuous incoming supply of cheap Mexican national labor. The latest waves of the latter were those of the braceros and of the hundreds of thousands of "wetbacks" who have played their part in the continuing low average economic status of the Mexican-American population.

Despite great obstacles, this population as a whole is clearly moving further away from lower-class Mexican traditional culture and toward Anglo-American middle-class culture, so that both its cultural status and its social-class status are changing. It is true that immigrants in many ways reinforce the traditional patterns locally, but they are coming from a changing Mexico much more urbanized and industrialized than the Mexico known to the immigrant of two, three, or four decades ago. The latest waves of immigration have come from socioeconomically higher, more urbanized strata of Mexican society. Mexican-American migrants also come in important numbers from other states of the Southwest, particularly from Texas and New Mexico. The communities from which they have come are generally more traditionally oriented than southern California Mexican-American communities. On the other hand, in the latter, particularly the urban ones, intermarriage and normal social relations among the various subtypes of Mexican-Americans are promoting their merger into a more homogeneous population.

MEXICAN-AMERICAN HETEROGENEITY

There have been no recent major published studies specifically concerning southern California Mexican-Americans, but the tacit assumption of general works or of studies of communities in other areas is that their conclusions apply with equal force to the former. Many reports have either concentrated on limited aspects of the group, or used source materials two or more decades old, or both.

The most competent documentations of traditional Mexican folk culture in both Mexico and in the United States often make the assumption that understanding this culture is somehow the key to understanding Mexican-American culture. The latter is frequently dealt with as if it were a variety of Mexican folk culture. The rejection of such an oversimplification does not imply, of course, that there is no value in understanding this "folk" or "preindustrial" culture with its close ties to the land, its different sense of time, its lack of emphasis on formal education, and a social structure based primarily on personal rather than impersonal relationships. At the same time, such concepts should not constitute a perceptual screen with which to view the current situation. It is important to note in this connection that in recent years Mexican-Americans in southern California have been categorized along with a number of other ethnic groups and social strata as "culturally deprived" or "economically disadvantaged." It is patent that the nature of the "cultural deprivation" or "economic disadvantage" of this ethnic group is primarily a handicap of class and not of culture, unless we specify lower-class culture. This point has been frequently missed by a number of observers. Kluckhohn, for example, has asserted that "Mexican orientations . . . *in our system* secure very little for individuals except a lack of mobility and a general lower-class status. Indeed the other group in America which has orientations most similar to the Mexican is the non-aspiring, generalized lower-class group." It is clear from the context, though not explicitly stated, that Kluckhohn is referring specifically to traditional Mexican lower-class culture. The middle-class Mexican immigrant and his descendants have not been ordinarily "culturally deprived" or "economically disadvantaged," unless they gravitate to a Mexican-American *barrio* with its particular culture. If they move into a predominantly Anglo neighborhood, as they usually do, their problems are normally no greater than those of middle class immigrants from other countries. Mexican middle class persons are more like American middle class persons in their general way of life and basic outlook than they are like lower class persons from their own country.

There is a reaction among educated Mexican-Americans and among some informed social scientists against the characterizations of Mexican-American culture to be found in authoritative books and articles on the subject. They feel that these sources tend to create stereotypes by which even well-trained and well-meaning Anglos will tend to perceive the group, not taking account of individual differences and achievements. Pride and sensitivity about the collective image remain important traits even among the most highly acculturated Mexican-Americans.

The type of characterization which is most unsatisfactory revolves about concepts of the Mexican-American population as largely engaged in migratory agricultural labor. The impression is given in a recent textbook on ethnic relations that the Mexican-American population is concentrated in rural areas: "Although there are great variations in the background and social position of the Mexican population in the United States, many Mexican families are concentrated in rural areas in the West and Southwest where a considerable number of them earn livelihoods as migratory laborers." The same authors cite a 1952 Broom and Shevky article to the effect that "Many of them work in homogeneous gangs, with few contacts with non-Mexicans: the kind of casual labor which they usually find means migration, unemployment, isolation in labor camps; the language barrier reinforces the other problems." Another recent text is even more definite on this point: "Their low incomes and low educational status is due, at least in part, to their principal occupational status . . . migratory farm laborers." The same text makes the statement that "Mexican-American children that do manage to attend school often do poor work . . ." This statement is supported by citing a book published in 1946.

Such broad generalizations as those quoted tend to blur the lines of distinction among the various social classes among Mexican-Americans. They further fail to differentiate clearly among a number of interrelated factors: the lower class, rural origins of the immigrants; the low average occupational status of Mexican-Americans at the present time; and the ways in which their present day problems are shared by the members of lower class groups, ethnic or otherwise. They further fail to take into consideration the broad rural-urban, class, occupational, educational, and regional differences of the Mexican-American population. A homogeneity is postulated or inferred where none exists. Even if we confine our attention to one broad geographical area, such as southern California, and examine the culture and social structure of this population, the homogeneity fails to appear.

The Mexican-American subculture in its most common variant is probably best regarded and understood as a variant of American working-lower class culture. This culture is, of course, affected by all the limitations of lower status in a predominantly middle-class society. The group's way of life is further conditioned by the effects of the reaction of the group to discrimination. If we accept the concept of Mexican-American culture, at least in its southern California variety, as a variant of the United States working class subculture, but influenced to a lesser or stronger degree by traditional Mexican folk culture, it follows that these people should be regarded as partially Mexicanized Americans rather than as partially Americanized Mexicans. No one who has carefully observed the way of life of rural and of urban lower-class people in Mexico, which would represent the original roots of most Mexican-Americans, would make the mistake of considering them the reverse.

RECENT SOCIOCULTURAL CHANGE

The forces of acculturation and assimilation working over a period of three or more generations have brought about the present situation. Most of the change has been slow and barely perceptible to many of the most-quoted authors in the field. Nevertheless, there was a major breakthrough during World War II of forces promoting change and the solution of problems confronting the Mexican-American community. At this time there was a great flow of people out of the *barrio* or Mexican-American neighborhood. Young Mexican-Americans took industrial jobs in increasing numbers, went off to war, traveled around the world, and were treated as individuals, some for the first time. During World War II Mexican-Americans volunteered in greater numbers and won more Congressional Medals of Honor per capita than any other ethnic group. Veterans especially returned to find themselves dissatisfied with the old ways, and many went to college under the provisions of the G. I. Bill. Occupational skills were upgraded because of wartime industrial experience, and because of the additional educational opportunities made available to younger members of the group.

Social change involves of course not only a realignment of individual perceptions, attitudes and actions, but also a reorganization of structural relationships within the community. It is important to note that the types of American communities, both rural and urban, into which Mexican immigrants and interstate migrants of yesterday and today have moved form a most heterogeneous congeries. Some of the differences found from one Mexican-American community to another are undoubtedly due to the varying natures of the several Anglo-American matrices in which the Mexican-American communities are imbedded. The rate of sociocultural change therefore varies widely from one southern California community to another.

Before World War II the Mexican-American population in the Southwest was largely rural, but by 1950 it was two-thirds urban, and by 1960 it was four-fifths urban. In southern California this population was 83.7 percent urban in 1960. With the tremendous rate of urbanization and metropolitanization of the region many communities that were rural towns or semi-isolated suburbs have now become thoroughly urbanized, with a consequent further urbanization of the resident Mexican-American populations.

One significant phenomenon occurring in these newly urbanized areas has been an attenuation of formerly very rigid interethnic lines of stratification. The older studies characterized Mexican-Anglo relations in southern California as of a caste or semicaste nature, with virtually separate Anglo-American and Mexican-American castes in the communities studied. The World War II and postwar periods promoted occupational and geographical mobility to such an extent that rigid caste barriers against intermarriage and equality of employment and housing opportunities have all but disappeared, particularly in urban areas.

Changes in the employment pattern in the Mexican-American work force appear to lie at the very confluence of forces promoting changes in this population. Closely related to the fact of increasing urbanization has been the shift from rural to urban occupations and the shift from unskilled to skilled jobs. These shifts have affected primarily the younger generation. Just over a decade ago Broom and Shevky had phrased the problem of studying Mexican-American social differentiation as one of determining to what extent people had left migratory labor and become occupationally differentiated. But California as a whole no longer has a Mexican-American population which to any significant extent engages in migratory agricultural labor. Only 14.9 percent of the Mexican-American labor force is engaged in agriculture, forestry, or fisheries, and only 12.2 percent are employed as farm laborers or foremen. Mexican-American field hands were largely displaced during the World War II and postwar periods by the huge influx of contract laborers from Mexico, the *braceros.* Having been displaced from agriculture, Mexican-Americans are not likely to return to this type of employment in large numbers now that the *bracero* program has almost completely been suspended.

From a preponderance of unskilled employment, Mexican-Americans in California have since World War II been concentrated primarily in blue-collar work of a semiskilled or skilled nature (46.3 percent) as compared to the total number of unskilled (farm laborers and foremen, other laborers, and private household workers: 23.4 percent). A significant proportion for the first time are now found also in entrepreneurial, professional, and other white-collar occupations (22.2 percent). Especially important has been the entry of Mexican-Americans into types of professional employment where they are in a position to assist in the efforts to solve the manifold problems confronting Mexican-Americans in southern California urban centers. Because to assert that Mexican-Americans have largely left behind the problems associated with migratory agricultural labor is not to say that they have no problems. It is rather that now their problems have become those of an underprivileged urban minority group.

CONTINUING PROBLEMS

The most serious problem undoubtedly lies within the area of education. In this connection it is important to recognize that Mexican-American children are not necessarily any more "culturally deprived" than are children of other low-income families. School authorities in southern California generally consider "bilingualism" as a handicap. Some teachers and administrators consider it as virtually tantamount to mental retardation. This is, of course, a misreading of the true meaning of bilingualism, which is equal fluency in two languages. The problem is obviously a lack of command of English, and not the ability to speak Spanish. Yet all poor and underprivileged people speak poorly and with an accent because they have not enough contact with the majority. True bilingualism, a potential asset in an increasingly international world, is actually discouraged, or at least it is not fostered, by the public schools.

Educational progress of the group as a whole has been relatively slow. Between the last two censuses of 1950 and 1960 the average number of years of schooling of the Mexican-American population in California increased by a little over one year (from 7.6 and 8.0 to 8.9 and 9.2 for males and females respectively). It is only in long range perspective that any impressive educational progress can be seen, e.g., the percentage of Mexican-Americans in Los Angeles who were completing junior college in 1957 was as large as the percentage of those completing the eighth grade in 1927.

Another focus for change among southern California Mexican-Americans lies in family structure. In urban areas of southern California at least, the traditional extended family group including siblings and their children is no longer found to any

significant extent. The *compadrazgo* or ritual co-parenthood relation no longer has any significance as a fictive kinship relation. Related to the increased emphasis on individualism is the move away from traditional Mexican values and toward the Anglo-American values of achievement, activity, efficiency, and emphasis on the future.

The breakdown of traditional Mexican family structure appears to be related to a relatively high incidence of juvenile delinquency for the group. At the same time, Mexican-American delinquency is on the downgrade because many of the neighborhoods which contributed to such conditions are slowly disappearing as a result of urban renewal and freeway construction. As a proportion of total state commitments, Mexican-American delinquents dropped from 25 percent in 1959 to 17 percent in 1965.

Housing discrimination has eased considerably in southern California urban areas and Mexican-Americans can now purchase or rent housing in many desirable areas formerly closed to them. This is not to deny that widespread discrimination still exists. It is ironic, therefore, that analysis of voting results in precincts with high proportions of Spanish surname individuals showed that in the November 1964 state election Mexican-Americans voted heavily in favor of the controversial Proposition 14. The latter, which passed, (although recently ruled unconstitutional by the California Supreme Court) put a provision into the state constitution outlawing antidiscrimination legislation in the housing field. Mexican-Americans apparently failed to realize that the measure was directed against them as well as against the Negro. Their political leaders had simply assumed that Mexican-Americans would vote against a measure which was self-evidently against their own interests. They had failed to reckon with the Mexican-American fear of Negro competition for housing, and the latent hostility between the two groups in some residential areas.

Some Mexican-American neighborhoods have disappeared through forced urban renewal, that is, without the consent of the persons displaced. Some Mexican-Americans have come to refer cynically to urban renewal as "Mexican removal," since for the families concerned no problems are solved by urban renewal. In a number of southern California communities in the past two or three years, Mexican-American leaders (notably in Pico-Rivera in 1964) have been able to muster enough political power, with the assistance of sympathetic outsiders, to prevent urban renewal programs from uprooting them from their homes to higher priced housing elsewhere. It is now unlikely that a situation, such as that of Chavez Ravine, will be repeated. The latter was taken over several years ago by the city of Los Angeles for a housing project, but sold for $1.00 to the Los Angeles Dodgers for a baseball stadium. The highly publicized forcible removal of several Mexican-American families from the ravine left an indelible impression on the public, Mexican and Anglo alike.

Anglo professionals tend to perceive Mexican-American problems as connected with various forms of social disorganization. Mexican-Americans, on the other hand, perceive their problems primarily in terms of the blocking of their aspirations. While biculturalism and bilingualism are viewed by most Anglos as problems, they are not so viewed by most Mexican-Americans. On the other hand, these two characteristics do in fact lead to problems in a society ostensibly committed to cultural pluralism but in reality sustaining the melting pot ideology. There have always been cleavages and factionalism in Mexican-American communities, but never before has the issue of whether to assimilate or not to assimilate been so clearly placed before Mexican-American public opinion.

SOCIAL AND POLITICAL ACTION

The major goal now presented to the Mexican-American community by its leaders is no longer simply the abolition of discrimination as it was in the nineteen-thirties and nineteen-forties, but rather of allowing the Mexican-American to make the best use of his abilities, including the opportunity to capitalize on his bilingualism. Formerly the community was drained of talent as trained, professional people left the ethnic enclave and became integrated into the dominant society.

Now they are finding that by moving professionally back into the *barrio* and working on Mexican-American problems they can advance their own careers and become recognized as community leaders. The community is therefore no longer losing its potential leadership as it once did. The old conservative Mexico-oriented leadership has been giving way to a new leadership of college educated professionals who are thoroughly at home in the Anglo world, but who have retained their ethnic roots.

Current changes appear to indicate a metamorphosis of the group from a lower ethnic caste to a minority group resembling a European immigrant group of a generation or two ago such as, for example, the Italian-Americans in New York, Boston, or San Francisco. Thus, for the first time since the 1850s Mexicans in southern California were appointed to public policy-making positions during the recent administration of Governor Edmund G. Brown. These political appointees in state and local government have been in a position to help open up employment opportunities to other Mexican-Americans and have also provided for better communication between various state agencies and the people. Similarly, Mexican-Americans now have their own political organizations such as The Mexican-American Political Association (MAPA) and have emerged as a political force in their own right. At election time the Anglo-American power structure has become increasingly cognizant of this new political force. Mexican-Americans for their part have learned that if they want such benefits as streets paved and kept in good repair, street lighting, adequate schools, Mexican-Americans on teaching staffs and on the police force, they have to make their power felt at the polls. As a result, a significant number of officials have been elected. There are at latest count 15 mayors, 56 city councilmen and 20 school board members of Mexican-American origin throughout the state, the great majority in southern California.

Another indication of increasing Mexican-American political strength was the recent defeat of the bracero program, for which Mexican-Americans are taking a great deal of the credit. Their leaders had long fought this program which they felt had undermined efforts to establish minimum wages, adequate housing, and schooling for farm workers and their families.

On the national level, one result of the 1960 and 1964 campaigns was that numerous political patronage opportunities were opened up to professional Mexican-Americans in the Peace Corps, the Alliance for Progress, AID, and in the War on Poverty. Mexican-American leaders are increasingly becoming concerned not only by what they can do for their own ethnic group but also for their country as a whole. They are especially eager to utilize their unique abilities and skills in promoting United States goals in Latin America, to which area they will no doubt continue to be sent in increasing numbers. Southern California, where the largest urban concentration of Mexican-Americans in the country is found, has produced and no doubt will continue to produce more than its share of such leaders, as this population as a whole moves ever closer to the mainstream of American life.

FERNANDO PEÑALOSA

From SOCIOLOGY AND SOCIAL RESEARCH *Vol. 55,*
(October, 1970).

Recent Changes
Among The Chicanos

The term "Chicano" is rapidly replacing the term "Mexican American" as the self-chosen term for the group especially among its more militant and better informed members. A stronger sense of community is developing among the Chicanos, at the same time that pride in the *barrio* subculture is increasing and a renewed interest is manifested in Mexico's scientific and humanistic achievements. Social and political action is taking more militant forms. Some of the most significant recent gains have been in higher education, with the increase in Mexican American enrollment and the institution of Chicano studies programs.

Introduction. Recent changes among the Mexican American population in southern California and elsewhere have made necessary the modification or even invalidation of certain conclusions arrived at by the author in an article published in this journal three years ago.

Pending receipt of the results of the 1970 United States Census, it is difficult to quantify some of the changes that have been taking place, although the most significant new developments are more qualitative than quantitative in any case. These changes will be discussed under a number of headings: (1) terminology, (2) sense of community, (3) Mexican American subculture and assimilation, (4) social and political action.

Terminology. One term referring to the Mexican American population which has now gained considerable ground among the more militant and more articulate leaders of this ethnic group is "Chicano." This term is used as a mark of ethnic pride and is considered preferable by those who stress its use for reasons among which are its popular origin and the fact that it was chosen by members of the group itself. That is, it was not imposed on the group by Anglo-Americans, as were such terms as "Mexican American" or "Spanish American." The parallel between the differing uses and connotations of "black" vs. "Negro" is of course obvious. A somewhat less strong tendency is the use of "brown" and of "La Raza," both with their connotations of pride in a mestizo racial heritage. The somewhat circumlocutious and euphemistic Census Bureau term "White persons of Spanish surname" on the other hand currently strikes many Chicano leaders as amusing.

The tides of change are reaching even that stronghold of resistance to Mexican identification, New Mexico. Nancie Gonzáles found it necessary to add to the second edition of her *Spanish Americans of New Mexico* a new chapter titled "Activism in New Mexico, 1966-1969." Mrs. Gonzáles indicates that the terms "Mexican American" and "Chicano" are used with increasing frequency in that state.

The new Chicano leadership has been drawn from what the author previously distinguished as "Mexican Americans" (those enculturated in the barrio or ethnic enclave) and "Americans of Mexican descent" (those brought up in a largely Anglo environment). This distinction however is increasingly hard to justify as the level of ethnic consciousness and participation rises in both groups.

Sense of Community.   While the postulation of the "existence" of a Mexican American community may be tantamount to reification of the concept, it is apparent nevertheless that a sense of such community "existing" is increasing among Chicanos. This is manifested by an increase in the public use of the terms "Chicano community" or "Mexican American community," the increasing number of persons identified as "community" leaders, the increasing use of collective action and mutual help in such situations as confrontations with school authorities in Los Angeles and Pomona or in the Coachella Valley grape strike, demands of Chicano college students that their education be made relevant to and productive of social change in their community, and increasing intercommunity and interstate visits and

activities of leaders, which receive wide publicity. Furthermore, a recent study carried out by the author revealed that 50.9 percent of a random sample of persons of Mexican descent in San Bernardino, California, felt themselves to be a part of the Mexican American community "very strongly" or "for the most part."

Subculture and Assimilation.   The direction of cultural change among Mexican Americans is no longer entirely certain, if indeed it ever was. It is becoming clearer, however, that for many persons upward social mobility does not require a complete shedding of ethnicity. As a matter of fact some of those who are now experiencing the most rapidly possible upward mobility (i.e., in government or higher education where ethnicity has suddenly become a valuable asset) are among those most assertive of their pride in their own subculture. They would maintain that it is no longer necessary to become a "Tío Taco" (brown equivalent of "Uncle Tom") to get ahead.

On the other hand, the relationship between the resurgence of Mexican American ethnicity and the steady erosion of linguistic assimilation on the use of Spanish in this population is theoretically and pragmatically a highly problematic phenomenon. Thus, for example, the survey mentioned above showed that 11.1 percent of the first generation adults spoke "mostly English" to their children, 67.6 percent of the second generation, and 81.8 percent of the third. Furthermore, 30.2 percent of the children spoke "mostly English" to their parents of the first generation, 81.6 percent to second-generation parents, and 93.8 to third-generation parents.

In another important development, Anglo educators and others are gradually learning to use the term "culturally different" rather than the offensive (to minority groups) "culturally deprived." Chicano leaders of both lower class and middle class family origins are increasingly prone to affirm their similarities rather than their differences, and at least symbolic loyalty to the barrio *subculture*. To assert that Mexican Americans "should be regarded as partially Mexicanized Americans rather than as partially Americanized

Mexicans," as the author did in the previous paper is at best a gross oversimplification.

There is a current resurgence of interest in the culture of Mexico (in the nonsocial science sense) with the sharp upturn in Chicano enrollments in colleges and universities largely due to the recent inauguration of special admittance and assistance programs such as E.O.P. (Educational Opportunities Program), and with the burgeoning development of Chicano or Mexican American studies departments and curricula, particularly in California. Young Chicanos are reaching out beyond the barrio subculture to learn about the history of Mexico, its architecture, its literature, its classical and modern music, its philosophers and historians, and its world-famous achievements in tropical medicine, cardiac medicine, fundamental education, and mural art. Mexican intellectual and artistic heroes such as José Vasconcelos, Alfonso Caso, Diego Rivera, Carlos Fuentes, and Carlos Chávez are being added to the pantheon which includes such Chicano militant heroes as George I. Sánchez, Ernesto Galarza, Julian Nava, César Chávez, Reies López Tijerina and Rodolfo "Corky" González.

Furthermore, there has been an accelerating cultivation of barrio art, literature, music and drama (e.g., the *Teatro Campesino* and the *Teatro Urbano*). In the forefront of this resynthesis of barrio and Mexican culture have been the dozen or so "underground" newspapers, members of the Chicano Press Association, published in various cities of the United States, and the activities of Quinto Sol Publications in Berkeley, California, particularly its intellectual journal *El Grito; a Journal of Contemporary Mexican American Thought*.

Social and Political Action.   While many of the targets of social and political action, and much of the strategy and tactics remain the same, the past few years have brought about a change in the rhetoric and in the demands which can best be summed up in the phrase "Chicano liberation." This refers to the idea that Chicanos should have control over the institutions which affect them most closely, or at least to have an active role in the relevant decision making processes. Spokesmen for the movement reject what they consider mere concessions made to them or favors doled out to them by the majority society.

Recent examples of the new trend include such activities as the high school walk-out led by Sal Castro in Los Angeles in 1968 demanding greater community control over the type of education given the Los Angeles Chicano school population, the largest in the nation. Another concerns the 1970 public demonstrations of *Los Católicos por la Raza* in an attempt to force the Catholic church to relate more relevantly to the concerns and problems of the Mexican American community. Then largely as a result of the agitation and plain hard work of student organizations such as UMAS (United Mexican American Students), MECHA (Movimiento Estudiantil Chicano de Aztlán), and the Brown Berets, Mexican Americans Centers and/or Mexican American or Chicano Studies Departments have been set up or are in the process of being established in every major college and university in California, as well as in a number of smaller colleges and junior colleges. These centers and departments are being administered and staffed by Chicanos with wide experience in social action programs, academic work or both.

A group called the "Chicano Coordinating Council of Higher Education," which consists of Chicano student and faculty representatives for institutions of higher education throughout California, has recently issued an ambitious plan for Chicano higher education. This volume consists of a collection of working papers describing the desiderata for Chicano studies programs, recruitment, admission and support of Chicano students, political action, and community involvement. It might be claimed that more than equality is demanded. For example, more autonomy is demanded for Chicano studies than is normally enjoyed by other academic departments. Furthermore a quota system is suggested: "Institutions must immediately accept and establish the principle of proportional representation for Chicanos—students, faculty, staff, and employees—in all areas and all levels of higher education. For example, the percentage of Chicano students enrolled at those institutions located in areas with a significant Chicano population must equal the percentage of school-age Chicanos in those areas ... Those colleges and universities situated in areas with few or no Chicanos must refer to the percentage of Chicanos in the state to determine the percentage of Chicanos students they must enroll. Presently, the Chicano student-age population in the state of California is approximately seventeen percent." Such a policy would of course result in numerical over-representation.

As curricula are being developed for Mexican American studies programs, existing text materials are being carefully scrutinized, with the result among others that the works of Anglo sociologists and anthropologists are being carefully reevaluated, with highly critical conclusions. Such works as Celia Heller's *Mexican American Youth* and William Madsen's *Mexican Americans of South Texas* have been singled for especially stringent criticism, as well as some studies sponsored by the University of California at Los Angeles Graduate School of Education. No longer may Anglo sociologists study Mexican Americans and expect to enjoy immunity from criticism by their subjects. Chicano sociologists have learned well what their Anglo Professors taught concerning ethnocentrism and are now beginning to turn upon their former mentors with some very penetrating questions about the validity of existing sociological studies of the Mexican American. Anglo sociologists have not yet begun to respond, but the resulting interchange should prove most healthy in forcing all concerned to reexamine their unstated, unconscious, theoretical, and ideological assumptions.

FRANCES L. SWADESH

Frances Leon Swadesh (Curator of Ethnology, Museum of New Mexico Research Laboratory, Sante Fe) has had a varied career in both academic and government service. Dr. Swadesh has published two articles dealing with the Alianza movement as well as a number of other articles in scholarly journals. In 1968 she delivered this paper on the Alianza at the annual meeting of the American Ethnological Society and it later appeared in that organization's PROCEEDINGS. *In this article Dr. Swadesh evaluates the Alianza as a native cultural phenomenon.*
By permission of the author and the University of Washington Press.

The Alianza Movement: Catalyst For Social Change In New Mexico

A series of dramatic incidents, set in the spectacular surroundings of some tiny mountain communities of northern New Mexico, have made familiar to countless people in the United States, Mexico and other countries such terms as "Tierra Amarilla," "Canjilon," "Coyote," "The Alianza" and "Reies López Tijerina."

These terms first burst into front-page headlines on June 5, 1967, when some twenty men entered the Rio Arriba County courthouse at Tierra Amarilla, bent on making a "citizens' arrest" of Alfonso Sanchez, district attorney of New Mexico's first judicial district. Grounds for the attempted arrest were that Sanchez had banned a public meeting at Coyote, where land-grant heirs were gathering for a fresh assertion of their claims to lands granted their ancestors by the governments of Colonial Spain and Mexico. Sanchez had arrested a number of leaders and members of the Alianza (renamed "Confederation of Free City States" but still better known by the original name), which is the main organization of land-grant heirs. He had arrested these people both in Coyote and on the highway, and had seized Alianza records and called Alianza leaders "Communists."

Alfonso Sanchez was not found in the courthouse at Tierra Amarilla, but the wrathful men who sought him held the courthouse for two hours. They shot and wounded a state policeman and a jailor, drove a judge and various county employees into closed rooms and shot out many of the courthouse windows before they departed. The last men to leave loaded two hostages into a police car and made a spectacular getaway.

That same day, 350 New Mexico Guardsmen, 250 State Policemen, 35 members of the Mounted Patrol, with horses, tanks and helicopters, mobilized for a historic manhunt. Eventually, thirty people were charged with crimes, including kidnaping, a capital offense. At preliminary hearings on these charges in early 1968, charges were dropped against all but eleven and the kidnaping charge was reduced to "false arrest," a fourth degree felony.

The accused, however, were not all rounded up for a number of months. The first targets of the manhunt were women, children and elderly members of the Alianza, who were camped out near Canjilon. They were seized and held overnight at the point of bayonets, under conditions of physical hardship and personal indignity.

News photographs of mothers with babies in their arms, teenagers and elderly cripples being herded by the National Guardsmen drew swift intervention by the Human Rights Commission and by the New Mexico Civil Liberties Union. Liberal Anglos became uncomfortably aware that the Spanish-speaking people of their state might have some cause for feeling rebellious.

Behind the sensational headlines of June, 1967, and the even more sensational headlines which have announced subsequent events in northern New Mexico, there is an ongoing process of social change, constantly accelerating, of which the Alianza is the chief catalyst. This process has been described as a "movement fully within the category of those described elsewhere as nativistic cult movements" by Nancie González. This interpretation follows the analysis of revitalization movements made by Anthony Wallace in his 1956 article of that title. Dr. González, throughout her report, refers to Reies Tijerina as the "prophet" of the nativistic movement and stresses all revelational and dream-inspired aspects of his rise to leadership among the grant heirs.

THE PROBLEM

The question is, does the Alianza actually fit within Wallace's revitalization concept? It is my contention that, despite many early developments in the organization which lend themselves to that interpretation and the strikingly charismatic nature of its leader, the answer is no, on the following grounds:

(1) Revitalization movements described by Wallace share with other movements for social change such a characteristic as deliberate innovation functioning as their principal motor force, rather than the chain reaction effect of evolution, drift, diffusion, historical change or acculturation.

(2) On the other hand, the principal goal of a revitalization movement is to transform the culture, to make it more satisfying. Such a process is largely internal, whereas other movements for innovative change strive to change the conditions of existence of subordinated groups by directly challenging the controls exercised by the dominant group. Such a process is largely external.

For instance although the Ghost Dance Religion had the expressed goal among others, of causing the White Man to disappear, the focus of the movement was internal and the steps taken to achieve the above goal were symbolic rather than practical. On the other hand, the mystique of the American Revolution was not unlike that of a revitalization movement, yet its main objective was to challenge control exercised by the British Empire.

(3) The dynamics of revitalization movements, their directional processes vary from those of other innovative movements. Even Christianity, one of the most widely influential movements cited by Wallace, involved a process of cultural divergence, the splitting off of the first Christians

from the Judaic tradition. The Alianza, on the other hand, while originally a movement of divergence, early embraced principles and organizational methods which changed its direction, and brought it into participation in a much larger movement.

(4) The principal revitalization movements cited by Wallace were religious movements. In assessing the Alianza, the pervasive religiosity of New Mexico's Hispanos is evident. In the Alianza, however, religion does not affect the motor force for change, in fact the dynamic for change, as I shall demonstrate in a later paragraph, operates *despite* religious factors.

(5) Finally, Wallace lists six revitalization types: Nativistic, Revivalistic, Cargo, Vitalistic, Millenarian and Messianic. If the Alianza really is a nativistic cult movement or any other revitalization type, how is it possible to explain its vital part in a new cross-ethnic alignment of subordinated groups in the United States whose declared intention is to challenge domination by the "White-Anglo-Saxon-Protestant" system? It should be added that this is not a movement of cultural or racial exclusiveness, as many "WASPS" are a part of it.

Below is a documentation of the innovative characteristics of the Alianza as they have emerged in its brief history. Each is linked with the problems they have been forced to solve and with the results of the innovative experience.

INTRODUCTION: CHANGES DESIRED BY HISPANOS

The Alianza was founded to deal with grievances which are wide-spread and deep-seated among the Hispanos of New Mexico. Specifically, these grievances stem from alleged violations of the Treaty of Guadalupe Hidalgo. Under that treaty, signed in 1848, Hispanos became citizens of the United States, but citizens with special rights acquired through previous governments, such as the right to their grant lands. Historical evidence supports the allegation that citizenship has been only nominal and that deprivation of the grant lands has forced a large percentage of Hispanos into chronic poverty. Economic loss has been accompanied by loss of cultural rights, especially the right to use the Spanish language in the environment of the school and the State Legislature.

The grievances are founded on facts, and many interested observers of the early 1960s conceded that something ought to be done about them. The prevailing opinion about the Alianza in its formative years, however, was: "Those people won't get anywhere."

The reason for this scepticism was the isolated and rustic character of the Hispano communities. New Mexico's 269,000 Hispanos constitute only 30 percent of the total state population, and are the most isolated and atypical of the more than four million Spanish-speaking people dwelling in five southwestern states. Despite occasional published opinions that the Hispanos are politically the most active of all Spanish-speaking groups and that, in the counties where they constitute a majority, they have "complete control of the power structure," the reverse is more nearly the case.

What passes for "Hispano political activity" is largely the activity of a handful of precinct leaders and henchmen who are deeply involved in the power structure but are far from controlling it. Any small base of power, in a social setting where so many are impoverished and powerless, can be used to control voting and other political behavior with a minimum of promises, bribes, threats and sanctions.

This is an attenuated continuation of the semi-colonial system originated during New Mexico's prolonged Territorial period. Hand-picked Hispanos served in the Legislature as junior partners to those who really held the reins. Their official task was to represent the overwhelming majority of the population, but in practice they helped keep this majority under control.

Control is still maintained, much as in the late nineteenth century, by garbling as much as possible the information which reaches Hispano communities and by taking advantage of the extended kin system to control entire groups by controlling their key members. This system is today the foundation of precinct politics in Albuquerque, a city of some 300,000, in every precinct with a high percentage of Hispano residents. Leaders and candidates build their influence through their relatives, affines and compadres and win support of other kin groups by extending small favors or handing a few dollars to key members.

In communities where the tendency for social enclavement is strong, the plea of ethnicity is useful as a last resort. Of many a Hispano incumbent who has proven himself incompetent or worse, the saying goes, "He's a bastard, but he's *our* bastard," since it is assumed that any Anglo in his place would be worse. To satisfy this sentiment, the New Mexico power structure allots certain slots to Hispanos whom they can control.

Along with this system goes widespread factionalism, dividing the smallest as well as the largest communities, mainly into rival kin groups. While this system can decide the vote in counties where the Hispanos constitute a majority, and is important in counties where their united vote can constitute a balance of power, it provides them with little say on the issues and with very narrow choice in candidates. Political lag will continue in New Mexico, along with its regressive system of taxation upon the backs of the poor, until Hispanos learn to form coalitions around issues of common concern with other ethnic groups.

SCHEDULE OF INNOVATIVE CHANGES

The Alianza has existed as a formal organization since 1963, but its organizational roots go back somewhat further:

1959

Reies Tijerina was invited to give his views on the land-grant problem to a meeting of the Abiquiu Corporation of Tierra Amarilla Grant heirs. The meeting was broken up by fighting between factions of the Corporation, some insisting that non-members had no right to speak. Tijerina, assisted from time to time by his brothers and other supporters, spent much time during the next five years collecting data on the Spanish and Mexican land grants of the Southwest in the National Archives of Mexico.

1963

Having completed his researches in Mexico, Tijerina returned to New Mexico and promptly founded the *Alianza Federal de Mercedes* (Federated Alliance of Land Grants), whose first annual convention held during the Labor Day weekend, was attended by some 800 delegates. The Alianza was incorporated under Federal and State laws as a non-profit, non-political organization. Its constitution, adopted by the convention, represented a new approach to the grievances of the Hispanos.

a) *United Action:* Most previous efforts to press land grant claims had been initiated on behalf of individuals, families or factions on a single grant, often in opposition to other heirs. Never before had representatives of many grants united to press their claims.

b) *The Common Lands:* Common, or *ejido*, lands constituted the greatest acreage by far of all community land grants. The principle of *ejido* has been no less dynamic in New Mexico than in Post-Revolutionary Mexico, where it continues to serve as the basis for land reform and the establishment of producers' cooperatives. Until the Alianza raised the issue, however, the very existence of *ejido* lands in the southwest had been obscured.

A large percentage of the New Mexico *ejido* lands had been assigned to the Public Domain by the Surveyors General of the period 1854–1880, because they paid no attention to claims other than those made on behalf of individuals. Some of the *ejido* lands were later opened up for Homestead entry, but a much larger acreage was incorporated into National Forest lands in the early years of the twentieth century.

The heirs were largely unaware of these transactions, due to isolation and the language barrier, and only reacted when fences were erected on these lands, cutting off their access to grazing and firewood. The history of violence in New Mexico is closely linked with the fencing off of *ejido* lands, from the Lincoln County outbreaks in 1876 to those on the Sangre de Cristo Grant at the Colorado-New Mexico border in 1963.

c) *New Legal Strategy:* Previous to the formation of the Alianza, heirs had repeatedly sought relief through the courts. There, case after case had been lost while the lawyers reaped fortunes. For instance, the lawyer who represented the heirs of the Canyon de San Diego in 1904, managed to get confirmation of 80 percent of the original 110,000 acres, then took half the acreage as his fee. A quiet-title suit on behalf of some Tierra Amarilla heirs undertaken by Alfonso Sanchez shortly before he became district attorney won nothing for the heirs but brought Sanchez into ownership of some Tierra Amarilla real estate.

The Alianza took the position that no competent legal decision on the grant lands could be made below the level of the Supreme Court. Early efforts were made to persuade the Attorney General of the United States and the New Mexico Senators to work for a Congressional bill to investigate the facts. In case this tactic should fail, recourse to the United Nations was mentioned in the Constitution of the Alianza. The Constitution also invited the moral support of all individuals and organizations with a disinterested concern for human rights.

1964

By the time of its second annual convention, the Alianza claimed a membership of 6,000 land grant heirs from the five states of New Mexico, Colorado, California, Texas and Utah. Some out-of-state delegates attended the convention, giving New Mexicans the sense of a common cause beyond their individual and community problems.

a) *Contact with Indians:* Friendly contact with members of several Indian Pueblos developed following the 1964 convention. The potential for joint efforts with the Pueblos began to be considered, since the documentary basis for both Hispano and Peublo land claims was the Spanish and Mexican Archives. With this thought in mind, when Taos Pueblo began to press its claim to the Blue Lake area, the Alianza voiced its support. By so doing, it lost potential supporters among the Hispano population of the Taos area, due to the attitude of envy which has characterized the His-

pano view of Indian gains in this century. Having once taken this position, the Alianza has continued to seek further for friendly relations with Indians, and the number of Pueblos represented has risen with each annual convention.

b) *Direct Action:* Some Alianza members had scant hope that Congressional action would be taken, despite continuing efforts toward the introduction of a bill. Some Tierra Amarilla Grant heirs began posting notices against "trespassers" on what used to be the Tierra Amarilla ejido lands, by which they meant Anglo ranchers who had bought tracts, built ranches and claimed ownership of these lands. A new *Mano Negra* scare was born.

Ever since 1912, when fencing was begun on the Tierra Amarilla common lands, a vigilante organization called the *Mano Negra* (Black Hand) had intermittently cut fences, slashed livestock and set fire to barns and haystacks. Lately, it has been rumored that some ranchers have set fire to their own premises so that they could whip up sentiment against the *Mano Negra* and, by implication, the Alianza, while collecting insurance on the damages.

Hispanos have had to resort to vigilante action whenever they have lost hope of securing justice through the government or the courts. Most Hispanos will not condone vigilante action, neither will they condemn it under certain circumstances.

1966

This was a year of accelerated change for the Alianza. Many of the older members were hesitant about making the changes, but in this year the total membership claimed for the Alianza rose to 20,000.

a) *New Leadership-Membership Relations:* One of the reasons the Alianza has been described as the core of a Hispano nativistic movement is the personality and background of its founder and leader, Reies López Tijerina. His charisma, rhetoric and visionary references to dreams all fit neatly into Wallace's portrayal of the "prophet" of such a movement. His background as a travelling preacher of the Assembly of God sect, during his years as a migrant worker, only adds to the image for the outside observer.

Focusing on the attitude of the Alianza membership toward their leader, one is forced to a differing view. This point first came to attention when Tijerina went to Spain in the spring of 1966, to study colonial archives in Seville. Long before he was due to return, many members began to be so fearful that he had taken his travel money and disappeared for good that they went to Alianza headquarters every day to check on the news. In view of the fact that Tijerina's bride of a few months had been left at home, such a likelihood appeared remote.

Conversation with some of the members revealed that, since Tijerina was Texas-born and a Protestant to boot, many of his Catholic New Mexico followers accorded him the distrust with which they meet "outsiders." Even his rhetoric, while greatly admired, was often not fully believed. Distrust was so deep that the Alianza membership had voted to put Tijerina on a very slim budget which often failed to cover expenses. Sometimes, a concerned member would buy his groceries.

When Tijerina returned from Spain in the early summer of 1966, he assessed the mood of the membership and resolved to build confidence by deeds rather than by words. He turned to a program of action and participation which placed him in the position of a participant-leader and began to develop leadership skills among the more promising members.

This tactic was productive. While no other Alianza leader compares with Tijerina as a public speaker, the pace of work continues during his increasingly lengthy absences, whether out of state or in jail. The Alianza has become a functioning organization, although its style of work is too spontaneous to impress outsiders as anything but chaotic.

b) *Self-Identity:* Over the 1966 Fourth of July weekend, a large delegation of Alianza members marched from Albuquerque to Santa Fe, many camping by the roadside at night and 125 assembling in Santa Fe to seek an audience with Governor Campbell. After a long wait, the delegation was able to present the Governor a petition asking his support for a Congressional bill to investigate their land-grant grievances. On this occasion, the inaction of Senator Montoya was criticized openly for the first time. For many Alianza members, this was their first taste of group demonstrative action.

Although the official purpose of the march fell short of accomplishment, in that no substantial help came from the Governor, its enduring effect on the membership was to change their perception of themselves. Through the public action they had jointly taken, they affirmed their identity as members of "La Raza," or what Reies Tijerina calls "a new breed," the people of New World Hispanic culture with its many increments from indigenous sources.

This broadening and firming-up of group self-identity gave Alianza members pride and tranquil self-confidence to a degree which is uncommon among Hispanos of today. Like members of other groups who are subject to lifelong social discrimination, maddeningly covert when it is not blatantly overt, Hispanos have tended to feel painfully ambivalent about themselves. Questionnaires which they have to fill in our prevalently racist land leave them wondering whether they are "white" or "other non-white." The language question is a constant thorn, since few of today's adults have escaped the ordeal of initiation into a school system where the use of English is forced upon pupils who can often barely understand it, let alone speak it. Such situations feed feelings of inadequacy and timidity—and also burning resentment against the dominant Anglos.

c) *Changing Role of Women:* Women, from the start, had been devoted members of the Alianza. The fund-raising dinners they prepared and served were vital supporting activities, yet no women had assumed a public role in the organization until the march to Santa Fe. Since then, their activist role has unfolded, sharpened by the experience of arrest, of the jailing of their husbands for weeks at a time and of visits by FBI agents. More and more women have taken these events in their stride and have emerged as fluent spokesmen for their organization.

d) *Youth Roles:* No formal youth group has been formed in the Alianza yet, informally, the teenage and young adult sons and daughters of active Alianza members have made a place for themselves in the organization. Many of them participated in the July, 1966, march to Santa Fe and an increasing number have participated in subsequent activities of the organization. In addition to the arrests which followed the Tierra Amarilla uprising, some very young people were charged in the original indictment. Perhaps because of the stresses voluntarily incorporated into their lives, these young people appear more poised and purposeful than is common for their age-group. Despite the police surveillance with which they are surrounded, none of these youth have been mentioned in the records of pick-ups for marihuana and drug use which are constant among youth of their income level. Disorder and brawling at Alianza dances are unknown.

e) *Renewal of Community Ethic:* In October, 1966, convinced that only by direct acts of civil disobedience could they force official attention to the land issue, Alianza members began to spend weekends in a National Forest campground located on *ejido* land of the *San Joaquin del Rio de Chama* (or Chama Canyon) Grant. Its area totalled some one-half million acres bestowed upon a group of settlers in 1806. The land shark, Thomas Burns, won his claim to the entire grant in the Court of Private Land Claims in 1904, but Congressional confirmation was denied because the Carson National Forest was created at this time and included the San Joaquin Grant area.

The heirs to the grant continued to live there, mainly in Canjilon at the northeast corner. For years, they were unaware that their grant had been taken away from them.

The Alianza campers took possession of the campground in the name of the San Joaquin Corporation, whose legal existence as the governing body they proclaimed. They refused to buy the required camping permits, cut a few trees for firewood and forbade the Forest Rangers to trespass on their grant.

Not all the campers were heirs to this particular grant. Some had come from as far away as California to participate in the "test case." On the other hand, the San Joaquin Corporation was real enough. This corporation had been re-activated under a constitution dated February 9, 1940, and

for twenty-seven years had been dedicated to the following goals:

> . . . to protect the society which is encompassed by said Corporation against the injustices and tricks of tyrants and despots, of those who insult us and seize our lands; to seek Law and Justice; to initiate lawsuits; to acquire, hold, possess and distribute through proper legal channels the rights, privileges, tracts of land, wood, water and minerals which were deeded to, and bequeathed by our ancestors, the heirs and assigns of the Grant of the Corporation of *San Joaquin del Rio de Chama* (ms, translation by F. L. S.).

On October 26, the Forest Service proceeded against the Alianza by placing a stop sign at the campground entrance and stationing uniformed personnel there. When the Alianza caravan drove into the campground without stopping, the Rangers followed them and demanded that they pay up or vacate. At this point, the Rangers were seized, their trucks and radios were impounded and a mock trial was conducted, in which they were charged with violation of the laws of the grant.

Participants in these proceedings who came from nearby communities and had deep-seated personal resentments against the Rangers would have preferred to carry matters much farther, but they were restrained by leading Alianza members. The Forest Service trucks and radios were returned and the Rangers were instructed to depart.

One year later, Reies and Cristobal Tijerina and three others were convicted in Federal Court of having "assaulted" Forest Rangers and of expropriating Government equipment. The verdict is being appealed.

The experience of living together under the community legal code and customary rules of their ancestors, often wistfully recollected by their grandparents, revived among Alianza members a sense of the vitality of their traditional value system. The feeling for solidary relations of the community, reaching beyond the ties of the extended kin group, was expressed by many Alianza members after the San Joaquin experience, and has become crystallized in strong ties of loyalty and affection among the members. These sentiments bring to mind the theme of Lope de Vega's great drama, "Fuente Ovejuna."

f) *Quest for an Alliance with Negroes:* While Alianza leaders had, in the past, stated that they did not intend to adopt the militant direct action methods of the Negro movement, their admiration for the organizational strength and effectiveness of this movement had grown with time and experience. Dr. Martin Luther King was invited to be a featured speaker at the 1966 annual convention of the Alianza. When he declined on the grounds of a previous commitment, Stokely Carmichael was invited. Carmichael accepted but was called elsewhere at the last moment.

A young Negro staff member of the local Poverty Program agreed to pinch hit. Despite his hastily prepared speech, delivered in broken Spanish, he was cordially thanked for his expression of Negro sympathy for Hispano aspirations.

Alianza members had hitherto been trying to win the sympathy of people in power for their slogan, "The land is our heritage: Justice our credo." Now they had come to realize that they would not be heard until they had the strength to force a hearing and that, to have this strength, they must seek allies among other subordinated peoples.

1967

The "uprising" at Tierra Amarilla has been described in the opening paragraphs of this report. What remains to be discussed are the innovative changes it produced:

a) *Recognition by Other Spanish-Speaking Groups:* Since June, 1967, "Tierra Amarilla" has become a rallying cry as well as a place name. From Denver came Rodolfo "Corky" Gonzales, leader of the Crusade for Justice, to hail the Alianza members for having "had the guts" to take their stand. A few weeks later, Bert Corona, leader of the Los Angeles Mexican-American Political Association ("MAPA"), made a like pilgrimage to Albuquerque. César Chávez, leader of the migrant farm workers of the Southwest, was in-

vited to Albuquerque to address liberal organizations, but took time out to attend a regular meeting of the Alianza. There, after an effusive greeting by the membership and a public embrace with Tijerina, Chávez announced that, if he were a New Mexico resident, he would sure be an Alianza member. He hoped all Hispanos of New Mexico would join, because the issue of the land is crucial to rural Mejicanos and reflects the cruel injustices to which they have been subjected. Chávez predicted no early victories, but spoke soulfully of the road of sacrifice that would have to be travelled by those who are committed to the struggle, sacrifice in atonement for the sins of others. The membership responded with heartfelt "Amens," for Chávez had touched the wellspring of Penitente thought which is still so alive in northern New Mexico.

b) *Partnership with Negroes:* The 1967 annual convention of the Alianza was attended by a busload of *Mejicano* and Negro activists from Los Angeles. The culminating point of the convention was a "Treaty of Peace, Harmony and Mutual Assistance" jointly signed by the Alianza leaders and leaders of SNCC, CORE, Black Panthers and other Black Power organizations. The members of the Alianza, with the ringing approval of all present at the convention, thus identified their movement with the objectives of Black Power, no longer on the basis of temporary and conditional "mutual self-interest," but in the context of "full brotherhood" (see center-page spread in *La Raza,* Los Angeles newspaper, 10/20/67).

1968

a) *Impact on Youth:* Partly inspired by the "Black Beret" and "Brown Beret" movement of Los Angeles activist Negro and *Mejicano* youth, the Alianza youth are starting to move out in new directions. In Albuquerque, it will be hard to build unity between "Black and Brown," as the two groups are now identified, because of the record of poor communication between the groups and of clashes between their youth. The coolness is partly the product of conservative trends in the local

Negro leadership which, in the future, is likely to be stimulated to new trends or else to be replaced.

On April 22, 1968, students of an Albuquerque junior high school called a strike. Under the slogan, "We want Education, not Contempt," the students charged that the educational curriculum of the school was adequate only for its few Anglo students, no effort being made to compensate for the educational handicaps of the Hispano majority and the Negro minority. Other student demands were an end to hitting the students, punishing them for speaking Spanish on school premises and displaying prejudice against Hispanos and Negroes. Forty of the students were arrested while marching to recruit students from other junior high and high schools to form a joint delegation to the School Board. Among those charged with "littering," "loitering" and "truancy" were two Tijerina offspring.

An ambitious plan has been written for a free summer workshop for fifty Spanish-speaking youth, to provide them with a background in all the knowledge of the world of today that they will need in order to become effective leaders. Included in the proposed curriculum are history, philosophy and the arts. Sponsorship and funding for the project are being sought.

b) *Leadership Role of the Alianza:* Paradoxical as it may seem, the relatively small Alianza with its widely scattered and largely rural membership occupies a central place in the regionwide united movement of minority groups. As such, the Alianza has become significant on a nationwide scale. The Tierra Amarilla episode so stirred the imagination that the Alianza has become standardbearer for the entire Southwest.

The authentic leadership of the Alianza in the ranks of the poor caused Dr. Martin Luther King to invite Reies Tijerina to the planning conference for the Poor People's March, held shortly before his assassination. King also chose Tijerina to be mobilization director for New Mexico and to be one of three leaders representing Mejicano-Chicano-Hispano demands in Washington.

Predictably, the implementation of these decisions produced hostile editorials in the New Mexico press and anguished wails from some liberals. While the mobilization commanded strong sup-

port from poor people and many middle-class liberals, measures to paralyze Tijerina's leadership were promptly taken.

On April 27, Reies and Cristobal Tijerina were arrested and warrants were out for the arrest of eleven other Alianza members on an indictment issued by the Rio Arriba County Grand Jury. The indictment reversed the decisions of the preliminary hearing on the "Tierra Amarilla Uprising" and reinstated the kidnapping and other charges which had been reduced or thrown out of the case by judicial decision. No new evidence was cited. Bond for most of the defendants was set at $24,-500.

The national leaders of the Poor People's March expressed their conviction that these arrests were an attack on the March itself. They demanded through the Justice Department's intervention release of the accused by writ of Habeas Corpus.

The State Attorney General and District Attorney Alfonso Sanchez, however, cling to the expressed belief that, once the Alianza leaders are behind bars for a long stay, the Hispanos will once more relapse into apathy. The State Attorney General has taken the position that the Alianza is part of a Communist plot and that elements at the University of New Mexico and in the Poverty Programs are in league with the plot. The State OEO director was dismissed as a result of the allegations, and covert investigations have been made of a number of Community Action programs. It is not known whether the recent firing of several University deans is connected in any way with the State Attorney General's campaign.

c) *Progress:* Despite the storm of controversy and accusation which surround the Alianza, it is considered a real political force in the upcoming elections. While no direct, overt concessions may be made on issues which the Alianza has raised, behind-the-scenes promises are expected, as in the gubernatorial elections of 1966. Very quietly, action is being taken to soften Hispano grievances and to still the protests. It is said that the Forest Service has opened grazing facilities to Hispanos to a greater extent than at any time since the 1930s. In addition, projects funded both publicly and privately are centering on the economic problems of the northern counties. Producers' cooperatives have been established in several communities, with promising results. Whether or not these concessions will still Hispano demands remains to be seen.

SUMMARY AND CONCLUSIONS

The development of the Alianza in less than five years since its foundation in 1963 is notable for the changes in the very process of change itself which can be traced. At the start, the organization had many of the characteristics of a nativistic cult; the charismatic leader, the goal of restoration of socioeconomic forms to a prior state, the search for ethnic identity and the renewal of the traditional community ethic. Had these been the only characteristics of the organization, the Alianza might have become a revitalization movement according to the definition of Anthony Wallace.

The main direction of such a process of change is toward cultural divergence or, in the evolutionary theory of Sahlins and Service (1960), "Specific Evolution." This apparently, is the main direction of many nativistic, cargo, messianic, etc. cults.

The Alianza, on the other hand, included from its inception innovative changes such as unity of purpose and action on a scale long unfamiliar to Hispanos, the linking of human, ethnic and political rights with those of property and, finally, the transformation of the action program from a base in traditional vigilantism to active participation in today's major national sweep for social change.

Here, I think, is an example of deliberate innovation that does not fit the revitalization concept. As an analogy, the emergence of a divergent sect of "Christian" Jews with a revitalized religious concept can be compared with the early Christian Church and its relation to the transformations between the time of the late Roman Empire and the emergence of the Medieval State. The latter changes seem to fit the stagewise advance to a higher level which Sahlins and Service call "General Evolution".

The Alianza movement is as yet very young, yet the changes it has stimulated make possible a new direction for the Hispano rural communities. Presently under severe stress of rapid acculturation and forced emigration for livelihood, they could restabilize if the conditions of existence for which the Alianza presses were met. It has already been noted that some avenues of economic development have been opened as a result of the Alianza's campaign. It should be added that those Hispano communities which have the resources for self-support (Chimayo, for example) possess both cultural stability and the flexibility to incorporate elements of the majority culture which are compatible with Hispano values.

Can it be said that cultural revitalization and social revolution are alternative aspects of the same process of deliberate innovative change? If so, it is logical that a revitalization movement may develop into a revolution, and that an aborted or detoured revolution may become a revitalization movement.

In setting criteria for predicting the success or failure of a revitalization movement, Anthony Wallace implies that "success" might be equivalent to social revolution:

> While a great deal of doctrine in every movement (and, indeed, in every person's mazeway) is extremely unrealistic in that predictions of events made on the basis of its assumptions will prove to be more or less in error, there is only one sphere of behavior in which such error is fatal to the success of a revitalization movement: prediction of the outcome of conflict situations. If the organization cannot predict successfully the consequences of its own mores and of its opponents' mores in a power struggle, its demise is very likely. If, on the other hand, it is canny about conflict, or if the amount of resistance is low, it can be extremely "unrealistic" or extremely unconventional in other matters without running much risk of early collapse.

While cultural change was not an objective of the Alianza, some cultural changes are occurring due to the easing of the cultural enclavement of the rural communities. This, then, is a by-product of the past struggles. Yet, within the movement that is sweeping the country, the greatest cultural change that is sought is one in the dominant culture. As Dr. Martin Luther King stated shortly before his death:

The American people are infected with racism—that is the peril. Paradoxically, they are also infected with democratic ideals—that is the hope. While doing wrong, they have the potential to do right. But they do not have a millenium to make changes.

It is in the light of this national perspective that the social changes of which the Alianza is the catalyst should be viewed.

JOAN London + Henry ANDERSON

Joan London (Publication Editor for the California Labor Federation) and Henry Anderson (Farm Labor organizer and presently employed by California Department of Public Health) have both written about, and worked extensively for the cause of California farm labor. Mr. Anderson has written three books on migrant workers, and Ms. London is the author of a biography of her father as well as numerous pamphlets and articles on labor issues. They collaborated upon SO SHALL YOU REAP *(1970), and the following selection about Ernesto Galarza and his early farm work for AWOC comes from that book. This highly sympathetic portrayal of Galarza outlines the continuous problems that union representatives face in fighting an oppressive system and in keeping in the vanguard of the movement. From* SO SHALL YE REAP *by Joan London and Henry Anderson, Copyright © 1970 by the authors and Thomas Y. Crowell Company, Inc.*

Man Of Fire: Ernesto Galarza

Among the extraordinary persons who have made the farm workers' cause their own, one of the most exceptional is Ernesto Galarza, a wiry man with a shock of graying hair and penetrating eyes under full black eyebrows, a brilliant speaker and writer, a doctor of philosophy from Columbia University.

Galarza fought, at times simultaneously and almost single-handedly, the power of agribusiness, federal and state governments, and Big Labor. In

the uneven contest, he may seem to have lost, as the world usually reckons winning and losing. But social movements have their own secret reckonings. Galarza kept alive the embers of the farm labor movement in California during a long night in which they came close to being extinguished altogether.

Ernesto Galarza was born in Tepic, Nayarit, on Mexico's Pacific Coast, at about the time the Mexican revolution was being conceived in secret

278

meetings led by Francisco Madero and others. In 1910, the revolution reached the shooting stage; Galarza's parents fled the country. One of his earliest memories is of crouching on the floor of a train bearing them north to the border as bullets spattered on the outside.

The Galarzas settled in Sacramento, where Ernesto had the opportunity, denied many a Mexican child before and since, of attending school regularly. In the summers, he did farm labor of various types.

A group of his high school teachers insisted that he go on to college. The leader of this group was an alumnus of Occidental, a small liberal arts college in southern California, and Galarza was turned in that direction. He obtained an academic scholarship, and in 1923 entered Occidental College. Since his scholarship did not meet room, board, and incidental expenses, he waited on tables, mowed lawns, and did whatever other work he could find. Periodically, he drove to Sacramento in his Model A Ford to help with problems of his brothers and sisters; as the eldest, he had become head of the family upon the death of his parents.

He went to graduate school at Stanford University, where he majored in economics, but then and throughout his life, he creatively combined an interest in the humanities and the social sciences. When he writes on economics, "the Dismal Science," it is with a grace, wit, and style which are rare in any field.

During his year at Stanford, Galarza met and married Mae Taylor. After he received his master's degree, they left for Columbia University, where he had won a fellowship to pursue his doctorate. He was almost certainly influenced by the School of Education at Columbia University, although he did not study directly under John Dewey. His entire adult life has been marked by a special concern for education. It was no accident that when the time came to choose a title for himself in the farm labor movement, it was Director of Research and Education.

By 1934 Galarza had satisfied all the requirements for his doctor of philosophy degree except the dissertation. He needed full-time employment; by now, he and Mae had two daughters. For

something over a year, he was employed by the Foreign Policy Association as a specialist in Latin affairs. Then, in 1936, he was offered a job with the Pan American Union as a research associate in education. He accepted gladly, since the position seemed an ideal outlet for several of his skills and interests, including his belief in education as an instrument of social change. Through his association with the Pan American Union, he hoped to help bring justice to the Spanish and Portuguese Americas without the kind of violent revolution he had witnessed in his childhood in Mexico.

During his years with the Pan American Union, Galarza worked on his dissertation, a study of the electric light and power industry in Mexico. It was completed in 1943, and Galarza received his doctorate from Columbia in 1944.

On Galarza's recommendation, a Division of Labor and Social Information was created within the Pan American Union in 1940, and he was made its first director. The job gave him a modest voice in policy recommendations, allowed him to travel rather extensively throughout the hemisphere, and supported his family in comfort. Later he said, "I would be there yet if I had been willing to turn to stone like the building we were housed in, and the diplomats who came there to keep us from accomplishing anything. Animated marble busts!"

In 1942, the World War II version of the *bracero* program was enacted. As a labor agreement between two member nations of the Pan American Union, it fell within Galarza's portfolio. He obtained permission to conduct an investigation of the program from the standpoint of its effect upon relations between the "good neighbors," Mexico and the United States.

Galarza bypassed the snares of bureaucracy and conducted the investigation in his own way. He went directly into the camps where braceros were housed and talked with them about their concerns: wages, food, medical care, recreation, their families, whatever. On the basis of visits to twenty camps, detailed interviews with two hundred of the workers, and brief discussions with hundreds more, he wrote a "Personal and Confidential Memorandum on Mexican Contract Workers in the United States." In effect, he concluded that the contract labor program, far from being administered as an instrument of neighborliness, was being used as an instrument through which the larger neighbor exploited the smaller.

Galarza stayed nearly eleven years with the Pan American Union. The break came in 1946, precipitated by an event which he summarized before a Senate committee six years later, in a characteristic mixture of anger, eloquence, high principle, and humor:

> I resigned voluntarily . . . on account of illness. I suffered a stroke of nausea when I observed at close quarters the betrayal of Bolivian miners and farm workers by the United States Department of State. This betrayal led to the installation in Bolivia of a coalition government composed of four parts tin barons, three parts corporation farmers, and two parts Communist Party. Sinister in its origin, hypocritical in its execution, and tragic in its ending, this obscure but significant diplomatic incident has yet to receive the attention it deserves.

For a time Galarza was "at liberty." He could have had any of a number of academic or bureaucratic positions, some of them paying handsomely, but he was looking for something which would permit him to come directly to grips with social justice, and he was willing to wait for the right opportunity.

For some years, Galarza had known of H. L. Mitchell and the Southern Tenant Farmers Union, which, in 1945, had become the AFL's National Farm Labor Union. In 1947, Mitchell received a grant which made it possible for the NFLU to move outside its base in the South into California. It soon became apparent that the drive in California needed a Spanish-speaking organizer; a coming-together of the man and the job took place. In 1948 Galarza and his family moved to California, where the long NFLU strike against the Di Georgio Fruit Company was already in progress.

The Galarza family home was established in San Jose, but Ernesto spent most of his time in the field, familiarizing himself with the changes in California agriculture since he had last done farm labor in the early 1920s. He was the very model of diplomacy, staying in the background while the Di Giorgio strike director, Hank Hasiwar, continued the activities which were already in motion. When Galarza eventually became his own strike director, Hasiwar returned his consideration with a loyalty rare in organized labor.

By 1950, Galarza felt ready for a major move. He was the principal organizer of an NFLU local in the area of Tracy, San Joaquin County, where most of the canning tomatoes in California were grown. The membership and staff decided to call a strike in September, 1950, to protest a wage cut in tomato picking.

Perhaps as many as three thousand workers became involved. Other unions and community groups did not respond as generously as they had three years earlier in the Di Giorgio strike, but one man did: Father Thomas McCullough. Years later he recalled, "We all fell in love with Ernie. The rest of us had been kind of fumbling around with the problem, and here was a man who really knew what he was doing! Boy, we thought, this is it! He was so dynamic. Such a grasp of the field. And how he can capture an audience! We thought, here's the leader we've all been waiting for!"

Large numbers of wetbacks were employed by the tomato growers at that time, but Galarza felt he could deal with the problem. "Despite all their handicaps, wetbacks are freer than braceros," he said. "They can walk off their jobs. Braceros can't." Some observers felt that the refusal of Teamster truck drivers to respect the NFLU picket lines was the most crucial factor in breaking the strike, but Galarza did not agree. "It wouldn't have made any difference if they drove through our lines, if there had been nobody behind the lines picking the tomatoes. What broke us was two thousand braceros, sent in to pick under Highway Patrol and police escort."

By the spring of 1951, Galarza was ready to try again. In many ways, the Imperial Valley was the most improbable of places for a fledgling union to try to organize agricultural workers. It was just across the border from a practically inexhaustible supply of cheap labor, and it was the bastion of an especially lawless brand of union-busting. Even today, there are those in health, welfare, law, and other fields who shrug their shoulders and say, "Imperial County? It's not part of the United States. It's another country."

At the same time, there were good reasons for going into the Imperial Valley. For nearly a quarter-century an undercurrent of Mexican self-organization had existed there, and Galarza was now confident of his ability to galvanize the latent militancy of Spanish-speaking workers. An even more important reason for the move was later expressed by Galarza in this way:

Theoretically, it may have seemed that we should have stayed in Tracy, but we weren't able to operate on the basis of neat logic. We had to be fluid; we had to move wherever the wetback or bracero tides were running the highest. If we hadn't shifted here and there, plugging this weak spot in the·dike, and then that, there wouldn't have been any dry land left anywhere in the state. By 1951, it was obvious that the major port of entry for the tide of Mexican nationals, legal and illegal, was Imperial County. The most useful thing we could do for the workers of the Tracy area, and every other part of the state, was to try to plug that hole.

The NFLU struck the Imperial Valley cantaloupe harvest in April, 1951. The immediate grievance was that the work, which had been done for years at piece rates, enabling skilled local crews to make fairly good earnings, had been shifted to a straight seventy cents an hour. Since Mexican nationals could survive on this, while American citizens could not, local workers were rapidly being forced out of the area.

When the U.S. Border Patrol proved lax in rounding up wetbacks, the union members made citizens' arrests of illegal entrants, and guarded the border to prevent their re-entry. Once again, however, the union underestimated the potentialities of the bracero system. On a number of ranches, braceros took the places of the wetbacks the union had removed; sometimes wetbacks were simply legalized on the spot by federal agents.

In the sense that the strike did not gain wage increases or contracts, it failed, but as Galarza explained:

Many of our strikes had objectives other than the usual ones. If we talked in the usual terms, that was because the labor fakers back East didn't understand any other kind. In fact, the strike was quite successful in its underlying purpose, which was to get rid of the wetback traffic. The stink we raised played an important part in getting the Texas labor movement to pay attention to the problem, in getting a number of exposés published in national magazines, in getting some Congressional hearings, and in getting the entire Immigration and Naturalization Service reorganized in 1954.

In the summer of 1951, Congress enacted Public Law 78, placing the bracero system on a more permanent basis than before. The NFLU fought the law from its introduction at a Department of Labor conference in February, 1951, to its passage in July. Once the law was on the books, however, union strategists felt that until it came up for Congressional reconsideration in 1953, the best that could be done was to try to find ways to turn it to their advantage.

Galarza noted an obscure clause in the treaty with Mexico which implemented Public Law 78: "No Mexican workers shall be assigned to fill any job which is vacant because of a strike or lockout." He had confidence in a society of laws, and this treaty was part of the supreme law of the land.

With this confidence, Galarza returned to the Imperial Valley in May, 1952. He found the local farm labor force already almost decimated by the effects of Public Law 78. From nearly five thousand the year before, the number of local cantaloupe pickers had shrunk to fewer than a thousand. He did his best to rally those who remained, and proceeded with his test of the treaty between the United States and Mexico.

More than half of the local workers walked off the job. Under ordinary circumstances, this would have been economically effective. Public Law 78 was no ordinary circumstance, however. It was a simple matter for members of the growers' association who had more braceros than they could use —a common condition throughout the life of the system—to transfer their excess workers to fellow members who were being struck. Galarza complained to the authorities that this was a violation of the law. They promised to "investigate," but that was the last he heard of the matter. In June, the cantaloupe harvest was over; so were Galarza's illusions about government agencies, including those which were theoretically "labor-oriented."

During much of 1953 and 1954, Ernesto Galarza was in Louisiana helping to organize sugar-cane workers and small strawberry tenant farmers, whose earnings were often lower than those of argicultural workers in California.

The 1953 effort was defeated by court injunctions. California growers have often obtained, from judges who are sometimes growers themselves, injunctions which limit the number and location of pickets. In Louisiana, however, injunctions prohibiting all picketing were obtained by corporate agricultural interests from their friends on the bench. The union's painstaking work of organizing two thousand people, and inducing them to leave their jobs, was nullified overnight.

Although the injunctions could not be set aside in time to save the union's 1953 efforts, the union appealed, hoping to keep the legal precedent from being used against it at other times and in other places. The Louisiana Supreme Court upheld the injunctions with these memorable words: "The guarantee of freedom of speech, even if picketing and speech are held to be identical, cannot be maintained in the face of such irreparable injury to property." Lacking the resources to appeal the decision to the United States Supreme Court in the usual manner, the union filed a pauper's oath, and a volunteer attorney, Daniel Pollitt, handled the case. Two years later, the Supreme Court set aside the injunctions on First Amendment grounds, but the damage to the union could not be undone.

Subsequent organizing efforts in Louisiana were destroyed in an even more remarkable manner. The rural-dominated state legislature enacted a "right to work" law in 1954. It was evidently a reprisal against the Louisiana labor movement for having supported the 1953 agricultural strike. The newly merged state AFL-CIO organization launched a campaign to repeal the "right-to-work" act, with strong support from the now renamed National Agricultural Workers Union. A repeal bill was introduced in the spring of 1956.

Without the knowledge of the NAWU, an agreement was worked out between the state labor federation and representatives of the American Sugar Cane League: the League would use its powerful influence to repeal the 1954 act—and substitute one applying only to agriculture.

In the legislative process, grower lobbyists and their beholden legislators amended the definition of "agricultural labor" to include cotton ginning and compressing, rice milling, sugar refining, and other work not included in the original agreement. Despite even this, the state AFL-CIO called the amended law "good legislation."

As Galarza pointed out, this put Louisiana in a distinguished position. Many states had many kinds of discriminatory legislation against farm workers, but Louisiana alone had a "right to work" law applying exclusively to agriculture. Furthermore, Galarza wrote, it "is the only so-called 'right to work' law on the books of any state in the Union which carries the endorsement of organized labor, AFL-CIO."

Galarza and H. L. Mitchell sought to have the national AFL-CIO repudiate Louisiana labor's position. They journeyed to a resort in the Pocono Mountains of Pennsylvania, where the AFL-CIO executive council was meeting in the fall of 1956. From the standpoint of the embattled little farm workers' union, the resort, owned by the International Ladies Garment Workers Union, was ironically named: Unity House. The NAWU's appeal was rejected.

The president and executive council of the AFL-CIO appeared wedded to a philosophy of labor Darwinism, under which the rule, survival of the fittest, applies to the evolution of trade unions as well as organic species. Given this philosophy, the position of the Louisiana AFL-CIO seemed perfectly reasonable: It is our job to look out for the interests of workers who are already organized and paying their dues; it is not our job to look out for anyone else; if the weak lose out, it is too bad, but it is their own fault for being weak.

To speak of turning points in men or movements is always something of a falsification. Such moments are always preceded by an accretion of experiences which point toward the eventual change. If the scales had not fallen from Galarza's eyes at Unity House, they would have fallen before long somewhere else, just as his final disillusionment with the U. S. Department of Labor would have taken place sooner or later if it had not occurred in the Imperial Valley in 1952.

Galarza left the Pocono Mountains with a burden under which a lesser man would have buckled. He was convinced now that in the task of organizing agricultural workers, he and his relative handful of co-workers were confronted with no fewer than three major classes of obstacles: first and most obvious, agricultural employers; second, the U. S. Department of Labor and state public employment services, with their control of the bracero program giving them a kind of power in labor-management relations never before or since wielded by government in this country; and third, organized labor itself.

The last of these obstacles was the most galling. It was not that labor, by and large, was hostile to the organization of agricultural workers. Scores of resolutions containing eloquent words about the "plight of the farm worker" were passed at conventions representing millions of organized workers. This rhetoric, however, only irritated Galarza, because it was so much less than he felt he had a right to expect from avowed friends. " We don't want their fine words," he said in a 1957 interview. "We want their support: financial, political, moral. When we go before a Congressional committee, for instance, we want to know that we're not being traded away in the back cloakroom. . . . We do not have that kind of assurance now."

Galarza undertook, simultaneously, to destroy the alliance between growers and government bureaucrats, and to shake organized labor out of its complacency. All the while, insofar as he was able, he maintained contact with farm workers in the Imperial Valley and other areas where the union had established footholds. He had neither large numbers of supporters, nor finances, nor friends in high places. His weapons were highly personal: the shield of research and analytical thought, the sword of the written and spoken word. Armed with these, he set forth to do battle with the fortified feudal cities of the bracero system, and the indifference of organized labor.

His basic tactic was to document the flouting of laws—the abuses, the corruption, the debasement, the scandals inherent in the bracero system—and to publicize his findings as widely as possible. If the growers and the government fought back, so much the better. Keep the controversy going, keep the pot boiling, keep the issue in the public eye: that was the most that could be hoped for in the short run. As long as the issue was open, there was always the possibility that some scandal would prove so odious, some salvo so explosive, that public indignation would be aroused and the somnolent democratic conscience stirred into action.

To be truly effective, the technique of *j'accuse* requires that the accuser have enough "troops" that the accused must pay attention. But Galarza was caught in a cruel moral dilemma. He could have gone to any number of places throughout the state and induced the local farm workers to protest visibly against the bracero system. This would have strengthened his hand in the mass media, in the halls of Congress, and in labor circles. It would also have left those workers defenseless. Under the bracero system, there was no way a strike could be won. The strikers would lose working time, with neither strike fund nor unemployment insurance as a buffer, and when the strike was over they would find their jobs permanently filled by braceros.

Galarza resolved this moral dilemma in the only way his conscience would permit.

I made up my mind that, until the law was changed, I would never again ask a farm worker to stick his neck out where it could be chopped off by one stroke of the pen—a pen held in the hand of some bureaucrat in San Francisco or Washington, D. C.—certifying more braceros. For me to ask farm workers to go out on demonstration strikes that they could not possibly win would have been using them for other purposes. I would rather see the union die than use human beings in that way.

Now, if a group of workers asked me to come in and said they had already made up their minds they wanted to walk off the job, and wanted my advice, the situation was different. I would tell them, in full detail, the consequences of what they were doing, as I saw them. If they still insisted, I would give them all the assistance I could. There were situations like this now and then. The workers always lost, but there are times when men grow so desperate they would rather take actions they know will lose, than to continue to endure the unendurable.

Galarza consistently personalized his opposition, a technique which was not widely understood or accepted even by his friends. Unlike Father McCullough, he did not believe it was enough to belabor an abstraction, such as the "evil bracero system." In order to educate farm workers, and to arouse the general public, Galarza believed it was necessary to translate the abstractions into real acts by real individuals. Whenever he spoke of the abuses of the system, therefore, he tried to use as an illustration a specific bracero or a specific domestic worker who had undergone a specific type of treatment at the hands of a specific foreman or other official at a specific ranch on a specific date. Beyond that, he tried always to trace the abuses to the ultimate seats of responsibility: he named names of state and federal administrators he considered particularly culpable.

Unlike some critics of the system, Galarza did not believe that the bracero program was inherently unadministrable. Elimination of the program was the goal, but as long as it remained on the books he felt there was much latitude for administrators to make it better or worse. Convinced that administrators were systematically using this latitude to the detriment of agricultural workers, he reserved for these men a contempt beyond anything he felt toward growers, merchants, chiseling doctors, insurance companies, pushers, drivers, labor contractors, and others who took advantage of the helplessness of farm workers in general and braceros in particular. Although he despised it, he could understand the behavior of an agribusinessman whose motive was frankly to make as much money as possible. But he could not understand the public servants whose salaries were paid by American taxpayers, whose duty, by law, was to protect and advance the interests of American workers, but who (so it seemed to Galarza) betrayed their duty, not for money, but for the sake of betrayal itself.

Among the public officials he considered particularly responsible for the maladministration of the bracero system, Galarza identified Robert Goodwin, Director of the U. S. Bureau of Employment Security; Don Larin, Chief of the BES Farm Placement Service and later the California Department of Employment's highest farm labor official; Glenn Brockway, BES Administrator for the Western States; and Edward Hayes, head of the California Farm Placement Service. Hayes resigned in 1960, after the state Attorney General's office proved Farm Placement representatives had been discriminating against domestic workers and accepting gratuities from bracero users. He immediately became chief executive of the Imperial Valley Farmers Association, one of the nation's largest bracero-user groups.

Among those who have manipulated the fate of farm workers over the years, there is a game with generally well-understood rules. Heads of government agencies who administer foreign and domestic farm worker recruitment programs, and heads of labor groups who ritually criticize these programs, have far more in common with each other than either group has with agricultural workers. Within the rules of the game, it is tacitly understood that, whatever public pronouncements may be called for by the role of one or the other, there are no serious animosities, and it is bad form to hold a grudge. Established trade unions and the Department of Labor have a symbiotic relationship and neither is going to jeopardize it over an issue as peripheral to their traditional interests as farm labor.

Galarza understood this minuet, was repelled by it, and refused to dance to it. The following reminiscence is characteristic:

. . . I attended one of these conferences with state and federal people. You know the type. 'We're all interested in basically the same things here. Let's be reasonable.' The chairman was some unctuous bum who had made a career out of knifing farm workers in general and our union in particular. In a polite way, of course. He looked around the table and said, 'We can be on a first-name basis here. You call me So-and-so, and I'll call you Ernesto.' I said to him, 'You are quite mistaken, Mr. Chairman. I will call you Mister So-and-so, and you will call me *Mister Galarza*.'

The players of the game did not know how to deal with someone who refused to play by their rules. In the end, they had to choose between radically rethinking their assumptions or ejecting this maverick from the game. They chose to eject Ernesto Galarza, and had no trouble constructing justifications which they found entirely convincing.

Galarza fought back. As his personification of the opposition grew more refractory and his attacks more envenomed, some of his friends were unable to follow him. It seemed to them that his attacks were assuming the aspect of a vendetta. Galarza denied that it was a matter of personalities: "I may want to destroy a man's power in certain areas, but not the man himself. . . . It would be absurd for me to hound a person after he was removed from the kind of position in which he could make decisions harming farm workers."

From time to time, the president of the NAWU, H. L. Mitchell, whose headquarters were in Washington, D. C., asked Galarza to modify his attacks on government officials and labor bureaucrats: "After all, Ernie, I have to work with these guys back here." But Galarza felt that his candor made it easier for Mitchell to function: "Let me be the one they hate, Mitch. By comparison with me, you will be a model of sweet reasonableness."

The bracero program's administrators developed a standard tactic of turning the barbs back upon Galarza. In a radio interview in February, 1959, for instance, Secretary of Labor James Mitchell exemplified this technique: "Galarza is an able person and I may agree with some of his objectives, but he hurts his own cause with his extreme, unfounded allegations." Labor leaders who were stung by Galarza's shafts picked up the same patronizing line: "Too bad about Galarza. . . . "

Galarza continued to believe that his technique of trying to pinpoint responsibility for the bracero system was a sound use of his limited time and resources. But subsequent events showed that the system had a momentum of its own, sufficient to carry along with it anyone who might be in a given administrative position at a given moment. When Edward Hayes was removed from his key position, the newly elected governor, Pat Brown, put "liberals" in charge of the California Department of Employment and its farm labor functions. Yet throughout Brown's eight years in office, braceros remained in California. During the last two of those years, California was the only state in the Union to import any braceros at all.

Galarza's enemies carefully cultivated the legend that he was "Mr. Farm Labor"—that the farm labor movement began and ended with him—in the belief that if they could destroy his reputation the movement itself would be destroyed. One of their gambits was to smear him as a Communist. Galarza declined to honor this calumny with any reply. He assumed that his record would speak for itself. Throughout his adult life, he had been fighting all forms of totalitarianism, not with empty words, but by building democratic structures. He confided to a friend, almost in bewilderment, "Can't they see? I love this country in a way that people don't if they are born here, and take it for granted, and have never seen what things are like anywhere else. I love this country because, for all the things wrong, it comes close—close enough to glimpse what the good society might be like. The best way I can possibly imagine to show my respect and affection is to come closer yet—to help get over that remaining gap."

So long as the red-baiting was directed solely at him, Galarza remained silent. But when his wife was drawn into the smears, Galarza's chivalry and family pride compelled him to take steps.

After teaching in the San Jose school system for nearly three years, Mae Galaraza was abruptly told that her contract would not be renewed. Sus-

286 The Beginnings Of Bronze Power

pecting pressure from local growers, Galarza demanded the right to inspect his wife's personnel file. In the course of the controversy, the superintendent of the school district publicly called Galarza a "Red." Galarza brought suit, in one of the first actions of its kind; this was at the time Joseph McCarthy was still riding high. Galarza won the case. Although only token damages were awarded, the message was apparently passed along the growers' network. Ernesto and Mae Galarza were not publicly attacked in this particular way again. But Mrs. Galarza's job in the San Jose schools was never restored.

It would be an exaggeration to say that Galarza stood entirely alone during the middle 1950s. He had friends; he could not have done things he did without their help. He had friends in a Joint U.S.–Mexico Trade Union Committee, which included representatives of the AFL, the CIO, the independent United Mine Workers, and various railroad brotherhoods. He also had friends in the Fund for the Republic. Late in 1955, Galarza received a grant-in-aid from the Fund to write a report on the bracero system. For four months he gathered evidence, from the impoverished villages of Mexico to the rich fields and orchards of California.

A report of several hundred pages, illustrated by scores of photographs, was submitted to the Fund for the Republic. With the help of John Cogley, former editor of *Commonweal,* Galarza condensed this material into an eighty-page booklet, and in July, 1956, *Strangers in Our Fields* was published by the Joint U.S.-Mexico Trade Union Committee. It was the most damaging bombshell to hit the institution of braceroism up to that time.

The institution was hurt. There is no other way to explain the way in which its functionaries reacted. Rather than ignoring the report, as they had ignored other criticisms, they ordered field representatives of the California Farm Placement Service to search for evidence to discredit Galarza. This enterprise probably cost tens of thousands of tax dollars. The quibbles were sent to Ed Hayes and through him to Glenn Brockway. In August, the San Francisco regional office of the Bureau of Employment Security mimeographed a long critique of *Strangers in Our Fields,* with every intention of making it public. At the last minute, however, Department of Labor officials in Washington concluded that it would be the better part of valor not to joust with Galarza openly.

In his field work, careful as he might be, Galarza was not always able to avoid receiving misinformation. For instance, he unearthed some check stubs which appeared to show that a bracero working for the Southern California Farmers Association had net earnings of $6.48, $6.03, and $2.88 for three consecutive weeks' work. These stubs were reproduced in the booklet, over a quote from one of Galarza's interviews with a bracero: "You work one day, and another—no. We spent much time counting the flies, as the saying is."

The government agencies had access to payroll records; Galarza did not. They found he had been misinformed. Each of the checks was for one *day's* work. With this and a handful of other discrepancies, the agencies sought to bring the entire work into disrepute and to paint its author as a shoddy researcher at best and perhaps even a deliberate liar.

As anyone walking through a bracero camp with his eyes open could have verified, braceros did indeed spend "much time counting the flies." For that matter, it is difficult to see how $2.88 for a full day's work is much more defensible than $2.88 for a week's work. By keeping the argument on their own terms, however, proponents of the system were able to persuade themselves and some innocent bystanders that Galarza was irresponsible.

Acutally, much of Galarza's treatment of the bracero system, then and later, was understated. In *Strangers in Our Fields,* he said almost nothing about "health insurance" which constituted one of the system's major rackets; almost nothing about the subsystem of so-called "specials" under which Lyndon Johnson and other favored employers were able to obtain "predesignated" braceros.

Galarza was fully aware of the need for factual accuracy and careful documentation. He knew that proponents of the system placed all the burden of proof on its critics. He knew that they would search exhaustively for some trivial misstatement in order to bring a carefully built edifice of research tumbling down. Even a professionally trained researcher like Galarza found it almost impossible to prove a charge against the bracero system beyond any cavil. Employers' records were closed to him. Wage and hour data were altered. Potential witnesses were hustled back to Mexico.

Nevertheless, *Strangers in Our Fields* proved one of the outstanding successes of Galarza's career. It received widespread publicity, even in media, such as the Los Angeles *Times,* which no one had ever accused of pro-labor prejudice. The booklet went through two editions and 10,000 copies. Condensations of much the same material appeared in at least three national magazines. Urban liberals were slowly being weaned from the misconception that the "farm labor problem" in California was still a matter of jalopies, and Joad families played by Jane Darwell and Henry Fonda.

Galarza's booklet also helped stir into wakefulness some elements of the labor movement. Early in 1957, the AFL-CIO's Industrial Union Department, headed by Walter Reuther, gave the National Agricultural Workers Union $25,000, with the understanding that about half of it would be used for organizing in California.

Pitiable as the amount was, this was the most money Galarza had ever had to work with. Husbanding it carefully, he made it last over a year. He opened offices, sometimes rent-free in private homes, in Yuba City, Tracy, Stockton, Modesto, Hollister, and San Jose and began to "develop local people." As he later put it: "Obviously, you aren't going to organize a statewide union with that kind of money. I looked upon it as a demonstration project. . . . I wanted to prove that Galarza wasn't the only potential organizer in California. Over the years, I would estimate that I have found at least two hundred people in this state—field workers—who would be first-rate organizers, given the chance."

The key problem facing Galarza was this: around what axis can you organize, when your members' jobs will almost certainly be filled by braceros if they try to rise above the braceros' wages and working conditions? To an extent, Galarza answered this question in the same way as Father McCullough and César Chávez, although

there was little exchange of ideas among the three. The union proved its value to its members by performing services they lacked the time or expertise to perform, and which did not involve a premature collision with employers. For instance, Galarza's San Jose local discovered that, although agricultural workers had become partially covered by the Social Security Act in 1955, growers and labor contractors often pocketed the payroll deductions rather than sending them to the Social Security Administration. One union member who had worked for a single employer all year, and had earned close to $2,400, was credited with only $427 by the SSA accounting office in Baltimore. A union representative was able to get the "error" corrected.

Galarza felt that an NAWU local should also perform a quite different type of function. In effect, he trained his cadres to operate as he himself was operating: as sleuths for abuses under the bracero program. He was still convinced that there was little point in ordinary union activities as long as Public Law 78 was intact, and that the best way to obtain its modification was to ferret out the most flagrant scandals and publicize them.

In August, 1957, Galarza was sure he had a case which would "blow the whole thing out of the water." Thousands of American fruit pickers were gathering in the northern end of the Sacramento Valley, around Marysville and Yuba City, in anticipation of the peach harvest. Due to unseasonably cold weather, the peaches ripened late. While waiting, the Americans looked for jobs as box-spreaders, limb-proppers, and whatever else might be available in the area. They found all such work being done by braceros, although this was contrary to the letter of the braceros contracts and to the spirit of Public Law 78.

Galarza had complained of this type of violation on many other occasions, only to be told in so many words, "Oh, really? Prove it." Under this peculiar institution the standards of evidence required of critics of the system would have taxed a Blackstone, but Galarza gleefully accepted the challenge on this occasion, because he felt the evidence was irrefutable. Accompanied by a notary public, he went along the ditch banks and under the bridges of Sutter and Yuba counties, and obtained nearly two hundred sworn affidavits, complete with names, dates, places, every detail, from American workers who had vainly sought employment in the pre-harvest period. The northern California press carried the story as front-page news for days. Galarza called for a withdrawal of braceros, and for an investigation of the entire Farm Placement Service.

Governor Goodwin J. Knight rode out the storm, saying that the state Department of Employment, parent agency of the Farm Placement Service, should "be given an opportunity to look over the situation." By the time the Director of Employment had conducted his "investigation," exonerated himself and his department, and declared Galarza's charges "completely without merit," the peach harvest was half finished, American pickers were either working or had drifted from the area, the media no longer considered the incident newsworthy, and Galarza's salvos was bursting in air unseen and unheard.

Galarza began writing a series of open letters to the Governor on the bracero scandal-of-the-week. He called them his "Knight letters." It is doubtful that the Governor ever read them; the letters were intended primarily for newsmen, church and political groups, and friends of the farm labor movement.

When Democratic victories in the 1958 elections ended the public career of Goodwin Knight, Galarza turned to writing straight press releases on the endless irregularities he and his representatives were uncovering in the field. A typical release began: "Death took a turn as compliance officer for the Department of Labor in Imperial Valley, pointing a bony finger at one more routine violation of Public Law 78 . . . "A bracero had been killed while driving a tractor, an activity prohibited under the master contract, but commonplace. The Department of Labor, in "an indecently hasty whitewash," alleged that the bracero was operating the tractor only "as a special favor" to the regular driver, and as a consequence there was no violation. Galarza demanded a full investigation at once, "before the truth is lost forever under a cloud of malathion and bureaucratic servility." As usual, his eloquence was ignored.

In time, weary of researching, writing, mimeographing, and distributing releases which were seldom if ever used, Galarza turned to writing essays which were apparently more for his own pleasure than anything else, although he distributed them to a small circle of friends.These essays are worth reading not only for their content but for their sardonic wit and verbal felicities. In a representative example of the Galarza style, he characterized the government's disciplinary measures against violators of Public Law 78 as "ten lashes laid on with a half-cooked noodle."

An essay entitled "Labor's Back Yard" is especially significant. Galarza charged that labor leaders "offer only token opposition while [their] most solemn pledges on human decency and democracy are denied one large segment of the brotherhood of labor." In conclusion, he warned:

If democracy, freedom of organization and collective bargaining are principles, they apply to all. The struggle to realize them must be pressed into every corner of the land, their enjoyment denied no worker, however destitute or ignorant he may be.

Otherwise, Otherwise, labor's long, bitter and often tragic commitment to humanity becomes a game of odd-man-out. The odd man must always be the low man on the totem pole. Once the "right to work" men have laid the axe to the base . . . no trade unionist need ask: "For whom does the axe fall?" It falls for him.

Galarza's near-despair was understandable. He exhausted the small grant from the Industrial Union Department early in 1958. He prepared a careful proposal to the IUD, calling for $250,000. With that amount, he was sure he could build a self-sustaining agricultural workers' union in California. He said later, "They didn't even have the courtesy to reply. For eight months I waited. I made three trips to Washington trying to build a fire under them. I had to close some union offices, disband some locals, and borrow $3,000 from friends to keep the others going."

The principal reason for the mysterious silence from Washington was that wheels were beginning to turn at the highest echelons of the national AFL-CIO, with motive power altogether different from Galarza's $250,000 program. The decision-makers involved did not feel it necessary to seek the advice of the one man who had had most experience organizing agricultural workers in California or even to notify him that plans were under way. Convinced that farm labor had been forgotten, Galarza became increasingly caustic in his comments about the California Labor Federation and the national AFL-CIO. In one of his gentler anecdotes, he said:

"Why is it that labor fakers always look so well fed? One time I was at a meeting with three or four of them. It was at one of these plush motels. It would be beneath their dignity to gather in a working-man's place. There they were, around the pool, overflowing their swimming trunks, wallowing around in the water for all the world like a bunch of great white whales. I felt like Captain Ahab making the discovery of his life! If I had had a harpoon handy, I would not like to be responsible for what might have happened."

Galarza's verbal harpoons helped to ensure that when the plans of the national leadership were completed he would be denied any significant role in them.

In February and March, 1959, when Jack Livingston, AFL-CIO Director of Organization, was looking for someone to head the new Agricultural Workers Organizing Committee, Galarza was never seriously considered. To the extent that his name arose at all, the decision-makers in Washington invoked the usual incantation, "Too bad, but he's lost his effectiveness." The most logical choice for the directorship of the Agricultural Workers Organizing Committee was, with only H. L. Mitchell's voice raised in his behalf, bypassed in favor of Livingston's old crony, Norman Smith.

The situation was as unfair to Smith as it was to Galarza, but each tried in good faith to make the best of it. In AWOC's early days, many magazines and newspapers assigned reporters to the story of "Big Labor's all-out drive in agriculture." Many reporters went first to Galarza; he invariably referred them to Smith. For all the general public might have divined from the resulting stories, the organizing drive was a one-man undertaking, with Norman Smith as the new "Mr. Farm Labor."

Giving the lie to those who said he was a "prima donna," constitutionally incapable of "playing on a team," Galarza functioned as a training officer for AWOC. Each day, he traveled to a different area—Stockton, Modesto, Hollister, Yuba City, other far-flung points—to preside at a staff meeting of local organizers and stewards, asking and answering questions, anticipating problems likely to arise in the field.

As time passed, it became clear to Galarza that Smith was strategically adrift, with no coherent idea of how agricultural workers might be organized. In addition, Galarza believed that Smith was wrong in many tactical details, such as a tendency to rely on the assurances of politicians, while Galarza mistrusted all of them. But he held his peace. The staff meetings continued through December, although in the absence of any organizing plan it became increasingly difficult to train a staff. The break came in January, 1960, precipitated by jurisdictional and philosophical problems which had long been simmering in the farm labor movement.

Norman Smith used to say in all seriousness, "I don't care if the Devil himself comes to earth to organize farm workers, as long as the job gets done." Although he might have drawn the line at the Devil, Father McCullough also subscribed to this general theory, on the assumption that even if the union were initially undemocratic or otherwise unsavory, it could later be reformed from within.

Ernesto Galarza did not accept the proposition that any farm labor union at all is preferable to none. Both principled and practical considerations influenced his position. The only proper objective of the labor movement, he felt, is "the kind of human being it produces." He was not interested in the kind of union which produces dependent, manipulable people, even if they are well paid and well fed. He was interested in a union which would help people become more autonomous, more responsible, better able to weigh alternatives and make decisions for themselves. He feared that such a potential for human development would be lost if farm workers were absorbed by some larger union.

At the more "practical" level, Galarza doubted that a merger of agricultural workers with any other union would serve even to "put pork chops on the table." He had long since concluded that established union leaders, no matter how sincerely they might try, could not think within a framework which was relevant to farm workers' problems. "Organized labor just doesn't have any answers to questions like 'What do you do about braceros?'" he pointed out, "because it has never had to deal with foreign contract labor in any other union."

Galarza could not resist noting, furthermore:

"There is no love for the NAWU in the labor movement. We are an embarrassing stepchild. We embarrass them simply by existing. We are a constant reminder to them of things they should have done, but did not do. . . .

"And I'll tell you another way we stand to embarrass the fakers. . . . If we succeed, we'll precipitate a political crisis in the State of California. There'll hardly be a politician in the state who'll be safe. We were instrumental in electing the first Mexican-American councilman in the history of Brawley when we were active in that area. We have upset well-entrenched regimes in the Arvin-Lamont area of Kern County and in Sutter County, And this was done on peanuts.

"If the AFL-CIO gives us the support we have been crying for all these years, we can stand the State of California on its ear. Naturally, this makes a lot of people nervous. Very nervous. Including a lot of people in the labor movement, who have worked out some very careful living arrangements with incumbents—in both parties."

Fairly early in the history of AWOC, Galarza and H. L. Mitchell began to suspect that AFL-CIO officials were bent on dismantling the NAWU in favor of the United Packinghouse Workers of American. In their efforts to preserve what they considered the legal and moral jurisdiction of the NAWU, Galarza and Mitchell said and did things which some observers interpreted as an attempt to bring down the whole farm labor movement in a general Götterdämmerung. Such an interpreta-

tion was as superficial as it was uncharitable. Some personal feelings were involved, to be sure. Galarza and Mitchell would have had to be immune to normal human emotion if, after holding the fort so long, they had felt no resentment at being elbowed aside by Johnny-come-latelies. Basically, however, they fought to preserve the jurisdiction of the NAWU because they felt it alone represented the best interests of agricultural field workers. They had serious misgivings about the political backgrounds of some UPWA leaders. But they would have been equally reluctant to see farm workers delivered into the hands of Teamster leaders whose politics were at the other end of the spectrum.

In an attempt to retain the integrity of the NAWU, Galarza and Mitchell clawed with tenacity. . . .

RENASCENCE OF FARM LABOR

Something of a renascence of the farm labor movement, and of Galarza's career within that movement, took place in 1963. On May 29, the House of Representatives unexpectedly voted to discontinue the bracero program. Although the action was rescinded a few months later, it was a serious blow to the aura of invincibility which Public Law 78 had long enjoyed, and it counteracted some of the despair into which many of the friends of farm labor had sunk.

Then, on September 17, the California farm labor movement was electrified, and the gloaming of braceroism was hastened, by the bloodiest in a long series of catastrophes traceable to the insensitive way in which foreign contract-labor gangs had always been handled. In this case, the driver of a rudely converted truck full of braceros drove into the path of a speeding Southern Pacific freight train near the tiny town of Chualar in the Salinas Valley. Thirty-two of the workers were killed.

The old fires flared again in Ernesto Galarza. It was the kind of scandal he had long believed could be used as the springboard for a full-scale Congressional investigation, which in turn might disgrace the bracero program's administrators and sound the death knell of the entire system. His cries for an official investigation had never come to fruition, but now he roused himself for a last effort. Bringing into play all his skills of speaking, writing, flattering, badgering, maneuvering, he persuaded the large Mexican-American population of San Jose to back him solidly in asking the House of Representatives Committee on Education and Labor to investigate the Chualar disaster and to appoint him as staff director.

In some respects, Galarza's luck was good, in others, bad. Fortune in both cases, revolved around the personality of the chairman of the Education and Labor Committee, Adam Clayton Powell. A more politic chairman would not have hired the " controversial" Galarza in the first place, or kept him on in the teeth of the gale which his appointment aroused. Congressman Charles Gubser, a grower and a major user of braceros, had represented Galarza's district for some years. Protected by Congressional immunity, Gubser took to the floor of the House with unprecedented personal attacks on both Ernesto and Mae Galarza. Ignoring the opposition, Powell told Galarza to proceed with his report and let the chips fall where they might. The report appeared in the spring of 1964: one of the most thoroughly researched and best-written reports ever to appear under the imprimatur of a committee of the United States Congress.

At this point, however, it became evident that Powell's commitment to agricultural labor was no more than skin-deep. There was no follow-up to any of Galarza's recommendations in terms of legislation, although in its documentation of employer negligence the report was useful to attorneys for the survivors of the dead braceros. Instead of the settlements of $1,000 to $1,500 which had initially been made, settlements totaling over $2 million were eventually obtained.

Powell's lack of any real interest in agricultural labor also worked against the realization of a dream Galarza had entertained for years. He was not given the authority to put under subpoena his old enemies, ask them the questions they had always ignored or evaded, and require them to answer publicly from the witness stand under penalty of perjury. About a year later, though, acting on his own with the assistance of a volunteer attorney, James Murray, Galarza came close to realizing this long-standing desire.

The Di Giorgio Corporation, in 1960, had sued a number of AWOC officials for showing the old film, "Poverty in the Valley of Plenty," which allegedly libeled the corporation. Galarza had been named a defendant, although he not only had had nothing to do with the showing but was not even associated with AWOC at that time. Galarza filed a countersuit, claiming malicious prosecution. In the course of this countersuit, he and Murray were able to obtain a number of depositions revealing interconnections between agricultural corporations and the government agencies which supposedly regulated them.

The verdict, rendered late in 1964, was another partial victory or partial defeat, depending on the perspective. The jury found that Galarza had had nothing to do with the showing of the allegedly libelous film, but it awarded him none of the damages he had asked.

Galarza retired to his writing, completing his analysis of the bracero system, for which Alaska Senator Ernest Gruening, an old friend, wrote the foreword. As its title implies, *Merchants of Labor* is an account of that portion of the agribusiness complex which deals in workers, rather than growing or selling fruits and vegetables. In particular, it is the story of bracero-user associations and the government administrators who catered to them. Although 1964 was the climactic year in the political struggle over Public Law 78, publishers still considered Galarza's book "uncommercial." He borrowed $1,500, paid to have this book printed by a San Jose firm, and undertook his own publicity and distribution. Orders came in; the first printing was sold out. In time, there was a second printing.

Then things were quiet again. By now there was a definite economic as well as psychological pinch. With many a wry comment, Galarza found a job with the War on Poverty. It required that he move to Los Angeles, but he did not give up the house in San Jose. In a little more than a year he was back, living on savings again, free to say what he pleased on any subject.

He is in some demand as a consultant—to the Ford Foundation, for instance, on a project having to do with Mexican-Americans in the Southwest. He appears frequently as a speaker at "brown power" conferences, where increasingly politically conscious Mexican-Americans are attempting to formulate a philosophy and program around which they can rally. He has published another book, entitled *Spiders in the House and Workers in the Field,* dealing with the 1947-1950 strike against Di Giorgio, and its aftermaths—including the part played by then Congressman Richard Nixon.

Galarza's contact with the farm labor movement is now minimal. He has no illusions about returning to the movement in which he invested so much of his life. In January, 1967, he journeyed to Delano, but came back to report that César Chávez was too busy to see him. Other times, other leaders: that is the way of social movements. Ernesto Galarza—fiery, loyal, brilliant, proud, organizer and doctor of philosophy—would no doubt agree.

Luis Valdez

Luis Valdez (Chicano author) writes for many American publications, among them the New Left periodical, RAMPARTS. Mr. Valdez argues that the CAMPESINO and not the urban dweller will guide LA RAZA. Furthermore he firmly rejects the belief that the melting-pot is beneficial. He sees no advantage in denying one's heritage merely to blend with the faceless mass of anglo society. It is for this reason that those who still maintain their ethnic identity, the exploited workers of all races, will be the vanguard and the soul of the effort to revolutionize America.

The Tale Of The Raza

The revolt in Delano is more than a labor struggle. Mexican grape pickers did not march 300 miles to Sacramento, carrying the standard of the *Virgen de Guadalupe,* merely to dramatize economic grievances. Beyond unionization, beyond politics, there is the desire of a New World race to reconcile the conflicts of its 500-year-old history. *La Raza* is trying to find its place in the sun it once worshipped as a Supreme Being.

La Raza, the race, is the Mexican people. Sentimental and cynical, fierce and docile, faithful and treacherous, individualistic and herd-following, in love with life and obsessed with death, the personality of the *raza* encompasses all the complexity of our history. The conquest of Mexico was no conquest at all. It shattered our ancient Indian universe, but more of it was left above ground than beans and tortillas. Below the foundations of our Spanish culture, we still sense the ruins of an entirely different civilization.

Most of us know we are not European simply by looking in a mirror—the shape of the eyes, the curve of the nose, the color of skin, the texture of hair; these things belong to another time,

293

another people. Together with a million little stubborn mannerisms, beliefs, myths, superstitions, words, thoughts—things not so easily detected—they fill our Spanish life with Indian contradictions. It is not enough to say we suffer an identity crisis, because that crisis has been our way of life for the last five centuries.

That we Mexicans speak of ourselves as a "race" is the biggest contradiction of them all. The *conquistadores,* of course, mated with their Indian women with customary abandon, creating a nation of bewildered half-breeds in countless shapes, colors and sizes. Unlike our fathers and mothers, unlike each other, we *mestizos* solved the problem with poetic license and called ourselves *la raza.* A Mexican's first loyalty—when one of us is threatened by strangers from the outside—is to that race. Either we recognize our total unity on the basis of *raza,* or the ghosts of a 100,000 feuding Indian tribes, bloods and mores will come back to haunt us.

Just 50 years ago the Revolution of 1910 unleashed such a terrible social upheaval that it took 10 years of insane slaughter to calm the ghosts of the past. The Revolution took Mexico from the hands of New World Spaniards (who in turn were selling it to American and British interests) and gave it, for the first time and at the price of a million murders, to the Mexicans.

Any Mexican deeply loves his *mestizo patria,* even those who, like myself, were born in the United States. At best, our cultural schizophrenia has led us to action through the all-encompassing poetry of religion, which is a fancy way of saying blind faith. The Virgin of Guadalupe, the supreme poetic expression of our Mexican desire to be one people, has inspired Mexicans more than once to social revolution. At worst, our two-sidedness has led us to inaction. The last divine Aztec emperor Cuauhtemoc was murdered in the jungles of Guatemala, and his descendants were put to work in the fields. We are still there, in dry, plain, American Delano.

It was the triple magnetism of *raza, patria,* and the Virgin of Guadalupe which organized the Mexican-American farm worker in Delano—that and César Chávez. Chávez was not a traditional bombastic Mexican revolutionary; nor was he a *gavacho,* a gringo, a white social worker type. Both types had tried to organize the *raza* in America and failed. Here was César, burning with a patient fire, poor like us, dark like us, talking quietly, moving people to talk about their problems, attacking the little problems first, and suggesting, always suggesting—never more than that—solutions that seemed attainable. We didn't know it until we met him, but he was the leader we had been waiting for.

Although he sometimes reminds one of Benito Juarez, César is our first real *Mexican-American* leader. Used to hybrid forms, the *raza* includes all Mexicans, even hyphenated Mexican-Americans; but divergent histories are slowly making the *raza* in the United States different from the *raza* in Mexico. We who were born here missed out on the chief legacy of the Revolution: the chance to forge a nation true to all the forces that have molded us, to be one people. Now we must seek our own destiny, and Delano is only the beginning of our active search. For the last hundred years our revolutionary progress has not only been frustrated, it has been totally suppressed. This is a society largely hostile to our cultural values. There is no poetry about the United States. No depth, no faith, no allowance for human contrariness. No soul, no mariachi, no chili sauce, no pulque, no mysticism, no *chingaderas.*

Our *campesinos,* the farm-working *raza* find it difficult to participate in this alien North-American country. The acculturated Mexican-Americans in the cities, *ex-raza,* find it easier. They have solved their Mexican contradictions with a pungent dose of Americanism, and are more concerned with status, money and bad breath than with their ultimate destiny. In a generation or two they will melt into the American pot and be no more. But the farmworking *raza* will not disappear so easily.

The pilgramage to Sacramento was no mere publicity trick. The *raza* has a tradition of migrations, starting from the legend of the founding of Mexico. Nezahualcoyotl, a great Indian leader, advised his primitive *Chichimecas,* forerunners of the Aztecs, to begin a march to the south. In that march, he prophesied, the children would age and the old would die, but their grandchildren would come to a great lake. In that lake they would find an eagle devouring a serpent, and on that spot, they would begin to build a great nation. The nation was Aztec Mexico, and the eagle and the serpent are the symbols of the *patria.* They are emblazoned on the Mexican flag, which the marchers took to Sacramento with pride.

Then there is the other type of migration. When the migrant farm laborer followed the crops, he was only reacting to the way he saw the American *raza:* no unity, no representation, no roots. The pilgrimage was a truly religious act, a rejection of our past in this country and a symbol of our unity and new direction. It is of no lasting significance that Governor Brown was not at the Capitol to greet us. The unity of thousands of *raza* on the Capitol steps was reason enough for our march. Under the name of HUELGA we had created a Mexican-American *patria,* and César Chávez was our first *Presidente.*

Huelga means strike. With the poetic instinct of the *raza,* the Delano grape strikers have made it mean a dozen other things. It is a declaration, a challenge, a greeting, a feeling, a movement. We cried *Huelga!* to the scabs, *Huelga!* to the labor contractors, to the growers, to Governor Brown. With the Schenley and DiGiorgio boycotts, it was *Heulga!* to the whole country. It is the most significant word in our entire Mexican-American history. If the *raza* of Mexico believes in *La Patria,* we believe in *La Huelga.*

The route of the pilgrimage was planned so that the Huelga could reach all the farmworkers of the San Joaquin Valley. Dependent as we were on each farmworking town for food and shelter, we knew the *raza* would not turn us down. *"Mi casa es suya,"* is the precept of Mexican hospitality: "My house is yours."

The Virgin of Guadalupe was the first hint to farmworkers that the pilgrimage implied social revolution. During the Mexican Revolution, the peasant armies of Emiliano Zapata carried her standard, not only because they sought her divine protection, but because she symbolized the Mexico of the poor and humble. It was a simple Mexican Indian, Juan Diego, who first saw her in a vision at Guadalupe. Beautifully dark and Indian in feature, she was the New World version of the Mother of Christ. Even though some of her worshippers in Mexico still identify her with Tonatzin, an Aztec goddess, she is a Catholic saint of Indian creation—a Mexican. The people's response was immediate and reverent. They joined the march by the thousands, falling in line behind her standard. To the Catholic hypocrites against the pilgrimage and strike the Virgin said *Huelga!*

The struggle for better wages and better working conditions in Delano is but the first, realistic articulation of our need for unity. To emerge from the mire of our past in the United States, to leave behind the divisive, deadening influence of poverty, we must have unions. To the farmworkers who joined the pilgrimage, this cultural pride was revolutionary. There were old symbols—Zapata lapel buttons—and new symbols standing for new social protest and revolt; the red thunderbird flags of the NFWA, picket signs, arm bands.

There were also political rallies in the smallest towns of the San Joaquin Valley. Sometimes they were the biggest things that had ever happened in town. Every meeting included a reading of *El Plan de Delano,* a "plan of liberation" for all farmworkers in the language of the picket line: ". . . our path travels through a valley well known to all Mexican farmworkers. We know all of these towns . . . because along this very same road, in this very same valley, the Mexican race has sacrificed itself for the last 100 years . . . This is the beginning of a social movement in fact and not in pronouncements . . . We shall unite . . . We shall strike . . . Our PILGRIMAGE is the MATCH that will light our cause for all farmworkers to see what is happening here, so that they may do as we have done . . . VIVA LA CAUSE! VIVA LA HUELGA!"

The rallies were like religious revivals. At each new town, they were waiting to greet us and offer us their best—mariachis, embraces, words of encouragement for the strike, prayers, rosaries, sweet cakes, fruit and iced tea. Hundreds walked, ran or drove up to the march and donated what little money they could afford. The countless gestures of sympathy and solidarity was like nothing the *raza* had ever seen.

The NFWA is a radical union because it started, and continues to grow, as a community organization. Its store, cafeteria, clinic, garage, newspaper and weekly meeting have established a sense of community the Delano farmworkers will not relinquish. After years of isolation in the *barrios* of Great Valley slum towns like Delano, after years of living in labor camps and ranches at the mercy and caprice of growers and contractors, the Mexican-American farmworker is developing his own ideas about living in the United States. He wants to be equal with all the working men of the nation, and he does not mean by the standard middle-class route. We are repelled by the human disintegration of peoples and cultures as they fall apart in this Great Gringo Melting Pot, and determined that this will not happen to us. But there will always be a *raza* in this country. There are millions more where we came from, across the thousand miles of common border between Mexico and the United States. For millions of farmworkers, from the Mexicans and Philippinos of the West to the Afro-Americans of the South, the United States has come to a social, political and cultural impasse. Listen to these people, and you will hear the first murmurings of revolution.

CÉSAR CHÁVEZ

César Chávez (labor leader and Director of United Farm Workers Organizing Committee, AFL-CIO) has been without doubt the most charismatic labor leader to appear upon the American labor scene since Walter Reuther. In this autobiographical sketch from RAMPARTS MAGAZINE, Mr. Chávez recounts the early history of his career. Copyright Noah's Ark, Inc. (for RAMPARTS MAGAZINE) 1971. By permission of the Editors.

The Organizer's Tale

It really started for me 16 years ago in San Jose, California, when I was working on an apricot farm. We figured he was just another social worker doing a study of farm conditions, and I kept refusing to meet with him. But he was persistent. Finally, I got together some of the rough element in San Jose. We were going to have a little reception for him to teach the *gringo* a little bit of how we felt. There were about thirty of us in the house, young guys mostly. I was supposed to give them a signal —change my cigarette from my right hand to my left, and then we were going to give him a lot of hell. But he started talking and the more he talked, the more wide-eyed I became and the less inclined I was to give the signal. A couple of guys who were pretty drunk at the time still wanted to give the *gringo* the business, but we got rid of them. This fellow was making a lot of sense, and I wanted to hear what he had to say.

His name was Fred Ross, and he was an organizer for the Community Service Organization (CSO) which was working with Mexican-Americans in the cities. I became immediately really involved. Before long I was heading a voter registration drive. All the time I was observing the things Fred did, secretly, because I wanted to learn how to organize, to see how it was done. I was impressed with his patience and understanding of people. I thought this was a tool, one of the greatest things he had.

It was pretty rough for me at first. I was changing and had to take a lot of ridicule from the kids

297

my age, the rough characters I worked with in the fields. They would say, "Hey, big shot. Now that you're a *politico,* why are you working here for 65 cents an hour?" I might add that our neighborhood had the highest percentage of San Quentin graduates. It was a game among the *pachucos* in the sense that we defended ourselves from outsiders, although inside the neighborhood there was not a lot of fighting.

After six months of working every night in San Jose, Fred assigned me to take over the CSO chapter in Decoto. It was a tough spot to fill. I would suggest something, and people would say, "No, let's wait till Fred gets back," or "Fred wouldn't do it that way." This is pretty much a pattern with people, I discovered, whether I was put in Fred's position, or later, when someone else was put in my position. After the Decoto assignment I was sent to start a new chapter in Oakland. Before I left, Fred came to a place in San Jose called the Hole-in-the-Wall and we talked for half an hour over coffee. He was in a rush to leave, but I wanted to keep him talking; I was that scared of my assignment.

There were hard times in Oakland. First of all, it was a big city and I'd get lost every time I went anywhere. Then I arranged a series of house meetings. I would get to the meeting early and drive back and forth past the house, too nervous to go in and face the people. Finally I would force myself to go inside and sit in a corner. I was quite thin then, and young, and most of the people were middle-aged. Someone would say, "Where's the organizer?" And I would pipe up, "Here I am." Then they would say in Spanish—these were very poor people and we hardly spoke anything but Spanish—"Ha! This *kid?*" Most of them said they were interested, but the hardest part was to get them to start pushing themselves, on their own initiative.

The idea was to set up a meeting and then get each attending person to call his own house meeting, inviting new people—a sort of chain letter effect. After a house meeting I would lie awake going over the whole thing, playing the tape back, trying to see why people laughed at one point, or why they were for one thing and against another. I was also learning to read and write, those late

evenings. I had left school in the 7th grade after attending sixty-seven different schools, and my reading wasn't the best.

At our first organizing meeting we had 368 people: I'll never forget it because it was very important to me. You eat your heart out; the meeting is called for 7 o'clock and you start to worry about 4. You wait. Will they show up? Then the first one arrives. By 7 there are only 20 people, you have everything in order, you have to look calm. But little by little they filter in and at a certain point you know it will be a success.

After four months in Oakland, I was transferred. The chapter was beginning to move on its own, so Fred assigned me to organize the San Joaquin Valley. Over the months I developed what I used to call schemes or tricks—now I call them techniques—of making initial contacts. The main thing in convincing someone is to spend time with him. It doesn't matter if he can read, write or even speak well. What is important is that he is a man and second, that he has shown some initial interest. One good way to develop leadership is to take a man with you in your car. And it works a lot better if you're doing the driving; that way you are in charge. You drive, he sits there, and you talk. These little things were very important to me; I was caught in a big game by then, figuring out what makes people work. I found that if you work hard enough you can usually shake people into working too, those who are concerned. You work harder and they work harder still, up to a point and then they pass you. Then, of course, they're on their own.

I also learned to keep away from the established groups and so-called leaders, and to guard against philosophizing. Working with low-income people is very different from working with the professionals, who like to sit around talking about how to play politics. When you're trying to recruit a farmworker, you have to paint a little picture, and then you have to color the picture in. We found out that the harder a guy is to convince, the better leader or member he becomes. When you exert yourself to convince him, you have his confidence and he has good motivation. A lot of people who say OK right away wind up hanging around the office, taking up the workers' time.

During the McCarthy era in one Valley town, I was subjected to a lot of redbaiting. We had been recruiting people for citizenship classes at the high school when we got into a quarrel with the naturalization examiner. He was rejecting people on the grounds that they were just parroting what they learned in citizenship class. One day we had a meeting about it in Fresno, and I took along some of the leaders of our local chapter. Some redbaiting official gave us a hard time, and the people got scared and took his side. They did it because it seemed easy at the moment, even though they knew that sticking with me was the right thing to do. It was disgusting. When we left the building they walked by themselves ahead of me as if I had some kind of communicable disease. I had been working with these people for three months and I was very sad to see that. It taught me a great lesson.

That night I learned that the chapter officers were holding a meeting to review my letters and printed materials to see if I really was a Communist. So I drove out there and walked right in on their meeting. I said, "I hear you've been discussing me, and I thought it would be nice if I was here to defend myself. Not that it matters that much to you or even to me, because as far as I'm concerned you are a bunch of cowards." At that they began to apologize. "Let's forget it," they said. "You're a nice guy." But I didn't want apologies. I wanted a full discussion. I told them I didn't give a damn, but that they had to learn to distinguish fact from what appeared to be a fact because of fear. I kept them there till two in the morning. Some of the women cried. I don't know if they investigated me any further, but I stayed on another few months and things worked out.

This was not an isolated case. Often when we'd leave people to themselves they would get frightened and draw back into their shells where they had been all the years. And I learned quickly that there is no real appreciation. Whatever you do, and no matter what reasons you may give to others, you do it because you want to see it done, or maybe because you want power. And there shouldn't be any appreciation, understandably. I know good organizers who were destroyed, washed out, because they expected people to ap-

preciate what they'd done. Anyone who comes in with the idea that farmworkers are free of sin and that the growers are all bastards, either has never dealt with the situation or is an idealist of the first order. Things don't work that way.

For more than ten years I worked for the CSO. As the organization grew, we found ourselves meeting in fancier and fancier motels and holding expensive conventions. Doctors, lawyers and politicians began joining. They would get elected to some office in the organization and then, for all practical purposes, leave. Intent on using the CSO for their own prestige purposes, these "leaders," many of them, lacked the urgency we had to have. When I became general director I began to press for a program to organize farmworkers into a union, an idea most of the leadership opposed. So I started a revolt within the CSO. I refused to sit at the head table at meetings, refused to wear a suit and tie, and finally I even refused to shave and cut my hair. It used to embarrass some of the professionals. At every meeting I got up and gave my standard speech: we shouldn't meet in fancy motels, we were getting away from the people, farmworkers had to be organized. But nothing happened. In March of '62 I resigned and came to Delano to begin organizing the Valley on my own.

By hand I drew a map of all the towns between Arvin and Stockton—86 of them, including farming camps—and decided to hit them all to get a small nucleus of people working in each. For six months I traveled around, planting an idea. We had a simple questionnaire, a little card with space for name, address and how much the worker thought he ought to be paid. My wife, Helen, mimeographed them, and we took our kids for two or three day jaunts to these towns, distributing the cards door-to-door and to camps and groceries.

Some 80,000 cards were sent back from eight Valley counties. I got a lot of contacts that way, but I was shocked at the wages the people were asking. The growers were paying $1 and $1.15, and maybe 95 percent of the people thought they should be getting only $1.25. Sometimes people scribbled messages on the cards: "I hope to God we win" or "Do you think we can win?" or "I'd like to know more." So I separated the cards with the pencilled notes, got in my car and went to those people.

We didn't have any money at all in those days, none for gas and hardly any for food. So I went to people and started asking for food. It turned out to be about the best thing I could have done, although at first it's hard on your pride. Some of our best members came in that way. If people give you their food, they'll give you their hearts. Several months and many meetings later we had a working organization, and this time the leaders were the people.

None of the farmworkers had collective bargaining contracts, and I thought it would take ten years before we got that first contract. I wanted desperately to get some color into the movement, to give people something they could identify with, like a flag. I was reading some books about how various leaders discovered what colors contrasted and stood out the best. The Egyptians had found that a red field with a white circle and a black emblem in the center crashed into your eyes like nothing else. I wanted to use the Aztec eagle in the center, as on the Mexican flag. So I told my cousin Manuel, "Draw an Aztec eagle." Manuel had a little trouble with it, so we modified the eagle to make it easier for people to draw.

The first big meeting of what we decided to call the National Farm Workers Association was held in September 1962, at Fresno, with 287 people. We had our huge red flag on the wall, with paper tacked over it. When the time came, Manuel pulled a cord ripping the paper off the flag and all of a sudden it hit the people. Some of them wondered if it was a Communist flag, and I said it probably looked more like a neo-Nazi emblem than anything else. But they wanted an explanation, so Manuel got up and said, "When that damn eagle flies—that's when the farmworkers' problems are going to be solved."

One of the first things I decided was that outside money wasn't going to organize people, at least not in the beginning. I even turned down a grant from a private group—$50,000 to go directly to organize farmworkers—for just this reason. Even when there are no strings attached, you are still compromised because you feel you have to produce immediate results. This is bad, because it takes a long time to build a movement, and your organization suffers if you get too far ahead of the people it belongs to. We set the dues at $42 a year per family, really a meaningful dues, but of the 212 we got to pay, only 12 remained by June of '63. We were discouraged at that, but not enough to make us quit.

Money was always a problem. Once we were facing a $180 gas bill on a credit card I'd got a long time ago and was about to lose. And we *had* to keep that credit card. One day my wife and I were picking cotton, pulling bolls, to make a little money to live on. Helen said to me, "Do you put all this in the bag, or just the cotton?" I thought she was kidding and told her to throw the whole boll in so that she had nothing but a sack of bolls at the weighing. The man said, "Whose sack is this?" I said, well, my wife's, and he told us we were fired. "Look at all that crap you brought in," he said. Helen and I started laughing. We were going anyway. We took the $4 we had earned and spent it at a grocery store where they were giving away a $100 prize. Each time you shopped they'd give you one of the letters of M-O-N-E-Y or a flag: you had to have M-O-N-E-Y plus the flag to win. Helen had already collected the letters and just needed the flag. Anyway, they gave her the ticket. She screamed, "A flag? I don't believe it," ran in and got the $100. She said, "Now we're going to eat steak." But I said no, we're going to pay the gas bill. I don't know if she cried, but I think she did.

It was rough in those early years. Helen was having babies and I was not there when she was at the hospital. But if you haven't got your wife behind you, you can't do many things. There's got to be peace at home. So I did, I think, a fairly good job of organizing her. When we were kids, she lived in Delano and I came to town as a migrant. Once on a date we had a bad experience about segregation at a movie theater, and I put up a fight. We were together then, and still are. I think I'm more of a pacifist than she is. Her father, Fabela, was a colonel with Pancho Villa in the Mexican Revolution. Sometimes she gets angry and tells me, "These scabs—you should deal with them sternly," and I kid her, "It must be too much of that Fabela blood in you."

The movement really caught on in '64. By August we had a thousand members. We'd had a beautiful 90-day drive in Corcoran, where they had the Battle of the Corcoran Farm Camp 30 years ago, and by November we had assets of $25,000 in our credit union, which helped to stabilize the membership. I had gone without pay the whole of 1963. The next year the members voted me a $40 a week salary, after Helen had to quit working in the fields to manage the credit union.

Our first strike was in May of '65, a small one but it prepared us for the big one. A farmworker from McFarland named Epifanio Camacho came to see me. He said he was sick and tired of how people working the roses were being treated, and he was willing to "go the limit." I assigned Manuel and Gilbert Padilla to hold meetings at Camacho's house. The people wanted union recognition, but the real issue, as in most cases when you begin, was wages. They were promised $9 a thousand, but they were actually getting $6.50 and $7 for grafting roses. Most of them signed cards giving us the right to bargain for them. We chose the biggest company, with about 85 employees, not counting the irrigators and supervisors, and we held a series of meetings to prepare the strike and call the vote. There would be no picket line; everyone pledged on their honor not to break the strike.

Early on the first morning of the strike, we sent out ten cars to check the people's homes. We found lights in five or six homes and knocked on the doors. The men were getting up and we'd say, "Where are you going?" They would dodge, "Oh, uh . . . I was just getting up, you know." We'd say, "Well, you're not going to work, are you?" And they'd say no. Dolores Huerta, who was driving the green panel truck, saw a light in one house where four rose-workers lived. They told her they were going to work, even after she reminded them of their pledge. So she moved the truck so it blocked their driveway, turned off the key, put it in her purse and sat there alone.

That morning the company foreman was madder than hell and refused to talk to us. None of the grafters had shown up for work. At 10:30 we started to go to the company office, but it occurred to us that maybe a woman would have a better chance. So Dolores knocked on the office door, saying, "I'm Dolores Huerta from the National Farm Workers Association." "Get out!" the man said, "you Communist. Get out!" I guess they were expecting us, because as Dolores stood arguing with him the cops came and told her to leave. She left.

For two days the fields were idle. On Wednesday they recruited a group of Filipinos from out of town who knew nothing of the strike, maybe 35 of them. They drove through escorted by three sheriff's patrol cars, one in front, one in the middle and one at the rear with a dog. We didn't have a picket line, but we parked across the street and just watched them go through, not saying a word. All but seven stopped working after half an hour, and the rest had quit by mid-afternoon.

The company made an offer the evening of the fourth day, a package deal that amounted to a 120 percent wage increase, but no contract. We wanted to hold out for a contract and more benefits, but a majority of the rose-workers wanted to accept the offer and go back. We are a democratic union so we had to support what they wanted to do. They had a meeting and voted to settle. Then we had a problem with a few militants who wanted to hold out. We had to convince them to go back to work, as a united front, because otherwise they would be canned. So we worked—Tony Orendain and I, Dolores and Gilbert, Jim Drake and all the organizers—knocking on doors till two in the morning, telling people, "You have to go back or you'll lose your job." And they did. They worked.

Our second strike, and our last before the big one at Delano, was in the grapes at Martin's Ranch last summer. The people were getting a raw deal there, being pushed around pretty badly. Gilbert went out to the field, climbed on top of a car and took a strike vote. They voted unanimously to go out. Right away they started bringing in strike-breakers, so we launched a tough attack on the labor contractors, distributed leaflets portraying them as really low characters. We attacked one— Luis Campos—so badly that he just gave up the job, and he took twenty-seven of his men out with him. All he asked was that we distribute another leaflet reinstating him in the community. And we did. What was unusual was that the grower would talk to us. The grower kept saying, "I can't pay. I just haven't got the money." I guess he must have found the money somewhere, because we were asking $1.40 and we got it.

We had just finished the Martin strike when the Agricultural Workers Organizing Committee (AFL-CIO) started a strike against the grape growers, DiGiorgio, Schenley liquors and small growers, asking $1.40 an hour and 25 cents a box. There was a lot of pressure from our members for us to join the strike, but we had some misgivings. We didn't feel ready for a big strike like this one, one that was sure to last a long time. Having no money —just $87 in the strike fund—meant we'd have to depend on God knows who.

Eight days after the strike started—it takes time to get 1,200 people together from all over the Valley—we held a meeting in Delano and voted to go out. I asked the membership to release us from the pledge not to accept outside money, because we'd need it now, a lot of it. The help came. It started because of the close, and I would say even beautiful relationship that we've had with the Migrant Ministry for some years. They were the first to come to our rescue, financially and in every other way, and they spread the word to other benefactors.

We had planned, before, to start a labor school in November. It never happened, but we have the best labor school we could ever have, in the strike. The strike is only a temporary condition, however. We have over 3,000 members spread out over a wide area, and we have to service them when they have problems. We get letters from New Mexico, Colorado, Texas, California, from farmworkers saying, "We're getting together and we need an organizer." It kills you when you haven't got the personnel and resources. You feel badly about not sending an organizer because you look back and remember all the difficulty you had in getting two or three people together, and here *they're* together. Of course, we're training organizers, many of them younger than I was when I started in CSO. They can work 20 hours a day, sleep four and be ready to hit it again; when you get to be 39 it's a different story.

The people who took part in the strike and the march have something more than their material interest going for them. If it were only material, they wouldn't have stayed on the strike long enough to win. It is difficult to explain. But it flows out in the ordinary things they say. For instance, some of the younger guys are saying, "Where do you think's going to be the next strike?" I say, "Well, we have to win in Delano." They say, "We'll win, but where do we go next?" I say, "Maybe most of us will be working in the fields." They say, "No, I don't want to go and work in the fields. I want to organize. There are a lot of people that need our help." So I say, "You're going to be pretty poor then, because when you strike you don't have much money." They say they don't care about that.

And others are saying, "I have friends who are working in Texas. If we could only help them." It is bigger, certainly, than just a strike. And if this spirit grows within the farm labor movement, one day we can use the force that we have to help correct a lot of things that are wrong in this society. But that is for the future. Before you can run, you have to learn to walk.

There are vivid memories from my childhood— what we had to go through because of low wages and the conditions, basically because there was no union. I suppose if I wanted to be fair I could say that I'm trying to settle a personal score. I could dramatize it by saying that I want to bring social justice to farmworkers. But the truth is that I went through a lot of hell, and a lot of people did. If we can even the score a little for the workers then we are doing something. Besides, I don't know any other work I like to do better than this. I really don't, you know.

John Shockley

John Shockley (Danforth Intern, Earlham College) in these two original essays discusses the now-famous Crystal City affair. Professor Shockley tells of the coalition of Chicanos and teamsters that won control of the city council in 1963, and of events over the next seven years that strained this political alliance. Students should be interested in the rise of class-consciousness within the Chicano majority prompted by the electoral victory.
Both essays by permission of the author.

Crystal City: Los Cinco Mexicanos

A six foot high statue of Popeye in the center of town reminds all that Crystal City is no ordinary community. It is "the Spinach Capital of the World." As such it is the center of the Winter Garden Area of Texas, rich not only in spinach but in a number of other winter vegetables that can be grown in the area. But Popeye is only one aspect of the town's uniqueness—a uniqueness that is the cause for this study. It was here that in 1963 a group of five undereducated and poor Mexican-Americans were swept into office as city councilmen. Backed by the Teamsters who had organized the Del Monte spinach plant on the outskirts of town and supported further by the San Antonio-based Political Association of Spanish-speaking

People, the all-Chicano slate defeated the old Anglo establishment which had run the town since its inception in 1907. At the time this happened, Crystal City was the only community in Texas, and perhaps in the Southwest, where Anglos had been ousted from decades of rule. This study will attempt to understand why this revolution occurred, why it failed, and why it was so rare. The Chicano takeover in Crystal City proved to be a false start, but it can and has provided valuable lessons for the Chicano movement to draw on in later years.

At the time of the 1963 revolution, Chicano enthusiasts were proclaiming that Crystal City was merely the beginning of what was to happen in all

303

of South Texas and in other areas where Mexican-Americans were a majority of the populace. Instead of that happening, however, in the elections two years later the chicano slate was beaten. Not only had they failed to capture the rest of South Texas; they had failed to hold even their base of Crystal City. An examination of the situation and circumstances in the community, however, would have shown that the town was in several respects quite different from other communities in South Texas. These differences were absolutely crucial to the success of the movement in 1963. Because of the town's composition and because of particular historical and economic factors, the town was a powder keg of a unique kind.

First, the town was overwhelmingly Mexican-American to an extent that is not common even for South Texas. For the county of Zavala as a whole, the 1960 census showed 74.4 percent of its inhabitants were Spanish-surnamed. This ranked the county as seventh in the state of Texas in terms of percent Spanish-surnamed. The town of Crystal City, however, has been far more heavily Mexican-American than the rest of Zavala County. The most common estimates place the percentage of its 9,000 residents who are Mexicanos at around eighty-five percent. To find Mexican-Americans in such high numbers in a community the size of Crystal City is not at all common in South Texas.

But it was more than this concentration that was unusual about the town: it was the way the town was ruled, given its heavy percentage of chicanos, which made Crystal City such a powder keg. There were a few other moderate-sized communities in South Texas—Laredo and Eagle Pass being two—where such a high concentration of Mexican-Americans could be found. But these communities, both situated on the border, were older communities with well established Mexican-American families who had always played an important part in governmental affairs. Crystal City, however, was another kind of town. It was a twentieth century town, where Anglos had always dominated and where the Anglos had never been tempered by the need to compromise with the Mexican-American. The town was not founded by Spanish explorers or by later Mexican settlers. It was created by the break-up of the Cross-S ranch

in the first decade of the century. The decision to break up the ranch and the selling and the buying of plots of land were all carried out by Anglos. The town's founding fathers and civic leaders were thus exclusively Anglo.

As is most common with twentieth century South Texas towns, Mexicans were brought in and recruited by the Anglos to work the fields, perform menial labor, and provide the economic base off which the Anglos could make their money. The Mexicans were not supposed to be real citizens of the community. They were recruited to perform the tasks the Anglos told them to do, and if they didn't like it they could always "go back to Mexico." The Anglos themselves were aware of these differences between "their" Mexicans and those of the older, established towns along the border. As one Anglo said to me, "They look different, these Mexicans." Tending to be more Indian than Spanish, tending to be newcomers to the northern side of the Rio Grande, and often having come to Texas by less than legal means, these Mexicans made for much easier control than the old established families along the border. Desperately in search of work of any kind and hoping not to be deported, these Mexicans were not in a position to think of themselves as or to act like citizens of Crystal City.

The degree to which Crystal City was an Anglo-run community with such a heavily Mexican population made the town more nearly unique than general to South Texas. But this situation in itself was not explosive so long as the Mexicans did not think of themselves as people able to challenge the Anglos over issues, run for office, and in general partake in the running of a democratic society. With the levelling off of the economic boom to Crystal City and the whole Winter Garden area during the depression, however, the town's population began to stabilize. Mexicans from the south side of the Rio Grande no longer poured into the city in search of work. As employment opportunities slackened, more and more Mexicans began to take the initiative and head north for employment during the summer as a means of finding more work and of overcoming the seasonal nature of the work in Crystal City. By the 1950s it is estimated that close to one half of the Mexican-American community's population were migrant workers for at least part of the summer. Although many left the migrant trail to settle in other parts of the country, most considered the town their home and always returned in the autumn. But as migrants they began to encounter different experiences and different ways of being treated from those they encountered in South Texas. Being isolated during much of the year and earning wages elsewhere made them less susceptible to Anglo values upon their return. They were somewhat set apart in the community, more difficult for the Anglos to attempt to acculturate or to control.

Those Chicanos who remained in Crystal City all the year were at the same time improving themselves. More and better Mexican schools were established, and the Mexican-American population, both on its own and through the help of Anglos, gradually began to improve its position relative to that of the Anglo. Although there was not even a school for Mexicans until 1925, and through the 1930s there were almost no graduates from high school, by the late 1950s more than half of those graduating from high school were Mexican-Americans. And this occurred while the ratio of Anglos to Chicanos remained basically the same.

Related to the upgrading of the Mexican-American community in Crystal City, and with hindsight perhaps the most important economic development in the town, was the establishment after the Second World War of a large California Packers plant, later to be renamed Del Monte. This plant, which by its very magnitude centralized much of the vegetable growing in the area, was California-owned and was used to dealing with workers throughout the nation. In being owned from outside the area, the plant was subject to some very un-South Texas ideas. The most radical of these was the plant's decision to allow unionization, as all their other plants were unionized. By 1956 a small Teamsters union was established at the plant and was recognized without any friction by the company. The decision by Del Monte to move into Crystal City and establish a large plant, although it was welcomed by many in the city's agricultural-business establishment, ultimately weakened these local Anglos' ability to control the situation. Having a large-scale plant employing hundreds of workers and then allowing the workers the opportunity to unionize set Crystal City off even further from other South Texas communities.

Even with these three potentially explosive ingredients—an overwhelming majority of Mexican-Americans in the process of improving themselves relative to the Anglo, an Anglo-run community, and a Teamsters union—the situation in the community remained close to the same for nearly a decade. No doubt many Anglos realized that complete Anglo dominance could not continue forever, but taking the initiative to alter the status quo was difficult for farsighted Anglos to do. L. L. Williams, the city manager for three decades, was one of these who recognized that the situation would eventually change, and he set about in several ways to bring a few Mexicans into the government, if only to protect the Anglos from a more massive engulfment. By the early 1960s a small but growing Mexican-American middle class had developed and was being consulted on many matters. But it was still quite small, and owing to the history of the community, it was still quite fragile. Neither the Anglos nor the great majority of Mexican-Americans themselves looked to this group for leadership.

The spark that set off the explosion in Crystal City was in fact an Anglo. Andrew Dickens, a retired oil-field worker, moved to Crystal City in 1961 and thereby proceeded to set up a doughnut shop. This in itself was hardly a radical step, but it turned out that Dickens' shop was located on property the city wanted. Dickens considered himself to have been "taken" on his property lease by the city, and when he tried to get help in fighting the arrangement, he found that both the city government and the county government were in agreement. He could get nowhere. Outraged, he vowed to the mayor and the county judge that he would work to turn the place over to the Mexicans in order to beat the "machine."

As a start Andrew Dickens contacted the union at the Del Monte plant and talked to its business agent, Juan Cornejo. These two, together with several others from the union, talked over the idea of organizing against the city government. They then journeyed to San Antonio to talk with the President and Business Manager of Teamsters Local 657 of San Antonio, Ray Shafer. Until that time Shafer had not been interested in putting his union on the line in Crystal City, but when the possibility of success appeared, Shafer was interested and told the group to begin by launching a poll tax drive.

With the help of outside organizational expertise, consisting particularly of Carlos Moore and Henry Munoz of the Teamsters, and including bookkeeping which allowed some of the Mexicans to pay their $1.75 in installments, the poll tax drive turned out to be extraordinarily successful. At the end of January, a whopping 1,139 Mexican-Americans had paid their poll taxes while only 542 Anglos had. This contrasted starkly with the previous year's figure of 792 Mexican-American and 538 Anglo poll taxes. Thus it was not just that the Teamsters had been unusually successful in their drive; this had occurred at the very time Anglo poll taxes had remained stationary. A quirk of fate allowed the Chicanos to increase their registration greatly without any "backlash" in Anglo restraints, and this alone may have been enough to make the difference between victory and defeat for the Mexican-Americans. The able city manager, L. L. Williams, died in the fall of 1962 and was replaced by James Dill. Dill was not familiar with the situation in Crystal City as L. L. Williams had run it. Previously it had been the practice to watch very closely poll tax payments as they were coming in. The town's Anglos were quite aware that they were in a minority, and a group of the town's businessmen and agricultural leaders had set up a contingency fund to be used to buy Anglo poll taxes if the Mexicans began buying too many. As was related to me, more than once the mayor of the city and other city personnel asked the new city manager how the poll tax payments were coming, and he assured them that he would check and that things were under control. James Dill did not check. The result was the disaster of several hundred Anglos not paying their poll taxes at the very time Mexicans had dramatically increased their number of eligible voters.

When the results of the poll tax drive were made known, Shafer of the Teamsters became even more interested, as he and everyone else working on the drive now sensed victory. Shafer drove down to Crystal City and called the first of several strategy meetings. But the choosing of candidates to run became more difficult than they had expected. A number of people declined to run, some through fear for their jobs and some through fear for their families. At the same time apparently the middle-class Mexican-Americans in the community would have nothing to do with the movement. The organizers were thus forced to comprise a slate of those few candidates who were willing to run. The five candidates, called *Los Cinco*, were Juan Cornejo, the business agent for the Teamsters at the Del Monte plant; Manuel Maldonado, a clerk in the local Economart store; Antonio Cardenas, a truck driver; Reynaldo Mendoza, operator of a small photography shop; and Mario Hernandez, a real estate salesman. None was well-known in the community; none had graduated from high school. None was in any of the Mexican, much less the Anglo, middle class organizations.

Along with the selection of candidates, the strategists faced another major problem—how to play down the influence of the teamsters in the election. By 1963 the Teamsters were in serious trouble with the United States Government, and the mere mention of their name evoked horror to most of the Anglo community. Being a labor union was bad enough, but being the Teamsters was even worse. Ray Shafer and two of his most trusted lieutenants, Carlos Moore and Henry Munoz, devised a two-fold plan to try to deflect the focus in the election from the Teamsters. Although earlier they had tried to conceal the identity of Teamster organizers, Anglos had eventually discovered them. Something more geared to active campaigning was needed. First, a local campaign committee was organized, called the "Citizens Committee for Better Government." This local organization thus channelled most of the outside help. Secondly, the Teamsters approached the Political Association of Spanish-speaking People (PASO), which was a new, militant political organization that had originated from the Viva Kennedy Clubs during the 1960 presidential campaign. PASO had been having serious troubles following its disastrous attempt to wield influence in

Texas, and a number of its leaders believed that in order to establish a more solid base, the organization needed to concentrate its activities at the local level. Crystal City fit in with this strategy brilliantly. By commissioning the help of PASO, the Teamsters were able both to get valuable help and to deflect some of the attention from their own involvement. Albert Fuentes, the state executive secretary of PASO, and Martin Garcia, a district director who was employed by the Teamsters, became the main PASO contribution to the campaign.

With the naming of the candidates and the establishment of the local campaign organization, the campaign had broken out into the open. Although worried by the developments taking place in their town, the Anglos still had reasons to be confident. Not only was the weight of tradition completely on their side, but owing to the quality of the Mexican candidates, the middle-class Mexican-Americans were staying rather firmly in line.

After *Los Cinco* had filed, several of the community's most prominent Anglos approached the local Mexican Evangelical Baptist Minister, Arnold Lopez. Explaining to him that the five candidates running were unqualified and not representative of the "better Mexican element" in the town, they convinced the minister that he ought to run for office. Whether these men's motives were to be able to vote for a responsible Mexican-American who was also concerned for the welfare of his community, or whether they rather wanted to split the Mexican vote, is not clear. None of the Anglos who came to the Reverend, however, were close to the mayor and his administration. But when the minister began launching attacks upon the five candidates, charging that they were being managed and run from outside and that they were unqualified, it became clear that his support might come more from Anglos in the community than from Mexicans. At this point the same Anglos who had talked Reverend Lopez into running came to him again and urged him to withdraw because he was splitting the anti-Teamster vote. In refusing to withdraw at this point, he added an uncertainty to the Anglo problems of retaining control in the community. And this problem was heightened by the entrance of

another independent candidate, Dr. Henry Daly, who also refused to withdraw from the race.

These independents emphasized problems the Anglo establishment faced in trying to retain control of the community. The old leadership had never been seriously challenged, although a number of Anglos themselves felt that newer, more innovative leaders were needed. Like most small communities in America, its younger citizens often left the community to seek better opportunities elsewhere, thus perpetuating the old rule. Because of the form of government—a weak mayor and council with a strong city manager—the offices of mayor and councilmen were not very appealing and went unpaid. The current mayor had been in office since the Twenties, not so much because he wanted to continue to be mayor but because no one else in the Anglo community seemed interested in taking his place.

Little had happened in the town government in the decade before 1963. Only two developments had occurred which seem to have had an impact on the town's government. The first was the veterans land scandal, which was a statewide scandal involving several people high in the Shivers administration. A program intended to help veterans obtain land had instead been used by interested land speculators to buy land that the state thought was going to veterans. It had also been used to get the state to buy land for veterans from the realtors at grossly inflated land values. In Crystal City the scandal turned out to be a rather blatant case of Anglo land speculators using Mexican veterans to obtain more land or money for themselves by "buying off" the veterans' right to the land. More than one Mexican in the community mentioned that this scandal was the first time the Mexicans in the community had followed local government or had realized that the local leaders were engaging in activities which other Anglos considered to be illegal. The immediate results of the scandal were rather small, however. It was rather something for the Mexican community to remember at a later date.

The second development in the community over the decade preceeding the revolution was the city government's decision to apply for and use urban renewal funds for a renovation of the city. The town had long been one of the poorest in the state, with almost no streets in the Mexican sections paved and with less than half the town having sewage connections. In 1950 the average Mexican-American twenty-five years of age or older had received slightly over one and one half years of education, and their average family income was considerably less than $2,000 a year. The decision to apply for urban renewal and to float bonds was not prompted so much by these statistics, however, as by city statistics showing that the city was not dying but was growing more rapidly than at any other time since before the depression. The decision to adopt an urban renewal program was made in 1957-1958, but the program was proceeding at a snail's pace and was having only limited impact on the community by 1963. Nevertheless the reaction of many in the Mexican community to urban renewal was one of hostility toward the condemning of their homes and the relocations that might be forced on them. Most important of all, the city government was now making itself more conspicuous to the people, Mexican-Americans as well as Anglos, migrants as well as permanent residents.

Viewed from this perspective, both urban renewal and the land scandal were liabilities to Anglo rule because they dispelled apathy toward local government. And under any minority government such as existed in Crystal City, apathy is an essential element of stability, whether that apathy is caused by basic agreement with the way the government is handling itself or whether it is caused by a feeling of hopelessness regarding change.

The old Anglo elite in Crystal City quickly had to realize in 1963 that the traditional apathy toward local government was being shattered. Their reaction, which had been remarkably lenient throughout the poll tax drive, now stiffened. Here were outside agitators, Teamster agents and militant chicanos from San Antonio, coming into their community to stir up the Mexican-Americans, organize them, and forge them into a powerful challenge to the decades of Anglo rule. A series of incidents followed, testing the very foundation of a democratic order. First there was trouble in filing for the elective posts. When the five Mexi-

canos went to file for office, the city clerk had "run out of forms." *Los Cinco* surmounted this problem by typing their own forms, which were accepted. The most serious incident occurred at the Del Monte plant during March, with less than a month to go before the election. Several employees were dismissed "for wearing campaign tags." How this incident was handled provided another instance of the crucial role the Teamsters played. Normally in South Texas such firings would have been final, and the men would have been without jobs. Had these workers in Crystal City lost their jobs now, in the middle of the campaign, the morale of the workers would have plummeted and fear would have become central for all those involved in the campaign. But the Teamsters, now more than ever willing to put their prestige on the line, interceded with the company and warned the management that the workers would have to be reinstated. This victory for economic security in the face of political activity bolstered the campaign activities of *Los Cinco* and the morale of all their supporters.

While the harassment was proceeding, and perhaps partly because of it, the campaign began to take on a tone that was most unusual for a city election: the issue of discrimination was raised. Mexicans began charging that they had been discriminated against on city improvements, such as the paving of streets and sewage connections. They noted that no Mexicans had ever been members of the city policy force and charged that local justice was such that Latins were punished more severely than Anglos for the same offenses. Rumors spread that the city's swimming pool, which apparently had been segregated until recently, had been disinfected each time after the Latins used it. These charges put the Anglo community on the defensive, and they began denying that there was racial discrimination now, although many admitted that there had been in the past. But the Anglos did not stop here. They charged that outside agitators were coming into the community to stir up the Mexicans, and they argued for local control of the community.

Both the general charges of the Anglos and of the Mexican-Americans were essentially correct. The charges against the Anglos of discriminating against Latins on street pavement and sewage, however, would have been more correct had the Mexicans charged that there was discrimination against the poor rather than against Mexican-Americans. Crystal City's decisions concerning these matters was based upon the normal American practice in local government of determining whether or not one was rich enough to afford to pay for it. Of course in actual practice this meant that paved streets and sewage connections were located overwhelmingly in the Anglo areas of town, but it upset the Anglos greatly that the Mexicans should have charged discrimination based on race when in fact concerning these city functions it was discrimination based only on poverty.

As to the Anglo charges that outside agitators were coming into the community to mastermind the Latin campaign, this was patently true. Teamster and PASO expertise was being used throughout the campaign, and was crucial from the beginning. The five candidates had had no experience in running campaigns, and they were watched and coached carefully on what to say and what not to say at rallies. This understandably infuriated the Anglo community and was an embarrassment to better-off Mexicans.

Two further issues developed out of the campaign itself concerning questions of discrimination. During the campaign the local Lions Club announced that it would be supporting an all-Anglo Boy Scout troop. Whereas this normally would have proceeded with scarcely a stir, it was seized upon by organizers and used as proof of Anglo discrimination. A further incident occurred late in the campaign. Martin Garcia, the PASO-Teamster organizer, was asked to leave from a restaurant after having ordered a beer, and he immediately charged racial discrimination. In fact the incident was somewhat manufactured: the management did not serve beer without food, and when informed of this, Garcia asked for a piece of bread with his beer. At this the management asked him to leave. The management did of course normally serve Mexicans, but it was also most reluctant to serve the kind of Mexican that Garcia was. Realizing the value of such an incident, Garcia in effect created it. Both these incidents emphasized the difficulties the Anglo

community faced in confronting the Mexican campaign. If the campaign was to be run at all along democratic lines, without relying largely on intimidation, it meant that at the very time Mexicans were getting belligerent, Anglos had to be very careful not to engage in discrimination against them.

Discrimination, then, became the major issue of the campaign, as one would have expected with an all-Latin slate running in a community overwhelmingly Mexican-American yet governed by Anglos. But by 1963 the Anglos no longer ruled by blatant discrimination against all Mexican-Americans. Indeed there was already one Mexican, Salvador Galvan, on the city council, and another councilman, Ed Ritchie, was part Mexican. The schools, which had been segregated at the elementary level for many years, were no longer segregated on criterion of race. Thus the issue of racial discrimination was in several respects quite different from the more clear-cut, obvious discrimination existing in the South between Negroes and whites. In Crystal City discrimination revolved more around questions of class and of culture than of race. Anglos were quite willing to admit that social discrimination against Mexicans did exist. But the great majority of Mexicans were not concerned with whether discrimination was based on "subtle" distinctions of class, culture, and social factors rather than upon race. They knew they had been discriminated against, and that was enough.

As the campaign approached its last few days, both Anglos and Mexicans increasingly realized that los Mexicanos were becoming more and more involved: *Los Cinco* rallies were now drawing hundreds of supporters. In response Anglo women organized a telephone committee to get all 542 Anglos to cast ballots, and the Anglo leadership engaged in more harassing tactics.

They called upon the Texas Rangers to come into Crystal City to maintain order. For over a century the Ranger concept of maintaining order had been quite different from the Mexican-American's idea of what this should entail. Bringing in the Rangers might have panicked the Chicano community into being afraid to turn out for rallies and vote. But again in a brilliant tactical move the Teamster strategists decided to circulate the fallacious rumor that they themselves had requested the Rangers in order to insure that there would be order in the community for the rest of the campaign. This rumor was not as implausible as it might now seem, because talk had been circulating throughout the town that there might be wholesale violence against the Mexican activists. Although Captain Allee of the Rangers was extremely upset over the outside agitators in Crystal City, this fact was kept fairly well-hidden until after the election, both by Allee himself and by the Mexican activists whom he visited.

One final harassment occurred when the city government refused to allow poll-watchers during the election. There had, of course, never been any before, and the city saw no reason for them now. When Carlos Moore, who specialized in Texas election law, showed the city authorities that part of the election code which specified the right of candidates to have poll-watchers, the city relented rather than face legal action.

The campaign from the beginning had been a series of Anglo mistakes, caused first by overconfidence and later by inability to decide upon a coherent strategy to counteract the Mexican activists. And the campaign had been a series of victories for los Chicanos. Morale in their community was running high and confidence in their right and ability to challenge the city fathers was increasing by the day. The initiative had been so taken by the activists that middle-class Mexicans were beginning to feel pressured. Several even put up signs supporting *Los Cinco,* but the great majority of those better off continued to side with the Anglos against the "rabble" trying to run for office. In fact Mexican and Anglo businessmen were so closely aligned that the week before the election the Mexican Chamber of Commerce joined the Chamber of Commerce in sponsoring the following advertisement:

We believe that city government should be local, representative government.
We believe in continuing the excellent racial relationships we have attained over the years and are against tactics designed to create racial issues.

We believe in voting for men who through their education, knowledge, business experience and good judgment are best qualified to handle the city's affairs.

Although the advertisement did not specifically endorse the incumbents, it was obvious to all that if one's criteria for voting were going to be a candidate's education and business experience, there would be no contest at all.

The amazing aspect of the Crystal City election, and that which made it such a radicalizing election, was that the Mexicans of the city were not listening to their own "leaders." The historical weakness of the local middle-class Mexicans and the independence of the city's migrant workers were clearly being felt. Enthusiasm for *Los Cinco* and respect for their courage in challenging the Anglo leadership was increasing. By election eve the final campaign rally for *Los Cinco* drew somewhere from 1,500 to 3,000 enthusiastic supporters. Again outside support was prominent as leading San Antonio liberals such as State Representatives Jake Johnson, Rudy Esquivel, John Alaniz, and PASO organizer Albert Fuentes spoke to the crowd, increasing both their confidence and enthusiasm. A letter from Albert Pena, head of PASO and a county commissioner in San Antonio, was circulated which stated that *Los Cinco* were "the only true 'Mexicanos' in the race for the City Council." This remark caused tremendous resentment in the Anglo community. Anglos, who were already upset that their opposing candidates were all Latin, charged that Pena's letter was further proof that it was the Latins, not the Anglos, who were discriminating.

Election day was long and tense, but with no real incidents. Trying different tactics, Anglo agricultural leaders suddenly doubled wages for that day to $2.00 an hour for those working in the fields. Certainly the possibility of making $2.00 an hour presented a painful choice to families who had little money to spare. Del Monte also announced suddenly that it was going into overtime production on election day. In both instances because of careful organization and outside assistance, this did not prevent the Mexicans from voting. With Del Monte, the Teamster organizers pointed out that even on overtime the company had to allow the workers the opportunity to leave their jobs temporarily to vote. Not to do so would have been a violation of the contract and an invitation to legal action or a strike, as the Teamster organizers made clear to the management. Because the Teamsters were willing to use their muscle, the management complied. To handle the wage increases in the fields, the organizers made sure that all drivers were to return with their workers by the early afternoon, vote them, and then return them to the fields. By setting the time early enough in the afternoon, the organizers would have time to send someone else out to bring in the workers should the original driver be lured into staying. As it happened, however, all the drivers returned from the fields with plenty of time to spare. Election day was in fact an impressive show of organizational strength by the Teamster-PASO coalition. From poll lists to see who had voted, drivers to bring people to the polls, cards with the candidates' names, and even a marked string to help illiterates know which of the seven candidates to scratch out, the Latins were so well prepared for election day that as many people voted in the city council election as had voted in the entire county in the Nixon-Kennedy presidential race three years before.

The Anglos spent the day uneasily eyeing the long voting lines. The Rangers patrolled throughout the city, but did little more than make themselves visible. Late that night the results were made known, and they electrified the town and South Texas. Soon they received national and international publicity. Los Cinco had swept to victory in a close count, defeating all five incumbents. The results were as follows:

Manuel Maldonado	864
Juan Cornejo	818
Mario Hernandez	799
Antonio Cardenas	799
Reynaldo Mendoza	795
Ed Ritchie	754
W. P. Brennan	717
Bruce Holsomback	716

J. C. Bookout	694
S. G. Galvan	664
Dr. Henry Daly	164
Rev. Arnold Lopez	146

Unfortunately for those who had worked so hard to bring about the electoral victory, governing the community turned out to be far more difficult than winning the election. The nature of the victory—the inexperience of the candidates, the dependence upon outside help, and the vulnerability of the Mexican community in a town which had always been dominated by Anglos—came back to haunt all those who had worked for the success.

The day after the election, Manuel Maldonado, the top vote-getter on the ticket and the man ironically most respected by the Anglos, lost his job at the Economart store. Anglo pressure had been strong enough that his employer reluctantly caved in. Another member of *Los Cinco,* Antonio Cardenas, found that his wages were halved from $77 to $35 a week. Within a few days a third member of *Los Cinco,* Mario Hernandez, had turned against the other four and began echoing the charges the Anglos were leveling at the council-elect. Ranger presence not only continued in the town after the election, but it became obvious to all that the Rangers were most upset with the election results. Captain Allee remarked that he was only trying to keep outside agitators from coming into the community, but of course outside agitators were essential to the whole movement.

This vulnerability of the Mexican community also had its impact on the selection of mayor for the town. By tradition the candidate named mayor was to be the one with the highest number of votes. This would have been Manuel Maldonado. But after Maldonado was fired, the next highest man, Juan Cornejo, actively sought the post. Aided by his connections with the Teamsters and the job security that this afforded, Cornejo managed to persuade the rest of the council to elect him mayor. This came at a time when journalists from all over Texas, Mexico, and the nation were becoming increasingly interested in what was happening in Crystal City. From being a dutiful worker at the Del Monte cannery, Cornejo was thrust into international publicity with what turned out to be disastrous results. The sky now seemed the limit to him. But the city charter was constructed so that the city manager, not the mayor, ran the city. Although the Teamster-PASO coalition managed to find an excellent, independent Mexican-American engineer named George Ozuna to become the new city manager, he was to run into trouble from Cornejo. Cornejo could never understand why he, having been elected mayor, should not be running the city. In the struggle to follow, it became increasingly apparent how much the whole institutional procedure for governance was premised upon middle-class and business-oriented Anglo ideas.

In the face of overwhelming publicity and wholesale Anglo resignations from the city government in the hopes that the new government would topple, George Ozuna thought that his most important task was to keep the city government running and to prove to the Anglos and to the world that the Mexican-Americans could govern Crystal City efficiently and justly. Cornejo, however, looked upon his assumption of leadership and upon the Anglo resignations as an opportunity to put his friends into office. His concept of government was more that of a traditional boss politician, or *patron,* who was interested in establishing a machine of the sort that other areas of South Texas had known. . . . In the end George Ozuna and Juan Cornejo remained deadlocked because of certain procedural regulations in the city charter. Not only did the city charter provide that the councilmen should receive no salary, under the assumption of course that only sufficiently wealthy people would be councilmen; it also prohibited council members from being in debt to the city on any of their bills. Fired from jobs, unable to find work, and increasingly in debt, the council members had to face this crisis as best they could. The two who couldn't make it and were expelled from the council by the courts were part of Cornejo's three to two majority in favor of firing Ozuna. Thus the government stayed deadlocked with both Cornejo and Ozuna remaining in office. This struggle between Ozuna and Cornejo and the

two different concepts of government they represented went on until the end in 1965. This feud greatly weakened the strength and prestige of the new government and gradually reduced the image of Cornejo, who after the victorious election had been viewed as a hero and savior. . . .

The unity under which the whole electoral campaign had flourished so amazingly now crumbled under Anglo threats, inducements, and the wave of publicity that changed the lives of all the men involved. The city government was swept from one difficulty to another. And somehow lost in the personal squabbles and rivalries were the numerous improvements the city government had made in such areas as paving, lights, sewage, police policy, and job opportunities.

While this battle within the Chicano camp was raging, the Anglos were increasing their own activity. What overconfidence and inactivity they had displayed earlier during the campaign were quickly overcome. When an investigation of the election failed to turn up grounds for calling another election, the Anglos devised the strategy of forcing a recall vote. However, Texas law required that in order to have a recall election a majority of those who voted in the election must request that a new election be held. The Anglos could not hope to get this many people to sign for a recall. Instead they devised a plan which was nothing short of brilliant in its ability to weight the procedures of governance in their favor. Calling their petition not a recall petition but a "charter revision," so that only 10 percent of the voters would have to sign, the revision proposed to increase the number of seats on the council from five to seven. All five councilmen would be forced to run again with the added stipulation that the election was to be held on October 1st, before all the Mexicans working in the fields up north would return. Although the district judge agreed completely that the petition was a "charter revision" rather than a recall petition, legal appeals managed to postpone a decision until the October deadline passed and the question became moot.

Although stymied in this attempt to use institutional procedures to throw out the government, the Anglos also set up a new organization to prepare for the next elections. Realizing that they could no longer rule as they had before the revolutionary election, they assiduously began courting the favor of the "better Mexican element." They were aided in this strategy by the new government's inexperience in ruling and inability to keep together a winning coalition. For example, shortly after the election representatives from the Mexican Chamber of Commerce approached the Cornejo administration in a conciliatory manner. When they were rejected by the new government, which quite understandably resented these businessmen's support of the old Anglo administration, the middle-class Mexicans had little alternative but to combine with the Anglo leadership. Together they formed a powerful coalition. This in itself would probably not have been enough to bring down the new government had it remained united, but once the militants' organization began to crumble, the Anglo-Latin business team assumed a commanding position. By nominating a slate of three Mexicans and two Anglos, and by promising to bring stability and local control back to Crystal City after the two years of bickering and shattered hopes, the new coalition was victorious. Mayor Cornejo and his battered and divided forces were crushed by a united, confident coalition of Anglos and middle-class Mexican-Americans while the Teamsters and PASO stayed out. Shortly afterwards George Ozuna was asked to resign. In losing, however, Cornejo received more votes in 1965 than he had in 1963. A turnout even greater in 1965 than in 1963 signified that although Cornejo had lost, Chicanos had solidified their role as participants and that the *ancien regime* could not be restored.

The lessons of this first Crystal City revolution lie in the nature of the revolt. From the beginning the revolution was dependent upon outside support and assistance. Because of the lack of opportunities and consequent inexperience in the local Mexican population, the Teamsters and PASO shouldered the questions of organization and of strategy, at the same time devoting little time to the question of what kind of government the new government should be and what goals it should strive for once it was in power. When faced with choosing candidates to run, the organizers were forced to choose from the very narrow field of those willing to run. Both the Teamsters and PASO hoped they were getting candidates they would be able to work with and continue to advise, if not also control. But because of their very success, new factors came into play—questions of what type of government the city should have, and questions concerning the need to keep receiving advice and consent from these outside organizations. Much of the failure must rest on the shoulders of Juan Cornejo. . . . But to blame a man of such limited experience for failure to carry through under conditions of tremendous difficulty and extreme pressure, having to use institutions designed much more for Anglo businessmen than for a semi-literate worker, is somewhat misleading. The Crystal City story of 1963 was a story of failure more because of the very inexperience and lack of opportunity which had produced these very leaders. The lesson to be learned would seem to be that in the end force of change and of revolution is contingent upon the local people who must do the leading and the following. And here the vicious circle of inequality and inexperience cuts in, for the ability of the local people is conditioned by the type of rule they have known. For the Chicano political movement in the future, more effort would need to be spent building up local, indigenous organization and leadership. For outside expertise to slight this factor would invite disaster. The uniqueness of the Crystal City organizational base of Teamsters supported by migrants was enough to win an election, but it was not enough to govern. If it was the uniqueness of Crystal City that allowed for the revolution in 1963, it was its very similarity with the rest of South Texas—similarities regarding poverty, inexperience, and vulnerability—that brought about its downfall.

John Shockley

Crystal City: La Raza Unida And The Second Revolt

After the Chicano takeover of Crystal City in 1963, throughout South Texas the town became a symbol of hope and pride to Chicanos and of fear to Anglos. Although the town's political revolution ultimately ended in defeat, Crystal City was to continue to be a pace-setter for Chicano politics. A second political revolt, occurring in the spring of 1970, was destined to have a far greater impact upon the community and upon politics in South Texas than did the first. Clearer goals, a different organizational base with a different strategy for mobilizing the Chicano community, and a vastly different kind of leadership all seemed to make this revolution far more exportable to the rest of South Texas.

The first revolution, it should be noted, did have as its goals the elimination of discrimination and the securing of Mexican-American representation in the community. But between 1963 and 1969 throughout the Southwest a great deal of thinking about the purposes of a Chicano movement had taken place, spurred on in part by the rising militancy of the Black movement. Integration became

less of a goal than the recovery and protection of a Chicano identity. A rebirth in history led to an increased awareness of the Chicano's prior claim to the Southwest, which in turn led to an increased militancy and to a greater confidence in confrontations with "the gringo." In the process of seeking to become the "masters of their own destiny," new organizations were founded with new leadership and new goals. The most visible of these new organizations in South Texas was the Mexican-American Youth Organization (MAYO), which was founded in 1967. Composed of young militants, often quite well-educated, MAYO adopted as goals a program to fulfill "the destiny of La Raza." These goals consisted of forming third parties separate from either the Democrats or the Republicans, gaining control of the educational systems in Chicano communities, and ending Anglo economic domination by the development of their own businesses and cooperatives. Chicano experience and intellectual thought had thus developed a great deal in the six years between 1963 and 1969, and this had its impact on Crystal City.

314

The second revolt in Crystal City differed from the first in that it was organized around specific examples of discrimination in the school system. Instead of being based as in 1963 upon the anomaly of the Teamsters Union, the second revolution had its organizational base in school children and their families. By mobilizing the family, the new revolution utilized one of the central points of Chicano culture.

The second revolt further differed in that leadership was not based upon outside organizational expertise and inexperienced local representatives. The new revolution was led by José Angel Gutierrez, a young man far more ideological, far more confident, and far more competent than his predecessor, Juan Cornejo. As a native of Crystal City, Gutierrez had gone on to receive a master's degree in political science and had developed his political training and expertise as president of MAYO.

In noting these changes within the Chicano movement, it is still necessary to examine the nature of the rule in the community which La Raza was fighting.

Reacting to the developments in Chicano thought and action throughout the 1960s, Anglos not only in Crystal City but throughout the Southwest became more defensive and began to assert their interest in integration, albeit Anglo-style. With a community of the composition of Crystal City, the Anglos had always been faced with basically only three ways of ruling: outright intimidation, cooptation of certain Mexicans, and the creation and maintenance of apathy. Their rule from the beginning had been a mixture of all three, with a gradual increase in the need for cooptation as the Mexican community began to improve its lot. This was, I should add, not necessarily done either deliberately or viciously. It was quite natural for the Anglo community to begin to extend ties to those Mexicans who were becoming increasingly like Anglos in attitudes and life-styles. But the revolt in 1963 upset the Anglo routine and forced the process to become far more deliberate. From the time of the all-Latin sweep of the city council elections in 1963, the Anglos realized that they could no longer rule in the same manner as previously. Common, ordinary Mexican-American "rabble" were now used to voting and to participating in the government. With a fundamental and permanent change in the voting rolls and in Mexican political behavior, the Anglos realized as never before that they simply had to have Mexican support in order to win. What emerged was a coalition with the "better Mexican element" which allowed these Mexicans to shoulder as much of the visible concerns of the town government as possible. This coalition became all the more necessary as traditional means of intimidation became less effective, both because of changes in federal and state laws and enforcement, and because the Mexican community was becoming better able to counter this intimidation.

From the successful defeat of Cornejo in 1965 until the second Chicano revolt, a majority of the city council was always Mexican-American. The town's Anglo leadership always made sure that a majority of its council candidates were Mexican-Americans. But as time passed the elaborate organization the Anglos had developed with middle-class Mexicans in opposition to Cornejo gradually began to wither. This happened both because of Anglo overconfidence and through the increasing disenchantment Mexicans began to feel with the policies of the local government and the manner in which the Anglos still treated them. Realizing how much the Anglos needed them, many Mexicanos who had originally felt that a coalition was needed to get rid of Cornejo now began to feel used. They began to doubt the sincerity of Anglo claims of integration and coalition government, particularly via the issue of discrimination in the schools.

Throughout the history of the community, progress had taken place in the schooling for Mexicans. Anglos offered this as proof of their sincerity and benevolence and as proof that any Mexican who really wanted to work could get ahead. In the early days there was no school at all for Mexicans. After 1925 a series of small Mexican schools were set up around the community. Those Mexicans who continued beyond elementary schools were then able to enter integrated schools. After the famous Supreme Court decision in 1954, the Anglo elementary school was integrated with a few Mexicans and the tiny handful of Negro children in the community. But continuing up until 1960 the only integrated school in the community was the Anglo elementary. The other elementary schools were totally Chicano. In 1960 a protest over the policy of continued de facto segregation led to a breakup of the system, although Anglos still tended to be separated from Mexicans in individual classrooms. This protest, which involved around 500 Mexicans under the leadership of the Mexican Evangelical Baptist Minister, Arnold Lopez, and a mail carrier, Gerald Saldana, surprised the Anglo community. The board and administrators at first indicated intransigence, but once it became clear that Mexicans were protesting and that legal action seemed imminent, school authorities quickly gave in. Having accomplished its goal, the first mass action by the Crystal City Chicano community quickly disbanded.

At the same time as *Los Cinco* Mexicanos were running for the city council in 1963, two Chicanos also ran for places on the city school board. Jesus Maldonado and Lorenzo Olivares came within a few votes of ousting the two Anglo incumbents four days after the city council election. In this campaign, however, discrimination in the schools was not a primary issue. It was more a question of gaining representation for the Latins, who had never had a member on the school board in the history of the city. The fact that the school district also encompassed some rural areas of the county, made up almost completely of Anglos, is probably the main reason the Latin candidates lost the school board election in 1963 at the same time they were winning election to the city council. The closeness of the vote, together with the shock of having elected an all-Latin city council seemed to influence the all-Anglo school board. Within the year one member resigned his post and overtures were made to one of the defeated candidates to see if he was interested in being appointed. He told them that he could never accept appointment rather than election to the board because he would forever feel indebted to them. The Anglo board did finally find a Latin willing to be appointed, however, and from that time on first one and then two Mexicans were always on the seven-man board. This maneuvering seemed successful because through the rest of the decade never

again did a Latin slate run against the incumbent board, even as city council seats were hotly contested.

While this successful cooptation was occurring on the school board, the school faculty was gradually increasing its contingent of Mexican-American teachers. From a faculty around 10 percent Chicano in 1960, by the fall of 1968 over one fourth of the faculty were Mexican-Americans. The dropout rate for Chicano children also declined. Although for the 1951 entering class of first-graders only nine percent graduated from high school, of the entering class in 1958 17 percent graduated. So there was improvement, but to many Mexicans the rate of progress seemed slow indeed. A dropout rate of over 80 percent was by national or state standards phenomenal, and even as the faculty composition changed gradually, all principals remained Anglo. The faculty ratio itself also remained enormously unreflective of the composition of the student body, because as the dropout rate gradually declined, the student body became increasingly Chicano. By the fall of 1968 nearly 87 percent of the student body was Chicano.

The spark which set off the second revolt was the election of cheerleaders at the high school in the spring of 1969. For most of the history of the community cheerleaders had been elected by the student body. As more and more Chicanos began to enter high school, however, the system was changed so that a select committee of the faculty would choose who they thought were the best cheerleaders. Because the Anglos could afford to send their daughters to cheerleader training schools, judgment on the basis of competence almost always meant that Anglos were selected. An unofficial system was devised so that three Anglos and one Mexican girl were always chosen. In the spring of 1969 the normal, routine practice again occurred. This time, however, two of the Anglo cheerleaders had graduated leaving vacancies and a Mexican girl, Diana Palacios, was considered by the student body to be as good as any of the Anglos trying out. The Mexicans, however, already had their "quota" in Diana Perez, so the faculty judges again chose two Anglos to fill the vacancies. The system of discrimination in the selection was thus exposed to the student body in an unusually clear manner. Since the protest was over the retention of the status quo, however, this also indicated that along with the basic developments in Mexican-American thought in the 1960s, Chicanos were becoming increasingly rigorous in their definition of what constituted discrimination.

After the new cheerleaders were announced, a group of Chicano students protested to the high school principal. He considered the matter a bunch of "phooey." The students then went over his head to the school superintendent, John Billings, at the same time increasing their demands to other issues involving discrimination. Billings discussed the matter with the students and agreed to adopt an explicit quota system for cheerleader selection: three Anglos and three Chicanos. The other demands, concerning the election of twirlers, high school favorites, and the establishment of bi-lingual and bi-cultural education, were met either with more quota systems or with a commitment to "check" what other communities in the area were doing.

The reaction of the Chicano students to their meeting with Billings was mixed, but most of them were pleased with what had occurred. Open segregation with separate but equal treatment seemed about the best they could hope for. Although throughout this period of agitation there had been talk of a walkout, none occurred, and Billings considered that he had been successful in avoiding a walkout. Dampening the students' desire for a walkout as well, however, was the realization that since school was almost over they would have little leverage and might all be flunked. The Anglo reaction to Billings' concessions was generally one of concern and disapproval, and a group of Anglo students went to see him. The old method of cheerleader selection seemed fair to them, and they feared that by pandering to the hot-headed students Billings might be opening a pandora's box. That June in fact the school board nullified Billings' concessions to the students and also passed a resolution dealing sternly with student unrest. With school closed and with many students and their families on the migrant trail, nothing was done to protest the board's reversal of the superintendent's policy.

But this action seems to have strengthened the hands of radical students by exposing the weakness of the school superintendent and by making the board appear completely insensitive to Chicano students. Word spread among the students that the board had cancelled the agreements, and plans for a school boycott were again discussed.

That same month José Angel Gutierrez and his wife returned to Crystal City from San Antonio, at the close of his tenure as president of MAYO. They returned hoping to put into practice the principles of the militant youth organization and immediately set about re-establishing connections and recruiting a staff to coordinate the effort, not only in Crystal City but in the neighboring counties of the Winter Garden area. His timing was important. In the spring elections of that year, before the school agitation, the all-Chicano slate had made its poorest showing since its 1963 victory. To increasing numbers of Chicanos new leadership and new issues seemed necessary if they were to beat the Anglo-backed coalition.

But for Gutierrez becoming the leader in the Chicano community was neither obvious nor immediate. His ideas and those of his staff were examined and their leadership was tested in numerous discussions and meeting places around the community. Fundamental to their strategy was a Saul-Alinsky-type interest in direct confrontation, and through this they hoped to expose, humiliate, and "eliminate the gringo" as the Chicano community united.

Although the school system continued to be the issue to mobilize the community, that fall a new example of school discrimination presented itself. The Crystal City High School Ex-Students Association decided to have their own queen and court at the annual homecoming football game. In previous years they had always considered the football queen to be their queen as well, but to increase interest in the organization, the Ex-Students decided to have their own election. Again hoping to further interest among Ex-Students, and with possibly other motives as well, the organization established a rule that for a girl to be eligible to run in their election, one of her parents had to have graduated from the Crystal City high school. Chicano students, already restive over the unresolved issues of the spring, seized upon this issue as a clear-cut example of Anglo discrimination, and the ruling was quickly labelled a "grandfather clause." As the discussion of the history of Mexican-American education in Crystal City should have made clear, very few of the Chicano students were daughters of parents who had graduated from high school. In fact of the twenty-six eligible candidates, only five were Mexican-Americans. When Superintendent Billings gave the Ex-Student Association permission to have their coronation at the homecoming game, school board complicity in the discrimination seemed clear.

In early November Mexican-American students and parents presented to the board a list of grievances, headed by the demand that the Ex-Students not present their queen at a school-sponsored event because of the association's restrictive clause. At the packed board meeting Gutierrez, now a consultant to the students, threatened that if the crowning of the queen did take place, students would disrupt it. Under the pressure of disruption by an increasingly organized Chicano community, the school board reluctantly voted to deny the Ex-Students Association the right to the field. This granting of the students' most explosive demand did not take momentum out of their protest. Because the board had so clearly reversed itself only under Chicano pressure, it was made to look weak. Having won one of their demands, student attention now focused on those which had been objects of contention since the preceeding spring. The board had postponed a decision on the other demands until their December meeting, hoping no doubt that the protest movement would cool off over the ensuing month. Anticipating that the board would turn them down on their long list of demands, however, students began preparing for a boycott. Enthusiasm and determination among the students grew during this period, helped by numerous rallies and the reaction of the Anglo community. By developing a siege mentality, uniting in the face of such a hostile threat, the Anglo community seemed to support all the radical students' claims of discrimination. Although many of the Anglos thought the Ex-Students Association had made a colossal tactical blunder, even more thought the

board had "sold out" and knuckled under to the pressure, and scathing attacks were made upon those Anglos who were thought guilty of being soft. The minister for the most influential church in the Anglo community, the Reverend Kenneth Newcomer of the First United Methodist Church, had worked tirelessly in his two years in the community to develop a spirit of reconciliation in his totally Anglo congregation. Now, however, he was to see his congregation slowly but surely pull back from any form of compromise in the face of such an obvious radical threat. By reacting in such a manner, the Anglos were helping to polarize the community in exactly the manner the radical Chicanos wanted: "gringo" versus Chicano.

When the school board met in December, the board announced that it felt the charges of discrimination as set forth in the remaining demands were false, and that the board would therefore grant none of the demands. At this the students presented a new list of grievances, even longer than the first, and told the board it would have to face the consequences of refusing to act.

The next morning the school strike began. By the end of the first day over five hundred students were picketing and a number of parents had gathered nearby to protect their children and help keep them orderly. The boycott became larger and more effective with each passing day, and journalists and television commentators poured into the community. Parents were standing solidly behind their children. For both parents and children the concern was to prevent the children from suffering the indignities the parents had endured. In this manner the confrontation was strongly buttressed by a united family structure.

The school board realized that it would have to do something. The boycott was too effective to be ignored. Representatives from the Texas Education Agency in Austin were invited down and the board proposed to set up a meeting with parents of the striking students. The board refused, however, to talk to the striking students. To have sat down at a negotiating table with a bunch of teenagers, much less Mexican rabble, was too much for the school board to stomach. This angered the students, who felt that they should be the ones to discuss the matter with the board. They also realized that their parents would be more vulnerable to the board because of lack of education and fear for their jobs. Parents stood fast with their children and refused to attend the meeting, and conditions remained at an impasse. A churchman's committee was formed from Catholic, Methodist, and Baptist clergymen and laymen in the community to try to bring about dialogue between the two groups. In the end it was unsuccessful because of polarization within the group and the resentment of the school board and administrators towards the purpose of the group. With tensions mounting and the community divided, attempts by local people to negotiate became doomed.

Having chosen what to the Chicanos were clear-cut examples of discrimination in the schools, the radicals also increasingly succeeded in immobilizing many of the middle-class Mexicans who were in the city government. The moderates' sympathy with many if not all, of the students' demands left them paralyzed, unable and unwilling to help the intransigent Anglos. As a consequence the Chicano community was more united than probably at any time in the history of the community.

As the week passed, the boycott spread even to elementary school children and publicity grew. By the last day before the Christmas holidays, from half to two-thirds of the entire school enrollment were absent from classes, but still no negotiations were taking place. Bolstering the publicity and the morale of the strikers, educators from around the state converged on the community to teach the striking school children during the Christmas holidays. Through the offices of Senator Ralph Yarborough, arrangements were made to fly three of the boycotting students to Washington. There they met with Yarborough and with officials in the civil rights divisions of the Departments of Justice and Health, Education, and Welfare. The Justice Department eventually became involved through its community relations service and two mediators were sent down at the invitation of both the board and the students. Through several days of tense and bitter negotiations, the Justice Department mediators eventually hammered out an agreement acceptable to the students and the board. Continuing support and involvement by

the students and their families in the boycott led the school board to capitulate on practically all the demands. But also involved were the increasing publicity about the walkout, state and federal presence (if not pressure), and talk that Chicano supporters from the area were going to converge on Crystal City to add strength to *la causa*. With the resolution of the conflict, the most successful Chicano walkout in the history of Mexican-Americans in the Southwest had ended. No disciplinary procedures were taken against the striking students and they did not receive unexcused absences with resulting grade penalties. The board agreed to pursue the establishment of bi-lingual and bi-cultural programs in the school system, agreed to try to find new means of testing pre-school youngsters, and consented to cheerleaders and nearly all school favorites being elected by the student body. Dress codes and the censoring of the student paper were to be reviewed. The board even consented to the establishment of an assembly period on September 16th, the Mexican national holiday. Except for a few points, such as the election of twirlers, the students had scored a stunning victory.

As with the victory over the Ex-Students Association in the preceeding months, however, this success did not cause momentum to subside. The greater clarity and ideological nature of Chicano goals were again revealed when toward the end of the boycott, the Chicano community began a selective economic boycott. The targets were a Chicano school board member unwilling to support the strike and an Anglo business which had tried to pressure the students by firing two of his employees involved in the strike. Although the boycott did not last, this reversal of economic intimidation further threatened the security of the Anglo business community and also threatened Mexican-American businessmen who were not willing to help in the strike.

School policies, economic domination, and soon political offices were all involved in this broad movement to unite and bring self-determination to the Chicano community. Building upon their successes, the strike organizers continued to proceed after another MAYO goal, the formation of La Raza Unida party. School board and city council candidates not only filed in Crystal City, but in the neighboring counties of Dimmit and La Salle, where organizing efforts were also taking place. With school policies now so much in the forefront of political concern, mere Mexican representation on the board became totally inadequate. Control of the school system and redirection toward Chicano needs became the goal, and Gutierrez headed a slate running for the three positions up on the seven-man board. But a sweep of the five-man city council was no longer possible. Changing the political set-up so as to discourage a repeat of the 1963 disaster, the Anglo and middle-class Mexican coalition had successfully adopted a charter change to provide for overlapping positions on the council, alternating three seats up one year with two the next. For the spring elections in 1970, only two of the five council seats were up for election. As it turned out, La Raza Unida party was extremely lucky to have even two candidates running. Discouraging poor candidates, the city charter included a requirement that any candidate for the council must be a property owner. Shortly before the commencement of absentee voting, the city attorney and city manager disqualified Pablo Puente, one of the two Raza Unida candidates, because he did not own property. With help from the Mexican-American Legal Defense Fund the question was immediately taken to court. As the Anglo city fathers had no doubt expected, the Fourth Court of Civil Appeals ruled that the question of putting Puente's name on the ballot was moot because balloting had already started. Appealing the case to the federal courts, attorney Jesse Gamez of the Legal Defense Fund claimed that such a decision by the Court opened the door to fraud. Any community, he argued, could wait until just before the start of absentee balloting to deny a candidate a place on the ballot for any of a number of clearly unconstitutional practices and could do so successfully because the question would immediately become moot. With Puente agreeing to forfeit the absentee ballots, the Federal Judge ordered Puente's name placed on the ballot barely in time for the election.

The anti-La Raza Unida coalition, although demoralized by the school strike, fought vigorously, if not always completely legally. For the council the two incumbents, one Anglo and one Mexican-American, chose to run for re-election. For the school board, significantly, all three incumbents chose not to run again. Their position in being opposed to the Chicano demands and yet capitulating had left them in a peculiarly vulnerable position from both sides. Nominated to take their places by the anti-strike coalition were two Mexican-Americans and one part-Mexican, part-Anglo. This in itself was a further move toward accommodation of Mexican-Americans by the Anglo community, but again as in 1965 the Anglos had decided to run a slate with a preponderance of Mexican-Americans only after an explosive issue had mushroomed in the community. The reaction of the local paper throughout the election campaign was also indicative of greater accommodation. Whereas in 1963, 1965, 1967, 1969 the *Sentinel* editor had run front-page editorials warning of community disaster should non-business, unqualified candidates win, in the 1970 election the *Sentinel* had only a short, perfunctory editorial the last issue before the election. Because the owner, an Anglo, had long been identified with the ruling Anglo group, it was apparently felt that to have run editorials again would have been counter-productive. Increasingly in the community, far more so than in 1965, it was felt that Mexicans themselves would have to tackle the militants. More than ever before, Anglos had to work behind the scenes and through Mexicans who were sympathetic to their cause.

The town's industrial establishment, however, did place large unsigned advertisements in the local paper, in English and Spanish, saying that to improve the economic welfare of the town industry was vitally needed. This was something which nearly all residents could agree upon, but the ad went on to say that

Industry officials seek a community with harmonious relations and a stable government. They avoid areas where there is agitation by militant groups which could hinder their progress. The working people of Crystal City hurt themselves when they vote for candidates for the school board and city council who are associated with militant groups that are unfriendly to industry.

The implications contained in this advertisement referred not only to new industry but to current industry in the town. In 1963 after Los Cinco Mexicanos won office, one of the packing sheds in the city moved to a nearby town. Word was being spread by Anglos that the huge Del Monte corporation might close down if the city tried to make it pay any taxes. In fact this seemed unlikely to happen. Although Del Monte's profit figures were kept secret, their Crystal City plant reputedly had a higher margin of profit than any of their other plants in the country.

In the face of such activity by businessmen, one might have expected the Teamsters Union to have been in the forefront again in support of the candidates against the city's business establishment. But in contrast to 1963 the Teamsters Union at the Del Monte plant was completely inactive. Feeling within the plant and in the Chicano community at large was increasingly that the Teamsters were trying to use and to control the Chicanos rather than to help them. Although this feeling stemmed from the firing of Mayor Cornejo as business agent for the union in 1964, it was increased by the Teamsters' reluctance to stand up for Chicanos when their jobs and rights were repeatedly being violated. By 1970 the union had moved full circle into being dependent upon management, not workers, for support and encouragement in the face of efforts to de-certify it and form a local Chicano union.

Being thus based almost completely upon the local Chicano community made the second revolution both more remarkable and more far-reaching. In not having the resources of the union to call upon, the similarity of Crystal City to other communities in the area was emphasized more than the town's uniqueness. The issues of the campaign thus emerged as the school strike, the Raza Unida movement, and the character and ideas of José Angel Gutierrez, who increasingly became the most visible of all the candidates. But in opposing Gutierrez, his adversaries could not use the main arguments levied against the 1963 revolution. As a native boy well-known in the community, Gutierrez could not be called an outside agitator or labelled a puppet of anyone. Charges that he was inexperienced could hardly be made after the masterfully executed strike. Charges that he was uneducated and unqualified could not easily be made against his eighteen years of education and two degrees. Instead the opposition centered their attack around the claim that Gutierrez and the ideas of La Raza Unida were "un-American" and dangerously radical. . . .

To counter some of the charges during his campaign, Gutierrez showed at his rallies such things as autographed photographs from Ted Kennedy and George McGovern, and his invitation to the Nixon-Agnew inauguration. But his major issues were those that related to the school strike, the MAYO goals of self-determination, and all that the community had experienced in the last year.

In terms of campaign organizations and get-out-the-vote drives, both sides were extremely well prepared. As an indication of voter interest, the turnout was considerably higher than in the 1968 Presidential election. Gutierrez and his running mates, Mike Perez and Arturo Gonzáles, won with around fifty-five percent of the vote. Three days later Ventura Gonzáles and Pablo Puente, his name now on the ballot, were elected to the city council with margins of slightly over sixty percent. In nearby Carrizo Springs and Cotulla the results of La Raza Unida work also produced victories. These were perhaps more remarkable because neither town had ever gone through the political mobilization and trauma which Crystal City had known from 1963 to 1965 and during the school strike. Such victories in nearby towns confirmed the belief that the second revolt was based upon strategies far more exportable to other South Texas communities, but the degree of success in these other communities is not yet clear. At the electoral level, at any rate, La Raza Unida had been stunningly successful.

Although their electoral success was unquestioned and their intellectual competence and expertise were in marked contrast to the first election of Mexicans in 1963, there were again serious difficulties to be faced in governing. In the first place, only a minority of the total number of seats on the city council and school board were up for election. On both boards, however, a critical swing vote was provided which allowed La Raza Unida candidates to gain control of the governing bodies. In three years on the school board, Eddie

Trevino had gradually evolved into a quiet, one-man opposition to the board's policies. Although he was originally appointed by the Anglos on the board, he welcomed the victory of the La Raza Unida. Francisco Benavides, who had been an independent voice on the city council, also swung over into support for La Raza Unida. Although he had originally been asked to run in 1969 by an influential Anglo politician, he had never been closely associated with the dominant Anglo ruling group. These two men gave La Raza Unida a 3-2 majority on the city council and a 4-3 majority on the school board. Although these developments could be considered as strokes of luck, they were clearly more than that. In the aftermath of the strike there was considerable social pressure being brought to bear by members of La Raza. Benavides, as the owner of a grocery store, could not have been unaware of the consequences which might follow from his refusing to join forces with La Raza Unida.

The loss of Trevino and Benavides to the opposition, in marked contrast to what happened in 1963 when one member of *Los Cinco* became a renegade, demonstrated the fundamental problems Anglos faced in trying to co-opt Mexican-Americans into their leadership. If Anglos picked Mexicans that were absolutely trustworthy, they could also be sure that such Mexicans would carry little weight in the Chicano community. If they picked men who were independent and respected in the Chicano community, then Anglos would not be able to rely on them in critical situations.

La Raza Unida thus surmounted its first hurdle, gaining a workable majority on both councils. But the lame-duck council and the school board had both done their best to tie the hands of the incoming officials. The city council had quickly voted to grant the Del Monte Corporation a seven-year reprieve on being annexed into the city so that they could continue to pay no taxes. And the school board shortly before the election had hired under three-year contract a new school superintendent, John Briggs. To try to void each of these actions, the newly-elected officials had to become embroiled in legal controversies. In working to bring changes into the community, the new council and school board increasingly had to resort to legal pressure. Simultaneously they had legal pressure brought to bear against them by the losing Anglos.

The extent to which the legal system was crucial to determining the degree of change in the community was no more clearly illustrated than in the contest to take control of the county in November, 1970. In January of 1970, both for ideological and for practical reasons, La Raza Unida was organized as a third political party. If their candidates had chosen to run as Democrats, as the Cornejo slate had done in their losing attempt to gain control of the county in 1964, they would have had to pay expensive filing fees and would have had to run in May, when many of the migrant workers had already gone north. By running as a third party in the November elections, La Raza Unida hoped to avoid both these problems. But the Texas election code is unclear at best, and misleading or contradictory at worst, on what procedures a third party must use to get on the ballot in a specific county. When county officials refused to place the names of La Raza Unida candidates on the ballot, the party filed suit. After an enormous amount of legal maneuvering and appeals, the party still could not get on the ballot. The only action left was for the party to conduct a write-in campaign. Owing to the nature of the procedures for write-in votes under Texas law, such a campaign was doomed. Stickers could not be used; names had to be written in. In a community where many, if not most, of the Chicano community were functional illiterates, getting them to write all their candidates' names correctly and in the proper place was an insuperable task. All the candidates lost although in several cases the write-in candidates captured more than 40 percent of the vote. Doing this well may have been a symbolic victory for La Raza Unida, but the incumbent county commissioners and county judge, all Anglo, were re-elected. Because terms were for four years, La Raza Unida could not hope to gain control of the county for at least another four years. Thus in spite of all the activity, mobilization, and involvement in the Chicano community, with highly able and qualified leadership, all county commissioners and the county judge remained Anglo in a county which was three-quarters Chicano. County policy would continue as before. In terms of tax rates, police policy, and welfare policies, the county might have been important in upgrading Chicano life. Instead it stayed steadfastly opposed to the Chicano activists, just as it did in 1963. Without control of the county, one of La Raza Unida's most difficult but most important goals would remain impossible: that of land redistribution. At present almost all the land in the county belongs to Anglo farmers, ranchers, or absentee landlords. Several important Texas politicians, such as John Connally, are important absentee owners in the county. Only through high taxation could the Chicano community hope to get any of this land, or at least get money for improved services.

Significant changes, however, have occurred in Crystal City. In matters affecting the schools in particular, the system has continued to feel the effect of the successful strike. The faculty has changed considerably since the strike, and after resignations and the ending of some of the lame-duck board's contracts, it is likely to change even more. For the first time close to half the faculty is now Chicano. And many of the new teachers, both Anglo and Mexican, are quite different from their predecessors in outlook. Because the Crystal City school district is establishing itself as a beachhead for Chicano power, or as Gutierrez says, for "extending education to the Chicano," the teachers accepting appointment tend to be more or less sympathetic to the aims of La Raza Unida. Bi-lingual education has been started in the early grades, courses in Mexican-American history are being taught, a free breakfast program for children has been initiated and the free lunch program has been greatly expanded. The district is more aware of and more willing to accept federal aid. A Title IV grant has been accepted for the purpose of facilitating integration and increasing faculty sensitivity to problems Chicano children face in the school system. The school district has refused to allow army recruiters onto school premises or to permit any employee from serving as registrar for the Selective Service System. Further emphasizing their anti-military policy, the school board has hired a draft consultant who has had training with the American Friends Service Committee. In support of the César Chávez lettuce strike, the school board has refused to allow

non-farm workers union lettuce to be served in the cafeteria.

Although these policy changes are important, the school district remains severely limited in its financial resources. The problem has been compounded because Anglos in the community have begun to withhold their school taxes. Coming at a time when the board is trying to institute new policies, this has placed further limits on what the board can do. For example, textbooks not recommended by the state adoption committee must be paid for by the local district. In trying to counteract the traditional Anglo story of Texas history told in textbooks, and in trying to bring new books for Spanish and for bi-cultural courses, the board has found itself without the money for any extensive book buying. Although over one hundred Chicano dropouts have returned to school on their own following the change in administration, the board still has not been able to inaugurate a program designed to bring into the schools the estimated 10 percent of Chicanos who are legally of school age but who are not in school. Again owing to limited financial resources, building facilities remain overcrowded and inadequate. Any new building program would require the use of bonds, yet it is quite possible that given the nature of the school board, bond companies would be reluctant to buy the bonds should the local district approve their sales. Recent investigations by the Texas Education Agency found numerous deficiencies in the implementation of the migrant program. They further criticized several aspects of the school system in general, such as the absence of the teaching of patriotism in the schools. Because of the board's reluctance to use standardized tests on its children, alleging that they are discriminatory in favor of middle-class Anglo precepts, the school district has run into continued pressure from federal and state authorities. With the board employing so many new ideas and new personel, many disruptions of normal school activities have occurred, particularly concerning where and when classes would be meeting. At present, the goal of many Anglos is to get the Texas Education Agency to revoke accreditation to the district. This move would have a shattering effect upon the schools, among other things denying them federal and state funds. From this turmoil and example of mis-management, Anglos with sympathetic Mexicans might be able to oust the incumbent board members. But denying accreditation to the school system is most unlikely, partly because it is such a drastic step. The future rather seems to be one of continued innovation, severely circumscribed by the limited resources of the district, and by both the regulations and the rewards of state and federal resources.

In the city government important changes have also taken place. With the hiring of Bill Richey, a former VISTA worker and close friend of Gutierrez, as city manager in the early summer of 1970, the city had an educated, efficient administrator and a tireless worker for La Raza Unida. Richey's Anglo background made him an anomaly in Crystal City and yet made charges of "reverse racism" against La Raza Unida less credible. Since taking office he has improved the quality of the city's staff and police force and has hired and trained Chicanos to the extent that now Chicanos are holding positions they have never held in the city bureaucracy before. But the city itself has also been hampered in much that it is attempting to change. Their ability to annex the large Del Monte plant on the edge of town is still being settled in the courts, and in attempting to change policy in the huge urban renewal project they have also run into legal difficulties. The massive urban renewal program has poured millions of dollars into Crystal City. Throughout its existence since 1958 it has been run by Sam Anderson, a former relator. Although Anderson has been an able director willing to use the numerous funds from the federal agency, he is resented by the Chicano militants for his close ties to the Anglo business world and his reluctance to hire Chicano contractors. Also resented is the awareness that along with the progress, urban renewal has uprooted people and forced a number of families to move into other slums. How much this is the fault of the director and how much the fault of the program itself is more difficult to determine. As a step towards ousting Anderson as director, the new city council tried to appoint two new commissioners to the urban renewal board. The mayor, who was a holdover from before the spring election, refused to appoint the new members even though it was the wish of the majority of the council. In trying to oust the mayor so that their appointments would be valid, the Raza Unida majority was reprimanded by the federal authorities in San Antonio, who cut off all urban renewal funds. However the crisis is revolved, it is another example of the constraints put upon the activists seeking to change policy as well as personel.

In the area of attracting industry, the city administration was also trying to pursue a new policy. Richey claimed that the Crystal City Industrial Foundation and other business groups were interested in attracting only certain kinds of industries, those wanting cheap and non-union labor such as textiles. He has tried to get government contracts, especially through provisions of the Small Business Administration which allow for minority group businesses to get contracts even if their bids are not competitive. Citing the large amount of federal military spending in San Antonio, Richey hoped to attract some of these jobs to Crystal City. Attracting industry and jobs has remained a critical problem for the city and is compounded by the lack of opportunities for migrant workers in the north. Because of continued mechanization in the fields, the future for the migrant worker is dim. Hoping to stem the departure of the jobless from Crystal City to the urban ghettos, Richey has noted, "We've got to get industry or repeat the saga of the Blacks migrating to the cities." The success of this effort to attract jobs to Crystal City will take longer to determine, as economic development will take longer to bring about than educational reform or political change. But in terms of the future of the community, this will be the most important factor in determining the success of the revolution. As in most of rural America, young people of Crystal City, both Anglo and Chicano, have been leaving the community in search of better opportunities elsewhere. The decline in population for the county between 1960 and 1970 emphasized this problem. Certainly the new administration has been aware of the problem and has been trying to handle it in ways the Anglo elite either was not aware of or was not willing to try. But ultimate success will depend upon far more than the community's willingness to try new approaches. It will depend on industrial attitudes and on what kinds of federal programs are available. At this level between 1963 and 1970, however, important national developments have aided the reformers, particularly the tremendous increase in aid to education and the war on poverty. National foundations and churches have also become much more aware of problems of poverty and discrimination and have been willing to help out in Crystal City, in both public and confidential ways. These changes have made the leadership far less vulnerable to local economic intimidation than was the leadership in 1963, but these national organizations have at times also been quite concerned about the militancy of the leadership.

From this review of the school, city, and county governments, it should be clear that any assessment of the success of La Raza Unida Party in Crystal City, or its applicability to the rest of South Texas and the Southwest, must be qualified. In comparison with the first Chicano takeover in 1963, the current regime shows tremendous differences. Their goals are clearer and more unified. Their leadership is more confident and experienced. The community now has more resources available to it because of changes in federal policy and national awareness. But tremendous tasks still face the new regime. After a year in office the Chicano community is still dependent to a great extent upon José Angel Gutierrez and the outside people he has brought into the community. Second-level leadership in the Chicano community remains weak, although it is improving in experience. The egalitarian spirit of the revolution and the common struggle in the Chicano community have as by-products introduced women and children into the leadership councils of the movement. Tapping both these resources has already strengthened the leadership. Federal programs and national foundations have been helpful, but they have carried with them serious constraints in being designed much more for incremental change than radical innovation. Owing to these and to further institutional constraints which are placed upon protest organizations, La Raza Unida has been thwarted in important ways even as it has also won astounding victories. It should also be remembered that in Crystal City there are peculiarly auspicious circumstances for revolt: the history of settlement, the Chicano-Anglo population ratio, the heavy concentration of migrant workers, and the large Del Monte canning factory with its historically important but currently defunct Teamsters Union. With these points in mind, it would be both naive and adventuristic to say that the experiences of Crystal City can be duplicated elsewhere. In communities such as the older border towns, where Mexican-Americans have always had an important role in government even as their substantive policies have been oppressive, it is difficult to see how the Crystal City strategy can work without important changes. In communities where a majority of the population is Anglo, not only must the strategy be modified in important ways, but the impact of the rhetoric of Crystal City militants may be damaging to those Chicanos who must work in coalitions.

Finally, even though the goals of La Raza Unida are far more carefully constructed than were those of Los Cinco Mexicanos, the regime will eventually be faced either through success or through failure with deciding upon what the whole policy of self-determination for the Chicano community really means. Just how to relate to Anglo cultural domination, whether and how to blend with it or to fight it or to isolate themselves from it, are questions and are solutions which remain unresolved. How much should the Chicano movement be one of separate cultural nationalism, and how much should it be one which will eventually prepare Chicanos for integration with Anglos as equals? These questions are not unique to Chicanos of Crystal City, of course. They involve fundamental questions facing all cultural minorities and all oppressed peoples. In fact they involve all human beings, who must in the end decide as individuals what their identity should be.

But the example of Crystal City on its own indicates two points which may be applicable to more of American society: the veneer of democracy, with explosive concerns suppressed beneath this veneer, and the extent to which integration has not only failed but has been used, for good or for evil, to mean cultural domination by one group over another.

In facing all these problems and difficulties, however, the Chicano community can call upon the very resources which were opened up by their struggle in Crystal City: the confidence, the pride, and the feeling of community. Their successes have brought a feeling of control over their own destiny that is simply not measured in terms of dollars spent, legal suits filed, or theoretical problems which must be resolved. The stereotype of a fatalistic Juan Tortilla, a loyal servant happiest when he is stooped in the fields picking spinach, has been shattered for both Anglos and Chicanos. As the Chicano community goes about trying to overcome the enormous problems they must face, this faith in themselves may be their most valuable possession. It will mean that the choice will be theirs to a greater extent than it ever has been before.

David M. Fishlow

*David M. Fishlow is a young newspaper editor in McAllen,
Texas, committed to social and economic equality. This
impassioned account of what Mr. Fishlow believes to be
police brutality is an example of the moral indignation, and
a new type of hard-hitting journalism coming from the more
radical newspaperman.
Copyright held and reprinted by permission of the* TEXAS
OBSERVER.

Pancho Flores Is Dead

Pancho Flores is dead. He was standing on a sidewalk in Pharr, Tex., with his hands in his pockets, on Saturday night, Feb. 7. Half a dozen witnesses say he was shot by a policeman.

"Full Scale Rioting Sweeps Pharr Streets" screamed the *Valley Morning Star* the next morning. "Massed Police Quell Youth Riot at Pharr" said the *McAllen Monitor.* Even the more reliable *Corpus Christi Caller-Times* had a double-column, front page story headed "2 Policemen Hurt in Clash at Pharr."

No policeman had been shot in the events that occurred on Saturday night, but when it was all over, Alfonso (Pancho) Loredo Flores, a 20-year-old construction worker from Pharr, was dead. Thirty-one people had been arrested and released on bail. And Pharr, the Hub City of the Valley, was a frightening place to live.

Since the "riot," the people have been waiting. Eight hundred of them marched silently in Poncho's funeral. The streets are quieter at night than before, especially in the *cantina* district along North Cage (U.S. Highway 281). Rumors scamper around town like malevolent rats, stopping to gnaw first at one soul, then at another.

It started out as a normal, hot day. Saturday morning is a busy time in most places, with business bustling and traffic heavy on the main streets. Pharr, where Hwy. 281 crosses U.S. Hwy. 83 before proceeding on to Mexico, is typical. But on the north side of town, under the water tower, is the Pharr police station. It used to be a dirty-looking brown, with a poorly painted fist pointing to the "Entrance." Now that it has a fresh coat of white paint, it looks less like the *calabozo* from an Antonio Aguilar movie, but it is still a squat, graceless building.

On Saturday morning, there was a picket line out front. A couple of dozen people, mostly teenagers and young people, with a scattering of children and middle aged working people, strolled up and down carrying signs saying *"Más justicia y menos garrotazos"* ("More justice and fewer beatings"); *"No necesitamos policías salvajes"* ("We don't need savage policemen"); and *"Fuera con Sandoval y Ramírez"* (Get rid of Sandoval and Ramirez").

The picket line had been planned by a group of local people working with community organizer Efraín Fernández. The issue—police brutality—is an old-fashioned one, but one which permeates every kind of public activity here in Pharr. In this town, you don't muck around with the government or the police, and when you do, there is bound to be trouble.

Chicano families have long complained about beatings in the Pharr police station, and in recent weeks the complaints have been more frequent. Guadalupe Salinas, 24, is a slender warehouse worker who got picked up at a service station a couple of weeks ago, was hauled into the police station and came out with blood all over his shirt, cuts, bruises and a black eye. He told whoever would listen that he had been beaten by Sgt. Mateo Sandoval, a smooth-talking ex-Harlingen cop whose sworn testimony in federal court has been known to differ substantially from versions offered by other witnesses I believe to be reliable.

A week before Salinas made his charges, 44-year-old Manuel Mata of Pharr said his two broken ribs were the results of a beating by Sandoval.

Daniel Vasquez is a disreputable-looking Pharr man in his early thirties and with some serious emotional problems. He often walks around town with a briefcase and a necktie—neither very common around here—and announces himself as president of existing and non-existent organizations. Vasquez has complained on several occasions that he was beaten by Pharr police, and the attorneys who investigated the complaints believe that his charges are true.

Others, too, have complained of beatings and brutal treatment in the Pharr jail. Noé Rocha, 23, told a reporter from the Spanish-language paper *¡Ya Mero!* he once was sprayed with some kind of gas by the police, and after he was thrown in a cell the only water available to wash the stuff off was from the toilet.

Police Chief Alfredo Ramírez is a tall, white-haired sharpie who likes to appear in court in a bright green suit and red cowboy boots. He, like every other city employee in Pharr, is utterly dependent for his job on R. S. Bowe, the balding, 60-year-old mayor and, as the front man for the little political machine that rules here, the undisputed czar of this community.

Saturday's picket line followed several meetings among the Mexican-American community. Though the protest was ostensibly directed against Sandoval and Ramírez, the issue goes far deeper. Basically, there is no representation for the poor people who constitute the vast majority of Pharr's 15,000 residents. The city commission is a rubber stamp for Bowe; I have been unable to find in the city records a single negative vote on any issue whatsoever in the minutes of all meetings held since 1966.

Special meetings are almost as common as the regularly scheduled ones, and notice of commission meetings is sometimes forgotten. The only jobs in town or in the area are in the fields, and the agricultural interests pull most of the strings. The Bentsens and others own huge tracks of land in the area, and the gas and oil wells bring in money for the owners, but little gets to the people. Until a month ago, the head of the welfare department was an unsuccessful candidate for sheriff who spoke not a word of Spanish and had no training in social work.

For several years there has been a parade ordinance on the books which defines "one or more persons" or "one or more vehicles" moving down the street as a "parade," subject to the regulation of the Mayor, who has the option of issuing a permit if he approves.

Once Federal Judge Reynaldo Garza asked Chief Ramírez, "If two women from the League of Women Voters walked up and down in front of City Hall with signs saying 'Register to Vote,' would you arrest them?"

"I would," said the chief.

"Well," said Judge Garza, "we public officials may not like picketing, but people have a right to do it." He then proceeded to instruct the good chief in some basic principles of Constitutional government:

"If they want to walk up and down outside the federal building with signs saying 'Judge Garza is Unfair,' I may not like it, but there isn't a thing I can do about it." Not exactly an earth-shaking statement from a federal judge, but Mayor Bowe, Chief Ramírez, and their lawyer, looked stunned.

By Saturday, though, they evidently had decided that they, unlike Judge Garza, *did* have something they could do about it.

The picketing had been relatively uneventful all day. Though Efraín Fernández and 14-year-old Daniel Magallán had been arrested in December for picketing city hall, this time the police made no arrests.

All afternoon, they lounged in the doorway, slack-jawed and grinning, bellies bursting the buttons of their too-tight blue uniforms. Nobody in Pharr speaks English except on official occasions, and the cops made jokes in Spanish, laughed at each other's gross humor, and made cracks at the young girls on the picket line.

Chief Ramírez, in sporty-looking "civvies," paraded around with a camera hanging from his neck as he, Sergeant Sandoval, and other officers photographed the pickets. The chief left several times during the day, oozing his big, gold-colored Monte Carlo in and out of the dusty police parking lot as the pickets parted to let him through.

Mayor Bowe, the most elusive public official south of Austin, as usual, was nowhere to be seen. Though he is a full time mayor ($400 per month plus "expenses") he keeps no regular office hours, and is frequently hard to find.

As it grew later, a large crowd, perhaps two or three hundred people, gathered across the street and on the sidewalk east and west of the police station. Perhaps two thirds of the spectators were teenagers and children, who laughed and hooted at each other's jibes. By evening the picket line consisted of about a dozen adults and a dozen children. Mrs. Virginia Ramírez, a middle-aged lady, convinced one of her friends that they, too, should picket because *"sería más respectable tener unas*

señoras ahí. No es cosa de puros chavalos." (It will look more respectable to have some ladies over there. This isn't just a thing for the kids.")

The kids were singing some jingles they had made up for the occasion, none of them particularly respectful to the police, but certainly not obscene. One, in Spanish, was to the tune of "I've Been Working on the Railroad":

> *Que hermosos son los marranos;*
> *Que hermosos son . . . oink, oink.*
> (How beautiful are the pigs,
> How beautiful they are . . . oink, oink.)

Another was in English, and sung to the tune of "Who's Afraid of the Big Bad Wolf?"
Sandoval's a big fat pig, a big fat pig, a big
fat pig;
He likes to beat the people up, the people
up, the people up;
We have to stop the beatings now, the
beatings now, the beatings now,
and so on.

Then Daniel Vásquez, whom everybody in town knows as an amiable crank, began making up little ditties, and the crowd loved them. *"¿Qué te pasó en la cárcel?"* he sang, and then answered his own question: *Me caí, me caí, es todo."* ("What happened to you in the police station? I just fell down, just fell down, that's all.") The hooting and hollering grew louder, and the police started looking edgier, but there was no physical abuse of anybody, no rock-throwing; just noise.

About 7:30, Chief Ramírez came out of the station and approached Fernández. Since the conversation was official, it was in English:

"Mr. Fer-nan-deez, your people are being abusive. This is not longer a peaceful picket," Ramírez said. The picket line moved around him and Efraín as they talked. Efraín was furious, but determined to keep hold of himself.

"They're just yelling," he told Ramírez through clenched teeth. "That's how they feel, and they're just yelling." And then he added: "If you leave them alone, nothing will happen. Just leave them alone and nothing will happen. They're just yelling . . ."

Ramírez turned on his heel, and went back inside. Soon sirens could be heard and a couple of white Pharr fire engines from the station across the tracks pulled into position behind the police station. (The firehouse in Pharr is on the "right" side of the tracks; the police station and jail, of course, are on the "wrong" side.)

A police car pulled into the middle of the street, and from an unseen loudspeaker, like the voice out of the whirlwind, came the anticipated announcement:

"This is no longer an authorized picket," or something to that effect. "You are hereby ordered to disperse. If you fail to disperse, further action will be taken." Maybe a third of the people present—those who speak English and were old enough to know what "disperse" means—understood, but the crowd whistled and hooted its answer. The police car pulled away. Tension grew. As the door of the police station opened and closed, I could see a group of men talking to the police. They were the same bunch that had been drinking beer on the back porch of the nearby Texas Bar during the afternoon. Sergeant Sandoval came around the building as the fire engines moved up to take positions on either side of the police station, facing the street.

"Have they been warned?" he asked. Somebody answered "Yup." The pickets kept moving, but it was obvious what was going to happen. One picket went to lock a portable tape recorder in the trunk of his car.

Suddenly the high pressure nozzles were opened, and firehoses drenched pickets and spectators alike. All became chaos.

The kids in the crowd unloosed a barrage of rocks and bricks picked up in the vacant lots near the police station. The crowd surged back and forth, and the pickets ran from behind the parked car where they had taken refuge from the water and rocks. But *El Loco* Daniel stopped running, turned around, and started to throw a brick at the police car behind which the pickets had "hit the deck."

In the midst of the water and rocks, with hundreds of screaming kids to choose from, Ramírez ran out of the police station and jumped Daniel. He was joined by two or three cops, and they hustled the terrified, struggling Daniel into the jail.

Witnesses later said they literally threw him into a cell.

Most of the crowd moved west, toward the main highway. Suddenly the shooting started. We could see rifle barrels sticking up from behind the police car parked near the door.

"*Son tiros de salva!* It's blanks!" somebody yelled. The crowd flowed back and forth, with most of it ending up on 281, swirling up and down the sidewalks in the midst of the *cantina* district.

Ramírez, probably on the O.K. of the invisible Bowe, called for reinforcements, and he got them from everywhere, it seemed, except San Juan, the next town east. Soon Pharr was a crazy battleground with only one side armed. Texas Rangers, DPS officers in gray uniforms, local police from McAllen in riot helmets, Hidalgo County sheriff's deputies and others driving around, running through the streets with night sticks and guns, and clearing the *cantinas* and stores.

Bullets were being thrown around like confetti, and whoever had yelled they were blanks was a wishful thinker. As firing and tear gas filled the streets, the Saturday night crowd became reluctant to leave the bars. Soon tear gas was being fired into some of the establishments. An M. Rivas supermarket was cleared when it became filled with the choking fumes.

"Pepe" Saldaña and another man each had several shots fired into their pickups. Night sticks got plenty of use. But hardly any windows were broken; no policemen were shot; none of the people were armed.

And one of the cops shot Alfonso Loredo Flores. Witnesses are unanimous in saying Flores was a bystander. A newspaper photo of him lying in a pool of blood in front of Stan Ramos' barber shop, show his hands still in his pockets.

Now the people are waiting, and they are not overly optimistic about "justice" being done. Just two months ago, a Cameron County sheriff's deputy shot a 14-year-old kid, Victor Nava, in the back of the head. It was self-defense, the deputy said; he thought Victor was coming at him with a knife, which later turned out to be a stick about a foot long and maybe half an inch in diameter. Other kids testified Victor was shot as he ran away. The grand jury returned no indictment. The FBI is investigating. Sheriff Boynton Fleming said it was a fine example for other lawmen.

Now, another kid is dead. He was 20 years old. He had a wife and a daughter aged three months. He had just found a construction job in hurricane-ravished Corpus Christi and was commuting on weekends. He was in Pharr on Saturday night. He went to see what all the commotion was on North Cage. He was shot.

They took him to McAllen General Hospital, and from there to Harlingen, and they told the papers he had been hit with "flying missiles." He died Sunday night. The doctors dug the fragments of a lead slug out of his head. They were sent to a ballistics lab, but supposedly they are too battered to show the gun from which they were fired.

By early morning, 31 people had been arrested and taken to Edinburg for arraignment before Justice of the Peace Jim Wilson.

By the time the Monday papers came out, public officials all over the valley were covering their tracks. Just as the hole in Flores's head was supposed to have been caused "by a thrown brick," now dents in one of the fire engines "appeared to have been bullet marks, indicating lawmen weren't the only ones armed."

Chief Ramírez read invisible Mayor Bowe's statement for the TV cameras. The mayor was conducting his own investigation, and he therefore felt it was "inappropriate" for him or any of the police to comment about the events of Saturday night.

The papers were almost unanimous in saying the rock barrage started the whole thing. Eyewitnesses, including this writer, say that is nonsense.

Soon the wheels of federal justice began to turn, but mostly they were just spinning. Richard Avena, field director of the U.S. Civil Rights Commission's southwestern regional office, arrived Sunday night. Manuel Velasco of the Justice Department arrived Monday morning with his wife, and promptly announced that he was not here to investigate the Flores killing or the causes of the so-called riot, but rather to do followup work on the Nava case from Brownsville. He told assembled relatives of the victim and witnesses that the FBI was investigating, and then he went off to talk to some of his "good friends and buddies from law school," including Judge Jim Wilson and Pharr city attorney Ramiro Martinez.

Yet on Monday afternoon, the FBI told Avena they could not investigate until they got a formal request from the Flores family. On Sunday, Mayor Bowe said *he* was going to ask the Hoover boys to "make a complete investigation of the facts leading up to the riot, as well as the riot."

César Chávez was in town Monday for a speech at Pan American College and an evening rally for farm workers. What was supposed to be a razzle-dazzle rally was turned into a mournful memorial for Flores.

Chávez was cheered as he called for a boycott of Pharr's businessmen until Ramírez and Sandoval are removed and the police department is brought under control. *"Son los comerciantes que tienen el poder aquí."* (It is the businessmen who hold the power here,") he said, and he reiterated what he had said earlier at a press conference:

"All the people wanted was a hearing by city officials. (Fernández had tried for two weeks before the picket to meet with Bowe). Brutality is widespread on the part of the police and one life lost is too much. Such things have to be resolved peacefully, or somebody tries to resolve them the other way. Mexican-American policemen can be as brutal as Anglos."

That, of course, was the crux of the problem. Bowe is mayor by the grace of the real powers in Pharr: a handful of businessmen and growers who hold all the strings. Ramírez and the other cops are all chicanos and utterly dependent on the little Pharr machine for their jobs. In Pharr it is not just the Anglos against the *Raza,* but also the economically powerful against the unprotected.

On Tuesday, some of the businessmen had a meeting with the city commissioners. Father Roberto Flores of the Texas Conference of Churches, one of the three priests who had tried to mediate between youths and police Saturday night, attorney David Hall, who represents the Flores family, and attorney Ben Canales of Austin had been invited to the meeting by the man who owns the little taxi company. The three went to see what kind of communication could be set up between dissidents and the "establishment"; they got thrown out of the meeting.

Judge J. R. Alamia, whose 92nd District Court handles most local criminal matters, called the grand jury together, and charged them with making an investigation. "The scope of your investigation," the judge said, "should be such that no doubt will be left in the minds of anyone but that it was fair, impartial, complete, and conclusive so that it will impress upon people the fact that confidence and reliance can still be placed in our courts and our institutions."

That is going to be hard to do in Pharr. D. A. Oscar McInnis has already asked the D.P.S. to investigate. That, to the *chicanos*, means the Rangers are being called on to investigate the Rangers, and they remember how the big federal Ranger trial of three years ago got all kinds of publicity, but that no judge has even bothered to issue a decision. They also remember how reluctant McInnis himself was to prosecute State Sen. Jim Bates for pistol whipping a Mexican truck driver in 1969, though Bates was later convicted. They remember how Bates was fined a measley hundred bucks.

They are also worried that the grand jury, scheduled to convene Feb. 18, will end up indicting people for rioting instead of taking care of the Flores shooting.

San Antonio City Cmsr. Albert Peña came down quietly on Sunday, Feb. 14, to make a private investigation.

By Wednesday, Feb. 10, the day of the funeral, Pharr was still tense, though an inspection of the business district and the area around the police station would have revealed little evidence of a "full-scale riot" three days previously. The only broken window in view was in the front of the police station, obviously from one of the many rocks thrown after the water was turned on.

Business was back to normal, except that the police had ordered no beer sold after 6 P.M. on the day of the funeral, and the street in front of the police station was once again blocked off Wednesday night.

About 30 monitors were named from among the MAYOS and other young people in Pharr, and they supervised the funeral procession; eight hundred people walking four abreast behind the slow moving black hearse in total silence except for the tramping of feet.

The column moved from De Leon's Funeral Home to St. Margaret's Church for the mass, and from there to the cemetery. There was a collection for the widow, and you could tell the congregation was a poor one: the baskets jangled rather than rustled.

It was not a very elegant funeral by urban standards. Some of the pallbearers wore jackets which did not quite match their pants, and they scorned the fancy collapsible wheeled cart, preferring to carry the casket. The ladies, some of whom I had seen Saturday in the picket line, were more elegantly dressed, but they walked with the same tireless patience I had noted then. They have walked in too many parades and processions to expect much change from that one.

Lupe Salinas was there, wearing a black turtleneck and sunglasses. I had not seen him since he came to complain about Sergeant Sandoval; the bruises and black eye were gone. He, like most of the young people, was subdued, solemn and tired-looking. The only bright clothing around was worn by a TV cameraman from Weslaco, who chose a yellow shirt and white bell-bottoms for the funeral. Most of the women wore *mantillas.*

That night the staff of *¡Ya Mero!* worked late to get the paper out. It was on sale in Mexican grocery stores all over the valley on Friday, stores kept calling for more papers. *"La Raza pierde otro hermano. Alfonso L. Flores muere de bala en la cabeza,"* was the banner. ("La Raza loses another brother. Alfonso L. Flores dies from bullet in the head.")

Then on Thursday some elderly people, former melon strikers from 1967, drove the 40 miles from Rio Grande City to find out what had happened. They said Sheriff René Solís, convicted of election fraud and sentenced to 30 days and a $2,000 fine, was still the sheriff. Why wasn't he in jail? What do you tell people? We explained that his lawyer, Jim Bates, had appealed, and that it might take years before Solís went to jail, if he went at all.

Friday, nearly 200 people crowded into the weekly Colonias del Valle meeting to talk about what will happen now. Will the FBI arrest the cop who killed Pancho, they want to know? People glance at the Flores family as a speaker explains what a grand jury is. Maybe he will be arrested after the 18th. Maybe not? *¿Quién sabe?*

Someone says he read in the Reynosa paper President Nixon had taken a personal interest in the case, which would be solved soon. He is told the story is a fantasy; the Justice Department lawyer came on Monday and was gone by Tuesday.

You drive down Highway 83, past the Cactus Drive-in, familiar as the place where the crassest of skin-flicks are regularly projected across a giant outdoor screen, as drivers just miss crashing into each other while they rubberneck to catch a glimpse of technicolor flesh. You see they're still playing Saturday's feature: "A Bullet for Sandoval." Somebody tells you Sandoval and Ramírez have moved their families out of Pharr in fear of some kind of retaliation, though there are no rumors that anybody is planning anything. You know some of the community organizers are staying in San Juan to avoid the Pharr police. Efraín Fernández says he hopes if they come to arrest him they don't do it in front of his little girl.

You drive past the high school and remember reading of time when there was enough freedom for Fred Hofheinz to hold a great outdoor debate with the late R. C. Hoiles, owner of the Freedom chain of newspapers, which oppose public education as socialist. Twenty years later, the first *chicano* student body president, and an active MAYO, Armando Castro, is removed from office for circulating a petition asking for the freedom to circulate petitions. You remember the new president is named Joey Stockton. You can be sure he's no MAYO.

Two of the Flores brothers tell you they flew down from Chicago as soon as they heard the news, but Pancho never regained consciousness. Now they have to get back or lose their jobs. Do they have to stay for the trial? The lawyer tells them there will be no trial for months, probably. They look surprised; say nothing.

You remember talking to Sheriff Claudio Castañeda's badge-wearing secretary the Friday before the riot as you wait to interview the sheriff. She is a *chicana* named Mrs. Larson. She gives you a lecture about how the union is bad, because all the other Mexicans except her and her labor-contractor father are lazy. Her sister married a *chicano,* and boy, was she sorry. All he does is drink beer and lie around. If you raise wages, the people just drink more and that makes more work for the sheriff. You wonder how many of the deputies carrying guns on Saturday night felt the same way.

You remember your mother teaching you the policeman is your friend. She wasn't running a game on you either. She meant it.

And you wait. And the people wait, to see if anything will happen. Probably not, and you start crossing the street every time you see a cop.

What else is there to do?

Clark Knowlton

Clark Knowlton (see p. 232) participated as an expert witness in hearings conducted before the then titled Inter-Agency Committee on Mexican Affairs on June 9, 1967 at El Paso, Texas. Professor Knowlton testified on problems concerning land tenure in New Mexico. His testimony points out for the student the many ramifications of that long-simmering problem. Probably the Federal Government's belated concern for Mexican American grievances, as expressed by this conference, was an attempt to soothe Chicano discontent in the Southwest. Nevertheless the report of that committee, The Mexican American: A New Focus on Opportunity *(1967), serves as a valuable source for students interested in the Chicano movement in general, and the specific problems of land rights, and compensation.*
By permission of the Inter-Agency Committee on Mexican Affairs, and the author.

Recommendations For The Solution Of Land Tenure Problems Among The Spanish American

Mr. Chairman, honorable guests, Ladies and Gentlemen. Before making recommendations for the solution of land tenure problems among the Spanish American people of northern New Mexico and southern Colorado, I would like to make the following observations. The land question among the Spanish Americans is no longer a simple economic, political, or social problem subject to discussion, legislation, or economic analysis. It has become a fundamental moral issue upon

334

which all their hopes, aspirations, bitterness, resentments, and longings are focused. It is also a moral measuring rod by which they have measured the moral concepts of Anglo American political, economic, and judicial systems and found them wanting. The Spanish Americans as a people are profoundly convinced that they were conquered in war, forced to become American citizens against their will at the time, and robbed of their land and water rights by the Anglo Americans aided by some Spanish American accomplices. This massive theft was, they believe, aided and abetted by state and national politicians, judges, government employees, Anglo-American merchants, ranchers, and businessmen.

As a result the Spanish Americans are completely skeptical of the moral claims of American democracy. They have little faith in any American political party. They have no trust in the American judicial system. They have little confidence in any private or public state or national department or agency. As a people, they are more deeply alienated from the values and concepts of the predominant Anglo American society of the United States than almost any other ethnic or racial group in the country. The Spanish Americans have the psychology of a conquered, dispossessed, and impoverished people who believe that they have suffered serious injustices at the hands of the dominant Anglo American society.

Until they, as a people, experience the physical return of all or a good part of the land taken from them or receive what they define as an adequate compensation, the deeply rooted burning emotions of resentment and of having suffered historical injustice will continue to exist. The poisonous abscesses of alienation, rejection of Anglo American society, and poverty can not be eliminated. It is of utmost importance that these abscesses should be lanced. If they are not, the accelerating slide of the Spanish Americans toward rural violence cannot be halted.

Furthermore, the Departments of Interior and of Agriculture have a direct responsibility for heavy land loss among the subsistence Spanish American farmers located along the major river systems of New Mexico. The development of almost every major irrigation and flood control districts in the state such as the Rio Grande Conservancy District and the Elephant Butte and Caballo Dams drove thousands of Spanish Americans from their lands through their inability to pay the financial charges imposed upon their small farms. The policies of both departments are such that the majority of their programs benefit the larger commercial heavily subsidized Anglo American farmer and not the small more subsistence Spanish American rural village farmer.

One authority estimates that the Spanish Americans conservatively lost between 1854 and 1930, a minimum of over 2,000,000 acres of privately owned lands, 1,700,000 acres of communal or *ejido* lands, and 1,800,000 acres of land taken by the Federal Government without remuneration. This massive and still continuing land loss destroyed the entire economic basis of the Spanish American rural villages. It has played a major role in the formation of a large distressed area marked by high indices of poverty and social disorganization.

I would like to suggest that a high level Government Committee be organized by the appropriate departments to study the land question in depth in New Mexico, southern Colorado, West Texas, and other neighboring areas. The committee should begin its study with Spanish and Mexican land owning customs and practices established in New Mexico, the impact of American conquest upon the Spanish Americans, and the causes of continued land loss from that date until the present. The committee should be empowered to hold hearings in the Spanish American areas, to examine records, and to subpoena witnesses. The staff of the committee should contain Spanish American and Anglo employees familiar with the language, culture, and history of the Spanish American people. The committee should be directed to recommend ways of settling the land issue.

The formation of such a committee would undoubtedly arouse great concern and anxiety among Anglo American landholders in the Spanish American areas as well as in the offices of local state governments. Land values would be affected, and existing land titles might come into question. Nevertheless, these problems are not as ominious nor as serious as the rapid increase of unrest and bitterness among the Spanish Americans alienated from the Anglo American society. The leaders of some Spanish American groups are seriously considering violence as a means of bringing the land issue to the attention of the American people and to force the Federal Government to act.

As most of the land lost by the villages was grazing and timber lands taken from the *ejido* or communal village lands, the returned land should be added to the communal lands that remain. The villages receiving land should be required to set up a bonded governing board composed of resident village inhabitants selected by the resident village population. Provisions should be made in the deed for the management of the land, the payment of land tax, the settlement of disputes over land use, regulation of grazing and timber cutting to prevent erosion, and perhaps provisions for royalties if minerals are discovered. It is of paramount importance for the welfare of the Spanish American areas that title to the land should be vested in the village as a land owning entity and not in individuals or the land will ultimately be lost again.

Spanish American resentment and hostility are steadily increasing toward the management of the Kit Carson National Forest in northern New Mexico. This resentment is reaching the explosive point where the lives of Forest Personnel may be in danger. Spanish American bitterness has originated over three points. One: The majority of the inhabitants of the mountainous Spanish American villages located in and around the National Forests are convinced that much of the forest lands were taken by the government without compensation or purchased from large timber and cattle companies that had first stolen the land from the Spanish Americans. Two: The Spanish Americans are convinced that the management of the National Forests are trying to force the Spanish Americans out of the villages in and around the forests. Three: A sharp wave of hostility swept the Spanish American villages when they learned that forest personnel were used to guide police and national guard patrols searching for Spanish Americans involved in recent events in Tierra Amarilla.

I would recommend that a study be made of all the land acquired by the National Forests to find out if the Spanish Americans are right about land being taken from them to create the National Forest in northern New Mexico. The Spanish American villages around the National Forests are almost completely dependent upon forest lands, the villagers should be given priority in forest use in northern New Mexico. Furthermore, the Forest Service should develop an extension division to assist the local Spanish American people to improve their livestock herds, to develop privately owned and village owned woodworking and handicraft industries utilizing forest resources, and to develop village owned recreational facilities of the Swiss village type. Techniques learned in northern New Mexico could be applied to the economic and cultural development of mountainous forested lands over the world.

Where the land can not be returned to the Spanish American villages without serious injustice to numerous small Anglo American farmers or suburban dwellers, then the villages should receive adequate compensation. Some of the money provided ought to go to the heirs of the men who lost the land, but most of it should be reserved as development capital and utilized to improve, the economic, social, and cultural conditions of the Spanish American rural village population.

The heirs of private Spanish American landholders who were deprived of their lands have the right to receive compensation for these lands. This will require proof of heirship and registration of heirs. Let me say again, that unrest and dangerous resentments in northern New Mexico and southern Colorado can not be reduced until the Federal Government makes a serious and concerted effort, as it has with some Indian tribes to resolve the land issue to the satisfaction of the majority of the Spanish Americans.

Land without water is useless in a semi-arid environment. Water adjudication procedures now going on among the Spanish American rural population are arousing anxiety and hostility. The State of New Mexico is trying to pinpoint individual ownership of water rights. The state officials are applying Anglo American concepts of water use that are quite different from the traditional Spanish American practices. In the villages, water is traditionally owned by the village and allocated by the village or ditch water master selected by the water users. I would recommend that water rights be vested in the villages and regulated and utilized according to village tradition and practice.

The irrigation systems of the Spanish American villages are antiquated and hand made. Large amounts of water are lost every year, and the crops frequently wither away. It would be very easy to develop a program in which the appropriate federal agency could provide technical skills and the use of machinery to be matched by labor and raw materials provided by the village people. A secure water supply would definitely enhance the productivity of Spanish American farms.

Many undoubtedly will argue that the state governments of New Mexico, Colorado, and surrounding states should assume the responsibility of improving conditions in the Spanish American segments of their states. Perhaps they should. However, these state governments have been in existence a long time. During this period, the majority of their agencies and departments have seldom shown any interest or concern in the welfare of the Spanish American people. Time has run out. Neither the Spanish Americans nor the United States can await the awakening of state governments to their responsibilities. The situation now is too threatening and dangerous for long delays for a discussion to take place over whether the state or federal governments should assume responsibility.

The social fabric of the majority of the Spanish American rural villages has unraveled under the impact of poverty, out-migration, land loss, apathy, and social disorganization. Community organizers sponsored by VISTA and O.E.O. programs are just beginning to knit the fabric together in a few villages. I would like to recommend that state and federal agencies should send trained community organizers into the villages to assist the villages to overcome apathy and factionalism, to develop village wide organizations, and to train a local village leadership.

As the communal tradition is far stronger in the villages than the idea of individualism, the appropriate government agencies should encourage and assist the villages to develop producer and consumer cooperatives. Because of low volume and almost complete ignorance of market trends and of Anglo American business values, Spanish American farmers are now at the mercy of local merchants and jobbers. Credit unions would be an invaluable need for village population that is seldom able to secure credit at local banks.

The state agricultural extension programs should receive funds and encouragement to conduct research on methods of improving agricultural productivity on the small Spanish American landholdings. Irrigation facilities should be modernized. Agricultural machinery suitable for poor small farmers might well be developed by the U.S. Department of Agriculture or perhaps the Interior. Here the experiences of the Japanese could perhaps be studied with considerable profit. As much of the produce consumed in Albuquerque and Santa Fe must be imported from out of state, there is room for the development of truck, poultry, and perhaps even of frozen foods and processing plants in the Spanish American areas.

In the rural Spanish American villages a once lavish handicraft tradition is dying. It is hard now to realize that at one time the rural Spanish American villagers possessed a handicraft tradition as rich and varied as that of the Southwestern Indians. While the Federal and State Governments and private agencies have encouraged and aided the Indian artisans and artists through the establishment of special arts and craft schools, nothing has been done for the Spanish Americans. I would therefore recommend that a foundation or the appropriate state and federal departments set up a handicraft board to train Spanish American artists and artisans, set standards, assist them to secure raw materials, and help to provide a market for their products. Unemployment and underemployment are chronic in northern New Mexico and southern Colorado. While few Spanish Americans could ever hope to provide for their families from hand work, they could certainly supplement a scarce income in the long cold winter months through furniture making, metal working, jewelry, pottery, woodworking, and weaving. The Handicraft boards of India and Siam perhaps could be analyzed for ideas that could be applied to the Spanish American village.

The Spanish American areas are marked by deplorably poor roads. Many of the villages are almost completely isolated during winter months. Federal and State Funds could be provided to develop a network of roads linking the villages with each other and with the major highways that almost completely bypass the Spanish American areas. The roads would also assist in the establishment of industry, the transportation of village products, and inhance the ability of village people to find employment in nearby urban centers. The Spanish American areas are in the same condition as Appalachia and perhaps the Ozarks as far as isolation and lack of roads go.

I would now like to discuss some of the reasons why past present state and federal programs have not been able to materially assist the Spanish Americans to escape from poverty. Lessons derived from the failures of other programs can assist us to improve programs of the future.

The files of state and federal agencies are filled with studies of the socio-economic conditions and problems of the Spanish Americans. Few additional studies are needed. The basic needs and problems of the Spanish Americans have been identified for over twenty-five years. Unfortunately the majority of programs based upon these studies litter the Southwest as dead and dying hulks. They failed primarily in spite of the excellent intentions of their originators because they must learn when to use Spanish and when not to in communicating with the rural people. The Anglo-American employee who learns enough Spanish to communicate with the rural people can break down barriers, make friends, and win an acceptance of ideas and programs.

And still another problem that complicates planning and program development among the Spanish Americans is the decay of the traditional rural village social systems such as the patron system and the extended patriarchal family. Outmigration has carried away the younger adults. The majority of villages are afflicted with anomie and social disorganization. Among the village population there are very few individuals who have a working knowledge of American culture and society. Marked by apathy, land loss, poverty, malnutrition the village populations tend to be factionalized and exploited by local political leaders who control public employment in the region.

Partially anglicized families are found in all but the more isolated rural villages. These families are able to relate quite well to Anglo American professionals. The average Anglo who meets them tends to assume that because of their facility with English, their familiarity with Anglo American habits of thought, their possession of a higher material standard of living than the mass of village people that they are village leaders. Many of the partially anglicized are often able because of this assumption to exploit both the Anglo Americans and the village population.

Precisely because these people are somewhat anglicized, deprecate Spanish, and tend to look down upon the local people, they tend to be rejected by the Spanish American masses. The real leaders are often intelligent men and women who because of poverty, a lack of education, and an ignorance of the English language and of American customs lack the ability to provide adequate leadership even though they have considerable prestige in their own village circles. One of the most serious problems of the entire region is the lack of good Spanish American leadership.

Any comprehensive program developed for New Mexico, Colorado, and nearby sections should have a leadership discovery and training component as a major part of the program. The village leaders to be effective must be men and women who speak both Spanish and English, who are firmly grounded in local Spanish American values and yet who comprehend Anglo values and procedures. There are very few of them, but the welfare of the Spanish American people depend upon their coming.

The Spanish Americans are a very proud people. Extremely reluctant, even under conditions of extreme poverty, to receive charity they respond very readily to programs that they believe will improve the economic or social conditions of the village. It should here be underlined that they accept more readily programs for group welfare than for individual welfare. Programs designed for the Spanish Americans in view of these factors, wherever possible, should involve the Spanish Americans in contributions of donated labor and raw materials.

One of the most successful programs in northern New Mexico was a state financed and sponsored program to improve the simple archaic inefficient irrigation systems of a group of Spanish American villages along the upper Pecos River. The state provided technical services and equipment. The Spanish Americans enthusiastically donated raw materials and labor. Every dollar provided by the state was matched by five dollars contributed by the Spanish Americans. Unfortunately poorly informed Anglo American politicians brought the program to a halt before more than a small handful of villages had benefited.

The harsh refusal of the dominant Anglo American population and the Anglo dominated state legislatures to permit the expenditures of state funds for programs to assist the Spanish Americans is quite ironic in view of the fact that the Anglo-American population is far more subsidized by state and federal governments than the Spanish Americans. This statement is supported by an examination of the evidence. The network of superhighways constructed by state and federal funds somehow always bypass the Spanish American areas suffocated by an inadequate transportation system. Lavish airports seldom utilized by the Spanish Americans mark the Anglo American cities. The poor small subsistence Spanish American farmer seldom sees the enormous subsidies received by the commercial Anglo American farmer. The Federal Government has financed expensive flood control and irrigation projects that drove the Spanish American off of his land for the economic benefit of Anglo American city dwellers and farmers. Considerable funds are spent in the natural forests for the Anglo American hunter, fisher, and camper to the neglect of the grazing facilities needed by the small Spanish American

village livestock owner. And finally it is exceedingly curious that virtually all of the defense and military installations in New Mexico are located in the Anglo-American areas.

In closing I would like to state that the Spanish Americans can not escape from poverty living on small subsistence farms. However, if the villages can obtain the grazing and timber lands taken from their *ejidos,* grazing and forest activities can increase their income. If handicrafts and woodworking industries are encouraged, another source of income is added. If the villages are assisted to cater to the recreational needs of the larger society on a year round basis then additional revenue is provided. It is not at all impossible that industries suitable to the natural environment of the region could not be induced to enter the region. By the development of various sources of income, a viable way of life can be created for the Spanish American people of the area.

The alternatives are too drastic to consider. A laissez faire policy will mean that northern New Mexico and southern Colorado will continue to be one of the most serious regions of poverty in the United States. Extremely high rates of hunger, poverty, social disorganization, welfare and unemployment will continue. Out-migration will continue to send out of the region hundreds of poorly educated unskilled semi-acculturated workers to add to the social problems of our larger cities. It is far easier to struggle with the problems of rural New Mexico and southern Colorado than it is with the problems of the large slums and ghettoes of the Southwest, the Pacific Coast, and the Rocky Mountains.

And finally, I would like to stress with all the power of my command that time is running out. The land issue has reached a crisis point. If it is not resolved soon Spanish American desperation will increasingly find an outlet in violence.

Jorge Lara-Braud

Jorge Lara-Braud (Director of Hispanic-American Institute, Austin, Texas) heads an ecumenical organization that collects and develops materials that will aid Spanish-speaking communities in the United States. The Institute receives support from eight Protestant denominations in Texas and is deeply committed to the Chicano movement. The call for bilingualism by Dr. Lara-Braud is the official position paper adopted by this varied coalition.

By permission of the author, and THE HISPANIC-AMERICAN INSTITUTE.

Bilingualism For Texas: Education For Fraternity

OUR COSMOPOLITAN ENVIRONMENT

The Southwest is the most cosmopolitan region of this nation. No other area of the United States encompasses a wider diversity of races, religions, and national origins, or a greater variety of cultural development of the people who belong to them. California, Colorado, Arizona, New Mexico, and Texas contain together some of the largest groups of American Indians, virtually all U.S. Indians of hispanicized heritage and of Mexican origin, four-fifths of those whose Spanish surnames are this nation's uninterrupted link of four centuries to the legacy of Spain and Mexico, the largest groups of Orientals in the continental United States (two-thirds of the Japanese, two-thirds of the Filipinos, and over half of the Chinese), a third of the country's Asian Indians, Koreans, Polynesians, Indonesians, and Hawaiians, and some three million of the nation's blacks. As Professor Fred H. Schmidt states, "In the truest sense of the word, the region is cosmopolitan—its people belong to all of the world, and the ties of many with other parts of the world are still recent and unsevered, for here are found one-third of the nation's registered aliens."

340

Of course, what makes any cosmopolitanism functional rather than purely statistical is the survival of the language of each cultural group represented in the regional "cosmos" in coexistence with the lingua franca of the nation to which the region belongs. In this respect, nothing contributes more to keeping the Southwest cosmopolitan than the persistent confluence of Spanish and English. Figures from a pre-Census survey of the Spanish-American population of the United States in November of 1969 reveal there were in this country 9,200,000 persons of "Spanish descent," not including inmates of institutions and members of the armed forces. Spanish was reported as the mother tongue of 6,700,000, despite the fact that 72.6 percent were U.S. born. More revealing even is that 4,600,000 reported Spanish as their current language, that is to say, their primary language in the home (even though more than 80 percent are U.S. citizens and a larger percentage is quite likely able to use English for social, educational and occupational purposes with varying degrees of proficiency).

More than half of the 9,200,000 "Spanish-Americans" of the November 1969 pre-Census survey, were Mexican-Americans living in the Southwest. Nearly two million reside in Texas. Roughly one out of every five Texans is a Mexican-American. There are no recent published Census statistics to determine what percentage of Mexican-Americans in the Southwest (including Texas) would report Spanish first as the mother tongue and then as the home language. Based on inference from the pre-Census survey and other studies, and on extensive empirical observation, we estimate 85 percent and 70 percent would report Spanish as the mother tongue and home language respectively. Let it be remembered we are dealing with a group overwhelmingly non-alien. Some 90 percent are U.S. citizens, whose ability to communicate in English ranges from faltering to glittering.

The persistence of Spanish in the Southwest may be fascinating or perplexing to non-Spanish speakers. Perhaps nothing clouds the understanding of this phenomenon more than the parallels drawn between Mexican-Americans and other so called "language minorities." All other language minorities ceased to be replenished with the end of heavy immigration from the country of origin. More often than not immigrants left that distant country with no expectation or desire of ever resuming vital cultural ties with it. The ethnic enclave—with its concomitant survival of a foreign language—was seen, particularly from the second generation onwards, as a transitional stage in the process of assimilation within the unilingual national mainstream. The nation had quite early defined its pattern of cultural unity primarily in terms of the language, religion, folkways, and institutions of the dominant English-speaking Protestant founders and their descendents. There was no perversity in discouraging diversity. The youth and relative insecurity of the new republic virtually demanded a "melting pot" policy. This posed no insurmountable problem for those who could melt. It did create difficulties for others, ranging from annoying to intolerable, depending on how distant their difference was from the primordial founding community. That meant many would be regarded as less then American, and subject to permanent or protracted rejection, no matter how eagerly some sought to expiate for their unintentional deviancy.

THE GRANDEUR AND MISERY OF DIFFERENCE

Against this background, the parallel between Mexican-Americans and other language minorities turns out to be no parallel at all. Rather, the contrast stands out. By the time the Southwest became U.S. territory following the military conquests of 1836 and 1846 Spanish had been the language of population centers for the previous three centuries. The region, though sparsely settled, was pervasively Mexican, a rich blend of Spanish and Indian culture. The "Anglo" conquest was traumatic. The native Spanish-speaking inhabitants, theoretically protected from cultural or economic depredation by local gentlemen's agreement and international treaty provisions, within two generations had been reduced to hewers of wood and drawers of water. Their language, religion, skin-color-and above all their status as a conquered people—made them ineligible even for an invitation to the melting pot. They were by no means totally cut off. To be sure, social institutions left them little or no room to participate. But compassionate individuals in the dominant group, especially members of churches, mitigated their plight through numberless acts of friendship and redress. Others, less compassionate, found or created ways to capitalize on the enormous reservoir of cheap labor they constituted. It would be impossible to explain the existence of mining, railroad, cattle, sheep, and agricultural empires of the Southwest apart from the massive use of Mexican-American labor, often in conditions of virtual peonage.

Meanwhile, throughout the second half of the 19th century and the first third of the 20th, Mexico was intermittently convulsed by bloody social disorders. Mexicans headed north by the hundreds of thousands to the U.S. Southwest and by the thousands to the industrial cities of the Midwest. There, they were to swell the ranks of friends and relatives engaged in menial work. Bedraggled refugees could hardly enhance the image of a people long reduced to wretchedness. The massive infusion of steady arrivals did, however, immeasurably contribute to further Mexicanize the environment and to revitalize Spanish as the ongoing mother tongue of Mexican-Americans. A curious accomodation was made by the dominant Anglos, more instinctive than intentional. Since neither the Mexicanhood of the Mexican-Americans nor their language appeared to be on the wane, but quite the opposite, the unwelcome replenishment of their "foreignes" could be deflected to folkloric attraction. Accordingly, a spirited promotion of Mexican food, Mexican art, Mexican music, Mexican crafts, Mexican festivals got underway. This was happening precisely at the time when Mexican-Americans were frequently denied admission to public establishments, when they had been driven to avoid as denigrating the self-designation Mexican in favor of Latin-American or Spanish-American, and when speaking Spanish in school halls and playgrounds was an offense punished with suspension, fines, after-school detention, or even corporal punishment. Incidentally, alarmed at the escalation of anti-Mexicanhood in Texas, and the refusal of Mexico to send her nationals to replace in the fields men now in uniform, the State Legislature was driven to enact formal legislation in May of 1943 recognizing the people of Mexican extraction as Caucasian, and entitling them to "whites only" public services.

Ironically, it took a war, the Second World War, to create conditions more favorable to intercultural fraternity. Mexican-Americans earned the admiration of fellow Americans for their disproportionate record of casualties and heroism. No other ethnic or racial group earned a larger proportion of Congressional medals. The G.I. Bill provided heretofore denied educational opportunities for college careers. Many Mexican-Americans moved on to well-paid jobs formerly the exclusive preserve of Anglos. Vigorous associations came into being for the redress of cultural and civil rights. Many of the blatant barriers against Mexican-American participation in public life, particularly in social institutions, came down under Anglo initiative or Mexican-American attack, or both. There lingered, however, even among Mexican-Americans (especially "success" types of the immediate post World War II period) a definite discomfort about the continuing persistence of Spanish. A century of sustained anti-Mexicanhood had taken its toll in many ways, one being the suspicion that no Mexican-American could attain the *sine qua non* of true U.S. citizenship, mastery of English, until he ceased to speak Spanish.

In the meantime, Mexico and the United States, close allies in World War II, emerged out of the conflict enjoying an unprecedented degree of friendship. Both made great economic strides in the ensuing decades. Immigration from Mexico, even though subject to no quota, slowed down considerably. However, the international border, never quite so much a boundary as a gateway for two-way traffic, registered booming crossing figures in both directions. In the year 1967–1968, the U.S. Office of Immigration reported 135 million crossings from Mexico to the U.S. It is estimated by this writer no less than 100 million were made from the U.S. to Mexico. Added to these astounding figures, the vibrant quest of Mexican-Americans for their long suppressed identity, the renaissance of Spanish among them and in institutions of higher learning, and the shrinking of the world into a multilingual global village—all make for a drastic questioning of the unilingual tradition of education in a bilingual, multicultural Southwest.

BILINGUAL EDUCATION: MISCONCEPTIONS, DEFINITION, APPLICATION

The foregoing historical review throws light, we hope, on the human realities underlying the confluence of Spanish and English in southwestern United States. When we deal with language we deal with life at its core. It is the means by which an individual decodes the meaning of his existence in the world and encodes his experiences for creative dialogue with others. Memory, affection, aspiration, reflection, anxiety, discovery, religion and a myriad of other personal experiences are mediated through language. There is no other path to self-awareness and self-disclosure. It is no coincidence that in the Bible nothingness and chaos are turned into creation and order by the Word and words. Man's dominion over the earth begins as a function of language, the naming of created things. The holiness of language is not a concept of cultural chauvinism. Rather, it is a fundamental notion of the Judeo-Christian tradition.

This brings us to *the* issue before us. Where two languages coexist, no matter how socially distant may be the respective communities which speak them, a unique human chemistry has been catalyzed. Neither community has remained untouched by the other. Certain commonalities of history, environment, style and perception have resulted. Some appropriate them at the superficial level of folklore, others at the more basic level of biculturalism. The former, quite probably unilingual, have a low ceiling of tolerance for difference. The latter, quite probably bilingual, possess a high appreciation for diversity. Prejudice, not inevitably but frequently, flourishes among the first. Fraternity, not automatically but naturally, thrives among the second. The magnanimity of Mexican-Americans in forgetting and forgiving present and past indignities is not due to any inherent nobility. Rather, it has to do with their enlarged ability as bilinguals to decode much of the motivational world of the dominant group. Conversely, Anglos who have earned the affection of Mexican-Americans have been able literally to "communicate" beyond the limitations of one language and one culture. Both experience less discomfort with the culturally different at home and abroad than their unilingual counterparts.

Bilingualism, nevertheless, is still hindered among us by at least four quite prevalent misconceptions: 1) English cannot be mastered as long as the individual retains another language as the mother tongue. 2) Using two languages as mediums of instruction cause academic retardation and even psychological confusion. 3) The low educational achievement among Mexican-Americans is directly attributable to their retention of Spanish; 4) retention of a foreign language impedes the Americanization of those who speak it.

We might better deal with these misconceptions if we first define bilingual education. It is "instruction in two languages and the use of those two languages as mediums of instruction for any part of or all of the school curriculum. Study of the history and culture associated with a student's mother tongue is considered an integral part of bilingual education" education.

Let us now deal with the first two misconceptions. They are closely related. Mastery of English while retaining Spanish as the mother or home language has been accomplished by countless bilinguals in the Southwest, particularly if instruction in both languages began at an early age. The main reason why this fact is not readily apparent is that until 1963 it was a phenomenon confined to individuals. It was not an officially approved educational policy anywhere in the U.S.A. (except for schools in New Mexico throughout the second half of the 19th century following language educational provisions of the 1848 Treaty of Guadalupe Hidalgo). The heavy influx of Cubans into the Miami area led the Dade County Schools in 1963 to undertake a completely bilingual program in grades one, two, and three of the Coral Way School, with plans to move up one grade each year. There were equal numbers of English and Spanish-speaking children. Approximately half of the instruction was to be given in Spanish by Cuban teachers, and half in English by American teachers. Now on its seventh year, the program has proven an astounding success. Children speak the second language with little or no trace of an accent, while being fully proficient in both across the gamut of all subject matter taught.

In 1964 a quite similar program was begun in the United Consolidated School District of Webb County, outside Laredo. As in Coral Way, half the children were English speakers and half Spanish-speakers. The teaching in English and Spanish in all elementary school subjects has been done by bilingual teachers who are native speakers of Spanish and fluent also in English. The results equal those of Coral Way, not alone in academic achievement, but also in intercultural fraternity. A recent evaluation of learning of mathematics in this program is additionally revealing. The achievement is greater for both Anglo and Mexican-American children when the subject is taught bilingually rather than in English alone.

Convincing results from programs such as these and from others equally successful, though different in implementation, and in some instances with English and a language other then Spanish as mediums of instruction, greatly contributed to make possible enabling federal and state bilingual education acts. On January 2, 1968 the Bilingual Education Act, with bipartisan sponsorship led by Senator Ralph Yarborough, passed by the United States Congress On May 22, 1969 the 61st Legislature of the State of Texas passed *unanimously* a similar bill. These legislative landmarks underscored bilingualism as a sound educational concept and committed the nation and the state to enlarge its dimensions.

Interestingly enough both bills dispell the misconception of possible retardation and confusion as a result of the use of two languages as mediums of instruction. The two pieces of legislation imply that non-English speakers will more readily attain mastery of the national tongue if they are first taught in the language of the home. Confirmation of this insight comes from a group of international experts gathered in Paris under UNESCO auspices in 1951 to study the uses of vernacular languages in education. Here is their consensus: "It is axiomatic that the best medium of teaching a child is his mother tongue. Psychologically it is the system of meaningful signs that in his mind work automatically for expression and understanding. Sociologically, it is a means of identification among the members of the community to which he belongs. Educationally, he learns more quickly through it than through an unfamiliar linguistic medium."

The experience of some Indians in Latin America at one time speaking only their tribal language proves very instructive in this regard. Those who were taught Spanish and Portuguese without first mastering the basic skills of reading and writing in their native tongues went on to record apalling statistics of social maladjustment. In contrast, those who were fortunate enough to have their native tongues reduced to writing by linguistic anthropologists (notably missionaries known as the Wycliff Translators), and then taught to read in a script corresponding to the sounds inherited from their ancestors, had little or no problem learning the national tongue. Their psychological and social adjustments were remarkably favorable. The crucial difference in experience is not hard to explain. When people are denied the continued use of their language, they are also denied their personhood, their history, their memories. One cannot adequately decipher the meaning of his reality through the mute subtitles of someone else's tongue. The foreign tongue ceases to be foreign only when it is filtered through the familiar sounds and signs of one's own.

Here is the logical point to deal with the misconception that the low educational achievement of Mexican-Americans is attributable to their retention of Spanish. There is no denying that the group has the lowest index of school years completed in the entire nation. Their dropout rate of 80 percent with respect to high school completion is the highest in the country. Earlier in this paper we reviewed the history of animosity to their linguistic and cultural difference—particularly the concerted effort to eradicate Spanish as a functional language in the Southwest. Would not the evidence suggest that their massive educational destitution is directly attributable to the school's failure to capitalize on their bilinguality? Could it not be that the educational process has been so conceived and implemented as to unwittingly penalize the Mexican-American in direct proportion to his attempt to remain bilingual? Could it not be in fact that much of his social maladjustment rather reflects the maladjustment of a society so misguided as to regard a functional second language as a liability instead of an asset, while in the course of such folly inflicting untold psychic, social and economic damage? The irony is that all along the teaching of Spanish as a *foreign* language was encouraged in high school and colleges when it was too little and too late for either Mexican-Americans or other Americans. This absurdity was forcefully pointed out to the Special Subcommittee on Bilingual Education of the United States Senate in 1967 by Bruce Gaarder, Chief of Modern Foreign Language Section of the U.S. Office of Education: "It is as if one said it is all right to learn a foreign language if you start so late that you really cannot master it. It is all right for headwaiters, professional performers, and the rich to know foreign languages, but any child in school who already knows one is suspect." By the way, on that occasion Dr. Gaarder also observed that the greatest unfulfilled need for Foreign Service personnel and Fulbright - Hays lecturers and technical specialists sent abroad was for those able to speak French or Spanish."

The last major misconception is that which assumes retention of a foreign language impedes the Americanization of those who speak it. The misconception, to begin with, implies a sadly provincial view of patriotism as unilingual conformity. The nation may have at one time discouraged diversity for the sake of consolidating its youthful existence, but even then the plurality of its origins was regarded as the genius of its universality. The melting pot has been proven more myth than reality. The country is richer for its failure. More visionary patriots have favored such imagery as a "mosaic of minorities" or the "symphony of mankind" to denote the blend of peoples and languages from all over the world which undergird the American Dream. No country in history has ever attained a more farflung influence on the face of the earth through the presence of its citizens and institutions. In the light of the country's multicultural genesis, multiethnic population, and multinational commitments, loyalty to it may well require a repudiation of its long held contradiction

of unilinguality. A more cosmopolitan view of the national experience to date suggests that bilingualism is a minimum requirement for true Americanhood. Texas is fortunate to provide a natural laboratory to put these notions to the test. Our neighborhood with Mexico and Latin America makes the need to test ourselves successfully a matter of hemispheric responsibility. Let us not forget that by the time this year's first-graders are in their middle thirties, English will have become a minority language in the hemisphere. Native speakers of Spanish and Portuguese together will number roughly twice as many as those will be native speakers of English. Spanish surnamed U.S. citizens will then number approximately twenty million, of whom about four million will be Texans.

If the evidence produced, the statistics quoted, and the arguments marshalled thus far are in any way credible, we can no longer waste time arguing whether bilingualism is a sound educational concept for *all* children in this state, whether their mother tongue is English, Spanish, Czech or German. Of course, the need for such education is greatest among children for whom English is not native. There, the backlog of educational dereliction requires urgent and massive corrective measures.

Psychologists agree that more than half of the growth of intelligence in an individual's lifetime occurs prior to the age when children normally begin school. We are, then, talking about an ambitious undertaking which goes much farther than our traditional school time tables. Ideally bilingual education should begin no later than the third birthday of a child and extend as much as possible beyond the end of the present sixth grade. We are also talking about monumental tasks of specialized teacher training, development of new teaching tools, expansion of in-service programs, and considerable expenditure of additional resources. The Texas Bilingual Educational Act appropriated no fresh monies for its implementation. It assumed the use of federal appropriations. Nevertheless, the Texas Education Agency has created the Division of International and Bilingual Education under the able direction of Dr. Severo Gómez as Assistant Commissioner of Education. The Bilingual Education Act of January 2, 1968 authorized fifteen million dollars *for all the nation* for the fiscal year ending June 30, 1968. Actually no appropriation was made until the year ending June 30, 1969. Even then, of the authorized thirty million dollars, only ten was appropriated nationally, of which Texas received only two. For the present fiscal year of 1970–71, our state will share only four million of the total national appropriation. These amounts are obviously inadequate. In 1969–70 only 10,003 Texas students could benefit from the national Bilingual Education Act appropriation. For the year 1970–71, the beneficiaries nearly doubled to 20,000. Even then, they continued to be almost exclusively Mexican-American, out of a total potential Mexican-American elementary and secondary school constituency of some 600,000! The challenge of supplementing the national appropriation is even more staggering if bilingual education is to be made available to the total Texas primary and secondary school population numbering in 1970 some three million. Since we have couched the concept of bilingualism in the context of fraternity, it is not unfitting to remember the Biblical word, "For where your treasure is there will your heart be also."

This writer happens to be one of those fortunate bilinguals educated by Church institutions. Across his twenty-three years of intimate knowledge of Texas, he has learned that its resourcefulness, often expressed in ingenious practices of prejudice, is even more ingenious in its practice of fraternity— and that it is willing to pay the price of any challenge if it is convinced of its worth. Let us hope it will no longer be dubious about the rich dividends of bilingualism as education for fraternity.

JESUS LUNA

Jesus Luna (who presently holds a Ford Foundation Grant in Mexico City, Mexico) came from a migrant worker's family to earn a B.A. from Pan American University and a M.A. from East Texas State University. "Luna's Abe Lincoln Story," chronicles Mr. Luna's early life "on the road of hope" and gives some insight into the New Chicano consciousness. The goal of the Mexican American is not simply faceless assimilation, but rather they now demand cultural acceptance, and their rightful place as "equals" in a society of equals.
By permission of the author.

Luna's Abe Lincoln Story

For many years the word Chicano had a derogatory meaning, but today the term has acquired a new meaning and the new *breed* of Mexican Americans uses this term to designate themselves as a proud minority group. In the context I do not consider myself a Mexican or a Mexican-American, but a Chicano. My parents Gustavo and Antonia Luna were born in Texas, but my grandparents were born in Mexico; thus I am of Mexican descent but I am an American. Being an American is what constitutes one of the problems that the second largest minority group in America is faced with today. My ethnic group, which consists of over six million Chicanos, has not received the benefits that were guaranteed to us in 1848 under the Treaty of Guadalupe Hidalgo that ended the Mexican War. Since 1848 the Anglos in Texas, southern California, New Mexico, and Arizona have looked at the Chicanos condescendingly and have never treated them as their equals. Today, in the 1970s, the decade of the Chicanos, the White Anglo Saxon Protestant (WASP) establishment recognizing the growth of self identity among Chicanos, has suddenly become aware of and wary of a new feeling among Chicano groups in the United States—especially where Chicano concentration is high. As usual the Anglos are still trying their piece-meal tactics to appease the "ig-

347

norant dirty greasers" and many of the *tio tacos* band with the White Establishment to sell their own brown brothers' votes. However, it is my hope that in the 1970s the new breed of Chicanos that went to college in the 60s will not buy the Anglo's loaf of bread but instead sell a new program to their people and keep the interest of the Chicanos in mind.

The following is an account of my life as a migrant child. To those who have argued that the Chicanos were happy, I reply with a resounding *NO.* I was never a happy child; in fact I never felt that I was a child since I had to work from an early age. My recollections of the migrant life are sometimes vague and brief, other experiences are touching, and a few have left their mark on me and have scarred me for life.

I, Jesus Luna, and my family were migrant workers in the 1950s. But our migrations finally came to a halt after I persuaded my parents to stop migrating for the sake of their children so that we could attend school. Since my father was and is a sensible person he agreed and the dreaded cycle ended. Today I am a Ph.D. student at North Texas State University.

There are eleven children in my family, six brothers and five sisters. Most of my family live in Edinburg and the majority of them still live close to my parents on 28th Street in Edinburg, Texas. I guess this in a way illustrates the closeness of the family in the Chicano way of life. My two older brothers, who never finished high school, work as foremen in a meat dehydrating plant outside of Edinburg. Both of them live on 28th Street. My four older sisters are married. The eldest lives in Elsa about five miles away from Edinburg; two others live on 28th Street, however, they and their husbands still migrate to California to pick grapes. Another sister also lives in Edinburg about five blocks away from home. Of the rest of the family; two of my younger brothers are sophomores in college; the youngest is in the seventh grade; and my other younger sister is a sophomore in high school. One thing that should be noted is that before I finished school none of my brothers or sisters had finished school. Today, however, I believe all my younger brothers and sister will finish high school and obtain a college degree. This is the present condition of the Luna family. My father still works as a farmer but owns his home, and my mother is perhaps the best housewife in the world.

The present status of the Luna family varies radically from the Luna's of the 1950s. In 1950 my father, Gustavo, bought a little one room shack behind his mother-in-law's house, here my parents and eight children lived. Dad's economic situation at the time was very bad and since he worked as a farm laborer he was only paid 60 or 70 cents an hour, hardly enough to feed eight kids much less clothe them and provide for medical attention. My two older brothers helped out however, by going out and picking carrots or oranges, or doing almost any job that would bring in a few cents to supplement the family income. Our family was too large for its income and it must have been extremely difficult for my father, who lived close to his in-laws, to see us go without many of the things we needed.

Faced with a difficult economic situation Dad decided to migrate. Our poor economic condition left my father no alternative but to follow the cotton harvest and employ his children as cotton pickers to increase the family income. Now we had always picked cotton in the Valley but after the cotton harvest was over in the summer of 1950 we migrated north. Dad had an old 1946 red pickup, a Ford, I think, and he persuaded several families to migrate with us that first year. Trying to get the people together was a little difficult, and in the evening after work Dad would go and talk to several families like the Melchors, the Granados, and the Aguilar's explaining to them the benefits of going on migration, how the trip would take place, where we would go from Edinburg, how far it was, the nature of the harvest at our destination point, and the conditions of the homes we were going to.

When he finally persuaded them to go everything was set for the day of departure. This was a big day for everyone. The kids would be running around the trucks, joyful because they were going on a trip, the adults would be well dressed and the few belongings were packed into the pickups and cars. Usually Dad's pickup and later on his truck would be the lead automobile. It reminds me today of Wagon Train, and I'll never forget my father giving instructions and wearing his light brown Stetson. Just before we left those relatives or friends remaining behind would gather around the caravan to wish us well. After the cars were checked, tires, oil, water, etc., the migration began and everyone waved goodbye and well-wished one another. We left the X Valley with a prayer asking God to grant us a safe journey. (It was in search of a better economic standard that we migrated. The search of the dollar was the reason that a man with a large family migrated during the cotton harvest.) For us kids it meant two or three months away from school and we enjoyed it until we were out in the cotton fields.

On a labor migration many factors came into play which are not usually experienced by most people. As a child, for example, at the age of six or seven I felt like a young adult because I was part of a group that provided for our family. I know that I did not contribute much but nevertheless I contributed my share. There was really no childhood that I can point to because it was circumvented by work. Often during the migrations many of the families which consisted of seven or eight children had to live in a two or three room house. As a result many of the children either had to sleep with their parents or in the same room, or crowd together in another room. Many a time we had to sleep with our uncles who also traveled with us. These two uncles, Morito and Jose Maria, were Mom's brothers and she washed for them and fed them; in return they paid her fifteen or twenty dollars a week for laundry and meals.

As migrants once or twice we had to live in houses of one or two rooms with dirt floors and in most of the places there were no bathrooms or running water, outhouses were the way of life—sometimes outhouses with two holes. Poor housing, inadequate sanitation, and poor drinking water were among the major problems that we faced as migrants. The adults did not seem to mind very much if they drank water from a flowing stream or a well, but many migrant babies became ill with the water given to them. Another bigger problem was the contempt shown towards us by the Anglos in many of the towns where we stopped. In Robstown, Kenedy, Palacios, Floydada, and many other towns the Anglo community looked at us

with disgust. Many migrants suffered the misfortune of having to pay rent for the sheds where they were staying, or being asked to leave immediately after the harvest. In general the conditions that migrants lived through were terrible.

Picking cotton was no fun job. I can distinctly remember my experiences as a young migratory worker. We used to start the cotton harvest in the Lower Rio Grande Valley and after the season ended in the Valley we would start our trek from Edinburg to Robstown and on up the state of Texas until the final stop in west Texas around Lubbock or Petersburg. On this journey along the "road of hope" one would always witness broken down cars, other migrants sleeping in trucks or city parks, and countless other migrants, usually Chicanos, seeking *Patrones* or bosses to work for.

My first experience in picking cotton was in the lower Rio Grande Valley. I thought that my family was making a lot of money because we were getting paid two or two dollars and fifty cents for every hundred pounds we picked. Since we were a large family we earned roughly from thirty-five to forty-five dollars a day. As a kid I thought this was a lot of money and did not question anything. The only catch involved in picking cotton was that you had to be a darn good cotton picker to pick 300 pounds of clean cotton from sun-up to sundown.

After the cotton season ended in the Valley we would move to Robstown. I hated the town and especially the farm where we usually picked, and every year we went to the same place. This is one thing that should be noted: My father had a contact in Robstown, his brother-in-law, Fabian Vasquez. We always went to pick for his boss because Uncle Fabian would get permission from his boss to allow us to live in some of his houses (actually sheds) while we harvested his cotton crop. My father considered the contact man to be very important. Before we were ready to move after completing one harvest, he would write to one of his previous bosses or *Patrones* farther north in Palacios or Port Lavaca to see if the cotton was ready. If we did not have a *Patron* to write to then the only solution was to go to the town square of a particular town and look for a job. The town square or city park was a sight to witness. Usually the park would be filled with small caravans of trucks, pickups and cars. The rancher who needed hands to harvest his crop would come to the park. Here he could take his pick from the several groups. His decision on whom to hire was based on how much of a crop he had. For example, a caravan of forty or fifty adults would not go with him if he did not have enough houses or sheds and if he only had twenty-five acres of cotton to be harvested. If a group liked the farmer's proposition then the head of the caravan plus several other adults, usually the heads of the other families, would go and look over the crop and the houses. Back in the park the kids would wander around and talk with some of the other groups there. Some of them we knew and others were from the surrounding towns in the valley.

Getting back to Robstown, I hated the place because of its drinking water. Some of the houses here were halfway decent but some of the people who came with us to pick cotton had to stay in sheds where the farm machinery was stored because of a shortage of houses. My antagonism towards the place was based mostly on the taste of the water which was very, very salty. The only way I could drink it was if it was very cold. Sometimes Dad or someone else would drive into town and get distilled water for the babies and it was from this water that I drank most of the time while we were there. I hated myself for drinking this water since it was supposed to be for the babies, but I had resolved that I was not going to suffer.

From Robstown we usually went to El Campo or Palacios. As I mentioned it seems that every year we ended up in the same place and the same old houses because once we had picked for a "patron" Dad would write to him in advance and he would notify my father when to bring the group up. This way Dad could discover the best time to arrive and assure that we would have a job and "housing." Of course housing for migrants entitled one to four walls, a floor—sometimes a wooden floor—if we were lucky, a roof and the usual outhouse with its nest of yellow jackets. The reason Dad usually went back to the same farmer was that housing for the group that traveled with us was provided. Housing although poor was a major problem. Sometimes, some of the farmers for

whom we had picked the previous year did not wait for Dad to write and hired another group. In one such instance in El Campo we had to spend several days sleeping under the stars while Dad tried to find a *Patron* who would provide work and housing for us. During these three or four days my mother cooked in a "kitchen" which Dad constructed by tying a tarp to a tree and driving stakes into the ground. I almost want to cry now when I think about these experiences that we went through. El Campo I did not like because of the mosquitoes which would not let one sleep at night. Also this town is near the Gulf of Mexico and we spent many a day playing poker because the rain did not allow us to perform our daily labor. Sometimes we were out of work for a whole week while the rain continued, yet, we had to survive and were never subsidized by anyone.

From El Campo we usually went to Hillsboro or Waxahachie. The places we picked at in Hillsboro were always hot—that is one of my few recollections of that area other than that in the early 1950s Johnny Cash's song, *I Walk the Line,* became very popular. While we lived in Waxahachie I remember that there were some cool underground springs that flowed near the old house we lived in. I also remember the adults talking about a big city near by and I remember how I pictured Dallas lit up at night, with millions of people in the streets, all of them very happy and buying things. Most of the people that I imagined were *gringos* because I always knew that all *gringos* were rich.

From Waxahachie, West Texas would be the final destination in our "trail of tears." Petersburg or Lubbock or the surrounding towns were the places we picked in West Texas. Dad had another relative in Petersburg who was again his contact man and he would always find out and inform Dad when it was best to come up.

I have some vivid memories of Petersburg. It was here where I saw my first real snow, and the snowman that we used to read about in story books. However, it was in this northern part of Texas where I almost froze to death one cold morning when I insisted that I wanted to go with Dad to pick cotton. I was only six at the time. West Texas also provided many funny experiences: it was in Petersburg where a skunk peed on Pepe, the son of Don Inez Melchor. It was funny to us but Pepe did not appreciate it. However, this was typical of the life of the migrant cotton picker. And whether he was bitten by a snake, peed on by a skunk, or stung by a yellow jacket, he usually had no insurance to take care of him. Most of the time, to save money, we would not go to see a doctor; the only thing to do was to recover and get back to work. No one, except the migrant and his immediate family, gave a damn for the migrant's well-being. Usually when someone in the group was sick home-made remedies were used on him. If these did not work then and only then would one of us go to a doctor. This was the last resort because we could not afford to be under medical attention. In Petersburg an unusual event occurred that relates the importance placed on herbs and superstitition by the migrants.

One evening after a long day in the fields most of the men were gathered around a fire talking and telling ghost stories. One of my uncles, who was married and who migrated with us that particular year had sent his son, Alonzo to get him a pack of cigarettes. It had rained that evening and as Alonzo was coming back he slipped and fell. Since he had always had problems with his bones because of the lack of vitamin D, Alonzo broke his leg when he fell. He was immediately rushed to a hospital. That evening my older brother, Gumaro, just before going to bed went out to urinate and later claimed that he saw (or envisioned) Alonzo who told him, "Cousin, give me your hand, I have hurt myself." My brother knowing that Alonzo was in the hospital walked back in and did not say a word to anyone but was badly frightened.

The next morning his whole body was swollen. No one knew what was wrong and at first Mom would massage him with volcanic oil and give him hot teas made out of lemon leaves and other household remedies, but the swelling would not go away. Finally after two days Dad took Gumaro to two or three doctors in Lubbock and none of them could do anything to cure him. After the third trip to Lubbock an old man in our group said that Gumaro had been badly frightened by someone or something and that he could cure him. My dad agreed and allowed the old man to treat Gumaro for three consecutive nights. The old man

would place him on a flat surface, cover him with a white sheet and sweep over the sheet. After the three nights were up the swelling went down and Gumaro was his normal self. Unbelievable but true. I was a witness to this and call it witchcraft or what you may but it worked and this is what a lot of the migrants practice either for "evil eye" or other maladies.

The injustices one suffered in the form of low pay for back breaking labor were minor compared to the degradation one suffered psychologically. The shacks where we lived as migrants were fire traps in the worst of shapes. The Luna family, however, usually obtained the best "home" when we went to a certain area because my Dad, as head of the group and owner of a truck, which he bought in 1952 in Hillsboro. was considered as the *Troquero* or *jefe* (leader). Since Dad carried almost everyone's belongings in his truck free of charge it was only natural that his family get the best residence. The only other compensation Dad received for being head of the group was that when we started to pick for a *patron,* the pickers would get a certain price for the pounds of cotton they picked, while Dad received 25 cents per hundred pounds for weighing the cotton and hauling it to the gin. Our group was an unusually small group and Dad and Don Melchor and the other heads of the families usually would not pick for a farmer unless housing was availabe. Most of the time the houses we stayed in were better than those of most other migrants, but they were still sub-standard. Ants, yellow jackets, cockroaches and often rats were the most common pests present in our make-to-do homes. Complaints to the owners were infrequent and were usually not voiced because of the fear of being asked to leave. Being insecure migrants striving for a livelihood four or five hundred miles from home, our parents usually suffered terrible conditions silently.

I guess the worst kind of abuse suffered by the Chicano migrant was direct embarrassment. Though most of the farmers could not speak Spanish and few of us spoke English, direct embarrassment could and did occur even to those who did not understand the English language. I suffered this embarrassment at the age of nine or ten and it scarred me for life. I will never forget when on the migration trail we stopped in a central Texas town while Dad and the other heads of families went to look at some cotton fields that this particular farmer wanted us to pick. It was in 1953 or 1954, anyway we were parked at the city park, and while Dad and the other men were gone an older member of the group and I went into a restaurant to eat breakfast and to bring back some breakfast and coffee for others. The man with me knew no English so I went along to order. At the restaurant we got a sneer from the waiter and after serving others who got there after we did he finally waited on us. I asked him very politely if we could have some breakfast. His reply was, "Sure you can have some breakfast but you will have to eat it outside." I called him a few choice words and the older man and I left the joint. From this time on I began to ask myself, why do these people hate us? Why do they treat us differently from other men? They want us to work for them—often cater to us during the harvest season—but after the harvest season is over they no longer want us around. They do not want us to talk to their daughters and even their sons adopt a condescending attitude toward us. They are willing to take our money at restaurants, and merchants and supermarkets open their doors to us on pay day yet they treat us with contempt and show no respect toward us as humans. WHY? WHY?

I could never understand this attitude towards the Chicanos as a young boy or a young man. How were they different from me? As far as I was concerned there was no human difference between us. True I had to pick cotton for a living while other farm boys my age drove their dad's tractors. The attitude of the *gringos* bothered me, but I never said much to my parents. I began to mature quicker because working for a living seems to make a person grow a little bit older. In the beginning the life of the migrant seemed to be a lot of fun and I envisioned ourselves as roaming gypsies. Yet as I started growing older and the same routine was followed year after year, the fun of migrating disappeared and disappointment and dissatisfaction set in. I realized that I was getting older, life was passing me by, and we had little other than sore backs to show for our work. I realized at the age of ten or eleven that the only way

to make a living comfortably was to get an education. Yet as migrants we attended schools only when the local authorities forced us to do so. The bosses we worked for never cared whether we went to school or not and never encouraged us to do so. Even when we did go to school while we were away from the Valley, we left very quickly because the work ended or because of the ridicule we suffered. Usually the Anglo kids would make fun of our clothes, our accent, or the beans and tortillas that we took to school for lunch. One time in West Texas I was involved in a fight in school because an Anglo kid made fun of the clothes my sister, Lucia, was wearing. That day we walked home and refused to go back to school. Afterwards we would pick cotton until about 8:30 in the morning, go home, and at 3:30 when school was out we would go back to the fields and pick cotton till dusk. This was the basic migratory pattern of our way of life from about 1950 until 1959. Dad would organize our uncles and the different families that were going to travel with us and every year the same route and routine were followed. During these years my older brothers and sisters married and for a while some of them traveled with us. Also one of my uncles, Jose Maria, married one of the daughters of the Melchor family, and more and more the group became interrelated. During these years Dad not only managed to buy a truck, in 1952, but he also purchased the two lots in Edinburg where my parents now live. This was done following the first season of migration. Afterwards he moved his one room house to its present site and he began to add to it. Sometimes my father would be the carpenter and he did as much of the plumbing as possible. Since 1951 our home has gone through several phases of "remodeling" with Dad splitting some of the work with a hired carpenter. Today our home is a frame home composed of three bedrooms, a bathroom, kitchen, and living room. At Christmas time of 1970 more remodeling was being done to the house by my father. Anyway after our migration in 1958, I noticed that I was beginning to have a more difficult time in school. So when 1959 rolled around I was the oldest child in the family still living at home. I told my mother that if they planned to leave for Robstown that year that they could count me out.

I was not going with them. If they left, I told her, I would stay with one of my aunts and go to school. My mother was furious and shocked at this obvious show of disrespect and only commented, "But you have always managed to pass." After a few minutes of debate with her I persuaded her that I was right and eventually the message was conveyed to my father who never said a word to me. My Dad is a silent type of person who speaks seldom, but since 1959 the Luna family never has migrated.

I had made up my mind that I wanted to go to school and graduate because I wanted to learn and also due to the fact that no one else in our family had really had the opportunity to go to school and to concentrate on getting a high school diploma. My two older brothers were forced to withdraw from school so they could work and help support the family and as far as my sisters were concerned, all they seemed to want was to get married, perhaps because they never did get a fair chance while in school. Too, they were constantly told by Mom to stay home and do the wash or the dishes or take care of the kids.

When we stopped migrating I began to concentrate on my studies. Dad would often take us to work on Saturdays but never did pull me out of school. I guess he began to realize how important education was. As far as his economic condition; it did not really improve. He was still getting paid seventy cents an hour on the Valley farm where he had always worked, and the only supplement to his income was the meager five cents a tree he was paid for hauling trees in his truck. Often he was allowed to be a share cropper but this was not enough to support a family of five plus a wife. However, Mother somehow or other squeezed those forty or fifty dollars Dad brought in per week and made them go a long way. Her favorite expression when we complained about the beans that we had to eat everyday was, "give thanks to God that you have something to eat."

After the migrations ceased our economic status did not improve a great deal, and it was around this time, when I was in the eighth grade, that I began to resent my father at times because he could not give us what middle class kids had. At the time I did not know how lucky I was, but I did know that other kids had better things and that was what I wanted. No, I never could understand that it took money and lots of it to feed seven people, pay bills, pay a mortgage on a house, clothe and send five children to school. Many other people, including myself perhaps, would have looked for an easy way out and would have perhaps gone to the local bars that dot highway 107 in Edinburg—El Matador, El Farol Verde, Robert's Drive Inn—or the countless other bars in Edinburg which would have been perfect places to seek refuge. Dad never did.

The only entertainment he allowed himself was a couple of beers on Saturdays and sometimes on Sundays. On Saturdays he would leave the house around 5:30 in the afternoon and return around 8:30 P.M. a little red in the cheeks, feeling high and friendly, and he would always give my little brother or sister a nickel or a dime or perhaps even a whole quarter. Everyone knew he had been drinking but no one blamed him since this was all the entertainment he obtained after working six days a week at hard labor. My Dad either dug citrus trees, or drove a tractor and for the money he was and is still paid, it is not worth it except to a man that has pride in his family. I call it pride but I really do not know what it is that has kept him going this long.

I guess I never really learned to love and appreciate my father until I moved away from home. As a teenager I resented him in a way for not being the provider that I expected. Later when I began to play in organized sports I resented him even more because he never showed an interest in what I was doing. Whether in sports or academic work my father never really seemed to care about me; yet today I know that he did and when he speaks to others about me he states with pride that I am his son.

When Dad stopped migrating he began to work full time with his old boss, Mr. B. Dad always had a job. He would work for Mr. B. before we left for the cotton harvest and after we came back he returned to his old job. Actually this is another peculiarity which made the Luna family and those that traveled with us different from many other migratory groups. Most of the people that traveled with us had a job to come back to when the cotton harvest was over; this was unlike many other migrants who came home and had no jobs and as a result in the two or three months that they were out of work they would spend their savings. Another peculiar thing about the Luna family and the other families that traveled with us was that all of us owned our homes while many other migrants only rented shacks in Edinburg or outside of Edinburg at a place called *La Hielera* (ice box). During the migration our group was also different in that we seemed to obtain better housing then most migrants and the decision on whether to work for a particular farmer or not was made by all of the heads of families and not by one single individual. Each head of a family had one vote and each individual adult who did not have a family but who traveled with the group had a vote. Usually the man with the largest family was the most influential. Our group was also different in regard to traveling accomodations. Dad never charged anyone to carry him or his few belongings in our truck as other truck owners did. Also my father never did operate like the labor contractors in California, the so-called *coyotes,* who contract people to work in a certain field and take a percentage of their earnings. Indeed it was an unusual group.

Today all of the eleven children of Gustavo and Antonia Luna are still living. Seven of us have married and only three boys and a girl remain at home with my parents. My father still works for Mr. B. and this coming year will mark the twenty-seventh year that he has worked for him. At the present he earns $1.00 per hour. My parents still regard Mr. B. as a nice old man who has helped them in time of need and as one who has loaned them money when they have needed it. They get upset when I tell them that Mr. B. has exploited the Luna's for years because even Dad's father worked for Mr. B. Yet Mom gets furious when I explain to her that the Luna's have made Mr. B. a wealthy man. The system used against my father is that of a landless man who has a family to support and the only thing he knows is farming. Mr. B. takes advantage of this and lends Dad money when he is in need, but all he has to do is call on Dad when he needs a job done and whether the temperature is 35 degrees or 110, Dad will work

for Mr. B. because he feels indebted to him. Even my mother to this day around Christmas time makes tamales to give to Mr. B., otherwise she feels that Mr. B. will not give them a $20 Christmas bonus. I constantly tell them that they have repaid Mr. B. a thousand times over because by paying them low wages Mr. B. has become a rich man. Yet, because they have drunk deeply of the old Chicano spirit that dared not raise its voice, they say nothing and still call Mr. B. a nice old man who has helped them.

This is part of the change that the Luna family has gone through since the migrations stopped in 1959. My father has settled down. Another change has been that the kids have been gaining an education and also Dad and Mom now take an interest in how the children are doing in school and who is running in local politics.

In comparing the Luna family to other migratory workers I would say we were extremely fortunate. Comparing the Luna family today to the rest of the families which migrated with us indicates that the Luna family has done much better than the rest. If we compare the Luna's and the Melchor's who were the two largest families in our group, an interview with Mr. Melchor reveals that none of his sons finished high school. He did state that they continued to migrate to West Texas often by themselves and often with another *jefe* until 1963 and by then most of his children had married. But of his eight children who used to go along with the Luna's, three of his girls married, though one later got a divorce, and the fourth girl never married and until today she helps around the house. Ramiro, his oldest son got busted for Marijuana and passing hot checks and since he was a naturalized citizen he was deported to Mexico and is currently living in Monterrey. Pepe who was about my age is a foreman in a packing shed. Of Don Melchor's two other sons, one is still a migrant and one just got out of the service. Don Melchor himself today works for a lumber yard and is an old man who forgets things easily. Thus in comparing the Melchor's and the Luna's, the Luna's appear to have done very well since 1959.

As far as the other families are concerned, my uncle, José Maria, who married one of the Melchor uncle who used to travel with us never married and is a sick man who only works part time. I never really knew what happened to the Aguilar's and as far as the Granado family, I did know one of their sons who finished school and enrolled in college.

This was the kind of life I went through in the 1950s when we migrated from town to town suffering humiliation in more ways than are mentioned. However, today in 1970, the decade of the Chicanos, times have changed and the new breed of Chicanos like me who are coming out of the colleges and universities will not accept the second class status to which our ancestors were relegated. We are willing to fight if necessary to break down the injustices done to our people. Today the new breed of Chicanos are a proud group who will not stand for stereotypes. We are a group of people who will no longer beg or request changes, instead we will demand them.

I firmly believe that in the 1970s many changes have to be made before this newly emerged group of brown people is pacified. Young Chicanos like myself who did not know any better in the late fifties and early sixties have seen and know a better way of life—a life that can be obtained only if we are offered an equal chance and treated as equals. Today especially in the United States there is much dissent and President Richard Nixon bores his audience with his pleas for unity. Well, I feel that this unity among Americans will come but it will not come; especially here in Texas, until the Anglos realize that there were Mexicans both inside and outside the Alamo. When this realization takes place perhaps a better understanding of the Chicanos and Anglos can take place in Texas. We do not want all of the pie, but we would sure like to know what apple pie tastes like. The Chicanos of the 1940s, '50s, and even early 1960s might have accepted things as they were, but today this new group of beautiful brown-skinned people who are in the universities and in the fields demand a change.

5.

THE URBAN EXPERIENCE

The Urban Experience

The last section concluded by pointing toward the emergence of a new Chicano dedicated to Bronze Power. Precisely where the movement will go no one knows, but there are weather vanes showing revolutionary winds blow strongest in the urban areas. The migration from rural America to the city has increased each decade, and Chicanos are part of this trend. The city offers excitment, jobs, and very frequently for minority groups, disillusionment. Thus new leaders will emerge from the cities and the urban areas will increasingly become the vanguard of the struggle.

To maintain that poverty in the urban areas will spark protests does not mean that rural Chicanos have a life free of poverty and exploitation. The whole thrust of previous section proves the opposite. Rather, the city presents unique circumstances that allow skillful leaders to foment change. In political terms the urban *barrios* will increase their political strength commensurate with population growth. Either politicians listen to minority votes in the cities or they become ex-politicians. Moreover, newer Chicano leaders realize that many Mexican American problems are not unique, but are a manifestation of the general problems of urban America. Consequently, look for Black and Brown coalitions forming to force change. The key to this "New Politics," as current political scientists call such coalitions, is spreading the word. In the city easier access to communication media exists, and therein lies the method to expand and improve a base of political power. The base is spreading because the Chicano continues to break out of the Southwest and concentrates in other areas of urban America as well. Hence, students need now to understand the urban experience.

The beginning selection by Arthur J. Rubel discusses Chicano attitudes in a small city in South Texas. It should point out two themes to the student. First, a city does not require a population of a million or so to create an urban experience, and secondly, *barrios* in Los Angeles, Albuquerque, or New Lots have more in common as far as economic and cultural conditions than most urban dwellers suppose. Such phenonmena as riots, then, may soon sweep small as well as large cities. The Kerner Commission Report states that poverty created the discontent that led to riots in the Black ghettoes. Consequently, a contemporary article from the thirties in the *Monthly Labor Review,* and Albert Pena's statement corroborates Rubel's findings. They demonstrate also the continuing poverty and the widespread geographic dispersal of the Chicano in the urban areas. The possibility of riots and their backgrounds, is discussed in Ralph Guzmán's report to an American G. I. Forum in Denver, and Richard Griego and G. W. Merkx's discussion of New Mexico.

Rioting has been only one manifestation of urban minority discontent. Another has been the take-over of the inner city by minorities and the confidence this dominance has given them. Elroy Bode writes of the death of an Anglo high

359

school because of a population shift in El Paso, Texas. His picture of the type of Chicano that this shift has produced offers some hint of Chicano politics of the future. Each must make his own predictions, but a reading of James Officer's and Donald Freeman's accounts of politics in South Tucson in the 1960s, where the Chicano has been a majority of the population for some time, and Guzman's sketch of California politics might help. But, the editors leave the student with Rodolfo Gonzáles' query: "What political role for the Chicano Movement?"

Arthur J. Rubel

Arthur J. Rubel (Associate Professor of Sociology, Notre Dame University) has written a well conceived account of a Texas barrio—ACROSS THE TRACKS: MEXICAN AMERICANS IN A TEXAS CITY *(1966). The excerpt reprinted below describes the attitudes and economic life of Chicanos in the* EL PUEBLO MEXICANO *of South Texas. From Arthur Rubel,* ACROSS THE TRACKS: MEXICAN AMERICANS IN A TEXAS CITY *(University of Texas Press, 1966).*

Two Sides Of The Tracks

New Lots is a city bisected by the railway of the Missouri Pacific. In 1921, the town's first year, the north side of the tracks were allocated by municipal ordinance to the residences and business establishments of Mexican-Americans, and to industrial complexes. Mexican-Americans refer to the north side of the tracks as Mexiquito, *el pueblo mexicano, nuestro lado;* even the traffic light north of the tracks is referred to as *la luz mexicana.* The other side of the tracks is spoken of as *el lado americano, el pueblo americano,* and other similar terms. Those who live south of the tracks also distinguish the two sides: "this side" and "the other side," "our side," and "their side," and "Mexican town" are all descriptive terms heard in the city of New Lots.

The north and south sides of the railway are far more than geographical zones useful for purposes of description. Each side of the tracks is a society with its own characteristics; each has a peculiar rhythm. Each side acts on the basis of understandings that were founded on separate traditions. Finally, each side of the tracks reacts to its social universe in terms of a distinctive framework of experience.

The parental generation of New Lots attempts to bring up the children with a sense of right and wrong, one of which is rewarded, the other pun-

361

ished. The right and wrong of one side of the tracks, however, may conflict, and often does, with the sense of propriety of those of the other side.

Until 1946 all of those who lived south of the tracks were subsumed under the term Anglo-Americans, while those residing north of the railway were known as Mexican-Americans. The terms and their equivalents perpetuated the concept that the city was divided into two mutually exclusive zones—this side and the other side, *el pueblo mexicano and el pueblo americano.* (Exceptions to the general nature of the north-side population were provided by about twelve Negro families, who existed as an encapsulated community with its own elementary school and a small church. Furthermore, several Anglo-Americans married to Mexican-American spouses lived surrounded by the Mexican-American community.)

On the south side of the railway the descriptive "Mexican" or "Mexican-American" may often be used pejoratively, but such is not always the case. These terms may simply be used to help describe some presumed or actual general characteristic of the group to which the person referred to belongs; it lends context to the remark. For example, "That Mexican boy who works for me" may simply refer to the only bilingual employee of a business firm. Of course, it may also be meant in a derogatory way, pointing out some characteristic which that employee presumably shares with others of the Mexican-American group, a characteristic not possessed by Anglo-Americans. The critical feature of the utterance, therefore, is not the word "Mexican," but the relative stress which the speaker places on that word. If he stresses the word "Mexican," thus differentiating it from the rest of the statement, it can with a great deal of justice be considered an aspersive remark. On the other hand, if "Mexican" is accorded the same relative stress as the other words, we may rest assured that it is meant as a specifier, not as a depreciative. In any case, the person to whom reference is made will almost surely consider the remark pejorative because of the use of the word "Mexican," however it may be stressed. Such is the manner in which the nuances of language keep alive antagonism and mutual hostilities between the two ethnic groups.

In New Lots, Mexican-Americans almost always attach an explanatory preface to a description of the actions of someone else of the city. This preface places into a larger context the actions of the individual mentioned by intimating that so-and-so performed this action in such a manner *because* that is the way in which the generic Anglo-American does things, or because that is the fashion of the Mexican-American.

A number of other descriptives are used to imply a different way of life as perceived from one side of the tracks about the other. The north side of the railway is spoken of as Mexiquito—Little Mexico—or Mexican-town. *That* side is contrasted with *this* side, and *their* side with *our* side. When an Anglo-American speaks of the Mexican-American segment of the population, he says "they," "them," "the Mexicans," or, more politely, "the Latins." Use of any of those terms encompasses all those residents of New Lots whose background contains some Mexican or Spanish ancestry. The terms are therefore inclusive of a varied group of individuals, for its members are by no means genetically homogeneous, nor possessed of a common citizenship status. A Mexican-American of New Lots may be a tall person of slender stature with blue eyes, blonde hair, and a nose structure either long and slender or snubbed and slender. The term will also subsume those whose pigmentation is dark, whose stature is short and stout, and whose features include brown eyes, straight black hair, a wide nose, and a trace of epicanthic fold over the eye.

A large proportion of the 9,000 Mexican-Americans have either immigrated to the city from the Republic of Mexico in recent years, or are the children of immigrants. Many of the north-siders, however, are individuals from families which have lived for the past two hundred years on the Texas side of the international boundary. Nevertheless the terms used by Anglo-Americans to describe the Mexican-Americans of New Lots refer to citizen and noncitizen alike; to recent immigrant and native-born American; and to those who speak only Spanish, those who are bilingual, and the small number who speak only English. In New Lots the most common denominator of those recognized as Mexican-Americans is the possession of a progenitor of Mexican or Spanish descent.

Today's Anglo-American group of New Lots also represents a variety of distinctive social, religious, and racial backgrounds. The term Anglo-American is umbrellalike and covers a variety of hyphenated Americans: German-Americans; Swedish-Americans; English-, Irish-, and Scotch-Americans; Italian-Americans; and even Japanese-Americans. Persons in these categories are *never* spoken of in terms of their subgrouping, and the subject comes up only during discussions of parental and grandparental backgrounds. By contrast, those with one or more Spanish or Mexican ancestors are *always* designated by Mexican-American, Latin American, or a similar term.

The approximately 6,000 Anglo-Americans in New Lots belong to a number of different religious persuasions. Some are Catholics, but they are relatively few, as the overwhelming majority are Protestants. The churches with the largest memberships are the Baptists and the Methodists, but there are also strong representations of Presbyterians, Christians, Episcopalians, and Seventh-Day Adventists. The Reorganized Church of Latter-Day Saints and a number of Pentecostal groups, supplemented by a small Christian Science institution, complete the roster.

Although the founding stratum of Anglo-American society in New Lots was composed of well-to-do emigrants from small towns of the north-central and north-eastern states of this nation, as well as from Canada, they were joined by a later influx of poor Southerners from East Texas, Louisiana, Mississippi, and Georgia. Each segment contributed its mores to the Anglo-American society of this city. But the alternative ways of behavior of the many strands in the south-side Anglo society tend to be minimized, and the more universal aspects of the "Anglo way of life" are maximized in the face of the numerically more important Mexican-American segment of the town. From the commencement of social life in New Lots the Anglo-American group has striven to protect its mode of living from Mexican-American influences, while assuming at the same time that the Mexican-American way of life should and would be changed.

Today in New Lots, Mexican-Americans speak of the others as *anglos, angloamericanos, bolillos, gavachos,* and *gringos.* When speaking of themselves, the Mexican-Americans speak of the *chicanos* or *la raza;* they also employ two other terms, the *mexicanos* and the *latinos,* or *latinoamericanos.* The last two are utilized only in the presence of a *bolillo* with whom one is not acquainted. *La raza* groups together all those in the world who speak Spanish; it implies both a mystical bond uniting Spanish-speaking people and a separation of them from all others.

The manner in which a Mexican-American attacks a problem, or the way in which an individual chicano conceptualizes a problem, is generalized to indicate that that particular coping behavior or conceptualization is peculiarly chicano. Mexican-Americans are wont to speak of generic attitudes or behaviors uniquely chicano. Quite often the contrast between a presumed Mexican-American solution to a problem and that which an Anglo-American would elect is set forth in the form of a self-turned witticism. For example, Mexican air-conditioning is described as the emptying of a sack of dry ice in the rear seat of an automobile. The self-turned witticism takes other forms as well. At times when the very popular tune "Mexico! No hay dos" blares from the jukebox, a wit exclaims "Gracias a Dios!" (There is but one Mexico! Thank God!)

The numerous stories and the often-quoted witticisms expressive of ambivalence and inconsistency—supposedly inherent traits of the Mexican-American—are tokens of the cultural and social fact that the Mexiquito Mexican-Americans are across the tracks from the Anglo-Americans, and across the frontier from the wellsprings of their traditional culture. Neither fish nor fowl, they are at home with neither of the groups that are significant to them. A young man who is a native-born citizen of the United States, as are his wife and children, posed the poignant problem of identity: "The other day my boy came home from school and asked me, 'Daddy, am I an American citizen?'"

As one walks across the tracks along the main thoroughfare of the city, he leaves one kind of scene and enters another. North of the tracks the whirring sounds of the mechanical belts, which bring the crates of packed vegetables and fruits from packing shed to motor truck and railroad car, are heard throughout the day and often until midnight. Interspersed with this north-side sound is the raucousness of the *ranchero* tunes from the juke boxes of the thirteen *cantinas* of that side of the tracks. These bars along the thoroughfare form the most popular type of commercial enterprise owned by Mexican-Americans, with the exception of food markets. Ten grocery stores front on the Boulevard on the north side, and more than fifty small neighborhood grocery stores are distributed in the residential areas. Although they are conveniently located, their stock is small; most of the smaller groceries cannot sell either fresh meat or milk products, for example, because they lack refrigerating facilities. Consequently, here the forgetful housewife purchases an onion, a single tomato, or a loaf of bread. The major family shopping is done in one of the larger grocery stores, where beans, flour, and rice may be purchased in sacks weighing twenty or fifty pounds. On Friday and Saturday nights the sidewalks in front of the three largest groceries north of the railway are thronged with shoppers; with boxes of groceries and sacks of staples, the families await the truck or station wagon provided by the store to carry them home to the peripheries of the north side, or to the vegetable farms where their cabins are located.

Three of the largest stores fronting on the main street sell work clothing. Prominently displayed in the show windows are high rubber boots, so useful for those who must work in the irrigation canals; denim and gabardine shirts and trousers; and the characteristic wide-brimmed straw hats, which deflect the rays of the sun from the face of the agricultural wage laborer. Two of the large clothing stores on the north side are owned and managed by European Jewish immigrants who escaped from the Polish *pogroms;* the other is the property of a Catholic chicano, who is so devout that he is called Jesusito—Little Jesus.

Four of the shops along the north Boulevard specialize in lending money to Mexican-Americans at usurious interest rates: 50 percent of the principal for short-term, small loans. A number of retail outlets sell used furniture and household appliances. In fact, more stores sell used articles of clothing and furniture than sell those goods new. Although one of the three drug stores of the north side boasts a licensed pharmacist, all three are heavily stocked with well-advertised patent medicines, which are supplemented by an inventory of brightly packaged *medicinas caseras*—home cures. Mostly balms made from herbs, barks, roots, and oils, these are wrapped in the colorful emblems of Don Pedrito or La Palma, the two wholesale distributors, whose traditional *remedios* are sold throughout South Texas. These remedies are retailed in New Lots at two other shops on the north side as well, both of which also sell Spanish-language periodicals and books. *Policía,* the Spanish equivalent of the Police Gazette, rests between volumes on how to learn English in just a few weeks and a book of instructions in the art of bewitching and beguiling by means of charm and incantation. In addition, traditional remedies are sold in several of the ten grocery stores along the Boulevard.

The remaining frontage on North Boulevard is occupied by a movie house dedicated to the showing of Spanish-language films, by seven restaurants, seven gasoline service stations, three bakeries, a tortilla factory, two photographic studios, a window-glass shop, a shoe repair store, a beauty shop, and a dry-cleaning establishment. All of the restaurants and bars are licensed for the sale of beer, a prodigious amount of which is consumed during the oppressively hot, humid months between April and October.

In Mexiquito, New Lots' north side, is a total of five elementary schools. One is attended exclusively by Negro children; another is a Catholic parochial institution attended by 575 students, of whom 25 are Anglos. The remainder of the grade schools are attended exclusively by Mexican-Americans. It is estimated that the Mexican-American students in the elementary grades total 3,100, but the number of registrants varies markedly according to the migratory work cycle. For example, in the 1957–1958 school year 400 more children were registered in the eighth week of the term than in the first week. During the same year there were 40 more registrants in the tenth week than in the eighth.

Of course, the growth cycle of the fruits, vegetables, and cotton, on which most of Mexiquito's families are dependent for a livelihood, varies from year to year, and school registrations reflect those variations in crop cycles. For example, there were 133 fewer registrants in the eighth week of the 1958–1959 term than in the previous year, and 10 fewer in the tenth week.

In Mexiquito, where most of the students do not continue in school beyond the primary grades, officials estimate a drop-out rate of 75 percent at the sixth-grade level. Because relatively few of those who attain a sixth-grade level ever participate in activities of the senior high school, the administration has originated a special certificate of achievement to be awarded those who discontinue their studies at this time.

There are a number of factors which mitigate against continuance of studies in senior or even junior high school for the bulk of the Mexican-American youngsters. Undoubtedly, the most important single problem is that posed by financial hardship in the families dependent on wage labor in agriculture and other unskilled employment. Furthermore, it is unquestionably true that many of the children are simply not motivated to continue studies past the sixth-grade level, as is true of many others who are not Mexican-Americans. But there are factors which are peculiarly applicable to the bicultural circumstances found in New Lots, factors which discourage students from Mexiquito.

Teachers and administrators of the city school system place an extraordinary emphasis on what might best be thought of as "civic responsibilities" and "personal hygiene," or "citizenship," if you will. This emphasis is apparent in all grades of the school system, but its intensity is exaggerated at the junior- and senior-high-school levels. The New Lots school system is organized to make of its students mirror-images of contemporary Anglo society, a type of society in which one's primary orientations, even if only on the surface, are toward responsibilities to civic and religious groups in which one holds membership. Later sections of this volume will point out that such orientations contrast with the basic values of the Mexican-American society. In many instances it seemed

that the personnel of the school system were intent on developing Anglo-Americans out of young Mexican-Americans as a primary goal, and paid far less attention to their academic achievements. For example, an administrator commented as follows about the admission procedures with regard to the transfer of Mexican-American children from the elementary school in Mexiquito to the junior high school located south of the tracks.

We try to get kids' hair cut, get 'em to look like the rest; cut off the *pachuco* style, and the bowl-type haircut. You've been down to Old Mexico where they go around with their shirts unbuttoned all the way down to the navel, and then they tie it around their waist. They think it makes them look sexy. We can't have that here.

Another said:

I don't know what you think about it, but we screen our kids before they are admitted to the school. If a kid wants to stay he has to get a good haircut, cut off the sideburns; we don't allow any mustaches in this school, once the subject has begun to shave.

Despite such hazards a growing number of Mexican-American youngsters enter and graduate from junior and senior high school. Education has assumed major importance as a criterion of achieved social status among young people of Mexiquito. They are quite aware that education, in particular English-language skills, is a prerequisite for attainment of improved occupation and income in the New Lots society. Increased income gained from steady, "clean" employment is the prize won by those who have gained fluency in English.

During the Second World War and the conflict in Korea a number of chicano servicemen received training as clerical workers, mechanics, and technicians. After the wars many returning servicemen took advantage of veterans' benefits to continue their education. Today's work force in Mexiquito, unlike that of former years, contains a significant proportion of laborers engaged in occupations other than "stoop" or "dirty" work. Some chicanos are engaged as physicians, teachers, nurses, pharmacists, and ministers of religion. Many others are salesclerks, and most clerical positions in New Lots—north and south side—are filled by qualified chicano men and women. Furthermore, several retail businessmen today compete successfully with their Anglo counterparts.

These chicanos aspire toward life goals which include social equality with Anglos. Some distinguishing features of this aggregation of mobile Mexican-Americans are its aspirations toward such status symbols as regular income derived from "clean," that is, nonagricultural, employment, English-language skills, high-school and college education, and possession of such other status markers as automobiles, refrigerators, television sets, and barbecue "pits." Among chicanos the status marker which excites the most comment is the type of house in which an individual resides, and the neighborhood in which it is located, that is, whether it is found in *el pueblo mexicano* or *el pueblo americano.*

Within Mexiquito one fails to discover neighborhoods marked by distinctive life styles indicative of social-class differentials. If one strays from the main Boulevard the dust of the unpaved side streets clings to face, hands, and clothing during the hot, humid spring and summer months. In autumn and winter the passage of pedestrian or automobile along these side streets is made difficult, or sometimes impossible by mud and standing water. Homes are generally impoverished and unpainted, with here and there a brightly painted building surrounded by a high wire fence. The residences of the north side range from one-room shacks, consisting of corrugated paper stretched around four posts and covered by a roof of planks, to multi-room structures of wood or plaster, handsomely maintained and painted in bright colors of blue, green, orange, pink, or white. In these, a visitor finds the appurtenances of middle-class life: a bright new refrigerator, a large gas stove and oven, an electric mixer for cooking, an electric washing machine, a suite of well-padded furniture, and, sometimes, a cocktail bar. Homes such as these are scattered throughout Mexiquito's

neighborhoods, where they house teachers, pharmacists, salesclerks, successful businessmen, commercial truckers, and supervisory employees in the packing sheds.

The buildings just described, and the material goods which they contain, are in marked contrast to most of the homes in any Mexiquito neighborhood. Most households north of the tracks clearly show the effect of a prevailing wage of fifty cents an hour; that is, when work is available. Most of the populace of Mexiquito are dependent on seasonal work as agricultural laborers. As a consequence, incomes in Mexiquito tend to be low, seasonal, and undependable.

In this neighborhood, as in South Texas generally, most Mexican-Americans are occupied as agricultural wage laborers. Approximately two thirds of the residents of the north side are employed as field laborers, most of whom are forced by dire necessity to migrate between March and December of every year in search of employment. A study of the earnings of wage laborers residing in South Texas shows that the average daily earnings of a farm worker were as low as $4.02, and that the daily wages earned by seasonal workers while employed in nonagricultural tasks averaged $5.03. These estimates are based on a sample of 594 chicano workers. During late fall and early winter, when agricultural workers reside in this region, the average daily earnings amounted to $4.91. The wage scales which reign here rank among the very lowest in the nation.

Independent calculations made in Mexiquito during the course of the present study fully support the reports by Metzler and Sargent. According to our figures, seasonal workers seldom earn more than $4.50 for a full day's work in the fields around Mexiquito, and even those who are employed as delivery truck drivers, package-boys in grocery stores, and other work of that ilk, earn between $3.50 and $4.00 for a full day's employment. Moreover, those who have been able to secure "clean" nonagricultural, jobs consider themselves peculiarly fortunate because of the regularity of the employment. The low wage scale is not the only serious problem which seasonal workers confront while at home base; as has already been implied, *under*employment in Mexiquito is at least as important! During the period in which they are not migrating in the northern states, chicano agricultural laborers are insured employment only three out of six work days in any single week. The study by Metzler and Sargent found underemployment of laborers to be a problem of utmost gravity throughout the south of Texas.

As a consequence of the underemployment and depressed wage scale, which characterize the Valley economy, almost all residents of Mexiquito who are employed as farm laborers must migrate periodically to other sectors of the nation to augment their income. In 1958 a total of 7,637 migrants left New Lots and a nearby smaller town in search of work during the spring, summer, and fall months of the year. The sum represented approximately 90 percent of the total of interstate migrants, and 60 percent of those who migrated within the boundaries of Texas. In 1956 an incomplete tabulation reported that 4,005 migrants had left the city in search of work elsewhere in the nation. Based on a sample of thirty Mexiquito households, the average earnings per migrant household amount to $2,400 in a prosperous year (1957).

The depressed wage scale which characterizes agricultural employment in Mexiquito affects the wage scale of nonagricultural employees as well. Only those employers of New Lots who are engaged in interstate commerce offer employment which pays laborers one dollar an hour, the minimum federal wage. Most of the work available to the unskilled and semiskilled workers of Mexiquito pays between forty and seventy-five cents per hour. Despite the comparatively low wages, steady, nonagricultural employment in New Lots is at a premium. Those who earn as much as $40.00 per week comment that "We're never going to be millionaires but we've come a long ways," while a young family head who earns $27.00 for a sixty-six-hour work week recalls that when he received his first pay check, "I thought I was rich."

There are some Mexican-Americans in Mexiquito who earn well above $30.00 and $40.00 per week, but not many. Among them are one physician, thirty school teachers, approximately twenty successful merchants, some commission-salesmen, and ten municipal employees other than teachers. Those chicanos who do not regularly migrate from Mexiquito regard themselves as a fortunate few, and are so regarded by others. Although their wages are by no means high when compared with wages elsewhere in the nation, their employment is steady and not dependent upon the vagaries of the weather.

Several reasons are advanced by employers for the low wage scale which prevails in the city. Some assert that their trade will not permit an increase in the wages of those whom they employ, and others claim that they do not raise wages of their employees for moral reasons. "Some of those who know the Mexicans best tell us that if we *have* to raise their wages, to do it slowly because their moral fiber can't stand too much money all at one time," according to one Anglo employer.

There are, however, more compelling factors which contribute to the unusually low rate of pay in this city. New Lots' location, just across the international boundary with Mexico, makes it very attractive to illegal immigrants. Inasmuch as the dollar is worth more than twelve times the Mexican peso, wages in dollars seem incredibly high to the "wetback." One young, native-born citizen of the United States described the economic situation succinctly.

The bad thing about New Lots is that people are always wanting to work for less than you are and take your job. Jobs are hard to get; suppose Mr. Smith went up to a boy on the street, one who spoke English, and said to him: "Do you want a job in a store?" "Sure!" he would say. "You bet!" Maybe he wouldn't even ask what the pay was, but if they offered him $18.00 or $20.00 and I'm getting $35.00 he would take it like that!

Then Mr. Smith would come over to me and say: "Well Telésforo, things are slow at the store, and I'm afraid that we're going to have to let you go." That's the trouble with the Mexican people; we need the money so bad, we have to feed our kids, we have to get frijoles into the house. Any job is good; we need the money real bad, and we'll work for anything!

Take that Señora Filomena, she works for any money. One of us—people who were born here in this country—will be working for an Anglo as a maid and getting $8.00 a week, ironing. She'll work from eight in the morning until two in the afternoon. But when someone like Señora Filomena comes around from Mexico she won't even ask what the Anglos will pay her. She'll work from seven until seven and when they hand her $3.00 at the end of the week there's nothing she can say about it. All she wanted was work so that she could get some food in the house. You see, that's the trouble—we don't even have any way to be sure that we have a job. Our people will work for anything, they'll take your job away from you.

Between 1946 and 1957 some, but not all, status-conscious and upwardly mobile young veterans of the Second World War moved across the tracks to the Anglo side. In 1957 a census counted 150 such mobile families. During 1958 four intimate acquaintances of mine made inquiries of realtors about property located on the Anglo side, and so the trend continues. Some of those chicanos now living south of the tracks reside in elaborate two-storied homes, or in more recently constructed ranch-type houses. These tend to cost a sum which amounts to more than $10,000. On the other hand, some who have moved across the tracks now reside in square, weathered, board buildings. In any case, the monetary value of the residence is of far less importance than is the fact that it is located in *"el pueblo americano."*

Some generalizations may be advanced about those chicanos who have elected to move south of the tracks. They are less than fifty years old; the rarely encountered oldsters prove to be widowed parents residing with a married son or daughter. The great majority of those who have moved from the north side are veterans of either the Second World War or the Korean conflict. Those who corss the tracks take advantage of federal veterans' legislation to facilitate the purchase of their house lot, and the construction or remodeling of

their homes. The young men are all bilingual, but some of their wives speak only Spanish. None of these south-side chicanos work as "stoop" laborers in agricultural season labor, and their annual income ranges from $2,400 to $20,000. However, the *sum* of the income is of far less significance than its dependability. All chicanos living across the tracks today are either salaried or self-employed. In many families both husband and wife work; their unvarying income, regardless of its total worth, permits them to engage extensively in credit buying. It is a generally acknowledged fact that one need not possess a handsome income in order to make expensive purchases. Chicanos who move to the Anglo side of town represent an aggregation of upwardly mobile young people with steady incomes.

Those who move south of the tracks and others who seriously contemplate the action share significant objective indicators of social-class status. They have completed elementary or high school, are employed in "clean" occupations, and boast dependable incomes; they also share corollary indices of class position, for example, substantial homes, relatively new automobiles, and such indoor appurtenances as television sets, refrigerators, ovens and stoves, and indoor plumbing.

Not all those who possess these material and cultural goods elect to move to the Anglo side of the tracks. Some decide to erect new homes and bring up their children in one of Mexiquito's neighborhoods, while others leave the city entirely. Whether it is appropriate to move across the tracks and be associated with the *bolillos* is a debate which stirs strong sentiments among chicanos whose acquisition of the aforementioned prerequisites of status mobility makes such a move attractive. Those electing to leave Mexiquito contend that one's obligations are restricted to himself and his family, and that a move to the other side will show Anglos that chicanos are as good as they are. Those who remain in Mexiquito, on the other hand, express the point of view that the more successful chicanos have an obligation to show or demonstrate to the less motivated how to achieve a "better" mode of life. However, from information garnered in private conversations, it appears that those who elect not to leave Mexiquito, although financially capable of doing so, feel less adequate and more timid about moving into *el pueblo americano.* In some cases a wife or coresident mother speaks little or no English, or one of the parents fears that his children's darker pigmentation will invite open hostility from the new neighbors. Hostilities are not, however, unidirectional, for some of the aspiring Mexican-Americans give as their reasons for not moving across the tracks the undesirability of living next door to "white hilly-billies," or to "white trash."

The apprehensions of those chicanos whose aspirations for enhanced social status urge them to leave Mexiquito, but who elect instead to remain, are nurtured by the evident unhappiness and disillusionment of those who preceded them across the tracks. Today, Anglos continue to lump together as "Mexicans" or "Latins," or "Latin Americans," all those with a Spanish or Mexican ancestor, regardless of the side of town on which they reside. The entire *chicanazgo*—laborer and professional alike—is lumped together by Anglos into a subordinate group based on ascribed characteristics. Those chicanos who move across the tracks prove unsuccessful in their attempts to engage Anglo neighbors in fruitful personal relationships. To an objective observer the discouraging response is less a failure by Anglos to validate the newly achieved status of the aspirant than a reflection of the manner by which Anglos organize social life. Among Anglos, friendships derive from consociation in formal corporate groups, such as Lions Club, Rotary, Optimists, Volunteer Fire Department, Chamber of Commerce, Beef Trust, Bible-Study Class, and others too numerous to mention here. By contrast, chicanos incorporate formal groups on foundations of informal associations with acquaintances or *palomillas.* Inability to engage Anglo peers in friendship relations is bitterly galling to upwardly striving chicanos. They interpret the "rebuff" as discriminatory and liken it to the rejection of Negroes by whites. Although there is no doubt that a number of fraternal clubs and church organizations are closed to chicanos, others do cultivate their participation, where as they do not cultivate that of the Negro. When the Mexican-Americans fail to join the organizations open to them, or to participate actively in them,

reluctance is interpreted by the Anglos as unfriendliness, and is considered diagnostic of a lack of civic responsibility. In the final analysis, whatever may be the objective reason why chicanos do not participate with their Anglo neighbors in activities both formal and informal, the chicanos conclude that a ceiling has been placed on their access to higher social status.

As one consequence of the assumed "rebuff," chicanos who reside in Anglo neighborhoods do not cut their ties with Mexiquito; they continue to interact with Mexiquito-based *palomillas* with the same frequency and intensity as before they moved across the tracks. The high frequency of interaction between those on the south side and those who remain in Mexiquito deters crystallization of social-class sentiments in the Mexican-American society. One young couple, who recently moved to the other side of the tracks, offer a representative example of the feelings of insecurity felt and voiced by the mobile young chicanos of New Lots. Both man and wife speak perfect English as well as Spanish and each is a high-school graduate. The young husband manages a retail store, and his wife is employed as a salesclerk elsewhere. The wife is bitterly disappointed with life "over there." "What's the matter with our people?" she asks. "Nobody comes to visit us, and we haven't made any friends over there." The disenchantment of this young couple with life across the tracks is brought forth by other young chicanos as ammunition to support their position that the more affluent and better educated chicanos should remain with "our own people."

The ethnographic evidence reveals the lack of clearly defined social classes among chicanos. Distinctions between ranked categories are at best tenuous and ill-defined, but such concepts are not totally absent from the chicanos' frame of reference. Furthermore, those sentiments seem to be increasing in significance. More explicitly, chicanos on the south side have not developed a sense of solidarity which excludes those who elect to remain in Mexiquito. Mexican-Americans motivated toward upward mobility do not conceive of themselves as filling a unique status vis-à-vis Anglos. One *never* hears south-side chicanos speak of "we," "us," "our," or similar terms to distinguish them from residents of the north side of the tracks.

Two terms, "high Mexicans" and "low Mexicans," were invented by the editor of a neighborhood news sheets to refer to those who move to the south side and to those who remain northsiders, respectively. The former term is being utilized in opprobrium, for a person mentioned in the newsheet as a "high Mexican" is one considered to have "turned his back" on the chicano way of life, though he need not be a person of either affluence or prestige. A "low Mexican," on the other hand, is one who remains a resident of Mexiquito, regardless of income and influence. Neither of the two terms has gained any currency among the chicanos, and their usage appears to be confined to the editor of the newssheet and his family.

Once a very acculturated chicano described as a "bracket" some men whom he planned to invite to an exclusive social function, but I never again heard the term. Similarly, those who perform low-paid "stoop" labor in agriculture are sometimes derogated by the adjective *tomateros* (literally, those who work with tomatoes). However, in a search for verbal symbols of social distinctions, although it proved possible to elicit the term from informants, I never heard *tomateros* used in conversation with others, or in discussions that were overheard.

New Lots today reveals two kinds of stratification, one of which is based on ascribed features, the other on achievement. In the first place, Anglos interact with Anglos, chicanos with other chicanos. For example, employees of a retail establishment, Anglo and chicano alike, may banter, bet on the outcome of sports contests, and discuss world affairs in animated fashion. But, at the coffee break or the lunch hour, members of one cultural group separate from fellow employees of the other group, whether or not English is a means of communication commonly shared. Little League baseball games draw enthusiasts throughout the season. The stands are not segregated (nor are any other publicly owned facilities) and chicanos sit right next to Anglo rooters, but an incredible lack of communication between chicanos and Anglos is evident although they may oc-cupy adjoining seats throughout the season. These are several examples of chicano-Anglo relations, but the list is too extensive to include all observations here. In New Lots one continues to be an Anglo or a Latin, a chicano or an *americano.* The society is stratified on the basis of ascribed characteristics into two cultural groups, Anglo and chicano.

Within the chicano group are present more subtle stratifications, based mainly on the kind of occupation in which one engages. Those employed as agricultural field laborers do not interact with others not so occupied, nor do members of each of the occupational groups attend public dances in the plaza on the same evening. Observations of behavior in Mexiquito indicate that the schism between agricultural laborers and others is widening, but further status distinctions within the Mexican-American society have been slower to emerge.

An emergent sentiment of class identification by status seekers who share certain symbols, in particular, type of employment and English-language skills, heralds a new phase in the history of group relations in New Lots. Upwardly mobile chicanos aspire to a life goal of equality with Anglos, whose status symbols they have acquired. If aspiring chicanos continue to feel "rebuffed" by dominant Anglos, and if they continue to feel their aspirations are capped by status ceilings, either of two results may be foreseen. Either the socially ambitious will leave the city in an attempt to resolve the perceived status inconsistency or else the qualities of alienation and anxiety, which figure so prominently in their attitudes, will increase in intensity. However, if upwardly mobile chicanos find that ceilings on their status aspirations have been removed, they will channel their energies to achievement of the social status which they seek.

SUMMARY

From its very inception the city of New Lots has been divided into two clearly demarcated neighborhoods. The north side of the railway was assigned to industrial plants and the residences of Spanish-speaking families, while the south side was allocated to English-speaking families. Over the course of the years each side of the tracks became clearly identified as either the Mexican or the Anglo side, *el pueblo mexicano* and *el pueblo americano,* this side and the other side. The lives of those on one side of the tracks were different from those on the other side; each of the neighborhoods preserved its own linguistic, educational, social, and dietary habits.

Today, as one crosses the tracks from one neighborhood to the other, a considerable change is evident from what is reported to have prevailed in the 1920s; yet each side remains distinctive. In part, the differences to be found today are due to the traditional cultures which guide the lives of those who live north and south of the tracks, respectively, but, also, the differences reflect the low income characteristic of Mexiquito families in contrast to the relatively high income of those living in *el pueblo americano.* Furthermore, the level of income is clearly associated with the amount of formal education one has achieved.

In Mexiquito there are five elementary schools, of which three are attended by Mexican-American youngsters, another exclusively by Negroes, and, finally, the fifth, a Catholic parochial school is attended by 575 children from Mexiquito and by 25 others from across the tracks. Beyond the sixth grade the relatively few children from Mexiquito (approximately 25%) who continue their education converge with their Anglo peers on the junior and senior high school, both located south of the tracks. Over the years, and especially since 1946,

increasingly large numbers of Mexican-American children have attended high school. The manifest goals of these highly motivated youngsters are English-language competence and "clean," steady employment, which is its correlate.

Moreover, beginning in 1946 the south-side bars on Mexican-American residents were lifted, and one now encounters approximately 150 such families in what was formerly an exclusively Anglo neighborhood. Characteristically, the adults of these newcomer families are young, are competent in both Spanish and English, possess a high-school or college education, and are engaged in occupations other than agricultural field labor.

Despite the differences in income, level of education, occupation, and bilingual skills, which set apart those chicanos now living south of the tracks from their counterparts in Mexiquito, no sense of solidarity binds together those on one side and excludes chicano residents of the other side. The failure of such a sense of solidarity to develop may be traced to two factors, of which the most important is that many chicanos, who are high-school and college graduates, who are employed in regular clean jobs, and who control English as well as Spanish-language skills, choose *not* to leave Mexiquito for the other side of the tracks. Secondly, those who have so elected to cross from the north to the south side have not yet been assimilated into the Anglo way of life. In New Lots, cultural differences continue to divide Anglo-American from Mexican-American, no matter on which side of the tracks a family resides.

The MONTHLY LABOR REVIEW *(see p. 178). This article, too, is based upon the writings of Paul Taylor. It tells of recruiting and conditions of a Mexican labor colony at Bethlehem, Pennsylvania from 1927 to 1930. This colony can be considered a typical one.*
By permission of THE MONTHLY LABOR REVIEW.

Mexican Labor Colony At Bethlehem, Pa.

The Mexican colony in Bethlehem, Pa., was built up mainly by the transportation from the Southwest of Mexican workers under contract with the Bethlehem Steel Co. In 1923 the settlement reached its peak population of about 1,000. Since then its numbers have rapidly declined, and in 1929 there were probably 350 or 400 in the colony, with those arriving and leaving about balancing each other. A monograph dealing with this colony forms the sixth of the published researches made by Paul S. Taylor on a grant from the Social Science Research Council and issued by the University of California. He made three visits to Bethlehem—the first in the early part of 1928 and the last in the early part of 1930.

Previous to 1923 there were only a few Mexicans in Bethlehem. In the spring of that year, however, there was an industrial revival and the steel company's idle furnaces were again started up. In order to meet the increasing demand for labor, efforts were made to secure Mexicans, with the result that between April 6 and May 30, 1923, there were 912 Mexican men, 29 women and 7 children transported from Texas to Bethlehem. Mexican workers were also sent to other plants of the company.

The recruiting was done through Texas employment agencies, cooperating with the Mexican consulate general in San Antonio. One of the company's Spanish employees was detailed to

Texas to aid in procuring and handling the desired labor. A representative of the Bethlehem Steel Co. and the Mexican consul general in San Antonio signed the contract covering the Mexican nationals shipped out of that city, as the latter wished to protect his departing countrymen.

According to the agreement, the cost of transportation was to be deducted from earnings in semimonthly installments of $3.50 each, but those who remained in the employ of the company one year were to receive back all deductions. The transportation of families was paid by the company without reimbursement. Quarters and board were provided in company houses for $1.10 a day. Wages were to be a minimum of 30 cents per hour, for such hours as were permitted by Pennsylvania statute, and were to be the same as those of men of other nationality doing the same work. Mexicans were not to be discharged without just cause, and any who might become public charges for whatever cause were to be returned at company expense to San Antonio. Under the latter provision the company did return some injured Mexicans, not only to San Antonio but to their homes in Michoacan.

The boarding house at Bethlehem was run by a commissary company which used Mexican cooks. Certain families did their own cooking. A Mexican with a small store sold groceries and other commodities which his countrymen desired, and for awhile was protected against bad debts by company deductions from wages.

The coming of the Mexicans was without doubt a shock to the people of Bethlehem and gave rise to exaggerated statements about this newly imported labor. It was rumored that these workers were strike breakers taking the places of natives who were reported to have left the plant demanding higher wages. Some weeks before there had been danger of serious labor disturbances. The company representative, however, regarded these reports as propaganda to keep Mexicans from coming to Bethlehem and denied the existence of a strike. An investigation was made by the Mexican consul at Philadelphia, who found conditions satisfactory to the imported laborers.

In 1929 a minor official of the company said, in reference to the attitude of the other workers toward the newcomers: "The other employees knew there was a shortage of labor, so they accepted the Mexicans." That the Bethlehem workers were not pleased at the advent of the Mexicans is quite obvious, however, the writer thinks, from a newspaper item published about the time of their arrival. The claim that there was a dearth of labor at this period is corroborated by the Pennsylvania State employment office report under date of March 15, 1923, that "in the iron and steel industry it is impossible to supply the needs for unskilled workers."

In order to avoid the importing of diseased workers to Bethlehem, prospective recruits were required to submit to a physical examination in Texas.

LABOR RELATIONS

Some Mexicans come to Bethlehem in search of work because they hear of the large steel mills in that locality. If they get jobs they stay, if not, they leave. Considerable numbers of them have come to Bethlehem because they had relatives already employed in the town. Frequently, money has been forwarded to Mexico or Texas to enable them to make the long trip. A remarkable instance is that of one of the group shipped from Texas in 1923, who has been followed by 7 brothers and 3 sisters, together with the families of those who were married, making a total of 30 persons.

As soon as the Mexicans reached Bethlehem in 1923 they began to scatter to look for more attractive jobs than the steel company offered. The greatest number on the pay roll of that company in any month of those who were originally brought from Texas in 1923 was 790 in May of that year. By the middle of the summer there were 24 percent less, by November the number was 53 percent under the maximum, and by the close of the same year 71 percent.

In the spring of 1930 only 46 Mexicans who were known to belong to the original group shipped in 1923 remained on the company's rolls.

Estimates of the total number of Mexicans employed in 1930 range from 90 to 150. Including Mexicans born in the United States, the writer considers 125 a conservative figure.

Upon arrival in Bethlehem the original contingents of Mexicans were concentrated in bunkhouses in a labor camp. In a little over a year, however, the scattering of Mexicans to other localities in the East, their return to the Southwest or Mexico, and their dispersion to other domiciles in Bethlehem depopulated the camp. The company then ceased to provide special arrangements for boarding Mexicans. Some of the solos were already boarding with Mexican families; now they are found boarding with Polish, Wendish, Slovak, Spanish, and Mexican families. Some of them live in groups, renting and housekeeping for themselves, each man buying his own food and doing his own cooking. Most of the Mexicans live in town houses, but a number, both of families and solos, still live in company-owned houses at the coke plant.

The greater number of the Mexicans of Bethlehem live scattered about the southern front of the works. They are not segregated in such clearly defined districts as characterize Mexican colonization in the southwestern part of the country. Early in 1929, about 124 Mexican men, women, and children were living in the neighborhood of the coke works, according to an estimate made by two Mexicans. This group included 17 families with 56 children and 34 unattached persons.

There are also a few Mexican workers who are not employed by the steel company, 4 having become machinists and 3 machinists' helpers in Allentown which is close to Bethlehem. In Bethlehem itself there were probably 2 or 3 Mexican men who are not employees of the steel company. There are 7 or 8 Mexican girls working in a cigar factory, while a couple of boys and a few girls are employed in a silk factory. A 5-and-10-cent store has a Mexican clerk, and a hotel steward employs a Mexican boy part time.

Almost all of the Mexican employees of the steel company are laborers. There are, however, a very few skilled mechanics and semiskilled workers among them. According to a statement of a Mexican, there are artisans among the Mexican laborers—carpenters and machinists—but they are not asked to follow their trades. This informant added, however, that these men do not speak English.

On the whole, the comments of numbers of executives on the Mexicans' industrial qualities were favorable. One executive, who had more direct experience with Mexican labor than some of the other reporting officials, made the following statement:

I don't think that the Mexicans are inherently different from other people. They are very easy to handle if they are given just treatment and are greeted with a smile. We rule them, but we are just. We tell them what to do and expect them to do it; but we don't worry them with what not to do. I take a personal interest in each Mexican, and have obtained their confidence. If they are sick or in trouble of any sort, they usually come and tell me. If they are sick, we send them to the hospital.

The Mexicans were reported as not standing the cold as well as other nationalities, but as being especially good for hot work on the open-hearth or blast furnaces. The rapid scattering of the Mexicans shipped to Bethlehem in 1923 to other employment led to the report that these workers were unreliable. Their "steadiness," however, was said to have increased. Possibly this latter observation was due to the departure of the more nomadic employees as much as to the better adaptation of Mexicans to industrial regularity. The following observations of a Mexican are of interest in this connection:

The foremen like the Mexicans. The American people don't like to work; the Mexicans do anything. The family men are steady and like steady work. The single men say, "Let the married fellow work. To hell with the work, we are going to have a good time."

The survey showed that the proportion of families has increased.

In making comments upon their employment the Mexicans noted both favorable and unfavorable conditions. The following observations were made by a group of Mexicans:

There is no discrimination in movies, restaurants, barber shops, but there is in the work. The bosses give protection to their own race. They give the most dangerous work and the lowest-paid jobs to Mexicans. The Mexicans get less. Yes, if they are doing the same work they get equal pay. The Americans do not make distinctions. The Americans are superintendents.

Even before the steel company had recourse to Mexican labor an attempt had been made to scatter nationalities and place a neutral, if possible an American, in charge.

We try to keep them split up pretty well; we think we have a little better control over them then. If we have a Slavish foreman on one shift, we put a Wendish foreman on another. The Slavish foreman would put most of the work on the Wendish, and vice versa.

SOCIAL RELATIONS

Prejudice against Mexicans in Bethlehem because of their color apparently was not strong and only occasional, if it had any existence. No color distinction was reported in the case of the few Mexican children in the schools.

In 1927 a characteristic mutual benefit society was organized but expired. It was succeeded by another which in 1930 claimed a membership of 120. The initiation fee was 50 cents and the monthly dues $1. After a waiting period, sick benefits of $8 a week are paid for 13 weeks and longer if the society votes approval. The death benefit is $100 plus a collection of $1 from each member.

Only a very small percentage of the Mexicans living in Bethlehem or in other parts of the United States have become American citizens, most of them expecting to return to Mexico. However, in Bethlehem they learn English more rapidly and adopt the characteristic American urban garb more readily than in the rural Southwest. In 1929 four Mexicans had bought homes in Bethlehem. The town also had a Mexican grocery, a barber shop, a pool hall, and a stand for selling Mexican newspapers. A considerable number of the Mexican workers buy company stock.

No criticisms were made in Bethlehem concerning the cleanliness of Mexicans, and the record of Mexican children in school, according to the reports of teachers and school officials, "was at least equal to that of the other children, a large proportion of whom were of European parentage."

Mexicans take little part in politics. Voting is restricted to the few, 18 in number, according to a report made early in 1930, who are naturalized citizens or were born in this country.

Apart from their grievances against foremen of European stock, little friction existed between Mexicans and other nationalities except the Poles. Intermarriages of Mexican men with women of other nationalities were reported as comparatively frequent. None of the Mexican women had intermarried. The Mexicans have some sense of kinship with other Latin Americans living in Bethlehem. Some Mexicans were included among the members of a Spanish club. Spaniards were eligible for membership in the Mexican society, although when the inquiry was made in the early part of 1929 none had applied for admission.

While the northern climate has without doubt been a factor in the departure of many Mexicans from Bethlehem, others have become accustomed to the colder temperatures.

THE FUTURE

Whether or not additional supplies of Mexican labor from the Southwest will be drafted for Bethlehem, the author thinks is a question not to be answered at present. The colony in that town, however, has proven that it is able to maintain itself at a long distance from its source without recurring shipments by the company. With or without such importation it is, according to a subordinate executive, "a nucleus for the future."

Albert Pena

*Albert Pena (Politician, San Antonio, Texas) is an excellent
example of a successful Mexican American politician who
retained his militancy while working within the system.
Pena has always spoken for the dispossessed of San Antonio,
and in this article he asks for a Marshall Plan for the
Mexican American of the Southwest.
By permission of the author.*

The Mexican American
And The War On Poverty

First of all, Mr. Shriver, one of the young ladies advised that you looked like Governor Connally. I told her that's where the similarity stopped. I told her also that I would very much like Johnson to take Connally to Washington and send you to Austin.

I want to apologize to you, Mr. Secretary, for not having sent you a transcript. I just made up my mind three days ago to attend. I was reluctant to attend. I couldn't reconcile myself to attending the conference sponsored by the Federal Government concerning Mexican American problems when the Federal Government back home is the worst offender.

I talk specifically about Kelly Field and I am sure this is true of other Federal installations throughout the Southwest and throughout the United States. This is one of the reasons why I thought I would not attend, so you will please forgive me for not having sent you a transcript.

The fact of the matter is that, being last, my speech has already been delivered three or four times, so we'll try to hit some of the highlights, some of the things that I believe we can do to help accelerate the war on poverty.

Perhaps I'm the least qualified to speak on this subject. I'm not a social worker and I have systematically been kept out of all the anti-poverty committees for some reason or other. Basically, I'm a politician, and I accept this conference and I think we all should as a political fact of life. We came here to say something, all of us have, in one way or the other, and we hope that in Washington and in Austin, they are listening because if they're not listening now, we won't be listening next November.

I know that is as subtle as a meat axe but I don't know how to say it any other way.

I want to be completely democratic so I'll address you as ladies and gentlemen and others . . . and if you're half Anglo and half Mexican, neither, but this is one of the things that has always concerned me, the image, the Mexican American image. We're called so many things we don't know what we are. We're called Mexican Americans, Spanish speaking, Spanish Americans, Americans of Mexican descent. I think some nut called us Iberian Americans. So I have come to this conclusion, that I am three things and in this order: first of all, I'm an American because I was born here. Second, I'm a Texan because I was born in Texas, and third, I'm a Mexican without a mustache because no one will let me forget it.

It's very difficult for Anglos to erase from their mind the stereotyped serape draped Mexican sleeping in the shade with an empty Tequila bottle to his side and with the burro over here waiting for him to wake up.

Every time I meet an Anglo for the first time, or most of them, they try to impress me first with the fact that they made a trip to Mexico and that they love Tequila, they like bull fights, they like Mexican food, and some of their best friends are Mexicans.

Now, this leaves me pretty cold because, first of all, I don't like Tequila. I like scotch, and second, I don't like bull fights. I like a good professional football game, the Washington Redskins. But I must confess that I love Mexican food and Mexican women.

The point I'm trying to make is this, that—and we have heard this many times—that we are proud that we are Americans, but we are also proud that we are Mexicans and don't let anybody forget that.

We've got to learn how to identify as a group because when you do this, then you're going to find out that we're going to have more unity. My friend, Maury Maverick, Jr., told me one time, he said, you know what's wrong with you Mexicans and I said, what, "They made white people out of you and now you don't know what the hell you are." Well, we ought to know what we are. We ought to identify with our people. We ought to identify as Mexicans and the problems that are peculiar to Mexican Americans in the United States.

I would like to also mention just for a few minutes the significance of the Delano grape strike and the significance of the Valley farm march here in Texas.

Here in Texas, I know that the Valley farm marchers that marched from Rio Grande City to Austin had more impact than all the groups, LULAC, GI Forum, PASO, and what have you. I'm not criticizing them because I belong to all of them.

But this march had more impact in those few weeks than all the other things we've been trying to do. Why? Because they not only spotlighted the problem in Rio Grande City but they spotlighted the overall problem of the Mexican American in Texas and throughout the Southwest. And recognition of our problems has been a long time coming. So these are crucial times for us. These next eight or nine or ten or eleven months are very crucial for us. Maybe we should all have stayed home and helped you just a little bit more, Mr. Shriver, and helped with our voter registration drives. This is important. Maybe we could do more good back home today going door to door and knocking on doors and registering people in the barrios because they are the people, these are the unorganized people and we must see that they vote. . . . The only way that they're going to be heard is through the votes. The only thing politicians understand, and I know because I'm one, is votes. They'll talk to people who have votes. And I think here in Texas, and there in Washington, they only understand votes. We need more understanding politicians. The only way that they are going to understand is for you to vote and register everybody in your communities. That's the only way that you're going to do it. It's the only way you're going to do it.

The Valley farm march spotlighted the problems we've been talking about, the high illiteracy rate, job and wage discrimination, the high tubercular rate in our communities, high infant mortality rate in our communities, poverty and injustice, all of these things were spotlighted. This is why it was so important. But there are solutions. I'm confident that there are solutions.

Think, for just a minute, and just imagine an island ninety miles off the United States, not Cuba, with eleven million people of Mexican descent dedicated to our democratic principles and way of life, and they had all these problems that we talk about, illiteracy and poverty and injustice, lack of jobs and high unemployment, all of these things. What would the United States do? They would give them foreign aid. They would give them massive sums of money to take care of that. This is the type of programs we need for the Mexican Americans. We need a Marshall Plan for the Mexican American throughout the Southwest.

These are the only things that I have reduced to writing and I'll try to explain here what I mean by this Marshall Plan.

What South Texas needs, what the land all along our Southwestern border needs, is a new climate, a political, social, economic climate in which the people, the Mexican Americans, can live decently. We need new outside capital to create new jobs. We need new education systems. We need new faces on the political scene and we need ideas. How are we to obtain this change? I'm not sure but I do know that unless the Federal Government begins soon to take unbreached steps towards creating the new climate, something is going to happen. It is inevitable that things will change. Hopefully, change would be orderly. I don't see how this would be possible without the massive assistance of the Federal Government. The State Government, particularly here in Texas, cannot, will not do the job. Most of the local governments up and down the border have but one function, to protect the status quo. In the past, I have called for a Marshall Plan for South Texas with massive aid, with massive loans, with massive technological assistance. What we got was the war

on poverty, too little and too late. I'm not criticizing the war on poverty. What I'm saying is, this is an extension of the war on poverty.

For example, we have some very fine programs in San Antonio. I think we have one of the finest youth organizations, SANYO.

We have the greater San Antonio Federation of Neighborhood Councils and . . . they are beginning to do battle with the power structure, so I am not criticizing. I'm saying that the war on poverty as it exists now is not enough. We need to create a new climate.

The Federal Government certainly has the resources to change the atmosphere in the border lands. We saw, after World War II, the demonstration of this when the United States Government converted the economically, politically, and morally destroyed people of Western Europe and Japan into democratic prosperous allies. Why not this for the Americans who live along the border?

I said we need capital. We need it to create jobs which would create the resources for educational and political changes which would pull South Texas and the border land up and we need the capital on this side of the border. If we can subsidize American capital flowing into Mexico, why can't we subsidize American capital flowing into South Texas?

If we can create jobs for Mexicans in Mexico, why can't we create jobs for Americans in America? If we can fight a fifty billion dollar a year war to free the Vietnamese in Vietnam from political tyranny, why can't we do the same for Americans in America?

I want to conclude by outlining what I think the role of government should be, what I believe is the philosophy of *la causa*. I delivered this to a SANYO meeting and also to a PASO convention.

My philosophy, and I am sure that most of yours, are the results of two great men. These two men were dedicated men. They were sincere men. They were good men. They were religious men. One was the leader of a great nation and the other was the leader of a great religion. One died a very young man. The other died a very old man. And both their names were John. One was John Fitzgerald Kennedy and the other was Pope John XXIII. The two Johns wrote many things and they said many things. Pope John wrote *Pacem in Terris*. John Kennedy wrote *Profiles in Courage*. And basically, they believed this. They believed, first, that all men are created equal in the image of God. They believed that every man was entitled to a good job, decent wages, an education, medical care, and decent housing, but more important than that, they believed that every man should have the equal opportunity to obtain these things and such was the impact of the two Johns that when John Kennedy died, even Republicans, conservatives who never voted for him, cried unashamedly, and when Pope John died, Protestants and Jews declared a week of mourning. Such was the impact of the two Johns. Both said, in different ways, that this generation of Americans has been handed the torch of freedom. Think about that for just a minute. You have been handed the torch of freedom but you're not going to get it until you stop asking for it and demand it.

Ralph GUZMÁN

Ralph Guzmán (Associate Professor of Politics and Community Studies, University of California at Santa Cruz) is co-author of THE MEXICAN-AMERICAN PEOPLE *(1970) as well as many other studies in the area. He served as associate director to the Peace Corps in Venezuela. For Dr. Guzmán the question is not "whether Mexican Americans will riot," but whether violent confrontation will become a permanent fixture on the socio–political landscape. Dr. Guzmán also raises the haunting spectre of a white middle-class riot which could indeed prove more violent than anything previously experienced.*
By permission of the author.

Mexican Americans In The Urban Area: Will They Riot?

Magic was the means by which primitive man made the world meaningful to himself. Modern America is on the verge of resorting to magic because the ideas and information available to it no longer explain the reality of its own life. Part of this phenomenon reflects an attempt to explain urban complexities with agrarian symbolism and value systems.

The real revolution of our time is not only the upsurge of the Negro toward dignity; it is not merely the rebellion of children against their parents; it is not just the erosion of eternal verities; it is not even the fantastic rate of technological development and redevelopment. The real revolution of our times is all of these, in juxtaposition to one another, and more.

380

One of the sad features of our modern society is that those who gained the most from this age of affluence have never asked: "Who lost?" In a sense, most of the facets of this age of unlimited expectations, this age where nothing seems impossible, is that the revolutions of our generation seem to be separate and apart from one another. But, the distance between the middle-class American who complains about his teen age children and says: "We don't speak the same language" is about the same as that of the Mexican American parent who regrets that his child refuses to learn Spanish. The distance is more apparent than real.

The arid phrases, normally used to describe the transformation of American life in the last decade, obscure rather than reveal the remarkable impact this revolution has had on individual lives and destinies. To say that this revolution has technological aspects does not explain to a 45-year-old man with family responsibilities that he is too old to learn a new trade and too young to vegetate for the rest of his life. Technological unemployment reveals nothing of the despair of an illiterate adolescent when he finds that he is economically irrelevant— or in short that he can't get a job. The words generational gap fail to convey the dilemma of a man who has sacrificed everything to give his children security only to find they reject it.

Fundamental anti-intellectualism in American society has over-shadowed the fact that in the arts, the sciences and the humanities, every tradition has been toppled and supplanted. The fight between college and town is a reflection between different views of the universe. In California the insistence that the university conform to the taxpayer's idea of a university stands in direct contrast to the idea that a university should be a place for the search of truth, however outlandish and antagonistic to the interests of the taxpayer.

Our society has still not assimilated the full implications of the change of the role of the government from that of the necessary evil to that of a force for positive good. This leaves liberals with visions of omnipotence and conservatives with nighmares of disaster. Neither view, of course, accords with reality. Governmental activism cannot resolve all problems; for these are problems that are rightfully beyond the reach of governmental purview. Neither is governmental intervention an automatic evil; for there are some problems that only government can reach.

Even as the churches have up-dated their rituals and theology, America is long overdue in renovating its supply of ideas. Symbols and values relevant to an agrarian past must be re-cast for our urban present. Notions of community solidarity; I-thou relationships; salvation through work; the Horatio Alger myth must be discarded. We must recognize and cope with the solitude; the privacy; the mobility and the restlessness of the city. For the city is not just a network of freeways. It is not just the decisions of the zoning commission. It is not merely a marble and concrete mechanism. It is a totally new way of life; an organism of immense complexity. It teems not with millions of cogs and wheels but with millions of people.

And for those millions of people the revolution of our time has been dangerously encapsulated in the equation; Negro equals riot equals revolution. For above all, minorities in these United States have been affected adversely by the onslaught of this new age of affluence. Both its victims and its prisoners; they have been the forgotten losers in the game of material acquisition. In the miles and miles and acres and acres of housing developments, few minority members are found. In the myriad expansion of services and luxuries, few minority people benefit. In the explosion of information and learning that circles the earth our ethnic minorities remain a mystery. They have been the most conspicuous of those who have not shared in this era of plenty. But along with the majority they have shared the loss of those psychic comforts associated with a simpler society. For, if the sense of rootlessness afflicts the Negro, it also afflicts the inhabitants of split-level ranch houses. If the loss of identity causes anxiety for the Mexican American he shares that problem with the bulk of American youth. If the break-up of the family exacerbates the problem of the poor let it be known that homes for the aged are not filled with the elderly of the poor and of the minorities.

This community of concern, that faces all Americans, has been strangely twisted into the problem peculiar to the racial and ethnic minorities of our country. Nowhere is the lack of intelligent comprehension of what this nation is, more evident than in the utter lack of knowledge shared by the majority and the minority about each other. Because of this simplistic equation, the search for concepts and solutions has been the province of a thin strata of the American establishment.

No one can say that the problems of the poor have not been researched, studied, examined, handled, committee-ed, anachronimed, and sloganed. There is hardly a letter of the alphabet that has not been used to form an abbreviation for an agency. Government has created OEO, CAP, EDA, MDTA, and HEW. All of these are part of the vast arsenal that comprise the invested personnel and resources in job training programs designed to diminish poverty. Church groups have been conspicuous in the attempt to enliven the conscience of the country about conditions related to poverty and race. In the 1930s the Rockefeller Foundation could deny a grant to aid the Mexican American poor on the grounds of insufficient data about these people. Today, it and other foundations eagerly encourage innovative programs to alleviate poverty and prejudice. But, let there be no mistake, this activity, this flood of concern engages but a minute percentage of the total population. This empathy is restricted to the elite of the American establishment. Between the vast majority and growing minority there exists a gulf of understanding, of information and knowledge that will never be bridged by the jargon of the elite.

Let there be no mistake. Programs designed to help the poor and the deprived have been the product of the top layer of American society. These programs have been created by them, administered by them, supported by them and, in some instances, even thwarted by them. They have been a meager response to the threat of violence. Their existence is predicated upon that threat. Consequently, they have no roots beyond this threat of social disruption. Therefore, the vast majority of the American people have absolutely no involvement intellectually or emotionally in any program designed to aid minorities that is not based on force and the restoration of the old order. This antipathy, on the part of the overwhelming majority, can be directly laid to blame at the door-

step of American leadership. For if one of the functions of leadership is to educate; to help make understandable the events of a nation's life, our leadership is largely talking to itself.

Perhaps this is most evident in the employment of a special new language devised by the elite and debased in popular usage. A term such as "hard-core unemployed" means to the elite an individual who lacks the necessary skills to perform minimum tasks in a highly developed technology. It also includes assumptions about value orientations and environmental disabilities. To the poor it means they can't get a job. Surprisingly enough, they knew this before someone told them they were "hard-core unemployed." But, to most Americans hard-core unemployment means: "to lazy to work." Another term that indicates myopia of the elite is "culturally deprived." One suspects that 97 percent of the entire population of the world would fall into that category. It is a term with meaning only to those who assumed that they have culture. Lumped together, as beyond the pale, are both those with a different culture and those without season tickets to the opera. The net result has been to increase the ignorance of various sectors of American society about each other. In a way the elite have ministered to the poor in a fashion not alike preachers riding circuit in the past. By day they travel to the ghettos of despair and at dusk they return to the security of their suburban retreats. They have become the buffer between the miserably poor and the misunderstanding many.

For the poor the application of terms to their economic circumstances does not increase their ability to escape. For if the poor really knew the causes and remedies for their poverty they would surely choose them of their own accord. Instead, however, they become cases, objects and problems. They themselves are called upon to play a passive part in their own rescue. The traditional values of the poor: suspicion, hostility, mistrust, doubt, hopelessness—all of these are re-enforced by the paternalism of the elite and the contempt of the majority.

The fact that so many of the poor are also ethnic and racial minorities has consequences for both the elite and the white middle classes. For the elite the reigning paternalism is increased by the fear of the mob. Thus what started out as a response to a single aspect of violence has become a defensive maneuver designed to maintain the urban peace; to preserve law and order; to keep the people quiet. For the white middle classes contempt has mingled with fear producing a tension level unparalleled in recent history. For the white middle classes are scared. They expect violence and their only substantive response, thus far, is repression. This misunderstanding of the revolution of our time; by all participants; by the elite; by the poor and by the white middle classes; has produced an atmosphere of terror and anxiety that certainly does not augur well for the future of our democracy. In the effort to repress violence the poor will never miss traditional civil liberties; for they have never had them. And it is increasingly clear that the white middle class will gladly trade traditional liberty for false security. Moreover, this dangerous equation: Negro equals riot equals revolution, has left many groups of people, who are part of this revolution, with neither the benefits of those efforts that have been made nor the goodwill of the society. The Indian and the Mexican American are the preeminent examples of the lost children of the urban revolution.

Right now no one knows exactly how many Mexican Americans there are in the Southwest. Estimates range between six and seven million. We do know that the median age of this group is 19.5 years; that the average family size exceeds that of the white majority and the Negro minority. However, modern statistics cannot reveal the context in which this group has developed. To the people of the Southwest the region itself is a closed book. Movies and television have projected an image of the Southwest in which numerous Nietzchean supermen constantly ride off into the sunset, clutching their saddles, after another sortie against savage Indians and/or villainous Mexicans. We Americans are a strangely historic people. By this I mean that the actual history of the Southwest; the history of violence and exploitation; the lessons of the conqueror and the conquered; the harsh combat of all against an inhospitable land— all these are forgotten, if they were ever known.

Conflict and guile guided the development of this area. Law was the weapon of the strong against the weak. And few people confused law with justice. In their role as conquered, Mexican Americans became prisoners of a popular stereotype of a triumphant and rampant mythology. They became a sideshow; a humorous diversion in the struggle of the victor against nature. Considered as foreigners they were excused their ethnic eccentricities. As peasants they were not supposed to be too bright. As idol-worshippers they were an American brand of basically inferior heathens. Even today the legend persists in the minds of many southwesterners, and practically all who are not from the Southwest. Despite the popular stereotype, however, the Mexican American has felt the urban revolution of our time—no less than his Anglo counterparts.

Technological developments have reduced his employability. First, the increased emphasis on formal language and social skills has erected a formidable barrier to upward occupational mobility. Second, the concommitant decrease in the need for unskilled labor has created a surplus of Spanish surnamed unemployed. Thirdly, mechanization in the agricultural sector has augmented the surplus and the exodus to the urban ghettos. Thus, while fewer jobs are available to the Mexican American in the cities hundreds of thousands stream toward the large metropolitan centers in search of nonexistant, unskilled jobs.

With more than a four hundred year history in the Southwest—more than European immigrants, only recently, in the last 25 years, has the majority of the Mexican American people become a part of the urban reality of this region. Long a rural people, this minority is today 87 percent urban.

Many now live in these cities armed with inadequate attitudes and social skills of an agrarian past. Desperately, against tremendous odds, many seek to maintain crumbling idylls that have no roots in the urban reality. Such is the impact of the social forces within the city. Nor have ethnic intellectuals been much help. First, because their numbers are limited. Second, because many are ideologues who look to the restoration of a lost grandeur while obsessively denying the presence of ragged poor. Every day the irrelevance of the latter becomes more apparent. For the Mexican American population of the Southwest is not foreign and archaic but overwhelmingly American by birth, young and grossly disadvantaged.

Moreover, the generational problem in the majority society is more than matched among Mexican Americans. If the old ideologues have little to say to their peers they have nothing to say to the young. Young Mexican Americans are living the urban revolution thus the values of the parent generation and the visions of the offsprings are as sharply contrasted within this minority group as they are in the larger society. The neglect of the young by both the old ideologues and the larger society has left them disillusioned, bitter and deeply resentful. While some may seek an artificial identity with the Che Guevarra and Negro militancy, others withdrew into an anguished apathy. Still others, the majority of the young, await viable direction for their destiny. The majority of them ignore their parents and await for one of their own to articulate grievances and direct social energy.

We cannot expect the young to remain polite and powerless. We cannot expect them to continue saying thank you for nothing. Social disorder is a function of the young. They question contracts established before their birth. And they challenge forces applied to maintain these contracts. The whole litany of inherited problems will never again be accepted as part of the natural order of things.

Still many Mexican American leaders bring up these problems in the same strident tones of their Negro opposites. They call for caution and patience; for thought and logic, and for ethnic unity built upon deference to age. All this is rejected by the young, particularly those who stand in envy of the Black Power movement. For most of the young want to escalate the drive for social change.

The question: "Will the Mexican American riot?" is probably irrelevant. Answering the affirmative or the negative sheds no light on the problems of this minority or this nation. Regretfully, present programs, conceived merely as a response to a threat of social disruption, whether continued or expended, probably will not prevent violence in the streets. For, given the rapidity and intensity of the revolution convulsing our country, the question is not *whether they will riot or when they will riot.* For all of us the question is: "Will riots become a permanent and enduring part of our national existence? Will riots become the only means to affectuate meaningful social change? Or, because of intelligent and reasoned application of resources will urban anarchy pass away into a footnote to history?"

Finally, there is one group that is not well-known. It has not been well-studied, but we do know that it has a propensity for violence exceeding that of either the Negro or the Mexican American. It too, has been equally a victim of revolutionary developments in our history. Any total response to the urban revolution of our times must include programs to assuage the fears of the white, middle-class American who has not yet rioted in full force. For it is this sector of our society whose history of hysterical outburst portends tragic consequences for the future of this country. We would be unwise and unrealistic: all of us Americans, minorities and non-minorities, if we ignore the white, middle class. After all, most members of this strata of our society have rarely displayed either the rural patience of the Negro or the agrarian politeness of the Mexican American.

Richard Griego + Gilbert W. Merkx

Crisis In New Mexico

Amid the breathtaking sweep of New Mexico's mountains, deserts, and river valleys the grim final stages of a long tragedy are unfolding. Sunshine and scenery in this "land of enchantment" are the setting for the death of a people and their way of life. These people are Mexican-Americans, bearers of an Indo-Hispanic culture that is older than the United States, older than Mexico itself, and far older than "New" Mexico. They are the victims of economic and social forces alien to them and of little concern to other Americans.

New Mexico is the heartland of Mexican-American society. Nearly six million Chicanos or Mexican-Americans live in the Southwest, distributed from California to Texas. But only in the geographic center of this region, which lies in northern New Mexico, are Mexican-Americans still a majority of the population, owning and working

385

land of their own while maintaining Chicano culture in non-ghetto circumstances.

Despite the legal fiction that New Mexico is the nation's one officially bilingual state, this *patria chica,* or little homeland, is rapidly disappearing. Anglo-Americans who pride themselves on New Mexico's "tradition" of cultural pluralism conveniently ignore the fact that they are presiding over a cultural destruction less violent but no less effective than that perpetrated against American Indians. Mexican-Americans are being driven from their rural homeland into urban slums and migrant labor camps throughout the Southwest.

Six counties lying north between Albuquerque and the Colorado border are still largely Spanish-speaking: Santa Fe, San Miguel, Guadalupe, Taos, Mora, and Rio Arriba. The most Chicano county of these is Mora (85 percent of the people were Spanish-surnamed in 1960), and the least is Santa Fe (54 percent). A seventh northern county, Sandoval, lost 37 percent of its Mexican-American population during the 1950s, dropping from 52 percent Spanish-surnamed in 1950 to 32 percent in 1960. The region as a whole lost 15 percent of its Chicano population during those ten years because of a disintegrating rural economy. This exodus began during the Second World War and has been accelerating in recent years. Mora county alone lost 45 percent of its population between 1940 and 1960; between 1960 and 1968 it lost an additional 13 percent.

The impact of this emigration has been felt in the urban centers of New Mexico, particularly Albuquerque, as well as in the area losing people. Albuquerque has grown from 35,000 in 1940 to 310,000 in 1968, partly due to an influx of Anglos attracted by the climate and defense employment, but also due to the yearly arrival of thousands of displaced Chicanos from the northern counties. Albuquerque now has large and growing barrios or slums sprawling along the banks of the Rio Grande and afflicted by considerable poverty. A recent sampling of Albuquerque residents designed by one of the authors found that 60 percent of the Chicanos had moved to Albuquerque from rural counties, 15 percent were from out of state, and only 25 percent were born in Albuquerque.

The destruction of the rural base of Mexican-American society and the proliferation of urban slums are two sides of the same coin, or two different aspects of the social inequity which characterizes the American Southwest. This inequity, which has been rapidly worsening in the period since the Second World War, is the underlying cause of the militant Mexican-American protest movements which have attracted so much public attention in the last three years. Chicano militancy takes several forms, which we will attempt to explain, but all represent a desperate attempt to save Indo-Hispanic culture from disappearing into a dominant "American way of life" which many Mexican-Americans find distasteful and with which they are ill-prepared to cope.

The ecological base of Mexican-American society in the northern counties is a mixed rural economy of small farming, orchards, and small-scale sheep and cattle raising. Unlike the Anglo or "Texan" ranchers and farmers who are competing for the same land, the Chicanos do not live on their land, but in small communities located in river valleys, which date from the days in which land was chartered to such communities by the Spanish Crown. Life in these villages is so attractive to the residents that they will stay under conditions of extreme poverty, and the dream of most migrants in the cities is one day to return to their community.

Nevertheless, the Chicanos are losing their lands to Anglos, and increasing numbers of Mexican-Americans find it impossible to survive in their homeland. Between 1949 and 1964 the acreage under crops in New Mexico declined 45 percent, while about the same area of land was added to Anglo ranches. In the seven northern counties the total number of farms dropped from 4,302 to 2,614 in only five years between 1954 and 1959. Small farms of under 10 acres almost cease to exist (in 1954 there were 2,025, but by 1959 only 662 remained.) Yet at the same time large enterprises of over 1000 acres actually increased in number from 769 to 835.

The tragedy of this destruction of small farming in New Mexico is that it represents not only the passing of inefficient economic units, but also the disintegration of a society and the creation of another urban underclass. As long as their communities are even marginally viable, Chicanos will remain. Some have stayed by taking employment in the cities, commuting long distances so as to live with their own people. Too few are able to find such employment, however, and the result is that these villages contain poverty, malnutrition, and a hopelessness made heart-rending by the stunning beauty of the region and the dignity and warmth of the people.

Some idea of this poverty can be gathered by looking at family income. Median income of Chicano families in six of the counties ranged in 1959 from $1,951 in Mora County to $2,864 in Guadalupe. Only in Santa Fe county, which contains the state capital, did median family income exceed the $4000 poverty line, and there it reached only $4,062. In contrast, Anglo median family income was $6,592 in Santa Fe, $4,605 in Guadalupe, and $3,463 in Mora. These median figures, which represent families in the middle of the income range, do not reflect average income, which is probably lower for Chicano families and considerably higher for Anglos, a number of whom are millionaires.

Those public officials on a local, state, and federal level who might contribute to the economic revitalization of Mexican-American society have done the opposite. New Mexico politics are dominated by a coalition of ranching and oil and gas interests which accept some progressive influence from military-industrial enterprises in Los Alamos and Albuquerque. Politicians of Mexican-American ethnicity are usually committed to these interests or do not challenge them in return for control over patronage in their shrinking local fiefs. Thus the political structure in New Mexico encourages ranching and mineral extraction in the countryside and aero-space and scientific investment in the cities. Anglo leaders in the state are either openly hostile towards Mexican-Americans or regard hastened destruction of small farming and the emigration of Chicanos as an ultimately beneficial phase of modernization. Should their vision predominate, New Mexico will soon resemble Arizona and lower California, where urban slums in the center cities house a marginal underclass which provides servants and menials for the endless acres of ranch-house suburbia.

The claim that Mexican-Americans in the state are sharing in the benefits of modernization is demonstrably false, despite the existence of a fair percentage of assimilated middle-class Mexican-Americans (the self-styled "Spanish"). Overt discrimination against Chicanos in the south and east of New Mexico, known as "little Texas," resembles the most vicious practices of the American South. Even Albuquerque, the most modern city in the state, evidences social inequalities that are as dramatic as those in rural counties.

Unemployment in Albuquerque has been the lowest in New Mexico for years, fluctuating between 4.1 percent and 4.8 percent from 1963 to 1968, while median family income nearly doubled between 1950 and 1960 (increasing from $3,451 to $6,621). But these figures conceal the increasing relative deprivation of the Chicano population. Employment opportunities have benefited highly skilled Anglos, not the native New Mexicans (43 percent of the Anglos in Albuquerque have been there less than 10 years). The harsh reality of Chicano life in Albuquerque can be seen in the fact that in the sample of Mexican-Americans, 20 percent of the heads of Mexican households were unemployed.

Not only are nearly a fifth of Albuquerque Chicanos unemployed, but also those who do find employment do not do very well. While 44 percent of the Anglos have professional, business, or managerial occupations, only 11 percent of the Chicanos have such employment. Most of the Mexicans are either unskilled manual laborers (41 percent) or machine operators (13 percent), while only 21 percent of the Anglos fall in these two categories combined. Essentially, the Albuquerque pattern is that Anglos are the bosses and Mexican-Americans the workers; Anglos work with their minds and Mexicans with their hands (when they find work).

This state of affairs reflects the inherent discrimination of a state educational system that operates exclusively in English despite a constitutional requirement that teachers be bilingual. The disregard for Chicano language and culture are such that most Mexican-Americans are, in the words of political scientist Ralph Guzmán, "force-outs" rather than drop-outs. Only 12 percent of Anglo heads of households in Albuquerque had not completed high school, compared with 60 percent of the Chicano heads of household. Over half (52 percent) of the Anglos had some education beyond the high school level, as opposed to only 15 percent of the Mexicans.

These depressing statistics are summed up in the figures for the income earned by Anglo and Chicano heads of household, which are shown in Table 1.

Table 1.   Annual Income of Albuquerque Heads of Household, 1967

Income	Anglos	Spanish Surnamed
Over $7,000	57%	20%
$4,000–$7,000	30%	47%
Under $4,000	13%	33%
Total	100%	100%

Source: "A Demographic and Attitudinal Study of the Albuquerque Standard Metropolitan Statistical Area," (Operation SER, Santa Monica, California), Advance Report No. 1, p. 12.

While only 13 percent of Anglos earned under $4,000 annually, 33 percent of the Chicanos were below this poverty line. At the opposite extreme, 57 percent of the Anglos earned over $7,000, as compared with only 20 percent of the Chicanos. *Per capita* income figures are even more skewed, since Mexican-Americans have larger families than Anglos. It is small wonder that 80 percent of the Chicano respondents agreed with the statement that "Mexican-Americans have to work harder than Anglos to get ahead."

The impact of 124 years of United States rule over New Mexico can therefore be summed up as follows. The original inhabitants of the state have been driven off their land except in a handful of counties where Chicanos still cling to an increasingly marginal existence. Those Mexican-Americans who have emigrated to New Mexico's cities are condemned to slums and unskilled, unsteady employment. Cast out from an Anglo-oriented school system, they are often functionally inadequate in two languages and lacking the skills necessary to benefit from the economic development of the region. Unless an economic and cultural revitalization of New Mexico is undertaken in the next decade, there may be nothing left to save of what was once heralded as a mutually-enriching combination of two cultures and two ways of life.

THE MILITANT REACTION

The exacerbation of social inequity and the deterioration of Chicano society in the last few years have touched off a major wave of Mexican-American militancy. The nature of the militant reaction varies from group to group according to whether the members are rural or urban, middle or lower class, youth or adults. But the common thread running through all militant organizations is belief in the cultural integrity of the Mexican-American people. They view the Spanish language, a close-knit family structure, a sense of interdependence, and an emphasis on human values rather than on money as aspects of the Mexican way of life that should be maintained. The militants are unanimous in their contempt for what they consider to be the sterility of middle-class Anglo values.

The *Alianza Federal de Mercedes* (Federal Alliance of Land Grants) is the main vehicle of Mexican-American protest in New Mexico. The issues and attitudes projected by the Alianza closely reflect the history of Indo-Hispanic culture in New Mexico. Elder Alianzistas still remember the times when their people had an economically marginal but stable life and were free to graze sheep on their forefathers' land. They have seen gringos come with fences and legal entanglements to cut them off from their grazing lands; the elders recount the disintegration of a way of life in bitter detail and their message is not lost on younger Alianza members.

The issue of land is at the very heart of rural New Mexican problems, since loss of the land destroyed the economic base of most northern villages. The Alianza was organized in 1963 by its leader, Reies López Tijerina, to press for the return of or compensation for millions of acres of land which it claims were wrongfully acquired by the federal government. The Alianza bases its claims on the Treaty of Guadalupe Hidalgo of 1848 which ended the war between Mexico and the United States. The treaty gave citizenship to Mexicans who stayed in the conquered territories, and it stated that land grants given to New Mexicans by the Spanish and Mexican governments were to be "recognized in the tribunals of the United States." Those tribunals invalidated 94 percent of the land claims made by Mexican-Americans, opening the way for their expulsion from the land. The Alianza is primarily concerned with the village land grants owned communally by the heirs of the original grantees. It does not lay explicit claims to land grant acreage now in private hands, but focuses on land appropriated by the federal government, much of which has been declared national forest.

Frustrated in attempts to get recognition for its claims, the Alianza turned to a strategy of direct confrontation with the federal government. The Alianza planned to reoccupy various land grants, in effect seizing what the U.S. government considers federal property. After all, according to Tijerina, the land grants had not ceased to exist; they were real entities that the Alianza would merely reactivate. This device was to bring the government into court, thus forcing recognition of Alianza claims. The strategy brought the Alianza into conflict with the government on several occasions. It culminated with the famous raid on the Tierra Amarilla courthouse in June, 1967, when Alianzistas attempted a citizens arrest of a district attorney who had allegedly violated the rights of Alianza members. In the trial which followed, Tijerina won acquittal on kidnap charges while acting as his own attorney. Since then, however, Tijerina has been convicted on a number of lesser charges related both to the citizens arrest and to the burning of a sign on national forest land. He is now in federal prison.

Unlike the Alianza, the Brown Berets deal with problems of urban Mexican-American poor and draw their members from youth in the city barrios. Brown Berets were organized in Los Angeles, but similar organizations now exist in cities throughout the Southwest.

The Brown Berets in Albuquerque were organized mainly through the efforts of Gilberto Ballejos, an articulate spokesman from the barrio who identifies closely with other *batos* (guys) in the barrio despite the fact that he is a college graduate. These *batos* find it hard to identify with the heritage of land the Alianza emphasizes, and they do not remember rural life as do the Alianza members. The Berets concern themselves with typical problems of the urban ghetto such as police brutality and education. They are currently active in organizing Chicano high school students. Nevertheless, while the Berets do not internalize the values of the Alianza, they generally support the goals of the Alianza. They too are concerned with restoring cultural dignity to la Raza, and chose the color of their berets to symbolize the brown skin of their people.

The Brown Berets' organizational structure is more sophisticated than that of the Alianza. The Alianza has been largely a one-man operation; everything revolved around Tijerina and sometimes it was difficult to separate Tijerina, the man, from the movement he led. The Brown Berets are careful to point out that there is no single leader of their organization. Ballejos, the current spokesman, was chosen by a six-man board that coordinates activities of the individual Brown Beret barrio organizations. Each board member is the equal of the others and each board member is responsible for organizing his own barrio. The individual barrio organizations are somewhat autonomous and the details of membership are known only to the organizers of the individual groups in an effort to guard against infiltration. Despite such efforts, police success in using informers has tended to drive the Brown Berets further underground and to intensify their suspicion of outsiders.

The Berets gained recognition in Albuquerque when they protested the killing of a Chicano youth by an Anglo policeman. The Berets and other groups demanded a police review board to handle complaints from the community. The review board was not accepted by the city commission, but a three-man police community relations task force was set up consisting of an Anglo, a Chicano and Black policeman.

A third militant organization, the United Mexican-American Students (UMAS), consists of Chicano college students from more middle-class urban backgrounds. The students in UMAS are capable of "making it" in American society, and are to a large extent acculturated to American ways. They are the hoped-for products of their parents' striving to be accepted in American society. But these sons and daughters of la Raza refuse to be absorbed. They insist on the viability of Mexican culture in modern America and openly identify with their Indian heritage, emphasizing the fact that they are not "pure white Spaniards." Their use of the term "Mexican-American" is itself controversial, since the word "Mexican" has had derogatory connotations in New Mexico. UMAS students embrace "Mexican-American" and even "Mexican" as cultural terms which accurately describe who they are, despite their parents' preference for the term "Spanish-American."

UMAS has mounted a campaign, already partly successful, for the inclusion of more Mexican and Indian studies in the curriculum of the University of New Mexico. They forced the student government to "Mexicanize" the annual student festival, ironically called "Fiesta." Students in UMAS also joined the Black Student Union in a controversial clenched-fist salute during the playing of the national anthem at a basketball game, as a protest against the allegedly racist policies of Brigham Young University. When the University of New Mexico president suspended a Black teaching assistant who was under community attack for using supposedly obscene poems in class, UMAS was the first organization to ask the President's resignation (acting before such militant organizations as the Black Students Union and SDS).

Following the poem controversy, UMAS touched off another major dispute by alleging university discrimination against Chicano physical plant workers. Despite administration denials, an HEW investigation of UMAS charges found them to be substantially correct. The university was forced to order changes in its personnel policies.

Probably the most significant long-term achievements of UMAS has been their successful drive to establish a Chicano Studies program at the University of New Mexico. This program has recently begun operation under a faculty coordinator but retains extensive student participation.

The differing social bases of the Alianza, the Brown Berets and UMAS help explain the differences in issue-emphasis between each group, as well as differences in style of articulation and approach.

The Alianza draws rural-based, northern New Mexican adults for its membership. They represent some of the most traditional elements of Chicano society in New Mexico. The Alianzistas are closely tied to the land as shown in their slogan *La Tierra-Nuestra Herencia, La Justicia-Nuestro Credo.* Outside a typical meeting at Alianza headquarters in Albuquerque numerous pick-up trucks of *campesinos* will be parked. Spanish is the language of the meetings, although some English will be heard, especially among the members' children. Tijerina is a dynamic speaker. His green eyes flash as he exhorts his audience in the style of his Pentecostal upbringing. Frequent applause and exclamations from the audience punctuate the proceedings. After the speeches, refreshments and Mexican food are served, and a *norteño* band plays ranchera music for dancing. The atmosphere is one of a church rally or family reunion.

Most of the Brown Berets would be called "hard-core ghetto youth" by Anglos. Some are high school drop-outs and others are Vietnam war veterans. But all are from the barrios, children of the working and welfare class. The Berets say they are willing to try nonviolent means to achieve their aims but if that fails they will be forced to revolutionary alternatives. In the words of James Kennedy, a regional SDS organizer, the Brown Berets "come closer to forming a revolutionary vanguard organization than any other group I have seen or talked with or studied in this country."

Few of the families of UMAS students are well off financially, though they come from the middle and lower middle strata of Mexican-American society. These strata are more economically insecure than their Anglo equivalents. Nevertheless, UMAS students have middle-class educational values, viewing higher studies as a vehicle of improvement for themselves and their people. UMAS students are likely to be willing to work within the system, since their education gives them the means to address Anglo society on its terms. The Brown Berets do not have access to such means and hence are more ready to attack the system and force change by radical methods.

On a cultural level UMAS and the Brown Berets have much in common. Their members are products of the Chicano urban culture. Their Spanish is liberally sprinkled with *pachuco* expressions. The *pachucos* were Mexican-American urban youngsters of the 1940s and 50s who were caught between traditional Mexican-American society and Anglo-American life. They responded by rejecting both societies and forming a subculture of their own, complete with slang, unusual dress, and a unique life style. Although the pachucos no longer exist as an identifiable group, they passed on a heritage and spirit of rebellion to contemporary Chicano youth.

The term "Chicano" is another word that implies rebellion against the older generation. "Chicano" is a transformation of "Mexicano" and it has not until recently been accepted as a formal or "nice" term to describe Mexican-Americans. The more traditional Alianzistas prefer "Mexicano" or "Indo-Hispano" to describe themselves in Spanish. "Indo-Hispano" is a term popularized by Tijerina, who uses it to emphasize his people's Indian heritage, thus further legitimizing their claim to the land by linking them to the original inhabitants. Perhaps the only term accepted by all Spanish-speaking people of the Southwest (indeed by all of Latin America) is "La Raza." It carries a deep feeling for the blending of Spanish and Indian cultures which produced a mestizo race. The concept of la Raza in a real sense represents all those elements which unify the militant movements of New Mexico.

CONCLUSION

The desperate efforts of Mexican-American militants from the rural heartland, the urban barrios, and the university to save what remains of the Indo-Hispanic culture and the New Mexican way of life constitute the last chance for the United States to undo the destructive results of its acquisition of the American Southwest. Chicano leader-

ship now exists in varied forms, and this leadership offers the promise of combining the traditional strengths of Indo-Hispanic culture with economic viability in contemporary America. But such a promise cannot be realized without an active response from Anglo-American leadership.

The choice which confronts the United States in New Mexico is very similar to that which faced Sweden and Norway in the decades following the First World War. The Scandinavian rural economy, based on small mixed farming like that of New Mexico, began to disintegrate rapidly, and urban planners found themselves faced with massive emigration from the countryside. As in New Mexico, this exodus was even more disturbing since the nexus of Scandinavian folk culture lay in the rural heartland.

The Liberal-Labor governments of Sweden and Norway chose to disregard conventional economic wisdom by investing heavily in the deteriorating areas. Schools and public services were upgraded, and small industry was introduced and encouraged with government aid, which included cheap electricity and transportation as well as massive credit. The rural population was given an opportunity to supplement farm income with factory work and other employment. Even today the usual pattern in rural Scandinavia resembles that which is incipient in New Mexico: a farmer is likely to combine his agriculture with several supplementary incomes from fishing, forestry, manufacturing, and civil service employment. Like the rural Chicanos, rural Scandinavians forego the various advantages of life in the cities in favor of an economically inferior but culturally more rewarding life in the countryside.

The rural way of life in Sweden and Norway remained economically marginal in the Sixties, even as it was marginal in the Twenties. Nevertheless, it is *successfully* marginal, and in real terms the quality of life has greatly improved. The benefits of this rural viability to Scandinavia have been great, though not in the American sense of providing massive agricultural surpluses. The slowdown in rural emigration permitted Scandinavian planners to eliminate slums and absorb the marginal underclass. Perhaps even more important, the maintenance of vital culture in the countryside has done much to give Sweden and Norway their uniquely egalitarian and Scandinavian way of life, so different from that of the more centralized and industrial German state.

The choice in New Mexico seems all too clear. If present trends continue, the last remaining basis for a viable Indo-Hispanic way of life will disappear. The American Southwest will be characterized by an urban underclass of second-class citizens, Mexican-Americans lost in a cultural limbo. Crammed into the ghettos of the cities, Chicanos will cling to an ethnic identity that serves only to stigmatize them and add to their inability to escape the too-well-known vicious cycle of urban poverty. The chasm which already separates prosperous suburban Anglos from barrio Chicanos will become unbridgeable.

On the other hand, a program of economic investment in the Chicano heartland of New Mexico, where both a population majority and a land base continue to exist, offers the very real possibility of saving the *patria chica,* given the determination of Mexican-Americans to remain there if they can find any way of doing so. Reduction of the rural exodus would then offer the chance of improving conditions in the urban barrios and reorganizing educational curricula so as to treat Spanish fluency as an advantage rather than a defect. The current generation of Mexican-American militants could be given the opportunity to take their rightful place as leaders of a cultural and social revitalization rather than being forced to become bitter and defiant organizers of desperate guerilla movements.

Perhaps most important, such a program would offer the United States one more chance to realize that ethnic differences can be a source of strength, not a weakness, that cultural diversity enriches rather than impoverishes, that pride in a people's heritage is a better basis for citizenship than flight from identity. New Mexico stands as an indictment of the United States, but it might still become a source of national hope. To bring this about we must recognize the gravity of the crisis in New Mexico and begin to act while time remains.

Elroy Bode

Elroy Bode (Author, El Paso, Texas) is a well-known author in Southwestern literary circles. This excellent account of the cultural impact of changing population patterns on a former upper-middle class Anglo high school won a 1971 Texas Institute of Letters Award.

Requiem For A WASP School

They stand in their tall, glassed-in picture frames, looking out from the uncomplicated 1940s to the crowded main hallway of El Paso's Austin High School. Small gold plates beneath the frames give the identifications: Walter Driver, State Champion, Boy's Single Tennis 1940; Billy Pitts, State Championship, Declamation 1942; Robert Goodman, First in State, Sliderule 1948. Holding their rackets and winners' cups, wearing their double-breasted suits with wide lapels and wide pants that sag around their shoes, they are reminders of the Days That Were: the days of Admiral Nimitz and General Patton and Ernie Pyle; of Glenn Miller and the Andrew Sisters and "Kokomo, Indiana"; of Jarrin' John Kimbrough and Betty Grable and "One Man's Family." They remain there behind glass, representing the Jack Armstrong-Henry Aldrich-Elm Street America that is gone forever.

It is easy, of course, to understand how rich in memories, how painfully nostalgic, these and other hallway pictures are to an old-timer at Austin High. Why, to him the 1940s mean—well, just about everything that was decent and sensible in American life. They mean kids who weren't perfect, of course, but who nonetheless respected rules and obeyed adults and knew how a human being cut his hair; they mean juke boxes and soda fountains and hayrides on Saturday night. They mean getting a lump in your throat listening to a glee club sing "The Halls of Ivy" because even if you weren't Ronald Coleman standing before a fireplace in college you understood exactly what that kind of song was saying: it was saying that Our Country Was a Grand 'n Glorious Place and Our Youth Were the Hope of Tomorrow. . . . And such an old-timer only has to turn from the pictures on the wall and gaze about him to feel an even

393

greater sense of pride, and of loss. For can't he look at thirteen showcases full of cups, plaques, statues, medals that have been earned by the hard-working students of Austin over the years? And over there—although no one ever stops to read them anymore—aren't those still the bronzed words of Theodore Roosevelt: "What we have a right to expect of the American boy is that he shall turn out to be a good American man"?

... "The American boy," the old-timer can muse: that's the key to the glory that once belonged to Austin, and to our country. And now look who we have filling these sacred halls: Mexicans.

Austin High School—the name is rich with associations for many El Pasoans. Over the past 40 years it has been a symbol of quality education, of good students from good homes, of traditions to be proud of. Students in nearby elementary and junior high schools looked forward to their freshman year at Austin with a certain amount of trembling, respect, and awe, for Austin meant everything a high school was supposed to mean: a long, elegant, two-story stone building for unsure freshmen to get lost in; teachers who presided over difficult courses that "prepared you for college"; a Panther football team that everyone could get excited about in the fall; homecoming assemblies and class officers and DAR essays and clubs and honors and prestige. Austin was the kind of all-around good school that lawyers, architects, businessmen wanted their sons and daughters to attend.

And then it happened. The '40s and '50s wandered innocently into the explosive '60s, and Austin High found itself with a problem on its hands: social change. The image of an Anglo-American, college-oriented student body began blurring into the image of a racially-mixed, academically varied student body that was more than half Mexican-American. A highly regarded middle-class WASP high school was becoming a gathering place for *chicanos*.

To understand this change it is necessary to know something about the geography of El Paso and the location of its high schools. Juarez, Mexico, lies south of the Rio Grande from El Paso; thus traditionally the heaviest concentration of Mexican-Americans has always been on the South Side.

Jefferson and Bowie High Schools, located in South El Paso, have for years been comprised mainly of Mexican-American students. In contrast, El Paso and Austin High Schools, located in the central part of town, have largely had Anglo enrollment along with a scattering of typically middle-class Mexican-American students. The newer suburban high schools—Andress, Irvin, Burges, and Coronado have also had, with the exception of Burges, relatively few Mexican-Americans. Technical High School, in the center of town, was changed this year to Technical Center—a school which next year will no longer offer academic courses or a high school diploma. Thus, since regular classes were being phased out, a number of students—largely Mexican-Americans from south El Paso wanting to enter "A Tech"—were forced into the halls of Austin High School last September even though they wanted to go elsewhere.

Here they came, the slow-walking girls of the freshman class. They moved along sidewalks toward a building which they had always considered "the gringo school on the hill," the snob school with its fancy golden dome, the school that—so rumor had it—didn't really like Mexicans. They came with their dukes up, not willing, in 1969, to let anyone put them down. They walked onto the campus in groups, they ate lunch in groups, they shouted in Spanish at boys from crowded doorways in groups, they waited in groups for whatever action might develop at the nearby Dairy Queen. And they were not Americans, in their own minds: they were Mexicans, they were *la Raza*. Their ties were to Mexico—its language, its culture, its dress and mannerisms.

They were the first class ever to enter Austin High expressing openly the attitudes and behavior patterns of a subculture world (and there seems to be little reason for their younger sisters and brothers to be thinking any differently in '71 and '72). They were not concerned with their "future," these stubborn, defensive South Side girls. Why should they be? They had on their block-heeled shoes, a transistor radio was pressed against their ear; their hair was hanging long and black and loose past their shoulders. Their skirts—brief triangles and handkerchiefs of color—revealed a long, mod stretch of legs halfway up the body.

They were like aliens in a hostile territory, not bothering to care about Austin's Most Beautiful Girl (—it certainly won't be a Mexican, they told one another) or the Select Scholar's list or the "Let's Really Yell it Now, Y'All" that the blonde cheerleader was getting red in the face about down on the gym floor. And they didn't care when they were warned during the morning p.a. announcements that they would "seriously jeopardize future freshman assemblies unless their conduct was more in line with that Austin expected of its student body."

They weren't interested in what Austin expected of them any more than they were interested in diagramming or reading *The Odyssey*. They were simply prisoners being held in an Anglo jail and they would continue to stare out sullenly through their granny glasses until the sentence was lifted.

It has long been the custom of school boards to select principals and other administrators from the ranks of coaches. It is not unusual, therefore, that the principal of Austin High is a former football coach; that the coordinator of instruction and guidance—presumed by many to be the successor to the principal when he retires—is an ex-coach also; and that the counselor most influential with the Austin administration is a former basketball coach. (Indeed, Austin is such a sports-and-coach oriented school that teachers in the good graces of the administrators are likely to be addressed by them as "coach." Thus the most unathletic math or government teacher finds himself being called "coach" as he requests an overhead projector or discusses a class load, for *coach* is the official password, the casual sign of camaraderie, the measuring stick of status).

It is safe to say that the principal and coordinator love Austin High School—that they consider it to be at the core of their life's work. It is also safe to say that both are sincere, intelligent men who are doing their jobs as they see them and who want perhaps more than anything else to keep Austin's image as a Good School from being damaged.

But sincerity, intelligence, and love-of-school—certainly adequate equipment for administrators during the less complex era of the '40s—are not enough to cope with the unsettling seventies. What is also needed are a high degree of flexibility in responding to potentially explosive situations which did not exist thirty years ago; a willingness to understand and trust student leaders who ask for change; and perhaps more than anything else, empathy with persons of minority groups—especially, in El Paso, Mexican-Americans.

High school administrations are generally conservative by nature; Austin's administration is perhaps more conservative than most. It thus views hippies, Reies Tijerina, César Chávez, black militants, anti-war demonstrators, college long hairs, etc. with a wholly unfriendly eye. The faculty, however, shares in large part this same conservative view. (Austin's Teacher of the Year for 1969–70—selected by Austin Teachers—had a sticker on his car reading "Register Communists, Not Firearms"). Whether the teachers' conservatism is directly related to age is conjectural, but the fact that out of a staff of over 100 probably less than half are under the age of forty does suggest that the majority of the faculty is far from being attuned to the strident harmonies of today—especially those voiced with a Spanish accent.

During the past year there was mild racial tension—mainly in September when a *chicano* walkout was threatened and Mexican and Anglo groups fought several afternoons after school; there was an awareness that the "melting pot" togetherness which Austin had begun priding itself on during the last few years had gradually begun to disappear; there was a feeling among many of the Mexican-American students—not just the reluctant freshmen—that they were the Unseen and Ignored Majority as far as honors, offices, awards, etc. were concerned. There was also a grim little war concerning censorship of the student newspaper, the *Pioneer*.

At the beginning of the year an administrative staff member had been assigned the extra duty of censoring the *Pioneer*. (Such censorship by an administrator rather than the journalism teacher was a city-wide policy). In October the administrator censored a letter-to-the-editor by junior journalism student Cecilia Rodríquez. The letter which dealt honestly with Mexican-American experiences and attitudes in typical school situations, was subsequently printed in the UT-El Paso college newspaper, the *Prospector*.

In April, a group on the *Pioneer* staff wanted to devote a entire issue to the concerns, problems, and culture of Mexican-American high school students. After much discussion—in which a few of the more secure Mexican-American students themselves balked at being singled out for special attention ("We're all Americans, aren't we?")—it was agreed that a single page of Mexican-American features would be run. When copy was submitted to the administrator, he cut the four lead articles: "Brown Misery"; "La Huelga," an article about César Chávez and the California farm workers' grape strike; an article on the origin and significance of the term *chicano;* and "the Race United," an article on the newly formed political party in Texas for Mexican-Americans.

It was a typical student-administration conflict. The administrator, in keeping out of the *Pioneer* what he considered to be extremist or inappropriate material, felt, one can be sure, that he was fulfilling his role as censor and was doing what was best for Austin High. What he did also, of course, was frustrate—once again—the efforts of some of the most creative, conscientious, and morally sensitive students at Austin—both Anglo and Mexican-American. ("Change this school?" said one depressed student afterward. "Never. You see how much trouble we had getting just one lousy, watered-down page in the *Pioneer.*" Another student added: "They say their doors are always open —yet every time you go to see them their minds are always closed. You can just see *No* staring at you before you even open your mouth.")

Thus the staff member added another footnote to an already familiar tale: high school administrators ironically helping to create the very college radicals whom they dislike, as well as stimulating the possibilities for an underground press. For the students finally end up believing what they really, at first, do not want to beleive: that the administration *doesn't* really care to understand what they are trying to say, *doesn't* realize that times have drastically changed, *doesn't* care about the quality of people's lives if those lives are led by blacks or browns; *doesn't* care to admit to the reality of a world which exists right outside the classroom

doors in the streets, on the television sets, in the books available at every drugstore. Such students who try to express their idealism, and fail, simply resign themselves rather bitterly to their high school fate and wait for college—when they feel they can get rid of all their pent-up frustration in orgies of action.

Thus, at a crucial moment in its history; Austin seems to be maintaining a steady course of drift. Apparently, the official policy is: Business as usual. Don't rock the boat if you want to be considered a good fellow. And don't stir up any trouble about problems which you feel are mounting—wait and see if they don't go away as they always have in the past.

But what is buried at the heart of the problem? Why *should* Austin teachers sigh at the prospect of their high school being filled with Mexican-Americans? Why, really, should Mexican-Americans be less academically capable than Anglos? Who is to blame?

The problem is many-rooted and complex, of course. Yet if there is an answer to the question, Who has been at fault, it should be arrived at after considering these points:

1. For too long Mexican-Americans have been offered the least and the worst of everything that is available in Texas, from jobs to housing to education to social status. They have been forced to live on the bottom rung of society and adopt the survival rules of what Daniel Moynihan has called the "underclass." They learn at a very early age not to believe in the "better tomorrow" of America's Protestant ethic. They learn not to believe they will get ahead by merely studying hard and saying yes-sir and going by all the rules. They learn not to hope, or to save up nickels for a rainy day. They learn not to be open and trusting and optimistic. Indeed, they learn many things which do not help them get A's in government or spelling.

2. A study of underprivileged children, by Norma Radin (condensed in the September-October, 1968, issue of *Children*), has this to say about the "hidden curriculum" which is available in middle-class homes but which is generally absent from homes of the disadvantaged: "Shapes, colors, numbers, names of objects, words on signs, etc., are part of the continuous input to the child. . . .

Books are read, stories are told, intellectual curiosity is rewarded, and efforts perceived as school-oriented are praised. These activities are not part of the mother's role in the lower-class home." The study also states: "A large fraction of the intelligence of a child is already fixed by the age of five. No amount of environmental change beyond that point can affect the intellectual capacity to any significant extent."

3. Granting the difficulty of trying to do alone what society as a whole should do, and granting the possibility that some Mexican-American children by age five are already too severely handicapped to compete on an equal basis with Anglos, the public school administrators of El Paso should nevertheless be held accountable for failing to implement—years ago—a program of bilingual education for elementary grade Mexican-American children. Chances are the school system will not remedy these children's needs until officials decide to give them massive assistance and the highest priority: until they decide that not only the bright Debbies and Bills from middle-class homes have the right to become surgeons and bankers and civil engineers but also the Rogelios and Alicias from south of Paisano Street who have typically grown up not able to read and not seeing much point in learning how to anyway.

The school system must try bold new approaches in order to break the miserable chain of failure which has linked each successive wave of Spanish-speaking students. The traditional methods have not worked, and Head Start—which gets children after the first crucial five years—is simply not enough. Therefore, if the school system does not wish to perpetually deny children from Spanish-speaking homes a chance at the greatest possible success our society offers, then it must implement programs which will allow a child who speaks no English in the first grade to nevertheless become proficient in writing and reading English in a reasonably short time.

4. The voting public bears part of the blame for school ills: One group generally wants "safe" school board members—those who will go slow—instead of concerned, progressive individuals who understand the need for change. The other group refuses to vote at all: it always lets conservatives have their way at the polls and determine important elections with a few hundred votes.

5. Many nervous parents transfer their children from the inner city schools to those in the suburbs—leaving the inner-city schools to become, finally, all Mexican-American. This happens because the typical middle-class Anglo parent is unwilling to run the risk of having *his* child receive less than what he conceives to be the best education—that is, the parent refuses to let his child pay the penalty for society's failure to educate Mexican-American children so that they are on a par with Anglos. Thus he sends his son to the suburbs—hoping the kid won't get on pot or acid—and leaves such schools as Austin and El Paso High to sink or swim with the many black eyes and brown skins. (Classic example: For many years El Paso High School was attended by students from the affluent Kern Place and Rim Road sections "on the hill" above the school, as well as by students from modest homes in the flatland below. It was a relatively successful mingling of rich, poor, and middle-class. Then Coronado High School was built in northwest El Paso, and school authorities gave parents the choice of sending their children to Coronado or El Paso High. The Anglo rush toward a lily-white school began and thus El Paso High—finally cut off from the Rim Road and Kern Place areas through obvious gerrymandering—has had its enrollment to drop by approximately 1,000 students.)

If school administrators genuinely want to educate students for the lives they will be leading in the '70s and '80s—rather than just keeping them quiet and off the streets—they must provide courses and teachers that are meaningful to both the highly motivated academic students and the indifferent, withdrawn couldn't-care-lessers. They must also determine which teachers do the incredibly difficult job of plunging into their subjects and making them exciting, challenging, alive—and which teachers merely show up for work, "keep order" with a deadening fervor, and then go home again.

And the principals: they should be energetic, widely read men who are conversant with the issues of the times and the problems which face students in their schools. They should be men who are constantly mingling with the students—staying in touch, hearing what they have to say in this era of intense social concern and audacious questioning of the status quo—rather than presiding over their desks in their offices. They should be "shirt-sleeves-rolled-up" administrators of the '70s, moving among students the way Mayor Lindsay moves through the people of New York. They should be courteous, open-minded, contemporary men whom the students feel are on their side—which of course, they will be if they are successful principals.

. . . The pictures on the wall at Austin High will continue to look out from a simpler time. Whether it was also a better time more just, more democratic—more American—time is still to be decided. If we truly wish to educate everyone and not just an elite—and if we find ways to turn that wish into a reality—then the glory that was yesterday will pale beside the glory of today.

James Officer

James Officer (Coordinator of International Programs and Professor of Anthropology, University of Arizona) studied urban Chicanos in the barrio of Tucson. In this excerpt from his Ph.D. dissertation, "The Joining Habits of Urban Mexican Americans" (1964), Professor Officer evaluates from his personal experiences the leadership and reasons for the Tucson Chicanos' considerable influence in local elections. Professor Officer has a good deal of knowledge of politics and government, having served both as Assistant Commissioner of Indian Affairs (1962-1967) and as a special assistant (1967-1969) to the then Secretary of the Interior Stewart Udall.
By permission of the author.

Politics And Leadership

During the period of my fieldwork, representatives of the Tucson Mexican colony were successful in winning election to two of Pima County's most important political offices. A Mexican-born lawyer in 1958 was named one of four judges to the county superior court and another young lawyer in 1960 was chosen as one of three county supervisors. The Mexicans had never before had a county judge and only one other member of the colony (Mariano Samaniego) had ever been a county supervisor. However, through the years Mexicans, at one time or another, had occupied most of the other county elective offices; had served on the city council and on the school board of Tucson District No. 1. The Alianza during its early history, and later, the Spanish-American Democratic Club, served the colony well in helping it to become politically sophisticated and aiding it to organize in such a way as to make its influence felt at the polls. Interest in politics among Tucson Mexicans was quite high, even the women taking part in political campaigns.

For many of those in the colony, politics was not so much concerned with choosing the candidate most qualified for office, as with selecting the one most likely to fulfill patronage promises. There was an expression which was frequently used to describe the plight of the individual who had aided a politician and got nothing in return. He was said to have been *muy mal paga'o* ("very poorly paid") for his efforts. Tucson's Mexican-Americans were not the only ones who were guided by such a philosophy, but they were more likely openly to acknowledge the motivation which underlay their voting behavior.

Feeling that Mexican votes, through patronage promises, could be "purchased," Anglo politicians literally swarmed through the *barrios* in election years seeking out the centers of influence and authority. During the election campaigns of 1958 and 1960, I was privileged to have a ringside seat in the *cantina* operated by one of the small Mexican political *jefes* in South Tucson. Anglo office-seekers who would not have deigned to enter his establishment in the "off" years all but established headquarters there while running for office.

Except for rare occasions when a severe crisis confronted the colony, it was split into many factions and no single individual or group could properly presume to speak for all. During the 1960 elections, there were at least five recognizable political factions within the colony, all related to the Democratic Party. At the outset of the campaign, Faction "A" led by the Anglo who held the county's most important political post appeared to be the most powerful. The nucleus of Mexican membership in this faction came from county employees and their families, and its focus of operations was the Latin-American Social Club. (Several of the former leaders of the Spanish-American Democratic Club had been associated with Faction "A", but by 1960, one of the most important had died and another was in such poor health that he could not make much of a contribution.)

Faction "B" was headed by a Mexican notary public who had formerly served in the state legislature. This man was a highly controversial figure in the total community, having attracted much attention to himself through publishing a small pamphlet in which he attacked the editor of the morning newspaper, the chairman of the county board of supervisors, the mayor, and several other Anglo notables. He drew most of his support from disgruntled lower class elements in the *barrios,* and received financial assistance from wealthy individuals, both Mexican and Anglo, who were opposed to the city and county administrations in power.

Faction "C" consisted of a small handful of the most loyal followers of the supreme president of the Alianza. In previous elections, this faction had supported many of the candidates endorsed by Faction "A", but, feeling that the influence of this group was waning, the supreme president in 1960 put up a separate slate of candidates. He was not seconded in this decision by all of the Aliancistas, since some of the candidates he chose to back were running against members of the Alianza lodges.

Faction "D" also included as its nucleus a small group of leaders from the Alianza. These were young men in their late 20's from the Alianza lodge known as the Monte Carlo Men's Club. They were mostly veterans and university graduates and their greatest political strength came from the Menlo Park district, and the *barrios* of El Río and Hollywood. They concentrated much of their attention on electing Mexicans to the state legislature and on capturing control of the county machinery of the Democratic Party.

Faction "E" was a coalition group, including among its organizers several small *jefes* who had defected from factions "A" and "C". Some were dissatisfied county employees and others were individuals with an extreme dislike for the supreme president of the Alianza. They gave their support to a young Mexican lawyer in the race to overthrow the Anglo head of Faction "A".

In the 1960 elections, the honors went to Factions "D" and "E." The Anglo who headed Faction "A" was soundly defeated by the young lawyer, and many of the candidates supported by the Alianza president also lost.

Through the years Mexicans had been less successful in winning elections than in helping elect Anglos who could be relied upon to fulfill campaign patronage promises. Many Mexican *jefes* concerned themselves less with the ethnic and racial backgrounds of candidates than with the likelihood of the latter to provide jobs for chicanos. The feeling of these politicos was summarized for me early in 1961 by the man who had been the leader of Faction "B." (At the time he had just been convicted in Federal court of falsifying an immigration document.) According to his observation: "It doesn't make much difference whether a candidate is a *gringo* or a *chicano.* One can screw you (*Uno le puede chingar*) just as bad as another. The thing that counts is whether he'll deliver what he says he will when he gets into office."

Although a woman of Mexican descent had been the Pima County Recorder for many years, women from the colony did not often seek political office. However, many contributed to the political life of the community and several, through politics, had moved into important city and county offices. For example, the city clerk was a Mexican woman, as was the clerk for the county board of supervisors and one of the deputy county attorneys. Those men from the colony who involved themselves in politics often called upon their wives and other female family members for aid. "Women have the time to work," one of the Mexican *jefes* told me in 1960, "and without their aid a Mexican candidate hasn't got much chance." Several of my informants reported that during the elections of 1958, a prominent U.S. Senator on a visit to Tucson sought out and spent several hours with two middle-age Mexican women who were *madrecitas* of large families.

Just as it was important in other areas of colony life, the kin group played a significant role in the realm of politics. Family members were expected to stand together in support of a candidate (they did not always do so,) and the Mexican political chieftains tried to enlist the support of persons from large extended families whenever they could do so. An informant reported that during the 1958 elections a Mexican who had previously supported one of the prominent Anglo politicians switched his allegiance to another candidate and brought with him the votes of more than 100 close relatives.

Those who played major roles in colony politics were not the only individuals of influence. A survey which I conducted during 1958-59 revealed several other areas of leadership. One of the most

important of these consisted of the Spanish-language radio announcers of the city. One man especially had a tremendous following among the lower middle and lower class Mexicans. An immigrant from a small mining town in the state of Zacatecas, he had come to Tucson in the 1930s after working previously in the copper mines at Jerome, Arizona. In addition to mining, he had conducted a radio program in Spanish on one of the Jerome stations, and was able to arrange a similar broadcast in Tucson. Despite the fact that he was an "outsider," he quickly gained a following among Tucson Mexicans, and the volume of advertising handled by his program helped the radio station to survive the depression. By the time I began my fieldwork in 1958, this man had become a local legend and was doing both radio and television broadcasts.

Two other radio announcers were also very influential within the *colonia* at the time of my research. Both were immigrants, one being from Nogales, Sonora, and the other from Ciudad Juárez, Chihuahua.

Either individually or collectively, the radio announcers often sponsored *colectas* (fund raising campaigns) on their programs to aid colony residents faced with crises of various kinds. In this endeavor they were often helped by the Mexican formal voluntary associations.

The successful Mexican businessmen constituted another influential element of the colony's population. To the Anglos, these men symbolized the Mexican upper class, and although some ignored the daily round of the colony, when they did become interested in its affairs, they could quickly find followers. Among the most highly respected and influential of the Mexican businessmen was a bank vice-president who had served on the city school board a few years before I began my study. This man's father had continued to reside in Barrio Libre despite his sons's prominence and success.

Several Tucson druggists were men of influence. Foremost among these was the Anglo-Mexican who for many years had owned the city's largest drug chain. Although he had sold his business and retired a few years prior to the beginning of my fieldwork, he was still being sought out for advice on matters of particular interest to the Mexican population. Another prominent druggist, whose store was located in the downtown district, was the community's principal supplier of medicinal herbs and was much respected by the lower class population of the colony. He was one of the few Mexicans who took an interest in such groups as the Tucson Council for Civil Unity.

Barbers, butchers and bartenders also contributed importantly to the formulation of opinion within the *barrios*. The latter especially were influential with working class males who spent much of their leisure time in the *cantinas*. Politicians were well aware of the role of the bartenders *(cantineros)* and devoted much attention to winning them over in election years.

Apart from the church, the beauty parlor was a significant moulder of opinion among the women of the colony. Two such establishments which were especially influential came to my attention in 1959. One, located at the edge of Barrio Libre, was owned and managed by a woman from a pioneer Mexican family, whose husband was a druggist. She had been president of the Drachman School P.T.A. and of the Club Camelia. She was also active in the auxiliaries to a veterans' organization and an occupational association.

Another beauty parlor which played an important role in opinion making among the women of the colony was located in Barrio El Río, and managed by a young woman whose brother was an official of the Democratic Party. As I was completing my fieldwork, this woman and her Anglo sister-in law were talking about relocating their business to an Anglo neighborhood, a move which certainly would have reduced its influence on colony affairs.

Some years prior to my study, the newspaper *El Tucsonense* went into a majority of the Tucson Mexican homes and may be presumed to have contributed significantly to the thinking of the *colonia*. However, it was forced to discontinue publi-

cation in 1959 upon the death of its elderly editor. Another paper, called *La Voz*, was put out by the head of the *Sociedad Mutualista Porfirio Díaz* who owned a small printing shop. It was an advertising "throw away" and not widely circulated throughout the community. For a short time during the period of my fieldwork, the head of political faction "B" prepared and distributed an inflammatory pamphlet of political tone known as *Arizona P-M*. Its greatest appeal was to the lower class families of Barrio Libre. Just beginning to emerge as I finished my research was a paper called *La Prensa*, published by a young Mexican-American university graduate from California. Its influence on the thinking of the colony remained to be determined.

Despite the fact that its affiliated lodges did not always follow the leadership of its supreme president, the Alianza was unquestionably the most influential Mexican formal voluntary association. On political matters the Latin-American Social Club had been influential with many males of the lower middle and lower classes, but following the defeat of its candidate for county supervisor in the 1960 elections, its future role remained to be determined. With certain groups, the *Sociedad Mutualista Porfirio Díaz* and the *Cocío-Estrada Post* of the American Legion were important opinion-making collectivities.

Probably the most influential of the women's associations were the Club Camelia, the Ladies' Auxiliary to the Club Comwolei, the *Damas Auxiliares de la Logia Fundalora* (the women's auxiliary to the founding lodge of the Alianza,) and the Ladies' Auxiliary to the Benefit Sportsmen's Club.

Prior to World War II, the Mexican Consul had been a major influence on the Mexican Colony, but this was not so in 1959. The Consul's closest friends in the community were the persons who retained the greatest patriotic interest in Mexico and these were declining in numbers at the time of my study.

Donald Freeman

*Donald Freeman (Chairman of Political Science
Department, University of West Florida, Pensacola, Florida)
has co-authored a textbook,* POLITICAL PARTIES AND
POLITICAL BEHAVIOR *(1966) on the workings of the
American political system. In this paper read at the
Southwestern Social Studies Association in 1967, Professor
Freeman uses the tools of the political scientist to attempt to
determine the political patterns of the large Chicano
population in South Tucson.
By permission of the author. From a paper prepared for
the Annual Meeting of the Southwestern Political Science
Association, March 1967.*

Party, Vote,
And The Mexican American
In South Tucson

South Tucson is an incorporated city, completely surrounded by the city of Tucson. The little municipality (population of 7,004 in 1960, and about one square mile in land mass) is now twenty-seven years old, and apparently South Tucsonians continue to enjoy their separate existence. Incorporation was a tactic to avoid the taxes and regulations of Tucson. Over 60 percent of the population of South Tucson is Mexican-American, and Mexican-Americans dominate the government of the city today.

South Tucson was chosen as the universe for study because of the concentration of Mexican-Americans there, because the land area of the city could be covered easily in a survey, and because of its location only a few miles from the campus of

403

the University of Arizona. Since South Tucson is relatively small, we were able to use a two-stage, strict random sample. The research design and supporting interview schedule for the study were prepared to replicate substantial portions of the Voting Studies of the Survey Research Center of the University of Michigan and the study of Southern voting behavior done by Matthews and Prothro at the University of North Carolina.

THE SAMPLE AND OPERATIONAL DEFINITION OF "MEXICAN-AMERICAN"

Largely this paper is based on simple descriptive and comparative analysis, describing the political behavior of the Mexican-American and comparing it with the political behavior of known populations and a control group. There is little bivariate analysis presented here, and no multivariate analysis. The number of respondents in the sample produces very small "N's" in cells if very elaborate analysis is used. This study was designed and carried out as a pilot project, with hope that a much larger sample would be secured in a more extensive research project at a later date.

The sample is, I am convinced, an excellent sample of South Tucson. According to the 1960 census, 61.1 percent of the residents of South Tucson had Spanish surnames. The proportion of Mexican-Americans in our sample of South Tucson is 64.9 percent. One major fear of survey sample designers is an over-sampling of females, especially in marginal communities like South Tucson where the interviewer may be misperceived as a bill collector or a policeman. Our sample is composed of 53 percent females and 47 percent males, a remarkable balance when you consider that a number of the households in South Tucson are headed by women.

One of the most difficult tasks faced in drawing up the research design was defining the term "Mexican-American." Interviewer observation would ask the interviewer to make a very doubtful and difficult judgment. A direct question about ethnic background might offend the respondent, and Spanish surnames are not always indicative of Mexican-American stock. Therefore, we have used the following operational definition: any re-

spondent is Mexican-American if he or she, or his or her spouse, or any parent or grandparent of either the respondent or the respondent's spouse was born in Mexico. We also collected an interviewer perception of the ethnic background of the respondent, and this agreed with the operational definition in 185 of the 188 cases. On the basis of interviewer perception, three respondents were classified as Indian though they were born in Mexico. Operationally we have included them in the Mexican-American group. Our sample breakdown was as follows:

Mexican-American	64.9% (122)
Anglo	27.7% (52)
American Indian	4.3% (8)
Negro	2.7% (5)
Oriental	.5% (1)
TOTAL	100.1% (188)

In the balance of this paper we will group the Anglo, American Indian, Negro, and Oriental components of the sample together as "Others." The "Others" grouping is obviously a heterogeneous one, but it has a certain unity about it in being the non-Mexican-American population of South Tucson, and as such, is the best control group, based on similarity of setting, which we could use.

The major problem faced in the fieldwork for this project was the nature of the community to be studied. South Tucson is made up almost entirely of low income people who are largely outside the social mainstream of middle class America. The political world of such people is a limited world. As voting studies have demonstrated, most American voters live all their political lives with a limited awareness of issues, parties, politics, and governmental operations. The people who exist at the bottom of the status ladder (of whatever sort of measure you wish to use) attain a level of political knowledge far more limited than that of the mass public. Awareness of functional specialization within the world of politics may well escape the deprived and disinherited in our society. How meaningful are issue questions to these people? Are interviewer and respondent communicating with each other? Are concepts taken for granted by the research designer understood by the respondent? We were very conscious of this problem. We worked hard to gain complete acceptance in the South Tucson community, used screening questions on all major issue and behavior items, and had available to the interviewer check boxes for "didn't understand" in many sections of the questionnaire. In large part, we feel that we were able to measure lack of understanding and avoid incorporating it as a bias into the survey results.

SOCIAL CHARACTERISTICS OF SOUTH TUCSON

A drive through South Tucson will quickly convince a social scientist that he is observing a distinctive sub-population in society. One strip of retail and service establishments runs right down through the middle of the city. The balance of South Tucson is probably best described as humble, simple, or marginal housing. There is a substantial number of trailer-dwelling units in South Tucson. The motels have mixed temporary and permanent residents. There are many small houses in South Tucson which would never pass the building inspection laws of a modern city, but the city should not be described as a slum and a ghetto. It is more appropriate to think of it as a predominately Mexican-American enclave, with a number of substandard dwelling-units. Some houses in South Tucson that would have a very low tax evaluation are kept so well that they have a neat and attractive appearance.

Ninety-one percent of the Mexican-Americans in South Tucson are Catholics, compared to 37.9 percent of the Others category. One National Opinion Research Center sample taken in January of 1964 found the American general public to be 26.0 percent Catholic. The commitment of the Catholics in South Tucson to their church is not as great as you would find among Catholics in New England: 31.9 percent said they seldom or never attend church, and 37.7 percent said they are not strong Catholics.

Relying on the three best objective measures of socioeconomic status, we can draw a more detailed picture of the social and economic opportunities available to Mexican-Americans. Using occupation of the head of the houshold we find that only 3.3 percent of the Mexican-Americans hold white collar jobs (professional and technical, managers and officials, self-employed businessmen, clerical and sales), while 24.2 percent of the Others in South Tucson hold white collar jobs. The largest single occupational category for Mexican-Americans is unskilled labor, 28.7 percent. Eighty-two percent of the Mexican-Americans hold blue collar jobs, compared to 63.7 percent of the Others grouping.

The opportunity to break out of the blue collar occupational category is simply not available to the Mexican-American, since the educational background to make the move has not been acquired. Slightly over 10 percent of the Mexican-Americans have had no education at all, and a total of 57.4 percent of this ethnic group in South Tucson has had no more than a seventh grade education. The lack of education at the higher levels for Mexican-Americans is even more striking: no Mexican-American in our sample has completed college. If you add together all categories of education from completed high school on up, you find that just under 10 percent of the Mexican-Americans have a high school education or better. The Others grouping has been considerably more advantaged in education level. Only 25.7 percent of the Others have seven or less grades of schooling, and 30.3 percent of the group has a high school or better than a high school education.

There is no statistically significant difference between the Mexican-Americans and the Others on the basis of total family income. Twenty to 25.0 percent of the respondents did not give information on family income, which makes it impossible to do an accurate comparison between these and other sets of data from national studies. Most of the non-responses were "don't knows" and appeared to be genuinely based on an inability to determine the family income. Roughly one-third of the Mexican-American families have a total income of less than $3,000 a year, and over two-thirds of the families earn less than $7,500 a year.

The Mexican-Americans are quite aware of their social and economic condition. One fifty-three-year-old, second generation Mexican-

American, who had five grades of school was described by the interviewer in these terms:

> Respondent had strong feelings about any inequality because of race or wealth. She kept remarking about how no one cares about the poor—they are thrown into jail. And she was often not hired because she was Mexican. 'But we are free and have our health, so I can't complain.'

She is a housewife and a hospital kitchen aide; her husband is a laborer with Southern Pacific Railroad. For another example, a second generation Mexican-American male, forty-five-years-old, with one-half a year of education was described by the interviewer in this quote:

> Respondent had very strong opinions and was quite articulate, but he kept apologizing about how he talked. Said he wished he could express himself well, but didn't go to school and felt his English was poor. It really wasn't. He used some words like cooperate, etc., and used them properly. He said the fellows where he worked kidded him about how he talked. Really, most frustrated he was. Said he would like to tell a lot of people how he felt, and was glad to have this interview, but thought he still wouldn't get across what he meant. He is very bitter about government in a way. Said he used to be quite interested, but not any more—all he gets is promises and nobody will help.

In the party response section of this same interview, the respondent was asked "Is there anything in particular that you don't like about the Democratic party?" His answer speaks of his economic condition and reveals something of the operations of the Democratic party in South Tucson:

> Nothing to say against them—But, the guys after us for voting—get elected, and all that you just talk to me and we'll fix you up—get you work—8 to 10 days a month. They never did—I went to talk to [Mexican-American South Tucson Democratic Councilman]—out of work one and one-half years—losing

house—sorry nothing for laborer. What's the use of voting if they won't help us—even if he is Mexican, I'd rather go for white people even if I'm a Mexican.

In sum, there is ample evidence to convince the social scientist that the Mexican-American is disadvantaged socially and economically by his ethnic status.

POLITICAL PARTIES IN SOUTH TUCSON

The two great political parties in the United States are venerable institutions, with rich images and traditions which permit the voter and even the non-voter to relate through them with the world of politics. In *Political Parties and Political Behavior* this description of the mass public's image of parties appears:

> The images of the Democratic and Republican parties have remained rather stable for three decades. The Democratic party is the party of prosperity, war, creeping socialism, bureaucratic red tape, the little man, the laboring man, the Negro and minority groups generally, the welfare state, Franklin D. Roosevelt and John F. Kennedy, the South, and internationalism. The Republican party is the party of peace, responsible administration, depression, free economy, the businessman, the better classes, the white Protestant of English origins generally, Dwight D. Eisenhower, and Herbert Hoover, "Americanism," and cautious internationalism.

The images of the two political parties for Mexican-Americans and South Tucsonians generally fit rather well into research findings on the mass images.

The image of the Democratic party for South Tucsonians and for Mexican-Americans is quite positive. For South Tucson as a whole, 181 favorable comments were made about the Democratic party and only 49 unfavorable comments were made, a ratio of better than three favorable to one unfavorable comment. Mexican-Americans volunteered 112 favorable remarks to 22 unfavorable ones, a positive Democratic ratio of five to one.

Group Related responses account for 31.9 percent of South Tucson's image of the Democratic party. Traditional ties with the Democratic party (personal, family ties or affective comment) account for 24.5 percent of the remarks, and the Domestic Policies of the party account for another 14.1 percent. It is rather remarkable that Party Leaders drew only 10.1 percent of the volunteered remarks. Government Management is a cipher in the image, evoking about an equal number of positive and negative comments, while the Democratic party's Foreign Policies are a clear liability for its image.

For Mexican-Americans only, the image is even more clearly dominated by the Group Related, Traditional, and Domestic Policy components. Slightly over seventy percent of the Mexican-Americans volunteered positive remarks falling into these three categories. Only 21.3 percent of the Mexican-Americans volunteered remarks falling in all the other four categories.

The image of the Republican party among people in South Tucson is much weaker in detail, and substantially negative. The number of volunteered negative remarks is greater than the number of volunteered positive remarks, 72 to 50 for all of South Tucson and 35 to 22 for Mexican-Americans only. However, the negative feeling toward the Republican party appears to lack intensity—there appears to be an abbreviated or disinterested view of the Republican party. For South Tucson as a whole, the three leading components of the anti-Republican image are Group Related (11.7%), Party Leaders (10.1%) and Traditional (6.9%). Only the order changes when we talk about Mexican-Americans alone: Group Related (9.8%), Traditional (5.7%), and Party Leaders (4.9%). The pro-Democratic and anti-Republican views are not mirror images of each other; because Domestic Policy is supplanted by Party Leaders when you move from the pro-Democratic to the anti-Republican side of the data. An overwhelming proportion of the Group Related responses favoring the Democratic party and opposing the Republican party were couched in these terms: the Democratic party is the party of the common man, lower income people, working-class people, and the average man, while the Republican party is bad for these groups or good for big business, the upper classes, the rich and the powerful.

More than a few Mexican-Americans have no knowledge of political parties and politics—they are apolitical. One eighty-one-year old lady who was born in Sonora, speaks only Spanish, is not a citizen, and is a widow, could not distinguish between parties and government. We asked her what she likes about the Democratic party and she replied: "I am very happy in this country. I'm an immigrant and they have treated me with kindness." And some have only a limited view of the parties. For example, here are the statements from a twenty-seven-year old, second generation Mexican-American (he had seven grades in school, works as a dishwasher in a drug store, and there are eight adults and seven children in the household he heads):

Like about Democrats: "Some people say it's better than Republicans. I feel the same way as others."

Dislike about Democrats: "Seems all right to me."

Like about Republicans: "No."

Dislike about Republicans: "Just don't like them."

The affection for the Democratic party, and the positive image of the Democratic party, transcends generational and social differences among the Mexican-American people in South Tucson. Below I shall quote the party responses from several Mexican-Americans of different circumstances.

A. Female, forty-nine years old, she and her husband are second generation Mexican-Americans, nine grades in school, and she has voted.

Like about Democrats: "Democrats are mostly the poor people—they are more interested in helping the poor people—lots of Spanish-speaking people get jobs from the Democrats—not from the Republicans."

Dislike about Democrats: "No, nothing."
Like about Republicans: "No, I really don't like the Republican party very well."
Dislike about Republicans: "They are the party of the big fish; we are the little fish."

B. Male, fifty-seven years old, he was born in Arizona but his wife was born in Mexico, three grades of school, speaks only Spanish, has voted.
Like about Democrats: "Always provides jobs and supports."
Dislike about Democrats: "No, no idea."
Like about Republicans: No response.
Dislike about Republicans: "Yes, the Republican president in 1929 allowed the people to starve. Ever since then I have always disliked [them]."

C. Male, eighty-three years old, born in Mexico and came to this country in 1890, has been a citizen since 1946, two years of school in Mexico, retired from Southern Pacific Railroad, and has voted. Respondent speaks only Spanish.
Like about Democrats: "Democrats working man's party. Republicans for the rich. Democrats best for him because he is a working man."
Dislike about Democrats: "Nothing in particular."
Like about Republicans: "I don't like a thing. Some speak well of them, but I won't change my affiliation." All candidates promise much but do nothing. Once in office won't comply with campaign promises. All parties' candidates do this, no exceptions."
Dislike about Republicans: "Nothing in particular except they are the party of the rich."

D. Male, thirty-eight years old, he and his wife born in Mexico, is not a citizen, is trying to learn to speak English but now speaks only Spanish, has six grades of education, he is a laborer with a construction company, and has not voted.
Like about Democrats: "Its more on the side of the poor—makes a better chance for one."

Dislike about Democrats: "No."
Like about Republicans: "I don't know. The Democrats pull a little more to the side of the poor—it is convenient for one."
Dislike about Republicans: "No."

E. Male, twenty-nine years old, he was born in Mexico but his wife was born in Arizona, he is not a citizen, speaks only Spanish, has seven years of school, is a mechanic, and voted in Mexico but not in the United States.
Like about the Democrats: "They give more opportunities to the worker. They help."
Dislike about the Democrats: "No."
Like about the Republicans: "No. They don't help as much."
Dislike about the Republicans: "No."

Political Scientists have attempted to measure the voter's relationship with his political party in a variety of ways since the earliest voting behavior research. The most successful technique of measuring the voter's psychological relationship to his party is that designed by the Survey Research Center at Michigan. The SRC party identification scale classifies the voter at one of seven points along a continuum running from Strong Democrat through Independent to Strong Republican, or, if the person completely rejects party as a meaningful concept to him, he is designated as Apolitical. Party identification, as measured by the SRC scale, is a powerful independent variable which explains a substantial proportion of a person's partisan political behavior.

The party identification of Mexican-Americans in South Tucson is distinctively pro-Democratic. About one-half of all American voters are strong or weak identifiers with the Democratic party, but roughly two-thirds of all South Tucsonians are strong or weak Democrats. The Mexican-Americans are significantly stronger in their identification with the Democrats when compared to either a national sample or the Others group from South Tucson. Forty-three and four-tenths percent of the Mexican-Americans are strong Democrats, while only 0.8 percent of this group are strong Republicans. The proportion of weak Democrats to weak Republicans is 23.0 percent to 1.6 percent. As might be expected, given the Mexican-Americans' background and lack of socialization in this political system, 13.1 percent of the group is Apolitical, a figure much larger than one could find in a national sample.

The voting consistency of Mexican-Americans in all presidential elections reinforces the picture we are drawing of this group's attachment to the Democratic party. Thirty-six and one-tenth percent of the Mexican-Americans always vote Democratic in presidential elections, compared to 0.8 percent of the group that always votes Republican and 8.2 percent which votes for different parties. Mexican-Americans are distinctively more Democratic in the consistency of their voting than either the 'Others' group or the SRC 1964 national sample, and they are substantially under the 'Others' group and the SRC 1964 national sample in voting Republican and voting for different parties. The significantly large proportion of Mexican-Americans voting Democratic over the years is made even more remarkable by the fact that 47.5 percent of the Mexican-Americans have never voted and were thereby not distributed in the party voting frequency cells.

The extensive literature on American voting behavior that has developed in the last twenty years has revealed that party attachments for the individual voter are largely inherited from the voter's parents. We asked our respondents about the voting behavior of their parents and found that 72.1 percent of the Mexican-Americans either had parents who did not vote or they didn't know whether their parents voted. The socialization literature largely rests on parental party identification, not voting behavior, however there is an indication in our data that much of the party identification of Mexican-Americans cannot be attributed to parental political orientation. Only 23.0 percent of the Mexican-Americans had one or both parents who voted Democratic. As our party identification data would predict, only 2.4 percent of the Mexican-Americans had one or both parents voting Republican. The Others group divides much as you would expect a low-income population to divide: 45.5 percent had one or both par-

ents who voted Democratic, 6.1 percent had parents who voted for different parties, and 12.1 percent had one or both parents who voted Republican.

There are actually more strong Democrats, 44.4 percent, among those Mexican-Americans who said their parents did not vote or didn't know whether their parents voted than there are among those who said that one or both parents had voted Democratic, 42.9 percent. This would lead us to minimally hypothesize that the strong ties of Mexican-Americans with the Democratic party flow in part from the ethnic group to which they belong.

VOTING BEHAVIOR IN 1964

The most important observation one can make about Mexican-American voting behavior in 1964 is that 51.6 percent were not eligible to vote and 13.9 percent who were eligible did not vote. In other words, roughly two-thirds of the Mexican-Americans in South Tucson did not vote. Johnson outpolled Goldwater among Mexican-Americans 30.3 percent to 0.8 percent. About one-fifth of the Others group was ineligible to vote and another fifth was eligible but did not vote. The Others group divided its vote in favor of Johnson, 47.0 percent to 9.1 percent.

If we consider the voting decision of voters only in 1964, the distinctiveness of the entire South Tucson support for Johnson is quite clear. Johnson drew 97.4 percent of the Mexican-American vote and 83.8 percent of the Others vote in South Tucson. The comparable percentage from SRC's post-election reported vote from the nation as a whole was 67.5 percent. At least in South Tucson, Mexican-Americans voted for Johnson about as heavily as Negroes across the nation. Even allowing for an over-reporting of vote in favor of the winner in a post-election survey, this is a remarkably high level of support for President Johnson.

When voting behavior in 1964 is checked by party identification, there appears to be a clear relationship between the two variables, however, one must be very careful about interpreting these data since most of the cells in the table are empty or contain very small frequencies. Johnson received the votes of 43.2 percent of those Mexican-Americans who identified themselves as either strong or weak Democrats, 11.2 percent of the votes of persons who identified themselves as independent Democrats, Independents or independent Republicans, and none of the votes of the three persons who identified themselves as weak or strong Republicans. The persons who identified themselves as weak or strong Democrats appear to be more clearly integrated into the political system; of all the party identification categories, they have the smallest proportion who did not vote. All of the Apoliticals were ineligible to vote, as might be expected.

POLITICAL PARTICIPATION IN SOUTH TUCSON

One of the simplest measures of the voter's involvement in the political system is the voter's level of interest in politics. The low level of interest in politics on the part of all South Tucsonians is only one indication, among several which we shall now marshall as the conclusion of this paper, of their lack of integration into the American political and party system. There is no statistically significant difference between the Mexican-American and 'Others' categories; both have a low level of interest in politics. Just under one half of both groups say that they are "somewhat interested" in politics. Roughly four Mexican-Americans say that they are "not interested at all" in politics to every one who says that he is "interested a great deal" in politics. The Others group does have a substantially larger proportion saying they are "interested a great deal" in politics.

We have checked Mexican-Americans against Others in South Tucson on six types of political activity. In every case the Others group has a larger proportion of persons saying they have engaged in the activity. Because of the small frequencies involved in the cells of tables under analysis, there is no significant statistical difference between Mexican-Americans and Others in two of the six activities, however, the overall difference between the two groups is impressive. Only 52.5 percent of the Mexican-Americans *have voted* at some time in their lives. Eighteen per-

cent of the group have *attended political meetings and rallies.* The same proportion of the Mexican-Americans, 13.1 percent, say they have *made a financial contribution to a party* and *worked for a political candidate.* Fifteen and six-tenths percent of the Mexican-Americans *have tried to influence another person's voting decision,* and 2.5 percent *have held a government or party office.* The level of political participation of Mexican-Americans is quite comparable to the level of political participation of Southern Negroes in 1961 on three of the activities: attending meetings and rallies, making a financial contribution, and working for a political candidate. In 1961 only 41.0 percent of Southern Negroes said that they had voted at some time in their lives, significantly lower than the comparable 52.5 percent for Mexican-Americans in South Tucson.

The cause of the large non-voting population in South Tucson should be explored, since 47.5 percent of the Mexican-Americans and 19.7 percent of the Others group have never voted. Some non-voting exists all through our political system, and the traditional explanations one receives from the non-voter are: illness, not old enough before, military service interfered, work interferes, or my religion forbids any political activity. Only 17.2 percent of the non-voting among Mexican-Americans can be explained by one of these traditional "excuses," and the comparable figure for Others is 46.2 percent. Students of voting behavior also expect to find a segment of the public which lacks interest in politics or can give no reason for not voting; 22.4 percent of the Mexican-Americans and 30.8 percent of the Others give these explanations. The largest single explanation for non-voting given to us by Mexican-Americans is tied directly to the group's ethnic status; they say they are not citizens of the United States, they are immigrants and they don't relate to the system, or that they do not speak English. One of these statements explained non-voting for 41.4 percent of the Mexican-American group. Another 3.4 percent are illiterate.

The research design for this study was drawn up with the expectation that Mexican-Americans had been barred from the ballot box and had been victims of discrimination against them in the political system. A battery of questions to measure political discrimination in voting used by Matthews and Prothro in their study of Southern politics was included in our questionnaire. Not one indication of discrimination is to be found in our interviews. Throughout the interview schedules the respondents say they were treated well, fine, or great when they went down to register. Some respondents indicated that the mobile registration unit had come to their home to register them because they were not physically able to go down to register. In the language of one Mexican-American respondent, they treated him "well—they gave him full honors—first class." The precincts which serve South Tucson overlap areas of Tucson as well and may be staffed by non-South Tucsonians, however there is excellent evidence here that Registrars have not discriminated against Mexican-Americans.

There is ample evidence in the data we have already presented to demonstrate that Mexican Americans are poorly related to and only partially integrated into the political system. There is every reason to expect that the Mexican-American in South Tucson lacks information about the political system and that the government and its leaders are vague, only partially understood referents in their lives. We sought to test this hypothesis by including a simple political information test in the interview schedule. Six of the seven items used in our test were replicated from the Matthews and Prothro Southern political behavior questionnaire.

On five of the seven questions in the test a substantially smaller proportion of the Mexican-Americans answered the questions correctly compared to the Others group in South Tucson. On the other two questions, the proportion of both groups answering the questions correctly was small, and the margin of the Mexican-Americans over the Others was one and two percent. A summary table was prepared comparing the scores of the Mexican-Americans and the scores of the 'Others' group. Three Mexican-Americans for every one 'Others' group member answered none correctly, and more Mexican-Americans than Others answered one correctly, but at each of the other levels, from two correct to six correct, the Others group had a larger percentage of its members answering questions correctly than had the Mexican-

Americans. The mean score of correct answers for Mexican-Americans is 2.025; for the Others the mean is 2.939.

In each of the six directly comparable political information questions asked to Mexican-Americans and to Southerners, the proportion of Mexican-Americans answering the question correctly is smaller than the proportion of Southern whites answering the question correctly, and, in general, the Southern Negro scores higher than the South Tucson Mexican-American. The proportion of correct responses to the question "Do you happen to remember whether Franklin Roosevelt was a Republican or a Democrat?" was 54.0 percent for South Tucson Mexican-Americans and 57.0 percent for Southern Negroes. Forty-three percent of the Mexican-Americans could name the governor of their state, compared to 68.0 percent of the Southern Negroes. Only 18.0 percent of the Mexican-Americans could give the length of their governor's term of office, whereas 65.0 percent of Southern Negroes could give this information. Eight percent of the Southern Negroes and 4.0 percent of the Mexican-Americans knew that there are nine Justices on the United States Supreme Court. The two items on which the Mexican-Americans in South Tucson did better than the Southern Negro were: length of term of United States Senators (12.0 to 8.0 percent) and naming the last two states to enter the union (45.0 to 35.0 percent). I am hoping that our coders did not code as correct the several responses we received that a United States Senator must serve for a long time or life because "Hayden there always." This response does have a ring of truth to one who has lived in Arizona. It is likely that the Mexican-American margin over Southern Negroes on the last states entering the union is due to a passage of time and the greater proximity of Arizona to Alaska and Hawaii physically and historically in statehood.

CONCLUSION

We have only begun, in this brief paper, to sketch the broad outlines of the political behavior of Mexican-Americans in South Tucson. These sketches have been basically descriptive and comparative. Explanatory models of any level of sophistication are absent from this paper.

The picture we have drawn is of a people who are economically and educationally deprived, who see the Deomcratic party as an aid to the underprivileged and poor, who have a strong commitment to the Democratic party demonstrated in psychological identification with it and in a strong tendency to vote for it, and finally, who reflect their ethnic background and lack of integration in the political system through low levels of political participation and low levels of political information. All of these components of our picture are true despite the fact that these Mexican-Americans have their own city, governed by Mexican-Americans, and that there is no indication whatsoever that they have suffered discrimination at the ballot box. Mexican-Americans have held public and party offices at every level of Arizona state and local government, but probably not in proportion to their potential or real voting power.

Our data describe South Tucson. Do they describe all of the 3,344,000 Mexican-Americans in the Southwest? We don't know. Our social and economic data have been confirmed in other studies, but there has been a fantastic lack of attention to Mexican-American political behavior. The behavioral sciences must, in my opinion, turn their research attention to this ethnic group. Research using aggregate data on a large scale is underway; a few small-scale studies based on survey research have been conducted; large-scale, significant research on Mexican-American political behavior, using the most powerful research tools and techniques available (and of course calling on our foundations to open their coffers) is certainly in order at this time.

Ralph Guzmán

Dr. Guzmán (see p. 380) in the following essay discusses the softening of political campaigns for limited ethnic goals. Professor Guzmán then turns to seven selected organizations that work for The Mexican American's assimilation into American society and politics.
Ralph Guzmán "Politics and the Policies of the Mexican-American Community." From CALIFORNIA POLITICS AND POLICIES, Dvorin-Misner, (eds.), Reading, Mass.: Addison-Wesley, 1966. And by permission of the author.

Politics In The Mexican American Community

POLITICAL PARTIES

Like voting, political party membership before World War II was not well understood. Mexicans were not voters and they were not involved in party politics. Consequently, contact between the Mexican people and the two major parties was insignificant. Without contact, conflict did not exist.

Nevertheless, Mexicans who lived during the 1930s held definite images of each party. The Republican Party was the party of Hoover, and the Democratic Party was that of Roosevelt. Beyond this, Republicans were often identified with the heavy hand of authority that denied food and demanded conformity. On the other hand, Democrats always conveyed an image of liberalism, generosity, and understanding. The generalizations, while not always correct, remained as myths through the war years, to be revived in the late 1940s and the 1950s.

Political party recruitment in the Mexican communities of the Southwest was unknown and unnecessary, again with the possible exception of the

413

State of New Mexico. Mexicans had neither votes nor money. When the direct efforts of groups like the Community Service Organization (CSO) gave thousands of Mexicans the voting privilege, Republicans and Democrats took note of the political emergence of the Mexican people. In 1965 an important member of the hierarchy of the Los Angeles Democratic Party raised the question, "How can the Democratic Party become more effective in the Mexican community?" A Republican official commented: "If you try to move in, you meet a great deal of resistance, whether you are a Protestant missionary or a Republican. Mexicans really couldn't care less. . . . they just don't want to get involved politically."

METAMORPHOSIS

World War II accelerated the change from a predominantly rural to an urban orientation. Many of the young people had gone off to war. Those who stayed behind included young and old, men and women as well as citizen and noncitizen. Almost all of these people found employment in defense or related industries. The rural pursuits of the past were abandoned for better paying urban jobs.

In East Los Angeles, the *enganches,* contract labor crews, frequently organized among members of only one family, became less evident during the war. The migratory worker cycle that started in areas like Belvedere, and went north to the prune and grape country and back again to the walnut orchards of Southern California, was gradually brought to an end. The new caravans were exclusively male and were composed of Mexican nationals, contracted in Mexico under an international labor agreement between Mexico and the United States. For years to come, Mexican nationals, popularly referred to as *braceros,* were to dominate the agricultural fields where Mexican-Americans once labored.

Throughout the Southwest, the war fever of the majority group was picked up by Mexicans. War songs, the counterparts of famous American World War ballads, were composed in Spanish. One song, with an improvised arrangement of taps, the evening bugle call, began: *"Vengo a de-cirle adios a los muchachos porque pronto me voy para la guerra . . . "* ("I come to say goodbye to all my friends because I shall soon be going off to war . . . "). When the New Mexico National Guard was trapped in Corregidor, the war was brought closer to many Mexicans. Thousands of youngsters volunteered for combat. The Marine Corps and the Paratroopers, in particular, attracted Mexicans from the urban slums of the Southwest. In California 375,000 Mexicans joined the Armed Forces during World War II. In Los Angeles, where Mexicans made up 10 percent of the total city population when Pearl Harbor was bombed, Mexicans accounted for 20 percent of all names on the war casualty lists.

Both new-found urban employment and involvement in the armed forces contributed to the change from rural to urban life. Within the postwar urban *barrios, colonias,* or ghettos, further changes took place. Increased social interaction with non-Mexicans opened new social vistas and new ethnic goals. Unknown to many members of this minority group, the process of acculturation had increased its effect on the members of the urban Mexican community.

Social change seemed to be greatest in residential areas where Mexicans were well-integrated with other peoples, including so-called Anglos. On the other hand, neighborhoods that were predominantly Mexican reflected less rapid social change during the early postwar years. East Los Angeles provides a graphic illustration. The first significant postwar political activity took place in the Boyle Heights community, where Mexicans lived side by side with other minorities. On the other hand, social change came about more slowly in the predominantly Mexican enclave of Maravilla, located on the outskirts of the Los Angeles urban area.

THE GAME OF POLITICS

Increased contact with Anglo society during the War, together with the new-found urban status of the Mexican, gave rise to commensurate political activity throughout the Southwest. However, most of this activity was local and of a protest nature. Often, discrimination and other majority group pressures forced the creation of new organizations that were later to reach national prominence. One such organization was the American G.I. Forum organized in Corpus Christi, Texas after a local cemetery refused to accept the body of a Mexican serviceman who died during World War II. In California, Pomona and San Bernardino Valley veterans, ranch hands, industrial workers, and railroad laborers formed Unity Leagues in order to deal with local problems, e.g., street lighting, sanitary conditions, street repairs, and politics. Throughout the Southwest, both old and new organizations emphasized the ballot as the most important method for bringing about social change.

Political organization was rarely exclusively Mexican in plan and execution. Considerable financial and organizational support was given to the Mexican people by sympathetic Anglos. Anglo groups like the Race Relations Council, the Industrial Areas Foundation, the Fund for the Republic, the Marshall Trust Fund, and many labor and church groups made substantial contributions. In addition, minority group organizations like the Legal Redress Committee of the National Association for the Advancement of Colored People (NAACP), the Urban League, the Anti-Defamation League of B'Nai B'rith, the American Jewish Committee, the Japanese-American Citizens' League (JACL), and several other groups provided funds and/or organizational knowledge to Mexican groups, particularly to the Mexican-American members of the Community Service Organization (CSO).

Mexicans were a disadvantaged people who recognized their social problems but who knew little about means for solving those problems. The concept of community organization, working together and finding allies among non-Mexicans, was not a familiar one. Invariably, community goals were defined with great difficulty. And when agreement did prevail, the implementation of proposals suffered from lack of full-time personnel and funds with which to pay them.

In California, the efforts of the American Council on Race Relations, and later the program of the Industrial Areas Foundation, emphasized (1) voter registration of Mexicans by Mexicans, (2) articula-

tion of community needs by members of the community, and (3) continuous participation at the polls. The task was *not* how to induce a sense of community (an ethos), but rather how to organize Mexicans so as to recognize and achieve a priority of goals.

Voter registration of Mexicans by Mexicans forced community people to articulate organizational goals at the screen doors of their neighbors. Mexicans learned to walk the pavements and to ring doorbells. Many learned to sell American democracy at the doorstep in both English and Spanish. Mexican voter registrars were best equipped to establish instant rapport in the Mexican *barrios,* thus helping to bring about permanent social change.

Whereas, in the past, social workers and well-meaning private citizens had tried to articulate the ethnic goals of Mexicans, the Race Relations Council and the Industrial Areas Foundation emphasized indigenous expression. Mexican Laborers, their wives, and their children learned to speak up at community meetings.

Organizational efforts were not always successful. Enormous apathy and self-denunciation blocked early postwar attempts to organize the Mexican community. Heavy clouds of cynicism, distrust of the Anglo, and fear of other Mexicans enervated the Mexican people. Anglos were suspected of ulterior motives, of trying to use the Mexicans, and of being insincere. Mexican leaders, on the other hand, were equally suspect. Too many of our leaders, the people said, betray us once they are in power.

Ultimately, post-war organizational efforts in California and in other parts of the Southwest resulted in improved relations between the Mexican people and governmental agencies, other minorities, and with the majority group. Ethnic goals became more clearly defined.

ETHNIC GOALS AND ANGLO POWER

After World War II, Mexicans tested the boundaries of the Anglo political world. Some, like Gustavo Garcia in San Antonio, ran for elective office in the school system and won. In other areas, Mexicans filed for political office, ran, and lost. Few had precinct-level experience and fewer still knew how to deal with "entrenched" Anglo politicians. Like Don Quixote, postwar Mexicans were convinced of the "justice of our cause." However, pure ethnic politics was seldom successful. Invariably, Mexicans were confronted by the majority group's political power structure, which was not always understanding and accommodating. In 1963, the Mexican community of Crystal City, Texas, aided by the Political Association of Spanish Speaking People (PASSO), the Teamsters Union, and other groups, won control of the home town's political system. Two years later, in 1965, a coalition slate of Mexicans and Anglos defeated the all-*chicano* group.

In California, two political campaigns, both organized in East Los Angeles, reveal how campaign strategy was adjusted in order to achieve limited ethnic goals. The campaign of Edward R. Roybal, when he first ran for Councilman in the Ninth District of the City of Los Angeles, is one example. A second is Leopoldo Sánchez' campaign for Municipal Court Judge in the East Los Angeles Judicial District. Both candidates were resisted by Anglo politicians. And both men wore the ethnic label. Yet each resolved the conflict of ethnic goals and Anglo power in different ways.

Roybal's effort was set in Boyle Heights, an east side community where there was much interaction between Anglo and Mexican and also a substantial amount of conflict. On the other hand, the Sanchez judicial campaign was launched in Belvedere, where there was little Mexican-Anglo interaction but a great deal of conflict. Another important difference is time. The Roybal campaign was initiated shortly after World War II, when Mexican social issues, sometimes provoked by the Los Angeles police, were immediate and urgent. By contrast, the Sánchez campaign took place in the late 1950s after great political momentum had been gathered and when police brutality, discrimination in housing, unequal educational opportunities, and other social problems seemed less urgent. However, it is in the area of ethnic goals that the greatest disparity between Roybal and Sánchez is seen. Roybal, recruited by a group of Mexican businessmen as an ethnic can-

didate to replace an aging Anglo in City Hall, dispensed with pure ethnic politics early in his campaign. Sánchez, on the other hand, maintained an ethnic platform in which he stressed that the majority of the people who came before the east side judiciary were Mexican, and that a Mexican from the local area could best administer the law for Mexicans.

While Roybal's district was heavily Mexican, the Mexicans were widely interspersed with other minority groups. Consequently, victory for Roybal depended on the successful blending of minority voting blocs (i.e., Mexican, Jewish, Negro, Oriental) along with pockets of Anglo votes. The Roybal strategy, to which no Mexican Democratic Party campaign organizer contributed personally, deemphasized the image of a Mexican politician.

Sánchez' East Los Angeles Judicial District included a heavily Mexican section (around Belvedere and Maravilla), several neighborhoods where Mexicans were interspersed with Jews, and a heavy concentration of Anglos in the Montebello area. In terms of voting blocs, Sánchez faced a more difficult path to victory than Roybal.

Ethnic goals in the Sánchez campaign, while clear from the beginning, were placed in sharp relief by opposition from Governor Brown. And, unlike Roybal who had the invaluable services of a professional Anglo organizer, Sánchez counted on a few friends, mostly from the American G.I. Forum, a Mexican civic action group. Reconciliation of ethnic goals with Anglo political power came early in the Roybal campaign because the issues were specific, e.g., discrimination in housing, in employment, and before the law. For Sánchez, the issues were vague, e.g., the need for Mexican representation and the need for justice. Sánchez noted that "bread and butter issues are not at stake in a judicial campaign." In the Roybal effort the issues concerned a candidate for a legislative post.

Today, several years later, both men remain important ethnic symbols. However, neither seems exclusively concerned with the ethnic goals that appeared sharp and urgent at the outset of their campaigns. Both seek effective involvement of Mexicans in the American political system.

ETHNIC GOALS AND ETHNIC ORGANIZATION

Civic organizations have been vehicles for the accomplishment of minority goals. However, American society has changed, and so have the goals of the minorities. The result is that new models of the vehicles of social change have emerged.

The following typologies of Mexican organizations is useful to the understanding of the creation of Mexican organizations and of the shifting patterns of ethnic goals: (1) assimilation into American society, and (2) participation in the American political system. Seven selected organizations illustrate this pattern of changing group goals. These organizations, arranged chronologically in terms of the period in history when they were created, are as follows:

1. The Mexican Liberal Party (MLP), organized September 28, 1906;
2. The Order of Sons of America, founded circa 1920;
3. The League of United Latin-American Citizens (LULAC), established in 1927;
4. Community Service Organization (CSO), chartered in 1947;
5. American G.I. Forum, organized in 1948;
6. Mexican-American Political Association (MAPA), founded in 1959;
7. Political Association of Spanish Speaking Organizations (PASSO), founded in 1960.

Concern for social assimilation as expressed in the constitution of the organization, recruitment pamphlets, house organs, news releases, and public statements by elected officials are used to classify organizations in terms of high, medium, or low intent to become socially assimilated. Some groups, for example, express organizational goals of complete integration into American society, with small concern for retention of things Mexican or a Mexican way of life. At the other extreme, some organizations emphasize retention of things Mexican or a Mexican way of life and only small concern for integration into American society.

In addition to general social goals, all organizations seem to have a high, medium, or low intent to become politically partisan. Some groups, for example, are highly active politically. On the other hand, some organizations are studiously nonpolitical.

THE MEXICAN LIBERAL PARTY (MLP)

Organized in St. Louis, Missouri, the Mexican Liberal Party of 1906 was oriented toward Mexico. Like the Cuban expatriate organizations of today that plan for the recovery of their island homeland, Mexican refugees established centers of resistance in the United States. Assimilation within American society was not a group goal. Nor was political participation in the American political system. The MLP exemplifies a Mexican organization functioning within the United States with little or no intent of belonging to American society or of participating in the American political system.

When members of the MLP intervened in the politics of Mexico, the neutrality laws of the United States were breached and MLP members were placed on trial in a Los Angeles Federal Court. Mexican residents, according to McWilliams, demonstrated great interest in the legal proceedings. Each day, supporters of the MLP would appear in court wearing the red arm band, the symbol of the organization; the visual effect was that of a solid phalanx of red. However, no evidence exists that the MLP's completely Mexico-oriented goals survived the trial and later the death of Ricardo Flores Magon, the principal defendant.

THE ORDER OF SONS OF AMERICA

During the early 1920s, a number of Mexican organizations had goals whose social intent seemed to be complete assimilation into American society, accompanied by some disturbance of the political seas. The Order of Sons of America *(Orden Hijos de America),* organized in Texas, was such a group. They did not demand "a complete equality either among the Mexican-Americans themselves or between them and the Anglo-Americans." Group goals for the Order of Sons included:

1. Elimination of racial prejudice;
2. Equality before the law;
3. Improved educational opportunities;
4. A reasonable share of the political representation in the affairs of the community, State, and Nation.

In order to achieve these social and political goals, the organization placed great emphasis on learning the English language and on the acquisition of naturalization papers. Indeed, the Order of Sons of America declared that their membership was restricted "exclusively to citizens of the United States of Mexican or Spanish extraction, either native or naturalized."

LEAGUE OF UNITED LATIN-AMERICAN CITIZENS (LULAC)

By 1927 the Order of Sons of America split and the League of United Latin-American Citizens, commonly referred to as the LULAC organization, emerged in the State of Texas. Like the Order, LULAC reflected a serious intent to become assimilated into American society and moderate concern for political participation. LULAC documents from this founding period are difficult to obtain. Douglas Weeks reports LULAC goals which reflect high intent to assimilate into American society. However, little is said about political intent. The following assimilation goals seem designed to reduce potential Anglo apprehension:

1. To develop within the members of our race the best, purest, and most perfect type of a true and loyal citizen of the United States of America.
2. The acquisition of the English language, which is the official language of our country, being necessary for the enjoyment of our rights and privileges . . . we pledge ourselves to learn and speak and teach same to our children.

Other LULAC goals similarly focused on ultimate assimilation. Unlike the Mexican Liberal Party, the LULAC organization did not create conflict between Anglo and Mexican. Whereas members of the MLP invaded the Mexican Republic from bases in Los Angeles, the LULAC and its antecedent, the Order of Sons of America, were concerned with peaceful entry into American society.

The MLP attracted intellectuals and individuals whose interest in the United States was transistory and based on the hope that they would someday return to Mexico. On the other hand, both the LULAC group and the Order of Sons of America had a permanent interest in the United States and, at best, only a casual concern for Mexico.

COMMUNITY SERVICE ORGANIZATION (CSO)

The aftermath of World War II brought with it the first significant alteration of previous sociopolitical goals. Throughout the Southwest, marked emphasis on political participation was seen. New organizations like the Community Service Organization (CSO) in the State of California called for increased political involvement of "the masses." "the grass roots," and the people of "the *barrios*" in American democracy. CSO organizers talked in terms of "the people in city hall" and the "need for more Spanish surnames on the voter registration lists downtown." Beginning on an intensely high level of political participation, as the partisan supporters of Edward R. Roybal's campaign for City Councilman, CSO members reduced their activity to nonpartisan civic action. The CSO focused on the community and less on individual candidates. Though members had once seriously considered calling their organization the Community Political Organization (CPO), they agreed that the connotations of this name were "too political."

Significantly, the social intent of the CSO seemed to balance the political intent. CSO members selected a name for their organization that did not have Mexican connotations. Social assimilation, therefore, clearly seemed a concomitant goal with political participation. Indeed, CSO campaigns for integrated public and private housing supported an implicit intent to assimilate into American society.

Whereas the Order of Sons of America and the LULAC organizations had earlier pointed to goals similar to those of the postwar CSO, the older organizations had couched their sociopolitical intent in more cautious phraseology. An early preamble of the CSO constitution (1949) set the following aims:

1. To guard and further our democratic rights.
2. To become aware of our responsibilities as citizens.
3. To better discharge our civic duties.
4. To coordinate our efforts for the common good of the community [12, p. 2].

Unlike earlier organization, the CSO did not restrict membership. Use of the English language and American citizenship were not prerequisites to membership. The CSO focus was on an economically and socially deprived sector of American society that happened to be Mexican, and all persons with concern for the people who lived in these deprived sectors were accepted as members. Consequently, the membership base became vast and heterogeneous. Members ranged from the very old to the very young, and from the recent immigrant from Mexico to the highly acculturated Mexican-American professional. When necessary, the Spanish language was used in order to improve communication, not to preserve a culture.

Like the Order of Sons of America and LULAC, the CSO also stressed American citizenship. When the Japanese Americans Citizen League (JACL) succeeded in its efforts to include a section in the Walter McCarran Immigration Law of the early 1950s that would enable immigrant "old-timers" to become naturalized in the language of their birth, the CSO launched a highly successful citizenship drive. Classes in Spanish, taught by CSO members, brought full American citizenship to thousands of old-timers in their sixties.

THE AMERICAN G.I. FORUM

The changing context of American society affects the goals of minority groups. It may be hypothesized that minority communities in the United States organize because (1) they want something, e.g., increased sociopolitical involvement, or (2) they want to defend themselves against an immediate majority group threat. In both instances undercurrents of conflict are present, the heritage of the past.

The genesis of the American G.I. Forum in Three Rivers, Texas supports the hypothesis of defense. In this respect, the American G.I. Forum, in large part a veterans' organization, is singular among Mexican organizations. Like the Order of Sons of America and LULAC, the American G.I. Forum was formed in an area of the Southwest where the heritage of conflict was severe and omnipresent. Unlike the Community Service Organization in California, the American G.I. Forum's home grounds appeared to be much more hostile.

In 1947, when the body of a Mexican-American G.I. was returned to Three Rivers, the use of local mortuary and cemetery facilities was refused. Mexican-American G.I.'s met to protest the discrimination. Telegrams and letters were sent to Congress and to the press, making the case of the deceased Private Felix Longoria well known throughout the country. Ultimately, Private Longoria was buried in Arlington, Virginia, through the intercession of then U.S. Senator Lyndon B. Johnson. Months later, Mexican-American G.I.'s met again to protest discrimination and poor service at a veterans' hospital in Corpus Christi, Texas. At this second meeting, identified as a public forum for the discussion of problems facing Mexican-American G.I.'s, the American G.I. Forum of Texas was born.

In spite of the fact that it had been organized out of urgent necessity and in response to restrictive pressure from the majority group, the ultimate social goals of the Forum reflected a balanced image which seems to be at once very American and very Mexican. For example, the format of American G.I. Forum meetings, the ceremony and the dialogue, is not unlike what is seen at an American Legion meeting or at some other veteran groups, Forum members wear campaign caps with the rank and home town of the wearer embroidered in gold lettering.

Unlike other veteran organizations, the language of American G.I. Forum members occasionally lapses into Spanish. A casual visitor to a Forum function may get the impression that the Mexican personality of the Forum is more pervasive when the meetings adjourn and informality returns.

Politically, the American G.I. Forum goes to the brink of partisanship. Like the CSO, the Forum is explicit about its political intent. It calls for increased political participation and openly encourages potential leaders to run for office or to seek political appointments. Though professing political neutrality, it is a predominantly Democratic organization. Many Forum leaders enjoy close personal friendships with members of the hierarchy of the Democratic Party.

While skirting the edge of total partisanship, the Forum ranks high in political participation in the American political system. Unlike other organizations, it has a full-time lobbyist in Washington, D.C. and a monthly newspaper that constantly emphasizes social legislation on the State and Federal levels. In 1960, Forum members figured prominently in the Viva Kennedy Club movement that helped to win the Mexican vote for John F. Kennedy.

Where other organizations have failed to weld regional interests into functioning national organizations, the Forum has succeeded. Forum chapters exist in every southwestern state, and several more groups have been organized in other states of the Union.

The American G.I. Forum's sociopolitical goals are partially reflected in recruitment literature that pledges to

1. Develop leadership, by creating interest in the Mexican-American people to participate intelligently and wholeheartedly in community, civic, and political affairs.
2. Advance understanding between citizens of various national origins and religious beliefs.
3. Present and advance the basic principles of democracy.
4. Aid needy and disabled veterans.

THE MEXICAN-AMERICAN POLITICAL ASSOCIATION (MAPA)

The balance between social and political goals achieved by organizations like the American G.I. Forum and the Community Service Organization (CSO) after World War II kept both organizations on the edge of partisanship. A curious political contradiction emerged during the 1950's. Organizations like the Forum and the CSO armed the Mexican people, a predominantly Democratic electorate, with the franchise, thereby increasing the Democratic Party's strength. Yet few effective efforts were made by Anglo Democrats to integrate the emerging Mexican community into the formal structure of the Party. For years, Democratic Party organizations throughout the Southwest appeared unable or unwilling to reach Mexican political activists. Consequently, many Mexican organizations and Mexican individuals remained outside of the organized life of the Democratic Party. Mexicans with political experience in labor unions, civil rights groups, and civic organizations sought participation in the formal structure of the Democratic Party. They considered this a logical move for a minority group emerging within the American political system. Unsuccessful efforts to open gateways into the Party structure convinced some ethnic leaders that "we are taken for granted." Meaningful participation in politics thus became a matter of paramount concern.

In 1959, after Henry P. Lopez, a Harvard-trained Mexican-American lawyer, became the only casualty on an otherwise victorious California slate of Democratic candidates, a convention was called in Fresno to consider means of protecting Mexican political interests. At that convention, the Mexican-American Political Association (MAPA) was formed.

Unlike other ethnic organizations, MAPA made explicit its serious political intent and small concern for social assimilation. MAPA members chose an ethnic organizational name that was clearly Mexican. The organization's political goals were similarly stripped of ambiguity. Mexican candidates were sought and heartily endorsed. Public positions were taken on issues affecting Mexicans. Other forms of political participation included voter registration drives, get-out-the-vote campaigns, and visits to elected and appointed officials to lobby for Mexican political interests. Within a relatively short time, the politically militant tactics of MAPA made it well known in California politics.

To judge from public positions taken, MAPA focuses more on politics and less on the sociological question of acculturation. Nevertheless, MAPA's name and political stance make it appear highly political within the American political system, and yet distinctively Mexican within American society.

POLITICAL ASSOCIATION OF SPANISH-SPEAKING ORGANIZATIONS (PASSO)

The genesis of PASSO reflects political change within the Mexican minority and the Anglo majority. By 1960, most Mexican organizations were involved in politics. Political activity ranged from cautious support of voter registration efforts to explicit advocacy of particular campaigns. In California, old-line organizations supported the nonpartisan recruitment of new voters. At the other extreme, the Mexican-American Political Association (MAPA) urged the voters to vote and to be partisan.

MAPA's activity attracted attention throughout the Southwest. In Victoria, Texas in 1960, a group of individuals organized a Texas counterpart of the California MAPA. The Texas organization was called Mexican-Americans for Political Action; its initials, of course, were also MAPA. The Victoria, Texas MAPA was overshadowed by a sudden mushrooming of *Viva Kennedy Clubs* after the late President won the Democratic nomination in Los Angeles. The *Viva Kennedy Clubs,* organized outside the regular framework of the Democratic Party, drew members from most of the active organizations of the Southwest, and captured the imagination of the Mexican electorate everywhere in this region. Apparently, both the widespread attraction and the intense political activity of the *Viva Kennedy* movement coopted the Texas MAPA's purpose and area of action.

After John F. Kennedy's Presidential triumph, *Kennedy Club* members and representatives of the California MAPA gathered in Phoenix, Arizona. Political activists from each of the five southwestern states met for the purpose of form-

ing a national organization. *Viva Kennedy Club* members included political activists who were also members of other Mexican organizations. Some of those other organizations were the League of United Latin-American Citizens (LULAC), the Community Service Organization (CSO), the Alianza Hispano-Americana (AHA), and the American G.I. Forum.

Throughout the convention, the California members of MAPA urged that the format of the proposed national body be comparable to that of MAPA, and recommended explicit identification as a *Mexican* political organization. The MAPA position was, however, rejected.

A consensus prevailed that Puerto Ricans and other Latin Americans who, it was argued, lent significant support to the *Viva Kennedy Club* movement merited some concern. Opponents of the MAPA strategy, which called for clear ethnic identity, suggested that a less ethnically partisan name could conceivably reattract non-Mexican Latin-Americans. Ultimately, the Political Association of Spanish-Speaking Organizations (PASSO) became the name of the new national organization. In California, however, both MAPA and the CSO refused to subsume their activities beneath the PASSO label.

Today, PASSO maintains a high level of political participation, mainly in the State of Texas. Like MAPA in California, PASSO concentrates on direct political action. Recently, in 1963, PASSO, joined by the Teamsters' Union and other organizations, helped to elect a completely Mexican slate of city officials in Crystal City, Texas. The Crystal City victory appeared to be a high-water mark of political activity for PASSO.

Like MAPA, the Texas-based PASSO does not seem to have much concern for social assimilation. PASSO, again like MAPA, reflects explicitly partisan political goals, in spite of the apparent ambiguity that its organizational label proclaims. A woman orator at a PASSO rally said:

Los Mexicans han estado en el back seat for *muchos años* (The Mexicans have been in the back seat for many years.) Let's get in the front seat and go. We, the Mexicans, deserve a few paved streets and a little self-dignity, and we're going to get it.

PORTENTS OF CHANGE

It has been said that the majority group determines the behavior of the minority. This relationship is evident in the politics of the Southwest. The California context is different from that of Texas. In California, Mexicans were able to organize the Mexican American Political Association, an unquestionable Mexican organization with untarnished ethnic goals. On the other hand, a clear ethnic identity in Texas was possible only briefly, when the Mexican-Americans for Political Action was formed. In California, prejudice against Mexicans is considerably less than it is in Texas and in other parts of the Southwest. It is easier (and safer) to say "Mexican" in California than it is in other states. In Texas, for example, "Mexican" has unmistakable pejorative implications derived from a heritage of conflict.

POLITICS

The political effectiveness of MAPA and PASSO is much debated by Mexicans and non-Mexicans alike. Among Mexicans it seems generally agreed that both MAPA and PASSO perform an essential gadfly function that has on occasion caused the donkey to bray and the elephant to trumpet. However, a significant section is concerned lest the image of a stoical, uncompromising Mexican supplant that of the docile *bracero.* One non-Mexican, a defeated officeholder in Mathis, Texas, said:

I don't know what it is they want. These people on the other side have got so bitter. I asked one of the Mexican leaders, "What are you people up to? What have we done?" All he could say was, "We want to get on top."

VOTING

Mexican leaders at a 1965 meeting in Los Angeles said: "The Mexican vote, once a monolithic Democratic vote, has shrunk and so has our political effectiveness." The voting strength of the Mexican in California has, indeed, dropped. Massive voter registration drives, once common in East Los Angeles, have been replaced by occasional specialized and narrowly focused efforts in selected Spanish-surname precincts. Out of a 1960 potential voting population of more than 600,000 Spanish-surname people in California, less than 20 percent were registered voters, and fewer yet were brought to the polls. In Los Angeles County a potential Spanish-surname vote of 256,000 was never activated. An estimate of comparative voting strength between Negro and Mexican voters (U.S. citizens only), based on 1960 Census data, suggests a potential Negro vote on the State level of 454,000 and a Mexican vote of 633,000. In Los Angeles County, the population of U.S. citizens in both groups is more nearly equal. Negro voters are computed at 243,400 and Mexicans (Spanish surnames) at 256,800. The combined potential of these two enormous minority groups has long been a prominent point in majority group conversation.

RACE RELATIONS

Substantial support has been given to the Mexican people by other minority groups and by members of the Anglo majority. That Jewish organizational know-how and Jewish funds have helped the Mexican people of California is slightly known. Less known is the political and financial aid that was rendered by the Negro community.

In California, there have been two examples of Negro cooperation and assistance to the Mexican community. One involved a group of Mexican and Negro citizens from El Centro, California who, in 1955, jointly filed a class suit in a Federal district court in an effort to end school segregation in California. The case, called *Romero vs. Weakley,* was sponsored by the Alianza Hispano-Americana and the National Association for the Advancement of Colored People (NAACP). Several other organizations, among them the American Civil Liberties Union, the American Jewish Committee, and the Greater Los Angeles CIO Council, filed an *Amicus Curiae* (Friend of the Court) brief supporting the Mexican and Negro plaintiffs. A news release from the Alianza Hispano Americana announced:

This *case* marks the first time in U.S. history that the Negro and Mexican communities have joined hands, as American citizens, to fight for a common social problem.

Three years later, in 1958, a Negro woman lawyer, representing a coalition of Mexican and Negro politicians, nominated Henry P. Lopez, a Mexican Attorney, for the office of Secretary of State at a convention in Fresno, California. That same year the Democratic Minority Conference, a predominantly Negro association, organized and financed an intensive voter registration drive among Mexican and Negro voters that netted 25,-000 new voter registrations within a three month period.

Comparable cooperation between these two massive minorities no longer prevails. Mexicans and Negroes have long shared similar economic and social distress in the large urban centers of the Southwest. And yet today, meaningful dialogue between responsible Mexican and Negro leaders is not heard. However, with the increasing pressure of the Negro Civil Rights movement, it seems likely that Mexicans will eventually seek renewed contact with the Negro people.

IMMIGRATION

Outside of the Southwest, majority group members view Mexicans in the same way as they do other American immigrant groups. For example, at the 1965 White House Conference on Education a participant commented that "Mexicans will cease to have problems when they become better acculturated, just like the Poles, the Italians, and other immigrant groups." This facile solution, unfortunately incorrect, ignores the historical factors that differentiate the Mexican from other minorities: the symbiotic relationship between the American Southwest and the Mexican northern area, and the difficulty of guarding the border. Most of all, it ignores the millions of Mexicans who have long had roots in this country. Given these conditions, it seems highly probable that the Mexican community will for a long time remain an emerging social complexity with a very real, and unresolved, heritage of conflict.

RudolfoGONZÁLes

Rudolfo Gonzáles (boxer, poet, author, politician, and social activist) heads the Crusade for Justice in Denver, Colorado.
Mr. Gonzáles certainly has had a wide enough range of experiences to ask the Chicano if he intends to work within or out of the system. The student must answer this question, too.
From "What Political Road for the Chicano Movement?" in: THE MILITANT *(March 30, 1970). Reprinted by permission of the publisher and the author.*

Chicano Nationalism: The Key To Unity For La Raza

Corky Gonzales: I reserved getting involved in some of the sensitive issues here. There are so many things that go through my mind, I know I can't make a short statement and really answer the questions raised, for example, the questions raised by the young ladies who took their positions up here. [At the beginning of the session a demand was made to have women be represented on the panel and two women, including Isabel Hernandez, were seated.] I've many thoughts on that line as I mentioned here last night, and I might mention a few of them here again today.

We understand and realize after having been involved in many kinds of movements, what the

strength of a woman is, and what her strength is to the movement. We also recognize, watching many of our college students here, one of the things that the young lady said at the end of the table, that we can intellectualize and we can rap, but that we must also get down to the grass roots. Which comes to the use of the tools which Froben mentioned here, which comes to the question of how do we start this political party?

Before I get into that though, I want to get back to the women's situation, not to get into an argument, because I don't want one unless we have an hour and a half or two hours. I want to say only this: That one of the problems that I see, as one of

424

the grass roots people that came out of the *barrios,* as someone who worked in the fields, is that I recognize too much of an influence of white European thinking in the discussion. I hope that our Chicana sisters can understand that they can be front runners in the revolution, they can be in the leadership of any social movement, but I pray to God that they do not lose their *Chicanisma* or their womanhood and become a frigid *gringa.* So I'm for equality, but still want to see some sex in our women.

So I want to rap. I want to tell you about some of the things we feel. I think that Tony Camejo hit on some very important points that we should analyze. I mentioned last night that we have to stop falling in the same old traps, stop being affected by the same commercial stuff that the majority of this idiotic society is believing—like the fact that if you used enough Hai-Karate you would have so many women after you that you would have to walk over a mattress of women to get the one you want. You know this is the type of thing that brainwashes the whole community. So we have to understand that all these false ideas they have put before us are illusions. That these false ideas are the same ones they have always used to control. The symbol of Anglo superiority has got to be destroyed. And the burden of Chicano inferiority has got to be destroyed. So, in doing these things, we want to control and develop our own leadership, and to politicize people—not just make politicians—but to make people aware and teach them. This has got to come through actions, not words. We understand that.

I don't want to get involved in discussing personality. But, because I'm very nationalistic, I'm very glad to hear Tony Camejo say that if we had a Chicano party, he would be willing to run as a Chicano in the Chicano party. I'm very proud of that and very thankful that he said that, realizing that his expertise and his professionalism, his brains, can be utilized within the Chicano community to help create that liberation that's important. Not to be dominated by white society that has set up every type of political party that exists today.

You know we had communalism and socialism hundreds of years before the white man ever hit these shores. And so did many of the other countries that were occupied but not "discovered" until the *gringo* got there with a cross and a gun.

Now we want to talk about how we are going to create action in the people. What are the common denominators that unite the people? The key common denominator is nationalism. When I talk about nationalism, some people run around in their intellectual bags, and they say this is reverse racism. The reverse of a racist is a humanitarian. I specifically mentioned what I felt nationalism was. Nationalism becomes *la familia.* Nationalism comes first out of the family, then into tribalism, and then into the alliances that are necessary to lift the burden of all suppressed humanity.

Now, if you try to climb up a stairway, you have to start with the first step. You can't jump from the bottom of this floor to the top of those bleachers. If you can, then you must be "super-*macho.*" (I don't talk about super-man.) But, you can't, so you start using those tools that are necessary to get from the bottom to the top. One of these tools is nationalism. You realize that if Chavez, or any popular figure in the Mexicano scene decides to run, and if he ran for any party, as popular as he is, then out of nationalism we would even vote for an idiot. If his name was Sanchez, if his name was Gonzalez, you would walk in and vote for him, whether you know him or not, because you are nationalistic. And we have elected too many idiots in the past out of nationalism, right?

Now, let's take that common denominator, that same organizing tool of nationalism, and utilize it to work against the system. Let's use it to work against the two parties that I say are like an animal with two heads eating out of the same trough, that sits on the same boards of directors of the banks and corporations, that shares in the same industries that make dollars and profits off wars. To fight this thing, you look for the tools.

Now, if Tony is a socialist, if my brother here is an independent, if my sister is a Republican—she might hit me later—if one of the others is a Democrat and one is a communist, and one from the Socialist Labor Party, what do we have in common politically? Nothing. We've been fighting over parties across the kitchen table, wives are Republicans and husbands are Democrats, sometimes, and we argue over a bunch of garbage. And the same

Republicans and Democrats are having cocktails together at the same bar and playing golf together and kissing each other behind the scenes.

So you tell me then, what is the common denominator that will touch the *barrio,* the *campos* and the *ranchitos?* Are we going to go down there with some tremendous words of intellectualism which they cannot relate to, when they relate on the level of, "We need food. We need health care for our children. I need someone to go down to juvenile court with my son. There is no job for my husband." And the revolution of 15 or 20 years from now is not going to feed a hungry child today.

So what is the common denominator we use? It is nationalism. If someone wants to turn around and say, "That's a cultural bag," I tell them to go to hell. Because I know one thing—in our group we have dropped all the parliamentary procedure bull, we dropped all the *gringo* type of government, and we have a *concilio de la familia.* And a seven-year-old boy can get up and make his ideas heard and can influence a change that everyone else agrees with.

A woman who influences her old man only under the covers or when they are talking over the table, and then he goes in—if it's a bad idea—and argues for that, because he's strong enough to carry it through, is doing a disservice to *La Causa.* Any woman can influence a man whether she is weak or strong. So it's better for her to bring it out in the *concilio* and then all of us can take it and evaluate it as to whether it's right or wrong, good or bad.

All right, how do we start this? We start it and call it an independent Chicano political organization. We can use it as Tony mentioned also, under the FCC code, we can use it as a forum to preach and teach. We can gain the same amount of radio and TV time as any phony candidate. We proved it in Colorado. I ran for mayor as an independent, and I campaigned two weeks. Two weeks, because we were busy directing a play and busy in civil rights actions. But, we had the same amount of time on TV as anybody else, and on radio. We were able to start to politicize people. We were able to start to tell about an idea. We were able, even, to sue the mayor and the top candidates for violating the city charter, for spending more money than the city provided for under its constitution. We had that mayor and the most powerful Republicans and Democrats sitting on their asses down in the courtroom. Our method was to take them to court, to take them to task, to show the public that they were corrupt. And we proved that they were liars, over and over again.

We must start off by creating the structure—the concilio—by calling a congress sometime this spring, bringing together all those people that believe that it can be done. We understand that when we organize in an area where we are a majority, we can control. Where we are a minority, we will be a pressure group. And we will be a threat.

We understand the need to take action in the educational system. We understand that we need actions such as the "blow-outs," because the youth are not afraid of anything. Because the youth are ready to move. The whole party will be based on the actions of the young, and the support of the old.

Secondly, in the communities where we are a majority, we can then control and start to reassess taxes, to start charging the exploiters for what they have made off our people in the past. You can also incorporate the community to drive out the exploiters, to make them pay the freight for coming into the community, and sign your own franchises. You can de-annex a community as easily as they annex a *barrio* and incorporate it. You can create your own security groups, and place a gun here to protect the people, not to harass them, but to protect them from the Man who is going to come in from the outside. You can also create your own economic base by starting to understand that we can share instead of cut each others' throats.

Now what are the tools? We said nationalism, which means that we have to be able to identify with our past, and understand our past, in order that we can dedicate ourselves to the future, dedicate ourselves to change. And we have to understand what humanism really is. We can tie the cultural thing into it, but we also have to tie in the political and the economic. We tie these things together, and we start to use the common denominator of nationalism.

Now for those Anglo supporters, don't get uptight. For the Black brothers, they are practicing the same thing right now. And we understand it and respect it. And we are for meaningful coalitions with organized groups.

We have to start to consider ourselves as a nation. We can create a congress or a *concilio.* We can understand that we are a nation of *Aztlan.* We can understand and identify with Puerto Rican liberation. We understand and identify with Black liberation. We can understand and identify with white liberation from this oppressing system once we organize around ourselves.

Where they have incorporated themselves to keep us from moving into their neighborhoods, we can also incorporate ourselves to keep them from controlling our neighborhoods. We have to also understand economic revolution, of driving the exploiter out. We have to understand political change. And we have to understand principle. And the man who says we can do it within the system—who says, "Honest, you can, look at me, I have a $20,000-a-year job"—he's the man who was last year's militant and this year's OEO employee (Office of Economic Opportunity). And now he's keeping his mouth shut and he ain't marching any more. We have to understand that he is not a revolutionary, that he's a counter-revolutionary. He's not an ally, he becomes an enemy because he's contaminated.

You can't walk into a house full of disease with a bottle full of mercurochrome and cure the disease without getting sick yourself. That's what we say about the lesser of the two evils. If four grains of arsenic kill you, and eight grains of arsenic kill you, which is the lesser of two evils? You're dead either way.

We have to understand that liberation comes from self-determination, and to start to use the tools of nationalism to win over our *barrio* brothers, to win over the brothers who are still believing that *machismo* means getting a gun and going to kill a communist in Vietnam because they've been jived about the fact that they will be accepted as long as they go get themselves killed for the *gringo* captain; who still think that welfare is giving them something and don't understand that the one who is administering the welfare is the one

that's on welfare, because, about 90 percent of the welfare goes into administration; and who still do not understand that the war on poverty is against the poor, to keep them from reacting.

We have to win these brothers over, and we have to do it by action. Whether it be around police brutality, the educational system, whether it be against oppression of any kind—you create an action, you create a blow-out, and you see how fast those kids get politicized. Watch how fast they learn the need to start to take over our own communities. And watch how fast they learn to identify with ourselves, and to understand that we need to create a nation.

We can create a thought, an idea, and we can create our own economy. You don't hear of any "yellow power" running around anywhere. Because they base their power around their church, their house, their community. They sell Coca Cola, but their profits go to their own people, you see, so that they have an economic base. We are strangers in our own church. We have got *gachupin* (traditional term of contempt for Spaniards who ruled Mexico for 400 years) priests from Spain in our communities, telling us *vamos a hechar unos quatros pesos en la canasta* (let's throw four pesos in the collection dish). And then he tells you, "I'm your religious leader," and he tries to tell you how to eat, where to go, who to sleep with and how to do it right—while he's copping everything else out. You know, we're tired of this kind of leadership.

You have to understand that we can take over the institutions within our community. We have to create the community of the Mexicano here in order to have any type of power. As much as the young ladies have created power in their own community. But they have to share it with the rest of us. They have to be able to bring it together. And we are glad when they sit down instead of retreating. It means that we're all one people. It means that we're all one *Raza* and that we will work together and we will walk out of here in a positive fashion.

And then you have to think positive. Don't think it can't be done. If you think negative you won't get across the street. You think positive, because it only takes a minority to begin to win over and move a majority. It only took Pancho Villa and seven men to cross El Rio Bravo and end up with a hundred thousand men in Mexico City. It only took Castro 82 men, and they killed all but 15, and 15 men took a nation. It only takes an idea and a philosophy to carry it through, and if the philosophy is written with the blood of martyrs, it cannot be erased, and we can become a free people. Thank you.

6.

CONCLUSION

Conclusion

Just as politics and the Chicano ended with a hint and a question, so do the editors end with the same conclusion. In the general introduction, it was pointed out that what gave birth to this volume was the lack of adequate historical treatment about the Mexican American. The Introduction also stressed the need for evaluating Chicano history. Indeed someone eventually will, but the question is how and from what frame of reference? Many Chicano intellectuals believe that their history has been distorted, and that Chicanos should take great care to write their own story. The concluding essays by Joseph Navarro, Fernando Peñalosa, and Ralph Guzmán address themselves to these points, and offer possible suggestions to future historians.

433

FeRNANdo PeÑAloSA

Fernanado Peñalosa (see p. 255) expresses satisfaction that no longer will sociological studies of Mexican Americans be done exclusively by Anglos. But he warns, too, that before the Mexican American sociologist begins work in this nascent field he should try to define the extremely varied and complex nature of the group. Then Professor Peñalosa asks several questions about the Mexican American population and offers very tentative answers to the student. Reprinted from AZTLÁN-CHICANO JOURNAL OF THE SOCIAL SCIENCES AND THE ARTS, *Volume 1 Number 1, (Spring 1970), Aztlán Publication's, Chicano Studies Center, UCLA, pp. 1–12.*

Toward An Operational Definition Of The Mexican American

The sociological study of the Mexican American, until very recently almost the exclusive province of Anglo sociologists, is about to be launched into a new period of development that should certainly produce more fruitful, more realistic, and more relevant data and conclusions than have previously been forthcoming. Before we move into this new period, however, we would be well advised to map out somewhat more carefully the population

we are going to study. In developing a relatively new field it is not so important to attempt to produce immediately the right answers as it is to ask the right questions. If we ask simple questions we may get simple and probably misleading answers, particularly since our subject is not at all simple, but exceedingly complex. Mexican Americans may constitute one of the most heterogeneous ethnic groups ever to be studied

434

by sociologists. With reference to the scholarly study of the Mexican American we would be well advised to stop trying to find the "typical" or "true," and seek rather to establish the range of variation. Generalizations extrapolated from the community in which a Chicano writer happened to grow up or which an Anglo sociologist or anthropologist happened to have studied can be particularly misleading.

It is furthermore essential that we avoid simplistic either-or types of questions, such as, are Chicanos a people or not?, do they have a distinctive culture or not?, or is there such a thing existentially as the Mexican American community or not? Realistically we are handicapped in attempting to answer these types of inquiries in which the alternatives are already implicitly limited by the question itself. A much more productive approach might be rather to consider prefixing our questions with a phrase such as "to what extent ..." so that we ask to what extent Mexican Americans constitute a stratum, possess a distinct subculture, etc.

Scholars, both Chicano and Anglo, have furthermore spent countless hours debating the question of the correct name for our group, and then attempting to define the entity for which the supposedly correct name stands. Perhaps the time has come to move beyond terminological and definitional polemics to an examination of some of the dimensions along which we might explore our subject in an attempt better to understand its character.[1]

The method of procedure in this paper will be as follows: A series of questions will be asked about the Mexican American population. An attempt will be made to answer each one, based on the writer's admittedly limited perception of the current state of knowledge, and to point out some possible lines of future research along that dimension. *Some* day, when we have approximately adequate answers to the questions posed, we *may* have a more of less acceptable operational definition of the Mexican American. By way of overview, these are the questions which will be discussed:

1. To what extent do Mexican Americans constitute a separate racial entity?

2. To what extent do Mexican Americans conceive of themselves as belonging to a separate ethnic group?

3. To what extent do Mexican Americans have a separate or distinct culture?

4. To what extent do Mexican Americans constitute an identifiable stratum in society?

5. To what extent is it realistic to speak of Mexican American communities?

6. To what extent are differences in historical antecedents reflected among Mexican Americans?

7. To what extent are regional socio economic differences significant among Mexican Americans?[2]

Let us then direct our attention to each of these questions in turn.

To What Extent Do Mexican Americans Constitute a Separate Racial Entity?

A goodly number of Mexican Americans and others are confused as to the biological nature of this particular group. An Anglo American may carelessly divide people into whites, Negroes, and Mexicans, or a Chicano may assertively speak of "La Raza."[3] The recently increasing use of the term "brown" similarly represents pride in the group's presumed racial distinctiveness, analogous not only to the Negroes' newly-found blackness but also to "La Raza Cósmica" of José Vasconcelos. Although most Mexican Americans are of mixed Spanish, Indian (both Southwestern and Mexican), and Negro descent, a large proportion are not physically distinct from the majority American population hence the group as a whole cannot be characterized in terms of race.[4] "Race" is essentially furthermore a nineteenth century notion which is rapidly becoming obsolete in physical anthropology and related disciplines. In any case biological differences as such are no concern of the sociologist; only the ways in which notions of race influence people's behavior concern him. The topic of our discussion is therefore what social scientists refer to as socially supposed races. Regardless of whatever mythology may be involved, however, if the majority group considers Mexican Americans as a race, and insists therefore on continuing to treat them in a discriminatory fashion, then the consequences are nonetheless real: not only the deprivation and segregation, but as the progress of the Chicano movement has shown, racial pride. Not all the consequences of racism are necessarily negative.

Some historical perspective is needed here. With reference to color discrimination it was noted by Manuel Gamio that in the 1920s dark-skinned Mexicans suffered about the same type of discrimination as Negroes, but that medium complected Mexicans were able to use second-class public facilities. Even light-brown skinned Mexicans were excluded from high-class facilities, while "white" Mexicans might be freely admitted, especially if they spoke fluent English.[5] To what extent is such a type of scale still applied in public facilities or in other areas of public and private life, and what social factors affect its application? Furthermore we might well examine the extent to which differences in physical appearances are socially significant to Mexican Americans themselves. The fact that we live in a racist society where the primary factor affecting a person's status and life chances has always been the color of his skin, means that it is unrealistic to attempt to sweep an unpleasant situation under the carpet and pretend it does not exist.

To What Extent Do Mexican Americans Conceive of Themselves as Belonging to a Separate Ethnic Group?

Tentatively at least we might characterize an ethnic group as a sub-population which shares a common ancestry and which is distinguished by a way of life or culture which is significantly different in one or more respects from what of the majority of the population, which regards it as an out-group. Do Mexican Americans conceive of themselves in this manner? If they thus conceive of themselves, what is the degree of separateness perceived? It depends of course on whom you ask. But it may be hypothesized that answers would probably fall along a spectrum or continuum, of which it is not too difficult to identify three principal segments: those at the extremes, and one at or near the center.

These segments can be characterized according to varying self-conceptions and variations in self-identity. At one extreme are those who acknowledge the fact of their Mexican descent but for whom this fact constitutes neither a particularly positive nor a particularly negative value, because it plays a very unimportant part in their lives and their self-conception. At or near the middle of this putative continuum are those for whom being of Mexican ancestry is something of which they are constantly conscious and which looms importantly as part of their self-conception. Their Mexican descent may constitute for them a positive value, a negative value, or more generally an ambiguous blend of the two. At the other end of the continuum are those who are not only acutely aware of their Mexican identity and descent but are committed to the defense of Mexican American subcultural values, and strive to work actively for the betterment of their people. Tentatively I would like to suggest, without any implication as to their "correctness," that the terms "Americans of Mexican ancestry," "Mexican Americans," and "Chicanos," are sometimes used for those who closely resemble the three types suggested.

Research is needed to determine whether indeed such a continuum can be identified, and if so, what are the proportions of persons falling at various points along its length, and with what other social indices these positions are associated. Sample surveys would seem to be one of the most direct ways of attacking this problem.

To What Extent Do Mexican Americans Have a Separate Or Distinct Culture?

Mexican American culture or subculture whatever its precise nature, composition and structure, if such are even determinable, appears to be a product of multiple origins, as one would expect in light of its history. The focus of its synthesis and emergence is of course the barrio and it is here and not toward Mexico where we must focus our primary attention. At the same time we should not minimize differences between the way of life of Chicanos residing inside and of those residing outside the barrio.

Tentatively it may be suggested that the chief sources of Mexican American culture are four in number. First, there is the initially overriding but subsequently attenuated influence of what is usually called "traditional" Mexican culture, the way of life brought by most of the immigrants from Mexico during several centuries.[7]

Secondly there is the initially weak but subsequently growing influence of the surrounding majority American culture. Mexican Americans are subject to approximately the same educational system and mass media of communication as are other Americans and participate to varying extents in the economic, social, intellectual and religious life of the broader society. A careful comparison of the way of life of persons of Mexican descent in the United States with those of Mexico will help substantiate the notion that the former are first and foremost "Americans," and only secondary "Mexican Americans."

A third source of influence upon Mexican American culture is class influence. The fact that the bulk of the Mexican American population has been concentrated at the lower socio-economic levels of the society means that some aspects of Mexican American culture may have their source in behavior characteristic generally of lower-class people regardless of ethnic group. Thus, for example, the alleged relatively high crime rate (at least for certain types of crimes) among Mexican Americans can perhaps best be explained in terms of social class rather than ethnicity, as well as in terms of the relative youth of the group as a whole and differential law enforcement practices. Apart from the question of Anglo discrimination, insensitivity and incompetence, Mexican American problems in education seem to be as much class problems as they are cultural problems. Educational studies comparing lower class Chicano students with middle class Anglos are as methodologically faulty as they are socially pernicious. Neither must it be forgotten that class discrimination is as real in this country as racial or ethnic discrimination.

The fourth source of influence on Mexican American culture results from the minority status of its bearers. The term "minority" is not properly a numerical concept, (Chicanos outnumber Anglos in East Los Angeles) but rather a term suggesting that the group has less than its share of political, economic and social power vis-à-vis the majority population and hence suffers from educational, social, occupational and other economic disadvantages mediated through the processes of prejudice, discrimination and segregation. Inasmuch as the concept of culture basically refers to the sum-total of techniques a people has in coping with and adapting to its physical and social environment, there have been developed some special cultural responses among Mexican Americans to their minority status, as occurs among members of other minority groups. These responses may be viewed as very important components of the admittedly heterogeneous and ill-defined Chicano subculture. An obvious example of this sort of trait is the Chicano Movement itself, which is both a response to the majority culture and society, and an outstanding component of Chicano culture itself. But even here the matter gets complicated, for it is necessary to recognize that the Movement has borrowed at least some of its goals, values, techniques and strategies from both the black and Anglo civil rights Movements.

It is suggested therefore that Mexican American culture is a multidimensional phenomenon and must be studied in terms of these four dimensions at least (there may be more), as well as in terms of its historical, regional, and ecological variants. It is highly unlikely that all the various strands will ever be completely unravelled and laid out neatly side by side for us to see, but neither must we lose sight of the heterogeneous origins of Mexican American culture, the nature of the varying continuing influences on it, and its continuously changing nature, as we seek to ascertain its differential dispersal, influence, and persistence among persons of Mexican descent in this country.

To What Extent Do Mexican Americans Constitute an Identifiable Stratum in Society?

A number of social scientists who have studied the relations between Mexican Americans and Anglo Americans in the Southwest have described these relations as being "caste-like."[8] That is, the nature of interethnic relations was said to bear some resemblance to the relations between castes in India and elsewhere. In the United States the situation which undoubtedly most closely resembles a color caste system is the traditional pattern of race relations in the South, with its supposedly superordinate white caste and subordinate Negro caste.

Although Mexican-Anglo relations have never been as rigid as black-white relations there may still have been a resemblance, particularly in certain communities, strong enough to characterize them as "semi-caste," "quasi-caste," or "caste-like." That is, there would be manifested a strong degree of segregation, blocking of entrance to certain occupations, political impotence, ritual avoidance, and taboos on intermarriage stemming from notions of "racial" or "color" differences. Intermarriage is an important criterion, for marriage implies social equality between partners. The idea that Mexicans and Mexican Americans are not whites was certainly more prevalent before the World War II period, or at least people expressed the idea more frequently without worrying whether or not anyone might take offense. The current situation in this regard is unclear.[9] It may be that the continuing low rate of intermarriage, the tacit or explicit superior-inferior nature of ethnic relations, and the concentration of Mexican Americans in certain jobs and their virtual exclusion from others, means that Mexican-Anglo relations still approximate semi-caste, although increasingly less so.

If Anglo-Mexican relations appear to be moving away from a caste basis to a class basis, and the evidence is definitely pointing in this direction, the internal stratification of the Mexican American population looms increasingly more important. With a few exceptions, our knowledge of Mexican American stratification has had to depend so far primarily on the rather impressionistic accounts of a handful of Anglo social scientists. We know that, generally speaking, Mexican American rural populations have less differentiated social class structures than the urban ones, that is, the status spread is greater in the city than in the country. We know some of the variables associated with socioeconomic status and self and community perception. Much more we do not know.

Impressionistic accounts and reworking of U. S. Census data in the manner of the UCLA Mexican American Study Project have not been enough. Careful original sample surveys to study the interrelations of "objective" stratification variables as well as the study of the "subjective" perceptions by Chicanos of their own internal stratification systems are urgently needed. Only thus will the myth of the class homogeneity of the Mexican American population be thoroughly discredited and its heterogeneity adequately documented.

To What Extent Is It Realistic to Speak of Mexican American Communities?

One badly neglected area of research is the extent to which Mexican Americans have a feeling of belonging to an identifiable Mexican American community and the extent to which their participation in its organizations and other community activities enable us to identify leadership roles and a social structure as well as a body of sentiment. Regional and ecological considerations are of primary importance here. Degree of community feeling and participation undoubtedly varies as among such places as East Los Angeles, Pomona, Tucson, Chicago, or Hidalgo County, Texas, to mention but a few. It varies between those who live in the barrio and those who live outside. Rural-urban differences are likewise significant. Rural Mexican Americans were never able to establish true communities in California, for example, because of Anglo pressures and because of the migratory work patterns of most of the people, according to Ernesto Galarza.[10] The range and variation of "communityness" must be empirically studied, not assumed a priori, both within populations and among a sample of different locales reflecting the differential impact of relevant regional and ecological variables.

To What Extent Are Differences In Historical Antecedents Reflected Among Mexican Americans?

To a certain extent this question foreshadows the succeeding one inasmuch as the principal regional variations have emerged because of different historical antecedents, and hence it is possible to separate analytically but not empirically the geographical and historical dimensions.

The Mexican American population in the United States from 1848 down to the present has been continually expanded and renewed by immigration both legal and illegal from Mexico, a continually changing Mexico. Mexican immigrants who came for example, before the Revolution, during the Revolution, shortly after the Revolution, and more recently, each came from a somewhat different Mexico. Those coming in at the present time as permanent residents come for the most part from Mexico vastly more industrialized, urbanized, modernized and educated than the Mexico of our fathers or grandfathers. How well have immigrants from different periods of Mexico's history, and their children, fared in the United States? What have been the differential rates of mobility and/or assimilation? We should also raise questions about generational differences, and with reference to the differential composition of Mexican American local populations in terms of their historical antecedents. How are these kinds of differences associated with significant social indices, rates of acculturation, and self-perception and self-identity variables?

To What Extent Are Regional Socioeconomic Differences Significant Among Mexican Americans?

A number of Mexican American regional subcultures can probably be identified. The historical and geographical factors affecting the emergence of these subvarieties are of crucial importance in understanding their present nature. It is important to realize, for example, that the Hispanos of New Mexico and Colorado evolved their culture in isolated mountain villages fairly remote from Anglo civilization; that the Texas-Mexicans are not only concentrated along the border but are also located geographically in the South with its unique tradition of discrimination and prejudice; whereas the Chicanos of Southern California have been caught up in a changing situation of rapid urban growth.

In all areas of the Southwest, the shift from rural to urban has been a highly significant trend. The overwhelming majority of Southwestern Mexican Americans now live in urban areas. These Mexican American urban settlements have grown primarily through migration from the countryside, so that the bulk of the adult residents of those communities have not yet completely adjusted to urban life. The kinds of problems they face therefore are quite different from those they had to face in the small towns and rural areas from which they came. Simple agricultural skills are no longer enough for the security of employment. The kinds of job opportunities available are primarily of an industrial nature and increasingly require a high degree of either manual dexterity or intellectual skills or both. The needs of automation are furthermore constantly raising the level of skills required in order to compete successfully in the job market. So the urban Mexican American is pushed further and further away from pre-industrial skills, habits, and attitudes and directly into the modern industrial social order with all its complexities and problems.

At the opposite extreme, Mexican Americans in such a place as rural Texas score the lowest on all the social measures. It is in this area where the permanent residences of many migratory agricultural laborers are concentrated. There is perhaps less social differentiation of Mexican Americans here than in any other area of the Southwest, and the most vigorous preservation of so-called tradional Mexican rural culture.

The Spanish Americans, Hispanos, "Manitos," or "mejicanos," are the descendants of the original racially mixed but Europeanized settlers of New Mexico and southern Colorado, when this area was under Spanish rule, but administered and colonized from Mexico. Traditionally most of the Hispanos lived in isolated rural areas and were economically and socially handicapped. In recent years they have become increasingly urbanized as many have been forced off their lands by the more competitive Anglo farmers, or as mines were closed. Many Hispanos left New Mexico and Colorado during the World War II and post-war periods. Many came and continue to come to Southern California and other areas of high urbanization. Here we have another case of attempting to unravel the strands, as Chicano urban populations are increasing in heterogeneity with reference to interstate geographical origins. The sociological study of the Mexican American should include both the *systematic* comparative examination of regional variants of the admittedly hard to define and identify Chicano culture and community (and not just a series of monographic reports, each one on a separate community), as well as the way in which these differences are being gradually obliterated in the urban milieu.[11]

In summary, seven questions were posed with reference to the Chicano population, some tentative answers were given, and some areas for future research indicated. It is not the writer's intention to imply that a series of adequately documented answers to these questions would constitute the corpus of Chicano sociology. There are a number of other extremely important unmentioned questions and topics which are obviously part of such a sociology, such as those relating to family life, value systems, power relations, bilingualism, educational questions, and many others. Rather, the explicit intention and hope is that the answers to these questions will help in the formulation of a sociological definition of our subject population before we tackle the multitude of difficult intellectual and social questions which lie ahead of us.

REFERENCES

1. The terms "Mexican American" and "Chicano" are used here for convenience as equivalent and interchangeable, without any implication of their "correctness" or of the "correctness" of any other term or terms that might have been used in their place.

2. The careful reader will have detected that the writer's philosophical bias is strongly nominalistic, that is, that he conceives of "culture," "community," "ethnic group," etc., not as "things," but rather as labels which refer to abstractions conjured up by the social scientist or others as a convenience in handling the data they are trying to understand. For example, the latest issue of *El Chicano,* a newspaper published in San Bernardino, carries the headline "Mexican Community Demands Dismissal of Judge Chargin." This is a figure of speech, of course, inasmuch as if the community is indeed an abstraction, it cannot demand anything; only individuals or organized groups can demand.

3. Readers of this journal are undoubtedly acquainted with the fact that throughout the Spanish-speaking world Columbus Day is referred to as "El Día de la Raza," the word "raza" in this context referring to all persons of Hispanic culture, as it does in the motto of the National Autonomous University of Mexico: "Por mi raza hablará el espíritu." Nevertheless, in matters social, words mean what their users *want* them to mean.

4. Cf. Marcus Goldstein, *Demographic and Bodily Changes in Descendants of Mexican Immigrants.* Austin: Institute of Latin American Studies, University of Texas, 1943, and Gonzalo Aguirre Beltrán, *La Población Negra de México 1519-1810* (México, D. F.: Ediciones Fuente Cultural, 1946).

5. Manuel Gamio, *Mexican Immigration to the United States* (Chicago: University of Chicago Press, 1930), p. 53.

6. The writer is currently carrying out a random-sample survey of the Mexican American population of San Bernardino, California, with reference to internal social stratification, self-identification, and perception of community and subculture. Hopefully the results will throw some light on these questions.

7. The pitfalls of stereotyping in this area are very great, as so ably pointed out by Octavio I. Romano-V., "The Anthropology and Sociology of the Mexican Americans," *El Grito,* II (Fall, 1968), 13-26.

8. Walter Goldschmidt, *As You Sow* (New York: Harcourt, Brace and Co., 1947), p. 59; Paul Schuster Taylor, *An American-Mexican Frontier, Nueces County, Texas* (Chapel Hill: The University of North Carolina Press, 1934); Ruth D. Tuck, *Not with the Fist: Mexican-Americans in a Southwest City* (New York: Harcourt, Brace and Co., 1946), p. 44; Thomas E. Lasswell, "Status Stratification in a Selected Community," unpublished Ph. D. dissertation, University of Southern California, 1953; Robert B. Rogers, "Perception of the Power Structure by Social Class in a California Community," unpublished Ph.D. dissertation, University of Southern California, 1962; James B. Watson and Julián Samora, "Subordinate Leadership in a Bi-cultural Community," *American Sociological* Review, 19 (August 1954), pp. 413-421; Ozzie Simmons, "Americans and Mexican Americans in South Texas," unpublished Ph. D. dissertation, Harvard University, 1952; William H. Madsen, *The Mexican-Americans of South Texas* (New York: Holt, Rinehart & Winston, 1964).

It may be argued that since the authors of all these studies are Anglos they may have had a slanted view of the situation, yet it should be understood they are reporting Anglo residents' perceptions of the social barriers they themselves have set up.

9. After the 1930 Census, in which Mexicans were listed as a separate "race," persons of Mexican descent were subsequently put back into the "white" category largely because the Mexican American leaders of that time insisted Mexicans were "white." Similarly the Chicano population is substantially the same as the 1950 and 1960 Census category "White persons of Spanish surname." Understandably therefore the recent emphasis on "brown"and "La Raza" has some Anglos confused. With reference

to the possible relevance of the caste model, it should be pointed out that the nature of the discrimination against Chicanos has been primarily social rather than legal, as has been the case for blacks in the South.

10. Lecture in the University of California Extension Series "The Mexican American in Transition," Ontario, California, Spring, 1967.

11. One of the findings of the writer's "Spanish-surname" sample survey of Pomona was that in every case in which a household contained a "Spanish American" adult, that person was married to a "Mexican American." It may be hypothesized on the basis of this admittedly flimsy evidence that in urban Southern California Hispanos are more likely to marry children or grandchildren of Mexican immigrants than they are Hispanos because there are no real barriers between the two groups and the statistical odds are therefore against the endogamy of the smaller group. To what extent this may be true of other areas of the country it would be hazardous to guess.

Joseph NAVARRO

Joseph Navarro (currently working for the doctorate in history at The University of California, Santa Barbara) surveys the present state of Mexican American History, evaluates the need for further research, and discusses some of the problems "inherent in the study of Mexican American History."

By permission of the author and THE JOURNAL OF MEXICAN AMERICAN HISTORY.

The Condition Of Mexican American History

Unlike the Anglo, the Spanish-American or Mexican-American is likely to be strongly oriented toward the present or the immediate past. He is not a visionary, with his eyes on the golden promise of the future. Nor is he a dreamer brooding over the glories of the past. Rather he is a realist who is concerned with the problems and rewards of the immediate present. The past, since he comes from a folk culture with no tradition of writing, was not carefully recorded, contained little that was sufficiently out of the ordinary to justify recording, and has been almost forgotten. The future, since for hundreds of years it brought almost nothing different from what he already had, offers no particular promise and is neither to be anticipated with joy nor feared. But the present cannot be ignored. Its demands must be coped with, its rewards must be enjoyed—now.

(Lyle Saunders, *Cultural Difference and Medical Care.*)

INTRODUCTION

The purpose of this paper is to examine the condition of Mexican-American history, which in this paper is defined as the history of Mexicans in the United States in the period from 1848 to the present. More specifically, this paper will consider

443

problems inherent to the study of Mexican-American history, and examine the most useful and representative literature. This report makes no claim to finality, but is offered for consideration in the hope it will stimulate thought, profitable dialogue, and relevant criticism.

To begin with, very little has been written about the history of Mexicans in the United States, and almost no effort has been made to tap and index primary sources in the archives and wherever else they might be found. These serious limitations explain why teachers are plagued by problems of organization and periodization: they want to know when their subject begins and what to include. Some students have asked if some distinction should be made, in the study of Mexican-American history, between history and social science, and whether some distinction should be made between history and journalism. These questions are raised not only because some writers have failed to make a distinction between history and other branches of knowledge, but have gone so far as to obscure the difference between history and social science, and also, the difference between history and journalism. It is true that bibliographies of Mexican-American history contain more works in social science than history, and more works of current events or journalism than developments which took place before World War II. In part, this is because little Mexican-American history has been written, because more Mexican-American literature is found in the social sciences, and because publishers and the news media have given increasing attention to current Mexican-American history, especially the Mexican-American Civil Rights Movement led by César Chávez and Reies Tijerina. Nonetheless, it should be made clear why social science studies and journalism are included in a bibliography pertaining to Mexican-American history. If Mexican-American history is to advance professionally, it must not only be defined clearly but it must also be made clear how Mexican-American history as history and as a specialized area of history, is related to other branches of knowledge, and also, how it is different from them. This is not to say that the serious student has to become deeply involved in the controversies over history and social science, in epistemological questions in the philosophy of history, etc., but he should know what most historians recognize as the distinguishing essentials between history and other studies of man.

The foregoing generalizations and problems will be examined and discussed further in the following manner: first, a discussion of the problem of defining Mexican-American history and how that problem is related to other fundamental questions; second, a critical review of the most useful and representative works on Mexican-American history; third, a discussion of the characteristics of history generally accepted by professional historians, and a brief comment on how history relates to other branches of knowledge, especially to social science and journalism; and finally, concluding suggestions on how the critical and scholarly study of Mexican-American history can be advanced.

DEFINITION: A PROBLEM OF LABELS, AREA, AND PERIODIZATION.

Since so little has been written about Mexican-American history, those who have to think about the subject for the first time are apt to be puzzled by a number of fundamental questions.

There is, to begin, a problem over what label should be used to refer to all Mexicans in the United States. Those who speak Spanish in New Mexico and southern Colorado prefer to be called Hispanos or Spanish-Americans. This is because they had little contact with Mexico, and because they identify with the early Spaniards. Those Mexicans whose ancestors came to the United States in the 1900s prefer to be called Mexican-American; the word Mexicano is generally accepted even by those who come from Mexico: some Mexicans will fight if they are called anything other than American; the label Spanish-speaking has been used by some writers because to them it appears to be the least offensive label; and the news media has popularized the label Chicano which some Mexican-American activists have adopted. There are other labels and preferences. It is enough here to point out that it is difficult to find a label which refers to all Mexicans in the United States, and which, at the same time, is pleasing to everyone, especially to all Mexicans.

Having noted that the label Mexican-American will not please everyone, it should also be pointed out that the definition of Mexican-American history used in this paper will probably be received with the same lack of unanimity. As already explained, this is because little thought has been given to the questions: What is Mexican-American history? What area(s) and period(s) of time does Mexican-American history encompass? My own experience with high schools, colleges, history conferences, and interviews reveal that teachers, writers, social scientists, and historians have different ideas about the definition of Mexican-American history. Not only do they use different labels to refer to all Mexicans in the United States, but they differ, also, on the proper area(s) of study, and they have different answers to the question of periodization. For example, some present the history of Mexicans in the United States as an extension of the history of Mexico; others organize Mexican-American history around both the history of Mexico and the United States. There are other combinations. This is not to say, however, that because pundits differ over the matter of labels, over the proper area(s) of study, and over the question of periodization, the definition of Mexican-American history must be arbitrary. The serious student will see that the definition of Mexican-American history need not be so arbitrary as to have no basis in history.

As indicated above, the definition of Mexican-American history in this paper is *limited in area to the United States and encompasses the period from the end of the "Mexican War" or more precisely from the signing of the Treaty of Guadalupe Hidalgo on February 2, 1848, to the present.* The label Mexican-American was chosen because it is now commonly known that it refers to "citizens of Mexican origin." Mexican-American history began with the signing of the Treaty of Guadalupe Hidalgo because this Treaty extended citizenship, albeit second-class citizenship to all Mexicans who lived in the conquered territories of the Southwest; prior to this Treaty there were no Mexican-Americans in the United States, at least, as we know them today. Further, in this report, the term Mexican-American refers to all Mexicans in the United States, including those few who are not citizens. It should be made clear that the choice of

terminology and definitions in this paper are conventional or conservative; Mexican-American history is regarded as ethnic history, an area of specialization within United States history. And it is probable that if professional historians ever take interest in Mexican-American history, they will define Mexican-American history along lines which have been expounded in this report. This is not to say that there is no room for imagination. It is conceivable, for example, that some thoughtful student might define Mexican-American history as the history of Mexicans in the Southwest beginning, say, in 1540 when the Spaniards began to colonize the area. In this system, the signing of the Treaty of Guadalupe Hidalgo would mean a continuation of the history of Mexicans in the Southwest under new conditions: the conquest of the Southwest by the United States and the decline of Mexicans from power to cheap labor and second-class citizenship. In brief, the definition of Mexican-American history used in this paper is conventional, unencumbered by exploratory theories of periodization or intricate schemes recommending the study of overlapping areas—happily, this is left to the next generation, which might have more information to work with.

It is important, also, to include with the definition of Mexican-American history given in this paper, some explanation of the value of four histories: the history of the North American Indian, of Spain, Mexico, and the United States. All of these histories are useful as background to the history of Mexicans in the United States. The history of the North American Indian should not be confined to the glories of the Mayas and Aztecs which is often done by popular and superficial writers; special emphasis should be given to the Indians of the Southwest. The Spaniards learned much from the Indians whom they intermarried with to create the Mexican people. The history of Spain should devote special attention to the contribution of the Romans, Moors, and Jews because their contributions were carried to Mexico and the Southwest, where they are permanent cultural features. The history of Mexico is not only useful as background (especially the background to the so-called "Mexican War"), but also because it helps explain why Mexicans are constantly migrating to and from the United States. Moreover, Mexican history sheds light on the social and economic conditions which influence Mexican immigration, and to some extent, how that immigration affects the lives of Mexican-Americans. The political instability of the Mexican Revolution helps explain why large numbers of Mexicans migrated to the United States, and as usual, this immigration affected the lives of Mexican-Americans: in some areas where large numbers of immigrants settled, Anglos became apprehensive and intensified their hostility and discrimination which was not limited to the immigrants only, but extended, also, to the Mexican-Americans. As for United States history, it, too, is useful as background to the "Mexican War." Needless to say, Mexican-American history has been a part of the history of the United States since 1848.

Those who study Mexican-American history in the manner recommended in this paper should be able to perceive that the concept of *mestizaje* applies to Mexican-American history. *Mestizaje* refers to the long history of racial and cultural mixing which Mexican-Americans and their ancestors have experienced in Spain, Mexico, and the United States. *Mestizaje* is the Mexican-American heritage.

In sum, the matter of defining Mexican-American history, at this time is in a state of confusion, owing to the fact that little thought has been given to the subject, or Mexican-American history is just beginning to be studied seriously. To be sure, the matter of defining Mexican-American history is apt to be hotly debated for some time. No doubt, the definition used in this paper adds to the confusion or lack of consensus, but it has to be entered in this discussion for the sake of clarity and to distinguish it from others. Finally, those who are struggling for a judicious definition of Mexican-American history are admonished to treat their terms provisionally, and to treat the definition of their subject like a probable hypothesis, flexibly defined so as to leave plenty of room for improvement.

THE LITERATURE AND ITS LIMITATIONS

The number of useful works on Mexican-American history can be counted on one's fingers, and the number of scholarly histories of Mexicans in the United States is considerably less. With rare exceptions, professional historians have paid no serious attention to Mexican-American history. The bulk of the literature has been written and continues to be written by amateur historians, i.e., journalists and to a lesser extent social scientists. This is probably why Mexican-American history tends to be ahistorical, and why more attention has been devoted to recent developments. From these initial comments, I should like to move on to the literature, beginning with the only general survey of Mexican-American history, and then move on to more specialized works.

The only comprehensive work on Mexican-American history *North From Mexico* (New York, 1948) was written by Carey McWilliams, who is not a professional historian. He is, however, a talented man of letters and distinguished journalist. His books on minorities, especially *North From Mexico,* were destined to have a long life because he was among the first to write ethnic history. It is still largely true that one has to start with McWilliams when undertaking the study of some ethnic groups, especially the study of ethnic groups in California. McWilliams wrote *North From Mexico* as part of the "Peoples of America Series" under the general editorship of Louis Adamic. A brilliant literary form and mastery of the best sources assured the popularity of McWilliams' survey in wide reading circles, especially among specialists and the intelligensia.

Fortunately for Mexican-American history, its only survey has many remarkable qualities. Although the author likes Mexican-Americans, an attitude which easily comes through in *North From Mexico,* he is not blind to problems Mexicans have among themselves. For example, he understands the generation gap between native and foreign-born Mexicans, and how this gap is manipulated by Anglos against the Mexican community. He perceives keenly the tendency of Anglos to work with the least representative or lighter-skinned Mexican; he mentions the frivolous nature of some Mexican organizations; and he also presents some telling facts on the matter of class differences among Mexicans. The book not only appreciates the contributions and cultural influence of Mexicans in the Southwest, but presents also an unusual analysis of the cultural and historical interaction of Spaniards, Indians, Mexicans, Mexican-Americans, and Anglos in the Southwest. There is more to this general history. It is perhaps the first thoughtful exposition on how to organize Mexican-American history. In the Foreword, McWilliams grapples with the question: who are the Spanish-speaking people (Mexican-Americans)? He explains that the Southwest and the relations between Anglos and Mexicans are important parts of the story, but to stress the region and Anglo-Mexican relations would divert attention from "the people, their origins, and ordeals, their struggles and experiences." He, therefore, decided to structure the story of the Spanish-speaking people in terms of a "process" or "movement north from Mexico." This process or movement suggests "an extension of a way of life . . . a oneness of experience if not of blood or language or ancestry; a similar movement within a similar environment." McWilliams is aware of the difficulty of trying to find a suitable label to describe accurately such a diverse ethnic group as the Mexican-American people. He notes that the Mexican border is regarded as "invisible" by Mexicans who are constantly crossing back and forth. He explains that Mexicans are not immigrants: they were in the Southwest long before the Anglos conquered them. *North From Mexico* is an excellent model of how social science and current events can be useful to history. At no time while the author uses information from the social sciences, or when he refers to the present, does he discard the historical perspective. While the movement of the narrative is chronological, the author is able to move back and forth in time; he never becomes topically redundant. It is an excellent balance of chronology and topical analysis. Those interested in research will find in *North From Mexico* numerous suggestions and hints.

Although the author respects Mexican-Americans, he is not as uncritical as Ralph Guzmán suggests when he writes that *North From Mexico* is a "passionate apologia of the Mexican people. And there seems to be some exaggeration in Russell Fitzgibbon's review where Fitzgibbon presents McWilliams as "counsel rather than judge . . . the zealot rather than dispassionate researcher shows up on every page. Flaming indignation is the tone

of the book." Fitzgibbon is probably right when he concludes that *North From Mexico* is a "book to make many of us blush." Nonetheless, the book is not perfect: it is poorly documented and poorly illustrated. For example, McWilliams claims the Treaty of Guadalupe Hidalgo provided for the teaching of Mexican culture to those Mexicans who would become citizens in accordance with another provision of the same Treaty. Yet, despite exhausting efforts, the author of this report has failed to locate such a provision in the various and final draft of the Treaty of Guadalupe Hidalgo. As for illustrations, there is only one map in the whole book.

As one moves away from McWilliams' resplendent general history to more specialized studies, it will become evident that the topics investigated are uneven, that many gaps exist, and that some of the information is only partially relevant to Mexican-American history.

The image of the Mexican as seen by Anglo-American writers is admirably documented in Cecil Robinson's *With the Ears of Strangers* (Tucson, 1963). Robinson has a good sense of history, that is, his study begins with the Conquest of Mexico and moves on chronologically to the present, analyzing the continuity and changing attitudes of Anglo-American writers. Early Anglo-American writers did not hesitate to show their disapproval of Mexicans. They disapproved of the "dirty" Mexican, the Mexican's preoccupation with pleasure, his laziness, the Mexican's technological backwardness, his morbid sense of death, the Mexican's willingness to marry Indians which deprives him of his right to be called "white," his cowardice, his violent tendencies, and several other attributes associated with the early stereotype. But in the early part of the twentieth century, as American Writers became more critical of the pace of American life, of the "rat race" and crass materialism, they expressed a more respectful attitude toward the Mexican life-style. One group of Americans expressed nostalgia for the Spanish past in the Southwest. To be sure, they romanticized the past, and longed for those bygone days which Ray Billington describes as "the charm of life in Mexican California, where a bountiful nature, a genial climate massive nature, and the home government's neglect allowed man to bask in an atmosphere reminiscent of the garden before Adam's fall." In this mission culture fantasy, Anglo readers could satisfy their cravings for a serene pastoral past. At the end of the nineteenth century, there emerged another group of Anglo-American writers, such as Oscar Lewis, whose writings on the Mexicans demonstrated critical and scholarly depth. Despite their new romantic and realistic attitudes, Robinson concludes, North American writers still do not understand Mexicans; they continue to perceive "with the ears of strangers."

Although Manuel Gamio's studies on Mexican immigration are anthropological and have been supplemented by more recent investigations, they are useful and give us insightful information about Mexican immigration before the depression decade. Gamio, a distinguished anthropologist, was selected by the Mexican government to cooperate with Social Science Research Council in undertaking the study of Mexican immigration during the period 1926–27. The first volume, *Mexican Immigration to the United States* (Chicago, 1930), indicates that low pay and unemployment in Mexico encouraged Mexicans to migrate to the United States where they work as cheap labor. Gamio points out that most Mexicans were not at home in the United States, where the hostility and discrimination of the Anglo tends to make immigrants more patriotic. The book has some valuable chapters on the mentality, religion, and songs of the immigrant. It should be mentioned, also, that since Gamio had undertaken a pioneer study, it was necessary for him to engage in extensive field work to obtain his information. The companion volume, Gamio's *The Mexican Immigrant, His Life Story* (Chicago, 1931) is based on interviews collected from 57 immigrants. It indicates that the Mexican Revolution was an important reason for migrating to the United States, that the immigrants distrusted native-born Mexicans, that they were loyal to Mexico, and that they usually planned to return to Mexico. Of interest, also, in these studies is Gamio's underscoring statement that he has been concerned only with the most representative Mexican immigrant or the dark-skinned Mexican with strong Indian features.

Gamio's investigation of immigrants is actually an investigation of Mexicans as cheap labor, a subject which has received more attention than most topics of Mexican-American history. One of the first serious studies of Mexican labor is Paul S. Taylor's series of monographs entitled, "Mexican Labor in the United States." Professor Taylor is an economist who, as we shall see, appreciates the historical perspective, which he uses judiciously in conjunction with field work and statistics. His researches not only tell us a good deal about Mexican farm labor in the Southwest (Winter Garden District, Texas; Imperial Valley, California; and South Platte, Colorado), but also the conditions of workers, on railroads, large industries and steel mills (Chicago and Calumet Region, and Bethlehem, Pennsylvania). His pioneer studies on "migration statistics reveal the difficulty of estimating illegal entries of Mexicans to the United States, and he points out differences between Mexican and United States statistics. Taylor's studies, like Gamio's, are fundamental and provide valuable information about Mexican labor before the Depression.

Recently, the migrant labor movement in the United States has received wide national and international attention. The famous strike in Delano has been covered satisfactorily by such writers as Eugene Nelson, *Huelga* (Delano, 1966), and such journalists as John Dunne, *Delano* (New York, 1967), and Peter Matthiessen, *Salsipuedes* (New York, 1970). In addition to these works, Ernesto Galarza has published several works on farm labor. In *Merchants of Labor* (Santa Barbara, 1965), Galarza presents a good historical background of the Bracero program, and then proceeds to a discussion of its adverse effects on domestic farm labor; the Bracero program prevented farm labor from organizing, the Federal government cooperated with agribusiness at the expense of farm labor interests, and Galarza explains that organized labor has remained remarkably indifferent to the plight and interests of farm labor. This study also describes how braceros were treated by employers, and how the program was administered by the government. Galarza's most recent book, *Spiders in the House and Workers in the Field* (Notre Dame, 1970), despite this funny title, is a fascinating history of the National Farm Workers Union's strike (1947–50) and how it was put down by Di Giorgio Fruit Corporation with the help of the Federal government, that is, with the help of such Congressmen as R. Nixon, T. Morton, and T. Stood, who sat in a committee which investigated the strike and drew up a document which condemned the union and its effort to organize farm labor.

Mexican-Americans, that is, United States citizens of Mexican descent, have not only distinguished themselves as cheap labor, but they have also been good soldiers. Those who read Raul Morin's *Among the Valiant* Los Angeles, 1963) will find out that Mexican-Americans received the largest number of Congressional Medals of Honor than any other ethnic group in World War II. *Among the Valiant* is a colorful book, illustrated with medal winners, and a glowing introduction by Lyndon B. Johnson. Although the author is not a professional historian, he has done extensive research and has been able to present his knowledge lucidly and historically; he notes social and economic changes which have affected Mexican-Americans from the Depression to the post-war period; and Morin gives an historical account of all the major campaigns in World War II and Korea. The author is optimistic about the future of the Mexican-American, and evinces an unusual patriotism. For example, on the last page, he exclaims: "our standard of living has improved 100 percent." This last exclamation is controversial and probably exaggerated. According to Professor Ralph Guzmán, who gave a lecture on the Mexican-American at the University of California, Santa Barbara in 1969, Morin is no longer alive. A member of the G.I. Forum of Santa Barbara has also confirmed that Morin is deceased, and that Morin lived in Santa Barbara. Of interest also is Professor Guzmán's statement that Morin could not understand why young Mexican-Americans did not share his patriotism. In any case, Morin felt that conditions had improved greatly for the Mexican-American since the Depression.

The book by Leonard Pitt on the *Decline of the Californios: A Social History of the Spanish-speaking Californians, 1846–1890* (Berkeley, 1966) is probably the most scholarly work on Mexican-American history. As the title suggests, the book deals with the removal of Mexicans from power after the "Mexican War," and the Mexicans decline to cheap labor, banditry, and second-class citizenship. This book is based on Pitt's dissertation which he completed in 1958 at UCLA, and bears the title "Submergence of the Mexican in California, 1846–90." Pitt not only details the illegal transfer of property or dispossession of Californios, the lynchings, and other forms of violence, but he also presents a good analysis of the Mexican social structure in California before the Anglos took over: he discusses class differences between the Californios, Mexicans, and Indians. Class differences and relations in Mexican California might be likened to class arrangements in the South: Californios might be likened to the planter class, Mexicans to the poor whites, and Indians to Black slaves. Of great interest, the author notes on page vii that the Californios "even in their heyday . . . were numerically too small and culturally too backward to contribute to mankind much that was new or original . . . the Yanks beat them badly and all but swept them into the dust bin of history." Moses Rischin, who reviewed the book, observes that Spanish language sources are very scarce and for this reason, Pitt had to limit himself to Southern California. Rischin is merely saying that Mexican sources are rare because the majority of Mexicans, then as now, were extremely illiterate. In any case, Pitt was able to find sources to piece together his story on the submergence of Mexicans to second-class status. He drew substantially from literate Californios whose recollections, memoirs, and accounts are stored at Berkeley in the Bancroft Library. Pitt also drew from a large number of books, newspapers, and some government publications and some theses and dissertations. The last section on the "schizoid heritage," explains lucidly the Anglo creation of a Spanish mythical past which, among other things, diverts attention from the embarrassing discrimination and poverty which Mexicans have been experiencing daily since their conquest one hundred and twenty-two years ago.

Cited in Pitt's bibliography is a very useful book entitled *The Life and Adventures of Joaquín Murieta* by John R. Ridge, who originally published the book in 1854 under the pseudonym of Yellow Bird. The Introduction to the reprinted edition (Norman, 1955), by Joseph H. Jackson, traces the origin and evolution of the Joaquín Murieta myth. Those writers who continue to refer to the existence of a Murieta would do well to read this book.

The historical literature on the Hispanos (Spanish-speaking of New Mexico) compares favorably with that of Mexicans in California, but is about as good as that of Texas and better by far the history of Mexicans in Colorado and Arizona—it would be no exaggeration to say that with the exception of brief mention in the general histories, the history of Mexicans in Colorado and Arizona is nonexistent. Like the Delano strike in California, the land grant conflict in New Mexico, under the leadership of Reies Tijerina, has received wide national attention. And like the Delano strike, Anglo journalists have been busy writing on Tijerina and the land grant conflict: Peter Nabokov's *Tijerina and the Court House Raid* (Albuquerque, 1969); Michael Jenkinson's *Tijerina* (Albuquerque, 1968); and now Richard Gardner's *Grito* (Indianapolis, 1970). All of these works supply a brief historical background and concentrate on contemporary social and economic problems. The same is true of Nancie L. González *The Spanish American of New Mexico* (Albuquerque, 1967) and George Sánchez' *Forgotten People* (Albuquerque, 1940). González' presentation is topical and concentrates on contemporary aspects of Hispano living conditions. She states that Hispanos experience less discrimination than Mexican-Americans in other parts of the United States. Sánchez supplies, in *Forgotten People,* a very brief historical summary, an in-depth analysis of social and economic problems in Taos, and concludes by suggesting that government intervene and solve the problems of his forgotten people. The tone of these studies is one of "flaming indignation," to use Russell Fitzgibbon's phrase: the emphasis is typically on the immediate which is detailed and followed by suggestions for reform. This impatience with the past deprives the reader of what Allen Nevins calls "a bridge connecting the past with the present, and pointing the road to the future."

Several analytic studies of Texas barrios have appeared recently. Their discussion is reserved below in connection with social science. Insofar as the writing of the history of Mexican-Americans in Texas is concerned, there are no good works.

The book by Beatrice Griffith, *American Me* (Boston, 1948) is not history, but it tells us a good deal about the grass roots Mexican-American in California cities during the 30s and 40s. It is unfortunate that this excellent book has not been reprinted, for the questions it raises and insights it gives into urban barrio life make it worthy of mention in any Mexican-American bibliography. Another similar piece, written about the same time, is Ruth Tuck's *Not With the Fist* (New York, 1946), is also out of print. It is a study of a small Mexican community "similar to other cities in Arizona and Texas," a small city with plenty of immigrants. In its introduction, Tuck points out that her book was intended for those who work directly with Mexican-Americans, e.g., police officers and social workers. Ignacio López, who wrote the Foreword, indicated that there has been "an appalling dearth of information" concerning the Mexican. "Of those studies made in years past," wrote López, "some were rigidly scholastic, coldly quantative things of charts and graphs." There was a "Mexican skeleton, but there was no flesh and movement. Still others," continued López, "were narrowly regional. ... Many, far too many, dripped with an overdose of sentimentality. ... much ado about that ... quaint ... Mexican." If this is true, and Mr. López is still around, he might be delighted with recent publications on the Mexican-American by Anglo journalists, having plenty of "flesh and movement."

Stan Steiner's *La Raza* (New York, 1970) is one of these books. There is no question that the author has demonstrated understanding of the contemporary Mexican-American movement, but the haste in which the book was written has led to several glaring errors. In the Bibliography, for example, he accuses professional historians of suppressing Mexican-American history because professional historians fear that if the study of Mexican-American history is undertaken it will disturb the historian's ethnocentricity and belief that Mexicans are inferior. There is no question that professional historians have neglected Mexican-American history, but Steiner should prove that historians have consciously tried to suppress it. It is true that scarcity of sources is one reason why so little has been written about the history of Mexicans in the United States. It may be however, that historians and other groups have discouraged either by silence or other means a vigorous search for documents. A discussion of how Mexican-American history might be abused, once it is written, should have been considered by Steiner. How would *La Raza* use or abuse Mexican-American history? How could Mexican-American history be abused by "Chicano" opportunists in the universities? Steiner might have speculated further and asked this question: How can the realistic study of Mexican-American history be advanced if *La Raza* demands that it be manipulated and used as propaganda? To what extent is this going on in "Chicano Studies" programs? Who in the United States should advance the serious study of Mexican-American history? Steiner of course is wrong in stating that a history of Mexican-Americans has not been written unless he does not regard Carey McWilliams' *North From Mexico* as a history of Mexican-Americans. He is also wrong in writing that a biography of Joaquín Murieta remains to be written. Apparently, Steiner did not look carefully into the Murieta literature, for if he had, he would have discovered that Murieta never existed, and the legendary biography was written for the first time in 1854. There seems to be some exaggeration in the statement that the general public did not have access to the Treaty of Guadalupe Hidalgo until 1967. There are other flaws but the greatest flaw of journalists like Steiner is the tendency to be uncritical and unduly sympathetic toward the Mexican-Americans. In one sense, this new attitude compensates for earlier disparaging attitude of Anglo-American writers, but like the earlier attitude, it serves more the interest of propaganda than of truth.

Although their professional level and scholarly value vary, most articles on Mexican-American history are superficial and poorly documented. The three articles which have been chosen for brief comment in this report were selected because they illustrate the kind of research which can and needs to be undertaken by serious students. Mrs. Jean F. Riss of Costa Mesa, California, was inspired into writing her article, "Lynch Law, Orange County Style" while reading Carey McWilliams' *Southern California Country*. She came across a passage on the lynching of a Mexican in her county. Intrigued by this local episode, Riss prepared a thoroughly documented paper on the lynching of Francisco Torres, apparently the last Mexican to be lynched in California. Riss' is an original contribution because she is the first to undertake this investigation, the first to bring most of the scattered literature together, and the first to tap primary sources relating to her study. The only major defect of the article is its failure to provide some historical background essential to any study, because it gives the reader what Allen Nevins calls "a sense of continuity."

The next article, "The White Caps in San Miguel County, New Mexico, 1889-91: A Study in Primitive Rebellion" was written by Andrew B. Schlesinger of Harvard University. Since Schlesinger's article will appear in this issue of the *Journal*, all that will be indicated for the moment, is that the article is a brilliant contribution to vigilante history in New Mexico, especially as that history relates to Mexican-American history in the late nineteenth century.

The third article is on the "Zoot Suit" riots of 1943. Ruben Cortez who researched the article has studied most of the available literature about Mexicans in Los Angeles. His investigation of the so-called "Zoot Suit" riots is remarkable not only because it is carefully researched and thoroughly documented, but also because of its keen sense of history: the story of the Riots is woven into the history of Los Angeles; Cortez gives the reader a better understanding of the Riots by reviewing briefly the evolution of the barrio in Los Angeles, and also, by reviewing antecedent conditions of the Riots. He concludes that little changed in Anglo-Mexican relations in Los Angeles, and refers to recent eruptions and the continuing poverty and discrimination.

In the social sciences, there are several studies which can be useful to Mexican-American history. Among the best of these studies are the advance reports of the Mexican-American Study Project, and Leo Grebler's *The Mexican-American,* which has appeared since the fourth draft of this paper one month ago. This bulky volume brings together all the findings of the advance reports, and has some additional topics on the Catholic Church, politics, and a majestic section on the "Historical Perspective." According to forecasts in high places, this handbook is a landmark in Mexican-American literature. The volume is based on over four years of research funded by the Ford Foundation. The information in the advance reports and Grebler's handbook are on the whole, "rigidly scholastic, coldly quantitative things of charts and graphs," lacking what Ignacio López calls "flesh and movement." The section on history (part two) is superficial and is based on old sources. It is not clear why a study which has only one Spanish-surname on its staff bothers to list almost every prominent Mexican-American in Los Angeles and San Antonio. (pp. xiii-xiv) In any case, it is to be hoped that the social science journals will be able to find judicious reviewers to tell us more about the value of this handbook.

Another useful social science study is Celis S. Heller's piece on Mexican-American youth. The book is not notably insightful, and contains only a three-page, poorly documented "Historical Profile." Heller's book, however, is useful because it supplies some basic information about Mexican-American youth. Margaret Clark's study of the San Jose *barrio* in California is also weak, as far as the historical dimension goes, but it provides some useful information on the health habits of that community. Of course, not all social science studies lack a sense of history. For example, Paul Taylor's study of Mexicans in Neuces County, Texas provides the reader with a brief historical discussion before illuminating on social and economic conditions of that area during the 20s and 30s. Another good example of a social science investigation which makes good use of history is Arthur J. Rubel's *Across the Tracks: Mexican Americans in a Texas City* (Austin, 1966). The author devotes a full chapter to what he calls "New Lots in Historical Perspective." Rubel uses good sources to document the history of his subject: dissertations, contemporary accounts, rigorous articles, and the best secondary sources.

There is an urgent need to study the various Mexican-American dialects. Little attention has been given to studies like George C. Barker's *Pa-chucho: An American-Spanish Argot and its Social Functions in Tucson, Arizona* (Tucson, 1950) which is an effort to understand the vocabulary of a "small minority of Mexican-American youth." Linguistic studies of this kind can be useful in a number of ways: first, it might put an end to some of the petty bickering among Mexicans over the origins and meaning of such words as "Chicano" and "Mexican-American," with or without the hyphen; and second, it could lead to the compilation of a dictionary and history of the Mexican-American language.

Finally, there are studies which justify the complaints which some historians lodge against the social sciences. I refer to the tendency of some social science studies to derive generalizations from a particular situation, and then proceed to apply those generalizations to all situations. For example, Lyle Saunders' *Cultural Difference and Medical Care* (New York, 1954) abounds in controversial generalizations about the Mexican-American; it is enough here to state that Saunders, from time to time, makes curt allusions to history in order to give cogence to his generalizations. Probably the best example, that is, the most odious and reckless example of social science generalization, is William Madsen's *The Mexican-Americans of South Texas* (New York, 1964). The fault of this work is not found so much in Madsen. He is careful enough and makes himself clear: "I will try to describe the socio-cultural condition of the Mexican-Americans in one county on the Mexican border today in order to provide some understanding of the stresses of acculturation process in this area." One could accuse Madsen of insincerity because the title of his study appears to refer to all Mexican-Americans of South Texas rather than those of one county. The fault, however, is found in those who recommend the book and read more into it then is actually there. For example, the Curriculum Guide used in one secondary school makes the following careless statement about Madsen's book: "Extremely valuable because the concepts examined and narrated are very valid and applicable to all Mexican-Americans in the United States." Octavio Romano's scathing critique in "The Sociology and Anthropology of the Mexican-Americans," assumes Madsen is referring to all Mexican-Americans, and reads perhaps too much into Madsen's generalizations.

HISTORY AND OTHER STUDIES OF MAN.

The final observation of this report on the condition of Mexican-American history relates to a subject close to my interests: the definition of history and how history is different from and relates to other studies of man. Specifically, this section is concerned with Mexican-American history as history; how as history it differs from and is related to the social science studies on the Mexican-American, and also, how it is different from and related to journalistic reports on current Mexican-American events. These distinctions and relations have been confused and obscured by several writers, which is one reason I have entered their discussion here. A second reason is to draw special attention to the affirmation that "history has a special mission to perform." If Mexican-American history is to advance from its present nascent stage to professional and scholarly levels, not only must it be defined clearly, but it must also be made clear how it is different from and related to other branches of knowledge. It should be mentioned that this section is not an effort to review every theory and definition of history. It is true that historians have a good deal to debate regarding the definition of history: the interest here, however, is their agreement.

Robin George Collingwood suggested that there are four characteristics of history generally accepted by historians: (1) history is an "inquiry:" (2) history inquires about past human actions; (3) history is a method which interprets evidence; and (4) history teaches "what man has done" and "what man is." Thus Mexican-American history asks questions about the Mexican-American past; in order to answer these questions about the Mexican-American past, it interprets evidence: and it teaches what Mexican-Americans have done and what they are.

This definition of history, however, does not tell us how history is different from other studies of man, especially how it is different from social science and current events. Of several works consulted on this matter, the final comments of T.R.

Tholfsen's *Historical Thinking* (New York, 1967) are useful and illuminating. Recapitulating the virtues of history, Tholfsen affirms "that in studying any human phenomenon it is necessary not only to identify recurring patterns and connected ways." He then tells us how history is different from social science:

Focusing on the event or idea or institution as it exists at a particular moment, the historian . . . cherishes peculiarities of time and place and resists any tendency to dismiss them as merely peripheral. He urges that general concepts be applied gently, so as not to do violence to the distinctive features of the phenomena. In addition . . . the historian inquires into the relationship between phenomena connected in time. He looks for continuity and change. He seeks the past that lies within every phenomenon. Above all, he analyzes the processes that brought it into being.

In other words, history is concerned with the analysis of change over time; the main responsibility of the historian is to find out what happened, "to identify events in sequence, to analyze the interrelationships among those events, and to discover how they occur in a given order." In this sense, Mexican-American history is an investigation of how things have come to be as they are in the barrios and wherever else Mexicans live in the United States. The subject matter of Mexican-American history consists of events which are worthy of being kept in remembrance, e.g., the Treaty of Guadalupe Hidalgo. Knowledge about these events is obtained by careful examination of surviving evidence. Thus, the explanation of the present condition of the Mexican-American involves a systematic study of the most important events which have taken place in the barrios since Guadalupe Hidalgo, and also the relationship of these events to conditions under which changes have taken place in the past. This means an analysis of the patterns found in the continuity of old forms, e.g., poverty and discrimination, and, also, an analysis of the patterns found in conditions under which changes have taken place. In short,

Mexican-American history is interested in continuity and the analysis of change over time. And it is this interest in the development of man over time which distinguishes history from social science and other studies of man.

There are, however, other characteristics which distinguish history from social science. A.S. Eisenstadt observes that the social sciences seek information for immediate use in solving social problems, and, also, that the social sciences tend to be reform oriented. History, on the other hand, has not traditionally been interested in social ills, and is usually conservative or part of the establishment. Social science is interested in formulating consistent patterns of human behavior while history is interested in differences between individuals and groups. The language of social science is supposedly impersonal, while the language of history reflects the personality of the historian and is, in a sense, a kind of poetry. According to Eisenstadt, both history and social science began in the nineteenth century in search of positive truth. History gave up the search in the twentieth century while the social sciences persist because if "they cannot claim to be furnishing society with certain knowledge arrived at by certain methods, they can claim nothing at all."

Although history differs from social science, it does not mean history cannot use social science information and methods. To be sure, both historians and social scientists agree that they have something to learn from each other. In its bulletin on *The Social Sciences in Historical Study* (New York, 1954), the Committee on Historiography of the Social Science Research Council encouraged historians to make use of the social sciences. *The Modern Researcher* (New York, 1970) claims: "history and social science are true sisters because the historian must again and again rely on the results of surveys, studies, and statistics gathered by his painstaking colleagues in the ologies; and because they in turn cannot breathe or move without adopting toward their material the attitude of history." Economist Paul S. Taylor believes that "history can serve social science—at least under many circumstances; history illuminates the contemporary social science study—and the reverse is also true."

Journalism presents the same problem as social science. For example, the increasing output of works on the current Mexican-American Civil Rights Movement, chiefly the work of journalists, is not history. This literature confines itself to current events with little or no consideration of the historical perspective; the subject is rarely perceived in terms of continuity and the analysis of change over time. More specifically, some writers confuse current events with history, and others cite works on current events in bibliographies of Mexican-American history without explaining how these works qualify as history. As in social science, the historian who uses information from current events or any other source, for that matter, should make clear how that information qualifies as history:

> Hence the historian who borrows most enthusiastically from the sister disciplines will take pains to use what he borrows 'historically' and maintains the identity of his own discipline.

The main point is not that history is superior to social science or any other discipline, but that history has certain advantages over social science— and the reverse is also true. The main point is that some writers have confused history with other disciplines and, also, they have failed to illuminate upon the specific interest of history: the development of the Mexican-American people over a period of time.

CONCLUSION

Although some of the works mentioned in this report have drawn extensively from archives, museums, libraries, field work, etc., it is still generally true that no serious effort has been made to tap primary sources. There are museums, archives, libraries, and other depositories which have never been catalogued and investigators have no way of knowing what sources on Mexican-American history are available. There must be a gold mine of information in the archives of the national, state, and local governments of Mexico and the United States. Further, a search for documents should not be limited to the Southwest because Mexicans also live in other states. It should be mentioned that written testimony by Mexican-Americans is rare, owing to the fact that the majority of Mexicans have been and continue to be extensively illiterate. Fortunately, there are Mexicans still around who witnessed much of their history in the period from 1850 to the present. Some scholars have considered the possibility of obtaining oral testimony from these survivors and utilizing the methods of ethnohistory to corroborate it. The process of searching for documents, cataloguing, indexing, editing, annotating, publishing, and making them available to serious students, if ever undertaken, will be expensive, requiring infinite patience, special skills, and years of labor. And if Mexican-American history is to advance in scholarly depth, it is imperative that this process be undertaken.

In this report, a discussion of the use and abuse of Mexican-American history by civil rights groups has been avoided. This is because sufficient information is not available. A terse comment, however, on the author's experience is perhaps not amiss. First, it is clear that the university which should be the vanguard of serious research, is not going to advance the serious study of Mexican-American history. This is so despite "Chicano Studies" as a publicity gimmick (to let the community know that the college is interested in "disadvantaged Chicanos"), and also, Mexican-American history is threatened in the universities by student politics and some professors who go along for reasons of personal advancement. And it is generally true that:

> When a community is at a crucial stage, just emerging from a time of oppression and second-class status, it is simply going to manipulate the past for its own purposes. One must expect this.

In other words, it is the opinion of this writer that the propaganda of the Mexican-American Civil Rights Movement, especially as it is used by the students is an impediment to the serious study of Mexican-American history. It is also sad, again, in the opinion and experience of this author, that foundations and government agencies also seem more interested in appeasing the vociferous than funding such critically neglected areas as Mexican-American history.

Also, in this report, no effort has been made to accuse professional historians of consciously suppressing Mexican-American history. The reason is simple: there is no evidence for such a charge or suspicion. Stan Steiner, as I briefly indicated, wrote in *La Raza* that "those who have written the textbooks of the Southwest have for one hundred years suppressed the history of La Raza." Steiner did not prove this serious charge. Henry Steele Commager, however, in his book on *The Nature and the Study of History* observes: "Over the centuries history has been written by the victors, not the vanquished. . . . One of the less amiable traits of victors, in the past, has been the deliberate destruction of enemy records and the silencing—often by death—of enemy historians. It is true that documents on Mexican-American history have mysteriously disappeared from certain depositories in the Los Angeles area, but this activity is not so widespread as to justify alarm. And no Mexican-American historian has yet been silenced, owing to the fact that there are none. Presently, it seems difficult if not impossible to train cadres of Mexican-American historians who: (1) are of Mexican descent, and (2) are independent of the politics and propaganda of the Mexican-American Civil Rights Movement. In short, there is no evidence which convicts professional historians of the suppression of Mexican-American history.

Mexican-American history, as defined in this paper, is just beginning to be studied seriously. Professional historians have almost paid no attention to the subject, and the bulk of the literature has been written and continues to be written by amateur historians, that is, by journalists and social scientists. Further, much of the literature has an indignant and reformist tone to it, and the recent literature, mostly the hasty product of journalists, concentrates on recent developments and ignores the historical perspective. The development of Mexican-American history, such as it is, has been far from smooth. It has proceeded unevenly; there are many gaps and most of the topics already dealt with in the literature require more profound study.

Ralph Guzmán

Ralph Guzmán (see p. 380); testifying before the U.S. Inter-Agency Committee on Mexican American Affairs in 1967, charged that scholars more interested in money than truth have taken government grants and reinforced racial stereotypes. The crux of Professor Guzmán's argument resides in what he considers the inability of academe in the pay of the government to look away from the minority group and into the majority society for the source of non-achievement.
By permission of the author.

Ethics In Federally Subsidized Research – The Case Of The Mexican American

All of the recent internal and external challenges to American values and power must not obscure the fact that we are in the midst of a most profound moral crisis. While most analysis of this crisis refer to questions of traditional moral virtues or business ethics or the behavior of the young, a largely unexamined arena is the question of the

relationship between the ethics of scholarship and the actions of government.

The importance and influence of governmental actions has been cited so often that it has become one of John Stuart Mills' "dead truths." In the field of minority research it is necessary to reemphasize that the programs of the government, in large

456

part, determine and fix for generations the conceptions, the images, the popular stereotypes of what the majority and the minority think of each other and of themselves. By the concepts it supports, by the programs it selects, and by the values it endorses, the government holds up a mirror of society. To the degree to which that mirror distorts, the society suffers. Society becomes imprisoned in irrationality and illusion. Men turn to magic rather than reason; they seek panaceas rather than programs to solve their problems.

The development of this crisis has been aided and abetted by American scholars; they are partially responsible for it. For American scholars have aborted the ethics of scholarship. They have participated in premature government programs; they have profited from the fears of isolated policy-makers; they have exploited the privation of the poor; in short, too many scholars have succumbed to the lure of profit and power and abandoned the acient obligation of their profession: The unremitting but unrewarded search for valid knowledge. Thus many have forgotten that the search for truth is not the same as the search for solutions of problems. Government operates; it is primarily interested in the question: "Will it work?" It must select among alternatives. But it is not primarily or preeminently interested in abstract truth and unrelated knowledge. As such the interest of government differs from the interest of scholarship. A working relationship between the two must be one of tension and co-existence—not merger. A strange symbiotic relationship has arisen between government officials who use the university as window dressing to validate their predetermined choices and the academics who use government grants, consultancies and contracts to validate their prowess in their pursuit of academic prestige. If this relationship were merely confined to the participants, it would only be sordid; however the ramifications of this symbiosis stretches the length and breadth of the land and as such affects the high and the low; the majority and the minority, in their respective quest for identity and dignity. And this is of particular significance in the Southwest.

Five and one-half million Americans of Mexican descent provide living testimony to repeated failures of the American conscience. The destiny of these people is inextricably entwined in the resolution of our internal moral crisis. The challenge posed by these people to American scholars and American political institutions has been largely unmet. The response has been ineffective, irrelevant and miserly, both in material and spiritual assistance. The consequences to the Mexican-American people echo like a medieval petition to a benevolent despot.

Many government officials and scholars have assumed the ideology of the past. At its highest level of conceptualization this tendency assumes that the problem of a minority group inheres in the minority group. It assumes that the larger society is without fault; if you could only find the fatal flaw in the character or the mores of the minority group the problem would be solved. The real question is not to "know the minority," but to know the failure of societal institutions to relate effectively to members of minority groups. The real emphasis should be placed in the malfunctions in the total system not on some supposed trait—really culpability within the Mexican-American. (It is this basic problem of *where* to focus—on the minority or on the society—that produced the government's agonies over the Moynihan Report.) This first basic error in where to look results in other fallacious assumptions. By this I mean that notions of racial inferiority; low intellectual capacity; social maladjustment; expendability in war and peace permeate official and academic circles. The more sophisticated camouflage these notions with phrases like cultural deprivation, lack of motivation, social alienation; marginality and lack of acculturation. The less sophisticated are more honest in their terminology. They talk about laziness and un-Americanism.

Tragically, these external social judgments have been internalized by many Mexican Americans. Recent surveys in San Antonio and Los Angeles show a tendency for Mexican Americans to agree with the negative judgments that the larger society passed upon them. Surely it is logically evident that if you treat people for generations as if they were inferior some will begin to believe that they are inferior and act accordingly when they are with you: if you treat people as if they were lazy some of them will respond accordingly to your demands; if you treat people as if they were unintelligent some will respond as if, indeed, they were unintelligent in performing your tasks. What this does to the chances of succeeding generations is not only morally but even criminally wrong; for it is a basic offense against human dignity. For scholars to participate in this process is to make them party to the destruction of human values rather than the fulfillment of them. This is a repudiation of their role as validators of the truth.

In another dimension this process generates social and personality patterns founded on fear—fear of the outside world; fear of competition; fear of social change; and fear of self in any but the safe, predictable world of the minority. The assumption that the intrusion of the "outside world" is a hostile event; the creation of categories of "we and they," not bridged by symbols named justice, democracy and consensus—these cripple the community. The young Mexican American scholar who is afraid to leave the *barrio* in order to compete; the immature mind that refuses to explore beyond the comfortable; the young adult that opts for social indifference rather than moral indignation—these are the heirs of the merger of government and scholar.

A romanticized picture of reality has obscured the salient problems of these people. Certain cultural anthropologists, among others, have unduly transmuted aspects of the Mexican-American people into presupposed patterns of behavior. They have swindled the American people into believing that the quixotic and picturesque represent permanent cultural essences. And they have also performed a grave disservice to the government as well as the community of scholars. To establish elaborate exegesis from the fact that some members of this minority group may have a rural sense of time; that some of them may remain dependent upon the local *curandera;* that some males remain obsessed with a notion of *machismo;* and that others have an overriding sense of social fatalism is not only disingenuous it is a cruel hoax. A quest for the quaint is not science; nor is it likely to be service to the United States government.

Having helped to warp the Mexican-American self-image American social institutions have not even been able to project an adequate picture of what the larger society really is. The legitimating myth of the American educational system posits a society in which achievement, loyalty and patriotism are automatically rewarded. No Mexican-American needs a college education to tell him that this is patently false. His own life experiences tell him that economic reward is not commensurate with educational achievement. His observations of the Negro teach him that a firm joining of the thumb to the nose produces more attention than patient supplication. Moreover, he knows that valor in war brings no vantage in peace. Both those who believe in the myth implicity and those who reject it completely share a gross misunderstanding of American society.

In the minority, this misunderstanding contributes to a disposition for unrealistic and irrelevant group goals. For example, the demand of some leaders, supported by some scholars, that the community *must* maintain a high degree of cultural solidarity and yet still be accorded the benefits of the affluent society is obviously impractical and an interference with a basic personal liberty. The Negroes wisely never accepted the idea of separate but equal. After almost sixty years the Supreme Court rejected the idea that separate facilities could ever be made equal. It should not take another sixty years to realize that separate cultural communities cannot be made equal either. Those who would impose group solidarity in terms of cultural pluralism merely re-state the old separate but equal doctrine. The point is that if an individual opts for one cultural identity or another that is *his* privilege, but for a government or its agencies to predetermine that choice is an easy concession to mutual racism. The concelebration of the Chamizal Agreement, and these hearings, presumes and assumes a relationship between Mexican Americans and the Republic of Mexico that exists largely in the minds of intellectual romantics. These El Paso agreements will not affect one school drop-out in Denver; they will not cleanse *Barrio Barelas* in Albuquerque; nor will they desegregate schools in Los Angeles; jobs will still be scarce for Mexican Americans in San Antonio, and houses in Phoenix will still have invisible but real signs that read: "For Anglos Only." In short, the problems that Mexican Americans face relate to the fact that they are American citizens. In the face of these problems of the Mexican Americans the disposition of the Chamizal is unimportant to the people gathered here.

The predisposition on the part of leaders and scholars to assert unrealistic and irrelevant goals naturally produces an excess of sweetheart leaders. Such leaders romance both the larger society and the Mexican-American community in their efforts to preserve the illusion of cooperation. Their concern for preserving this facade is maintained at the expense of genuine progress for all Americans.

All these things sustain a fatal dependency that destroys the effectiveness of legitimate government endeavors and impairs the ability of the Mexican American to enter a meaningful relationship to himself or to American society.

This dependency is fostered by improper and unethical scholarship. Mexican Americans have not been served well by those who purport to interpret them to the larger society. In a sense, they have been the victims of spurious relationships between the scholar, his subject and program builder. Some scholars, blinded by a passionate commitment to methodology or to their own attachments to Mexican Americans fail to see the real strengths and liabilities in the Mexican American community.

Many educators, for example, graciously concede the existence of a representative Mexican-American culture. However, in making this concession they seize the opportunity of defining its content. Naturally they also assume the responsibility for fitting every square peg of a Mexican American into the round hole of culture they have invented. There is no one so totalitarian as an educator confronted by a Mexican-American child who refuses to conform to the educator's notion of what a Mexican American child should be. Unique individuals are assumed to be non-real, non-legal or possibly non-Mexican. This diagnosis is *not* necessary. If necessary, Mexican-Americans can define their own culture.

There is an attachment to the method which sometimes transcends interest in its success. There are some, for example, so committed to adult edu-

cational television that they discount the weight of any impartial evaluation as to how it might be received in the *barrios.*

In another category are those that have a ready made diagnosis in scholarly findings about Mexican Americans. They admit that they don't know Mexican Americans well but emphasize that they are well-disposed towards them. These same individuals squeeze Mexican Americans into models based on previous ethnic experiences in different times and settings. Well-meaning, well-disposed scholars assume that Mexican Americans are only dislocated Puerto Ricans, merely lower class Cubans, a variant of the Black Power Movement, or simply Spanish-speaking Irish. These scholars suggest programs that have worked for other ethnic groups while ignoring the reality of the Mexican Americans. For example, bussing children into middle-class white neighborhoods may symbolize the aspirations of some parents of middle class Negro children. It does not follow, however, that the same program will cause the parents of Mexican-American children to rejoice.

Others have exploited this minority in the game of government grants-manship. Personnel from school systems that have failed to serve Mexican American children effectively are often the ones who receive government grants. Grantsmanship has widened the chasm between the pursuit of truth and the intelligent selection among alternatives. Some of the reasons for this are inherent in the system itself.

Those most skillful in securing government grants display their ability to communicate with grant-givers. It should not be necessary to note that there is no automatic relationship between skill in grant design and academic excellence. Too often scholars become smooth operators who maintain themselves by reinforcing the respective misconceptions of the power structure and the community. Not surprisingly, the ethics of some of these individuals relate to the profit motive associated with primitive capitalism; not to the rewards represented by a genuine contribution to either the total sum of human knowledge or the solution of pressing and immediate problems.

The point is that the relationship between the scholar and government is in disarray. At present the academic medicine man converges on Washington with special skills in packaging research programs. To place it in proper perspective the government should diligently and honestly seek scholars with integrity. The validation of truth may be unpleasant—it emphatically will not please all of the public but, if the scholar is not to be politicized, he must feel free to report unpleasant even politically unpalatable truths. Government, on the other hand, must realize that it is no business of the scholar to make American society feel better about itself.

When this necessary change occurs government and scholars can address themselves to the real research needs of the American people.

The President has requested specific guidelines for basic research in this area. The following areas demand urgent attention. Overall, there should be a focus on what has *changed* among Mexican Americans.

One, there is a desperate need for a history of the Mexican-American people which neither serves patriotic sentiments nor panders to the pride of the sub-group.

Two, there is a need for a comparative study of the peoples of the Southwest and their patterns of social interaction. The varying relationships between and among the several minorities and the dominant society in the Southwest must be related and the ongoing process probed in order to assess the viability of American political and social institutions on a broad continuum of past, present, and future trends. The difference between this approach and the more narrow approach is that scholars have conceptualized minorities as if there were no context of a larged society.

Three, the myth of an automatically assumed special relationship between the Mexican-American people and the Republic of Mexico must give way before research into the true relationship that has varied with time, place and generation and is continuously changing. For many scholars the proximity of Mexico has obscured the fact that problems of the Mexican Americans relate to American life. While grandfathers may dream of small villages in Jalisco the majority of the Mexican Americans cannot remember events before World War II.

Four, the border as a concept must be recognized for what it is: a political bludgeon used against Mexican Americans which alternately appears and disappears when agricultural interests dictate.

Five, nostalgic appeal to the rural communitarian past must be challenged by a continuing focus on the present-day urban reality of Mexican American existence, while the problems of the rural present begin to get realistic attention.

Six, and perhaps most important, while most research will remain concerned with things that are there must be substantial support for research that centers on "things that could be." In other words, government, more than anyone else, has a responsibility to support daring, imaginative and possibly outrageous research. Dare to follow with action research the implications of what has been done in Denver by Ozzie Simmons and his colleagues and by Lyle Shannon in Racine, Wisconsin. Dare to trust the poor to direct their own lives; dare to trust them to administer programs, establish direction, and to make decisions. Then study these processes.

Seven, there are two beneficial by-products of research that can justifiably be encouraged by scholars and government. One is research that represents a partnership between the scholar and the community. This not only helps the community to become more aware of itself, as it really is, it also helps the scholar to reformulate his conceptions as he meets real people, not cases. The other is the incorporation of Mexican-American youth into research activities as assistants and managers. This will sensitize these young people to become more confident American citizens; it will also produce scholars of the future who can match compassion and competence with insight.

Finally, a note of caution. There are real limitations to the scope of scholarship and the power of government. Neither can grant dignity to a proud people; for dignity is not granted, it is a product of a personal sense of achievement and esteem. Both the scholar and the government must realize that personal dignity and psychological well-being for the Mexican American cannot be secured through intervention by government. The lady bountiful complex, that has characterized the relationship between scholar, government, and Mexican Americans can only stifle the development of these people, suppress their political socialization and subvert their dignity. To those who have approached the Mexican American people as condescending fathers or anxious hucksters I can only warn you to walk warily for you walk in the dark corners of your own conceits.

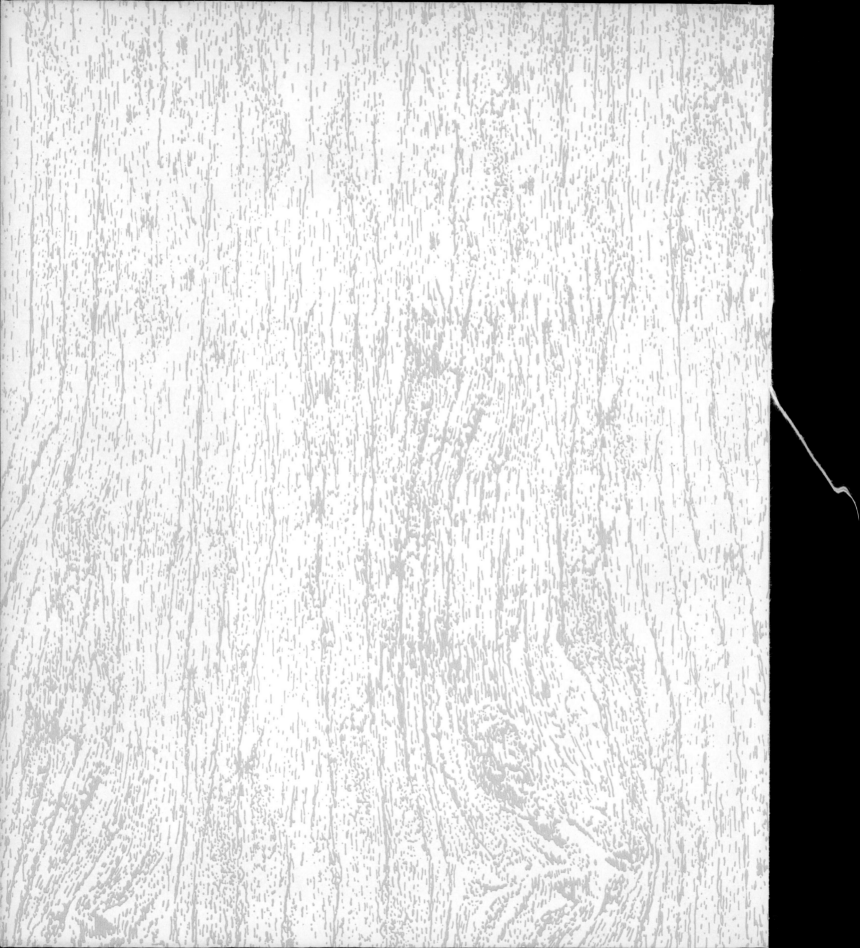